CONTROVERSIES IN SOCIOLOGY

Sylvia M. Hale

Custom Edition for SOC100H at University of Toronto Mississauga

Taken from:
Contested Sociology: Rethinking Canadian Experience
by Sylvia M. Hale

Controversies in Sociology: A Canadian Introduction, Second Edition
by Sylvia M. Hale

Custom Publishing

New York   Boston   San Francisco
London   Toronto   Sydney   Tokyo   Singapore   Madrid
Mexico City   Munich   Paris   Cape Town   Hong Kong   Montreal

Pearson
Custom Publishing
is a division of

www.pearsonhighered.com

ISBN 10: 0-558-23016-4
ISBN 13: 978-0-558-23016-6

LIST OF CHAPTERS

Chapters 1–4, 6-9, and 13–14 were taken from *Contested Sociology: Rethinking Canadian Experience,* Third Edition, by Sylvia M. Hale. Chapters 5 and 10–12 were taken from *Controversies in Sociology: A Canadian Introduction,* Second Edition, by Sylvia M. Hale.

CONTENTS

Chapters 1–4, 6-9, and 13–14 were taken from *Contested Sociology: Rethinking Canadian Experience,* Third Edition, by Sylvia M. Hale. Chapters 5 and 10–12 were taken from *Controversies in Sociology: A Canadian Introduction,* Second Edition, by Sylvia M. Hale.

The Sociological Imagination: The Promise of Sociology

The goal of sociology is to understand the social world and our lives within it. As a discipline it develops the tools to explore critical questions How does the social world work, how did it come to be this way and how is it changing, and how are our individual lives—our biographies and our life chances, created and stunted by the social world that we ourselves, collectively, produce? Sociology is the hub of all the social sciences. It forms the core discipline that underlies multiple specialized areas of study like political science, economics, criminology and native studies. It forms the foundation of many professions, including social work, education, policing, journalism, urban planning, and political policy formation and analysis. The insights of sociology are also central to contemporary literature, arts and drama.

The social world is not a tangible entity in the sense of a system that exists independently of the behaviours of the people who constitute it. People continually create and recreate the social world by the pressures or forces that we exert over each other and ourselves. Sociology is concerned with understanding the sources and the forms that these social forces take. During certain periods, as when countries go to war, or when the economy collapses, leaving hundreds of thousands of people adrift without jobs, forces may seem overwhelming, sweeping people along as helpless victims. Yet these are still human forces, pressures that people in groups bring to bear upon each other. Sometimes people resist, fighting back against such pressures and forcing changes. People continue to assert themselves, even within the most oppressive social institutions. Goffman

(1961a) describes how a patient, stripped of almost all autonomy in a large, closed ward of an asylum, still managed to assert himself against the system by urinating on the radiator—an ideal location for the act to produce maximum effect. People once harassed and criminalized for 'deviant' sexual orientation embraced their label as 'queer' and turned it into a mark of pride. Converging around slogans such as "We're here. We're queer. Get used to it," they and their supporters publicly celebrated their stigmatized identity in tumultuous Gay Pride marches. In Canada in 2005 they won the right to transform their partnerships into legally-recognized marriage.

In a brilliant essay, C. Wright Mills (1959, ch. 1) expresses the sense of ambivalence that people feel given their positions as both victims and creators of society. Mills observes that people often feel as if they are in a series of traps in their personal lives. They feel that they cannot overcome their personal problems, and in this they are often correct. Individuals do not generally control the forces that affect their lives. These forces are socially located far beyond the immediate, personal settings in which people live, and it is difficult for people to see beyond their own private reality: their jobs, their neighbourhoods, their families. The more that threatening forces transcend their direct experience, the more trapped people feel. How do fishers of Newfoundland feel when cod stocks collapse and the fishery is closed? Or Alberta beef farmers when one case of 'mad-cow' disease is used to justify closure of the Unites States border to live cattle? Or residents of a small town when its major employer, a **multinational corporation**, closes local operations and moves to the United States? Or parents who see their children's lives bombarded by war toys, pornography, drugs, sex, the threat of AIDS? All these forces are more or less beyond the immediate control of the people who are affected by them. Personal successes and failures occur within definite social situations and reflect the effects of modern historical changes.

The information revolution in the media has increased people's awareness of world events. Anyone who reads newspapers or watches the news on television cannot help but be aware that we are living in the middle of upheaval everywhere: in the Middle East, Afghanistan, Africa, Latin America, Northern Ireland, and at home in Canada. International terrorism, in the form of bombings, skyjackings, and assassinations have become a regular part of nightly news, especially since they happened so close to us in New York in 2001, Madrid in 2004, and London, England 2005. Suspicion,

fear, and heightened security concerns overshadow all public events. Each time we catch an international flight, we are reminded that someone might want to blow it up. People fleeing from civil war, dictatorship, and persecution abroad seek refugee status in Canada almost daily. Still more come seeking to escape grinding poverty at home, only to be faced with Canada's own unemployment problems. Stories such as those of people gunned down on Toronto streets, and of scores of murdered sex-trade workers, are brought into our living-rooms as we watch television.

While the media increase our awareness, they do not necessarily increase our understanding of events. When we are unable to understand what is happening or why, we desperately try to interpret these events in individual, personal terms. People often blame parents for anti-social behaviour by youth, suggesting that the youths had been badly brought up and should have been disciplined more when they were younger. Others view the beggars pan-handling on downtown streets, and lining up outside soup kitchens, as inadequate, lazy or alcoholic individuals who could pull themselves up if they wanted to. It is easy to see riots as caused by a few troublemakers, outside agitators who should be put in prison. But these individual explanations are inadequate to account for major shifts in patterns of behaviour affecting multiple communities.

When we as individuals are faced with forces that we do not understand and cannot control, we often react by withdrawal. We retreat into our private lives, stop listening to the news, tell ourselves that the problems are not our responsibility, and try to forget them and get on with our own lives. When we cannot avoid the threats, we tend to react with fear, resentment, and hostility. Moral insensitivity can result from people's sense of being overwhelmed by historical changes that they do not understand and that may challenge cherished values. It is easier to demand that national borders be closed to refugees and alien immigrants than to cope in our immediate lives with the reality of trans-national migrations prompted by global inequalities and war. Feelings of being overwhelmed by seemingly intractable problems of destitution in the midst of plenty, may help to explain why so many residents petition city officials to clear their downtown streets of panhandlers, and demand that toilets and park gates be locked so that homeless people cannot sleep in them. In some neighbourhoods, people have resorted to covering hot air gratings with barbed wire to stop derelicts from huddling over them. People do not want shelters for the homeless, for young delinquents, or mentally retarded adults built in their neighbourhoods. Fear of unemployment of inflation threatening a tenuous hold on a middle–class lifestyle makes people easy prey for get–tough policies and glib political slogans that promise easy answers.

People need much more than information to overcome their sense of being trapped. We live in the age of the information revolution, with satellite printing of national newspapers, instantaneous around-the-world coverage of events on radio and television, and a plethora of magazines. Media flood us with information, but they do not ensure that we have the capacity to handle it, make sense of it, and distinguish the reliable information from that which is misleading. In some ways mass media actively work against our deeper understanding of issues, because they are designed to turn all information into entertainment to please mass audiences and particularly corporate advertisers, and to offend no one. They bring us horrendous news one minute, followed by sports scores and other trivia the next. We live increasingly in a world of hyper-reality in which what we see on television can seem more real than reality itself. Bystanders interviewed at scenes of terrorism or destruction frequently catch themselves saying it was like being in a movie. For C. Wright Mills, the special promise of sociology as a discipline is its capacity to process information. He uses the term the **sociological imagination** to describe "a quality of mind that will help [people] to use information and to develop reason in order to achieve lucid summations of what is going on in the world and of what may be happening within themselves" (Mills 1959, 5).

The basic assumption of sociology is that our life chances as individuals are understandable only within historically specific social situations, which we can begin to grasp through comparisons with the life chances of others in similar situations. One's chances of getting a job, of getting rich, of dying from cancer, going to war, being a Catholic or a Protestant or an atheist, are socially situated. Sociology as a discipline tries to grasp the nature of this relationship between individual biography and social-historical forces within society. The way in which we tend to answer the question, "Who are you?"—in terms of our sex, age, profession, and ethnic background—situates us on a social map. Given information about people's occupations and incomes, we can predict a great deal about them: where they live, what kind of home and furnishings they have, what they read, what music they listen to, how they speak, how they vote, even whether they prefer sex with the light on or off (Berger 1963, 80–81).

This embeddedness of individual life chances within social structures becomes sharply visible for people living with special needs or disabilities (Dandaneau 2001, ch. 5). They live their lives at the intersection of laws and administrative rules that determine who will qualify for available supports or income assistance, networks of competing interest groups that set priorities for budget allocations, and shifting definitions of 'normal' that determine whether people like themselves will be accommodated within mainstream social institutions, with access to education and opportunities for meaningful work, or segregated out of sight in special facilities, or abandoned to cope as best they can or to die on the streets or in homeless shelters.

According to Mills (1959, 6–7), the sociological endeavour entails three broad categories of questions focussing on the structure of society, the patterns of social change, and the characteristics of the people who constitute the society. The first category includes such questions as: What is the structure of this particular society? What are its major parts? How are these parts—education, church, polity, economy—interrelated? How does Canada differ from other societies and why? All of us have immediate experience of how different elements of society affect each other. We know that the economy affects education, influencing decisions about whether to go to university or to take a job and about what course of studies to follow. Religion affects voting patterns, the numbers of children people have, the chance that one will commit suicide. Work life affects family life, dictating the standard of living and also the time available for parenting. As a total **social system**, Canada differs from other societies in multiple ways. It was founded as a predominantly white European settler society, with indigenous peoples pushed aside into reservations, and non-Europeans admitted only grudgingly and under unequal conditions. More recently, the makeup of Canadian society has become more visibly diverse, as patterns of global migration, policies promoting multiculturalism, and the Charter of Rights and Freedoms have loosened up the establishment.

This leads into the second major type of question emphasised by Mills: Where does our society stand in human history? How did it get to be this way and how is it changing now? How does any particular feature or episode of our society's history fit into the present situation? Sociology looks both backwards and forwards in an effort to understand contemporary society. Successive generations of people can be thought of as cohorts, people born around the same time, who struggle with the dominant issues of their time. For people who were young adults in North America during the 1930s, the dominant issue was the "Great Depression"—a period when one third of the labour force across North America were unemployed. This was followed by the turbulence and misery of the Second World War years, and then the economic expansion of the post-war years. Young adults during the '60s retroactively defined their cohort as the hippie generation, coalescing around struggles over civil rights, the Vietnam war, and feminism. They also lived under the cloud of the Cold War between 'East' and 'West' and the threat of nuclear war. Young adults in North America at the start of the twenty-first century find their lives shaped around new challenges. Among the dominant issues facing this age, my students listed international terrorism, globalization and competition over oil, global inequality, environmental degradation and global warming, and AIDS. This new millennium has opened with hard challenges facing humankind.

There are also powerful social changes closer to home. The lives and life-chances of university students in the first decade of the twenty-first century differ in critical ways from the previous generation of students. Thirty years ago in Canada higher education was considered a public good that society as a whole should pay for. In current political thinking, higher education is considered more an individual consumer product that individual customers should pay for themselves (Mueller and Reimer 2006). The result is that students are often graduating with huge debts that will impact heavily on their future life choices. Students graduating in the 1970s could reasonably expect to find professional jobs that offered long-term security and pensions. Students graduating now are being advised to expect to change careers several times, and to think of themselves as entrepreneurs with flexible packages of skills to trade in an ever-changing global marketplace.

The third type of question is, What kinds of women and men make up our society? How are people selected and formed? How are we liberated and repressed? How are we made sensitive or blunted? What does the experience of years of unemployment do to young people who are out of work, and what does the constant fear of possible layoffs do to people who are working? The 1960s were known for hippies, flower power, and campus radicalism, but students now seem more conservative and conformist than their earlier counterparts. We need to explore why these changes are happening. Young adults in Canada at the beginning of the new millennium grew up with the Charter of Rights and Freedoms, and with

the internet. As a cohort, they are more sensitized to issues of sexism, homophobia, and global inequalities, but at the same time, perhaps more cynical towards political involvement and more detached. Parents fear that the sensitivities of children are being blunted by violence on television or excited in negative ways by war toys, pornography and sexual predators on the internet. The feminist movement in many ways radically altered the lives of women and men. Yet there are signs that young women do not identify with the movement. Does this mean that feminism was only a passing fad? Or does sensitivity to feminism only comes with greater experience of the deeply gendered fissures that still run through the ruling institutions of society?

The student of sociology, Mills argues, has to be able to shift perspectives in imagination, to switch from looking at politics to looking at the family, the economy, and war, and to see their interconnections. It is not an easy discipline. The sociological imagination frequently makes the ordinary world look incredible. We commonly think of family relations, for example, as part of our uniquely private lives. It frequently comes as a shock to see how deeply these intimate relations are shaped by wider social forces. The basic message of sociology is that our society has not always been the way it is, nor is it inevitably this way, and it probably will not be so in the future. It can be different, and we need to understand how we can affect these changes through acting collectively. For this reason alone, the critical eye of sociology can often provoke opposition from powerful groups in contemporary society who benefit from the status quo and who do not want change or want it only in a particular direction.

An important distinction drawn in sociology is between personal troubles and public issues (Mills 1959, 8–10). Troubles stem from private matters that lie within an individual's character and immediate relations with friends and family. Issues, by contrast, go beyond the personal, local setting, to broader social forces that affect the life experiences of many people. An important part of learning to do sociology is learning to generalize from personal experience to broader social forces that this experience reflects. Consider unemployment. When only a few individuals are unemployed in a large city, it can reasonably be viewed as a private trouble, reflecting the particular problems of the unemployed individuals, and it can perhaps best be dealt with using an individual casework approach. But when fifteen million people are unemployed out of a nation of fifty million, for example, unemployment is a public issue. It cannot be solved by helping individual cases. The structure of opportunities has collapsed.

Similarly, one or two homeless people living on park benches can perhaps be seen to reflect personal trouble. But when hundreds of thousands of people are out of work, or entire industries collapse, and one-fifth of children grow up in households that look to foodbanks to meet their basic needs, helping individuals will not solve the problem. Something in the structure of the economy, or of families, or of mental health services has broken down. We have to shift perspectives to see these problems as a social issues, requiring changes in societal institutions.

Mills argues that the sociological imagination, the capacity to understand the relationships between elements of society and their impact on individual life chances, has become the central feature of modern society. It dominates how people think, how histories are written, the kinds of art we view and literature we read. Science and technology remain powerful forces in society, but they are no longer central to how people think, because they have failed us in important ways. In many respects, technology has conquered nature. We know how to get to the moon and beyond, how to grow food artificially, how to transmit thousands of conversations simultaneously on optical fibres, yet we are in a worse mess than ever. Technology has not solved our problems, but has become, instead, part of what traps us. Contemporary literature and art express the uneasiness that people feel, but they cannot provide answers, except insofar as they may suggest new ways of seeing. It is the sociological imagination that seeks to explain social processes, the nature of our traps, and the underlying structural factors that give rise to them (Mills 1959, 14–15). Sociological explanations are more difficult and more elusive than explanations in the physical sciences because society is not a tangible, fixed entity ready for objective experimental research. The very sociological knowledge we generate is likely to alter the sets of relationships we are trying to study. In another sense, however, sociology may be easier and more rewarding than the physical sciences in that we ourselves are part of it, creators of the societies in which we live, able to understand social processes subjectively as participants in their production.

Sociology and the Scientific Ideal

As a science, sociology is concerned fundamentally with the search for knowledge about society, but this search is both difficult and dangerous. It involves the study of people who, as members of a society, generate their own sense of truth about the social world. Socially generated ideas can be grouped into two categories. First, they take the form of common-sense understandings, or assumptions about how things work, and why, based upon immediate experience. Secondly, they involve more coherent ideologies, or systems of values that justify certain kinds of actions or ways of life, sometimes to the detriment of the interests of other people. These ideologies strongly influence the way we see social reality. They tend to sensitize us in certain ways and to blind us in others.

Sociological analysis must typically confront and challenge ideologies. A critical problem is that sociologists may be as blinded by ideologies as are other people, since they are themselves part of the society that they study, and they tend to accept the assumptions of people like themselves. Smith (1990,93-100) has conceptualized ideology, not as specific beliefs, but as a biased form of *method* of inquiry about society, a method that entails in its effects a systematic means *not* to know and *not* to see the situations of others. Our thinking gets caught up in patterns of circular reasoning, or what Smith calls 'ideological practices'. Children living on welfare appear to be failing in school because their mothers are stressed out and not coping well. Stressors in their mother's environment are identified as poor housing and socially disorganized neighbourhoods. Mothers' failure to cope better with these environmental stressors then seems to explain their inadequate mothering. The solution appears to be stress-management classes and parenting classes (Swift 1995). The active social practices that continually reproduce poverty for one-fifth of Canada's children, and continually reproduce 'mothers' as the site of primary responsibility for unequal educational outcomes disappear from view.

A similar ideological circle noted by Mueller and Reimer (2006), involves university students struggling with debt loads. Students appear to be performing poorly in their academic studies because they are stressed out about their student debt loads. Some are even so stressed that they drop their studies altogether. Debt load is this a major environmental stressor for students, and their attitude towards managing that debt is critical for their success. Hence, students are counselled in stress management to learn to adopt a more healthy attitude towards effective handling of debt. What disappears from view in this circular reasoning is the political decision-making that has changed higher education from public good into personal consumer product that students pay for. That students, or their parents, pay their own university fees, books, room and board appears only as social fact.

Given that sociologists are predominantly well-educated, reasonably well-paid professionals, and until recently were predominantly male, it should come as no surprise that the values of such people tend to be represented in sociology to a greater extent than those of less privileged people. Poorly educated women living on welfare or people working in unskilled jobs, for example, do not tend to publish much in sociology journals. The scientific search for knowledge in sociology entails a major struggle to see past the taken-for-granted understandings and justifications of the professional middle-class world.

It is always easier to see through the ideologies of other groups than to see through one's own. The Nazi ideology of the superiority of the Aryan race has been discredited, but the ideology of capitalism and the work ethic are harder for most Canadians to see through. The ideology of "free market" and "free trade," for example, implicitly justifies price wars to crush small competitors; the ideology of profit justifies charging higher prices to poor people who often do not have access to alternative markets; it justifies laying off employees when the going gets tough and charging higher interest rates on money that poor people have to borrow. The ideology that effort and ability lead to success justifies labelling the unemployed as lazy or stupid. The Christian ideology that "man" was made in the image of God and given dominion over the beasts justifies the exploitation by humans of everything on the planet. We cease to think about the lives of chickens in battery-egg-production factories at the same time as we become enraged at the news of a pet dog being mistreated.

It is important to remember, however, that we are not merely blind victims of ideologies. We are also their creators and interpreters, and we can learn to analyse them, to challenge them, and to change them. The major problem with common-sense interpretations of the world, and with most ideologies, is not that they are totally wrong, but that they can be biassed and partial. Common-sense knowledge is inevitably self-centred. It tends to deal with very narrow individual concerns, not with the broader interests of other people in other situations. Common sense is incomplete, based on limited personal experience with only a hazy idea of what other people's lives are like. Ideology, too, has its limitations and can lead to intolerance. We often have a great deal

invested in our beliefs, and it can be difficult to question and to change them, especially when change can have disturbing consequences. If we abandon the ideology that effort and ability lead to success, for example, it changes our responsibilities to the poor and the disadvantaged. We begin to feel uncomfortable about our own wealth and about the system that allows such discrepancies to exist.

Science, as a search for knowledge, attempts to provide explanations based upon impartial evidence. Impartiality is particularly difficult in the social sciences because people who are the subjects of research react to findings in a conscious way, and the theories themselves affect their behaviour. Even the physical sciences do not escape this social imprint because human society itself reacts with and alters the physical world. Socially learned values and ways of thinking also profoundly influence how research questions come to be asked.

In sociology, the problem of objectivity lies, in part, in the fact that sociologists cannot be impartial to what they study. Our own preconceptions and biases are hard to break. For example, part of the problem for prostitutes is that other people define them as a problem. There are alternative ways of looking at the subject. Perhaps the "real" problem is the sexual frustration of the men who seek out prostitutes, or the fact that soliciting is illegal, which makes the prostitutes prey to protection rackets and pimps. Perhaps the problem is the double standard, which leads to the arrest and prosecution of prostitutes while their customers go free. Perhaps there is no problem at all. Perhaps prostitution should just be seen as a service industry like any other and be left to operate freely as in the red light district of Amsterdam. Alternatively, perhaps the real problem lies in the much bigger picture of worldwide sex-trafficking in women from desperately poor countries, whose bodies are served up as toys for affluent male clients. How we come to think about an issue, and what we see as the immediate and underlying causes powerfully impacts on what we want done about it. What is far harder to see, are the social forces that structure what we think we know and how we know it.

Scientific Objectivity

Notwithstanding the values of researchers, a measure of objectivity is possible in social science. At root, it is not the values that matter so much as the research methods used to collect the evidence. There are many different techniques, some of which are discussed in chapter 3. None of them are foolproof in completely avoiding bias, but there are important principles of research that can reduce it.

The underlying philosophical assumption of all science is that it is relatively easy to find evidence to support an argument. Even stupid theses can usually be backed up by some examples. It is important, therefore, to test an argument by deliberately searching for information and evidence that, if found, would show the argument to be wrong. Consider, for example, a researcher who is interested in studying divorce because she strongly disapproves of it and feels that it harms children. Such a researcher could still provide impartial evidence by deliberately allowing for the reverse data, the possibility that dissolution of an unhappy marriage is a good thing for the children involved. A minimum requirement for such a study would be comparative data from four types of families: those where the parents describe themselves as happily married; those where the parents describe their marriage as unhappy but say that they intend to stay together for the children; divorced families that describe themselves as happier since the divorce; and divorced families that describe themselves as unhappier since the divorce. If data are gathered concerning children in all these sorts of families, the researcher allows for the possibility that children of divorced parents turn out to be happier and healthier than children living with parents in stressful, unhappy marriages. Useful research tests for the possibility that the researcher's starting assumptions might be wrong.

The critical element here is reasoned procedure, the disciplined, rigorous collection of evidence that deliberately tests for the opposite of the initial assumptions. Good research, of course, will attempt much more than this. Given that divorce, like marriage, does not always bring the same results, it is important to explain the conditions under which different outcomes are likely. Again, the ideal is that explanations will be tested, rather than assumed and supported with only selective examples.

In all scientific practice, regardless of the particular theories and methodologies adopted, three general principles are involved. The first is the need for systematic and public accumulation of experience and observations. It involves a search for materials and the incorporation of a variety of people's experiences, not just those of one's own group. It is critical to be clear about how the evidence was collected so that others can do similar research to check or challenge the results.

A second important principle of research is comparative investigation, incorporating data on people in different situations or different societies. A comparative focus is critically important in avoiding ethnocentrism, the tendency to assume that one's own group's way of doing things is more natural and proper than that of others. A sociological study of families, for example, might look at how family life is managed in other countries, other ethnic groups, or at other times in history. Through such comparative evidence, the study might explore the effects that different patterns seem to have on family members.

The third principle, and for philosophers of science the most important, is systematic doubt. Whatever the evidence looks like, it could be false, or misleading, or biased, or badly collected. Key factors may have been overlooked. Assumptions on which the research was based may turn out to be wrong. One may spend decades researching the effects of divorce upon children, only to conclude in the end that divorce is not the key issue at all; it is the poverty that so often accompanies divorce.

It can be very difficult to discover the "real" factors underlying a phenomenon. Some researchers spent three years studying the effects of illumination, rest pauses, and length of the working day on productivity of workers in a telephone assembly factory, only to conclude that these variables had next to nothing to do with productivity. The "real" factor was the attention that workers were getting from the researchers, which made them feel important and valued instead of just one of a mass on the shop floor (Mayo [1933] 1960). Sceptical researchers later disputed this result. They argued that the "real" factors influencing productivity were the onset of the economic depression of the 1930s and the desperate need of two of the five women in the experimental group for money to support extended families when other relatives were unemployed (Carey 1967).

Facts can be elusive things. The ideal approach is to scrutinize the evidence, to question the theories and assumptions of any research, and to ask how the research was carried out and whether alternative strategies or additional data might have made the picture look different. Science is essentially a style of rigorous, systematic, critical thought, not a collection of facts to be memorized.

In sociological endeavour, controversy is critical. Given the biases and blind spots of researchers, the goal of systematic testing for the opposite of one's beliefs is often not attained. Researchers are often more concerned with supporting their theories than with testing them. Scientific journals are reluctant to publish articles that seem to show that starting assumptions were proven incorrect, as if it somehow meant that there must be something wrong with the research. For a long time, the assumption of differences between women and men was so strongly accepted that research that failed to substantiate behavioural differences between the sexes was simply discarded. Nicholson (1984, 4) estimates that for every published study showing differences between the sexes, six finding no difference remained unpublished. It is important that research that challenges established theories, whether those of the researcher or of larger groups, be conducted and be available to other researchers.

While it is essential that individual sociologists test their own data and theories, it is also important that the discipline encourage controversy among sociologists. When researchers disagree among themselves, it leads to a search for new evidence. New questions that might never have been thought of from one point of view can be brought forward by another researcher who started with different assumptions. Mutually incompatible assumptions provide the best challenge to each other. If your theory says that village life is happier and less isolating, and my theory is that city life is best and villages are stifling, our combined evidence is likely to be the best test of each other's assumptions. This is true of all science, not merely the social sciences. The philosopher Feyerabend (1970) has argued that, whenever strong consensus emerges among a body of scientists that they have found the truth, the likely result will be dogmatism. More and more research will be done supporting the same assumptions, and it will be increasingly difficult for anyone to come up with alternative theories. Evidence that might well show the errors in the dominant theory is likely never to come to light because no one will be looking for it. In effect, controversy or lack of agreement over theories in sociology is not a problem, but an asset. It can even be argued that diversity in

theoretical perspectives is a precondition for creative research (Hale 1992).

Current sociology is in no danger of sinking into dogmatic consensus. As will be evident from the next chapter, there is no one theoretical approach that dominates sociological research, but rather a number of schools of thought that begin from every different assumptions and are often very critical of each other's work. To be valuable for science, however, controversy should be organized, not just shouted opinions. Organized controversy entails checking the assumptions of different perspectives and challenging them with alternative evidence. Clarity of basic assumptions is essential.

This book sets out to present the controversies of sociology in an organized way. The theories of classical sociologists are presented in detail. We explore their basic assumptions, the logic behind them, and the consequences or predictions to which they give rise. These consequences are then tested by looking at relevant evidence, drawn mostly from contemporary Canadian research. Controversy among different theorists is used to clarify the strengths and the limitations of different theoretical assumptions by comparing the research results from studies based on different perspectives.

As students, I hope to encourage you to react to, not to accept, the text. Challenge arguments by examining their underlying assumptions, thinking up alternatives, and exploring counter-evidence. The goal is to develop a capacity to shift perspectives and to question assumptions in a systematic way. Howard Boughey (1978, ix), in the introduction to his delightful little book *The Insights of Sociology*, comments that the beginning scholar in the Sanskrit tradition must have the capacity to be aware of eight things simultaneously. This text attempts the lesser version of exploring four approaches to a problem. The basic philosophy of the text is that it is more important for you to develop the capacity for critical questioning than to amass facts.

CHAPTER 2

Thinking Theoretically

This chapter provides the framework for the rest of the text. It sets out four major perspectives that sociologists use to analyse social issues: functionalism, political economy, social constructionism, and feminism. Perspectives are broad ways of thinking about society that structure the kinds of questions that different sociologists find important and that guide research. The most useful way to think about perspectives is not whether they are correct or wrong, but how useful they are for making sense of issues at hand. We will explore what assumptions sociologists make when they draw on different perspectives and the kinds of ideas and insights they provide.

You may well be wondering Why begin with theory? Why not begin with factual descriptions of broad features of Canadian society or personal experiences, and theorize later once we have some evidence? The answer is that we have to draw on theories even to produce a description. Whenever we describe something, we have decide what to pay attention to and what we can ignore, how we are going to organize and name features that seem important, and how to make connections between these features so that our description makes sense for others. Different theoretical perspectives give rise to such markedly different descriptions of aspects of society that even what constitutes a 'fact' can be a matter of dispute. If I were to begin this text with a description of

Canadian society, I would in effect be describing everything from my favourite perspective. After I had finished producing my description, the theory that would look like the best explanation for the evidence, would be the one I had been using to organize the evidence.

For example, I could describe Canadian society in favourable terms as a peaceful liberal democracy, governed by the rule of laws that are framed within an overriding Charter of Rights and Freedoms. Ours is a relatively egalitarian and tolerant multi-ethnic society, in which people enjoy freedom of thought and expression and civil rights. Women and men have guaranteed equality rights under our Charter. Our economy is mostly based on a free-enterprise, capitalist system that offers the large majority of citizens a very high standard of living, that is the envy of much of the world. Canada is one of the best, if not *the* best society in the world in which to live. There are minor problems, of course, including politically the separatist movement in Quebec, and the long-term problem of excessive poverty among Aboriginal or First Nations peoples within Canada. But these are problems that can be solved within our liberal democratic framework.

Alternatively, I could describe Canada in more negative terms as an unstable, branch-plant economy heavily dependent on the United States for our long-term economic survival. Our economy is based mostly on unsustainable resource extraction industries. Some industries, like the cod fishery in Newfoundland, have already collapsed, while other farming and mining enterprises are on the brink of failure. Everywhere, our environments are threatened by global warming, precipitated by the very industries on which we depend. Our privileged standard of living is extracted from misery of masses of exploited workers in other parts of the world. Our myth of equality is belied by the hundreds of thousands of Canadian-born children who live in dire poverty, and hundreds of thousands more whose life chances are stunted by racism and sexism.

I can also describe a Canadian society in which the immense concentration of mass media under the control of a few giant corporations render illusory the myths of democratic values and freedom of thought. We live increasingly in a postmodern world in which we experience only pseudo, managed 'freedoms'. Our emotions are managed to the degree that a season without hockey interests many of us more than news of millions of people dying of starvation and disease elsewhere. Ours is a democracy in which most young people respond to evidence of massive corruption in high places only with cynical disinterest. 'Real' wars happen for us only at the level of entertainment on the television. Meanwhile, our supposedly affluent and privileged society is awash in anti-depressants and illicit drugs. I could also describe a Canada in which men dominate all the important centres of power and influence in society, domestic violence remains one of our most pervasive and least prosecuted crimes, and the circulation of pornography is the most pervasive use of the internet. Described this way, Canada appears more closely akin to George Orwell's classic *1984,* than to a utopia.

Suddenly it does not seem so easy to describe "Canada". The goal of this text is to encourage you to explore the assumptions that give rise to these vastly differing descriptions of society that we come to know as Canada, and to search for and evaluate evidence for different viewpoints. Only as you develop the capacity to get behind any claims to describe 'social reality', to recognize and make explicit the theoretical assumptions implicit in them, and to challenge them with alternative ways of looking and new forms of evidence, will you truly have the freedom to make reasoned decisions for yourself. Each chapter if this text is designed to make visible the interrelationship between description and theory by presenting competing theoretical perspectives in turn and exploring how they shape our understanding of what is going on.

Science and Personal Choice

All social sciences grapple with the tension between freedom and determinism, between individual human agency and constraining social structure. If science succeeds in explaining broad patterns of social behaviour, what does this imply about personal freedom and responsibility to choose how to behave? The box labelled "Choice and Constraints" is designed to help you explore your personal sense of choice and agency—making decisions about your own future and working to achieve your personal goals, and some of the structural constraints that impact on your choices. Currently within Canada, roughly 30 percent of high school graduates go on to university, while 70 percent do not. Proportions of girls and boys who enter university is now roughly equal, although they are attracted to very different kinds of programs. Historically what we see now is vastly different from a century ago when far fewer young men went to university, and almost no women. Exploring the complex mix of personal choices and structural constraints that underlie these patterns will give you a sense of what the agency/structure debate is about.

Sociologists generally agree that what we call 'social structures' are best understood as produced by decisions and actions taken by people in the past. These structures include all the ways of organizing complex nation states like Canada—systems of government, law, administration, education, production, and so on. Few would argue that such structures emerged by themselves or have minds of their own, even though they might seem rigid and coercive at times. We also see these structures as maintained or altered by the decisions and actions of people in the present.

Having said this, we are still left with some big questions (Sharrock 1987, 126–27). We might agree that people make history, but in what ways is this true? We could say that the weight of history and social constraints are so great that people only have a marginal capacity to influence social structures or to make personal choices. The option of bowing to market forces or facing bankruptcy and ruin, for example, does not feel much like free choice. On the other hand, we could hold that people are capable of overcoming the limitations of the circumstances they find themselves in and reshaping those circumstances. But then we have to show how they are able to do this. Social organizations are human creations, but they are nonetheless capable of exacting conformity from vast numbers of people over long time spans and enormous geographic distances. The four major theoretical perspectives that are the focus of this text propose very different ways of thinking about how social structures dominate people and how people respond to, negotiate, change, and recreate social order in their everyday lives.

The remainder of this chapter is designed to give you basic conceptual tools for thinking like sociologists. It is divided into four sections that set out the basic assumptions behind each of four broad theoretical perspectives

in sociology. Sociologists draw upon these assumptions to explore social life and to generate questions about what is going on, why social relations seem to be the way they are, and what might be useful strategies for effective social action. Each section concludes with a discussion of the concept of *culture* to illustrate the striking differences between perspectives. We begin with functionalism, the perspective that dominated North American sociology for many decades.

Choice and Constraints:

If sociologists can predict with some accuracy what kinds of people are more or less likely to enter university, what does that say about your choice in the matter?

You can 'choose' to come to university, however difficult it might be, but how free are you to 'choose' the conditions under which you do it? Can you choose how much money your parents will contribute, or the size of the student loan you can get, the cost of tuition, books, computer, room and board? How free are you to 'choose' the grade point average at which you will be accepted or rejected? Alternatively, you can 'choose' to drop out of university, but how far can you 'choose' or even influence the consequences that would flow from this choice?—your future job chances, your future family income, your status in the neighbourhood?

You might insist that everyone in Canada has the chance to go to university if they are bright enough and work hard enough in school. But how much do you think your choice to continue in school might have been affected if you found yourself facing any of the following circumstances, either separately or in combination:
– there is pervasive hostility and violence in your school directed against people who look like you?
– your friends and family members scoff at university as a waste of time and money relative to on-the-job technical training?
– family life is so stressful that it leaves you feeling depressed and worthless, and unable to concentrate on school work?
– your family is desperately short of money and young children are looking to you to support them now, not four years from now?
– the fees double, and the student-loan program closes down?
– university places are cut and university entrance grades are set 15 points higher than they currently are?
– many people you know have achieved honours degrees but have since been unable to find work in their field?.

Try your hand at developing three lists:
– the factors that contribute to school life being experienced as enjoyable or as unpleasant or even a nightmare;
– the factors that contribute to university being comfortably affordable or extremely difficult;
– the likely financial consequences in your local area of a decision to leave school before grade twelve.

Which of these factors appear sufficiently important that they could change your decision to attend university or not?

Which of these factors can you change by your personal choice, perhaps with the help of your immediate family?

Which of these factors can local teachers or politicians change if they really want to?

Which of these factors are beyond the influence of local people? From where would the most powerful support for change, and powerful opposition to change likely come?

Theory Section One
Functionalism: Society as a Social System

When sociologists use a functionalist perspective, they draw attention to the long-term familiar and predictable character of large-scale social organization, barring only catastrophic events. By far the best predictor of what life will be like next year in your town and region is that it will be much the same as last year. The central assumption is that social life can most usefully be understood by thinking in very broad terms about society as a relatively self-contained and **self-maintaining system** of interrelated parts. This social system tends towards stability and balance over time through continual organizational adjustments between the parts. In other words, societies tend towards **dynamic equilibrium**. Sociologists are interested in how this overall structural equilibrium is maintained across generations, and they seek answers in the ways in which different parts of society are structured and functionally interrelated to meet the needs of the system as a whole. Parts, or the constituent organizations and institutions of society, are studied both for how they contribute to the system as a whole, and also how they are organized as sub-systems in themselves, comprised of functioning parts.

To get a sense of how to analyse society using a functionalist perspective, think about how biologists study an animal's body. Biologists think of a body as a system, with all the body parts or organs carrying out distinct functions that work together to keep the body healthy, that is, in a state of dynamic equilibrium. They study particular organs, such as a heart, to determine what its primary function is, and how it is structured to perform this function. This can lead to ever more detailed research into the specialized structure of heart muscle, electro-chemical impulses that maintain the precise heart rhythm, and the like. Medical researchers also probe further into what happens when a heart malfunctions, to identify structural problems and how they might be fixed. Biologists also study how specialized sets of organs are integrated into functioning subsystems of the body, like the circulatory system, the nervous system, the hormone system, and how these in turn impact upon and regulate each other.

Society as a functioning system

It is a daunting task to identify all the functional requirements of a healthy society, although there is some agreement about important needs. All societies must work with the natural environment to physically sustain its members and to pattern heterosexual relations to produce and raise children. Societies need some orderly means of allocating critical functions among competent members and ensuring that such work is performed regularly. This in turn requires adequate systems of decision-making authority, communication, and administration. Societies also need some means to teach and motivate generations of members to participate in society in appropriate ways, and to effectively control disruptive forms of behaviour and emotions (Adapted from Aberle et. al. 1950). Individual societies, in turn, can be analysed as subsystems functioning within an increasingly interconnected global system of transnational economic, political, and legal institutions.

Functionalist theory also draws attention to systemic dysfunctions, when the requirements of healthy social systems are not effectively being met. The state of civil war is a stark indication of the failure of political institutions within individual states; famine is an extreme measure of the failure of economic institutions; pervasive illiteracy a measure of the failure of educational institutions, and so on. At the beginning of the twenty-first century the staggering number of civil wars raging in societies across the African subcontinent, parts of South-East Asia, the Middle East, the former Soviet Union, and in Latin America, testify to the fragility of many contemporary social systems, as do widespread famines, the rampant spread of AIDS, and the millions of refugees and displaced persons worldwide. Closer to home, the 1995 Quebec referendum on sovereignty where Quebeckers came within one percentage vote of opting out of Canada, and rumblings of western alienation, remind us that Canadian political institutions are not functioning as well as they might. Many First Nations communities within Canada also show multiple signs of systemic dysfunction, with levels of poverty, family breakdown, substance abuse, suicides, and morbidity and mortality rates similar to those in the least-developed countries in the world.

Advisors to governments and to peace-keeping teams use functionalist analysis to guide the reconstruction of countries devastated by war or natural disasters. Typically first priority is given to 'humanitarian' needs for food, medicine, and clean drinking water. Then attention turns to providing law and order, governance, and all the complex organizations and institutions that sustain commerce, education, transportation, and so on. Directors know that if they fail to set priorities reasonably well, people may die from hunger, cold and disease, or the society collapse into chaos.

Most sociological work in the functionalist tradition focuses on more manageable questions of how particular institutions within a society are structured and the functions they perform. Policy analysts in many professions draw upon the insights of functionalist theory to address social problems (Burnett 2004; Curran 2003). Families, collectively referred to as 'the institution of the family', are generally considered the most basic organizing unit within any society. Families function to produce and nurture young people and to meet the intimate daily material and emotional needs of people. The broader education system, comprised of networks of schools, colleges, universities, school boards, text-book producers, and the like, builds upon the specialized functions of the family by teaching young people the knowledge they will need to perform adult work, and reinforcing collective values and standards of behaviour of the society. The economic system, with its myriad of productive enterprises, produces and distributes material goods and services. Political institutions organize collective goals and legitimate power relations, and so on. The multiple organizations that form parts of each of these systems can in turn be studied as functioning systems in their own right.

Complexities in functionalist analysis result from several related factors. Firstly, any one organization or social arrangement always functions as part of a wider network of related organizations, and hence full analysis requires concern with external relations as well as internal operations. Quebec and First Nations communities function as distinct societies within Canada, while Canada functions as a small, prosperous nation state in global networks of transnational institutions. Secondly, social institutions are multi-functional. Too simplistic a definition of core functions can cloud understanding of what is happening. You might argue that the intended function of a school is to impart knowledge and skills, with success measured by formal examinations. But it would be a serious error to assume that preparation for examinations is all that schools do. Others may argue that teaching cultural and religions values, and patriotic commitments are even more important than teaching technical skills. Schools also teach social skills. Severely learning-disabled children who cannot follow the academic curriculum may still have much to gain from being part of age-graded school classes. Distinctive functions may generate competing priorities and fierce struggles between subgroups over allocation of institutional resources.

Functionalists distinguish between **manifest** or intended functions of social institutions and **latent** functions, those that are less obvious and not directly intended, but which may still be important for society as a whole and for the people directly involved (Merton 1967, 73–138). Latent functions may explain the continuation of social organizations long after their intended function has become irrelevant or even devalued.

A sanatorium set up for people with tuberculosis may continue after the epidemic has passed, as people struggle to find new uses for the centre because the jobs bring money into the community. Similarly, universities may be financed by governments primarily to promote a highly qualified work-force, but many students come for very different reasons. Increasing numbers of retired people register for university courses, long after they have ceased to be concerned with career advancement, because they enjoy the intellectual challenge and camaraderie of campus life. The manifest functions of sports may appear to be physical exercise and entertainment, but their importance may be eclipsed by the powerful latent function of promoting community spirit and nationalism (Merkel 2003). Many Canadian universities devote surprisingly large proportions of limited budgets to hockey teams and athletics scholarships for these reasons.

Latent functions, the unintended consequences of actions, are not necessarily positive for all members of society. Collective organizations may have some effects that are **dysfunctional**. The sociological theorist, Robert Merton, has argued that perhaps the most important contribution of functionalist theory is to reveal unintended and unwanted consequences of social organization. The expansion of formal education, for example, has as one of its consequences, the enforced segregation of young people from adults and the adult world of work. It also prolongs the state of adolescence or 'childhood' well beyond physical and sexual adulthood. Can you think of some potentially dysfunctional aspects of this arrangement? From the standpoint of people within these organizations, Giddens argues (1984, 293), unintended consequences most often result from restricted knowledge of all the wider and longer-term consequences of choices. Students who quit school early to take jobs may see the autonomy, the adult status, and the fun that come with earning money, without seeing how they are trapping themselves into a lifetime of dead-end, low-skilled work. On the other hand, people who commit themselves to years of higher education may not see the consequences of heavy debt loads and delayed marriage and child-bearing years.

A further factor that complicates functionalist analysis is change. As we noted above, the functionalist perspective is primarily concerned with explaining how the social system is maintained in a state of equilibrium or balance. But this equilibrium is dynamic, not static. Any social organization that fails to change in response to changing external conditions risks becoming seriously dysfunctional. The functionalist perspective draws heavily upon biological sciences in identifying **differentiation** and **specialization** as fundamental processes involved in adaptive change of social systems. A classic example of functionalist analysis of systemic change is the gradual shift from family to school as the site of education. In less technologically advanced societies, families perform the major functions of nurturing children, educating them in the skills needed for adult life, and organizing economic production. However, as societies become more technologically advanced, the family is no longer adequate to meet all these system needs. The three primary functions of nurturing, educating, and producing become differentiated into different institutions. Families have become more specialized in performing the nurturing function, while schools specialize in education, and factories and businesses specialize in production. Similarly, in small organizations tasks may be relatively undifferentiated with a few individuals doing everything, but as the organization become larger and more complex, tasks are differentiated and divided among specialists.

In focussing attention on these adaptive changes in social systems, the functionalist perspective also points to important roots of dysfunction and conflict in failure to adapt to the needs of a changing environment. Conflict can be functional for a social system in promoting a willingness to change and thus overcoming rigidity in the system (Coser 1956).

Social Systems and Individual Members

A theoretical perspective that focusses on large-scale social systems must address the critical question of how to integrate individual people into the model without them appearing like mindless cogs in a machine, and also how such integration is smoothly perpetuated from one generation to another. The functionalist perspective conceptualizes this integration through the ideas of **role**, **socialization**, and **culture**.

Role

The concept of **role** focuses attention on typical and expected patterns of behaviour, particularly those regarded as appropriate and proper in specified situations (Biddle and Thomas 1966). The violation of these normatively valued expectations generate both surprise and disapproval. Institutions can be thought of as organized collections of interacting roles. An individual role can be thought of as the smallest unit of analysis for social institutions, the level at which actions of individual people are the central focus. No two individuals ever respond in exactly the same way in similar situations, but nonetheless it is rarely difficult to pick out common patterns. The idea of role draws attention to these patterns. Think about school teachers you have known. Each will be easily distinguished from the others, and each classroom experience different. Yet all teachers have certain behaviour patterns in common, certain expected and valued ways of behaving in classrooms, that make them recognizably teachers, and not janitors or secretaries, or parents who may have helped out in school classes.

Roles and role expectations are relatively easy to see in formal organizations like schools and businesses. They are typically defined by jobs and job descriptions. In bureaucratic organizations the expectations, obligations, and minimum standards for performance are usually set out in great detail. In informal settings, normatively expected patterns of behaviour are less precise but evident nonetheless. The role expectations for school teachers are more closely bureaucratically defined than the role of mother of school children, but teachers can nonetheless articulate a set of normative expectations they have for mothers. People similarly know the limits of acceptable behaviour in settings like churches, restaurants, ball games, or family gatherings, even though they are not written down.

Functionalist theory regards these mutually recognized sets of expectations as centrally important in promoting stability in social interaction over time. Functionalist analysis commonly uses terms like *actor* and *role-incumbent* to shift the focus of attention from individual personalities to patterned expectations for behaviour. Different individuals can come and go as teachers, but the role of teacher remains constant as a predefined and recognizable feature of the school context.

The concepts of **role-set** and **role strain** focus on how different role expectations interact and overlap. A **role-set** usually refers to the sum of all other roles with which the incumbent of one specific role interacts. A school teacher, for example, interacts with pupils in class, with parents of these pupils, with other teachers, the school principal, members of the school board, and others, in the course of performing the teacher role. The notion of role-set is also sometimes used to refer to the sum of all different roles that one individual performs. A teacher may also be a parent, a spouse, a child, a church member, city councillor, golf buddy, and so on.

The concept of **role-strain** or **role conflict** refers to the tensions that can occur when the expectations and obligations associated with related roles clash. Different actors in a system of roles may have conflicting expectations of what a particular role entails. Teachers, for example, may find that parents want different things from them as teachers than does the school principal, and so have difficulty keeping both satisfied. Also, teachers may find themselves juggling competing obligations and expectations as parent, employee, and church member.

Socialization

This theoretical focus on shared normative expectations for appropriate and proper role behaviour gives rise to a series of questions. How do people come to recognize and adopt roles? How do people learn role expectations? How are role expectations transmitted over time as different people take up and leave roles? What motivates people to conform to social expectations?

A basic assumption within the functionalist perspective is that participation in social systems is for the most part voluntary. The large majority of individual members must want to conform to social expectations for any long-term stability or equilibrium to be possible. Even prisons rely heavily on the willingness of prisoners to conform to the rules in order to function. So the big question is: What motivates most individuals to participate willingly, competently, and consistently in social institutions, and to conform sufficiently well to the patterned expectations associated with multiple roles, to bring about the long-term stable functioning of social systems? The functionalist perspective sees life-long processes of teaching and learning, termed **socialization**, together with a shared system of meanings and values termed **culture**, as the foundations of social order. What follows are some basic assumptions about how this socialization process works.

Children learn basic expectations for social behaviour primarily by watching and emulating the people around them. Parents are pivotally important as role models, but so are other care-givers, relatives, neighbours, teachers, and arguably also television characters. Favourite games for young children commonly include play-acting 'mommy' or 'daddy', and other familiar roles. Children and adults may imaginatively 'take on the roles of others'—imagining what it might be like to do different jobs, or to be in different social situations. Later, this role-play is likely to be supplemented by more formal role-training or instruction in what is expected. Over a lifetime we take on many roles, first as youngest child and sibling, older sibling, school pupil, child-minder, parent, breadwinner, citizen, and the like. Functionalists think of the sum of all these roles as together making up our social selves. The social roles we play are not merely external patterns to which we conform; they become part of how we come to see ourselves, part of our identity.

A further important assumption underpinning role theory is that, for the most part, people want approval and acceptance. We appreciate receiving approval ourselves and reciprocally we tend to give approval to others who behave as we expect them to. Over time, we come to **internalize** the expectations around roles that we play, to feel that they are right and proper. This internalization process explains an important anomaly in functionalist theory. While the perspective conceptualizes society in very broad systemic terms, the actual behaviour of people is explained primarily by reference to the attitudes and values that people hold, and to the family backgrounds in which primary values are learned.

Controls over Individual Behaviour

The two concepts of role expectations and socialization account for how most individuals conform most of the time, and for societal reactions to lapses in conformity. Social controls at the level of individual behaviour can be thought of as circles of constraints. (Berger 1963, 68–70). Voluntary conformity is sustained by the innermost experience of guilt. Individuals internalize their role expectations and feel a sense of personal failure when we do not live up to them. Our desire for approval from people close to us acts as a secondary circle of constraint. If these intimate pressures are not sufficient to ensure reasonable conformity, then economic sanctions usually come into play. Non-conformists can expect to find that rewards and incentives which normally go along with approval will be withheld. In particular, they may find themselves unable to get or retain jobs. Finally, if economic sanctions fail to check deviance, more overt punishments may be administered. Children who break family rules may find themselves grounded and their allowance withheld. Adults who break societal laws may end up in prison. However, any social system, be it at the level of a family or a nation state, that must rely heavily upon punishments and force to exact conformity from members, is inherently less stable than one whose members voluntarily conform.

Culture

The concept of **culture** is centrally important in the functionalist perspective, because it is understood as the central mechanism holding all the elements of social systems together. We will first describe it below as a concept within the functionalist theoretical model. Then we will return to it later to illustrate how it has been used as a tool within functionalist research to explore Canadian national and global relations.

In its broadest sense, the concept of culture refers to the overarching system of shared meanings, beliefs and values prevailing within a society, along with a shared material culture of scientific knowledge and technology. Shared beliefs and sentiments form the basis of moral order in society. The ritual practices that express these collective beliefs function to unite people together in a sense of community.

Culture is species-specific. All animals communicate with each other, but only humans communicate through abstract symbols, especially language. Language has critical survival value for humans, making possible advanced learning, and complex systems of cooperation. Within the discipline of anthropology, which focusses on simpler societies, culture is commonly defined as 'the whole way of life of a people', encompassing all that individuals would need to know to function as competent members of the society. In more complex societies, characterized by high levels of specialization and differentiation, shared culture is not so all-encompassing. Culture is viewed as a flexible system in which core values and meanings will be held in common by members of the society, but with much subcultural variation, reflecting distinctive social positions and experiences. This concept of **subculture** can be applied to distinctive communities within wider societies, such as villages,

neighbourhoods, clubs, members of particular professions or work-groups, and so on.

A form of subculture that functionalist theory identifies as particularly significant is that associated with ethnic minorities, people with distinctive origins who may share distinctive languages, religious traditions, and the like. These differences may vary from minor aspects of personal life, like dress, food preferences and family traditions, to broad patterns of private and public behaviour that set one group of people apart from others. The term **assimilation** refers to the process of change by which members of once highly distinctive subgroups come increasingly to adopt the cultural patterns of the wider social system.

Culture is transmitted across generations through socialization. The basic assumption here is that while members may not always live up to community values, they generally know what these values are and tend to use them to evaluate their own and others' behaviour. Through internalizing the generalized culture of their community, people are already oriented towards appropriate patterns of behaviour even before learning detailed expectations associated with particular roles. Culture is thus viewed as an essential mechanism serving to integrate roles within a society and to reduce friction between them. In complex societies, cultural values are widely codified into laws and religion and transmitted through media, literature, schools, religious organizations, symbols, customs and traditions.

Shared language forms the core of any cultural system. Saussure (1964) defines language as essentially a system of signs, comprising the *signifier*—the words or images used, and the *signified*—the object to which it refers. He stresses, firstly, that the relationship between signifier and signified is essentially arbitrary. There is no inherent link between the sound 'mother' and what this word refers to. Different languages use different sounds. Secondly, any word conveys meaning only in relation to an entire system of meaning or language, not in isolation. The word 'mother', for example, can be defined only in relation to the associated words 'child' and 'father'. Language is a system of grammar and symbols. Individual users must conform to this system in order to be understood.

Saussure argues further that language does not merely apply names to an already coherently known reality. Language actually organizes reality. As we apply names to chaotic sensory experiences we create some sense of meaningful order. People live in symbolic universes, experiencing the world as culturally constructed through language, and hence in some respects always unique to a given language system. For example, English words like 'left', 'right', and 'centre' work to organize a cacophony of political views into a semblance of coherent orientations. Words like 'adolescent', 'teenager', and 'retiree' are meaningful only within cultural systems that prolong 'childhood' well beyond physical puberty, and that end productive employment well before physical senility or death. Such terms may have no direct translation and make no sense in other cultural systems. The Mi'qmac and Maliseet languages have no word for 'boundary' (Bear-Nicholas 2004), reflecting the absence of a concept of ownership of land in pre-contact First Nations communities in the Maritimes. European meanings of terms for boundary and land ownership were not translatable into Aboriginal cultural systems, resulting in serious discrepancies in interpretations of the meaning of treaties.

Language usage differs also according to how well community members know each other and how similar their lifestyles are. In close knit communities members can talk in condensed or restricted ways and be readily understood, while more elaborate and detailed forms of communication are required to get meanings across among strangers. (Wuthnow 1984, 103–4).

The study of language—or semiotics—provides a model for studying how people convey meanings through a host of other non-linguistic signs and gestures. Bodily gestures like facial expressions, hand signals, posture—such as slouched or upright, and spatial distance between bodies, convey culturally specific meanings like welcome or disapproval, acceptance or rejection, insolence or submission. Travellers to foreign cultures are commonly warned to learn the locally acceptable signs to avoid inadvertently offending people. Mannette (1992) suggests that subtle differences in culturally-learned body language, reticence, clothing and demeanour, and tone of voice between Native defendants and non-Native jurors can convey dangerously flawed messages about probable guilt in criminal trials. Barthes (1971) analyses a famous photograph of a black soldier saluting a French flag to clarify how the flag signifies France, the man's clothing signifies the armed forces, the salute signifies notions of duty, service, and obedience, and the man's dark skin signifies the history of French imperialism and the subjugation of people in the colonies. The photograph is unique, but the system of signs, or shared meanings by which the photograph communicates complex abstract messages to viewers, is highly structured. Advertisers routinely utilize these cultural associations between visual signs and abstract mean-

ings to link their products to desirable states (Turner 1990, 21; Douglas 1979). The makers of *ski yogurt* show their product being eaten by people engaged in sailboarding, hang-gliding, surfing and skiing to create the image of yogurt as a life-style product associated with youth, vigour and health. People also routinely use these shared symbol systems to convey impressions about themselves to others, including complex messages around sexual availability, religious orientation, community of origin, institutional membership, and the like.

Ritual practices are also inherent features of cultural systems that function to signify membership in a society and in various sub-communities, and simultaneously to strengthen integration. In Canada, we have national holidays, complete with military music, flag-waving, and fireworks, hockey nights showing national teams on television, and a host of other staged political events that signify and strengthen national unity. At the local and intimate level, everyday rituals like tidying, cleaning, and putting things in their place, and serving particular kinds of food on particular occasions, carry similar symbolic meanings, reinforcing among participants a sense of belonging and conforming to a shared moral order in the home and beyond (Douglas 1966, 1979; Wuthnow et. al., 1984, 87).

Functionalist analysis of the integrative power of shared culture does not assume that all members of a given society will conform to the values, beliefs and expected practices associated with a cultural system. What it does assume is that competent members will learn through socialization to recognize and understand these core elements, and will recognize non-conformity as deviant.

Culturally shared expectations for behaviour may not always function in positive ways for all members of a society. They may have latent dysfunctional consequences, especially when they fail to adapt to changing external conditions. Core values of individual competitiveness, and striving for consumer goods, if carried too far, can undermine other community values like compassion and sharing, and promote long-term environmental degradation and depletion of natural resources. Striving to maximize efficiency and time management can foster dysfunctional excesses like a workaholic mentality, regimentation, and diets surfeited in fast foods. These conflict with other cultural values, such as collegiality at work, a family life, and community health.

The functionalist view of societies as comprising systems of inter-related parts fosters awareness of how excesses in one subsystem can lead to dysfunctions in another and give rise to pressures to reestablish balance.

Systemic Conflict and Dysfunction

Functionalist theory focuses attention primarily on mechanisms that account for dynamic equilibrium in social systems. Weaknesses or inadequacies in the functioning of these basic mechanisms are used to account for conflict and disequilibrium or the breakdown of order. At the level of role performance, shared role expectations are assumed to promote stability. Hence, divergent role expectations promote instability. The emotional, nurturing expectations of family roles, for example, may clash with the instrumental expectations of work roles whenever the two role sets are inadequately separated. Processes of socialization are assumed to explain conformity to role expectations and cultural values. Hence, faulty socialization explains deviance. Children whose parents are bad role-models are likely to learn bad practices. Violent parents breed violent children. Desire for approval promotes conformity. Hence, indifference to approval promotes deviance. Broken homes, or shallow emotional ties between children and parents promote shallow concern for parental values. Consistency among many salient role models promotes conformity. Hence, inconsistency weakens it. Exposure to media violence, or bad influences outside the home is likely to undermine other good influences. Hence, children who grow up in high-crime neighbourhoods are more likely to learn criminal attitudes and values than children in low-crime neighbourhoods.

These relationships are not viewed as deterministic, because there are multiple sources of socialization that may be inconsistent. The negative effects of dysfunctional families may be countered by more positive socialization from other sources, and vice versa. Nonetheless, family breakdown is considered a pivotal factor in social disorder.

Other kinds of social conflicts are assumed to stem from systemic maladjustments. Societal equilibrium is understood as dynamic and not static, because societies must continually change to respond to changing circumstances. Balance between functional subsystems of society promote overall integration. Hence, imbalance is assumed to weaken societal integration. Rapid change in any one part of a social system is likely to generate conflicts with other subsystems. A common experience is for economic subsystem to respond more rapidly to external pressures than the cultural subsystem, with such cultural lag generating high stress for individuals caught between discordant expectations. In such circumstances, conflict within the social system may be functional for pressuring more systemic adaptation to change and preventing excessive rigidity. Other systemic conflicts are generated by competing interests. Giddens (1984, 310–319) cites the examples of governments depending heavily on revenues from private business enterprise, and higher income earners paying more in taxes for publicly funded services like buses, schools and health care while they themselves use cars and favour private schools and clinics. Government institutions play a critical role in the management of such competing interests.

Summary

In Summary, we now have all the core assumptions that underlie the functionalist perspective. Society is seen as a system of interrelated institutions that function together as a dynamic whole. The voluntary participation of individual members of society is sustained through the core mechanisms of role expectations and socialization. The overarching cultural system of shared meanings, beliefs, values holds the entire social system together. Culture is internalized at the individual level through socialization, and it functions to integrate diverse roles at the institutional level and diverse institutions at the societal level.

The Functionalist Perspective on National Cultures in Global Society

This last section uses the concept of national cultures to illustrate the distinctive approach of functionalist analysis. We will refer back to this section later to show how strikingly different the descriptions and analyses of Canadian society are when viewed through other theoretical perspectives.

Canadian sociologists have long been interested in trying to characterize what is distinctively Canadian as against American national cultural values. This interest was promoted, Brym suggests (1989, ch. 1), by the large numbers of American sociologists who filled positions in Canadian universities during the 1960s. American sociologists working within the functionalist perspective have tended to view the United States as a leading example of political and economic modernity. Typically, they explain this in terms of the distinctive culture that arose from the common experience of frontier settlement by rugged individualists, many of them Protestant nonconformists fleeing persecution in Europe. These experiences promoted a system of cultural values that emphasize individualism, free enterprise, private property, and rejection of religious authority, tempered by an abstract 'civil religion' embodied in the Declaration of Independence, and presidential oaths of office (Bellah 1990). Canadians, in contrast, seemed more conservative than Americans, with a greater tendency to respect authority and hierarchy, and to accept state control over the economy. The people who emigrated to the colonies of Upper Canada and Quebec were more likely to be Anglicans and Roman Catholic, or British Empire Loyalists who left America after the revolution of 1776. Analysts suggest that these relatively hierarchical and authoritarian churches inculcated cultural values of deep respect for authority (Clark 1968; Lipset 1976, 1985; Porter 1965, 1979). Lipset further concludes that English Canadians are generally more elitist and accepting of class divisions, less entrepreneurial or achievement oriented, less willing to take risks, more oriented to collective than individual interests and more accepting of ethnic differences among people that are Americans (Brym 1989, 28). Horowitz further suggests (1985) that French Canada inherited a feudal political structure, and English Canada an aristocratic Tory political culture that conceptualizes society as a hierarchically ordered system rather than the liberal view of society as an agglomeration of individuals. These roots in different political cultures, Horowitz suggests, explains why a social-democratic party emerged in Canada but not in America.

Such sweeping generalizations about American and Canadian political cultures necessarily admit of many exceptions. But there is nonetheless a sense that it is meaningful to speak of different political cultures in the two countries. These differences are seen as reflected in far stronger support within the Canadian electorate for a federal medicare system, and for higher taxation to support a more generous social safety net. Cultural differences are reflected also in strikingly lower rates of violent crime in Canada. Different political cultures were also reflected in Canadian federal government decision not to support the American-led initiative to invade Iraq in 2003 without the prior approval of the United Nations. Kalberg (2003, 17) similarly argues that the appeal to missionary idealism "to establish democracy in Iraq" and to "liberate the Iraqi people" resonate with American people still deeply influenced by the cultural legacies of ascetic fundamentalist Protestantism. German people, in contrast, reacted with almost universal scepticism, assuming that the "real motives" must be more secular national self interest.

Cultural Integration in Multi-cultural societies.

The level of cultural integration in any society is seen as a particularly problematic issue from the functionalist perspective. A shared cultural system is assumed to be a central integrating mechanism in social systems. Hence, cultural diversity potentially threatens societal integration, risking division and conflict. Canada does not conform to this theoretical ideal of a cohesive community united through a single language and cultural system. Canada has two official languages—English and French, as well as some sixty or more First Nations languages and a host of heritage languages spoken in immigrant communities. These diverse languages reflect and reinforce a diversity of cultures. Relations between French and English Canada have been characterised as 'two solitudes' with strong political movement within Quebec pressuring for separate sovereign status (Nesbitt-Larking, Paul 2001, 264–9). The Quebec referendum on sovereignty in 1995 failed by a margin of less than 1 percent. Had it succeeded the discussion of Canadian cultural institutions and societal integration in this text might well be very different.

Many immigrant communities continue to have close contacts and cultural ties with their communities of origin, facilitated by the Internet, satellite radio and television, and telephones, and they continue to retain their mother tongue and other elements of culture. Even within the dominant white English-speaking majority it is difficult to speak of a single unified cultural system. A more accurate characterization is that of fragmentation, with a diversity of 'faith communities' including Christian, non-Christian and atheistic and a multiplicity of family forms and sexual practices. There is also an eclectic mixing of foods, clothing, musical and other artistic styles, borrowed from around the world. The global reach of mass media makes it impossible for Canadians to isolate themselves from these influences, even if they should wish to. The concept of *postmodernism* refers, in part, to this experience of cultural fragmentation and hybridization.

Globalization and National Culture

Two competing arguments have developed out of functionalist analysis concerning the future of national cultures, loosely referred to as neo-liberal and neo-conservative. The dominant neo-liberal argument is that globalization—the reality of global networks of communications and commerce, has already profoundly altered the nature of tradition and culture. Global systems of communications and global migration inevitably intrude on traditional cultures. In the face of this reality, Giddens argues (2000, 67) a shift in cultural values towards rational, tolerant, and cosmopolitan acceptance of diverse autonomous subcultures becomes essential for wider societal and global integration. Giddens sees the main threat to stability or equilibrium in cosmopolitan societies not as diversity, but as fundamentalism in religious, family or ethnic forms. He defines fundamentalism as 'beleaguered tradition', characterized not by the content of beliefs, but by how they are defended or asserted—the non-reflexive insistence on conformity to a pre-existing set of practices. Traditions, he argues, still play an important role in giving social stability and continuity to social life. But they are becoming more cosmopolitan and accepting of diversity, and also more obviously commercialized and contrived for the tourist trade. He predicts further that nationalist sentiments will decline as citizens identify more with super-national systems of governance like the European Union, and the North American Free Trade Agreement.

It is also widely predicted in functionalist analyses that modern cultural values will become increasingly defined in unifying secular and rational terms around values of political democracy and human rights, while potentially divisive expression of religious faiths will become privatized and separated from institutions of government (Berger, 1967). In Canada, such adaptation has taken the form of The Canadian Charter of Rights and Freedoms. The Charter endorses official commitment to bilingualism in English and French at the federal level, an official policy of multiculturalism, and respect for Aboriginal treaty rights. All government-run institutions are officially 'secular', and religious attendance within Canada has been dropping steadily over many decades (Bibby 1993; 2002).

Another line of theory developing from functionalist analysis, however, suggests that pressures of globalization may work to heighten commitment to nationalism and distinctive national cultures, rather than promoting cosmopolitan cultural values. One reason for this, Bernal suggests (2004) in his analysis of Eritrea's struggle for independence from Ethiopia, is the political recognition given to *nations* as sub-system units in the organization of global political and economic systems. It is specifically as nation states that small societies can claim a seat in the United Nations Organization, and

claim eligibility for assistance from international agencies such as the World Bank and the International Monetary Fund (ibid. 14). The added international clout that national status would confer over merely provincial status is not lost on the people living in Quebec. It may also play a part in the insistence by political leaders of the Aboriginal peoples in Canada that their communities be recognized as *First Nations*, and that their signed treaties with Canada be recognised as having international status (Bear-Nicholas 2004). More generally, the spread of global consumer culture has proven compatible with heightened interest in the celebration of local cultures. Quebecois and Acadian nationalism both reflect these patterns, as do the revival of heritage and First Nations languages and cultures.

A stronger statement of this position, sometimes referred to as neo-conservatism, is that national sentiments, associated with a strong core of shared religious values is essential for societal integration in the face of globalization. Strong national cultures function to promote the internalization of shared cultural values by the mass of citizens and so to promote social harmony and discourage anti-social, deviant behaviour. An essential function of political institutions—in conjunction with mass media, educational, and religious institutions, is thus the revitalization of a unifying national culture.

Canada and the United States have tended to take different positions between these two poles. Canadian political institutions have taken some steps to promote nationalism. The government-funded national radio and television networks, the Canadian Broadcasting Corporation (CBC), and the French-language equivalent, Société Radio Canada (SRC), have an official mandate to promote Canadian national unity and to reflect bilingualism and multiculturalism. The ill-fated sponsorship program launched by the federal liberal party under Jean Chretien after was intended to promote a federal presence at social and sporting events in Quebec after the 1995 referendum on separatism. However, these efforts have been largely perfunctory, with limited teeth or money invested in them.

In the United States, in contrast, there hare been far stronger pressures to promote national unity and a swing towards fundamentalism in family and religious values. The widely predicted shift towards secularism and privatization of religious expression has not happened in contemporary American society (Berger 1999, Diamond 1998; Kintz and Lesage 1998). Nor does it hold for many Islamic societies (Esposito 2002). We explore these issues further in many later chapters of this text, concerned with religion, family, and race and ethnic relations.

Theory Section Two
The Political Economy or Marxist Perspective

The political economy perspective challenges us to think about society in very different ways from functionalist analysis, to ask different kinds of questions and to pay attention to different features of society. As you will see, this perspective gives rise to strikingly different descriptions of what matters most about Canadian society.

It is useful at the start to clarify the distinction between 'conflict theory' as often described in North American sociology textbooks, and political economy theory, which has its roots in European sociology. Both fault functionalist analysis for failing to pay sufficient attention to issues of conflict, inequality and power within social systems. Both approaches concur in emphasizing economic inequality and struggle over access to economic resources as critical features of society, and they concur also in giving more attention to power relations in the maintenance of social order. Conflict theory typically focusses attention on institutions within society that manage conflicts over resources, including competing political parties, trade unions, labour laws, social safety nets, and the like. Political economy theory pushes us to go beyond this analysis of conflict management to explore the structural features of capitalist economies that routinely produce and exacerbate the inequalities that generate the conflicts in the first place. Theoretically, what most distinguishes political economy theory from conflict theory is the exploration of structural problems or 'contradictions' that are built into the way contemporary capitalist economies function.

Karl Marx (1818–1882) is the acknowledged founder of political economy theory. Marx devoted his life's work to an analysis and critique of the social conditions he saw around him in nineteenth-century England, during the early period of industrialization. The suffering of factory workers and their families inspired him to write *Das Kapital* [Capital], a scathing critique of the economic system now known as **capitalism**. What Marx saw in industrializing Britain was not a society in equilibrium but a society riven by conflict, inequality, and turmoil. His powerful writings analyse what he saw as a long historical process through which an emerging elite of manufacturers and businessmen amassed wealth and power, particularly through colonial expansion, and came to dominate and displace the old aristocracy. Meanwhile at the bottom, masses of impoverished people, dislocated from the land, were flooding into cities to seek wage-work in the factories as their only means of survival. Marx wanted to understand how this economic order had emerged historically, how it worked, and how it might change.

Economy and Social Order

The first assumption of the political economy perspective is that the economy is the central defining feature of all societies. Political economy theory shares with functionalism the view of society as a system of interrelated institutions, but with the economy rather than culture or family as the central focus How people collectively organize to exploit available natural resources and productive tools is the foundation that shapes all other features of society. As Marx expresses it, economy is the *base* and other societal institutions the *superstructure*. This does not mean that the economy is all that matters. It means rather that we need to begin with the economy to fully understand the functioning of other societal institutions. For Canada and most other contemporary societies this is the global corporate capitalist economic system. Political economics analyse political institutions, for example, from the standpoint of how they respond to and facilitate corporate profits, how they manage labour relations and defuse potential for revolt by economically disadvantaged classes of people. Legal institutions are studied for how they manage property relations, and how they function as arenas for struggle between employers and workers. Cultural institutions are analysed for how prevailing beliefs and values reflect the interests of the dominant economic class and work to excuse and justify economic inequalities. Similar questions can be raised for all societal institutions—education, religion, family, and the like. These are qualitatively different kinds of questions from the functionalist view of meeting systemic societal needs.

Why is the economy considered so central? Marx reasoned that people must produce in order to live. People need food, shelter, and clothing in order to survive. Hence, they must organize themselves collectively to work with the aid of productive tools to transform available natural resources into products that meet their needs. The concept of **economy** refers to the *mode of production*—how people organize to turn resources into food, and the *relations of production*—specifically the kind of relations between people that arise through this organization.

Marx was centrally concerned with the organization of power over access to, control over, and exploitation of productive resources, and thus control over the wealth or surplus generated human labour power. He argues that all history can be understood as the history of **class struggles**, the collective struggles of peoples subordinated within any particular system of production to overthrow that system and replace it with one that would be more productive and more widely inclusive.

Simple hunting and gathering economies, in which small groups of families cooperate to hunt wild animals and gather edible plants, was egalitarian in that everyone enjoyed similar access to resources available. Such economies, however, can only sustain small numbers of people at a low and uncertain standard of living. Settled agriculture, based on the domestication of cereals and beans, and herd animals for productive energy and transportation as well as for food, provided much greater scope for food production and thus sustained larger populations and more complex social organization (Diamond 1999). Inequalities emerged between elites who gained control over the productive resources of land and animals and managed the surplus produced, and the mass of people who worked the land. This feudal mode of production prevailed in Europe and much of Asia over many centuries. The industrial revolution transformed productive potential by harnessing the mechanical energy from steam engines and later fossil fuels to drive machines. Machines made possible the mass production of goods because energy was no longer confined by the limitations of humans and animal energy. Increasing surplus production in turn promoted a population explosion, and the development of cities in which most people no longer depended on access to land for survival.

Marx saw emerging private ownership of the means of industrial production or 'capital' as heralding profound changes in the organization of societies. Those who gained control over these productive resources—the capitalists, gained the capacity to generate and control enormous and potentially unlimited surplus production, while those lacking such resources have only their labour power to sell. They may be willing and ready to work, but without access to land or to productive machinery they have no means to produce anything, and so must sell their capacity to work to those who control the means of production, in return for wages. Hence,

Marx argues, two great classes of people emerge in capitalist societies, capitalists who own the means of production and wage-workers who do not.

In classical Marxist theory, the term **class** refers specifically to relationship to the means of production, not to income groups. Workers whose skills are scarce and in high demand by capitalists may command vastly superior incomes and standards of living than unskilled workers or those easily replaced. But when the crunch comes, these still depend on selling their labour power to capitalist employers. They still risk being laid off when corporations are downsizing. Small business enterprises enjoy some measure of freedom from large capitalists, but they too operate under the shadow of bigger corporate capitalists. Their survival often depends directly on contracts with bigger corporations, or on the purchasing power of corporate employees' wages.

Contemporary Global Capitalism

The global character of contemporary capitalism is qualitatively different from what has gone before. With the breakdown of the Soviet-style communist economies of Eastern Europe and the gradual opening of China to a market economy, the capitalist economic form now dominates across the world. Increasingly capitalism is operating as a single global system, organized into transnational trading blocs. These economic networks are increasingly integrated into global corporations that own and manage multiple levels of the production process, linked together through vast computerized networks that crunch the vast inventory of information, and facilitate instantaneous communications around the globe.

To grasp the immensity of contemporary global corporate capitalist economic networks it helps to focus on a few familiar consumer products and follow them through from production to purchase and consumption. Consider the blemish-free, look-alike tomatoes you may have brought home from your local supermarket (Barndt 2002). The chances are that they began life in the thousands of acres of monocrop tomato greenhouses in Mexico. The seeds themselves come from transnational corporate-owned scientific plant breeding centres, where they are genetically modified to produce harder fruit with longer shelf life, often with an antifreeze gene inserted from Arctic flounder to produce fruit better able to withstand long transit times in refrigeration trucks and warehouses. Once germinated, the plants must be continually treated with chemical fertilizers, pesticides, and fungicides. Genetically identical plants are preferred to ensure that they all ripen with minimal variation in number of days, and size of fruit to maximize efficient handling. When ready, workers have to pick them, sort them for ketchup, canning or fresh fruit, pack them and douse them with ethylene gas to begin the ripening process. Then convoys of trucks drive them the 20-hour trip to the Mexican-American border where more workers inspect them, store them in corporate warehouses, and ready them for another fleet of truckers to drive them to corporate food outlets across North America. Finally, at the level of individual grocery stores, workers unpack them, display them for consumers, and check them through barcode scanners that record sales for inventory and re-ordering. The slice of tomato in your lunch connects you as an individual consumer with a vast network of workers, including scientists in research laboratories, chemical factories, Mexican farm labourers, truck drivers, and cashiers, and these workers in turn are connected to the bankers and finance workers that manage the flow of money that keeps this system in continual motion, the computer experts that manage the inventory, the corporations that build and manage the fleets of trucks, the warehouses, the grocery-store chains and fast-food outlets.

If you have a cup of coffee with your tomato, this ties you in with another vast global corporate economic coffee-producing network that includes growers in coffee plantations in Central America and Africa, and the planters, pickers, packers, graders and truckers that manage them, chemical workers who produce the styrofoam cups the coffee is served in, or the forestry-product workers that produce the paper cups and coffee-filters, workers who grow and refine the sugar, farmers who supply the milk and cream, workers who produce and manage the supplies of clean drinking water that coffee is made with, and so on (Swift, Davies, Clark and Czerny 2003 Ch. 1). These integrated economic networks are so vast that it would be virtually a course in itself to analyse the entire trail in detail, and so far we have only looked at two food items. If you check the labels on your clothing there is a high probability that you are wearing at least one piece of clothing that was made in China. With its vast labour-force of ultra-cheap workers, China has become the leading country in the world for garment manufacture, from cheap Walmart versions to high-priced designer clothing. China's manufacturing economy has been growing at such a rate that economists widely predict that the economic output of the Chinese economy as a whole will rival that of the USA by the middle of the 21st century.

This shift in manufacturing from comparatively high-waged developed economies to low-waged developing economies corresponded with structural transformations in western European and North American labour markets from predominantly mass production and factory labour jobs to computers and electronics. Buzzwords for referring to the new economy include 'the information economy', the knowledge-driven economy, entrepreneurial cities, network economy, and the like (Fairclough 2003, 2). This restructuring of labour power in turn has profound implications for political and social relations. Relations between unionized labour and corporate bosses, and sources of profit or 'surplus value' are also qualitatively different in 'the new economy' where the dominant form of labour is professional and knowledge-based rather than manual. The income gap is growing between highly-educated skilled labour and unskilled workers in developed societies.

Globally, while workers find themselves increasingly enmeshed in common networks of corporate power, they experience enormous inequalities working conditions and material standards of living. Fluctuating coffee prices and cut-throat competition between small countries desperate to sell their primary export crop to corporate buyers may make the difference between coffee growers able to comfortably feed their families and send children to school, and near destitution. Workers in mass-production factories in China may be working on contract to middlemen suppliers for as little as 30 cents an hour, manufacturing clothes and shoes for which wealthy American consumers will pay hundreds of dollars. Migrant farm workers from Central America may be paid $1 an hour, compared with $7 minimum-wages for part-time cashiers and shelf packers in Canadian grocery stores. At the top end of the salary scales scientists and skilled workers may be earning more than $100 an hour, while Chief Executive Officers who run large corporations can command annual incomes in salaries, stock options and bonuses of millions of dollars annually.

Nation states in the developing world commonly lack the political clout to manage corporate investment capital or to challenge exploitative labour contracts. When corporate assets are measured against gross national products, roughly half of the top one hundred economies in the world are corporations. These giant corporations are largely self-regulating economies that determine capital flows, allocation of resources and labour across the globe. They have the power to shift investment capital and manufacturing contracts rapidly from one location to another to get the most profitable deals. Global financial markets are managed by trans-national agencies like the International Monetary Fund (IMF) the

World Bank, and the World Trade Organization (WTO). These developments are prompting new kinds of research into issues of how trans-national institutions manage the flow of labour and international trade and investment. These are new institutional forms conduct business in ways that are qualitatively different from treaties between nations. Nations no longer manage the global flow of capital, although they restrict the movement of labour (Hardt and Negri 2000, 3–10).

Environmental degradation on a global scale is another direct consequence of global capitalist production that few nation states or international regulating bodies have either the power or the will to curb. Monocrop agricultural production may be highly efficient, at least in the short term, for cheap mass production of agricultural goods, but with long term costs loss of biodiversity, soil depletion, and chemical pollution. As newly developing countries strive to catch up to western standards of living, and especially as China, and the countries in the former Soviet Union embrace capitalist production, the demand for finite resources of raw materials and especially fossil fuels on world markets is accelerating, reflected in conflicts and wars fought between rival claimants for scarce resources. The ever-increasing rate of burning fossil fuels is contributing to dual phenomena of global warming and global pollution. The large majority of natural scientists the world over concur in their measurements of global warming at a pace that is melting polar ice caps, threatening to disrupt warm ocean currents that moderate northern climates, and to cause a catastrophic rise in sea-water levels—sufficient to drown many coastal cities across the world. Political economists predict that such far-reaching geographic changes are likely to precipitate a collapse of our governing social institutions (Dandaneau 2001). Worst of all, scientists and business and political elites of all ideological stripes can see these processes occurring. They know in broad terms the economic practices that are producing them, but can see no economically viable way of stopping them. As Dandaneau expresses it, it seems easier to destroy our planet than to change our mode of economic production.

Contradictions of Capitalism: The Paradox of Wealth and Poverty

The capitalist mode of production has proven vastly superior in generating wealth and mass consumption goods and services compared to any other way of organizing economic relations that has yet been tried. State-managed centralized industrialization under formerly communist regimes in China and the Soviet Union failed miserably in comparison, and were eventually abandoned in favour of 'free market capitalism'. Yet Marxist analysis of the underlying logic of industrial capitalism in 19th century Europe, led him to predict that, in the long run, the capitalist system would itself fail under the pressure of its own internal contradictions. Capitalist societies, he predicted would be characterised by chronic instability and turmoil rather than equilibrium. They were destined eventually to be overthrown by mass revolt of workers struggling against their exploitation. Here we will sketch a brief outline of Marxist assumptions about how competition and profit motives work within the capitalist mode of production. A more thorough analysis is given in later chapters devoted to the work of Karl Marx and the political economy of Canada.

The first key assumption is that capitalist economies are oriented to production for *profit* through competition to sell products in the market. Capitalists invest in productive resources and hire labour power in order to convert raw materials into *commodities*—goods produced not for personal use, but for sale. Profits arise primarily through the gap between production costs which include all the various raw materials, machinery, wages paid to workers, and the like, and the market value of the finished commodities.

The second assumption is that the most effective way to increase profits is to reduce labour costs by investing in labour-saving technology. Capitalists certainly strive to pay the lowest wages possible, until workers refuse to work for them, rebel, or in a closed system begin to starve. Capitalists can also strive to get the cheapest input resources possible, until no one will sell any to them. The third method of raising profits, however, is at least theoretically unrestricted—that of raising productivity through inventing labour-saving technology. Those capitalists who are first to invest in new labour-saving technology will be able to produce goods more cheaply than competitors in the market, undercut them, and so make large profits.

The third assumption follows from this. Capitalists will find themselves compelled to keep investing in the newest labour-saving, productivity-enhancing technology. It is this compulsion to keep investing and to strive unceasingly to invent new productive technologies that most explains the wealth-producing potential of capitalism. The system never stops advancing. Capitalists who become complacent will fall behind in the competition, find themselves unable to sell their more expensive products, and eventually face bankruptcy. Their employees will find themselves laid off.

This reasoning leads to a fourth assumption of the model, namely the tendency for capitalist corporations to expand in size and shrink in number. Corporations that invest successfully in labour-saving technology will make high profits and be able to invest in still better technology. They will also be in a position to buy out smaller and less efficient competitors. The global economy is now dominated by multinational corporations whose sales in billions of dollars exceed the gross national products of many of the smaller nation states in which they do business. Yet no matter how large or powerful such corporations become they still cannot escape the competitive pressure to innovate further and cheapen or improve their products, or risk financial ruin. Not long ago General Motors commanded seemingly invincible dominance in the North American car markets. Yet in 2006 GM is fighting for survival, losing market share to more fuel efficient and lower-cost cars from Asia.

Contradiction and alienation in the lives of workers

What implications do these processes have for workers? Those who are employed within profitable capitalist enterprises at the cutting edge of new technology are likely to be among the more highly paid. The downside, however, is that labour-saving technology displaces workers so that high profitability can occur at the same time as competitive downsizing, rising structural unemployment, and increasing competition among workers for jobs. High unemployment in turn drives down wages as workers undercut each other to vie for limited employment options.

High unemployment predictably tends to generate crises of overproduction as purchasing power falls across the market. People may still want and need commodities but be unable to afford them. Capitalists can respond by dropping prices and thus cutting into their profit margins, cutting back production, or striving to produce cheaper goods with even less labour input. The result is recession. Eventually the economy tends to improve again as some technological breakthrough opens up new areas of production, stimulates capital investment and new employment opportunities and thus a new period of prosperity. But in the long run the cycle will predictably

repeat itself. The model predicts that capitalist economies can remain stable only by continually growing and expanding into new markets, and continually finding new sources of energy and raw materials to exploit. Even a slow-down in the rate of investment can create panic.

The relentless cycle of competitive innovation and cost-cutting under threat of bankruptcy has serious implications for social relations between employers and employees. The model leads to the prediction that **alienation** will be widespread in capitalist societies. Alienation refers to the lived experience of structurally-generated powerlessness in the face of economic forces largely beyond one's control. Work lacks meaning, relationships are shallow, and mutual obligations are limited to cash payment. Money seems to be valued over all else. The logic of capitalist relations implies that capitalists cannot afford to care too deeply about their employees or to feel obligated to them because it would impede their readiness to cut labour costs and downsize when necessary to remain competitive. Likewise, wage-workers would be unwise to commit themselves too much to their employers or their jobs when this is unlikely to be reciprocated in hard times. Caring deeply about the job one does makes little sense when products are only made for sale, and not for use and enjoyment by oneself or people one knows, and when profits from sales go only to employers, and especially if working faster and harder increases the likelihood of layoffs.

The model sketched out above is not by itself sufficient to make sweeping predictions for all circumstances. Rather, it works to highlight the contradictions inherent in capitalism and to guide research questions. Marx himself predicted that capitalist societies, characterised by sharp cleavages along class lines, would face an ever-present threat of revolt. Exploited masses, he reasoned, would always be ready to rise up and overthrown the entire capitalist system. This has clearly not yet happened, at least on the global scale that Marx once imagined. Many theorists take this as evidence that Marxist reasoning is itself flawed. Others argue that the Marxist assumptions about the inherent contradictions within capitalism are still valid, but that many factors have come into play that have so far managed to keep the system from spiralling utterly out of control. One such factor is that the predicted collapse of capitalism and the reasoning behind it are common knowledge to union leaders and business elites alike. This shared consciousness helps to stabilise the system by encouraging both sides to limit excesses of capitalist exploitation of labour, and to increase concern with legitimating capitalism as an economic system.

In any specific economic situation there are always multiple factors that influence how capitalist processes work. Here we can name just a few. The potential for innovative technology may generate new production and new demands for labour power, and so stave off crises of unemployment and overproduction. New markets may absorb excess production. Wars massively alter both the supply and the demand for certain kinds of resources and commodities. There may be local gluts and shortages of certain kinds of raw materials or labour power. Political interventions help to flatten out booms and slumps. Competing interests of locally-owned businesses and those managed from headquarters outside the country or region also impact on regional capitalist economies. Research into the contemporary Canadian economy explores these processes, as we will see in later chapters.

In summary, we now have the core assumptions that underlie the political economy perspective. The organization of the economy, both in the short-term and local situation and in the long-term and global context, has a decisive impact on the social organization of communities and the life experiences of individual members. The capitalist economic system, by the inherent structure of how it works, generates social systems characterized by extremes of wealth and poverty at both local and global levels, and relations of power and dependence, chronic instability, alienation, and conflict.

Political Economy of Culture

This last section returns to the concept of culture to illustrate the kind of analysis generated by the political economy perspective and to contrast it with the functionalist perspective described earlier. Both perspectives share the view that culture—the prevailing system of beliefs and values, functions to promote societal integration. But they differ greatly in their understanding of how this integration works. Political economists view cultural traditions as growing out of material conditions and how people organize collectively to produce, distribute and consume the goods and services that sustain life. Aboriginal peoples of North America traditionally organized themselves cooperatively to live from the land through hunting, fishing, and gathering, making the technology they needed, and trading among the communities. This cooperative economic system fostered cultural values of sharing, reciprocity and responsibility to others, and spiritual beliefs that see human beings as

integrally one with the natural world. People knew that their economic survival depended on their involvement in such cooperative networks. These cultures are remembered in the stories of the people and the written records of European settlers and missionaries. Only vestiges of them survived three centuries of colonial wars with invading European traders and settlers from the early 1500s to the late 1800s (Bear-Nicholas 2004). Reservation economies have widely been reduced to dependence on welfare handouts from the Canadian federal government, fostering cultural systems that reflect fragmented identities, despair, boredom, alcoholism and anger. Some of these communities are being drawn into the surrounding capitalist economy, establishing businesses on the reserves, and seeking off-reserve careers and wage-work. As discussed below, however, the cultural beliefs and values fostered by capitalism are so different that they threaten the very survival of Aboriginal cultures. First Nations communities across Canada are still struggling with the federal government to win land claims and treaty rights that might return their access to sufficient natural resources to make some restoration of communal economies possible.

The capitalist economic system is founded on private rather than communal ownership of productive resources. People exploit the natural world, extracting raw materials that can be manufactured into commodities for sale. The cultural values fostered by this economic system are those of domination over nature, competition, individual effort and achievement, personal consumption, and the amassing of personal wealth.

The classical Marxist theorist Antonio Gramsci developed the concept of **ideological hegemony** to explain how capitalist economic systems win consent and discourage revolt, in the face of obvious inequality and instability. Ideological hegemony refers to a mode of ruling or hegemony that is based on ways of thinking that legitimate the economic order, and account for inequalities in morally justifiable ways. The capitalist system appears both reasonable and inevitable, while alternative economies, like Soviet or Chinese-style communism, seem unworkable or worse. (Gramsci 1971; Giddens 1983,20, 90; Nesbitt-Larking 2001, 86–88). Hence revolt seems wrong-headed, misguided, naive and unreasonable.

Gramsci's theory reflects Marx's observation that the dominant values in a society are those of the dominant class. In feudal times the nobility were considered racially superior to common people, and their authority over lands as delegated through the divine or god-ordained right of kings. Colonial rule was similarly justified through beliefs about racial, cultural and technological superiority and the white-man's burden to civilize more primitive peoples. The emerging class of capitalists challenged the hereditary rights of king and nobles with new values of individual enterprise, effort, ability, and capacity to take risks, to innovate, and to succeed in a free competitive markets. Those who fail to get ahead were viewed as lazy or of limited ability.

These hegemonic ideas or ways of thinking typically blame attitudes, values, and motivation, rather than economic conditions, as the cause of economic inequality. Wealthy societies generally and wealthy individuals are represented as naturally superior—either born with superior qualities or having superior cultural beliefs, values and patterns of behaviour that result in their greater economic success. European colonizers saw themselves as bringing their more rational and superior civilization to more primitive peoples. Capitalists attribute their economic success to their superior cultural values—values of hard work, thrift, effort, ability, creativity, and the like. The poorest countries in the world appear to have clung too long to feudal communal values that stifle individual initiative, as do remaining communist countries. These countries have failed to make the adaptive cultural changes to promote scientific rationality and innovation, and individual entrepreneurial spirit that are required for capitalism to flourish. America represents the epitome of successful advanced capitalism. American cultural values are said to reward entrepreneurs, achievement, and risk-taking, and Protestant individualism to a greater extent than Canadian culture, with its more communal Catholic culture (Lipset 1976, 1985; Porter 1965, 1979; Brym 1989, 28)). Thus culture is said to explain why capitalism advanced more quickly and successfully in America than in Canada. Similarly, individual talents and work ethic are held to account for individual success while laziness and moral failure account for those who fall to the bottom.

Such explanations probably sound like commonsense. Where they fail is that they totally ignore and obscure the entire workings of the exploitative, profit-driven capitalist economic system that we discussed above. That is what makes such ideas *ideological.* Ideologies are belief systems that function as *means not to know* and not to see what is actually going on. Hegemonic belief systems that account for structurally-generated inequalities in terms of individual merit and cultural ethics like hard work, obscure the structural foundations of capitalism that generate the concentra-

tion of wealth, the compulsion to exploit cheap labour and raw materials on a global scale, the investment cycles that generate chronic instability and structural unemployment that condemn masses of people to poverty.

From the political economy perspective there are more convincing structural explanations for Canada's poorer status relative to the USA. Canada has a 'branch-plant' economy, dominated by corporations with their headquarters located outside the country. This means that Canadian managers have more limited opportunities for independent entrepreneurship than their American bosses. This is a reality that contributes greatly to the cultural differences observed by Lipset and others. What ruling ideas portray as natural and cultural superiority, political economy theory represents as the outcome of structural-generated advantages. Impoverished third-World countries face immensely greater structural disadvantages than does Canada, as we shall see later in the text..

Global Corporate Culture

The new world order of global corporate capitalism with almost instantaneous global communications is transforming cultures around the world. This does not necessarily mean the end of cultural diversity. Diversity may actually be good for business—opening new marketing opportunities. But what it does mean is that dominant values promoted by political and corporate elites around the world embrace capitalism itself as the only viable and legitimate mode of economic organization. These values are framed in the moral language of free markets, and individual freedom and initiative (Fairclough 2003). Capitalists everywhere promote what Sklair (2002, 36) calls the "culture and ideology of consumerism". People are encouraged to identify the good life with commodities they can buy, these products pushed incessantly with advertising. What consumerism as ideology obscures from view is the appalling costs incurred in global plunder of natural resources, environmental degradation, pollution, global warming, and the exploitation of sweatshop labour by transnational corporations driven to squeeze costs and maximize shareholder profits (Klein 2000).

Images of popular culture and traditions around the world are routinely harnessed by advertisers to sell their brand-name products. The gap between advertising and culture is becoming increasingly blurred, Klein argues (ibid. Ch. 3), as transnational corporations shift from sponsoring cultural events to actually buying artists and staging events, where the main point of the events are to advertise brands. Television stations like MTV are 24-hour advertising channels, packed with giveaways, contests, awards ceremonies, and the like, featuring luxury products. Teenagers are hired to report back on 'what's cool' so that these images can be built into advertising for such brand-name products as Nike sneakers and Hilfiger clothes. Truck-loads of sneakers and sports clothes are dumped on playgrounds in Black-American ghetto areas so that they can be seen 'on the right people' to impress teenagers. Rebellious teenage counter-cultures are readily incorporated into product marketing images. Teenagers around the world are incited to identify with the North American 'teen image' and the consumer products that go with it. Younger and younger children are targeted as consumers, incited to pressure their parents to buy such products as the big-Mac with the latest Disney toy. Klein laments that there is almost no public space left in North America that is not saturated with advertising.

The distinction between economic *base* and cultural *superstructure*, that we discussed above, is increasingly hard to draw in the contemporary knowledge-based economy. Knowledge and intellectual products are themselves becoming commodities for sale in global markets (Hardt and Negri 2000, 32) . Management theories, for example, and the 'social science' of business administration, are commodified—packaged as textbooks and courses for sale in global education markets. Corporate media giants sell culture to global audiences in the form of entertainment and news. These intellectual commodities affect us at very deep levels, influencing how we think about our self identity and our relations with other people. They have the potential to profoundly influence spiritual awareness of what it means to be human.

In conclusion, the political economy perspective promotes a particular kind of research that strives to bring to light features of capitalist economic relations as the foundations of contemporary society—national, regional and global. The perspective prompts research questions that would not arise from the functionalist perspective. Indeed, some political economists argue that the traditional functionalist perspective is itself a form of ruling ideology in that it functions to obscure deeply exploitative structures that underpin society and thus helps to sustain them.

Section Three: Social Constructionist Perspectives

Social constructionist perspectives begin from the core assumption that all social action is inherently meaningful. People reflect on situations and interactions and form subjective interpretations or understandings of what is going on. These subjective understandings guide how we respond. Unlike functionalist analysis, social constructionist analysis does not assume that shared meanings are given or fixed by pre-existing cultural norms. Instead people are seen as continually working up a sense of shared meanings—negotiating, constructing, sustaining or abandoning tentative definitions of situations as we interact with each other. Any sense we may have that social relations are orderly and meaningful, rather than chaotic and meaningless, depends on the work we do continually to actively sustain and communicate this shared sense of order and meaning. From this broad perspective, the work of doing sociology is itself meaning-constructing work. Any sense we have of 'society' as an orderly social system is thus seen as a *result* of such meaning-construction work. Society is never simply 'out there' to be studied in the way that biologists study organic systems. Rather, it comprises systems of shared meanings that we continually work up and shape through our reactions to them.

Essentially what you are being asked to do here is explore how you and others you interact with make sense of social relations. We can ask this question at roughly three levels of complexity. First, we can explore what are the subjective meanings or definitions of situations that different individuals use to guide their responses to social situations. We know that how people see a situation affects how they respond. You are likely to feel and respond very differently if you think someone spilt coffee on you accidentally or if you think it was done deliberately. A second level of questioning is more difficult. How do individuals come up with definitions of situations? What kinds of reasoning processes or 'sense-making practices' do individuals use in order to come up with their definition of the situation as accidental or deliberate? The third level of questioning is the most complex: How are authoritative definitions of social situations worked up? These are definitions of situations that large numbers of people in very different times and places are willing to accept as correct and use to guide their behaviour. The first level of questioning is associated with approach of *symbolic interactionism*, the second with *ethnomethodology*, and the third with *institutional ethnography*. We will add some further distinctions to these three broad categories or groups below as we flesh them out in more detail.

1) Symbolic Interactionism

Symbolic interaction explores the subjective meanings or 'definitions of the situation' that guide how people respond to situations. The core research assumption of this approach is that people experience social interaction as meaningful. We respond to situations in terms of their subjective meanings for us rather than unthinking or instinctual responses to stimuli. This assumption is captured by the classic concept of "definition of the situation". If we differ in our definition of a situation then predictably, our reactions will differ. This is because, subjectively we are not responding to the same situation.

An example of this is a short story by Averchenko (Bonner 1994, 225) in which the 'facts' are that one man hits another on the head with a brick after he was approached with a request to light a cigarette. As the man tells the story, he reacted with the brick because he saw the request for a light as a set-up for a robbery. His wife, however, saw what happened as a jealous reaction to attention that the other man was paying to her. The 'victim' later describes himself as having been attacked by a lunatic. A newspaper account describes paramedics being called to pick up a drunken man who had fallen and cracked his head on a brick. The role of the sociologist as observer, Bonner suggests, is not simply to add a fifth perspective to the story, but to facilitate the dialogue that makes possible a shared and mutual understanding of diverse interpretations of the stream of events. It is thus a critical and ethical endeavor. As sociologists we are not free to interpret the world whatever way we want, because we are constrained to continually test our assumptions against the resistance that others give when they talk back. Knowledge develops not by the 'discovery' method in which we amass objective facts about an external reality, but by inquiry into the life-worlds and interpretive understandings that people bring to their social lives (Bonner 2001).

Symbolic interactionism draws attention to the symbolism that people use when giving accounts of events, that shape our sense of what is happening and therefore what an appropriate response might be. Consider the debate that took place early in 2003 among government leaders around the world on whether to support the American-led proposal to use armed force to depose the government of Saddam Hussein in Iraq. The symbolism of 'weapons of mass destruction' proved pivotal. Those who saw the situation as involving a brutal dictator who was amassing weapons of mass destruction in blatant defiance of United Nations sanctions, and with the intent of launching terrorist attacks against Israel and the United States, were predisposed to use force. Such a scenario was particularly convincing for those people already predisposed to view the world as a dangerous place and their communities as vulnerable to terrorism. Contrasting definitions of the situation, portraying Saddam Hussein as essentially contained and powerless, and the Americans as more concerned with controlling oil supplies than worried about weapons, militated against support for armed intervention. Intelligence reports of mobile weapons factories, backed by grainy video evidence of truck convoys, proved unconvincing.

The Rodney King trial in Los Angeles in 1992 gives another example of how people with different definitions of the situation at hand can interpret the same evidence in sharply different ways. The trial focussed on a home video that masses of Americans viewing it on television interpreted as showing racist white police officers beating a helpless black man. Jurors for the trial, however, interpreted the same video as consistent with the defence lawyer's account of Rodney King himself as behaving violently towards the police and so instigating the police response. The lawyer's account was consistent with other views widely held among jurors that associate black males in general with criminal behaviour and police as generally upholding law and order (Lewis 2001, 29). These examples draw attention to the symbolism embedded in descriptions that shape people's sense of what is happening and thereby what constitutes an appropriate response.

Labelling theory is a branch of symbolic interactionism that explores how public labelling generates a spiral of reactions. People respond to how they feel themselves judged and labelled by others, and in turn judge and respond to others in terms of how these others are socially labelled. Much of the research from this perspective has focussed on micro-level interactions, exploring such issues as how judgements by parents and teachers influence the self concept and behaviour of children. Labelling theory is less concerned with the accuracy of the labels than with their impact, particularly in the possibility of self-fulfilling prophecies, as individuals feel pressured to conform to the public labels. Public labels tend to promote a spiral of action and reaction. People labelled as 'deviant' may find themselves subject to ostracism and distrust and react to such treatment with anger and withdrawal, which reinforces the original deviant label. Stigmatized people may gravitate towards other similarly marginalised people, and so promote the sharing of deviant subcultural norms and behaviour. Favourable labelling, on the other hand, may prompt a positive spiral of action and reaction.

At the macro level entire groups and classes of people, and even entire societies find themselves subject to the gaze of 'others' who have the power to impose labels and to act upon them. Edward Said (1978) analyses how the concept of 'oriental' is largely a figment of western colonial construction, but nonetheless extremely powerful in the political representation of cultures and peoples geographically positioned to the south and east of Europe. Historically, research and writings produced by European colonisers dominated international scholarship and commanded more respect than non-western research. As a result, scholars from Asia frequently find they need to travel to England to consult library sources on the history of their own societies. The characterization of Islamic societies by Western commentators and government leaders, often in painfully simplistic and derogatory ways, functions as a foil against which representatives of diverse Islamic societies struggle to redefine their nations in the global arena. People of Islamic cultural origin living in Western societies struggle similarly to portray a positive sense of themselves in the face of negative stereotypes. This was especially difficult in the strained political climate following the September 11th 2001 attack on New York, when the terms 'Islamic' and 'terrorist' were often juxtaposed in media summations of international conflict.

Lewis's studies of public opinion polls in the USA show how powerfully such generalized negative labelling works to influence electoral support for federal government policy initiatives on domestic and international issues. The term 'welfare' refers to government income assistance for people without other financial resources, but the term carries a negative stigma that predisposes people to assume the worst on virtually any issue with which the term 'welfare' is linked. Lewis reveals the extent of this stigma by asking students to estimate the average number of children that mothers receiving welfare have. Students wildly overestimated the correct average of less than two (Lewis 2001, 126). Students were also wildly inaccurate, although in predictable directions, in guessing the characteristics of for-

eign governments known to be allies or opponents of American foreign policy. Allies were assumed to be democracies and opponents dictatorships; allies were assumed to have exemplary human rights records and opponents bad records; opponents were assumed to endorse drug-trafficking while allies were clean, and so on (ibid. 130–134), These positive and negative associations were assumed with minimal reference to factual evidence, and they fostered easy support for aggressive government policies that targeted welfare recipients and stigmatized foreign governments.

The *dramaturgical model* is another branch of symbolic interactionism that explores how people actively present themselves to influence how others see them. Erving Goffman is particularly remembered for his use of drama and theatrical performance as a model for analysing social interaction. Rather than viewing roles as predefined expectations, he draws attention to how much freedom actors enjoy to negotiate their role performances. The bare outlines of role expectations may be culturally defined, but the details are not. Also, many social interactions involve informal encounters that do not take the form of predefined roles at all. Research in this tradition focusses on how people as actors in a social situation give and give off impressions through body-language, how they strive to influence how others perceive them, how they take cues from each other, how they collude together to create scenes, how they use clothing and other props to manage images and to convey feelings like surprise, anger, hurt, pleasure, and so on. In multiple studies of informal interaction, Goffman illustrates the practices of secrecy, deference and demeanour, team work, backstage collusions, and consensual performances before potentially critical audiences, that characterize these encounters.

We live in an era where our primary means of appraising political leaders and candidates is through watching them on television. In politics it is widely claimed that having a television presence can make or break the electoral chances of candidates. An entire industry has grown up around *public relations* or 'PR' with experts managing the television appearance of senior politicians and other public figures. Appearances by Canadian Prime Minister Paul Martin and opposition leader Stephen Harper are carefully staged. A notable example of political theatre was American President George W. Bush's 'Address to the Nation' on May 1, 2003 to declare active fighting over in Iraq. In the morning the President appeared in suit and tie, head bowed in prayer to lead the national day of prayer. In the evening he appeared wearing battle fatigues and carrying a helmet, on the deck of an aircraft carrier, with a backdrop of American flags, guns, fighter jets, and 5000 soldiers. The juxtaposition of religion and military power filled the newspapers the following day. Such presentations require extensive backstage management and collusion by a team of workers. As in the theatre, this work has to remain hidden. Exposing the backstage carries the risk that one may undermine the credibility of the frontstage performance, unlike the theatre, however, journalists and politicians from rival parties have vested interests in bringing about precisely such damaging exposure. Careers can be threatened by unguarded comments made "while the microphone is still running".

Cassin (1979, 1980) draws on Goffman's notion of flawed performance to suggest a partial explanation for why women generally do not advance as rapidly as men in public service. Men, she suggests, learn through conversation and socializing with senior managers how to present themselves as 'ready for promotion'. Her research shows how officials in junior government posts learned how to talk about the policy relevance of any work they were engaged in, without having to be prompted. In contrast, junior women were more likely to discuss technical details of their work, not connecting this to matters of policy unless specifically asked to do so. Women socialized less frequently with their all-male senior managers, and hence had less chance to learn how to talk the managerial talk in performance appraisals.

2) Ethnomethodology

Ethnomethodology begins from the same assumption as symbolic interaction, namely that individuals respond to situations in terms of their subjective understanding of what seems to be going on. But it raises more complicated subsidiary questions: *How* do people generate subjective 'definitions of situations'? How do people actively work at making interaction meaningful? How do we reason ourselves through routine everyday situations to achieve and maintain some sense of meaningful order?

The term ethnomethodology is derived from the Greek word for people, 'ethno', plus methods. It refers to the study of people's methods of reasoning which they use to make sense of social situations. The perspective emerged in the 1960s as a response to nagging questions raised by functionalist and symbolic interactionist perspectives. The challenge that Psathas (1980) raises

with respect to Goffman's work is that while he gives us wonderfully insightful descriptions of face-to-face interactions, he fails to show us, methodologically, how he comes up with his interpretations. Goffman imputes intentions to the actors he watches. He presumes to know what Actor A thinks about Actor B, and vice versa, but what Actors A and B are really thinking is not observable. Goffman does not stop the interaction in process to ask each actor to explicate in words precisely what each is thinking. Goffman must guess the thoughts and intentions of the actors from subtleties of the interaction.

In everyday interaction, when we discuss the motives that people might have for particular actions, we are effectively engaged in the work of producing a meaningful world, and producing our sense of being able to understand other people as acting in terms of motives (Bonner 2001, 273). This kind of 'motive talk', Bonner argues, has distinctive rules or grammar. For it to be considered adequate, and not merely chatter, it must meaningfully connect the stream of events with reactions. Ethnomethodological research explores these reasoning processes. It studies how actors and observers in any social situation come to a collective understanding of what is going on, including how they draw inferences about the thoughts and intentions of others and orient themselves to these meanings.

Harold Garfinkel (1967) is recognized as the true founder of ethnomethodology. He studied the functionalist perspective as a graduate sociology student and began to question the explanatory value of the concept of learned role expectations in predicting behaviour in social situations. Something important seems to be missing from the explanation. How do people come to know and to know in common, what 'roles' are going on, and therefore which role-expectations appropriately apply? Consider first the deceptively simple example Boughey (1978) gives of what he labels "cards night at a church". Commonplace expectations around the activity of card-playing might involve raucous laughter, back-slapping, competitive play, and the like, while expectations around church involve quiet, respectful behaviour. The question Boughey raises is: How do we decide which set of expectations to apply when the two activities merge— we are playing cards, but in a church? In Boughey's example much negotiating goes on among the participants. Men at one table engage in loud laughter but a woman at another table shushes them with the comment, "This is church, you know". The men retort "Na, but this is cards"! The central point Boughey is trying to get across here is that the participants cannot know in advance which set of pre-defined role expectations is going to govern the evening's interaction. Who is going to win this little battle for social control, and just how is it that their preferred definition comes to prevail? After the evening is over, functionalist analysis of role expectations can be fitted to the scene, but not before it happens. Boughey's further point is that people are not just playing their roles. They are actively negotiating them, sustaining or abandoning them as the evening wears on.

Boughey's example is a simple one where only two options are presented. Many social situations potentially involve far more than two options, and the stakes are much higher. Consider the complexity of role relations referred to above in interaction between junior male and female employees and more senior management. Participants' sense of what is going on can shift from minute to minute. What begins as an informal friendly conversation or having a beer together, may shift suddenly into a mentoring session as a senior manager coaches juniors in how to present themselves properly and what is important to know. The conversation can simultaneously include a covert evaluation of a junior colleague's management potential, a set-up to glean information, and a chance to make an impression or to gain favours. Those who are less adept at reading and manipulating these complex role interactions are less likely to climb the corporate ladder. In everyday interaction we are continually involved in making judgements about meaning that have far-reaching consequences for our lives. Susan Kreiger (1997, 196) describes her struggle to figure out the meaning behind how some students in a sociology class were responding to her. What did it mean when they seemed to avoid looking directly at her, or when they had trouble talking about the content of a text on lesbians? Was she a bad teacher, or was she feeling distant from the students, or did students simply find the material boring—or in retrospect, were they feeling afraid of her because they suspected she was a lesbian, or because they knew she had denied permission to a male graduate student to take her feminist research seminar the previous year and were punishing her? In her article she speaks of the nuances, the clues, the history of individually tiny signals that she believes add up to the invisible presence of homophobia that she senses without it being voiced.

Canadians have legal protection under the Human Rights Act, the Canadian Charter of Rights and Freedoms, and many union contracts, from discrimination on the basis of such characteristics as sex, race, religion and disabilities, and more recently also sexual orientation. The central problem facing all the people involved in such cases, is determining the *meaning* of the hurtful actions that have occurred. To gain legal redress the victims must prove beyond reasonable doubt that what they experienced as hurtful actions were instances of sexism, racism, or homophobia. Defendants, however, invariably argue that their behaviour was not discriminatory but based on legitimate and reasoned grounds. Was Susan Kreiger wrongly denied a permanent teaching position because of homophobia, or because she rebuffed the sexual advances of a senior male colleague? Or was she legitimately passed over because her teaching or her scholarship were of poorer quality than another candidate, or because she was an abrasive, dysfunctional colleague? How do jurors decide?

Breaching Experiments are a methodology widely used within ethnomethodological research. It involves deliberately violating commonsense expectations for behaviour in given situations, to expose patterns of commonsense reasoning, and how people respond when such reasoning is upset. The goal is to explore the commonsense knowledge that governs normal interaction, the tacit or seen-but-not-noticed rules of orderly relations that we competently use to negotiate our way through everyday activities. To do such research, sociologists must learn to 'suspend the natural attitude', to let go of the assumption that it is obvious what is going on, and to ask how is it that we, as competent members of our culture, know what is going on and what to do. Garfinkel devised the research method of *breaching experiments* to make visible the tacit rules governing some everyday behaviour by deliberately disrupting them (1967, 41–49). Students in his classes were instructed to select some simple everyday interaction, like exchanging greetings or getting on a bus, to act briefly in a way that contravened some tacitly expected behaviour in that situation, and report on how other people reacted. Students were amazed at how upset and angry people became when these small episodes of social order were disrupted. Garfinkel suggests that people became angry because an unspoken but powerful moral obligation was being violated—the obligation people have to mutually sustain meaningful social interaction.

Garfinkel also set up an experiment where students received random 'Yes' or 'No' answers to a series of questions they asked in what they thought was a social-work counselling session. Students readily made coherent sense out of these meaningless random answers. The experiment reveals how the students reasoned their way through this objectively meaningless exchange. They assumed without question that all conversation is intended to be meaningful, and they felt morally obligated to work at making the counsellor's comments make sense. Ethnomethodologists argue that this taken-for-granted work of making sense is the foundation of all social order.

Breaching experiments do not only happen in research laboratories. Giddens discusses how rebellious working-class boys in a school in England deliberately breached tacit rules of interaction to undermine the authority of their teachers. They conspired together to pretend not to hear or to understand anything their teacher said: "'Let's send him to Coventry when he comes", "Let's laugh at everything he says", "Let's pretend we can't understand and say, 'How do you mean?' All the time."'(Giddens 1984, 291, citing Willis 1981).

Lewis (2001, 185) uses trick survey questions in a similar way to Garfinkel's breaching experiment, to explore people's common-sense methods of reasoning in deciding how to vote in elections. One question asked American university students to identify whether Presidents Bush (Republican) or Clinton (Democrat) proposed a series of federal government policies. The vast majority relied on the 'informational shortcut' of associating right-wing policies (pro-business, law-and-order agenda) with Republican and left-wing policies (pro-labour, social services agenda) with Democrats. Only between 3 to 5 percent of students correctly answered or guessed that the two presidents took the same stand on all issues—both supporting right-wing policies and neither supporting left-wing policies. A series of similar questions show how pervasively students rely on abstract background understandings, or what Schutz would call 'recipe knowledge', to make sense of political affairs, and hence how readily they could be swayed by political slogans.

Conversation Analysis or CA is a branch of ethnomethodology that focuses research attention on people's methods of regulating normal conversation. It enjoins researchers to suspend the natural attitude that it is obvious how people manage to talk, and to explore the tacit known-but-not-mentioned background understandings that make talk manageable The central interest is with *how* talk is managed, not with linguistics or subject matter. The management of conversations both reflects and reinforces social inequality, with topics raised by subordinates less likely to be taken up by the

next speaker, their turns more frequently interrupted, and their contributions more frequently qualified as questions (isn't it? Don't you think?) than asserted as fact.

A central assumption of this perspective is that talk is *indexical*. An index in a book refers to subjects and information that are discussed elsewhere in the book but not in the index itself. Phrases used in a conversation similarly refer to background knowledge that participants are expected to have but that is not elaborated in the conversation under way. It follows then that the meaning of talk is not self evident, but embedded in the background understandings that participants bring to it. Every conversation balances the risk that participants may not fully understand these unspoken referents and so not fully understand the talk, against the counter risk that an attempt to clarify every reference in every sentence of a talk would result in infinite regress.

Consider the following conversation between two people:

A: "I have a child"
B: "That's okay"
A: "I also have a dog"
B: "Oh, I'm sorry"

An outsider to this conversation might well find the exchange nonsensical, but to participants who know that A is a prospective tenant and B a prospective landlord it is readily understandable. We know that many landlords place restrictions on people to whom they rent premises, often prohibiting pets, and sometimes children. The two parties to this talk do not need to refer openly to this background knowledge because both assume that they both know it. If A does not know this background information, then the response "Oh I'm sorry" would make no sense and might prompt the question "What do you mean—you're sorry I have a dog?" There is also much more background knowledge that may be pertinent to the conversation. One participant may know that there are some municipalities in Canada that do not permit commercial landlords to discriminate against people with children or pets. Such information will colour how A's comments and B's responses are heard. The actors may also be expected to know that race is not a legally permissible ground for landlords in Canada to discriminate against prospective tenants so that reference to having a child will be heard differently from reference to being black. None of this background knowledge is explicitly mentioned in the brief exchange quoted above. What has been said is quite sufficient for both actors to know, and to know in common, that A will not be renting accommodation from B.

Conversation analysis at the macro societal level explores how the management of talk is centrally involved in political influence, particularly in the contexts of public debates, media interviews, and the like. The inherent indexicality of talk means that there will always be some vagueness with respect to what key terms in discussions actually refer to, and such vagueness is amplified when people talk in abstractions like 'efficiency', 'enterprise', or 'left-wing' versus 'right-wing'. Vagueness allows for much leeway in interpreting and manipulating meanings. Lewis (2001, 136) describes how questions used in public opinion pools are commonly so vague that people with widely differing views give affirmative answers. Pollsters and their corporate or government clients can then impose their own interpretation on the question when citing poll results to claim that respondents support a favoured policy alternative.

3) Institutional Ethnography

Institutional Ethnography explores sense-making practices at the level of large-scale organizational settings where multiple participants are involved, and where most do not normally know each other, or ever interact directly (DeVault and McCoy 2002, 752). The central question is, how are common understandings generated and sustained simultaneously in many different work sites, that work to regulate and coordinate activities?

Within advanced industrial societies such as Canada, the meaning-construction work engaged in by people within formal organizations is particularly significant in generating shared meanings that guide behaviour over widely disparate work sites. This commonly involves the use of standardized forms and procedures to manage social interactions. People also draw upon the authority of professional training and status to claim expertise on which to legitimate and sustain authoritative definitions of situations. These professional ways of framing situations structure policies that become built into standardized procedures. Hence, the study of work practices by professionals in these organizational sites is central to the understanding of the social construction of power relations or **relations of ruling**.

Research in institutional ethnography typically begins with the experiences of an individual worker in a particular work site. The goal is to trace in meticulous detail the chains of activities that tie this work site to others. Typically, there are networks of texts, and particularly procedural manuals and standardized forms, files and records that workers must complete at one work site and transmit to another. These are analysed as critical mechanisms that generate common and authoritative definitions of situations for workers in multiple sites of activity. Research focuses on the indexical character of such texts, exploring how workers make sense of them, and how they condense the complex realities of people's lives into predefined categories. To do this categorizing, workers have to select, highlight, ignore and discard masses of jumbled information about individual lives to produce what will be officially recognised as 'knowledge' for practical purposes.

A key assumption of institutional ethnography is that these routine work practices, coordinated through networks of texts, are central to **relations of ruling**—that is, to the exercise of power and authority in contemporary society. Networks of standardized texts make it possible for officials at distant centres of power to exert detailed regulation over the activities of individual workers at a multitude of disparate local work sites. Managers within giant multinational corporations increasingly rely on electronic information networks to coordinate productive activities across the globe. Knowledge-workers, or professionals of all kinds, accomplish these power relations. They construct and disseminate most of the information on which others rely to make sense of what is going on in the world. In effect, they *produce* the culturally sanctioned appearance of social reality as most of us come to know and interpret it.

From this perspective, power and knowledge are inseparably connected (Foucault 1980). Knowledge-workers command authority based on their expertise to interpret 'the facts of the matter' which then becomes the basis for administrators, corrections officers, social workers and others to take action. The power wielded by experts works through persuasion rather than coercion. People who reject expert advice can readily be discredited as unreasonable. Political struggles of all kinds commonly involve struggles over meaning as subordinate groups challenge official ways of framing experience and try to propose alternatives. These struggles are variously referred to in literature as '*reality-defining contests* (Loseke 1987, 235) '*contestations over naming*" (McKendy 1992, 60) or "*the politics of interpretation* (Denzin 1992). One example is the struggle by the women's movement of the 1970s to re-frame the issue of *family conflict* as 'wife battery' to identify the underlying problem as one of male dominance rather than interpersonal frictions (Walker 1990a, 1990b). Successful shifts in representation mandate different courses of action. A 'family conflict' frame promotes family counselling as the preferred solution while the 'wife battery' frame promotes funding for Transition Houses for women and criminal prosecution for perpetrators. Environmentalists have similarly challenged the prevailing scientific representation of nuclear energy as clean, efficient and safe (Clow 1993), in the hope of promoting different policy options around energy production and use.

Discourse Analysis explores how people draw upon professional training to legitimate and sustain authoritative definitions of situations that work to determine policies, and to coordinate responses in multiple disparate sites of interaction. Professional discourses constitute part of the networks of power/knowledge through which relations of ruling work. Critical discourse analysis focusses research attention on how professionals frame issues and the relations of power embedded within these frames. Historical studies trace the links between shifts in scientific and professional discourses and shifts in cultural practices and state policies and legislation. Michel Foucault's work is famous for analysing how shifts in knowledge claims within the disciplines of law, medicine, psychology and psychiatry have impacted on the social labelling and treatment of behaviour associated with deviance, sexuality, child-rearing, schooling, and the like (1977; 1978). Other studies in the sociology of knowledge explore the influence of mass media in spreading particular representations or definitions of events, and how different audiences draw upon these representations in making sense of their personal experiences.

This view of knowledge as socially constructed does not reduce material existence to interpretation, nor reduce 'fact' to 'opinion', but it does assert that the lines between them are difficult to draw. The key distinction between 'facts' and 'opinions' is that facts are subject to verification by evidence, while opinions are not. However, while material evidence may be factual, the categories in terms of which we think about evidence, what we selectively notice or ignore, and how it becomes meaningful to us, are socially constructed, and what we believe about factual evidence powerfully influences our opinions. A powerful illustration of this mixing of fact, categories of thought, and opinion, is evident in what people generally know and think about income-assistance policies, better known as 'welfare' (Lewis (2001, 15). The question "How large was the Canadian

federal welfare budget in 2002?" appears to be a question for which there is a clear factual answer—"$ X-billion". But what is included and excluded from this amount—handouts to the poor, or salaries for the vast bureaucracy that administers welfare? And how large is this amount with respect to what? As an unqualified statement set by itself the amount may appear huge, but as a proportion of gross national product, or of all government expenditures, or in comparison with government assistance to industry, or to the military or civil servants' pensions, or comparable expenditures by governments in other developed countries, it appears much smaller. Stated as monthly income on which a welfare recipient must survive, compared with the cost of necessities like shelter, food, clothing, school supplies, bus fares, and the like, the amount appear minuscule.

What matters, Lewis argues, is not so much what we know as what we think we know, and *how* we know it. Facts never come to us devoid of interpretive framing, Pure 'factoids' devoid of any context are the most ambiguous and misleading of all. Most of what we know about our society beyond immediate personal experience, and especially at the levels of national and international affairs, comes to us second hand through texts—in the forms of mass media reports on TV, radio, magazines, films, internet websites, and the like. We can think about such issues only through informational frames or representations that others have worked up.

Seen in this way, evidence of cultural differences between the USA and Canada, as reflected in opinion polls, can be traced to sharply differing informational climates rather than to fundamental differences at the level of personalities. Mass campaigns in corporate-owned media against 'welfare' fraud and waste, and against incompetence and meddling of 'big government' are predictably reflected in subsequent opinion polls measuring widespread public support for welfare cuts and for private enterprise over 'big government' running things. However, if questions are worded very differently, in terms of support for low-income people, and for a public medical insurance scheme, measured responses are highly favourable (Lewis 2001, ch. 5). The responses are not self contradictory, Lewis argues. Rather, the questions trigger very different indexical meanings and tap into different informational frames. As noted above, the government and corporate sponsors commissioning the polls have the power to select the interpretive schemes most conducive to their preferred policy options, should they choose to publicize results. Sharply differing public opinions in the United States and Canada in support or opposition to the armed invasion of Iraq in March 2003 also coincided with sharply differing informational framing of the issues in government and media representations.

In summary, the core assumption that underlies all the perspectives included under social constructionism is that social reality comprises meaningful interaction. People reflect on situations and interactions to form subjective interpretations of what is going on, and guide their responses accordingly. All social life, including relations of authority, power and control, are constructed, negotiated, sustained or demolished through meaning-making work. Hence, the central focus of social constructionist analysis is on these subjective meanings, how and why they emerge as they do.

Culture and Identity as Social Constructions

The analysis of culture from the social constructionist perspective is strikingly different from the functionalist and political economy approaches. Instead of trying to describe culture, social constructionism explores how people continually generate, negotiate, sustain and challenge cultural meanings. Culture is thus an ongoing accomplishment not some fixed body of beliefs and customs that can be described. The discourses of professionals and leaders in politics and business, and how these are represented in mass media, form important parts of the network of practices that sustain cultural meanings. Social constructionist theory shares with *postmodernism* the view that all cultural meanings, and the sense of social identities that emerge from them, are essentially fluid and diverse. Attempts to describe or fix their characteristics freeze what is a dynamic process, giving at best only a short-term snapshot. In the post-modernist view of identity, individuals cannot be defined by such characteristics as nationality, race, religion, or even gender. This is both because we are all multi-faceted and because we continually re-think and re-define ourselves, depending on the contexts we find ourselves in and the experiences we have. Different facets of ourselves become salient or irrelevant in different situations, and in relation to different social and political struggles. We do not produce these self-images or 'narratives' about ourselves out of nothing. We draw on cultural resources around us, resources that are becoming increasingly diverse and globalized with mass communications. (Barker 1999, 3)

Barker recognizes the power of multinational corporations and media production conglomerates to spread capitalist consumer culture around the globe, but he stresses that people do not simply absorb these influences. They interact with them. The adapt and refashion some influences and reject or ignore others. Mass media productions do not convey identical meanings to people living in different social context. Neither is it only a top-down process of influence from people who dominate mass media to the rest of the world. Influence works both ways, with the result that people around the world are becoming more culturally homogenous in some respects, but simultaneously more diverse and hybrid in other respects. People's sense of themselves as being 'Moslem', 'Christian', or 'Jewish', for example, are continually being shaped by both local cultural influences and by global representations, and the contemporary politics of war and cultural imperialism.

The concept of *'identity politics'* draws attention to how people struggle to develop new ways of describing themselves, along with others who share these new representations (Barker 1999, ch. 7). Examples of people actively working up new descriptions of themselves include generating a new self-consciousness around the idea of being a born-again Christian, a feminist, a First Nations person with clout under the Canadian Charter of Rights and Freedoms, or as a person with gay and lesbian sexual orientation seeking Charter recognition and respect. For people who feel marginalized within the dominant cultural discourse, these struggles over redefinition and re-presentation have profound political consequences, for they challenge the grounds of social inclusion and justice.

Professional discourses are particularly influential in creating cultural meanings in contemporary society, including sociological perspectives. People draw upon sociological research and explanations that they come across in magazines and other media to make sense of their own experiences. The research process itself can become circular as people who are being interviewed by social researchers and reporters draw upon their own knowledge of sociology and psychology to frame descriptions of themselves (Denzin 1992, ch. 4). In Denzin's own studies, people he interviewed readily borrowed ideas from popular self-help psychology books, adopting such notions as 'adult-children-of-alcoholics' to talk about themselves.

It is difficult to recognize and resist power or relations of ruling that take the form of professional expertise and advice because it seems like commonsense.

Resistance takes the form of 'reality-defining contests' in which people struggle to establish competing interpretations of the way things are that support alternative policies for dealing with social problems. Within the social constructionist perspective the study of power relations and the study of culture and counter culture overlap. Competing sociological perspectives are important tools in resistance movements. The study of sociology thus contributes both to the authoritative creation of culture and to its deconstruction.

Section Four: Feminist Perspectives

The feminist perspective in sociology began to emerge as a distinctly recognized theoretical approach only in the 1970s, although it has roots in the long history of women's movements. Why the 70s? Universities across North American and Europe were expanding rapidly and opening their doors more widely to women, both as students and as junior faculty. More women than men are interested in gender, argues Paula England (1999, 263), so gender studies expanded as numbers of women expanded. This observation opens up a series of further questions, including: Why were universities overwhelmingly male preserves prior to the 1970s? How and why did this change? and Why are men less interested in gender issues than women? The feminist perspective focuses attention on questions such as these, and in so doing, it profoundly challenges the adequacy of conventional sociological research and explanations.

Central assumptions of the Feminist Perspective

A key assumption of feminism is that all features of social life need to be understood as gendered—not just the obvious area of family life, but everything—including the state, politics, the economy, education, universities, and the foundations of sociological discourse itself (Marshall 2000, 25). Gender is seen as a central organizing principle of social life. The Marxist perspective gives priority in explaining social structures to relations of production, or how people organize to produce material goods. Feminism gives priority to relations of **reproduction**, or how people organize to produce children

and nurture children, and more broadly to nurture and care for bodies throughout societies.

A second foundational assumption is that gender identities are best understood as social constructions, rather than the natural expression of biological differences. The concept of *gendering* refers to these social processes through which gender identities are accomplished—continually produced, reinforced, and struggled against in ongoing social structures and relationships (Marshall 2000, chap. 5).

A third assumption of feminism is that gendering is hierarchical (Nakano-Glenn 1997). Relations of reproduction are viewed as fundamental mechanisms through which inequalities of access to material resources, personal services, status, and power in society are organized. The work of reproductive labour, both in the narrow sense of bearing children and the broad sense of daily renewal of bodies, is pervasively feminized, privatized, and de-politicized, and located outside the organizational centres of social power (Acker 1997). Globally, women comprise about half the adult human population, yet they control only a tiny fraction of material resources. Culturally, those attributes associated with the 'feminine' are pervasively less highly valued than those identified as 'masculine'. It is still more complimentary to describe a girl as 'acting like a boy' than to describe a boy as 'behaving like a girl'. Structurally, young women and men are now equally represented in Canadian universities, although concentrated in different disciplines. Yet this has not translated into gender equality in future careers and incomes earned. Women are nowhere equally represented in offices and roles in society where political, economic and cultural power are wielded. Statistically, the category of women whose career achievements in the public arena most closely resemble those of comparable men, are women who remain single and childless, or a minority of elite women who are wealthy enough to hire nannies and housekeepers. Such partial equality is achieved at high personal cost.

The organizational practices that sustain and reinforce gender hierarchy are collectively referred to within feminist thought as **relations of patriarchy**. The feminist perspective encompasses both a positive and a normative project—a commitment to understand and make visible how gendering is accomplished, and a commitment to dismantle gender hierarchy.

A fourth assumption of the feminist perspective is that the production of knowledge is gendered. As a social process, the work of science is embedded in and reflects the historically specific contexts in which the struggle for knowledge occurs (Smith 1990). The profound shifts in sociology that occurred since the 1970s as more women entered the academy, indicates that what formerly passed as knowledge was not neutral but deeply gendered, reflecting male-centred interests and interpretive perspectives. Women scholars found that the prevailing concepts and explanations in sociology were inadequate to account for women's experiences. In the feminist jargon of the time, one could not just 'add women and stir'. Profound re-thinking was needed.

More recently, feminist thought itself is being challenged from within as reflecting white, western, professional, heterosexual women's experience, and not adequate to account for the situated experiences of more marginalised women. These challenges do not imply that scientific knowledge as impossible, but rather that all science is socially accomplished. The knowledge we derive from scientific work reflects the social organization of that work and needs to be interrogated as such.

The remainder of this section elaborates these basic assumptions of the feminist perspective and the experiences and reasoning behind them. The question raised above—why the feminist perspective emerged in the 1970s, still needs to be addressed. Part of the answer lies in economic changes. The 1970s was an era of relative prosperity for Europe and North America, with economic relations shifting increasingly from the mass-production factory system to information and service industries, expanding corporations, and expanding post-World-War-II welfare-state bureaucracies. This resulted in a high demand for women's labour as clerical and service workers. These new opportunities in turn encouraged women as well as men to seek higher education in unprecedented numbers. What remains to be explained is why so many young women scholars were so dissatisfied with the existing functionalist, Marxist and interpretive perspectives in sociology that they were driven to promote a paradigm shift in theory and methods. Karl Marx was driven to write his critique of capitalism by revulsion at the oppressive conditions of industrialization. What were these women struggling against in the 1970s and what were the experiences that they felt could not be accounted for by existing sociological explanations?

Feminism and Mainstream Sociology

A collection of life-histories of feminist sociologists (Laslett and Thorne 1997) throws some light on these questions. Women who studied sociology in the 1970s write of experiencing a sense of 'bifurcated consciousness', in that the sociological explanations they were learning about did not fit with or account for their lived experiences (ibid. 7). Women achieved access to higher education along with men but often under more difficult and highly gendered conditions. Women describe their emotional and physical exhaustion as they struggled with the relentless demands of managing relations of reproduction along with academic work. Laslett describes her own struggle with her children's illnesses, their sleeping problems, her own constantly interrupted sleep and interrupted studies, and her worries about childcare. Added to these worries were struggles to juggle the roles of graduate student, mother, wife and hostess to her husband's colleagues, and a marriage that was beginning to unravel. The functionalist theory that prevailed in American sociology in the 1970s posited a structural separation of 'public' work roles from 'private' family roles. Women's lived experience did not fit with this model. Emerging feminist research identified women's work in the home, and how women absorb the emotional and material work of reproducing bodies, as the essential but unacknowledged underpinning for the abstracted public realm of men's work (Acker 1997). The supposedly 'public' realm could not function if labour in the supposedly 'private' realm were to be withdrawn. Their artificial separation in mainstream sociological theory needed to be re-thought.

Feminist research promoted a methodology that begins not with an abstract model of social systems, but with the immediately experienced, concrete, material situation that individual women found themselves in. The research question then becomes : what are the organizational features and practices in the wider society that structure experience and sustain precisely this lived experience? This approach, which subsequently became known as institutional ethnography, was first used by women in sociology principally because there were so few resources for studying women's lives in the 1970s. The first *women's studies* or *sociology of women* courses offered in the '70s took the form of seminars in which graduate students and instructor together struggled to come up with questions, carry out their own research, and pool what they discovered. They could not begin with library research into existing theories because there was no body of academic sociological literature that could be studied. Seminar leaders struggled against the prevailing view that what they were doing was not scholarly and should not count for academic credit (Smith 1992a, 1992b). These seminars were the crucible in which much early feminist theory was formed.

The very absence of sociological literature on women fuelled questions about how and why previous sociological research had been so gender biased. This questioning leads back to the concrete material conditions of women's oppression. Historically, women have been systematically excluded from the creation of culture, along with other disprivileged people. Men almost exclusively occupied the leading positions in all the major professions such as medicine, psychology, law, sciences, theology, and all the disciplines pursued in the universities. When women began to enter universities and professions in large numbers, it was to find that the dominant ideas, paradigms, methodologies, and standards for evaluating scholarship already entrenched. These concrete conditions of gendered inequality are embedded into all the professions, including the social sciences.

Feminist Disillusionment with Mainstream Sociology

Many of the feminist sociologists who contributed their life-histories to the collection by Laslett and Thorne, describe themselves as initially attracted to Marxist sociology because of its focus on injustice and class struggle, and its commitment to radical social change. To students who came of age in the '60s and who were caught up in the American anti-Vietnam war movement, Marxist analysis of capitalism seemed to offer important insight. Feminist disillusionment with Marxism came from two sources, analytical and practical.

Analytically the central Marxist concept of *class,* rooted as it is in the abstract model of relations of production, excludes women (Acker 1997, 37; NaKano-Glenn 1997, 81–2). Efforts to fit women's domestic work into Marxist categories has largely failed. A powerful example of this failure is provided by Nellie McClung (1972, 91–2) in her autobiography *In Times Like These*. A farmer with a 1000 acre farm would be classified within a Marxist framework as wealthy business class with substantial capital resources. The farmer's wife and children would be classified as sharing his status. Yet the males and females within this family actually occupy very different class positions, measured by both property

and inheritance laws of the time. When the male farm-owner died, his three sons between them inherited all the farm. His unmarried 40-year-old daughter who had contributed farm and household labour all her adult life, got only $100 and one cow. His wife received merely "her keep with one of the boys". The three sons thus continued to have capital resources and could be classified as at least in the 'small business' class. The daughter, however, had no productive resources of her own, and if her brothers did not wish to keep her, she would have to seek wage-work as a household servant. The widowed mother was left virtually destitute, beholden to her sons for 'her keep'. The feminist critique of Marxist class analysis is that it only works for men. Classifying this farmer's wife and his unmarried daughter as 'wealthy business class' is ideological in that it obscures their actual dependent servant status. This would be true for all families where the business assets or career credentials are the property only of the man. But if this is true, then how should one classify 'homemakers'?

A second source of disillusionment with Marxism came from practical political experience. Women who became active in left-wing politics in the '70s often encountered rejection from men on the left (Smith 1977; Smith and Malnarich 1983). They found their struggles on behalf of women's oppression characterized as divisive and misguided, and their concerns trivialized. Women were widely seen as politically backward for not supporting the union struggles of their working-class husbands and, at worst, as class enemies for their greater willingness to work for lower wages than men. What the Marxist activists did not comment on was the structurally gendered reality of the total economic dependence of homemaker-wives on their husband's wages to provide a home and security for their children and themselves. It is her husband's work and his wages, not hers. If he should choose to drink his money with his friends, or should go on strike, or get fired or blacklisted for political agitation, her world comes crashing down, but it is still his business and not hers. Male activists, committed to the cause of class struggle, still largely failed to see women's oppression, and indeed sometimes actively contributed to the oppression in their personal lives.

Relations of Patriarchy

The multi-faceted character of women's oppression is illustrated in the account of the life of one woman living with an abusive husband, cited by Smith in her essay on the conflict between Feminism and Marxism (1977, 40).

Smith challenges her readers to figure out the nature of the trap that this woman, and thousands like her, found herself in. The trap has multiple dimensions, and all of them taken together constitute what feminists refer to as *relations of patriarchy:*

> [She] had endured a nightmare marriage for 30 years. Time and again she had tried to break out. She often went to her mother's but her husband had broken in there and taken her back. The police never did anything to stop him because it was a marital quarrel. Nobody else wanted to be involved. After all, she did have a roof over her head, didn't she? He always kept her short of money. She took a job once but had to work 12 hours to earn overtime to make her salary equal to a man's and that meant leaving the children alone in the evening. After six months of that she gave it up. Each time she and her children went back to her husband, he got her pregnant again. Each time they were treated worse because he knew they could not choose but take it. He used to taunt her with "Where can you go? What can you do"?

The challenge is to see how culture, socialization, the economy, class, schooling, childcare responsibilities, control over sexual relations, law, criminal justice, social services, welfare, and professional discourses are all interrelated in the lived experience of oppression that this woman endured. Culture and patterns of socialization are implicated in the assumptions people have about marriage and divorce, religious and moral obligations to sustain a stable two-parent home for children, differential responsibilities for parenting, and so on. These are revealed in the kinds of advice and support or rejection that women seeking to leave a relationship typically receive from various authority figures including religious leaders, social service workers, lawyers, and police, and also from relatives, friends and neighbours. The economy is certainly implicated, with a gendered labour market in which women's average earnings are far below those of men. The large majority of children who depend financially upon a single-parent mother live below the federal poverty line. The public school system and curriculum are also implicated in gendered career training, guidance, and role-modelling for girls. Relations of reproduction are especially significant in this trap, with women expected to take the bulk of responsibility for child-care. For the woman in Smith's example, taking a job with the long hours required to support her children financially meant leaving them alone in the evenings. The combination of her husband's total control over sexual relations with her, and her lack of access to reliable birth control technology or to abortion results in repeated pregnancies, and more children who depend on her care. The law, criminal justice, and the state, are also heavily implicated. Smith's article was written in the late 1970s, when police routinely refused to intervene in domestic violence, and laws against rape did not apply to husband-wife relations. People in the women's movement fought long and hard to get state funding for Transition Houses—safe places for women and children fleeing abusive homes. But even now, almost three decades later, getting an effective restraining order against an angry, abusive spouse remains very difficult. Smith suggests further that should a marriage break down and the husband/father leave the relationship, the true nature of the trap for the wife/mother becomes fully visible, because she is still in it. Women who walk out on their children are sanctioned in very different ways from men who walk out. The feminist concept of *relations of patriarchy* tries to name and so to make visible this network of interrelated social processes.

Gender Bias in Mainstream Social Science

The challenge that the feminist perspective raises for mainstream sociological theory is how to account for the relative invisibility of these relations of patriarchy—their unnoticed or taken-for-granted character. We need to ask what it was about classical sociology that made women's oppression so difficult to see. McRobbie's (1991) feminist revisiting of Marxist cultural studies in England reveals just how marked was this failure to notice women and the specifically gendered character of oppression (Cohen 1955; Willis 1981; Hebdige 1979). The studies focussed on working-class subcultures, but defined them entirely with reference to male behaviour, styles and values. Girls, if they appear at all, are portrayed only in marginalised and stereotypical ways.

The problem is not merely that male researchers choose to study young men rather than young women, but that the terms of reference are so narrowly defined that entire dimensions of the boys' lives are left out, and their brutally patriarchal orientation to sexuality ignored. What we learn about is public behaviour of Teddy boys, mods, rockers, and motor-cycle boys in the streets, and in relation to schools, work, and the criminal justice system. Girls are less free to be on the streets, less likely to be involved in violence, or to have sufficient disposable income to buy motor bikes, so they become invisible to researchers who focus only on the public world.

There is a structured absence of any attention to family and domestic life. We do not find out what happens when a 'mod' boy goes home after a weekend on drugs. The lads may get by with each other on the streets but they do not eat, sleep, or make love there (McRobbie 1991, 19-20). There is little recognition of the extent to which the symbolic and temporary flight of teds, mods, and rockers, from the 'family trap' takes place at the expense of women, especially mothers and girlfriends. Marxist researchers like Cohen (1955), Corrigan (1979), Willis (1981), and Hebdige (1979) highlight and even celebrate the aggressive masculinity through which the lads kick against the oppressive structures of capitalism. They ignore how the language of these macho styles is unambiguously degrading to women. Studies recount how schoolboys scorn their teachers as 'cunts', and voice their future goals as "fucking as many women as I can" (McRobbie 1991, 21, citing Willis 1981). Skinhead boys brag about hitting their girlfriends to keep them in line, and take the welfare cheques intended to support the girlfriend and her baby. Yet male researchers seemed oblivious to these blatantly patriarchal aspects of the lower-class youth cultures they researched. In their writings they frequently reproduced the comments made about girls by the boys they studied as if they were simply factual statements. Fyvel, for example, refers in his study of teddy boys to "dumb, passive teenage girls, crudely painted" (Fyvel 1963, cited in McRobbie 1991, 1). Willis similarly describes the unattached girls who hung around with the motor-bike boys as follows: "What seemed to unite them was a common desire for an attachment to a male and a common inability to attract a man to a long-term relationship. They tended to be scruffier and less attractive than the attached girls" (Willis 1981, cited in McRobbie 1991, 1–2). Willis also dismisses them as "unforthcoming, unwilling to talk and they retreat, in giggles, into the background". McRobbie suggests that such comments more accurately display the researchers' biases and their unconscious adoption of the attitudes of the boys they are studying than any accurate description of the girls themselves.

Within these classical sociological perspectives, the roles of men and women in reproduction tended to be seen as 'natural' or biologically determined, and thus not requiring sociological explanation. Such assumptions made the structural oppression of women difficult to see. Feminist theorizing challenged the taken-for-granted character of categories like 'male' and 'female', and 'masculine' and 'feminine', insisting that these are social constructions. These challenges to such fundamental notions of gender identity helped to foster *postmodernist* thought in sociology (Stacey 1997, 136; Marshall 2000, 68). **Postmodernism** refers to a contemporary approach within cultural studies and philosophy that focuses on uncertainty, impermanence, doubt, and the continual transformation and recombining of once disparate categories. Feminist scholarship was influential in fostering these new schools of thought.

Sociology looks very different now from what it did in the 1970s. There is now a vast body of sociological research and literature on women. But some feminists remain concerned that the critical edge and politicizing potential of the feminist perspective is being lost (Marshall 2000, 24). Few male sociologists, either faculty or students, show much interest in courses focussing on women or gender issues (Connell 1997). Much mainstream research includes women as a category for sorting data but without critical feminist analysis. Marshall's survey of six Canadian introductory sociology texts (2000, 30–33) shows that gender as a category is rarely referenced outside chapters specifically on gender and family. Feminism as a body of theory gets short shrift.

Diversity in Feminist Thought

Feminist theory has not emerged all in one piece. It is not uncommon to find alternative and sometimes contradictory arguments within feminist literature. As noted above, feminist research in sociology began with a focus on women as *objects,* asking such basic questions as where are women in relation to the situation or issue being studied, how are they differently situated from men, and if they are not involved, why not (Lengermann and Niebrugge-Brantley 1990). This remains the major form in which feminist work has been incorporated into mainstream sociology.

Feminist research gradually shifted to the study of women as *subjects,* investigating how a shift in perspective from typically male to female standpoint can radically alter our sense of what is going on. In an early study of union participation, male leaders criticized women as apathetic because they turned up irregularly for union meetings and mostly remained silent (Smith 1979, 16). From the standpoint of women, however, patriarchal union organization, not female apathy largely explained their limited involvement. Union meetings were routinely scheduled in late afternoon and evening time-slots—times when many women were otherwise occupied in picking up children from schools and day-care, giving them their dinner, and preparing them for bed. Women further complained that when they did speak up at union meetings their voices were not heard, and topics raised by them not followed up. Issues of particular interest to women, like maternity benefits, flexible hours, child-sick days, benefits for part-time workers, sexual harassment in the workplace, the wage gap between male and female workers, and the like, tended not to be taken seriously by male union members. They might be included in negotiations, but only to be traded off for percentaged wage increases which mostly benefited the already higher-paid male workers. What looks like apathy from one perspective looks like patriarchy from another.

Feminist standpoint sociology developed into the postmodern focus on multidimensional, shifting and situated standpoints, with the recognition that women do not form a homogenous group. People experience themselves simultaneously in terms of gender, class, race, ethnicity, age and sexual orientation. The relative salience of these dimensions of self varies with the situations and struggles people find themselves in (Marshall 2000 ch. 2). Consider how vastly different the experience of being a mother of a pre-school-aged child is for women in the following situations: an undergraduate student, a teenage single-parent with grade 9 education, the wife of a high-income professional breadwinner, a woman with a lesbian partner, a migrant woman working as a nanny in Toronto while her own children live in another country, a Native woman living on a reservation, a woman who herself holds a demanding executive position in a corporation. No one role description could meaningfully encompass all these experiences. Yet every situation is gendered, in the sense that the comparable experiences of women and men in equivalent situations would be markedly different.

Schools of Feminist Thought

Feminist theory varies with the assumptions that guide research and the kind of explanations that authors favour when trying to account for gender inequality. Five broad schools of feminist thought have been identified although in practice there is much overlap (Jaggar and Rothenberg 1984; Tong 1989). **Liberal feminism** begins from the assumption that discrimination against women is the central mechanism perpetuating gender inequality—initially in the form of legal barriers to

women's entry into higher education and the professions, and later in more subtle prejudices that work to reduce opportunities for women. **Marxist feminism** looks to the workings of capitalism to explain women's material subordination. It is in the interests of capitalists to divide workers along gender lines to facilitate the greater exploitation of women as cheap labour. Women's domestic labour is also exploited by capitalists as it cheapens the cost of reproducing and maintaining labour. **Socialist-feminism** favours a more dual-systems theory approach arguing that in addition to exploitation by capitalists, women as wives, mothers, and daughters are exploited by men. The bodily support services that women typically provide for men in their homes serve to free up men's time for greater leisure and public-arena activities, and so gives men a major competitive edge as employees. **Radical feminism** locates the arena of gender inequality and struggle more squarely in male control over female sexuality and reproduction, particularly through the threat of sexual violence. **Cultural feminism** locates the struggle more in discourse, and internalization of cultural meanings that stereotype and often denigrate the female and the feminine.

To gain a feeling for the usefulness of these different explanatory approaches you might try to apply each in turn to the situation described above of a woman who feels trapped in an abusive marriage. Different aspects of her situation are highlighted in turn, and all may play some role, although varying in importance for individual cases. Each approach has fostered political movements to struggle against these multiple dimensions of women's oppression.

As feminist theory has broadened to encompass recognition of the diversity of women's subjective positions, these theoretical distinctions are becoming less important (England 1999, 263). Theorists like Marshall (2000) advocate a re-thinking of feminist frameworks to move towards a more fluid understanding of gendering as a process rather than the attribute of a person. The concept of **gendering** refers to a view of gender identities as emerging out of different material situations that men and women find themselves in as they take up particular practical struggles. The assumption here is that we do not first identify ourselves as female or male, and then take up gender issues. Rather, we first encounter gendered issues like struggles over reproductive labour, or sexual violence, and then identify ourselves as female or male in responding to these experiences. Gender identity is thus accomplished, not something fixed or given for either male or female individuals. All women or all men will not always feel themselves lined up on opposite sides of an issue. In some circumstances, being a woman and not a man may be the single most salient feature of one's identity. In others, being a black woman may be sufficiently different from being a white woman that racialized identity takes precedence.

Where feminist theory differs from abstract postmodernism, Marshall insists, is that there is a material base to gendered identity. This material base is not the fact of biological sex difference. It is the fact of gendered relations of reproduction, together with the myriad of gendered inequalities in access to and control over resources and services, status, recognition, sexual freedom, and the like. It is the gendered character of social structures, not biology, that continually reproduces gender as a salient feature of individual identity.

The Politics of Feminism and Backlash

Feminist theories create a language through which it has become possible to see women's oppression. This language itself has become contested and politicized, with both feminists and non-feminist critics and opponents struggling over the meaning and definition of 'feminism'. The hegemonic view of feminism in mass media, Vavrus maintains (2002, ch. 1), is *postfeminist liberalism,* a view that works to depoliticize feminism by attributing all power differentials and under-representation of women in positions of status and influence to individual weaknesses, rather than to patriarchal societal structures. This hegemonic view accepts the right of women to work in formerly male-dominated jobs for higher salaries, and assumes that the 'level playing field' between women and men has been largely achieved. Consequently, if women are manifestly not achieving equal status with men, it must be due to different average abilities and efforts and to different lifestyle choices. Postfeminist liberals readily point to evidence that gender equality has been achieved in completion of undergraduate degrees in Canada since 2000, although women and men tend to choose different programs. Women have long outnumbered men in most liberal arts and humanities undergraduate programs, while men dominate in physical sciences, computer science, mathematics and engineering.

Postfeminist liberalism is not pro-patriarchy in the sense of favouring male dominance over women, but it is non-feminist. It suggests that problems based on sex and reproduction are largely resolved, and hence that feminism as a political movement is irrelevant or out of date. It represents feminist issues around relations of reproduction as matters of lifestyle choices, choices to prioritize having children and being with them over career ambitions. In this hegemonic representation, conflict between employment and home-making and child-rearing are best resolved by women prioritizing home-making roles while children are young, while men prioritize career and 'bread-winning' roles. Assumed within this representation is the functionalist view of role conflict and incompatible role demands, best resolved by some level of gender-role segregation. Rather than seeing 'the personal as political', postfeminist liberalism defines political struggles as private and personal matters. The structural features of gendered inequalities in all spheres of wealth, power and influence in society are reduced to issues of personal abilities and lifestyle choices. The more extreme anti-feminist 'backlash' position blames feminism itself for generating unnatural or unrealistic expectations among women. In this view, the women's movement foments competitiveness and hostility between women and men that feminism then denounces (Faludi, S. 1991; Vavrus ibid).

Theorizing Sexual Diversity

The assumption that gender identities are neither predefined nor fixed has opened space for more research into diverse and non-hegemonic forms of gendering, that Seidman (1996) loosely calls "Queer theory"—focussing on gay, lesbian, bisexual and transgendered identity formation, and the politics of struggles around which these identities emerge and coalesce. Queer theory challenges the binary categorization of gender into exclusively male or female, suggesting that this dualism is not natural, but rather the socially-constructed effect of its continual reinforcement within all societal institutions. In so doing, queer theory challenges foundational cultural assumptions about social institutions like the family, and the organization of relations of reproduction. A Marxist focus traces the linkages between the shift from feudalism to individual wage-work and the emergence of the possibility of distinctive homosexual communities, first for males and later for females (Kinsmen 1987, ch. 2; Frank 1987). The social constructionist approach, building on Foucault's (1978) seminal work traces how long historical shifts in conceptualization of sexual practices—as sinful activity, as specific 'types' of people, as psychological or medical illness, or as lifestyle choice, are associated with profound shifts in institutionalized responses. The approach of institutional ethnography traces how such responses, particularly in schools, function to reinforce hegemonic heterosexuality, and simultaneously to construct the everyday lived experiences and gendered self identities of people who live outside the hegemonic norm (Connell 1987; Khayatt 1992; Smith 1998). The postmodernist focus on identity politics explores how gendered subjectivities emerge and change in contexts of struggle around material concerns (Marshall 2000, ch. 2).

The feminist perspective, in its diverse forms, challenges us fundamentally to let go of images and stereotypes of essential 'maleness' or 'femaleness'. Feminist theory challenges the assumption that people can be meaningfully slotted into 'male' or 'female' categories, or that these categories constitute causes of subsequent behaviour. We are challenged further to resist thinking of 'gender' as to do only with women, and to recognize that masculinity is as historically specific and socially constructed as femininity. Feminism posits gender identity, along with other all other aspects of identity, as negotiated social processes, emerging from situated practical experiences, material interests and struggles, and informed by available social and cultural resources. In this regard, feminism has a close affinity with postmodernism

In summary, the feminist perspective places the social organization of relations of reproduction at the centre of sociological analysis. Reproduction is understood broadly to refer to the nurture and care of children and bodies generally. These relations are pervasively gendered and hierarchical, and systemically reinforced through all major societal institutions. They are also pervasively naturalized or biologized within mainstream (malestream) sociological perspectives, and thus rendered largely invisible or irrelevant to the discipline of sociology, or trivialized as obvious matters of private choice. Feminist theory struggles to make visible these gendered relations of ruling, with the wider political agenda of changing them.

Feminist perspectives on Culture and Representation

Feminist perspectives see cultural representations of male and female as highly politicized and saturated with power (Barker 1999, 22). Women have been relatively excluded from the creation of western culture (Smith 1975). Historically it was almost entirely men who occupied all the social positions associated with the creation

of culture—positions in higher education, the professions, law, politics, religion, art, and mass media. More recently women have entered these positions in far greater numbers, but the frames of thinking and criteria for evaluation have been pre-established. Women's contributions are judged by pre-defined male standards.

The male standard is particularly pronounced in psychoanalysis, the influential school of analytical psychology founded by Sigmund Freud. Freud argues that the origins of culture are biologically rooted in male sexuality and founded on "the Law of the Father" (Freud 1905; Grosz 1990). The most basic primal drive for infants, Freud reasoned, is the urge to possess the mother who satisfies all basic physical needs and pleasures, and who is the first love object. But this primal sexual desire is taboo. It brings a boy in direct conflict with his father arousing the profound anxiety that his more powerful father might retaliate and castrate him. Freud names this conflict *the oedipus complex*. The oedipus complex is resolved only by repression of incestuous sexual love into the unconscious, and the displacement of this powerful emotional energy into more acceptable motivations, recognized in the conscious mind as adult heterosexual love and the morals, values and commitments of family and community life associated with it. The incest taboo is thus the origin of culture.

Girls, Freud reasoned, do not experience these powerful drives of emotional repression and displacement associated with the oedipus complex, and hence do not contribute the same emotional forces to the creation of culture. Female infants also desire possession of the mother, but this cannot be realized. In Freud's view, this is not because of conflict with the father, but because they lack a penis. They are biologically incapable of expressing powerful sexual drives in the same way as boys, and so are destined to become more passive. They can realize these primal drives only vicariously through pregnancy and giving birth to a male child. Girls overcome their biological castration to achieve true femininity as objects of male desire.

In psychoanalysis the distinction between male and female is the most basic of a series of binary or either/or distinctions that characterize western culture—distinctions like presence/absence, active/passive, culture/nature, self/other, sacred/profane, public/private, and the like. In all these binary oppositions, the second or subordinate term is associated with female, and is defined through its relation to the primary male term. Woman is 'not man', defined by what she lacks. Freud's theories have had a profound impact on studies of culture. The anthropologist Claude Levy-Strauss posits the oedipus conflict as the principal universal feature of human culture, linked to the universal prohibition against incest, the principle of *exogamy* or rule that sexual relations and marriage ought to take place only outside the kinship group, resulting in the exchange of women across kin groups (Franklin et. al., 1991, 9).

Feminist theories of culture struggle both within and against psychoanalytic theories to achieve a more positive understanding of women and women's contribution to cultural life. Jacques Lacan (Lacan 1972; Grosz 1990, 96–7; Barker 1999, 21) replaces the biological determinism in Freudian theory with a theory of language as the origins of culture. It is not the penis as biological fact that establishes male power over female, Lacan argues, but its cultural status as 'phallus', as symbol of the social power that will accrue to male children but not to females. Our sense of ourselves as male or female is learned at the oedipal stage as we first learn to talk. In our conscious mind we are aware only of the culturally acceptable ideas and emotions. All the emotions and drives that language fails to express are repressed into the unconscious mind, experienced only indirectly through metaphors or associations.

Feminist psychoanalysts like Mitchell (1975), Kristeva (1986) and Irigaray (1985) draw from Lacan's reformulation of Freud the insights that gendered identities, even deeply felt emotional experiences of femininity, and motherhood, are best understood not as natural or biological givens, but as socially constructed through language (Turner 1990, 28: Barker 1999, 88–94). It follows that it might be possible to explore a more authentic pre-oedipal stage of life in which undifferentiated masculine and feminine characteristics are combined in infants, a stage before they are separated and hierarchized in language. It might also be possible to develop a woman's language without the phallocentric traces of western patriarchal culture. They sketch a vision of a women-centred language that privileges not the phallus, but women's reproductive power—their capacity to give birth and to suckle infants. They acknowledge, however, that it is almost impossible to create such a transformative language without the prior transformation of social order. In the meantime feminists struggle to express alternative representations while using existing phallocentric language. As the feminist poet, Audre Lorde, expresses it, "the master's tools will never dismantle the master's house" (1984, 110–113).

Where feminist cultural critique has been effective is in exposing the patriarchal roots of much of western culture. Patriarchal culture can be seen as rooted in male envy of female powers. Mary O'Brien (1981) takes up the theme that central religious images in Greek and Christian traditions are rooted in male envy of female reproductive powers. She cites the recurring theme of male gods who create offspring without female potency being involved, suggesting that such myths reflect efforts by men to compensate through culture for their alienation from birth and human continuity. The institution of marriage, with males defined as head of household and children named through their male lineage, can be seen as reflecting the same male drive to control reproduction vicariously through possession of a wife and her children.

Nancy Chodorow (1978; 1989) offers another materialist interpretation of psychoanalysis, suggesting that girls are more passive because they do not need to break from their mother as boys do. They can identify directly with her as female, while boys are forced to break away from their mothers to identify with their fathers and other men. Girls may experience 'penis envy' not as something they lack in a biological sense, but as a struggle for personal autonomy from mother and motherhood (Van Zoonen 1994, 23).

These feminist re-readings of psychoanalysis have been criticized in turn for assuming an *essentialist* version of gender identity—an identity that is fixed in infancy and thereafter unchanging (Van Zoonen 1994, 29-33; Barker 1999, 27-9). Others argue that our sense of ourselves as masculine or feminine emerges not solely in early childhood experiences but throughout life, in response to historical and social situations we find ourselves in. This shift in assumptions has prompted a critical focus on agencies of socialization—schools, religious institutions, and especially on mass media representations of femininity and masculinity. Researchers challenge pervasive cultural portrayals of women in stereotyped roles as homemaker, wife-mother, secretary, and nurse, or shopping for household goods while authoritative male voice-overs give advice. The challenge also the anorexic models used to sell beauty products for women, and the dangerous pornographic representations of women's bodies as sex objects for male pleasure.

Postmodern feminist critics have challenged this research in turn for implicitly assuming that there is some 'accurate' image of 'real' women, in relation to which media representations can be shown to be distortions (Marshall 2000, ch. 2). They also critique the assumption that there is a direct transfer from media messages or agents of socialization generally, to internalized identity.

Audience members can and do reject messages, ignore or reinterpret them, depending on their own situations and struggles. In this new view, gender identity work is understood as a continual process, in which people draw on available cultural images as resources for their individual identity projects. This project is itself embedded in practical material conditions with which people struggle. Feminist consciousness-raising groups growing out of the second-wave feminist movement of the 1970s have been critically important in sustaining an alternative feminist cultural identity (Staggenborg 2001). These cultural networks in turn provided the organizational foundation for collective political action focussed around such issues as equal rights legislation, shelters for abused women, rape crisis centres, reproductive choice, and most recently the right of lesbian and gay couples to marry.

Conclusion

Hopefully it is clear but now that there can be no one sociological description of Canadian society that precedes analysis. Different perspectives focus variously on integrating cultural systems, modes and relations of production, systems of knowledge production, or relations of reproduction. They highlight very different features of social experience, and alter the kinds of questions we think to ask about what we notice. The challenge of this course is to develop qualities of sociological imagination that will allow you to continually shift perspectives as you think about social life. The goal is to learn to recognize and articulate underlying assumptions, both explicit and implicit, in descriptions of social life that you read about, and that you produce for yourselves. This capacity gives you the freedom to decide for yourselves the usefulness of different perspective, alone and in combination. You will know why you are adopting one perspective rather than another, and more importantly, you will know what you are choosing not to pay attention to when you do this.

CHAPTER 3

A Critical Look at Methodologies

Sociologists use a variety of research techniques, adapting them for different kinds of research contexts and questions. An important distinction that is often drawn is between *quantitative* and *qualitative* methods. Quantitative methods, which include surveys and census data, try to generate statistical analysis of patterns and trends that apply to large numbers of people. Qualitative methods, which include observations and in-depth interviews, explore the subjective meanings that particular social settings have for members. While there is no fixed correspondence between theoretical perspective and methodology, certain combinations are more common than others. Theorists who favour functionalism, or systems theory, often emulate the physical sciences in stressing quantitative, objective data that can be analysed using high-powered statistical techniques. Political economists draw heavily on statistical analysis of economic data to document exploitative class relations. Theorists who favour interpretive approaches often deride such approaches as 'number crunching' which misses uniquely subjective features of

social life. Feminist researchers have tended to side with qualitative approaches, seeking to give voice to the intensely personal and intimate experiences of women who speak from the margins of society (Duelli Klein 1980; Kirby and McKenna 1989). However, these are not hard and fast divisions. Systems theory is also associated with the technique of participant observation in anthropology, in which researchers try to live as participants in another culture, learning from insiders how the complex web of social institutions comes together as a total cultural system. Many feminist researchers advocate methods to explore the systemic structures that generate women's experiences, that are not immediately visible to the people involved (G. Smith 1990). Yet other feminists have used surveys, census data, and statistical techniques to test generalizations about the situation of large numbers of women (Eichler 1985a, 632–33; Allahar and Cote 1998; Lochhead and Scott 2000). The important question is not which method one might prefer, but which is more appropriate for the particular kinds of evidence one is trying to get. As you will see below, no method is foolproof. Each has its particular strengths and utility, and its particular weaknesses and blind spots. The ideal, therefore, is to have a number of researchers coming at similar issues from different perspectives and starting points. Their studies then will not only complement each other and increase our overall understanding, but will reveal the limitations and blind spots of specific approaches.

The objective of this chapter is help you to become intelligent readers of research. You should not just passively absorb "facts". Rather, it is important to be constructively critical of research findings by developing an awareness both of the strengths of good research and of the inevitable limitations of knowledge.

Experiments

For researchers in the physical sciences, **experiments** are virtually the defining characteristic of the "scientific method". There is no better technique for testing precise causal relationships. The ideal experiment controls, or holds constant, everything that could possibly influence the phenomenon of interest, then allows one **variable** to change. If there is a change in the phenomenon, and the experiment was done properly, one knows that the manipulated variable, and only that one, caused the change. In the terminology of experimental research, the **independent variable** is the presumed cause. This is the one that is manipulated in the experiment to see the effect of its presence or absence. The **dependent variable** is the phenomenon that is thought to depend on or be influenced by the other variable.

One interesting sociological experiment began with the observation that students who habitually sat near the front of classrooms tended to get higher marks on average than students who habitually sat near the back (Dooley 1984, 20–23). Two plausible hypotheses were suggested. The phenomenon could be due to "self selection"; that is, that the more interested and able students chose to sit near the front. Alternatively, it could be that increased interaction and eye contact with the professor stimulated higher performance from students who sat at the front. An experiment was designed to test these theories The professor let students choose where to sit on the first day of classes, then asked them to stay in that place for the next three weeks until he gave the first test. Then he randomly mixed everybody up, with some of the back-row people moving to the front, and some of

the front-row people moving to the back. Three weeks later he tested the students again. The theory was that if self-selection causes the association, then making some of the better students sit at the back would make no difference to their test results. But if sitting at the front under the close eye of the processor was the real cause, then there should be noticeable changes in test results after student were moved. The results supported the self-selection hypothesis, showing that moving people randomly seemed to make little difference to the results. Good students choose to sit at the front while the weaker or less motivated students choose to sit at the back. It was interesting to note, however, that the level of participation, measured by their asking questions and getting involved in class discussions, did change as students were moved from back to front and vice versa. Closeness to the professor rather than personality characteristics of the students seemed to be the major factor in class discussion.

This study has all the elements of a true experiment. It includes a clear theory that either self selection or proximity to professors causes grades to be higher among students who sit near the front. In this experiment the dependent variable is grades. There are two independent variables—proximity to professor and self-selection. Two logical predictions are derived from this theory. If the theory of self-selection is correct, then moving the students will make no difference to their marks. If proximity to the professor is the correct theory, then moving students will make a clear difference. The researcher changes one variable—where people sit—and everything else is held constant. All students receive the same lectures and tests. The researcher observes what happens and decides which theory is correct on the basis of whether the results were as predicted.

Future researchers who wish to critique an experiment can first *replicate* or repeat it with different classes of students to see if the same pattern holds. You might try this experiment in your own sociology classes to see if you find comparable patterns. Researchers also need to closely examine the *measurement* of the dependent and independent variables to decide if there is a truly good fit between the original concepts and the measures used. If proximity to professor is a variable that works slowly, perhaps the three-week gap between first and second test is not sufficient to really judge its impact on grades. There may also be other hidden influences that were not entirely controlled in the experiment. Students may be reacting to the fact that they know what the professor is testing for.

A second experiment was designed to test the effect of different levels of severity in prosecution of domestic assault cases on likelihood of repeat offences (Sherman and Berk 1984; Sherman 1992). In this study the dependent variable was evidence of repeat offences, while the dependent or proposed causal variable was reaction by police to domestic assault calls. In cooperation with the Minneapolis Police Department, the researchers arranged for 330 assault cases to be *randomly* assigned to one of three conditions: arrest and charge the offending spouse, order the offender out of the house for eight hours but not arrest, or merely given a verbal warning. Random assignment means that treatment of each case was determined by chance or luck of the draw. Neither police nor researchers could influence which offender would or would not be charged. This was to ensure that police did not bias the study by arresting the more unpleasant offenders. Cases where injuries were serious, or where a spouse insisted that an arrest be made, were exempted from the study. Researchers measured the effect of different treatment by police records of repeat offences and by telephone interviews with victims every two weeks for the next six months. The results showed large differences by treatment. Only 13 percent of those arrested assaulted their partner again over the six-month period compared with 26 percent of those who were separated from their partner but not arrested. This group differed little from those who were merely given a verbal warning. Researchers concluded that the 'deterrence theory' was supported. Harsher punishment deters repeat deviance. This study was influential in changing police protocols in favour of mandatory arrests.

Replication of the study in six more cities, however, produced inconsistent results with four of them showing long-term increases in domestic violence among those arrested. A detailed examination of cases suggested a new explanation. Offenders who were married and employed were less likely to offend if arrested, but those who were unmarried and unemployed were more likely to repeat offenses if arrested (Schutt 1996, 50; Sherman et. al., 1992). Researchers proposed a new theory of social control. The shame resulting from a public arrest is a stronger deterrent when individuals have a 'stake in conformity', or more to lose from deviant labelling. This 'fits' the data, but has yet to be tested in a controlled experiment.

Critics of the original study suggest that measurement of the dependent variable is flawed (Dobash and Dobash 2000, 261). Both police records and victim's reports are well known to seriously underestimate the true extent of domestic violence. Perhaps the wives of employed men are also reluctant to face the shame of a second arrest, and victims may fear reprisals for talking with researchers. More than half the victims in the first study refused to carry out follow-up interviews (Schutt 1996, 48).

Experiments work best in specially equipped settings like **small groups laboratories** in universities, designed so that researchers can control key variables that influence behaviour, such as seating arrangements, lighting, noise, whether subjects in the experiment can or cannot communicate with each other, the exact task that subjects engage in, and so on. Archibald (1978, ch. 7) describes studies of coalitions and bargaining in competitive three-person games, and how all-male, all-female, and mixed-gender groups behave. The experiments suggest that in games with two women and one men, or with two men and one woman, the two members in the majority sex appear to compete for the member of the opposite sex. Each of the two men, for example, would try to get the woman on his side against the other man. All-female groups tended to be less egoistic than men, being more likely to form a three-way rather than a two-against-one coalition, dividing the outcomes equally.

Limitations of Social Experiments

The inherent limitation of experiments in such artificial and simplified contexts, is that it is risky to generalize from them to predict how people will behave in more complex and longer-term social situations. It is commonly students from large undergraduate courses in sociology and psychology who are used as subjects for experimental research because they are readily available and easily persuaded to participate. We cannot assume that how students play games in a research laboratory will accurately reflect the behaviour of people in far more complex settings like managers in business meetings. Archibald notes further that the competitive behaviour evident in these games may be culturally specific, reflecting how people have learned to behave in competitive capitalist societies rather than ones based on co-operative forms of economy.

When experiments are carried out in real-life settings like the classroom behaviour and the domestic violence arrest studies described above, researchers face major complications controlling the multiple and interconnected influences Students can readily guess the seating-grades hypothesis and strategize to change the outcomes.

Victims of domestic assault can exaggerate or cover up their experiences in anticipation that their abuser will be let off with a caution again or sent to prison, or they could refuse to say anything. Police officers can and did override their orders to randomize caution or arrest responses (Schutt 1996, 54).

Ethical Issues with Experiments

The evasive responses taken by police in the study of the effects of arrests on spousal abuse draws attention to serious ethical issues that arise in research involving people. Is it ethically acceptable for researchers to invoke the authority of the U.S. National Institute of Justice to force police officers to randomize whether they caution or arrest offenders, and to subject unsuspecting victims of domestic assault to such experimentation? The informed consent of police chiefs was gained prior to the study, but not the consent of individual officers who had to confront the families. Furthermore, the victims who call the police for help had no opportunity to refuse to participate in the experiment, or even to know that they were being experimented upon. This is notwithstanding the fact that how police respond to the domestic abuse call potentially opens victims to the risk of further assault. The counter-argument in favour of doing this research is that the resulting data was critical for guiding future police protocols and perhaps protecting future victims. How do we balance the risk of harm to unwitting families caught up in the experiment with potential benefits from the knowledge gained?

Consider also the ethical issues involved in the experiment linking where students sit with test results. Suppose I want to test the hypothesis that proximity to me in my introductory sociology classes has a long-term influence on students' grades, would it be ethically acceptable for me to force some of you to sit in the front or back rows for an entire semester against your own inclination, even if I have the power to make you conform? Remember that I am predicting that grades will be adversely affected by making people sit at the back.

The practical difficulties involved in manipulating people in social experiments, combined with serious ethical issues raised by such manipulation, has favoured the use of **quasi experiments** in sociology, rather than classical experiments. In quasi experiments, researchers rely on comparisons among naturally occurring settings where they do not try to randomize or otherwise control the people who are already involved. Research is weaker

in that problems of self selection and prior differences in kinds of people involved in different settings do impact on results, and other possible influences cannot be eliminated. On the other hand, the settings are more realistic and ethical concerns less pressing. Dobash and Dobash (2000) describe their study of two naturally occurring comparison groups of men prosecuted, found guilty and placed on probation for domestic violence. One group of men was ordered by the presiding judge to participate in intensive court-mandated offender treatment programs while the comparison group comprised men sanctioned in other ways, including fines, traditional probation, and prison. Knowing that the two groups were not equivalent to start with, the researchers tried to measure and control for these differences by comparing the men individually on more than 30 theoretically relevant variables. They also measured the effects of treatment by in-depth interviews and postal questionnaires with both men and their women partners at intervention, 3 months following, and 12 months following. They conclude that the court-mandated programs did seem to reduce controlling and intimidating behaviour and improve quality of life for both men and women partners over the 12-month period. Results were also more positive for men in state-sanctioned marriages and for those who were employed than those in the unmarried or unemployed categories. Researchers claim further that their in-depth interviews and follow-up questionnaires provide greater understanding of the subjective meanings and responses of the men and women involved, and hence of the true causal processes at work, than does the exclusively experimental work of Sherman and Berk. We explore these methodological approaches below.

Survey Research
Questionnaires

Survey Research is so commonly associated with sociology as to be virtually synonymous with the discipline in the minds of many people. Typically, surveys involve the use of **questionnaires** or structured interviews in which a series of questions is asked of large numbers of people. In theory, one could approach every person in a population when doing a survey, as when a census is taken. But in practice this is so expensive and time-consuming that usually only a sample of people is used.

A **sample** comprises a small proportion of people carefully selected from a wider population, On a university campus with 30 000 students, for example, a researcher might interview a selected sample of 300 students (a one-percent sample) to study aspects of student life. The goal is to use information gained from the sample to generalize to the wider population it represents.

It is very important that the sample be selected carefully so that it fairly represents the range of experience and characteristics in the population. The data garnered from a survey of 300 students in a local pub, for example, would not be representative of the student body as a while since these students differ in important respects from others who rarely or never go to pubs and hence would not be included in the sample.

The ideal way to select a sample is through a random process. A random sample is one in which every member of a population has an equal chance of being selected, leaving no possibility that researchers can select their friends or particular types of people who might be easily available. To draw a random one-percent sample of university students, we might get the registrar's list of students, close our eyes and stick a pin in the list to choose the first person for our sample, and then select every hundredth name thereafter, until we had the number of names we wanted for our survey. In practice, many surveys fall short of this ideal because randomized samples of people tend to be difficult to contact. While all students at one university are concentrated on one or two campuses, a random sample of the residents of Ontario would be spread over thousands of square miles and take years to contact in person. Sociologists have ways of stratifying or grouping members of such a huge population to make sampling more realistic while still being reasonably representative of the whole. Smaller, low-budget, exploratory studies often settle for a sample of people who are easy to get. The caveat is that while their findings may be insightful, they cannot be assumed to describe accurately the wider population.

One important advantage that surveys have over experiments is that they permit **multivariate analysis**. As we have seen, an experiment studies the effect of change in one variable while all others remain the same. Surveys, in contrast, can gather information about a number of variables at the same time and explore how combinations of variables influence the issue of interest to the researcher. In a survey of students, for example, we might be interested in finding out why some maintain a high grade point average while others fail or

barely scrape by. We have good reason to believe that no single variable can explain this. Multiple variables may be involved We might want to find out not only about students' IQs, but also about how many classes they attend, how many hours a week they study, how often they visit a pub, how many hours of paid employment they have per week, the family responsibilities they carry, and so on. Do less intelligent students who study long hours do better or worse on average than highly intelligent students who spend more time socializing than studying? What difference does it make if we also take into account that some students come to university straight from school while others have not been in full-time education for years? With the aid of computers and statistical techniques it is possible to see how sets of variables interact in combination.

One example of large-scale survey research that I was involved in explored patterns of immigrant settlement and race relations in an English city (Richmond et. al., 1973). It used a questionnaire with 172 questions, covering such topics as housing conditions and overcrowding, social and economic status, local slang and idioms, work experience, including discrimination in getting a job and possible prejudice experienced from fellow workers, satisfaction with the neighbourhood, interaction between residents of different ethnic origins, and continuing relations between immigrants and people in their country of origin. The survey also covered the topic of **acculturation**, the extent to which immigrants have adopted the culture—lifestyle, behaviour patterns, values, and attitudes—that prevails among local people.

Responses to a range of questions provided a wealth of material for understanding the life experiences of immigrants and their locally-born neighbours and allowed researchers to explore a multitude of hypotheses concerning how variables might relate to each other. Do relations with neighbours improve with acculturation? Are immigrants measurably worse off than indigenous people with respect to housing? Does the level of cooperation or conflict with neighbours vary with ethnic groups, social class, or family size and structure? Does it vary in terms of whether immigrants keep their houses in good repair?

Since a complete **enumeration** of the 2633 households in the chosen area was used as the basis for the sample, one can be confident that the results are based on a representative cross-section of the community, free from the biased coverage that would occur if any volunteers or personal friends and contacts of the researchers had been used a sources of information. This particular study was carried out by a team of researchers who went door-to-door, called back many times, took great pains to encourage people to be interviewed because it was so important to learn how everyone felt, and arranged for foreign-language interviews whenever necessary. Virtually no other research technique could have provided the quality of information derived from this survey. Even living within the area as a member of the community would have been less effective, since friendship patterns and acquaintances are invariably limited and selective. Mailed questionnaires or forms that people are left to fill in themselves could not have achieved this very high level of coverage. This survey in Britain provided the blueprint for a number of similar surveys in Canadian cities by the York University Institute of Race Relations in Toronto.

Not all survey research is conducted like this. Such exhaustive surveys take a great deal of time, skill, and money. Under the broad term *survey*, there is a wide variety of techniques that can be used to ask people questions. At one extreme, tightly structured questionnaires can be mailed out for people to fill in themselves and post back to the research headquarters. Such an approach may be particularly valuable for collecting data on topics that are sensitive or embarrassing. People may feel more comfortable answering questions about their sexual behaviour, for example, or suicidal thoughts and conflicts with parents, in an anonymous questionnaire than with an interviewer facing them. Mailed questionnaires are also quick, relatively cheap to administer, and can be mailed out simultaneously to very large numbers of people over wide geographic areas.

Limitations of survey research

A number of problems make self-administered questionnaires unsuitable for many kinds of research. Clearly, they cannot be with illiterate subjects. They are also unsuitable for many less-educated people, who, while able to read and write, may have difficulty understanding the language of the questionnaire and expressing themselves in writing. More generally, if the questions are the least bit vague or ambiguous, there is no way for the recipient to ask for clarification. Another common problem is inappropriate answer categories that do not fit the person's peculiar circumstances so that she or he is unable to answer accurately. Since recipients cannot explain to the researcher what the problem is, they are likely to answer randomly or pick an inappropriate response

and leave it to the researcher to work out what they meant. In addition, the researcher has no way of knowing what people answering the questionnaire meant by their answers and can only assume that what they meant is what the researcher would have meant. If you recall what happened in the experiment described in chapter 2, in which students made sense of the random utterances of a supposed counsellor, you can see why the major critique of survey research raised by interpretive sociologists is that researchers are simply reading into the answers the patterns that they are determined to find. In reality, these patterns might not be there at all, There is much evidence that the wording of the questions themselves can determine, at least in part, the kind of answers given. Public opinion pollsters are notorious for asking vague questions that lend themselves to interpretations favoured by those who hire them (Lewis 2001, 136).

Experiments designed to test how people respond to questionnaires suggest that people routinely try to read meanings into questions and construct appropriate answers, even when they cannot possibly know the answer. To oblige the researcher, subjects have been known to rank what, unbeknownst to them, were fictitious television programs. The resulting order is largely a product of the researcher's question, combined with vague associations that the wording raises in subjects' minds. It is entirely possible that other rank orders, such as ethnic preferences, may be equally artificial, with people creating a ranking to oblige the researcher, while actually having no particular preferences.

Other questions distort reality by imposing false answer categories or invalid combinations. Consider a question on the quality of relations between siblings that provides the following answer categories: (1) warm, co-operative, supportive relations; (2) helpful and co-operative much of the time; (3) strained, mildly competitive relations; (4) much competition and tension. The problem is that answer categories do not allow for the possibility that people may have very warm and supportive relations that are also very competitive, or tense relations that are not competitive. According to this question, competition is bad by definition, whatever the respondent might think.

Another problem with questionnaires is that the meaning of answers to questions is commonly context-dependent. For example, attitudes towards the desirability of large families depends heavily on whether one is thinking about family parties or education costs. The coded answer may be meaningless if interpreted out of context (Cicourel 1974). Similarly how one responds to a question on whether small towns are a good place to raise children will vary with the implicit frames of reference that different people use (Bonner 1999). Long-term residents may be positively valuing the closeness of their extended family members, while newcomers from the city may be positively evaluating their increased distance from interfering kin. Long-term members may be thinking of their commitment to their whole community, while short-term residents are evaluating their rational self interests in easier parenting. What matters more to them may be the sense that neighbours recognize their children and so will watch out for them more, and report back any bad behaviour. Also it is quicker to drive children to varied activities than in a city, thus making the job of parenting easier. Objectively the 'same' questionnaire responses can represent very different underlying worldviews.

Responses to scales that try to measure strength of attitudes are also heavily influenced by different comparative reference groups that people may be thinking about when answering. If asked to indicate on a 10-point scale my level of support or opposition to Canada joining the USA in the 2003 war in Iraq, for example, I may well use how strongly my immediate friends seem to feel as a gauge for the strength of my own feelings. Similarly, how strongly I would rate my involvement in delinquent behaviour as a teenager will reflect how I compare myself to others around me as well as how I actually did behave.

Distortions can also arise when researchers inadvertently build biased assumptions into a question. One question asked respondents to agree or disagree with the following statement: "If a married woman has to stay away from home for long periods of time in order to have a career, she had better give up the career" (Eichler 1988, 82–88). More working-class than middle-class respondents indicated agreement with this question, leading the researcher to conclude that working-class people hold more traditional views towards women's roles. Eichler, however, shows that this interpretation may reflect the biases of the researcher rather than the respondents. When a parallel question was added about whether married *men* had better give up their career, more working-class than middle-class people agreed with this as well. The two questions together suggest that what the responses of working-class people really show is a higher value placed on family life over careers generally for both women and men, while middle-class respondents were more inclined to value careers. The middle-class researcher had taken it for granted that a

married man's career would have to take precedence over spending more time at home, and hence not even thought to include the question.

In summary, surveys are only as useful as the quality of the questions asked. A critical reading of research must involve taking a hard look at the questions used to see whether the researcher's interpretation of the answers is warranted or whether some other meaning could reasonably be applied. Reports that provide respondents' answers but omit the questions asked or the context in which questions were embedded are particularly suspect.

Interviews

Interviews as a methodology involve face-to face discussion between researcher and individuals from whom we hope to learn information, these people variously referred to as informants, subjects, respondents, or participants. As these terms suggest, interviews can vary widely. At one extreme interviews involve reading standardized questions to informants with a predefined set of response options, and they are designed to generate quantitative data for statistical analysis. Interviewers are commonly carefully trained to ensure that they do not bias responses by altering the tone or wording of the questions or revealing their own opinions on topics. Much research has gone into how the gender, race, and class characteristics of researcher vis-a-vis respondent may influence responses, and how best to conduct an interview to minimize these effects.

At the other extreme interviews seek qualitative in-depth lifestory narratives focused around the research theme. Such interviews may last for several hours with neither researcher nor participant knowing beforehand all the issues that may be explored in the research conversation. Here there is no expectation of standardized responses. In a widely cited essay on feminist methods Oakley (1981) flatly rejects the standard textbook advice for conducting detached, formal interviews as assuming a 'masculine model of sociology and society' (ibid. 31). In her own research with women on their experience of childbirth she describes her interviews as deeply personal encounters spread over some 9 hours each. These interviews often involved intensely personal exchanges of information, advice, and feelings between herself and the women who participated or co-operated in the research.

Limitations of interview research

Interviews, no less than questionnaires, inherently raise problems of interpretation. Interviews have the advantage over questionnaires in clarifying meanings because the interviewer is there to correct ambiguities and misunderstandings. Response rates are commonly far higher. People may simply throw a questionnaire into the waste basket or never get around to answering it, but they will talk to someone standing in front of them, particularly if the researcher seems friendly and genuinely interested in listening to them. Researchers can also gather much additional, subtle information about confusion, disinterest, or worry, by watching respondents' facial expressions, body language, and so on. This sensitivity is mutual, giving rise to concerns that respondents may tailor their answers to fit what they sense will please the researcher.

Interview responses are often not authentic, in the sense of conveying truly deep, inner feelings and convictions about an issue (Silverman 1993, ch. 5). Respondents typically only have a few seconds to think up an answer to a question, and hence tend to respond by what immediately comes to mind. This is most likely to be standard culturally- expected, common-sense responses, or whatever they think will come across as an acceptable or meaningful answer. They may also offer self-explanatory answers that will avoid prompting a series of 'why do you think that?' type of follow-up questions.

The interview situation itself is also a social encounter in which respondents are necessarily presenting a public image of themselves to another person when being interviewed. Mothers of sick children discussing their encounters with medical practitioners routinely talked in ways that produced themselves as 'morally adequate mothers.' Part of such moral adequacy involved affirming that they thoroughly monitored their baby, and hence 'knew' something was wrong before the doctor told them (Baruch 1981, cited in Silverman 1993, 109). In the same study researchers noted that mothers often recounted 'moral atrocity stories' such as the callousness they noticed in doctors who would announce to them that their baby had a terrifying disability like cystic fibrosis and then not even give them time to ask questions. Videotaped recordings, however, showed that doctors routinely did wait for parents to ask questions, but parents were often experiencing too much shock to formulate any response. The discrepancies between the videotaped evidence and descriptions given by parents led the researchers to suggest that doctors tell parents about the diagnosis at one meeting and then arrange a later one for parents to ask questions.

The distortions that can occur between the meaning a person intends and what their comments are interpreted to mean by a researcher is evident in the reaction of one housewife to the race-relations survey discussed above. At first, she did not want to be interviewed because she felt that if she raised even legitimate complaints about immigrants, researchers would automatically jump to the conclusion that she was racially prejudiced. She explained carefully that she did not dislike immigrants but hated the way that the immigrant men living in rooming houses on her street would whistle and shout sexual remarks when she walked past them, as if she were one of the local prostitutes. She was also disturbed and intimidated by the noise these men made as they crowded onto the steps outside their houses on warm summer evenings. In this neighbourhood it was common for landlords to rent rooms to 8-10 men at a time, who had migrated from Pakistan without their families to find work in Britain. The female interviewer assured the woman that she could understand these feelings. But when the interviewer later discussed the conversation with a more senior male researcher, he responded bluntly that the woman obviously was prejudiced against immigrants and was merely rationalizing her responses. People would naturally be reluctant to express strongly racist views to a naive young white female interviewer, even when directly asked. Perhaps he was correct. But what if the woman meant what she said, that she was distressed, not by their racial characteristics, but by the sexual taunts from crowds of frustrated single men? There was no way researchers, out to prove that English people are prejudiced, would believe her.

Ethical issues in interview research

Important ethical issues arise in using interviews as a research tool. Codes of ethics for sociological research all emphasize the principle of informed consent. People being interviewed have a right to know in advance what the interview will be about and to refuse to be interviewed or to refuse to answer specific questions, and to terminate the interview at any time. Researchers also have an obligation to protect the confidentiality of informants. Beyond such standard advice, Oakley further reminds us that research can be an emotionally intense experience for participants who may be asked to relive powerful life situations like the birth of a child or being beaten by a partner. Research should not be undertaken lightly or carelessly. Hiller and DiLuzio (2004) describe how their research on internal migration within Canada became a catalyst for participants to re-think their entire migration experience, sometimes involving flight from family conflicts and unacknowledged feelings of loneliness and loss. Many spoke of how much they appreciated the opportunity presented by the interview to reflect on these experiences, but the interview could also be profoundly disturbing in opening old wounds and pain.

A group of women associated with the Canadian Research Institute for the Advancement of Women (CRIAW) got together in 1993 to draft a feminist code of ethics that makes explicit issues of power and privilege that arise in research and explore how more egalitarian relations between research participants might be achieved (Muzychka and Poulin 1995).

Participant Observation

Participant observation involves varying degrees of personal involvement in the everyday lives of the people being studied, sharing in their activities on a face-to-face level, observing, questioning, and learning how to participate in their world. This gives the researcher a uniquely valuable position to develop a sympathetic understanding of social reality from the perspectives of the people themselves. This is pre-eminently the methodology of anthropology, since it is ideally suited to developing an understanding of the total culture of a people, especially those who live in small, isolated communities. In sociology, participant observation has been adapted to the study of distinctive subgroups such as work teams, churches, group homes, special-interest organizations, and the like.

The degree to which members of the subgroups are aware that they are being studied has varied from minimal to total disclosure. In his classic study of jazz musicians Becker (1963) writes about his observations of the band in which he himself played, without openly adopting a separate role as 'researcher'. Hochschild (1973) studied a senior citizen's housing project while working as a reporter for the project's monthly newsletter. George Smith (1990) was an activist with the Toronto AIDS group whose political struggles he studied. Ammerman (1987) became of participating member of the Southside Gospel Church in Chicago. She informed the church elders that she was a sociologist interested in

researching the religious community, but the vast majority of congregation members knew her simply as one of themselves.

In other cases researchers have openly represented themselves in the role of researcher, this particularly in situations where they could not pass as a regular group member. Most western anthropologists who wish to study non-industrialized and non-western communities are obvious outsiders. Jean Briggs (1970) could not possibly pass as an Eskimo when she studied a nomadic Innuit community. In fact, members of the community she lived with had to go out of their way to look after her. When Whyte conducted his classic study of *Street Corner Society* (1943), the unemployed Italian men hanging out on the streets of Boston knew he was not one of them but were willing to have him participate in their daily activities. Warren (2003) sought the permission of the course instructors and students to sit in theatre classes and observe how students performed literature from diverse cultural backgrounds, and how, in the process, they performed 'race'. These researchers trade the risk that their presence will disrupt normal activities for the advantage that being known as a researcher gives them the freedom to ask questions and interview participants. Their common experience is that as time passes participants soon forget about the fact that they are being researched and pre-established routines of behaviour re-emerge.

Participatory research offers unparalleled depth of insight, but lacks some of the systematic controls and potential for replication and checking that other research techniques permit. Researchers learn about the groups and activities they are studying through unique networks of personal experiences, friendships and events. Another researcher, joining the group at another time, may have very different experiences. This raises the difficult question of whether one researcher is the more accurate, or whether the group culture itself may have changed over time. The famous anthropologist, Margaret Mead, has been accused of painting an overly harmonious picture of adolescent live in the Samoan community she studied, failing to see the teenage strife, delinquency, and illegitimacy that actually occurred (Mead 1928; Freeman 1983). The Samoans may have gone out of their way to hide this seamier side of community life. The quality of the final analysis in participant observation depends very heavily upon the personal resources and sensitivities of individual researchers. Warren (2003, 1–3) describes his excitement at his first tentative flash of insight into how 'performing white superiority' gets done, while listening to a white researcher describing scenes in schools with predominantly white or black students. His elation was crushed when comments from a black woman in the audience brought the realization that something he was barely able to sense, was obvious to her. His text is full of ethnographic descriptions of student performances through which he reads the active construction of racialization. Other observers of the same scenes, including students in the theatre classes, might well not notice these subtle nuances and patterns.

Ethical issues in participant observation

Participant observation studies, like other forms of research, raise difficult ethical questions. Do sociologists have the right to conduct research on or in a group of people without their prior consent or knowledge? Would it be different if people know that the research is going on but do not understand exactly what it is that the researcher is looking for? Contemporary codes of ethics stress the importance of informed consent, but this does not solve the question of whose consent should be obtained. Practical and political considerations usually dictate that researchers get the permission of leaders or elders in a group or community. But it is hard to argue on moral grounds that such people can legitimately speak for everyone else. Should negative votes by a few members be sufficient to terminate Ammerman's study of Southside Church or Warren's study of theatre students? There are no easy answers to such questions, but sociologists have an obligation to raise them and deal with them as best we can. At the very least, researchers have an obligation not to carry out research in ways that might reasonably be expected to harm their subjects.

Unobtrusive Measures

Among the arsenal of social science research techniques are some that avoid risks of interaction biases between researcher and subjects by focussing on secondary analysis of records that are collected for other purposes and traces of events that have already happened. Some of these are described below.

Census Data and Official Records

Census data are immensely valuable for social science research. These comprehensive surveys of the entire population of a country, carried out every ten years with government funding, and with the force of law to compel people to answer the questions, provides a wealth of information about the social, economic, and **demographic** characteristics of a people, on a scale that no other form of research can parallel. Many sociologists rely on census data as their primary source for studies of population change, hence making it a matter of considerable importance what kinds of questions are included in census forms. The omission of a simple question such as ethnic origin of parents, for example, would greatly hamper the study of migration, assimilation, and discrimination in the labour market. As noted above with respect to surveys, small changes in the wording of questions in census forms result in large changes in data collected. The 1961 census in Canada included the question "To what ethnic or cultural group did you or your ancestor (on the male side) belong on coming to this continent?" (Pryor et. al., 1992). In 1981 the clause "on the male side" was deleted and the naming of multiple ancestries permitted, in recognition of feminist interests in descent through mothers. In 1986 the clause "on first coming to this continent" was dropped, in recognition of the fact that many 'ethnic' groups, like Aboriginal, French Canadian, American, Quebecois, Mexican, and the like, have not technically come from outside the continent of North America. Also, the pre-defined categories or mark-off boxes were altered to include 'Black'. A series of tests in 1986 experimented with how to include 'Canadian' as an ethnic option in census forms. Responses varied from lows of 1 percent to 10 percent if 'Canadian' was not explicitly mentioned, to highs of 30 to 53 percent when it was included as an example of ethnicity and listed as a separate mark box. The great variation in responses reveals the context-dependent character of peoples' ethnic self identification. Shifting terminology in census forms also complicates any long-term analysis of trends in ethnic composition of the Canadian population.

Census data present problems for sociological analysis in other respects, in that the categories used to collect information may not be appropriate for research interests. The census, for example, records the total number of marriages for the period under consideration, but does not indicate whether a given marriage is a first or a subsequent one for the persons involved. It thus becomes impossible to determine how many **reconstituted families** may exist within a community. Similarly, the census records the number of single parents who have children living with them but does not record the number of men who have fathered children without a long-term attachment to the mother. Records of family income as units give no information on how much money the wife might actually have to call her own. Hence many interesting questions about family life cannot be answered using census data because the recording categories do not permit it (Eichler 1988a, 21–23). similar problems arise for sociological researchers that draw on records kept by other government and private agencies such as crime statistics from the Department of Justice, poverty statistics from the Department of Health and Welfare, numbers of people registering for assistance with local food banks, or international data collected by agencies like Amnesty International.

It is important to remember that such reports are generated by officials within bureaucracies who use particular kinds of forms to manage the practical activities of their organization (Smith 1999, 148–51). To understand what the statistics mean one needs to look carefully at how they are collected. Research problems often arise because it is not always clear how particular experiences are coded into categories used for the statistics. Different record keepers may make these decisions quite differently. Suicide rates for a particular region of Switzerland, for example, jumped by fifty percent in one year when government bureaucrats replaced Catholic priests as keepers of the rates (Douglas 1967). Researchers who mistake the apparent increase in counted suicides as evidence of a real increase in the numbers of people choosing to kill themselves may be building up complex explanations for something that never happened. A change in whether police are encouraged to lay charges for any and all incidents of fighting among youth or to calm the situation and leave will drastically affect youth crime rates (Schissel 1997) How clerks interpret rules for classifying medical problems for purposes of workers' compensation claims will drastically affect rates of 'workplace related' illness (Doran 2002), and so on. No statistical data should be accepted at face value without questioning how they were generated and for what practical purposes.

Statistical Analysis

Statistical analysis in sociology has reached a high level of sophistication. With the aid of computers, it is possible to measure the relative impact of many variables upon each other. It is important to gain some understanding of statistics and how useful they can be for modelling social relations. But, it is also important not to assume that just because evidence is presented in numerical form that it is somehow more scientific or rigorous or objectively true than any other form of presentation.

Statistical **correlations** also do not prove causality. It may be possible to show that two variables are correlated, in that as one variable increases so does the other, without there being any direct causal relation between them. Bernard Shaw once pointed out a strong correlation between age of British men at death and the type of hat they wore. Men who wore top hats seemed to live much longer on average than men who wore cloth caps. Does this mean we should all start wearing top hats if we want to live longer? Of course not. The association reflects the fact that top hats were worn largely by upper-class men who had much better living conditions and healthier diets than the working-class men who generally wore cloth caps. Time ordering can also be tricky. There is a close relationship between number of fire engines on the scene and size of fire but that does not mean that fire engines cause fires. There is also a relationship between age of women on marriage and number of children they bear. This could mean that delayed marriage causes fewer children through the biological mechanism of reduced fertility. However, the causal relation could be reversed. Reduced desire to have children causes people to delay marriage through the subjective mechanism of couples only wanting a legal marriage after deciding that they would like to have children (Uhlmann 2004, 82–3). In summary, statistics are a useful tool to show relationships between two or more measured variables but the causal processes that might account for such statistical evidence still need to be thought out. These processes include all the methodological practices that go into producing the measures.

Documentary and Textual Analysis

Techniques that focus on written documents provide opportunities for unobtrusive research into the social reality of the writers. Writing is an intentional form of communication of facts or records and impressions by the authors, often for specific audiences. Sociologists are frequently as interested in reading between the lines to explore the underlying assumptions of the authors as in reading the overt text. An early study by Thomas and Znaniecki, *The Polish Peasant* ([1919] 1971), used the letters and diaries written by Polish immigrants to America to piece together what life was like for these people. The inevitable limitation of such documents is that one cannot be certain that what the immigrants wrote was, or was intended to be, an accurate description of their experience. Immigrants may feel under pressure not to worry family members left behind, to make their accounts more rosy than their experiences really were, and to leave out references to activities of which relatives might disapprove, in the same way, letters that students write home may not be accurate accounts of what they have actually been doing at university. But what they do provide is evidence of the frames that the authors themselves bring to bear on their social reality as they try to make their experiences accountable to others. It is frequently this aspect, as much as factual data, that interests sociologists.

The technique of **content analysis** aids the study of written materials. In such analysis the content of samples of written materials such as newspapers, letters, or website documents, is counted into predefined categories determined by the theoretical hypothesis. Depending on the research focus, this may involve counting the number of times particular topics are raised within a given time frame, the number of column inches devoted to these topics, the number of positive or negative adjectives used to convey approval or disapproval of the topic, and so on. The same technique can readily be modified to count numbers of minutes devoted to certain topics on television. Chomsky (1988) used this technique to powerful effect to show how US mass media ignored violence perpetrated by dictators favourable to the USA while giving extensive coverage to similar violence by communist regimes. Hackett (1989) similarly counts minutes of coverage to illustrate the bias in Canadian television coverage of foreign news, vastly favouring news of the USA and Western Europe over the rest of the world.

Textual analysis involves a more sophisticated study of the form, as distinct from the content of particular pieces of writing, to reveal in detail how meaning is constructed within a text. Early work by Dorothy Smith (1974, 258–59) draws attention to how the factual property of statements is not intrinsic to them, but is conveyed by the social organization of the text itself. When a statement is prefaced by the words "in fact", or bluntly stated without qualification, as in "X is conservative", then the statement comes across as unarguably factual. Yet if the same statement is prefaced by qualifiers like "I think," "I believe," or "she said that X is conservative" it conveys the sense that the statement is an opinion that can be subject to questioning and interpretation. Official accounts of events convey the aura of facticity through depersonalized language as if it were aggregate

knowledge from no particular place or person. Bystander accounts, in contrast, are presented in the "I saw" or "it seemed to me" form conveying more limited, opinionated knowledge.

Another powerful tool for framing different versions of reality is the location of 'brackets' or cut-off points that mark the beginning and end of an account of an event. For example, if brackets are placed at one time frame, a confrontation between police and street people may appear as an instance of people throwing rocks at police who then have to defend themselves. But if the brackets are widened to include events several days or weeks earlier, then the same event may appear as police harassment of people who eventually fight back.

Conversation Analysis

Conversation analysis developed out of ethnomethodology, focusing on the intimate ways in which people accomplish a shared sense of order and meaning in conversation. The basic assumption is that conversations are structurally organized so that no order is accidental or irrelevant. A question structures any response as an answer, or as an evasion that needs some explanation. A greeting structures any response as a returned greeting or as some level of rejection that again needs explanation. Relations of equality or hierarchy are signalled by whose topics are picked up or dropped, who interrupts whom and whether signals of wanting to say something are acknowledged or ignored. Hesitations, qualifications, repetitions, and the like signal nuances of meaning. Tone of voice also contributes significantly to the implications of what is said (Opie 1992). These basic forms of interaction are regarded by ethnomethodologists as the foundations of social order. Orderly talk is required before any other level of meaningful interaction can take place. Techniques of conversation analysis are now part of the regular tools used by journalists and political analysts to comment on speeches by political leaders. Van Dijk (1993, ch. 3) uses this technique to interrogate political speeches for implicit racism, particularly highlighting qualifications as in "We do this, but they..." forms of speech. Internet chat-rooms and websites provide new sources of publicly available written conversations for research using combinations of conversation and textual analyses.

The ethical issues that arise in using already published materials as sources of data are less pressing than those that intrude into private thoughts and experiences. Mostly they concern the need to recognize that the materials being studied were produced for other purposes. We cannot be certain that what analysts find in materials was recognized by those who first produced them. A graduate student interested in discussions of childbirth experiences posted on the internet, felt it was ethically necessary to contact the writers first through posted email addresses to ask permission. Those who did not reply or whose email addresses no longer functioned, were omitted from her sample, even though this meant losing three-quarters of the potential sample (Nuernberger 2004).

Institutional Ethnography— putting it all together

Institutional ethnography is fundamentally a research methodology that begins with individual experience as an entry point for studying routine organizational practices that produce these experiences. Institutional ethnography as a theoretical perspective and methodological approach requires the simultaneous use of different techniques—observation, interviews, analysis of standardized questionnaires, textual analysis and conversation analysis—to explore how individual behaviour in one situation is tied into networks of control and power outside that immediate setting. So far we have been describing specific techniques in isolation, but often researchers use them in combination to get a more rounded understanding of their topic.

We will trace how these research techniques work together using the example of Ng's 1986 study *The Politics of Community Services*. The findings of this study are described in more detail in the chapter on Race and Ethnic relations. Here the focus will be on methodology. The setting is a service agency in Toronto devoted to helping immigrant women find employment. Ng begins her study with *participant observation,* volunteering as a counsellor who could work with Chinese immigrants. Taking up this role enabled her to experience the counsellor role for herself, and to know at first hand what she had to learn to get the job done. She was also positioned to *observe* closely how fellow counsellors were doing their work, and how they were visibly interacting with each other and with clients. She immediately encountered the *standardized questionnaire* used by counsellors to interview each new client. Ng learned what information was needed to translate Chinese qualifications and past work experiences and force-fit them

into the detailed categories on the employability assessment form. Techniques of *conversation analysis* alerted her quickly to power relations controlling the counsellor-client interaction. These were not ordinary conversations with standard turn-taking and signalling of topic shifts. Rather, counsellors routinely cut clients off in mid-sentence, and abruptly shifted topics. Doing the job made it clear that the standardized questionnaire almost totally controlled the conversation, dictating the order of topics and the precise details needed. Discussion of topics that did not fit the form were summarily cut off. Conversation analysis also alerted Ng to the unequal power relations between counsellors and potential employers who regularly telephoned the agency looking for cheap labour. Ng could hear the conciliatory and pleading tones used by counsellors when talking with employers, followed by mumbling and sometimes smothered rage after the phone was put down. She could also hear the bullying tones used to pressure clients to take available jobs whether they wanted them or not. Ng also learned rapidly that the standardized forms were essential to produce the weekly and monthly *statistical analyses* required by the government as a condition of funding. Standardized forms enabled counsellors to calculate precisely the number of clients served, their ethnic backgrounds and employment experiences, and the number of job placements made. Until these required statistics were calculated and provided to the satisfaction of the government liaison officer no-one got paid, office rental fees went in arrears, and even the coffee supplies were not replenished. She could also observe counsellors locking new clients out of the office for several days until the paper work was finished. *In-depth interviews* with counsellors enabled Ng to put the whole picture together. She could explore with them what the agency used to be like when it was staffed by volunteers trying to help immigrant women in their struggle to adjust to the city, care for their families and access jobs, and how drastically the agency changed once it received government funding and became incorporated. She could piece together how accountability to the government for funding required both the use of standardized forms and the generation of statistics demonstrating the placement of prescribed numbers of clients from approved ethnic backgrounds into employment. Keeping these numbers up in turn explained why counsellors resorted to bullying clients to take job openings and supplicating employers who were sometimes openly racist. Ng experienced, watched, and heard about the frustration and despondency that counsellors felt. By the end of her study she could pinpoint precisely how *relations of ruling* worked in a chain of command through government funding regulations, accountability rules, statistical records, standardized forms, restricted interaction between counsellors and immigrant women, and pressure on these women as 'clients' to fill undesirable job openings. The study made visible how counsellors were themselves an integral part of the chain, their roles transformed from advocates on behalf of immigrant women to de-facto government employees servicing the cheap labour-force requirements of local employers.

The exact methodologies associated with institutional ethnographies vary with each setting but they all entail a similar combination of finely detailed observation of how workers carry out some routine activity, close attention to workplace conversations through which workers communicate with each other their sense of what they are doing, close attention to standardized texts (either paper or electronic) that regulate how this routine activity is to be carried out and recorded, what happens to that text after the worker has finished with it, and in-depth interviews to draw on workers' expert knowledge of how and why they do things the way they do. All of these methodologies are focused on the specific question of how routine work gets done and the relations that rule them.

Ethical issues in Qualitative Research

The ethics of doing institutional ethnographies are complex. The research involves two levels of data collection—the particular setting, and the wider relations of ruling or chains of command that organize work within that setting. Gaining access to a research site can be tricky in that those who have the authority to give permission may be directly implicated in the research results without having control over how the research itself gets done (Campbell and Gregor 2002, 61–9). Issues of confidentiality may arise around the materials that employees work with, protecting the privacy of clients, disclosure of organizational information, disruptions to the efficient use of employee's time, and the like, can all raise concerns. Methodologically it is also impossible to know the boundaries of the project in advance, or exactly who needs to be interviewed or what texts or discourses need to be examined. University research ethics committees tend to be suspicious of research proposals that do not spell out such details in advance. There is also the question of who will use the knowledge gained into organizational practices and whose interests might be enhanced or damaged by such knowledge.

The issue of ethical procedures for qualitative research and ethnographies in particular remains hotly debated (Van Den Hoonaard 2001;2004). The *Tri-Council Policy on Ethics Involving Human Subjects* which came into force in Canada in 2000 covers Medical, Natural Sciences and Engineering, and Social Sciences and Humanities research councils in Canada. As a condition of being eligible to receive any research funding, every Canadian university is required to establish ethics-review committees to review all research, whether funded or not, to ensure that it meets the Tri-Council policy guidelines. At the heart of the debate is whether the biomedical research model is appropriate for sociological research. Medical researchers are required to give detailed information to subjects about exactly what procedures will be involved and all known or suspected risks, and to tell subjects that they can drop out of the research at any time. Signed consent forms are designed to ensure such full disclosure and to ensure that subjects have willingly consented to participate. Van den Hoonaard voices concerns of many social science researchers that these formal standards are not appropriate for the kinds of research they do and that they can actually be non-ethical if applied too rigidly. Research that begins from clear hypotheses and uses experiments and standardized questionnaires to gather data may fit quite closely with the medical model. Much qualitative and ethnographic research that relies on observation and fieldwork begins with a broad focus of interest. Specific research questions emerge and change over time through intensive observation and interviewing (Van Den Hoonaard 2001, 23; O'Neill 2000). Research ethics committees that require hypotheses and procedures to be defined in advance have made it extremely difficult for qualitative research to gain approval.

A second major focus of concern is signed consent forms. On the positive side, they ensure that the researcher has indeed properly informed participants of their rights, and of the nature of the research. But in practice consent forms may function more to protect the legal interests of the funding councils, universities and researchers, than to protect subjects. In many areas of research that involve sensitive issues and social problems people who are willing to participate in the research are fearful that signing their names to consent forms threatens their anonymity. It is now commonplace for researchers to ask for signed consent forms to be returned with 'anonymous' standardized questionnaires. Since social science researchers do not enjoy legal protection from court orders forcing them to divulge sources of information, signed consent forms could potentially get informants into trouble. In one case a doctoral student in Washington university was pressured to surrender field data on a radical animal-rights group, raising the real possibility that he might have to go to prison to protect his informants (Comarow 1993, A44, cited in Van den Hoonaard 2001, 26). Less dramatically, signed consent forms compromise the anonymity of surveys. As individuals fill out private and perhaps embarrassing information, they know that they cannot conceal their identities from researchers. A compromise approach is for researchers to sign a letter that they give to participants outlining their research interests, identifying research sponsors, providing contact addresses and a clear statement of how the identity of participants and the confidentiality of information learned will be protected. Taped interviews can then begin with a question whether the informant freely consents to be interviewed, to which the informant can answer "Yes", without otherwise identifying him or herself.

Yet another area of debate concerns what should happen to data once the research has been completed. Current guidelines suggest that all data be securely protected, and destroyed within one year. This protects data from being used for purposes other than those disclosed to informants when they consent to participate, but at the same time it prevents scholars from using the data for legitimate secondary analysis and future comparative research.

Research ethics for Carroll and for contributors to his collection of *Critical Strategies for Social Research* (2004) goes beyond Tri-Council concerns with informed consent, and disclosure of risk to the underlying power/knowledge relations within which all social research is necessarily embedded. From Carroll's perspective, standard social science research involves ethically questionable social relations—relations of power that reduce 'informants' to objects used by researchers to collect data that the researcher wants. Morally responsible research ethics, in contrast, entails that the researcher ask in whose interests is this research being conducted, and whose interests will be served by the knowledge generated? For Carroll, critical research is research that will empower subordinated and marginalized people to gain the knowledge that they can use to understand the social processes that structure their lives, and to act effectively to change their situation. Linda Tuhiwai Smith (2004) suggests twenty-five indigenous research projects that are explicitly designed to help generate the kinds of

knowledge that Aboriginal people need to promote their cultural survival, self-determination, healing from the wounds of colonialism and their struggles for social justice. Critical research methods, Carroll argues, should involve cooperating with subordinated people so that they themselves learn the methodological tools and skills they need to be able to conduct their own research.

Research generates knowledge that is legally defined under copyright law as belonging to the collector of that knowledge, unless by prior agreement, copyright has been legally signed over by the researcher to the informants. This law has profound implications for indigenous peoples. Over many years, bio-medical researchers have used indigenous informants to gain knowledge of traditional plants and medicines. Researchers have subsequently patented the information to profit themselves and the pharmaceutical companies funding the research. From the perspective of indigenous peoples, their knowledge has effectively been stolen from them to profit others. Another example of the theft of indigenous knowledge involves the collection of 80 tapes or 5000 pages of traditional stories recorded from Aboriginal informants over many years. Initially the researcher had agreed to turn over copyright to the First Nations bands that contributed the stories. However, when it became clear how valuable the publication of these stories could be, the researcher claimed that legally all the stories belonged to him as their collector (Bear-Nicholas 2006). The case was still before the courts some ten years later, in 2006, with First Nations lawyers arguing that the cultural knowledge belongs to the indigenous peoples and the researcher arguing that the collected stories constitute his private intellectual property.

Researchers are always enjoined not to cause harm to their subjects, yet this principle too is not always straightforward. People live in society not isolated individuals but as members of complex and often hierarchically ordered groups and communities. Knowledge about the social organization of these groups may simultaneously support the interests of one sector while compromising the interests of another. This recognition greatly complicates the issue of informed consent. Is it sufficient, for example, that an individual member of a First Nations band agrees to tell a researcher about tribal medical knowledge or to recount tribal stories, or should the consent of band council officials be sought first, or even a plebiscite of all band members? Bear-Nicholas (2006) recounts the example of government-funded research conducted under the auspices of a university department that interviewed First Nations people about their memories of land-use practices from the past. Respondents were offered inducements of $100 to participate in the research. It turned out later that this research on land use might be used by the government in a court case involving Aboriginal woodcutting rights. The Band fears that individuals may have taken the money and even fabricated memories of land use that will be used as evidence in court. First nations communities in New Brunswick, as elsewhere, have be actively involved in working out research ethics protocols that must be followed in all future research involving First Nations people. Of central concern in these protocols are issues of collaborative research, research designed to develop knowledge useful to First Nations peoples, and the vesting of that intellectual property with First Nations and not with external researchers.

In conclusion, research raises important ethical issues for which there are no easy answers. It is important to be mindful of the human dignity of the people we study, and at the same time not to exaggerate the very small potential for harm or risk to people from sociological research. The vast majority of people who participate in research enjoy the experience. As Hiller and DiLuzio note (2004) the people they interviewed often expressed their deep appreciation at the opportunity to share their migration experiences with others and were fascinated to learn whether their experiences were similar to those of others. Pecora (2002) points out that in contemporary western culture people compete in the thousands for a chance to appear on 'reality TV' shows and discuss their private lives on the media. Many thousands more display their personal lives on web pages that celebrate intimacy as public performance, while millions visit the web pages to look. In the postmodern fantasy world of mass media, Pecora suggests, "television is now doing the kind of social psychological research our universities no longer permit" (ibid. 356).

Loss of Community? The Rural-Urban Debate

The question mark in the title of this chapter is significant. It is a signal that what you will find here is not a collection of factual knowledge. Rather, you will confront conflicting evidence and interpretations concerning the nature of rural and urban communities, both now and in the past. This ongoing debate surrounding patterns of social change calls into question many fundamental assumptions about the nature of human communities.

The methodology of social science is a critical issue in this chapter. The first section traces the processes of formulating a theory, spelling out its basic assumptions, testing them against evidence, and framing conclusions about whether the original theory worked and how it might be modified or replaced by alternative theories that seem better able to account for the evidence at hand.

The classical loss of community thesis originated in the conservative worldview that prevailed in late nineteenth and early twentieth centuries in Europe. The assumptions implicit in this pessimistic worldview were spelled out in a theory concerning the characteristics of community life and how they were being threatened by forces of industrialization and urbanization. This theory has empirical consequences, and it is these consequences that can be compared with evidence collected through research. In principle, evidence that conflicts with the expected consequences challenges the assumptions on which the initial theory was based and so prompts its revision. In practice, however, this linear progress is complicated by the development of competing theories that search for very different kinds of evidence. What is particularly problematic is that theories can easily generate blind spots and distortions in the amassing of evidence. As a result, new research may generate more and more evidence that seems to lend overwhelming support for the prevailing theory. Competing theories face a major battle in reinterpreting what is perceived as existing "knowledge."

Loss of Community

The loss of community thesis is rooted in the belief that, from the nineteenth century onwards, communities in Europe underwent profound changes with the development of industrialized, urban centres. The thesis includes a nostalgia for the past and for a vision of a more humane form of community characterized by harmonious, integrated, and stable relationships and collective sentiments of loyalty and belonging. In contrast, the present social world is seen as characterized by growing individualism, with concomitant disharmony, disintegration, instability, disloyalty, and lack of sense of belonging. In effect, the thesis constitutes a basic critique of industrialization and urban life.

Gemeinschaft and Gesellschaft: Community and Association

The German theorist Ferdinand Tönnies was the first major exponent of the loss of community thesis, which was set out in his study entitled *Gemeinschaft and Gesellschaft* (1887). The term gemeinschaft can loosely be translated into English as *community* and gesellschaft as *association*. Tönnies argues that the pattern of social life that emerged with industrialization differed profoundly from what went before. Preindustrial society is characterized by what Tönnies refers to as "natural will." Relations among people are governed by natural ties of kinship and long-established friendship, by familiarity and liking, and by age-old habit and customary ways of doing things. Industrial society, by contrast, is characterised by "rational will." Relations among people are governed by careful deliberation and evaluation of means and ends, or the advantages that people expect to gain from others. Tönnies viewed the gemeinschaft community as akin to the natural community of a living organism. It involves an underlying consensus based on kinship, on residence in a common locality and on friendship. Relations exist for their own sake and cannot be arbitrarily terminated. Social position or status in such a community is clearly defined by birth, based on who one's parents and ancestors were, and on one's sex and age. Personal achievements, education, property, and the like, matter little compared with status ascribed by birth. Moreover, most people remain within the same status group, as peasants or nobles, throughout life. People are also geographically immobile, staying in or close by the same locality.

These stable communities are generally homogenous. People are descended from the same racial stock, and they share the same ethnic identity, religion, language, and way of life, all enforced by the central institutions of church and family. These institutions in turn derive their strength from the people's unquestioned acceptance of them as natural. Core values within this culture are the sanctity of kinship ties, solidarity as a community, and attachment to the locality. People share a sentimental attachment to conventions handed down through generations of ancestors. Their community operates through dense networks of interaction among people, who are highly interrelated through marriage, who know each other well, and who know that they hold cherished values in common.

The gesellschaft pattern of relations differs so greatly from this traditional form as scarcely to warrant the term 'community'. Tönnies refers to this form as an association of people based on principles of contract and exchange. He views such society as merely a mechanical aggregate rather than a living organism, an artificial society that is transitory and superficial, and emerges out of competitive struggles among individuals who do not feel themselves bound together by either kinship or religion. People are geographically mobile and, hence, tend to be heterogenous with respect to racial and ethnic origins and religious beliefs. Relations among individuals are impersonal, based on rational calculation of advantage. In such calculations the spirit of neighbourly love and the virtues and morality of community life are lost. People tend to collect in large-scale agglomerations rather than in small local groups.

Tönnies' vision of gesellschaft—the collapse of community life into an association of individuals motivated by calculated self-interest—was intended as a critique of the order of society underlying industrialization. The fundamental value of capitalism, the rational pursuit of profit and individual advantage, generates dehumanized and artificial relations. George Simmel, a German theorist who was a contemporary of Tönnies, modified Tönnies' ideas to apply more specifically to rural versus urban settings. Simmel identified gemeinschaft patterns with rural communities and gesellschaft with urban. He proposed further that a unidirectional process of change was occurring from rural to urban type. Urban life appeared essentially rational, with only weak emotional attachments. Diverse occupations and interests further weakened local controls. Simmel feared that this weakening of communal solidarity in urban areas would lead to the collapse of a stable social order. Rural community life appeared to be superior to urban lifestyles.

The overwhelming impression that comes through these theories of urbanism is a sense of loss and regress, rather than positive change for the better. The term 'loss of community' expresses dissatisfaction with the quality of contemporary urban life and a desire to return to a more humane society where individuals were integrated into stable and harmonious communities of family, neighbours, and friends. The past may well not have been as rosy as this idealized image of integrated community life. But the feeling of loss cannot be dismissed as merely misguided nostalgia, for what they articulate is a deep criticism of the present.

The Chicago School

A number of sociologists working together at the University of Chicago in the late 1920s and 1930s developed a broad body of theory and research into urban life that became known as *The Chicago School* of urban sociology. Louis Wirth, Robert Redfield, Robert Park, and Ernest Burgess are important individual theorists in this group. They researched stages in development of the city of Chicago in the industrial heartland of America. Successive waves of immigrants with diverse racial, ethnic and linguistic backgrounds, arrived from many parts of the world, attracted by expanding opportunities for jobs and commerce. The city thus provided an inexhaustible natural laboratory for the study of urban life. Park and others developed the *concentric zone theory* of urban development (Park 1932;1952; Park et al. 1925;1967). Typically, impoverished newcomers settled first in densely populated inner city areas where older, slum housing was cheap. Over time, they gradually moved outwards to find somewhat better accommodation while new immigrants took their places in the city centre. Longer term residents in the new zone were in turn moving yet further outwards to more spacious suburbs.

One of these Chicago theorists, Louis Wirth, in his essay "Urbanism as a Way of Life" (1938) set out a formal theory in which he suggests that the characteristics of the city *as a city* explain the patterns of culture identified by Tönnies, Simmel, and others. Wirth identified three critical variables as causal determinants of the gesellschaft type of community: size, density and heterogeneity.

The large *size* of urban centres inevitably gives rise to differentiation between people. It becomes impossible to know and to interact with everyone over a wide variety of concerns. Hence, interactions inevitably become limited and specialized, and therefore superficial, transitory, and anonymous. The result, suggests

Wirth, is the experience of individual loneliness within the urban crowd.

The second key variable is *density*. People are concentrated in a limited space, where they experience overcrowding and pollution. Like rats artificially crowded together in laboratories, people are forced into a competitive struggle for space. Laboratory rats, housed in a spacious cage, live peacefully together. But as more and more animals are crowded into the same space, their behaviour changes. They become increasingly aggressive and more likely to inflict injuries on each other (see studies by Hall 1966, ch. 1; Calhoun 1963; Michelson 1970, 6–7). Wirth reasoned that overcrowding in cities would generate similar antisocial behaviour among people.

The third variable is *heterogeneity*. People with different racial and ethnic backgrounds and different occupations and statuses are mixed together. In the face of such heterogeneity, people have divided allegiances and hence cannot form a secure sense of belonging, either to their locality or to the people around them.

In this model, the relation between urban setting and values reverses the original association proposed by Tönnies. For Tönnies, the values of rational, calculated self-interest led to the breakup of community life and to the impetus to gather in cities that offered economic advantages. In the Chicago School model developed by Wirth, it is the gathering in cities that leads to the loss of community values and to their replacement by calculations of individual advantage.

The Chicago School model draws on the same basic assumptions as the functionalist or systems theory perspective. In this perspective, shared culture and moral consensus are the foundations of social order. Culture comprises the complex of language, history, symbol systems, values, attitudes and behavioural expectations. Broad cultural values, along with patterned expectations for behaviour in specific roles, are internalized through early socialization within families, and reinforced by the institutions of church and school. The central social controls that reinforce conformity are internalized sense of guilt, and desire for acceptance and approval. These moral bases for order and control are weak or absent in the urban agglomeration. *Heterogeneity* of social backgrounds means that urban residents lack a common core of culture and moral consensus. Individuals cannot assume that other people have internalized the same behavioural expectations and values. Distrust and fear in interpersonal relations are the likely result of this unpredictability. Moreover, *large size* and the resulting prevalence of limited and specialized interaction among strangers, weakens traditional sanctions on behaviour. People have less concern with social approval and acceptance from strangers. The other variable, *high density*, increases frustrations and competition and so promotes aggression and crime. In terms of Berger's model of circles of social control (see figure 2-1), the intimate controls of guilt and need for social approval cannot be expected to work in this context. With these sanctions weakened, control increasingly has to take the form of force—the option of last resort.

Predictions that follow from the theory

Wirth's theory predicts that where population settlement is small in size, of low density, and relatively homogenous, as in rural areas, one can expect the sense of community to be strong and characterized by intimate co-operation, and a clear sense of security and personal identity. In contrast, in large cities such as Toronto and Montreal, and more so in metropolises such as Chicago and New York, relationships will be superficial and competitive, with limited sense of belonging to a cohesive and satisfying community. In effect, one can expect to find a rural-to-urban continuum with the sense of community being strongest in the smallest settlements and steadily weaker as the size of the city, overcrowding, and diversity of inhabitants increase.

It is important to keep in mind that while arguments may sound plausible, they are not necessarily correct. They need to be tested in a systematic way against evidence, and this includes looking for cases that might contradict the predictions and so reveal weaknesses in the assumptions. Evidence also has to be scrutinized for the biases and distortion that preconceived notions can impose. As we argued in chapter 2, the most useful and productive way to test a theory is to compare it with an alternative theory that begins from different assumptions and makes different predictions.

Marxist Theory: Community and Economy

An important alternative theory to the Chicago School model is the political economy perspective, which draws heavily on the work of Karl Marx. It starts from different assumptions and makes different predictions about the changing quality of rural and urban community life.

This theory finds the same evidence of dehumanization—loss of community and dissatisfaction among people in contemporary urban, industrial society—but explains this evidence in terms of different causes. Marx saw nothing inherently bad about the shift from rural to urban living. On the contrary, he saw city life as liberating people from mind-numbing subservience to land, and endlessly repetitive traditional patterns of life (Marx and Engels [1845] 1965,38; Marx and Engels [1947] 1970, 39–95; Bonner 1998, 166–170). In the cities people were free to think and work independently, and to develop more fully their creative and productive potential.

If city life were experienced as alienating, Marx reasoned, it was not due to factors like size, density, and heterogeneity, but to the dehumanizing effects of capitalism. Capitalism is a system of private control over productive resources that exploits human labour power for private profit. Conditions of poverty, unemployment and insecurity generated by capitalist organization of production, are identified by Marx as fundamental causes of dehumanization in urban society. This theory does not predict that people living in small towns or rural areas will be any more or less happy than people in urban areas It predicts rather that people who have economic security, and who control their own means of production, will develop satisfying social relations with others, while this sense of community will collapse when fundamental economic security is undermined. To the extent that villages are comprised of farmers or small producers who have both security and independence, such communities are likely to be contented and cohesive. But economically insecure rural poor are predicted to be as likely as the urban poor to experience a breakdown in sense of community.

Political economy theory is closer to the original ideas of Tönnies than is the Chicago School model. It implies an indictment not of cities as such, but of the values of rational, calculated self interest that pervade industrial capitalist society at all levels. The classical theorist Max Weber argued that this capitalist culture of rationalism would spread pervasively from cities to rural areas, obliterating any cultural distinctions between them. He noted that farmers across the great wheat-producing states in America have always had more in common with urban capitalists than with the traditional agriculturalists of Europe. In essence they were entrepreneurs, wedded to the values of competitive economic individualism, rather than to the folk communities of European villagers (Weber 1946, 364). Weber thus concurred with Marx in predicting that there would be minimal difference between the quality of community life in urban and rural areas.

In the following review of research in rural and urban sociology in Canada, we explore first the contribution of traditional theory to the analysis of precapitalist rural life in Quebec, followed by comparative studies of contemporary rural and urban communities. With respect to each broad area, we draw attention to evidence that seems to contradict the basic assumptions of the Chicago School model. Similar research contexts are re-examined from the perspective of political economy theory to test the extent to which it can account for these apparent contradictions. Later in the chapter, we explore the contribution of the social constructionist perspective and the closely related work of feminist urban geography.

Folk Society: A Test of the Chicago School Thesis

Robert Redfield (1947), another contributor to the Chicago School, elaborated an **ideal-type model** of **folk society** to contrast with urban society, drawing on the work of Tönnies, Simmel, and Wirth. An ideal-type model is designed as a tool for research to highlight typical features of the kind of society or social institution being studied. Any particular case may not have all the features listed in the model, but the broad characteristics should be visible. Redfield was particularly interested in the folk communities typical of relatively isolated rural areas. In his model he highlighted five key features: (1) folk communities are organized around family and kinship ties; (2) they involve intimate face-to-face relations; (3) they have minimal specialization or division of labour; (4) people are united by a strong sense of local identity, loyalties, and obligations; and (5) the members support a deep commitment to shared cultural values and ways of behaviour.

The model of an urban society incorporates the opposite of these key features, namely (1) weak family ties; (2) superficial relations between strangers; (3) a high degree of specialization of occupations; (4) limited cohesion; and (5) readiness to adopt new and changing values and ways of behaving. Redfield suggests that the typical differences between a hamlet, a village, a trading centre, and a city can be described in terms of a systematic and linear process of change from folk to urban characteristics.

Redfield (1930) found strong support for his thesis that rural communities are more cohesive than urban centres in his pioneering study of life in Mexico in the 1930s. He describes the small village of Tepoztlan as a homogeneous, smoothly functioning, well-integrated, contented, stable, and harmonious community. He compared it favourably with a neighbouring town, which he characterized as heterogeneous and faction-ridden.

This powerful support for his folk society model was not to go unchallenged, however. A study of the same village by Oscar Lewis (1949), conducted less than twenty years later, shattered the harmonious image, and with it, some of the credibility of Redfield's thesis. Lewis argues that Redfield biased his research by focussing only on co-operative and unifying factors. He charges Redfield with glossing over evidence of violence, cruelty, disease, suffering, poverty, economic and social maladjustment, and political schisms. Redfield later attempted to defend himself by arguing that Lewis had imposed his own value judgements on his research. Lewis wanted to find support for the Marxist argument that the low material standard of living in Tepoztlan gave rise to social maladjustment. Hence, he went out of his way to look for evidence of suffering and stress in the community, and then overemphasized the problems that he found. Whatever the validity of this response by Redfield, Lewis's work did challenge the image of the village as an ideal-type gemeinschaft community.

Quebec Folk Society

In Canadian research, studies of the folk society of rural Quebec offer powerful and convincing descriptions of life that accord closely with the gemeinschaft image. But these studies, too, have been subject to the criticism that researchers found just what they were looking for, rather than what was actually there. A widely cited study of French-Canadian folk society is that by Horace Miner (1939) on the parish of St Denis. Robert Redfield wrote the introduction th the book, and he leaves no doubt that he views St Denis as the epitome of a folk society: "Habitants live in terms of common understandings which are rooted in tradition. . . . Fundamental views of life are shared by everyone, and these views find consistent expression in the beliefs, institutions, rituals, and manners of the people" (Redfield 1964, 58). Sanctions have a strongly sacred character in St Denis. The way of life of the people is endorsed by the priest, but followed because of deeply felt convictions of the people themselves rather than due to any pressure from outside authority. The family system is also strong, pervasive, and certain in its effects. Almost all aspects of life—work, getting married, finding a career, politics—are largely determined by position in a family. There is minimal social disorganization.

Redfield and Miner acknowledge that the fact that St Denis is not an isolated peasant community, but part of a modern urbanized world, cannot be ignored. But this can be discounted in large measure. Although people do have connections with the city, and even relatives who live there, this exposure to alien influences is mediated by the Catholic Church, which "has stood between the changing world and the habitant, preventing admission of elements which she [the church] condemns and interpreting admitted elements in accordance with the faith, and with the local culture" (Redfield 1964, 60).When local ways are threatened, the church minimizes the influence of outside forces and so helps to preserve the folk character of the community.

The only threat to this way of life has come from the structural problem of land pressure (Miner 1964, 66), a consequence of traditionally large families, indivisible small farms, and limited supply of land. Farmers needed money to educate sons for alternative city jobs or to buy farms for them. The result, suggests Miner, was the gradual erosion of independent subsistence farming as a way of life. Farmers slowly became more dependent on the outside economy. The only other solution to the land pressure problems would have been to cut the birth rate, but Miner argues that this was strongly opposed by the Catholic Church, which has always played a vital role in the rural parish, Birth rates declined rapidly in urban areas during the interwar years, but not in the villages, suggesting to Miner that the old culture of religion and **familism**—or life centring on the family—was not disrupted.

Hubert Guindon (1964) and Marcel Rioux (1964) similarly defend the appropriateness of the folk society model as applied to rural Quebec until well into the twentieth century. They cite evidence of strong family ties, low geographic and social mobility, the central importance of inherited land, and the powerful moral leadership of the clergy in perpetuating the folk character of communities such as St Denis. Rioux characterises rural Quebec as made up of small communities, with few outside contacts, and with people bound together by organic ties of family, culture, and church. It is this folk cultural identity, Rioux suggests, that underlies contemporary Quebec nationalism and sense of French-Canadian identity. Although Quebec has an urban

population, Rioux argues that the province can still be characterized as essentially a rural folk culture.

Challenging the Folk Culture Model

It is Philippe Garigue (1964) who challenges the validity of this folk society thesis in the context of rural Quebec, notwithstanding the wealth of data in its support. Garigue, like Oscar Lewis, argues that the model has led researchers to overemphasize evidence that supports it, and to minimize the relevance of empirical data not related to the definition. He suggests that the concept of *folk society* is not valid in French Canadian history nor is it appropriate for contemporary rural Quebec. Historically, he argues, there never were the equivalent of close-knit self-contained, traditionalist, organic communities in rural Quebec. The land was colonized by a process of ribbon development out from small towns, which acted as colonial trading posts. Individual farms were established in parallel rows, first fronting a river and then on an interior road build for the purpose.

This pattern of settlement worked against the development of close-knit communities, suggests Garigue. Farmers were fiercely individualistic. They built houses in the middle of their own individual plots about three miles away from neighbours in either direction. Only much later did communities or villages begin to emerge, once a church was built in the district. The church provided an initial gathering place around which other buildings were established, Old people tended to move near the church when they retired, and the locality slowly began to function as a service centre for the district. Only at this stage could a village be said to exist. But the development of such a village centre did not substantially alter the private family individualism of Independent farmers. In 1663, Louis XIV of France tried, for administrative convenience, to force settlers or habitants to build houses in village groups rather than on their own land (Falardeau 1964, 20). But such edicts were strongly resisted. Farm families refused to move. People maintained social relationships with the families living on neighbouring plots, but had no desire to form village communities. Parishes were not formed until long after colonial settlement, and they constituted only huge administrative areas. Throughout most of Quebec's history, they could not be equated with rural communities.

Tenancies were frequently bought and sold (Garigue 1964, 126). This too, challenges the notion of cohesive, long-settled folk communities. In addition, one researcher found that entire families had moved away from parishes to seek their fortune elsewhere. Nobody seemed to find this unusual or regrettable (Gérin 1964, 36).

The structural constraints of large families, indivisible farms, and limited land meant that the majority of children in any large family could not settle near home. They had to seek a livelihood elsewhere. Thus, there was considerable geographic mobility within families, contradicting the folk society model, despite the near truism that there was low mobility among the people who stayed behind. Usually only the youngest son would inherit the family farm when the parents were too old to farm it themselves. Older sons left. Only the lucky ones among them got farms in neighbouring parishes, This accounts for the observation that rural families in the 1950s were not usually centred in one community but were spread all over the province of Quebec and beyond (Garigue 1964, 134).

Garigue challenges even the notion of an all-embracing church with a subservient flock of parishioners. He cites evidence of widespread accounts of laypersons who refused to obey their priests, or even the bishop, over such matters as building a church and paying dues (Garigue 1964, 129–30). Thus, in multiple ways, Garigue argues that rural settlement in Quebec does not conform to the folk society model. The concept, he suggests, is a myth, an ideology imposed on the data by the researchers. The intensely individualistic, independent farmers that Garigue found have more in common with the image of nuclear family individualism, characteristic of urban life, than with the Chicago School caricature of people embedded within an organic folk society.

The Myth of Quebec Motherhood

Another strong challenge to the notion of folk culture in Quebec comes from an unlikely source, a re-evaluation of fertility data. Marie Lavigne (1986) questions the image of the fertile French Canadian mother, dominated by the Catholic clergy and local political elites advocating a large French-speaking population. Québécois women have been portrayed as fertile mothers, responding not only to Catholic admonitions to have as many children as possible but also to nationalistic propaganda exhorting "the revenge of the cradle." Lavigne questions how we can reconcile this image with the history of the women's movement in Quebec from the nineteenth century onwards. Her answer is that this fertile mother image is largely a myth, applying at best to about one-fifth of all Quebec women from the 1850s onwards, when her data begin. Folk culture values, admonitions

from the clergy, lack of access to modern contraceptives, and their illegality prior to 1968 notwithstanding, the birth rate in Quebec fell steadily every decade between 1850 and 1961.

As table 4-1 shows, of the women born during the years 1887, 1903, and 1913, at least 25 percent never became mothers. Most of these childless women remained unmarried, and only a small minority of them became nuns. A further 15 to 25 percent of women made only a minimal contribution to fertility rates by having one or two children. At the other extreme, the ideal-typically large family of ten or more children was produced by less than one-fifth of the 1887 cohort. This ratio dropped to about one in fifteen women by 1913. The percentage of women having six or more children also dropped from almost 40 percent to just over 20 percent in the same period. This sharp drop indicates that many girls whose mothers had large numbers of children did not see this model of motherhood as the one they wanted to copy.

Clearly large numbers of women did practice contraception, regardless of the church's teachings on the subject. Interviews in 1950 with elderly women who had their families at the turn of the century, indicated that they had not been particularly influenced by church doctrine, despite outward conformity, They practised contraception and still went to church. Lavigne argues from these data that we have to revise our view of the influence of religion on family life in Quebec. It appears to have been considerably shallower than the folk culture model would lead us to believe. We only have to compare these data with Redfield's commentary at the beginning of the study of St Denis—with his references to the sacred character of sanctions, the deeply felt convictions of the people, and the family system as "strong, pervasive, and certain in its

Table 4-1

Birth Cohorts of Women by Marital Status and Number of Children, Quebec			
Number of Children	1887	1903	1913
0	10.8	13.7	11.9
1-2	15.8	21.2	25.2
3-5	21.9	22.8	27.4
6-9	19.7	16.3	14.7
10 or more	17.7	11.0	6.5
Unmarried women	14.1	15.0	14.3
Total	100	100	100

Source: Lavigne (1986). Calculations based on Henripin (1968)

effects"—to realize how significant a challenge Lavigne's work presents to taken-for-granted theories.

We still need to ask where the image of fertile French-Canadian women comes from, if the majority of women did not conform to it. Lavigne points out that the collective memory that all Québécois ancestors had large families derives from the fact that most people remember the same minority of women. For example, if hypothetically, ten women have one child each and one woman has ten children, half of the resulting twenty children in the second generation will have grown up in a large family, even though 90 percent of families did not conform to this pattern.

From Lavigne's article we learn that strong convictions, even when they appear well substantiated by evidence, may still give a false overall picture. The folk society concept of large families, inherited land, and overarching religious control by the Catholic Church is not wholly false, in that it does apply to a proportion of people, The problem is that it may not fit more than half the members of the community. The majority of women and men made decisions about their family size that conflicted with the teachings of the church. It cannot even be assumed that women with large families were mindlessly following church edicts. Lavigne suggests that economic factors, like the usefulness of child labour on farms and in the textile mills or the disadvantages of large families once schooling became compulsory, played a role in decisions about family size. Women make rational choices in historical-economic circumstances. Lavigne suggests, rather than conforming unquestioningly to cultural norms. It would seem, then, that the folk culture model obscures more than it reveals about life in rural Quebec.

Contemporary Rural Communities

The Chicago-School model predicts that village communities, characterized by small size, low density, and homogeneity, should be socially cohesive, with residents sharing attachment to locality and to a core of shared cultural values. Studies of villages draw heavily on this model (Strathern 1982; Rapport 1993). However, not all studies support this rosy image. Samuel Clark's controversial study of four villages in the Miramichi and Bathurst areas of New Brunswick conducted during 1972-3, describes social life as anything but well-

integrated and cohesive. The impression is one of people shut in on themselves, having little contact with the outside world, or with their immediate neighbours (1978, ch. 3). "No one ever visits," said one respondent. "Television ruined that," said another. "People visit less now, got no reason to visit. . . . I'm not one for visiting." Many residents complained about the lack of social activity in their area, yet they gave no indication of intending to do anything about it. "There's not much social life here. People don't try to get together," was a typical response.

Two sets of ties did have some meaning—kinship and church. Almost everyone in the communities was either a relative or a neighbour of a relative of someone else in the community, and few new people moved in. Yet Clark found that kinship obligations appeared shallow and rarely extended beyond the immediate family circle. In Catholic communities virtually everyone went to mass, while in Protestant areas church attendance tended to be associated with higher status. But in either case church did not form the focus of much active social life.

Apart from what limited social life developed around kinship and church, the communities had few organized social activities. A few residents said they belonged to clubs or bought a newspaper, but most did not. Clark concludes that what generally obtained was "what might be described as a state of anomie." Anomie is a state of social breakdown, characterized by weak bonds between people, a limited sense of meaningful relations, and the lack of any strong commitment to shared norms and regulations guiding interactions. Most residents expressed little sense of social obligation to their local community, and many gave vent to their grievances, discouragement, and at times despair. The dominant attitude was a fatalistic acceptance of things as they were.

The two other communities in the study, located on the outskirts of large towns, showed similarly impoverished social life. There was evidence of a good deal of animosity and little visiting among neighbours. One person described her neighbours as "a God-damned bad crowd—from way back in the woods where they never see no people, only bear and fox. Maybe is good people. We can't tell" (ibid. 92). Insecurity and fear of crime were widely felt in these communities. Interviewing was actually cut short because "the field-workers had reason to fear for their physical safety had they attempted any extensive interviewing in the more congested parts of the inner area." (ibid. 73). People were suspicious that interviewers on the project might be government agents, checking on them with the intention of cutting off their welfare payments.

Clark's study is not alone in finding that small size, low density living, and homogeneity do not ensure close community ties. The image of idyllic rustic communities may be part of our collective cultural mythology, but it is not part of the contemporary reality of village and small-town life. A 1983 study of towns and villages in Canada cites public opinion polls that record preferences for farm and small community living, and nostalgia for the peace and friendliness and simplicity of life in the countryside for city-weary, ecology-conscious, and independent urbanites. But the study itself found little evidence to support these images (Hodge and Qadeer 1983, 131). The study suggests that, while individual towns and villages differ widely from each other, patterns of daily life show minimal differences between rural and metropolitan centres.

The study further showed that small communities are not necessarily safer places than big cities. The per capita incidence of crimes of violence may actually be higher in small towns than in cities. To the outside world, small towns and villages may present a face of serenity, but internally they are communities with a fair degree of individualism and social division (ibid. 143). Smallness results in high visibility, and hence familiarity between residents, but this does not necessarily lead to sociability and friendliness. Often small towns harbour a hard core of poverty that is combined with a general indifference towards the poor. Prejudice is also often present. Racial and ethnic minorities may be tolerated, but they are often made to feel unwelcome.

These negative accounts of social disorganization in rural communities should not be taken to imply that all or even most rural communities are characterized by social anomie. Towns and villages vary widely, and many residents experience a satisfying community life. The critical point here is that smallness and homogeneity by themselves do not guarantee integrated community spirit. To explain such patterns we need more complex theories than the Chicago School model provides.

Political Economy Analysis of Small Communities

Researchers who begin from the perspective of political economy offer new insights into the economic determinants of loss of community and why such loss seems more in evidence in some contexts than in others. They focus not on the demographic characteristics of different localities, but on the surrounding economy and the destructive impact of economic insecurity, poverty, and exploitation. Political economy theory predicts that, regardless of size or location, the communities that will show the most evidence of social disorganization and demoralization will be areas of relatively severe poverty, or more importantly, where people are losing their basic sense of economic security and control over their life situation.

The study of villages in the Miramichi region of New Brunswick in the early 1970s give ample evidence of prolonged economic decline, which is consistent with the conditions of social anomie found by researchers. Clark suggests that the poor quality of farmland, with the exception of isolated pockets of fertile soil near rivers could support only a subsistence level of living. In other words, the farms might provide sufficient food, fuel, and building materials to meet the basic necessities of life for a family, but they provided little surplus produce that could be marketed. Most farmers depended on supplementing their farm income with part-time work as woodsmen, fishermen, or labourers. Some farms became more prosperous as the opening of nearby urban markets promoted commercial farming, but success was not possible for all, and many were ruined by debt (Clark 1978).

A collection of articles on primary producers in the Atlantic region (Burrill and McKay 1987) documents the extensive destruction of the rural Maritime economy to the state of near catastrophe for many communities. Between 1941 and 1981, for example, the number of farms in New Brunswick dropped from 26 000 to 4 000, as highly mechanized corporate capitalist farming took over the potato industry. What happened to the 22 000 displaced farmers and their families? Where did they go? Many of the young people with options migrated from the region, going to Alberta and Toronto. Many more people, who lacked the financial and educational resources to move long distances, drifted into the outskirts of smaller towns in the Miramichi area, forming the settlements described in Clark's study. They survived as best they could on intermittent, low-wage work and welfare. Thousands of families lived below the poverty line in the substandard housing that still dots the area. Small fishing communities in the Atlantic region fared little better as factory freezer trawlers threatened the survival of the small inshore fishery, and the centralization of fish-packing plants caused many of the smaller, local plants to close. Families that once survived on wage-work at the packing plants fell back onto welfare.

Clark himself tends to blame impoverishment, minimal levels of education, and lack of experience of industrial work for the apparent inability of many Miramichi residents to move in search of better opportunities. A few of the more enterprising people did get out, he suggests, but the remainder are trapped by cheap housing, unemployment insurance or welfare payments, and the absence of any social or educational skills that might equip them to survive in a city such as Toronto.

William Dunn, a sociologist who worked directly with Clark on the study, and who is himself a native of this area, disagrees strongly with Clark's historical-cultural perspective. While supporting the quotations, and the sense of anomie that the people expressed, Dunn argues strongly for a more critical neo-Marxist analysis of the findings. In particular he stresses the high levels of poverty and welfare that researchers found in three of the four villages studied. He comments "that the very poor should lack interest in literature is not surprising. When one struggles day by day to survive, there is not time for literature, or any other interests that middle-class folk take for granted" (*Miramichi Leader* 9 March 1988, 5). People on welfare, people who have lost their means of independent subsistence, do not tend to give generously to the local United Way. Nor do they generally show much interest in the arts. They cannot. They are victims of the system. From this perspective, the "social anomie' described by Clark has little to do with the culture of the people, or with "a few bad apple," says Dunn. Powerlessness, dependency, and loss of hope for the future breed anger, frustration, and sometimes violence. The underlying factor is fear. It was precisely such feelings that led residents in one community to threaten researchers, for fear that they might be collecting evidence that could be used to cut welfare cheques, the only source of meagre economic security for many local families in the early 1970s. These people had already lost their dignity as independent farmers, farm workers, and fishers. They probably could not take much more.

The Marxist theorist James Sacouman (1980, 1981) similarly rejects Clark's notion that poverty might be accounted for by an inadequate rural culture, arguing instead that the uneven development of farming, fishing and forestry in the Maritimes was the result of organized capitalist policies. This process he terms the semi-proletarianization of the domestic mode of production. What he means by this is that people who once worked for themselves as small farmers, woodlot owners, or small fishermen, or some combination of these activities, have been pushed into a situation where they have to take part-time wage-work to survive. The jobs made available to them are seasonal, insecure, and at the bottom of the wage scale, so that it is impossible to survive on wages alone. The fact that people in the region could provide for themselves, at least in part, through subsistence farming has meant that employers in big corporations have been able to exploit them, paying below subsistence wages or extremely low prices for the raw materials, Merchants also benefited from unequal exchange: they bought products from rural producers at low prices and sold supplies at high prices. The result was that merchants always came out on top, and the rural population was unable to accumulate any wealth.

The political economy thesis similarly predicts a high level of anomie in many First Nations communities, despite the structural advantages of small size, low density, and cultural homogeneity. Indian reserves in Canada are commonly so lacking in an economic base that they cannot provide a standard of living above welfare for the residents. Welfare dependency, loss of dignity, and the absence of hope for the future manifest themselves in exceptionally high rates of alcoholism, suicide and domestic violence (Muise 2003; Anderson and Lawrence 2003; Baskin 2003). We explore further below the long history of colonialism that generated these conditions.

Urban Communities: The Myth and the Reality of Anomie

Chicago School theorists viewed cities as made up of distinctive zones or "ecological areas" that emerged and changed as the population expanded in response to industrialization. Cities developed in the nineteenth century around manufacturing industries. Large factories were commonly located near railroads and waterways, and surrounded with cheap, housing for low-income workers. Better-quality housing for more highly-paid, skilled workers developed further out. Successive waves of migrants attracted by employment opportunities had to compete for space with existing residents. Economically dominant groups were able to command their space, or invade favourable new areas, while others were crowded out. The weakest groups thus tended to become concentrated in the poorest zones, close to the factories. More established working-class families occupied the somewhat better housing around this inner core, with middle-class homes located further out, and spacious higher-class housing farthest away from the deteriorating city core. These early ecological models—seeing people in relation to their distinctive habitat zones within cities—have been revised and adapted to the experience of individual cities, and have been used extensively to plot ethnic migration patterns (Driedger 2003).

By mid-twentieth century both the economic structure of major North American cities, and resulting ecological zones were clearly in transition. The economic era of mass-production manufacturing was in decline. Manufacturing and assembly work has been moving increasingly to developing countries where wages are cheaper, being replaced in the centres of capitalism by the post-industrial economy of high-technology, information and financial services, and mass consumption. This economic transition fostered very different kinds of urban infrastructure (Stevenson 2003). High-rise office buildings, often owned by giant transnational corporations, replaced factories giving rise to the now familiar city skylines marked by skyscrapers. Skyscrapers function both as cultural icons and art-forms, symbolizing man's conquest of nature, rising like towering cliffs with rivers of cars flowing below them. Inner-city redevelopment, often constructed on abandoned factory sites, replaced centres of production with centres of recreation and tourism for high-income consumers. Cities now compete in global markets to offer 'world-class' environments for 'festival market-places' and simulated local attractions, complete with museums, centres for expressive arts and cultural activities, upscale hotels, restaurants and shopping boutiques, and the like (ibid. 99–100). A facade of local attractions and 'historical interest' heritage sites usually complete the marketing image.

Behind the powerful discourse of civic pride and citizenship that accompany such developments has always been the social reality of inequality and exclusion. Increasingly these cultural centres promote rising land values in surrounding areas. Upscale highrise apartments and condominiums join the mix, and middle-class families, attracted by the recreational and cultural amenities, begin to buy up and renovate formerly working-class housing. Poor and working-class families who formerly inhabited these areas find themselves excluded, their homes bulldozed or priced and taxed beyond reach. The poor do not disappear from the inner cities, but they are crammed into devastated areas and subsidized slum-clearance housing, out of sight of the tourists (ibid. 97).

Ecological Zones and Urban Community life

The focus of this section is on testing Wirth's model of urbanism as a way of life, with respect to different residential zones. If many rural communities do not fit the folk image, can it be argued that the metropolitan environment characterised by large size, high density living, and heterogeneity, necessarily results in a loss of community? The thesis predicts that local neighbourhoods would decline in significance in urban centres. Nuclear families would be mobile and hence isolated, detached from stronger allegiance to kinship ties beyond those of husband, wife, and dependent children. Social disorganization would increase with the demise of traditional bases of social solidarity. Political economy theory, in contrast, predicts that symptoms of social disorganization will be concentrated in zones characterised by poverty and high levels of unemployment social disorganization. Demographic features of high density living and ethnic diversity are expected to be largely irrelevant, once levels of poverty are taken into account. The following review of research begins with the more outward zone of suburbs, and moves inwards through lower-middle class borough, a working-class area and finally the inner-city.

Suburbs

Descriptive studies of life in city suburbs suggest a closer fit to the gesellschaft model in the sense that relations among neighbours tend to be superficial, transitory, and limited to a narrow range of interests rather than forming thick or multi-faceted loyalties. Yet these relations are not necessarily experienced as anomic or unsatisfying. Dyke (2002) suggests that while people may hold ideals of family togetherness and close community life, these are hard to achieve. In most suburban families, both parents earn incomes to be able to afford the high property values, and commonly they both face long daily commutes to and from work. Individual families also tend to be highly mobile in and out of new suburban housing. Hence, neighbours are mostly strangers. People walk a fine line, Dyke suggests, between desiring to protect their family privacy from prying neighbours and desiring to avoid total domestic isolation (ibid. 106). Ideal neighbours are 'friendly' but not 'friends', pleasant but not intruding into one's private family life.

Dyke's own study focuses on how the involvement of children in organized sports provides a mechanism for their parents to associate with their neighbours, in what Dyke describes as compartmentalized but nonetheless enjoyable relations. Involvement of parents is voluntary and can range from superficial to dedicated. At a minimum, parents are expected to provide transportation for their children to and from practices and games and to support their children's efforts by showing up to watch them at least some of the time. The success of amateur sports organizations also depends heavily on some parents becoming more actively involved in fund-raising and coaching. As parents stand around to watch and to wait for their children, and to participate in special events, they come to know each other at least by sight and to share in common their children's sporting interests. One weekend bus trip to a track meet mixed together 20 adults and their children. Two-thirds of the parents had been born outside Canada, from a total of ten different countries, and most barely knew each other before the trip. This experience can be viewed very differently, depending on whether it is compared with the gemeinschaft or the gesellschaft model. Dyke describes it as 'a remarkably enjoyable and memorable experience' (116) that gives a limited and fleeting, but nonetheless meaningful sense of community. But it can equally well be described as 'pleasant' but nonetheless compartmentalized, limited and fleeting. In all likelihood fellow travellers on the bus trip will not crossing the boundary from 'friendly' to 'family friends'. Also, as children grow up, change schools, get bored with athletics and drift away from the club, their parents will likely not interact again.

In his many articles on computer-mediated relations, Wellman (2001) paints a similar picture of suburban life as comprising thinly connected and partial communities, but on the other hand offering opportunities for multiple, personally-chosen 'networks of interpersonal ties that provide sociability, support, information, a sense of belonging and social identity'(2001, 18). The days have gone, Wellman argues, when people visited by walking from door to door, limiting their social relations to a few blocks from home. Now people drive or fly from place to place and use the telephone to talk with each other. Entertaining takes place in people's homes more often than local pubs. Cell phones and wireless electronic messaging systems mean that person-to-person communication can occur almost anywhere, anytime. Family members can talk to each other even if they are all doing different things in different places. Community is liberated from location. Individual family members can each develop their own personal social networks and interact across multiple separate networks simultaneously. What appears to be isola-

tion and dis-connection from traditional viewpoints, can be experienced as socially rich and meaningful networks. Ironically, Wellman notes, the 'wired' individuals tended to know more of their neighbours than the non-wired, able to name 25 of them on average, compared with 8 for the non-wired. A study of an on-line bulletin board for the Queer Sisters organization in Hong Kong suggests that such boards help to promote off-line community by posting information, managing group activities, and facilitating discussion of issues (Nip 2004). Such boards can also function as places to chat with like-minded people, keep in touch, and even express passions and offer apologies and other difficult emotions that people find hard to say in face-to-face encounters. Nip concurs with Wellman in finding no evidence that on-line communications competed with or detracted from on-line communication.

The suburban experience can thus be argued both ways. From the classical functionalist perspective suburban life is much closer to shallow association than to close-knit community. From the political economy perspective, the relative economic stability enjoyed by families that can afford to live in suburbs, their access to telephones and computers, cars and air travel, their ability to enrol themselves and their children in exclusive clubs, means they can afford a quality social life without necessarily knowing any of their immediate neighbours.

Middle-Class Boroughs

Research in the Metropolitan Toronto borough of East York did not bear out the predictions of the Chicago School model (Wellman 1978; Shulman 1976). The major difference between suburbs and the borough is that borough residents are more long-settled. A study of a small sample of young, native-born, anglophone lower middle-class couples found a high level of social integration. Geographic closeness between generations was quite high. People valued being near to other family members and wanted frequent interaction with them. Three-quarters of the sample visited kin in the metropolitan area at least once a week. The minority whose parents lived farther away saw them less frequently. Couples expressed a sense of obligation to keep in contact with other family members. They regularly initiated contacts and participated in common ritual activities such as birthdays and anniversaries. Almost one-third saw their parents more than any other persons. The telephone was also a common means of contact.

The studies in East York note that mutual aid was very important between young couples and their parents.

Almost half the young couples had lived with one set of parents during the early years of marriage, before they could afford a place of their own,. Common forms of aid included young people caring for sick parents, and grandparents babysitting their grandchildren. Parents also gave financial aid in crises, while young adults helped their parents with house repairs and with other needs of older people. The prediction that urban life would result in the breakdown of kinship ties was not substantiated in East York.

The related prediction that high mobility would result in social isolation was similarly not supported by the data from studies in Fredericton and Montreal (McGahan 1982, 239–41). Geographic mobility did not reduce the size of the kin universe. The average number of kin contacted did not differ between the mobile and nonmobile urbanites. The nonmobile people had more face-to-face contacts, while the others used letters and telephones to keep in touch with relatives. There was no difference between them in the importance that they accorded to the kinship bond. The death of central connecting relatives was more important than mobility in terminating kin ties.

French-Canadian families provide a particularly valuable test of the thesis that family ties decline with urban residence, given the strength of the image of large, traditional rural families. One would expect city families to present a very different picture from rural ones. McGahan's data from urban Montreal, however, totally contradict the prediction that nuclear family isolation would be evident in urban areas. People in the Montreal sample were able to name, on average, 215 relatives. Women were generally able to name more relatives than could men, and wives could often name more of their husbands' relatives than the husbands themselves knew (Garigue 1956). Women had much greater knowledge of the affairs of the kin group and interacted with the group more frequently. Contact with both parents and siblings was sustained regardless of geographic location. In the French-Canadian community in St Boniface, Manitoba, mobility also did not disrupt kinship bonds (Piddington 1965). Instead, migrant kin tended to cluster together, and chain migration was common. Intermarriage among distant kin was not uncommon.

Working-Class Zones

Stable working-class zones in large cities show a consistent pattern of close identification with neighbourhood and kin. McGahan (1982) cites the example of

Toronto's Cabbagetown, a locality then inhabited predominantly by Anglo-Saxon, blue-collar, semiskilled and unskilled workers with below average incomes (Lorimer and Phillips 1971). Family roles were very traditional and were segregated along age and sex lines, but family ties were strong, with mutual support and obligations. Circles of close friends commonly included kin, often parents and adult children. The impression given by the research is that these working-class residents derived much satisfaction from living in Cabbagetown, and had a strong sense of community cohesion and identity with the neighbourhood. This was evidenced in their ability to come together in organized opposition to the city's urban renewal plans that threatened to disrupt their narrow residential streets.

This sense of cohesive community life closely matches the findings of similar studies. A famous one by Young and Wilmott (1957) focuses on the working-class area of Bethnal Green in East London. In the heart of one of the largest cities in the world, the authors found not an anonymous gesellschaft but a stable, homogenous, and very close-knit community. On a shopping trip, for example, one of their respondents met sixty-three people she knew, thirty-eight of whom were relatives. Herbert Gans (1962) found a similar pattern in the Italian neighbourhood in Boston. Gans calls his study *The Urban Villagers* to emphasize the similarities he found between urban neighbourhood life and images of rural folk society. Social life in Greenwich village in the heart of New York is similarly described as living up to its name in sustaining a village-like atmosphere of interactive pleasantness and familiarity on the sidewalks as residents habitually walked to do their errands (Jacobs 1961). Local shopkeepers functioned as "public characters' (ibid. 68) who would keep spare keys for their neighbours, watch out for their neighbours' children and warn parents if they were getting out of hand.

Wirth's thesis that cohesive community life could not be sustained in the context high density residence in the heart of large cities is clearly contradicted by these studies of long-settled middle and working-class boroughs. Two of the three predictors—size and density, are shown to fail, although the third predictor of heterogeneity might still be useful.

Over the past decades in many cities in Canada and the United States, the cohesiveness of these old working-class communities has been disrupted by the influx of middle-class renovators looking for the convenience of downtown residence. This process, which is known as *gentrification,* is examined in much greater detail below. In the context of Cabbagetown in the 1970s McGahan describes relations between long-term residents and renovators as 'cautious but edgy', with a mutual recognition that they are quite different types of people. Newcomers tend to be less noisy and "troublesome" than some working-class residents, but on the other hand these newcomers cause more annoyance by making a fuss about such things as the congestion created by neighbours parking on the street (McGahan 1982, 273).

Zones Within the City Centre

The strongest predictions of urban anomie and blight in the Chicago School thesis are directed at the inner city, seen as the locality with the highest density and the most mobile and heterogeneous populations. The rival political economy perspective makes a similar prediction, based on high rates of unemployment and poverty. The term 'inner city' refers to the central areas of older properties within large cities. These may encompass a wide variety of neighbourhoods, including the commercial core of office blocks, newly gentrified areas, stable working-class areas, slums and "skid-row." The focus here will be on urban slums.

Town planners commonly assume that social deterioration goes along with physical deterioration and that urban slums are dangerous areas that should be avoided. Yet even here researchers have found evidence of integrated social order based on loyalties to ethnic groups and to territory. One famous study was conducted in the mid-1960s in the Addams area in Chicago. This area comprised half a square mile and had a population of 20 000 people, including Italians, blacks, Mexicans, and Puerto Ricans (Suttles 1968, 1972). Even in this area of high density, heterogeneity and poverty, an underlying social order existed with territoriality and ethnicity providing bases for association and integration. A certain mutual trust and predictability developed among the various groups, subdivided by ethnicity, territory, age, and sex. Sectoral conflicts emerged from time to time but residents were also able to co-operate against a common enemy from outside the neighbourhood. Street life was critical for forming personal acquaintances. People got to know each other as they lounged on street corners or met informally in local businesses and corner stores. In effect, the mainstream view of slums as anomic was not supported by the residents themselves. For most it was a viable community with which they could identify. Residents in subsidized housing in two inner-city apart-

ment blocks in England knew that their area was stigmatized by outsiders as an aggressive, dangerous, crime-ridden neighbourhood (Foster 1995, 568) yet insiders came to think of it as "quite a family estate" where neighbours looked out for each other.

A study of hobos, or the men on skid row, reflects the same discovery that, behind the appearance of destitution and personal disorganization, there was nonetheless a recognizable and, in some measure supportive social organization (Harper 1979). When Harper spent two weeks living and travelling with a hobo companion, he found that the man had a network of lifelong friends, and that together they had their own complex system of stratification and moral obligations. African American street vendors who scratched a living on the sidewalks of Greenwich Village selling used books, or magazines retrieved from garbage, developed community networks of friendship and support both among themselves and with their customers (Duneier 1999). Many of the regulars thought of themselves and were generally regarded as "public characters" whose regular presence and watchful eyes on the street promoted a sense of security and community.

The limits of 'Community': Exclusion and Anomie

A note of caution here is that, just as Redfield and Miner found what they were looking for in describing harmonious village relations, so other researchers may be overemphasizing the sense of social organization in the slums, to the exclusion of tensions and hostilities. The fact that people manage to develop meaningful relationships and sense of home-place under difficult conditions does not mean that the sense of community is always experienced.

The zones for which there is most consistent evidence of urban anomie and social disorganization are areas to which people have been relocated after forced slum clearance programs, especially so where this rehousing takes the form of high-density highrise apartment blocks. Conceived by architects and urban planners as experiments in constructive social engineering, they have largely been experienced as massive social failures. Such areas are pervasively described as characterised by graffiti, broken elevators, wasted parklands and smashed windows (Stevenson 2003, 87; Jencks 1984, 9). Such repeated vandalism, often causing millions of dollars worth of damage, is interpreted by Jencks and others as expressions of resistance by the powerless to the oppressive power and values of the dominant developers who pushed them into these living quarters.

The failure of developers to recognize or to value the importance of local community networks plays an important role in the social anomie that has so often followed slum clearance projects. It may be that professional planners, used to suburban lifestyles, with non-localized social networks based on cars, telephones and electronic communications, have a learned incapacity to see the support networks that enable impoverished people to survive in urban slums. Forced relocation destroys these survival networks, moving isolated and impoverished people in among strangers. Public housing projects offer few advantages over the slums they replace. They are still overcrowded, the noise level intense, and services and facilities not maintained. The stigma of public housing creates a negative stereotype that residents feel deeply. Tenants may have improved accommodation, but they mostly viewed it unfavourably (McGahan 1982, 278–82), complaining of swearing, drinking, fighting, noisy and destructive people, and limited social controls, particularly over children. Controls are typically imposed from outside the area, by police and social workers. Thus, suggests McGahan (281) in the public housing projects "extensive solidarity is inhibited by mutual distrust, inability to cooperate, and subordination to external authorities." Residents lack control over their total life situation.

This sense of powerlessness, of being pawns in a game played by impersonal developers, government agents in the housing office, or in social work departments, may well be the most important element in the fatalism or "welfare mentality" often associated with residents in subsidized housing. Powerlessness, and not high-rise living conditions, is what residents of the remote Innu village of Davis Inlet in northern Labrador most have in common with slum-clearance residents in cities. The village made headlines in Canadian newspapers in the 1990s for the high numbers of adults addicted to alcohol and young children addicted to sniffing gasoline. In a failed Canadian experiment, the federal government allocated $150 million dollars to build a new village on the mainland, but these new houses were extensively vandalized even before people moved into them. Substance abuse appears as pervasive as ever (Moore 2003).

Aboriginal people inving in inner-city Winnipeg, many of them displaced from marginalised reserves by poverty and loss of status, conveyed a pervasive sense of being disconnected, disjointed, and fragmented at community level. The spoke of keeping to themselves to such a degree that few had even met fellow Aboriginals living in the same area. A typical comment was "For all these years I've been in here, I've never bothered nobody. Nobody bothers me, I don't bother nobody" (Silver 2006, 53). This is notwithstanding the fact that Winnipeg has the highest concentration of urban Aboriginals in all Canada. Barely any of those interviewed by Silver and his colleagues had had any contact with the local Neighbourhood Association, most believing they would be rejected there and stereotyped as unemployed, drunken Indians (ibid. 44).

In summary, the best we can conclude from these accounts is that results are mixed. Evidence of integrative community relations, local loyalties and kinship ties even in densely populated, mobile and heterogenous urban environments, challenge the classical functionalist thesis linking urban life to loss of community. Political economy theory accounts for some of the contradictory evidence in that people who are experiencing serious economic stress, whether in rural and urban communities, find it difficult to sustain cohesive social relations. Yet the study of the Addams area of Chicago shows again that poverty does not preclude cohesive community life, any more than wealth ensures it. The failure of these multiple field studies to find consistent evidence of either gemeinschaft-style folk communities in rural areas or gesellschaft-style shallow associations in urban areas has prompted efforts to move away from simplistic models and to re-think theories about community life.

Interpretive Perspectives: Re-thinking the Concept of Community

Interpretive perspectives in sociology challenge the implicit determinism in both the functionalist and political economy approaches to analysing community life. Structural characteristics of relative size, density, and heterogeneity, and relative economic well-being of residents, may be associated with different patterns of community life. But the subjective meanings that these characteristics hold for people can differ widely, reflecting diverse life-worlds.

Efforts to re-think the concept of 'community' in light of the failure of traditional theories has prompted what Amit terms 'a cacophony of definitions, descriptions, and claims' about community that have proven of limited analytical usefulness (Amit 2002, 1). In his influential text on *The Symbolic Construction of Community* (1985) Cohen suggests that 'community' carries mostly symbolic rather than descriptive meaning, conveying a sense of cultural boundaries or of similarity and difference. 'Community' signifies some boundary between people who share much in common and others who are dissimilar on some key characteristics. This idea of cultural or 'imagined' community has been widely adopted to refer to religious, ethnic and nationalist sentiments that link together large numbers of people spread over wide geographic areas, who do not know each other and never meet face-to-face (Anderson 1983/1991; Winland 1993; Driedger 2003). Driedger lists a series of studies of what he terms "classic clusters or communities": of the Chinese in Vancouver (Anderson 1991); Chinese across Canada (Li 1998); Blacks in Nova Scotia (Henry 1973); Jews in Montreal (Shaffir 1974); Portuguese in Toronto (Anderson 1974); Blacks in Toronto (James 1990); French in Calgary (Stebbins 1994); and others.

The problem with this concept of imagined community, Cohen argues, is that usage of the term 'community' has become so vague and imprecise as to be virtually meaningless. In his *epilogue* (2002) to Amit's edited collection, he strongly repudiates the ideas he set out in his 1985 text, even though the book was so successful. What concerns him is that the term 'community' is being applied to virtually any set of people. It "has become a way of designating that *some*thing is shared among a group of people at a time when we no longer assume that *anything* is necessarily shared"(2002, 169; emphasis in original). In everyday talk, 'community' implies more a moral idea, he suggests, than a description of reality. It reduces to a collectivity of parents who share in common the experience of adopting children from overseas (Howell 2002), or of having children involved in athletics (Dyke 2002), or people who 'know' each other only through 'visiting' the same electronic chat room (Wellman 2001). Sometimes, it carries no meaning at all, as in 'the community of nations' or 'fragile plant community' (Cohen 2002, 168). Reference to ethnic communities may sound superficially more meaningful, but when used in sweeping generalizations, as if to imply that everyone in Toronto who has an Irish ancestry belongs to the 'Irish community,' then it has no analytical value. The concept is not attached to any theory of how a sense of belonging to such an imagined community could be realized. What seems to be needed is a more subtle and nuanced understanding of what researchers mean by community, and what people mean

when they speak about or think of themselves as members of 'communities'.

Symbolic Interaction: Community as Life-World

Symbolic interactionist research reminds us that it is not possible to give one objective, neutral description of a town or a neighbourhood because the subjective meanings that people bring to a sense of place differ widely with their differing life situations and experiences. Residents of a small prairie town responded with disbelief to social science research data that showed no difference between city and small town locations on such measures as crime and incidence of domestic violence. "Does this mean we are all stupid?" they asked (Bonner 1999, 87). Their lived experiences as former urban residents who had moved to live in a small town belied the implied sameness. Surveys showed that fully 80 percent of small town residents concurred that small towns are a better place to raise children, and similar numbers of city residents agreed with them (ibid. 3). What parents of young children experienced was a greater sense of visibility and familiarity among small-town neighbours which encouraged them to feel more secure when their children were out by themselves. The felt that other residents knew their children and would watch out for them, and importantly, would inform them if the children were getting into trouble. Parents also much easier to drive their children to local activities, or to allow them to walk by themselves to events that they would have spent hours driving the children to in the city. The combination of familiarity, convenience and visibility in small towns significantly reduced their anxiety as parents and freed up their time, making small towns a better place than the city to raise children.

Other residents, with different life-worlds, experienced the same small towns in markedly different ways. For adults without children, or whose children had grown up and left, the same residential areas were experienced as more constraining and boring, with city life looking more inviting. Markedly different again were the subjective life worlds of 'hometowners', people who had grown up with their parents and grandparents in these small towns and rural areas, rather than moving into them from cities. These people drew on very different symbolic meanings to talk about their love for the place, reflecting images more closely tied to the classic sense of folk communities. They emphasised the importance of extended kinship ties, of having multiple family members living nearby, and a shared sense of unlimited obligations for care for their children, and the elderly.

The irony that was not immediately visible to newcomers who praised small-town life, was that the measures they applied to judging small towns as 'better places to raise children' were in themselves the displaced values of urban dwellers focussed on private consumption needs and pragmatic self interest, rather than folk-society values of community obligation. As they purchased property in the small towns they used, and were actively encouraged to use, real-estate values—saleability, amenities, quality of housing and services (Ramp 2001, 353; Bonner 2002, 6–7). Their privatized and instrumental orientation to small-town life threatened the very sense of community that attracted them. Can any place be that great, Bonner asks, if we have a purely instrumental orientation towards it (1999, 140)? What values are we teaching our children when we talk about place in such terms? The risk Bonner sees is that the values of objective social science measurement that permit comparative statistical evaluation of different living spaces both reflect and promote the same values of real-estate consumerism. Such 'objective' science risks undermining the alternative home-towner's folk-society or gemeinschaft worldview precisely as it tries to define and describe it (Bonner 1998, 183; 1999 ch. 8).

The physical infrastructure of place also invokes different subjective meanings and attachments for people who have lived different lives in relation to that space. Old streets and buildings carry special memory traces for long-term residents of inner-city spaces who remember them as once established working-class neighbourhoods. Residents of economically deprived neighbourhoods in six European cities described their sense of 'place' mostly through memories of how they came to be in that locality, where they would hang out and play as children, the small shops where neighbours would meet and exchange gossip, and local pubs where they could go for a laugh (Corcoran 2002). For them a sense of place is 'experienced rather than rationally examined or economically valued' (ibid. 51). These same streets held no intrinsic value for transient newcomers seeking cheap housing in de-industrialized areas of town, or for the families of professionals drawn to newly gentrified apartment and condominium complexes. Newcomers, often immigrants, refugees and asylum-seekers, tended to hang out in different spaces and to favour their own ethnic shops. Some of the long-established shopkeepers harboured deep resentment against newcomers, not simply because their small shops, already hit by supermarkets, were losing trade, but because they themselves were losing their centrality as public characters in the neighbourhood (ibid. 57–8; Wells and Watson 2005). The new 'gentry' also related to space in markedly different ways from old-timers, tending to segregate themselves behind locked gates, to shop outside the locality, and to come and go in cars, rather than spending time chatting on the sidewalks. They push up housing prices beyond the reach of the children of old-timers, and so contribute to the break-up of local extended families and the deterioration in the lives of ageing parents left behind (Corcoran 2002, 61).

City planners and developers tend to bring subjective meanings to urban space that are more closely akin to the 'gentry' than the old-timers. The irony is that they risk homogenizing space and thus destroying the very sense of specialness of place and urban-village community life that initially attracts professional families to the newly gentrified properties. Dublin and Toronto are cities with vastly different histories and infrastructures, yet city plans look and sound the same, with the same discourse of 'investing' in (rather than subsidizing) culture, to attract tourists, and a creative class of highly educated, bright and mobile residents (Dowler 2004, 25). 'Heritage' becomes an exercise in branding. The international financiers that invest in downtown development and gentrification and 'spectacularization' are themselves cosmopolitans who share the values of consumer capitalism and the globalized economy (Bonner 2002, 3). They expect the same services and lifestyles in cities across the globe. In this mindset, 'place' becomes merely interchangeable 'space'. How these financiers and planners conceptualise 'community' and 'place' matters in that they wield great influence over future city space, both to design new places and to shape how old places come to be seen as 'mere space' to be bulldozed out of the way.

Social Constructionism: Accomplishing 'Community'

The social constructionist perspective shifts the focus of inquiry to active practices of people as they engage in doing things that bring into being and sustain their sense of community, or alternatively behaving in ways that undermine those relations to generate what sociologists call anomie. Here we return briefly to the debate around how best to conceptualize 'community' and re-think the ideas as active practices.

If community implies 'boundary' or similarity among insiders and difference from outsiders, as Cohen suggests, then the issue to be explored is how people sustain this sense of boundary. What differences count as sufficiently or strategically 'different' to be foregrounded in exclusion of others? What differences can be ignored or viewed as inconsequential, and backgrounded to permit belonging?

If 'community' is not bounded by location, as studies of transnational religious and ethnic communities imply, then how do people sustain emotional relations across geographic space? How does location work in sustaining a sense of 'us' and 'not us', even when people do not live in the locations with which they feel some identification? How are boundaries located and negotiated in social relations, and how is this similar to and yet different from immediate physical location?

If communities are 'imagined', how do people realize this in everyday relations? How do they sustain emotions of loyalty, belonging, similarity, and identity in imagined social relations? Further, if individuals inhabit multiple, competing, and partial networks of relations, as Wellman's studies of computer-mediated networks imply, then how do people pull these together into a coherent sense of body and social space? How are boundaries, and sense of inclusion and exclusion negotiated and realized in practice?

Further, the questions can also asked in reverse: If community is actively organized, realized, and brought into being by what people do, then how is the loss of community actively produced? If community is understood as a deeply rooted feature of social life, then loss or anomie is not merely absence of community. It implies active destruction, brought about by dis-organizing and un-settling practices. These are practices of excluding, differencing, discounting, and ignoring of the colonized, the poor, the homeless, and the marginalized by which people come to experience themselves as not belonging.

Community Boundaries as Social Relations

From the perspective of social constructionist theory, locating community or home-place is not simply a matter of locating some administrative borough or village with pre-defined boundaries. It is a matter of how people who live there organize everyday patterns of interaction and how they move to and from home. In her study of a rural area northeast of Winnipeg Sprenger (2002) notes four administratively distinct localities on the local map: an Ojibway First Nation reserve, the Pine Falls Bush

Camp owned by a forestry company, a Francophone village, and a mill and company townsite. They each have long histories as separate settlements. They are also culturally and linguistically distinct, with English, French and Ojibway commonly spoken. Other smaller rural populations with distinct local names are dotted about the map, and include many family farms, churches, pubs, a liquor store, and what is locally recognized to be a brothel. At the intersection of two highways that cross the area is a Mohawk filling station and restaurant called Clark's Corner. The locality covers several hundred square kilometres. Sprenger tracks the routine everyday interactions of people from all these localities as they come and go through Clark's Corner restaurant. The constant banter across the tables indicate that the diverse residents recognize and interact with each other as locals, sharing the ingroup experiences that permit the truncated or 'indexical' speech patterns of people who know they do not have to explain the local jokes and references. Routine markers of community continually dissolved as fair-skinned men wore Native jackets, and Anglophone waitresses answered Ojibway customers in French.

One February night a dance or "community social" was sponsored by a Catholic Women's Church group as a fundraiser for a family whose house burned down. Truckers drove in from the bush camp some 200 kilometres away. Young people came from the nearby Indian reserve, others hitchhiked in from town; forest-workers and mill-workers mixed with Metis and francophones. In the parking lot, RCMP and Band constables broke up skirmishes between students from rival English, French, and Ojibway high schools. Police even participated in selling illegal hash oil which became part of the fundraiser. For all these people, Sprenger suggests, this is 'homeplace'. Community is defined by who attends, who is welcomed, who is turned away, who talks, dances or drinks together, and who fights with one another.

Sustaining Cultural Communities Beyond Spatial Location

Cultural or 'imagined' communities, as understood in the social constructionist perspective, are not located through pre-defined cultural attributes or characteristics that people can be objectively seen as having in common. Community is the outcome of active practices through which people organize social relations around particular similarities so as to generate and sustain a mutually recognized and experienced sense of belonging and membership. The focus of interest is thus on the practices that produce community, and not the characteristics of the members. There is no assumption that all people sharing particular similarities will think of themselves or be seen as members of a common community. The lifestory narratives of two men of Caribbean background living in England (Olwig 2002) shows that one thinks of his English village as homeplace while the other considers 'backhome' as the Caribbean. They share a common Caribbean ancestor, but experienced very different relations with immediate workmates and neighbours in England, and different non-local family ties. Olwig concludes that there is no such thing as 'a Caribbean diaspora' into which migrants fit. Rather, individuals continually construct for themselves networks of interpersonal relations through which a sense of belonging or not belonging emerges.

Communities can also be understood as continually coming into being in the face of changing personal situation and social contexts. Elderly people in an ex-mining town come together in social clubs for the 'active elderly'. They define what they have in common as being 'working-class', unlike the posh residents of surrounding suburbs; old-timers with long roots in the locality, unlike younger people who move away in search of work; and as able to live independently and are not incontinent or confused, unlike the senile people in nursing homes (Dawson 2002). Within these boundaries they sustain a viable community life, sustaining membership by covering for each other's slow physical and mental decline as long as possible. Cultural or imaginary communities are not necessarily bounded by location. Nor are they necessarily all-embracing, as the folk-society model would suggest. People can negotiate membership in multiple and partial communities, whose boundaries shift with context and activities. A study of Norwegian adopters of transnational children (Howell 2002) explores how many of these parents worked up a sense of community together. Before they met they had in common the emotionally harrowing experiences of struggling unsuccessfully to become pregnant, registering for adoption, being evaluated, and several subsequent years of waiting before a potential adoptive child became available. The transnational adoption agency first brought a number of these couples together for information sessions on adoption, and organized groups to travel together to a designated orphanage where they commonly waited several weeks to actually receive their child. The sharing of these emotionally intense experiences provided the basis for building a sense of commu-

nity. Many of the couples valued these relations enough to keep in contact and to travel long distances for regular reunions. The adoption agency also organized regular reunions of parents who had used their agency, and published magazines with updated pictures of the children. Parents constructed a sense of extended family ties from the fact of having travelled together or having children from the same orphanage. Parents often described these reunions as "for the children" but Howell notes that they also served important functions for the parents themselves. In this specific context parents foregrounded the biological fact of transnational adoption as what they all shared in common. Space and location also worked as important signifiers of sameness for parents of children from the same orphanage, or same region.

Parents also negotiated another community for their children among family members and neighbourhood where they lived, in which social kinship was foregrounded and biological differences backgrounded as insignificant. All the parents worked at 'kinning' their children as soon as they arrived home in Norway. This involved taking them to the location of their ancestral family roots in rural Norway—ideally the family farm or fjord to which they could trace ancestors. They took numerous photographs of children with extended kin in these locations, and commonly dressed the children in national costume and distinctively local styles of dress. Significantly, Howell notes that immigrants, who make up 20 percent of the population of Oslo, almost never gained sufficient acceptance from Native Norwegians to make this transition into local costume (2002, 93). When the first-ever immigrant woman was appointed to lead the preparatory committee for Norwegian National Day in 1999 she faced vocal hostility, and was explicitly denied the right to wear a local costume. The same difference of origin that was foregrounded to exclude immigrants, was backgrounded for transnational adopted children to include them as Norwegian through the kinship of their parents. A third potential community for transnational adoptees could be ethnic solidarity with fellow immigrants from the same origin country. Howell finds, however, that almost none of the adoptees pursue this, even though they often find themselves mistaken for immigrants by others. The largest majority actively distance themselves from immigrants, and also from other adopted young people. What they foreground is their kinship ties with the extended family of their adoptive parents.

In summary, membership in cultural communities cannot be read from spatial location, or from physical characteristics like skin colour or origin. The boundaries of sameness and difference, belonging and exclusion, are continually negotiated and sustained in different contexts of interaction. People's sense of belonging to a community of parents of transnational adoptive children is only one of a number of social networks to which these parents feel they belong. It is fully compatible with a sense of belonging to the local communities of ancestral village and residential neighbourhood.

Demolishing Community: Active Practices of Social Dis-location

When community life is understood as actively being organized, realized, and brought into being by what people do, it implies the converse understanding of *loss* of community life as also actively produced. The sense of community life as lost or as being lost does not reflect a structural feature of the community or the neighbourhood itself. Rather, it emerges as the outcome of active practices that continually break up relationships, undermine local organizations, and selectively exclude people from localities where they once felt a sense of belonging, or where they seek to be included. In the next section we will focus on active practices of community dis-location as they are experienced with respect to the colonized, the poor, the homeless, and unwelcomed newcomers.

Colonialism and the Settler City

The settler cities of Canada were all founded through varying degrees of violence as European settlers ignored the prior claims of indigenous peoples and drove them out of the way. The discourse of pioneers taming the 'empty' wilderness obscures the presence of complex systems of overlapping rights that guided how different peoples used the lands for hunting, fishing, gathering food, seasonal migrations to follow herds of caribou, bison and deer, seasonal settlements as winter and summer camps, and sacred places to bury their dead. Sometimes, as in the case of the Maliseet people along the St. John River in New Brunswick (Martin 2002, 232–3, citing A. Bear-Nicholas), this dispossession occurred through settlers blatantly taking over land that officials at the time knew had not been conquered by, ceded to, or purchased by the colonial government in Britain. Sometimes it occurred through the settlers' ignorance or lack of understanding of indigenous conceptions of use rights rather than 'ownership' over land. Within the prevailing European view of land, it was, and mostly still is, the presence of buildings,

fences and boundary markers that signify valid possession. Without such markers, land appeared as *terra nullis,* land devoid of people, rather than *terra populi,* occupied by settled communities (Blomley 2004, 92). Native peoples appeared as transients, not settled in one place, and hence having no enforceable legal claim to the place compared to Europeans who cleared the land, fenced it off, and constructed permanent buildings and roads.

European settlers enclosed ever-expanding territories for cities and towns, farms and ranches, industrial development and resource-extraction enterprises, reserving only bounded tracts of land for indigenous peoples to call their own. The active practices that continue to undermine and dis-organize communities on these reservations are well known. Canadian government agents exercise sweeping powers under the Indian Act to 'manage' governance, law enforcement, and economic relations within them, in ways that are foreign to indigenous practices. Most reserves were established historically in areas least desired by European settlers—areas with limited access to economic resources for viable community development. It is also difficult to calculate the enormity of the destabilizing impact on generations of parenting practices and kinship networks within aboriginal communities of the Canadian government policy of educating Indian children in residential schools. On some reserves it meant that there were no people present between the ages of 6 and 16. Young people raised in institutions lack the experiences of kinning and parenting that most of us take for granted. As families fell apart under these strains, ravaged by experiences of powerlessness and despair, poverty, anger and alcoholism, social workers from the 1960s onward removed many children from reserves to find foster homes and adoptive parents in non-aboriginal families. Aboriginal peoples continue to struggle to build satisfying communities in the face of these formidable challenges.

Colonial dispossession continues to be actively contested through Aboriginal land claims being pursued in Canadian courts. These include a specific claim filed by two First Nations Bands in 2001, to Native ownership of 4.2 hectares of land on which the British Columbia Legislature now sits (Blomley 2004, 107–8), and claims to lands occupied by Simon Fraser University in Burnaby (ibid. 135). These court challenges remain profoundly unsettling processes within the settler cities, as continuing reminders that historic injuries still resonate in ongoing tensions between descendants of settlers and aboriginal peoples. The confrontation at Ipperwash in 1995 when the native protester Dudley George was killed by a police bullet was one of many such struggles. In 1942 the Canadian government used the War measures Act to appropriate Stony Point on the shores of lake Huron for a military base. The Chippewas residents were moved over to nearby Kettle Point reserve where many families became destitute and unable to care for their children (Bressette 2003). The original promise was that the land would be returned after the war, but this never happened, as the military has continued to use it as a cadet training facility. Protracted negotiations continued over the next half century as residents tried to reclaim the lands, coming to a head in 1995 with a small group of natives, including Dudley George trying to occupy the barracks. In the context of an official inquiry into his death, which opened in July 2004, a native lawyer tried to explain to non-native judges that aboriginal peoples feel a continuing relationship with their ancestors so that they would not abandon the graveyards of their community (Galloway *The Globe and Mail* July 15, 04., A6, "Ipperwash inquiry given history lesson"). Meanwhile the Kettle Point reserve is torn by overcrowding and conflict between displaced Stoney Point families and original Kettle Point residents who had to give up lands to accommodate them. These conflicts are fuelled by the government's insistence on separating the claims of those relocated from the claims of those who gave up lands for the relocation (Bressette 2003, 33).

The colonial dispossession of aboriginals from urban lands is now largely complete, Blomley argues, but not their displacement from the cities. Recent Statistics Canada data (2003) estimates that half of all aboriginal people in Canada now live in urban areas, one quarter of them in ten urban areas, particularly in Prairie cities. Overwhelmingly aboriginals are concentrated in the inner-city cores of crumbling properties, cheap rooming houses and shelters. Here, along with others among the urban poor, they experience continuing quasi-colonial practices of dispossession and dislocation that are explored below.

Colonizing the Inner-City: 'Gentrification' and the Politics of Property

The politics of gentrification, Blomley argues (2004) are inherently colonial. The way developers typically talk when referring to the inner-city zones slated for bulldozers parallels closely the discourse of earlier European colonizers. They promise to 'clean-up' the area and tame the urban wilderness. From the viewpoint of developers, the poor people who inhabit cheap hotels and shelters look like transients, without commitment or roots in the

area, unlike property-owners who appear settled. Hence, even areas that are densely populated with poor people look 'empty'. Poor people are described as congregating in the zone only because services like community kitchens and shelters are provided there. Hence, the poor, along with the services they use, can readily be moved out.

Practices of mapping, almost always done by groups with authority, help in this process of emptying and re-allocating space. Landscaping, suggests Blomley, is a particular way of seeing that highlights particular claims while obscuring others. Maps produced by European settlers superimposed boundaries and grids onto space, dividing regions into plots that could be sold. The presence of indigenous peoples disappeared. Developers' maps similarly re-zone space in ways that make current uses invisible. In the Vancouver area of Downtown Eastside, Blomley tracks the multiple interests and use rights of hotel residents, shelter residents, and coalitions of homeless who inhabit the streets. None of these interests were represented in developers' maps. What locals saw as a park for community use near the waterfront, developers saw as "just weeds, rock and junk"(Blomley 2004, 47). New zoning regulations passed by city council to encourage owners to enhance the value of their properties and attract upscale tourists, resulted in large-scale evictions of poor people. One such resident, who became an icon in the local resistance movement, had lived in the same hotel room for 30 years. As a non-owner, his claims to residency, like thousands of others, are invisible.

Excluding the Homeless Bodies

Urban renewal in the interests of creating attractive public space for upscale recreation and consumption necessarily involves displacement of the most economically marginal. People who are homeless, who literally inhabit the public street, are routinely excluded from the definition of legitimate "public" as interpreted by city developers. They are constituted as a problem for the public rather than a part of the public (Kawash 1998). City parks that are intended to be attractive to tourists must be made off-limits to the homeless

The homeless person occupies embodied space, but has no place in which to be. In Kawash's harrowing description of embodied homelessness, a city map for a homeless person consists of sleeping places, warm places, eating places, safe places, panhandling places and especially toilet places. The corollary, excluding the homeless, involves systematically excluding from the city map the places where the homeless can be. Padlocking parks at night protect the legitimate public users from homeless bodies who might otherwise congregate there to sleep. Public toilets are routinely locked at night, when legitimate tourists are tucked into their hotels and restaurants. City by-laws prohibit sleeping on park benches or sitting on sidewalks, or panhandling anywhere which might be annoying to more affluent tourists. In a vicious circle homeless people who cannot find accessible public toilets eliminate bodily wastes in public places, evoking the very disgust that legitimates their being excluded from public places. People who cannot find accessible places to sleep, or to bathe or change their clothes, become filthy and obtrusive in public space, reinforcing the belief that the legitimate public needs to be protected from them. The homeless are especially unwelcome in "festival centres"—the gentrified city centres commonly built precisely on the sites of abandoned factories and slums which homeless people formerly inhabited. When special festivals of global significance are planned, such as the Olympic Games in Vancouver, homeless people are often herded up and dumped outside the city, with the warning that if they return they risk arrest and imprisonment for vagrancy. Kawash ends her article with the warning that the violence of the expulsion and containment of the homeless in ever smaller city spaces threatens to undermine the very public security that such containment is intended to protect.

The National Film Board of Canada's 1998 film *East Side Showdown* (Director Robin Benger, Producer Peter Starr) powerfully dramatizes the ongoing class struggle between homeless residents and people trying to gentrify the Toronto neighbourhood of Dundas and Sherbourne. On one side are close to a hundred people who live in large shelters in the area and many more near-homeless who live in overcrowded, cheap rooming houses. Many of these have lived in the area all their lives. They are supported by local church leaders, and anti-poverty activists agitating to gain access to boarded up industrial properties that could provide shelter. Lined up on the other side are better-off residents who have invested heavily to fix up down-town homes, and to open a bed-and-breakfast business catering to upscale tourists. They are increasingly desperate to clear the streets of people they sometimes refer to as 'scum'. Supporting them are the police, and developers with plans to convert abandoned industrial sites into upscale condominiums and offices. The destitute are driven a few blocks further east where their embodied and unwelcomed presence seems likely to precipitate another round of struggle.

The Un/settlement of an Urban Slum Community

The history of the black community of Africville on the Bedford Basin on the outskirts of Halifax is a long and chequered story of settlement, struggle, encroachment, exclusion, and eventually forced expulsion in a slum clearance project in 1964 (Clairmont and Macgill [1974] 1999; Nelson 2002). The community traces its beginnings to William Brown and William Arnold, who purchased about 13 acres of land from white merchants in the 1840 and established a church, elementary school, post office and a few stores. Black families had been moving into the areas over the previous 30 years as it offered some means of livelihood from fishing and wage-work in the city. They were mostly descendants of slaves and freed slaves who migrated from America after the War of 1812. Like indigenous peoples before them, they were allocated spaces to settle in "small lots of rocky soil and scrubby forest" (Clairmont and Magill 1999, 28) inadequate for people to survive off the land. By 1851 there were an estimated 54 blacks living in the Africville area. Their numbers had expanded to about 400 by 1964.

Active practices by city politicians and surrounding businesses, for over the 120 years of Africville's existence produced its characteristics as a marginalized slum. Despite the fact that it was within the city limits, the city flatly refused to provide even basic services like water lines, sewage, and garbage collection and denied police and fire protection. Roads into the area were unpaved and unploughed. Meanwhile the community became encircled with a host of businesses and activities that no other neighbourhood wanted, including night-soil deposit pits in 1858, followed by a bone mill, two slaughter houses, a leather tanning plant, a tar factory, the Rockhead prison, a hospital for infectious diseases, and an open city dump. By the early 1950s the overflowing dump was moved directly onto Africville land, 350 feet from the nearest house (Clairmont and Magill 1999, 109; Nelson 2002, 214–219). The area then readily became referred to as "the slum by the dump".

When the city decided in the 1960s that it wanted the land for industrial re-development, the practices that produced the area as a slum were obscured from public consciousness by the discourse of good intentions, and 'putting the community out of its misery'(Nelson 2003, 222). Bulldozing the properties could be characterised as compassionate relocation. Nelson describes the violence done to the community in the process of this 'benevolent' relocation. As with most slum-clearance projects, families were relocated as standard nuclear family units, without recognition that children might be cared for through alternative extended family networks and communities of support. Families that had more children than the norm for new housing projects had to divide up their children. In some cases single mothers were required to marry the fathers of their children to qualify for new housing (Nelson 2003, 225). Extended community support networks were broken up.

Economically, many families found themselves living in better housing but otherwise financially worse off than they were in Africville. After generations of inter-marriage and handing down of houses within families, many inhabitants lack clear title to properties and so did not qualify for home-owner compensation. Many found themselves paying rent for the first time. The assortment of illicit and semi-legal practices that provided income in Africville were lost, as was access to fishing for food.

The importance of what was lost can be measured in part by the tenacity with which these displaced residents and their descendants have clung to the memories of the Africville community more than forty years after their relocation. Oral testimonies of former residents, recorded at the North Branch Public Library September 1986 speak of communal bonds of religion and mutual self help, and of their well-kept gardens, their homecrafts, their music, and their memories of ministers, deacons, teachers, and elders (Clairmont and Magill 1997, 296). Annual reunions continue to take place on what is now the twenty-five acre Seaview Memorial Park. However, anything that might remind visitors to the park of the history of the area has been purged, with the exception of a small plaque. There are plans to build a swimming pool in the area where the city formerly refused to supply drinking water and sewer pipes. Nelson ends her article with the question—why was it that the Africville community was subjected to forced relocation in the interests of industrial re-development, when no such development ever occurred? Why was it so important to the white community of Halifax to remove a black community?

Community Life after Slum Clearance

Africville residents managed to sustain a sense of collective community identity after their relocation, focussed around demands for compensation that are still before the Nova Scotia courts. As individual families, however, most found they could not sustain the sense of kinship intimacy and independence that they enjoyed in Africville (Clairmont and Magill 1999, 232–3). The more general experience of people who are rehoused is that the quality of community life that emerges in slum-relocation zones is socially impoverished and unsatisfying, typically associated with high rates of vandalism, crime, and family breakdown. Economically disadvantaged people are uprooted and bundled together into subsidized housing complexes, under the patriarchal authority of government agencies. The relocation that turns them into "grateful" recipients of welfare housing, brings with it a powerlessness that promotes the social collapse that is subsequently attributed to the character of the recipients themselves.

Some tentative insight into practices that contribute to this sense of powerlessness comes from personal discussions with single-parent women who lived in subsidized housing projects. Among other experiences, these women described city housing officers giving them certain semi-legal privileges, such as paying them to do small jobs without having to declare the money as income. Once they accepted such a perk they were under obligation to the official, and also subject to the threat that disclosure could mean losing their accommodation. Several women felt trapped in a vicious circle of compliance, including providing sex, because they had accepted such favours. Also, women who were not certain of their rights as tenants were easily intimidated, and would not risk openly trying to assert control over their lives in the housing project, for fear of being evicted on some technicality. Teenaged children also face pressure to prove themselves as members of local gangs, or to face reprisals. Such comments suggest there may be systematic practices that sustain the powerlessness of residents in housing projects as ongoing accomplishments, but we need more detailed research to explore them.

Unwelcomed Newcomers: Subtle Practices of Exclusion

The borough of East York, as described above by Wellman (1978) and Shulman (1976) was a tightly cohesive urban folk community in the 1970s, held together by class and ethnic homogeneity and extended networks of kin and friends. Over the next thirty years, the composition of the borough changed with the significant influx of immigrants into the greater Toronto Area. Before 1960 most immigrants came from Britain and Europe, but since then the majority are from parts of Africa, Asia and the Middle East. By 2000, Toronto became home to some 200,000 Muslims, and many of them settled in East York (Isin and Siemiatycki 2002).

Negotiating the boundaries of sameness and difference, belonging and exclusion, in a changing residential area raise challenges for both long-term residents and newcomers. It is important to recognize that people living in the same city zone tend to have much in common, with the exception of areas undergoing rapid redevelopment, as described above. Family incomes tend to be similar, influenced by ability to pay going rents and real-estate values in a particular zone. People also seek proximity to, or easy transportation to places of employment. Position in family life cycle also tends to be similar. People with young children tend to gravitate towards suburban housing close to schools and playgrounds, while the young and single are drawn to apartments in areas with appealing night life, older people seek low-maintenance housing in quiet areas close to the services they need, and so on. The salience of differences that reflect origin, language, religion and physical characteristics of skin colour are negotiated in relation to these similarities.

People who are recent immigrants, and especially those experiencing language barriers, also value the social support of living close to others with whom they share language, religion and other customs in common (Simich 2003). These concerns tend to reduce with time, Bannerji argues (2000, 159), unless external pressures push people to turn inwards. As newcomers begin to spread across the city, they find it attractive to settle in places where they know someone already, or which have places of worship and shops that sell the kinds of food they like. Real estate agents often assist in directing them to such zones. Through such mechanisms of choice and attraction, it is common to find zones in every large city where there are relatively high concentrations of people with particular ethnic minority characteristics. They share similarities with, as well as differences from other residents, and these are reflected in negotiations over the use of space.

Groups of Muslim who settled in East York found themselves embroiled in stormy negotiations with the municipal council over space for a place of worship and an associated meeting place for social activities (Isin and Siemiatycki 2002). In principle any place where Muslims gather to worship constitutes a Mosque. Their efforts in 1995 to construct a special building, with traditional minaret and dome, on the site of a vacant factory building, meant more than just a place to worship. It signified the active inclusion of Muslims as a distinc-

tive community of residents within East York. What they came up against was a protracted struggle expressed as an issue about parking. New bylaws passed that same year required increased on-site parking, set limits on the maximum size of places of worship in industrial zones, and stipulated that no more than one place of worship be established within 500 metres of another place of worship on lots in industrial zones within 500 metres of residential areas. All existing places of worship were exempted from the new bylaws. Long-term residents argued that the bylaws were needed to protect the industrial tax base of their borough from too many tax-exempt places of worship, to protect their property values from the negative impact of congested street parking and excessive weekend use of a local park near the proposed new Mosque. Muslims argued that the bylaws were being designed and used explicitly against their community and their struggle for recognition in the borough. Churches were readily given exemptions to the regulations while mosques were not. Eventually the dispute was settled by the municipal council which gave approval for a smaller mosque, with part of the factory demolished for added parking, and no social hall. A survey of 24 full-service mosques in the Greater Toronto Area in 1998 found that eight of them had experienced zoning or planning difficulties, articulated as issues of location, size, and parking. The article provides no comparative data on zoning difficulties experienced by proposals for new churches. Many of the Muslims involved in lobbying for new mosques feel that zoning technicalities obscure the deeper concerns of non-Muslim neighbours about too many of certain kinds of people coming together too often in the neighbourhood. Muslims feel they are in but not fully included within the borough.

Ethnic Folk Community as Political Ideology

The Chicago-school thesis presents the folk society model as the ideal form of community, with people closely knit together by bonds of shared cultural values and lifestyles, with low social and geographic mobility helping to foster long-term ties of friendship and kinship. What is missing from this presentation are the active practices, both external and internal to the community, that promote and sustain such homogeneity and cohesion. Missing also is analysis of relations of power, inequality and sometimes oppression that internally divide folk communities. Nostalgia for Africville should not obscure the experiences of poverty and exclusion from white settler society that pushed black-skinned people into this marginalized settlement. The pride and resilience of Aboriginal peoples also should not obscure the colonial practices that established the reservations and that continue to support political structures governing First Nations communities that many members find oppressive.

The presence of ethnic folk communities in Canadian cities reflect ongoing negotiation of boundaries of similarity and difference by both insiders and outsiders. People who migrate to Canada, particularly when they first arrive, often seek out and enjoy the company, support and comfort of fellow migrants with whom they share origins, migration experiences, and common language, religious rituals, customs, food preferences, and the like. Practical help in finding accommodation and employment are also often found through these relations. There is little that distinguishes people from the rest of the world from European immigrants in this regards. What does distinguish them is physical visibility in the majority white settler society of Canada. As Bannerji expresses it, colonial meanings are written onto skin colour (2000, 160) signifying non-white as "Other"—as both different and traditional or pre-modern compared to how whites see themselves. State policies of 'multiculturalism' add to this sense of difference by foregrounding the separateness of ethno-cultural identities. Immigrants whose skin colour is other than white and whose cultural backgrounds are marked as different, experience "othering"—ways of being treated as different and as outsiders, to a greater degree than immigrants who fit the white-European mould. This othering, Bannerji argues, makes it harder for them to feel included in mainstream Canadian society, and fosters greater reliance on ingroup or ethnic folk-community. When people cohere for protection and support around mini-nationalities of ethnic communities, this has important consequences for internal community structure and politics. Elites within mini-nationalities exert political agency in Canada as spokespersons for their specific cultural community, so that their authority depends on maintaining the appearance of community solidarity and uniformity. Internal politics as well as external pressure combine to create and sustain a homogenized and rigidly traditional definition of community. Diversity of class, gender, and political influence within these ethnic-communities is obscured, and dissent stifled in the name of presenting a united front. Individuals who press for change in tra-

ditional practices, which are often strongly patriarchal, appear as disloyal and even subversive. Bannerji concludes that cultural nationalism and cultural community are very modern formations, in which a mythic and rigid picture of tradition is invented to sustain current political interests.

Feminist Theory: Gendered Community Space

The feminist perspective, and particularly feminist urban geography led the way in social constructionist analysis of community life. Feminist research drew attention to the close interrelationship between spheres of activity traditionally thought of as separate—the spheres of private and public, domestic and productive work, family life and employment. In exploring these relations feminist researchers developed innovative ways of seeing how community life was sustained through women's work. This section explores what women do to maintain farming as a way of live, women's practices in sustaining kinship relations, and how women's resource networks transformed suburban "dormitories' into centres of production.

Farm Life as Accomplishment

In the traditional model of rural or folk societies, farming is associated with almost mystical notions of a way of life, with farmers working their own lands in harmony with nature. Political economy theory shifts the focus from agriculture to agribusiness, where farms are pressured into becoming large-scale, highly mechanized businesses. Corporate capitalist farms manage heavy investment debts and large payrolls for hired labour. Rural communities disappear as thousands of small farmers sell out or go bankrupt.

What we do not see in either of these accounts are the active strategies and choices worked out by the families involved. Machum's study of women's work in potato farming in new Brunswick (1992) describes two very different survival strategies that hinged directly on the value that women placed on "the family farm" as a way of life. A shift in focus from *what* women do to *why* they do it was prompted by one of Machum's respondents exclaiming "Why are we doing this? Are we crazy?" (1992, 92). Love of farming as a way of life motivated this woman and many like her to do a tremendous range of income-generating and income conserving work to support the farm—planting several acres of vegetables, canning and freezing a year's supply of food, producing eggs, milk, and butter, participating in other farm work and often also holding a paid job to cover family consumption costs, and otherwise minimizing expenditures on household goods. These families actively resisted mechanizing their farms to hold on to these ideals, against persistent pressure from government and agribusiness.

When women withdrew this intensive level of unpaid labour, the entire character of farming changed. Families either left farming altogether, or invested heavily in machinery and additional land to focus on running a business. Women connected with these farms had largely ceased to be "farm women." They were more likely to have careers that were unconnected with the farm, and if they became involved in farm bookkeeping and accounting, they drew salaries. Their homes had all the modern equipment of an urban household. Their goal for their children was often not to continue the farm, but to "go where the money is." The preservation or demise of family farming as a way of life is thus neither automatic or inevitable. It is the outcome of active strategizing in which women's commitment is centrally important.

Doing Kinship

The descriptive studies cited above of East York, Montreal, and East London boroughs draw attention to the special roles played by women in sustaining social relations with kin and neighbours. Wives telephoned their parents more frequently than did their husbands, and organized most of the social events that brought people together. The extensive networks of kin and friends, sometimes estimated at upwards of 200 people, do not happen by biological accident. The have to be worked at. This is especially true when families are mobile and kin spread out geographically across provinces and cities where meeting would not occur by change. Older family members tend to be particularly important in forming the centre of networks of kin. Early studies only provide glimpses of the work involved in maintaining these networks—writing letters, making regular telephone calls, keeping track of birthdays, actively organizing get-togethers, and doing the extensive amount of food preparation associated with celebrating special events like Thanksgiving and Christmas. Bella (1992) describes how staging the magnificent family feasts and family gift exchanges around Christmas became both a moral imperative and a test of homemak-

ing skills for wives in Western Europe from the Victorian era onwards. Women's magazines and department stores like Eatons and The Bay focussed extensive advertising and promotions to persuade women to outdo themselves year after year in performing these kinship rituals. Wellman (1992; 2001, 25) refers to women as historically "the kin-keepers of western society" providing the extensive emotional and domestic support required to sustain kin networks.

Community relations have become more focussed around private and domestic venues rather than local pubs and clubs in walking distance from home, Wellman suggests (1992) now that most families now have cars and telephones. The result, Wellman argues, is that men more often spend their leisure time at home, and rely more on the informal social ties between couples that their wives develop. Women thus help to maintain many of their husbands' friendships through providing entertainment at home. They also do much of the work of sustaining community networks through minding each others' children and organizing sleep-overs and social activities among their children's friends.

Accomplishing Suburbia

Work in feminist urban geography during the 1980s uncovered the extensive practices through which women, trapped in the privatized realm of suburban homes, managed to change them into centres of production for themselves (Mackenzie 1986b, 87). City planners of the 1950s envisioned suburbs as centres of relatively low-density, single-family homes, with open spaces and parks. The prevailing assumption was that women as housewives and mothers would remain within the suburban home with children, while the husband father commuted to the city each day as family breadwinner. Transportation routes were designed to carry workers to work in the mornings and back in the evenings.

Suburbs worked as places to live, Mackenzie suggests, only so long as these assumptions held. The crunch came in the 1960s when the costs of purchasing and maintaining a suburban home became greater than one income could sustain. As women began to seek income-earning work that they could combine with raising children, they had to develop strategies to combat the segregating practices built into suburban layouts (Mackenzie 1986b, 92–3). Women who wanted to run small businesses from their homes had to convert rooms and garages into work stations—places in which they could manufacture crafts, food, or other goods for sale, or organize play centres, tutorial classrooms, drop-in centres, and the like. Domestic work became simultaneously income-generating work.

More and more women living in the suburbs began to seek out and set up networks to assist them in their dual homemaking/income-earning activities. Contacts among friends and neighbours were redesigned as working networks, sources of contact, advice and assistance. Such networks helped to advertise the quality of services offered and operated as referral systems, linking child-minders with mothers needing the service, and knitters and dress-makers with their clientele, for example. Women also organized mutual aid networks to develop facilities such as drop-in centres and playgrounds to support their "domestic-community work."

Women have also had to struggle with the implicit gender-role biases built into the organization of public transit. Women on average use public transit three times more frequently than men, but the system designs rarely take their needs into account (Michelson 1988, 89). Most suburban bus routes are designed to take workers from suburbs to city centre in the mornings and back in the evenings. This arrangement proved very inconvenient for women whose income-earning activities often require lateral movements from one suburban district to another at irregular hours. Women who earn money by selling cosmetics or clothing or other home-produced goods, or who do domestic work or child-care in other people's houses, or who tutor in evenings, are all likely to find the bus service extremely inconvenient if not useless. The Toronto transit system, with its interconnected grid of routes, very frequent services, and monthly passes that allow unlimited transfers, may be one of the few exceptions to this general pattern. Most urban transit systems do not permit the erratic and multistop movements women commonly need to make between child care, shops, children's teachers, and the like. It is perhaps only when one has tried to leave work, stop off to buy groceries, run other errands, pick up a child from day-care before it shuts, and bundle all this onto a bus to get home, that one realizes just how frustrating public transit can be. When families can only afford one car, it is typically the husband who uses it to get to work, leaving the wife to contend with all the inflexibilities of transit systems (Michelson 1998, 88).

Research into the working lives and the "hidden economy" of women's work highlights how different the experience of suburban living can be for men and women. People who leave the suburbs during the day to work elsewhere may develop few ties within the suburbs, while people who are trying to transform them into work centres may find them teaming with networks of support services and clientele (Mackenzie 1986a).

Organizing Community Economy

Women's work in organizing a domestic-community economy took on special significance in the community of Nelson in the British Columbia interior during the 1980s (Mackenzie 1987b). The resource-extraction economy of Nelson underwent severe economic recession with massive cutbacks in mining, smelting and forestry, and concomitant loss of jobs in industry as plants either closed down or "rationalized" their operations. Secure, highly-paid, unionized jobs for men disappeared.

Political Economy theory predicts that loss of community spirit is very likely to follow such economic recession, but this prediction does not take into account the tenacity with which people struggle to maintain a viable community life. What remained after the downturn in the industrial economy of Nelson, BC, was the once economically marginal activities largely done by women, such as caring for children, maintaining homes, cooking meals, growing food and manufacturing goods and crafts in the home. Mackenzie describes how women's community networks were expanded to form the West Kootenay Women's Association, to provide support and resources for small enterprises, including holding seminars on business management and skills development. The network mobilized people involved in the informal domestic-community economy to expand their operations to meet the economic crisis. The local Doukhobour community revived its farming and food processing co-operatives, largely inactive since the 1940s. They joined forces with the politically active feminist movement and back-to-the-landers comprising relatively well-educated people with city backgrounds, who were attracted to a self-sufficient rural lifestyle. Together they organized a variety of alternative employment, including woodworking, home renovation, machinery maintenance, food processing co-operatives, artisans' co-operatives, home child-care services, and related nursery education classes. They used the recently deserted university buildings to develop a Summer School of the Arts and to promote tourism and the sale of artwork.

The outcome, suggests Mackenzie, was a radical transformation of a formerly gender-segregated, resource-based male-working-force town. Definitions of public and private locations, and of what constitutes unskilled and private activity versus marketable and public skills broke down. Women gained prominence in community activities as the informal economy was transformed into the public economy, and in the process, kept the community of Nelson going when the formal economy pulled out (Mackenzie 1987a, 248–49).

Gendered Inequality in Community Life

Women, as primarily responsible for homemaking and childcare, are differently located from men in residential communities. They are also differently vulnerable to many of the practices described above that dis-organize and un-settle community life. Colonial practices through which white settler society displaced indigenous peoples onto reservations impacted especially hard on women, undermining their pre-contact status as community leaders. The Indian Act was explicitly patriarchal, recognizing only Indian men as carriers of native status, a status that they automatically conferred on their wives and children. Aboriginal women who lived on reserves held rights to residency and housing only through their fathers and husbands. Status Indian women who married non-status men lost their status as native, as did their children. Loss of status meant they no longer had the right to live within the reservation. Over the years this has resulted in large numbers of women and their descendants who consider themselves Native, but who have no community or land base—in a sense, no home (Lawrence and Anderson 2003, 12). Bill C-31, passed by the Canadian federal government in 1985, eventually revoked this rule so that Status-Indian women can retain their status on marrying out, but this does not automatically confer right to band membership or residence on reservations.

The "right" to live on reservations has also commonly meant living in communities ravaged by poverty, powerlessness, anger, alcoholism, and despair. Women have borne the brunt of this misery, expressed in levels of family violence and sexual abuse far in excess of non-Native communities (Muise 2003, 35). When families break up women are left without housing. Others feel victimized by rigid application of band policies that marginalize them as women. For these combinations of reasons—loss of tribal status, lack of housing and employment, and violence, women of aboriginal heritage have migrated into the cities in higher numbers than men.

Aboriginal people in the cities are even more marginalized. In the prairie cities of Winnipeg, Regina, and Saskatoon 60 percent of Aboriginal households live below the poverty line, rising to 80 to 90 percent of women-headed households (Razack 2002, 133). Ninety percent of aboriginal children in Regina drop out of high school before graduating. The population of impoverished and homeless people who inhabit the streets of inner-city slums are thus both racialized and gendered, as well as classed. Under these wretched conditions large numbers of Aboriginal women turn to the sex trade. Here they face harassment by police, often at the behest of middle-class property owners seeking to gentrify their streets and clear the neighbourhood of 'scum'. Forceful displacement and harassment combine to drive these women into concealed spaces where they are even more vulnerable to violence, a violence that is largely unwitnessed and unpoliced (Blomley 2004, 151; Razack 2003, ch. 5). Frightening numbers of women from such inner-city streets have disappeared or been murdered, with few arrests. As both Razack and Blomley observe, these women continue to be victimized by colonial practices of dispossession and patriarchal power.

Patriarchy in Ethnic Enclave Communities

The practices that encourage people to cohere around ethnic folk communities also differentially impact upon women and men. It is difficult for people to challenge or change oppressive practices within their community when they feel unwelcome in the wider host society—as when employers reject their non-Canadian qualifications, white neighbours make disparaging remarks about their skin colour or cultural habits, other children reject their children as playmates, neighbours object to having a mosque or other minority cultural symbols being built nearby, and the like. People come to feel safer turning inwards, presenting a united front to the outside. Elites within ethnic minority communities also have strong vested interests in sustaining the image of a united cultural front when their political agency or authority within wider political institutions depends upon their claims to status as spokespersons for their ethnic group. People may also feel a sense of belonging and commitment to a world-wide community of Muslims, espepcially at a time of international conflict . The combination of such external and internal pressures promote an exaggerated and rigid identification with tradition.

Women in these communities bear the brunt of such traditionalism that is commonly both patriarchal and anti-feminist. Women typically face powerfully-enforced expectations that they fit into traditional and pre-modern roles as nurturing and self-sacrificing wives and mothers within the patriarchal family mould. Within South Asian Muslim communities in Canada, Bannerji suggests (2000, 164–7), women are widely dehumanized as symbols, even as property of their community and their husband. Any movement towards change is readily criticized as violating the very authenticity of the community itself and therefore as intolerable. Bannerji argues that when religious and political elites within these mini-nationalities insist on such rigidity they are not reflecting tradition so much as inventing it as a political tool in the context of white settler society. She sees it as a very modern expression of colonial politics, in which the racist values of colonial and white settler societies that define non-white cultures as inherently pre-modern and primitive, are internalized and twisted into self-defining features of ethnic folk communities.

Within aboriginal communities in Canada, pre-contact traditional community structures are widely recognized as matriarchal. Yet even here the 'invented' traditions have a strongly patriarchal character, subjecting women to the authority of male elites in the name of preserving community values. Martin-Hill (2003, 114–5) describes the re-victimization of Aboriginal women by newly established male 'elders' who use their authority to scold women in public for supposed violations of "tradition" such as not wearing skirts or not observing elaborate rituals around menstruation. Maracle (2003, 77) similarly laments the rigid enforcement of gender stereotypes by elders who exclude women from learning to drum or learning the teachings. Both Martin-Hill and Maracle see these practices as reflecting the internalization of the values of the colonizers. Aboriginal women thus find themselves challenging their own traditions even as they draw upon them to build a positive spiritual sense of themselves as Aboriginal peoples (Blaney 2003, 167).

The active agency of women and the support networks that they establish are nonetheless recognized as centrally important in community life, and especially so within Aboriginal communities. Women come together under the very difficult conditions of non-status Mi'kmaq communities in Newfoundland to share what they know of tradition and medicines to bring healing to often traumatized families (Muise 2003). Urban Aboriginal women led the way in developing Native Friendship Centres (Maracle 2003, 72–3). First they opened their homes to shelter homeless newcomers to the urban centres. Then they organized small gathering places for tea and talk, and eventually established permanent Centres. These natural leaders, Maracle argues, were overwhelmingly women. The males who held formal authority within the band structures, were running to catch up the women who were at the forefront of urban community development.

The experience of 'community' is thus highly gendered and politicized. From the perspective of feminist theory, the concept of 'community' is ideological, in the sense that it implies a unity that obscures deep divisions along the lines of gendered class relations and inequalities in political power.

Conclusion

The study of rural and urban sociology has a long history, but many questions remain unanswered, and the developing approaches of social constructionism and feminism indicate that there are still many more questions yet to be formulated. The folk-urban thesis popularized by Chicago School theorists has not stood the test of comparative research. Rural communities are not uniformly or even generally characterized by the close-knit, integrated social life envisioned in the notion of folk society. Neither do urban neighbourhoods fit the image of shallow and detached associations between strangers. The predictions of political economy theory that link community integration with economic security have a better fit with evidence. But such explanations fail to take account of the tenacity with which people fight to hold viable communities together in the face of economic hardship. The practical activities of people involved in creating and sustaining community integration are now being more extensively explored, particularly under the impetus of feminist research. But as this research has expanded, the concept of 'community' itself is being challenged for obscuring too much. "Community" cannot be defined independently of the practices that continually draw people together into a sense of belonging, and simultaneously undermine these fragile social connections.

A valuable lesson to be learned from the classical loss of community debate is the importance of subjecting evidence to a critical evaluation. The folk-urban model sounds convincing. It fits the preconceptions that most of us have about simple rural life, where people care about each other, and about anonymous crowds in the city, where self-interest prevails, But however convincing this argument sounds, when the assumptions are systematically tested against the evidence, they do not hold up, it is essential to adopt the same critical approach to all other theories in sociology, and indeed, in all other fields of study.

CHAPTER 5

Gender Relations: Competing Perspectives

Gender relations are moving into the centre of cultural, social, and political struggles in the 1990s. Much of the taken-for-granted character of relations between women and men, and also between men and men, and women and women, have been challenged by feminist theory, the active politics of the women's movement, and emerging struggles around gay and lesbian sexual orientation, and men's liberation movements.

Contraception changed the character of intimate sexual relations, increasing the possibilities for sexual expression outside of procreation. But a host of new problems and questions have emerged alongside sexual liberation. The reduced risk of pregnancy has changed the moral debate around adolescent sexual activity, but the potential for "liberation" has also increased the potential for coercive and exploitative relationships as girls in particular find themselves under increased pressure to be sexually active and available. Medical concerns have arisen around the spread of virulent forms of sexually transmitted diseases, particularly the epidemic of acquired immune-deficiency syndrome (AIDS).

Other concerns have focussed around the commercialization of sexuality in advertising, pornography, and prostitution, and associated struggles around public definitions of morality, censorship, and freedom of speech. The 1980s were also marked by heightened awareness of the sometimes exploitative and violent character of sexual relations, reflected in the proliferation of accounts of battery within the home, sexual abuse of children, sexual assault and date rape, sexual harassment, and violent attacks against gay men, and also increasing anger and frustration directed against campaigns focussing on these issues.

Sexual politics have brought to light new patterns of power, interest, and conflict. Within the economy, struggles have focussed on employment equity policies, affirmative action, and nondiscrimination on the basis of gender and sexual orientation. These, in turn, are associated with a questioning of the appropriateness of traditional division of domestic responsibilities, child care, and breadwinning within families. Patterns of change have been neither unidirectional nor uncontested.

Alongside the politics of feminism and gay liberation are the politics of religious fundamentalism and the "New Right" concerned with the reinforcement of traditional family and sexual values.

These arenas of confrontation reflect profound confusion over the appropriateness of emerging patterns of sexuality and gender relations. The goal of this chapter is to explore this contested terrain of gender relations through four major theoretical perspectives within current sociology—functionalism, political economy, social constructionism, and feminism—comparing and contrasting the different explanatory frameworks.

The study of gender relations is particularly useful for giving a sense of how the focus of sociological analysis differs from approaches of biology and psychology. The sex dichotomy of male and female is commonly viewed as an immutable biological state, but contemporary analyses in sociology have challenged this assumption as ideological rather than factual, developing a different conceptualization of sex differences and gender relations as socially constructed rather than given. We begin this discussion with a brief overview of biological theories of gender as the background against which specifically sociological theories have developed.

Biology or Social Learning: The Foundations of Gender

Functionalist theory in sociology stays closest to the biological view of sex differences, but with an important qualification. Functionalism begins with the assumption that there is a biological basis to the specialization of functions for males and females in society, but it sees this specialization as structured by socialization. Typically, in functionalist writing the terms **sex** and **sex roles** are used to refer to differences in male and female bodies and reproductive capacities that are presumed to be universal. The terms **gender** and **gender roles** refer to socially acquired behavioural differences that vary across cultures and historical periods. In practice, as we will see below, much controversy surrounds this distinction.

Functionalist theory argues that the long dependency of human infants, necessitating many years of adult care, is the biological root of gender relations (Goode 1982). The reproductive strategy of having few offspring and caring intensively for them is held to predispose long pairing relationships in family settings, since the nurtur-

ing female depends on her male partner for support and protection. These biological imperatives are also seen as dictating fundamental differences in the roles of adult males and females. Females are seen as physically handicapped by long pregnancy and breast-feeding and are home-bound with dependent infants and young children. Hence, they are more tied to the domestic arena. This was especially so in the era before widespread use of contraception when women could expect to be either pregnant or breast-feeding for most of their adult lives. Males, in contrast, are freer to move away from the home, and since they are also physically stronger, they are best suited biologically to perform the roles of hunter and protector. With industrialization, the importance of physical strength declined, but males are still freer to work away from home every day as principal breadwinners while females are seen as biologically better suited to remain at home as principal caregivers for small children. These roles can certainly overlap with fathers giving some time to child care and mothers some time to work outside the home, especially when children are older, but the basic predispositions and principal responsibilities remain. In some feminist writings, particularly those of Shulamith Firestone, liberation for women is seen as ultimately requiring a technological revolution that would free women from the biological imperatives of pregnancy.

The thesis of Social Darwinism elaborates on the biological roots of behaviour, maintaining that many of the differences in average behaviour between men and women emerged through a long evolutionary process that selectively developed traits conducive to survival. While males and females produce both testosterone and estrogens, the higher average levels of the hormone testosterone in males compared to females is seen as predisposing males to greater aggressiveness, a trait that enhances their survival as hunters. Aggressiveness would not have the same adaptive value for females who do not participate in the hunt. Conversely, higher average levels of estrogens in females may predispose them to the more passive, nurturing behaviour necessary in caring for infants. Some theorists argue further that the relative sexual promiscuity of males reflects the biological evolution of traits that increase the survival of the male's gene stock (Dawkins 1976). Promiscuity has little reproductive value for females since they can bear only a limited number of offspring. Conversely, females have a strong need to form pairing relationships to support them during pregnancy and the care of infants. Lionel Tiger (1969) argues further that males selectively evolved the traits of teamwork and male bonding as adaptive to their survival as hunters, and this predisposition now gives males an advantage over women in business and politics, or other similar activities in the public arena that involve teamwork. The argument has been expanded to assert that patriarchy or domination by males over females in society, is biologically determined, since males have a competitive edge over females in all assertive, public leadership roles (Goldberg 1973).

Studies of differences in male and female behaviour among animals is widely cited as supporting evidence for the biological roots of human behaviour. A common example is Harlow's studies of infant rhesus monkeys who had been separated from their mothers. The males appeared to be naturally more aggressive, to engage in more rough and tumble play, and to initiate more games (Harlow 1962; 1965).

Current work in the field of **sociobiology**, the study of the biological bases of social behaviour, goes beyond speculative evolutionary arguments to explore differences in brain functioning of males and females. These include studies that suggest that girls on average are predisposed to be better than boys at verbal skills and the recognition of interrelated patterns. Boys are generally better than girls in thinking that involves linear logic and mathematical skills. The gender-inversion theory of homosexuality suggests that the hormones and brain patterning of homosexuals may be congenitally those of the opposite biological sex. This theory is held to account for the tendency of gay men to display "effeminate" characteristics and for their concentration in careers in the arts. Lesbians are seen as congenitally predisposed towards masculine characteristics.

The Limitations of Biological Explanations

Much of the early sociobiological theories concerning evolutionary traits cannot be tested scientifically against evidence. They are based on imaginative speculation, not biological research. Elaine Morgan, in her book *The Descent of Women* (1972), offers a critique that is partly serious and partly a parody of what she sees as essentially "male-centred" theories of evolution. She speculates that evolutionary functions can be thought up for all kinds of traits that distinguish women from men, with female traits generally having greater survival value for the species. Take, for example, the evidence that baldness is common among men but rare among women. Morgan speculates that during the prehistoric period

when our human ancestors lived in shallow coastal waters, it would have been very important for the survival of infants that their mothers had long hair. Naked apes are slippery when wet and the infants of bald mothers would be more likely to drown. Baldness in males would have no evolutionary consequences. Similarly, it might have been advantageous for females to develop fat on their buttocks since they would have had to sit on sharp rocks at the water's edge to breast-feed their young.

The main value of Morgan's work lies not in these proposals as such, but how they illustrate the speculative character and the male bias of more widely accepted versions of evolutionary functions. Whatever the appeal of certain arguments about evolutionary traits, their usefulness in understanding the contemporary social behaviour of men or women is minimal. The conditions under which male hunting packs had any survival value have long gone. So, at least within Western societies, have conditions under which women could expect to be pregnant and suckling infants throughout their adult lives. As Connell puts it, evolutionary theories are about 2 million years out of date (1987, 72).

Other aspects of sociobiology have been supported by evidence from studies of animal behaviour, but there are several serious problems with extrapolating from animals to humans. In the first place, the animals chosen are often selected to make the point in question. Rhesus monkeys, for example, are known to be a particularly aggressive primate species. Male baboons are much more docile and might be cited to support very different conclusions about innate male behaviour with respect to aggression. Analogies drawn between animal and human behaviour leave out what is most characteristic of the human species—the capacity for language, intellect, imagination, and learning. These attributes play such an overwhelmingly important part in the social behaviour of people that comparison with primates in which such attributes are minimal or nonexistent can have little explanatory value.

Efforts to link biological differences between males and females to differences in behaviour have generally been inconclusive. A common argument is that boys and men are generally more aggressive than girls and women because they have more of the hormone testosterone. But other evidence reverses this cause and effect relationship, suggesting that social context, and emotions of aggression and anger produce fluctuations in testosterone levels. Rather than the body determining behaviour, social relationships are seen as producing characteristics of the body.

The argument advanced by Goldberg (1973) that patriarchy is inevitable because males enjoy an aggressive advantage over women in competition is seriously flawed in other ways. It assumes that there is open competition between women and men and that women lose. The historical experience of women in most societies, however, is that they have never been given the opportunity to compete on equal terms with men for positions of power in society. The institutional arrangements that feminists refer to as "patriarchy" are precisely those that block opportunities for women to compete. Biological evidence of small average differences between women and men in hormones, body size, or mathematical abilities, even if taken at face value, are not adequate to explain why so few women are found in positions of major political authority and economic power in most contemporary societies. The extensive overlapping of characteristics and abilities among women and men would support the prediction of far greater social equality than is actually found.

In general, theories that try to account for gender differences by reference to biological factors tend to be both too weak and too strong. On the one hand, the connections established between biology and human behaviour are generally very weak. On the other hand, theories that rely on biological explanations assume a uniformity within the categories of male and female that cannot account for tremendous variation in gender behaviour. This variation is evident among people with homosexual orientations as well as heterosexual. The images of "butch-femme" women and effeminate men implied by the gender-inversion theory of homosexuality at best applies to only a small minority of people who would identify themselves as homosexuals. To account for such variation we need to shift focus from biology to social learning as the basis of gender relations.

Psychoanalysis

Psychoanalysis, as a branch of psychiatry, lies midway between biological and social explanations for gender relations. In the classic theory first proposed by Sigmund Freud (1856–1939), the biological fact that boys possess a penis, while girls "only" have a clitoris, is seen as a central determinant of different temperament and personality of adult males and females (Freud [1905] 1976). Freud suggests that during the phallic stage of development, beginning around three to four years of age, a boy experiences strong urges to compete with his father sexually for possession of his mother. He

learns to repress this drive, and later to displace it onto other women, out of fear that his father might retaliate and castrate him. Infant girls, in contrast, experience a sense of mutilation and sexual powerlessness at not having a penis, which accounts for their relative passivity.

Freud's work has been widely criticized for its deterministic, ahistorical, and male-biased assumptions. Contemporary re-reading of Freud's thesis suggests that what Freud interpreted as universal features of human sexuality are better understood as the historically specific characteristics of sexuality developed within late nineteenth- and early twentieth-century patriarchal bourgeois families—the family background of most of the patients that Freud treated for neurosis in his Vienna clinic. Mechanisms of repression and displacement of sexual drives that are central to Freudian theory, have been reconceptualized as deep psychological responses to power relations within families dominated by an all-powerful husband-father figure. Feminist reading of stories told by female patients suggest that these are not merely childhood fantasies, as Freud surmised, but accounts of incest. The neurosis displayed by these patients seems more likely to reflect the trauma of sexual abuse than displaced penis envy. Feminist psychoanalysis has generated further theoretical interest in the potential effects on gender-identity formation in families where a powerful father figure is absent (Chodorow 1978). The theoretical insights of psychoanalysis have also been incorporated into theories of homosexuality, drawing on the Freudian notion that children have inherently bisexual instincts and drives that are moulded and channelled into socially acceptable heterosexual forms through early childhood experiences within the nuclear family. The mechanisms of psychological repression and displacement are seen as controlling bisexual drives but never fully erasing them.

In general these re-readings of Freud's work retain the insights concerning the importance of the unconscious mind, and mechanisms of repression and displacement, but with a significant change in underlying assumptions. The explanatory focus has shifted away from notions of innate biological drives and toward a greater emphasis on the role of historically changeable family forms and patterns of culture in the development of adult gender identity. This shift in focus has facilitated the incorporation of aspects of psychoanalytic theory into contemporary sociological perspectives on gender relations.

A fuller discussion of contemporary readings of Freud's work and the importance of psychoanalytic theory in understanding patriarchal culture is presented later in this text.

Functionalist Theory of Gender Roles

Functionalist theory of gender relations incorporates a decisive shift to focus on social environment and social learning, an approach often referred to as *socialization theory*. Infants are assumed to have sex but not gender. Gender roles do not depend upon innate biological or psychological drives. They are learned through the processes of **gender-role socialization**. The basic idea of functionalism is that people in society can be thought of as occupying social positions, to which a set of expectations are assigned. These expectations or norms define which actions are appropriate to given positions. Individuals acquire and internalize norms and these guide behaviour, much like actors in a play conform to a script. Becoming a man or a woman means taking on a general role ascribed to one's sex, such that in almost all social contexts there are two distinctive sets of roles corresponding to different social expectations of males and females. Individuals are inserted into social relations through learning the role behaviour appropriate to their sex. Functionalist theory is centrally interested in the people and institutions responsible for this learning—the "agents of socialization"—including parents, family, teachers, peers, religious leaders, mass media, and the like. Research focusses on the scripts—the gender patterns and stereotypes that are taught, the different treatment of boys and girls, and the ways in which models of feminity and masculinity are conveyed to children. Deviance from acceptable gender behaviour is understood in terms of faulty socialization, especially in early childhood experience. This approach has the advantage over sociobiology of offering an explanation for both the variation and the consistency in patterns of male and female behaviour within a given culture. It also offers a policy for reforming gender relations through changing expectations, and challenging stereotyped attitudes.

Variations Among Cultures

Margaret Mead's (1935) classic study of three New Guinea tribes, the Arapesh, the Mundugamore, and the Tschambuli, emphasized the malleability of human gender-role behaviour and the importance of socialization over biology. She described marked differences in the specific behaviours ascribed to males and females in the three cultures. Among the Arapesh, both males and females were socialized to be gentle, nurturing, responsive, co-operative, and willing to subordinate themselves in the needs of others. Both men and women participated actively in childbirth. They were both said to "bear the child," and it was believed that only through the continual caring and participation of the father could the child grow in the mother's womb or continue into healthy adulthood. According to Mead, authority and aggression were repugnant to both Arapesh men and women. Arapesh men did not provoke fights, and rape was unknown. Among the Mundugamore, in contrast, both men and women were expected to be aggressive rather than nurturing. The people practiced headhunting, and emotions of hostility, hatred, and suspicion permeated their relationships. Even their families were organized on the basis of the theory of natural hostility among members of the same sex. Fathers and daughters formed one rival group against mothers and sons. Within the third culture, the Tschambuli, women were expected to be more dominant, impersonal, and managing than men, while men were expected to be less responsible and more emotionally dependent than women, in effect the opposite of feminine and masculine expected in Western societies. Later studies modified Mead's findings, suggesting that she overstated the cultural differences, but her general thesis that the gender-role behaviour of women and men are powerfully influenced by upbringing and cultural expectations remains.

Functionalist theory assumes that individuals come to internalize the gender-role behaviour patterns appropriate for their biological sex through socialization. Primary socialization occurs within the family. It is principally here that infants acquire language and gender identity, and learn the basic norms, and appropriate attitudes and values of their sex. Secondary socialization involves learning and teaching in the public arenas of school, church, work, and mass media. The two spheres of socialization are directly connected during childhood since parents commonly select the day-cares, churches, and schools that their children attend, and monitor their friendships and the mass media to which they are exposed. Socialization continues in some degree throughout adult life as individuals enter new roles and form new associations, but the influence of parents in early childhood learning is considered decisive in gender identity formation. We know from studies of young children that they learn to accurately define their own gender and that of others from a very early age (Mackie 1991, 79).

Behavioural Traits Within a Culture

Primary socialization into gender roles in Western cultures begins from the moment of birth as infants are assigned an identity as male or female on the basis of genitals. Sex-typing may begin even before birth, as parents speculate that an active fetus is most likely to be male and a quiet one female. From the first day of life parents tend to see, and to respond to, boy and girl babies differently. Girls are more often described as little, beautiful, cute, weak, and delicate, whereas boys are described as firmer, larger, more alert, stronger, and hardier. This occurs despite objective evidence that male and female babies are on average of equal size and activity level, and female neonates are generally more robust than males.

The behavioural traits identified as specifically male or female are actively promoted and reinforced by parents. For example, a study of the content of rooms that parents provide for children (Rheingold and Cook 1975; Greenglass 1992, 208) showed that boys' rooms tended to have vehicles of all kinds, building blocks, toy tools, sports equipment, machines, and military toys. Girls' rooms most often had dolls, doll houses, stuffed animals, and domestic toys of all kinds for playing house.

Activities and interests encouraged by parents commonly emphasize the same gender-typing. Domestic chores are commonly allocated to boys and girls differently. Boys tend to be encouraged more than girls to be independent, for example by being allowed to cross streets alone at a younger age, to play away from home for long periods without first telling parents where they would be, and using sharp scissors without adult supervision. There is no objective evidence that boys are any more advanced than girls at such skills. If anything, boys tend to be more impulsive and less mature (Hoffman 1977; Greenglass 1992, 210). Parents also see female toddlers as needing more help, encourage them to ask for more help, and restrict and supervise them more. As a result, boys and girls develop different kinds of competence and coping skills. As adults, men strive for success and take risks to attain it, while women are socialized not to take risks and to perceive risks as threatening failure. Early in life they learn not to have high expectations for themselves and so as adults they tend to be less self-confident, less assertive, and more timid than men. They tend to rely more on others than do boys, and have a greater need for social approval, and are more likely to break down or cry under stress. All these traits are seen as detrimental to women who try to function in adult work roles that require leadership or management skills (Hale 1987a, 491; Hennig and Jardim 1981; Fenn 1980; Larwood and Wood 1977). On the positive side, girls are encouraged to be more nurturing, to display emotions, to be open to others, to be skilled listeners, and more empathetic than boys, traits that prepare them well for adult roles as caregivers.

There is much evidence to suggest that gender-typing is more rigidly enforced for boys than for girls. Boys are under greater pressure not to be "sissies" than are girls not to be "tomboys," and boys are subject to much more physical and nonphysical punishments, as well as more praise, in pressuring them to behave in a "masculine" way. Fathers are also more likely to emphasize gender-typing in their interaction with chil-

BACK BENCH

Problems in Family Socialization

From the perspective of socialization theory, failure to exhibit appropriate adult gender-role behaviour can be accounted for primarily by faulty upbringing, especially within the family. A central cause for concern in studies addressing the notion of a "masculinity crisis" is the gender confusion that boys may experience when appropriate male role models are absent from their families (Brittan 1989, 25–26). Young boys may scarcely see their father when he is working away from home all day or working very long hours. High levels of unemployment may mean that fathers are home for longer periods, but inability to hold a steady job undermines a father's ability to provide an appropriate male role model for his sons. The erosion of the father's authority and status within the home may be further exacerbated if the wife-mother is employed. Of particular concern within research on socialization is the growing numbers of single-parent female-headed households. In functionalist theory this deviation from the traditional nuclear family form is seen as likely to result in deviant psychological development, especially for boys. The fear is that fatherless boys may find it difficult to achieve proper gender identity, and may act out their resulting insecurities and anxieties in negative ways, through delinquency, violence, and hostility towards women. Chodorow (1978) and Dinnerstein (1976) link psychoanalysis and functionalism in their theory that the masculinity crisis may be generated by the extreme differentiation and specialization in gender roles in Western societies, which leave mothers almost totally responsible for child care. Boys, they suggest, are engulfed in the overflowing influence of women, the combination of maternal care and discipline that translates into power over boys. They suggest that boys resent and try to escape from women's power, rather than struggling to repress oedipal conflicts with respect to an all-powerful father figure. The key problem is not a too-powerful father, but a weak or absent father, or a too-powerful mother.

The challenge of raising sons to be appropriately masculine is a difficult one for feminist mothers. Van Gelder and Carmichael (1975) studied the attitudes of mothers, including those in leadership positions in feminist organizations. As many as one-third of these mothers worried that they might unwittingly be responsible for their sons "unnecessarily" becoming homosexual. None of them worried that a liberated or feminist upbringing would turn girls into lesbians, but they feared that it might turn boys into homosexuals. They gave

Gender traits are often promoted by parents who encourage boys to play with vehicles, tools, machines, and sports and war toys.

dren than are mothers (Greenglass 1992, 209; Lynn 1974; Mackie 1991, 109–10). Fathers worry when boys seem unaggressive and unwilling to defend themselves, while they do not worry about unaggressive girls. David and Brannon (1976, 12) summarize the traditional requirements of the masculine gender role as (1) no sissy stuff—with a stigma on all stereotypically feminine characteristics; (2) the big wheel—the need to be looked up to and to have symbols of success and status, especially as a breadwinner looked up to by his wife, if no one else; (3) the sturdy oak—portraying a manly air of toughness, confidence, and self-reliance; and (4) "Give 'em Hell"—the aura of aggression, violence, and daring. The most important of all is no sissy stuff—not behaving like girls. Boys are socialized to suppress emotions that suggest vulnerability, and especially not to cry. The involvement of boys in sports is widely cited as critical in the development of appropriate masculinity. Male athletes commonly report feeling pressured, even bullied, into participation in sports by their fathers (Messner 1992). Teamwork, competition, winning at any cost, and aggression, are important aspects of organized sports for boys. There is no comparable pressure on girls to become involved in sports, and if they do, the aspects of having fun tend to be stressed over competition and winning.

serious thought to nonsexist child-rearing for their girls, but not for their boys. Among their peers, boys who fail to display appropriately masculine behaviour, who are unathletic or bookish, or who enjoy "effeminate" activities like dance, knitting, or even cooking, are likely to be taunted by such gibes as "What are you, a fag?" Such homophobic taunting seems to function as a powerful technique for enforcing conformity to stereotypically masculine gender-role behaviour (Fine 1992, 138; Lehne 1976).

Those concerned with promoting the advancement of women in prestigious and better-paid careers in business and management see the prevailing pattern of socialization for girls as a critical limiting factor. Studies of women in management roles suggest that competitive team sports, particularly football, are important in socializing boys into skills of leadership and teamwork, and notions of planning, tactics, strategies, and playing to win (Hennig and Jardim 1981; Fenn 1980; Larwood and Wood 1977). Girls who have no comparable socialization experience are severely handicapped as adults if they try to enter roles in politics, business, and management, where skills of leadership and teamwork are very important. Liberal feminists, working within the functionalist perspective, have focussed attention on restrictive stereotypes of adult roles for women, especially in mass media and school textbooks. They stress the importance of nontraditional role models for girls in changing the distribution of gender roles for women and men.

The Limitations of Socialization Theory

Socialization theory offers major advantages over biological explanations for gender relations in that it provides a workable explanation for broad differences between cultures and it places at the centre of analysis the specifically human characteristics of social learning. It is, however, open to criticism as an overly simplistic form of explanation that ignores much of the complexity of gender relations.

The model relies on an implicit notion of normal male and female gender-role behaviour, and implies that there is consensus among agents of socialization as to what these norms are. Critics argue that neither assumption fits the evidence. There seems to be too much variation in how women and men behave. If we were to use what we know about normative expectations to predict actual behaviour of males and females in specific situations, we would be wrong more often than correct. A

study conducted in rural India tried to predict women's responses to new employment opportunities on the basis of prevailing norms for women's behaviour that emphasized domesticity and strict seclusion within the home (Hale 1988a). All the predictions failed. Cultural norms did predict what women thought other people thought, but not at all what the women had internalized as standards for themselves. This discrepancy between the prevailing culture and what women actually wanted to do, calls into question the meaning of "culture" as the accepted set of norms, attitudes, and values of the people. It suggests that the culture of rural India reflects more how men want women to behave than the internalized values of women themselves.

There is also extensive evidence of inconsistencies, conflict, and contradictions between different agents of socialization that belies the notion of normative standards. They may teach conflicting messages about gender-role expectations to children. What parents teach may differ from school teachers, and both may differ from mass media or peers, or religious teachings. Consistency among all socialization agents in a given community may be the exception rather than the rule. Moreover, individual agents are themselves often inconsistent in what they teach. Studies of families suggest that contradictory pressures and demands are routinely placed on children (Connell 1987, 192–93). Mass media similarly offer contradictory messages about appropriate gender-role behaviour. The notion of distinctive patterns of socialization for boys and girls also seems to have been overdrawn. The body of research on parent-child interaction with babies and preschoolers that was reviewed by Maccoby and Jacklin (1974) failed to find clear-cut differences in either the amount or kind of parental talk or nurturing behaviour toward sons and daughters.

The unquestioned assumption within functionalist theory that there are distinctive male and female gender roles has promoted extensive research into differences in upbringing and behaviour of boys and girls. As we noted in chapter 1, however, for every published study that confirms expected differences, several more are discarded as flawed because no significant differences were found. Connell suggests that were it not for the powerful influence of gender-role theory on research, we would be focussing on sex similarity studies rather than sex differences (1987, 170).

Critics also challenge the assumption that deviation from normative standards for gender-role behaviour can be accounted for in terms of faulty socialization (Brittan

1989, 23–24). The bookish and unathletic boys, the male ballet dancers, the women with leadership and management skills, cannot all be explained away by reference to malfunctioning socialization. The assumption that children mechanically internalize standards that they are taught ignores both choice and resistance in human behaviour. Children may reject what they are taught, or they may choose to mix gender traits in ways that conflict partially or perhaps fundamentally with how they were brought up. The theory that homosexuality is the result of faulty parental role modeling loads unnecessary guilt onto parents, without any evidence of specific parenting practices being linked to the sexual orientation of children. It also denies any agency to individuals who come to identify themselves as homosexual.

There is, furthermore, a strongly conservative ideology embedded in the assumptions that specific feminine and masculine gender identities are necessary for psychological health and that boys who lack immediate male role models will be disturbed and deviant in their own self-identity. Such assumptions imply that there is only one way to be psychologically healthy and all other patterns are sick.

There seems to be something seriously wrong with the theory. It seems that normative standards do exist for male and female behaviour. Most of us know what they are and can list them when asked. Yet the majority of people we know do not seem to have internalized them in the way that the functionalist theory of socialization predicts. The normative pattern of the nuclear family with male breadwinner and female homemaker is not the prevailing form of gender-role behaviour. Connell suggests that what we begin to see here is that what is "normative" is not a definition of normality, but a definition of what holders of social power wish to have accepted (1987, 51–52). Yet this analysis of power is precisely what is missing from functionalist theory.

We do not speak of "race roles" or "class roles" because in such relations power differentials are obvious. But the assumption that gender roles reflect natural differences between women and men functions to obscure the dimension of power in the structuring of gender relations. Socialization theory implicitly assumes that all problems of inequality in relations between women and men can be accounted for by upbringing, with the corollary that if society were to alter the prevailing role models all such inequities could be eliminated. Critics reject such arguments as simplistic at best, and at worst as ideological distortions that legitimate inequality. Critics argue that the pervasive inequalities

in occupational status, income, and political influence between women and men cannot be reduced simply to learned psychological predispositions; all the difficulties encountered by the token few women in management positions cannot be meaningfully attributed to lack of experience on football teams. Nor can the prevalence of pornography, violence against women within families, or rape be accounted for simply by boys' resentfulness at the authority of mothers during their infancy. Such explanations ignore the vested interests in the maintenance of relations of domination and the active strategies and power dynamics that shore them up (Connell 1987, ch. 9; Brittan 1989).

Once we come to see gender-role stereotypes as embedded in power relations, we are led to question the interests that structure and maintain them. Socialization theory describes how males and females are supposedly trained to fit the mould of acceptable masculine and feminine behaviour, but it does not address the question of why the moulds have the characteristics that they do. Why are boys raised to be aggressive and competitive? Why are girls not also raised like this? Such questions point to issues of social and economic structures that are not addressed within socialization theory itself. The force of such criticism is not that socialization has no influence on adult behaviour or gender relations, but that it is too limited and too individualistic in focus to account for complex structural patterns of gender-based inequality in society. A different kind of analysis seems to be needed to explain the structural patterns of gendered inequality.

The Political Economy of Gender Relations

Political economy theory focusses on patterns of economic organization and their importance in shaping all other social relationships, including gender. The contemporary Canadian economy is part of a global system of advanced corporate capitalism. This means that it is characterized by private enterprise that is dominated by giant corporations that compete on world markets to sell commodities for profit, with smaller sectors of small-business people and primary producers in farming, fishing, and forestry. The majority of people in Canada's labour force do not work for themselves, but find careers in corporations or state bureaucracies. An individual's social class is defined in terms of their relationship to the system of production, whether they own or control capital, and their situation with respect to the labour market.

A central argument within political economy theory is that the attitudes and values that people hold are shaped by their immediate practical experiences in the daily processes of survival or earning a living. Attitudes and values are thus effects rather than principal causes of behaviour. Analysis of gender relations, and the different attitudes, values, and behaviour of women and men, is embedded in the understanding of class relations within capitalism.

The Influence of Gender on Class Situation

Frederich Engels, a long-time collaborator with Karl Marx, suggests in his classic essay on the rise of private property, the family, and the state ([1884] 1978) that in the earliest hunting and gathering economies, authority and descent within kinship systems were probably organized around women as the only known parent. Men most likely played a secondary role within extended matriarchal households. However, Engels argues, this probably changed dramatically with the introduction of more advanced means of production, such as domesticated animals and cultivated land. As men gained control over these means of production they would have been able to break the authority of women and organize descent and inheritance through the male rather than the female line. Men would have been in a position to control and enslave women because women and their children would be economically dependent upon them. Women's work was still essential, but socially subordinate. They worked for their husbands. Engels refers to this point in history as the world historical defeat of the female sex, and the first example of class relations. The solution to the subordination of women to men, in Engels' view, would be to draw women into the labour force, and to abolish the bourgeois pattern in which men control the family wealth. **Communism**—the communal ownership of all means of production—promised ultimate equality for all members of society.

Prior to industrialization, most economic production took place in households, with no clear division between domestic and productive work, or between family production and consumption. With the rise of industrial capitalism this pattern changed dramatically. Production shifted into centralized factories, and households became units of consumption. Increasingly, men went out of the home to work for wages, while women remained within the home, taking principal responsibility for child care and domestic work. This shifting pattern of economic production is widely seen as decisively important in structuring gender relations. It liberated many people from the confines of the old households and made possible new forms of independence and sexual expression, but it simultaneously trapped others in a narrow private realm.

Women's involvement in the paid labour force has varied greatly with the economic situation of their families and shifting labour demands. But such involvement has not provided a basis for economic independence for women, with the exception of a minority in professional careers. With the development of industrial capitalism, women from the wealthier capitalist and upper middle classes were expected to remain within the home devoting themselves to domestic duties, the management of servants, and the care and moral upbringing of children. For women from the poorer classes, however, some means of supplementing family income was essential. Men's wages were commonly so low that it was impossible for a family to survive on them. While the cult of gentile domesticity for women and notions of childhood as the age of innocence prevailed as ideals among the upper classes, working-class women and children were more likely to experience the drudgery of working appallingly long hours under bad conditions and for very low incomes (Synnott 1992, 196–97).

Historical records of women's employment in Canada are sparse and unreliable (Wilson 1986, ch. 5). There were generally no records kept of women's unpaid farm labour in the preindustrial rural economy. In the cities, until the beginning of the twentieth century, the two major occupations open to working-class women were domestic service or labour in their own homes for the developing textile and clothing industries. Under the "putting out" system, women and children sewed in their homes or in small shops for a middle man who sold the completed goods to a manufacturer. Women could supplement the family income through such work, but could not achieve any financial or social independence. Women who worked in domestic service had no privacy and were under the constant control of their employers. By the end of the nineteenth century, textile and garment factories were expanding in Canada, while demand for domestic servants was declining with the introduction of electricity and home appliances. Accounts suggests that women gladly traded the isolation and controls of domestic service for factory work, but conditions of work and levels of pay remained abysmal. A Royal Commission on the Textile Industry, published in 1938, described women and young girls working seventy-five to eighty hours a week in conditions thick with dust, heat, fumes and gases, and for weekly wages of fifty cents to three dollars, often cut on the pretext of "flawed work" (Wilson 1986, 86–87). Such wages were insufficient to live on, even as a single person.

There is scattered evidence of women's involvement in unions and strikes in the nineteenth century, but efforts to improve working conditions for women were isolated and of short duration (Prentice 1988). Women were concentrated in unskilled jobs, or scattered in small workshops or in domestic service, which made it very difficult for them to organize collectively. Most reformers of the day, together with trade unionists, employers, and fellow labourers saw women's labour-force participation as undesirable at best. Government policies to regulate women's employment focussed on morality, and the importance of segregating women from men in the factories. Working conditions and wages were ignored. Employment for women was described as temporary and secondary, and their incomes merely supplemental to the man as the main family breadwinner. The cheap labour of women and children was generally seen as unfair competition that dragged down men's average wages. A few voices were raised in favour of the argument that equal pay for women and men would eliminate this problem (Prentice 1988, 137). But most unions focussed their efforts on attaining **family wages** for male employees so that women would not have to work. The plight of women who had no male protector was overlooked.

Women from the lower middle classes who had access to some education had a somewhat wider range of employment options. Many found work as nurses and teachers, but at the turn of the century these were not the kind of professions we think of today. Nursing schools were connected to hospitals and provided a constant source of unpaid labour. In the early 1900s, for example, the entire nursing staff of Toronto General Hospital were unpaid nurses in training. This meant there were limited jobs for graduate nurses—they mostly did home nursing, with sporadic employment and very low pay (Wilson 1986, 84). Women teachers were paid half of a male teacher's salary, on the excuse that they were temporary workers who would soon quit their jobs. In many jurisdictions this was ensured by legislation that prohibited hiring married women as teachers. The assumption

was that women ought to be supported by husbands. The plight of women who had to support themselves was not addressed.

Current patterns of employment for women in Canada emerged during the period of prosperity following the Second World War. The growth of corporate capitalism and the associated expansion of bureaucracies and government administration increased demand for labour in offices, sales, and service. Women were available to meet these demands. While the number and range of jobs available to women increased, however, the organization of the dual labour force has changed little. By the mid-1980s, approximately two-thirds of single women and half of married women with children were employed. But women remain concentrated within a much more limited range of jobs than do men. In 1983, 60 percent of all women worked in three occupational categories, clerical, service, and sales, all of them relatively low paid. A further 15 percent worked in medicine and health, and teaching. Only a tiny minority of women work as executives or in positions of decision-making power within corporations. The 1982 figures show that average salaries of women employed full-time equaled about 64 percent of average salaries for men. Professional women fared the best but they are far from typical. Women working in factory and service jobs earned only 54 to 56 percent of men's wages. Moreover, a quarter of all women are employed only part-time so that their actual incomes are very low. Most of those working part-time are married. Half of all married women are not employed at all: they are full-time homemakers.

What these figures mean is that notwithstanding all the changes in labour-force participation, the majority of women remain dependent on a man's wages to maintain a decent standard of living. They either are not employed at all, work part-time, or work in jobs where they do not earn sufficient income to support themselves and one child. Legislation requiring that women and men receive the same pay for the same job has little effect in a system where most women are employed in jobs that men rarely do. The lives of women who have to support themselves continue to be very difficult, particularly when they have children. Single mothers are often considered a welfare problem. Unless they are part of the small minority of women who have professional careers, the kind of jobs they can expect to get will provide an income little better than welfare if they have to deduct child care, medical and dental expenses, and pay for clothes and transportation to get to work.

Government policies focus on trying to force absent fathers to pay maintenance. The question of whether women with children ought to be dependent on men is rarely raised. It is taken for granted.

The institutionalized organization of women as secondary members of the paid labour force assumes that all women are tied to men, and that they are financially dependent upon men. These structures and their justification in social values constitute what is termed **heterosexism** in lesbian politics. For a woman to declare herself publicly a lesbian means to accept that she will not be tied to a man, and will therefore have to support herself for the rest of her life. It means learning to cope in a society that is not materially organized to incorporate women alone (Bunch 1975). The gendered character of class relations has a special immediacy for lesbians, Bunch argues, because its impact is inescapable. Lesbians need to develop political consciousness as a matter of survival,

not merely idealism. Women who are tied to men by material interests may be committed in principle to fighting discrimination against women in the job market, but tend to back away when it is their man's job prospects that are threatened by feminist hiring practices. Women who have experienced marital breakdown may experience the force of heterosexism with similar intensity, although it is easier for ex-wives to shift blame onto individual men rather than onto the institutionalized structures of heterosexism.

The rise of capitalism in Europe is closely associated with the historical emergence of homosexual men as a distinct social category (Kinsman 1987b, ch. 2). Kinsman argues that capitalism afforded these men avenues for personal freedom that were not available to lesbians. By separating work from household, capitalist relations created social space in which young men could earn their own discretionary income and live autonomously. This made it possible for men who engaged in same-gender sex to congregate, and to develop networks that provided places where they could meet for sex and where they could develop a distinctive identity and self-awareness. By the early eighteenth century, such networks of gay men were clearly established in London and Paris. Opportunities for young women to achieve financial autonomy from the household were much more restricted. Kinsman estimates that it was only towards the end of the nineteenth century that equivalent lesbian networks began to emerge.

The Influence of Class on Gender Relations

A central idea in Marxist thought is that it is not consciousness that determines existence, but rather existence that determines consciousness. The notion of existence refers to experience of the daily struggle to survive, while consciousness refers to how people come to understand the social world around them and the attitudes and values they have towards it. Marx also argued that the dominant ideas in any society, those that receive public backing and support by agents of socialization, are the ideas of the dominant class.

Prevailing gender stereotypes can be linked directly to how different classes of women and men experience the struggle for economic survival. The idealized version of masculinity described in functionalist theory incorporates many of the values pressured into executives within the corporate capitalist system, where competitiveness, aggression, and hard-nosed, unemotional decision-making, are considered good business practice.

Lesbians need to develop political consciousness as a matter of survival, not merely idealism.

Ruthless executives who are capable of firing fifty men at a shot and imposing their will on subordinates are widely admired (David and Brannon 1976, 27). Young executives are expected to prove themselves by fitting into the corporate image and working long hours, including evenings and weekends. Men who break the stereotype by balking at decisions that hurt others, not being highly competitive, and especially by avoiding working overtime to give more of themselves to family and children, risk jeopardizing their careers and their family's economic future. Currently only a very small proportion of all corporate executives are women, but the same pressures apply to them. Many find it extremely difficult to meet these demands and to cope with the pressures of running a home and raising a family (Maynard and Brouse 1988).

Working-class factory jobs carry different pressures. They commnonly entail endless days of physically demanding work, often under conditions of dirt, fumes and noise, and demanding mindless obedience to machine-paced tasks. Typically, factory work forces have been segregated on gender lines, with textiles and light assembly work overwhelmingly female and heavy industry overwhelmingly male. Gray (1987) suggests that male blue-collar workers typically develop shopfloor cultures that value toughness, swearing and rough behaviour, and exaggerated maleness that gives their work status as "man's work." The alienation generated by such work, and by the emotional coldness of competitive capitalism, has been cited as an important factor in domestic violence, as men displace repressed emotions and anger onto weaker targets in the home (Luxton 1980, ch. 6). The wretched conditions endured by women in nineteenth-century textile factories, however, were not cited as precipitating abusive behaviour by women.

The application of political economy theory to women's behaviour draws attention to how particular conceptions of "feminity" are organized into work requirements in many of the jobs that are typically considered "women's work" (Connell 1987, 103; Hochschild 1983). Receptionists, secretaries, flight attendants, and others in similar jobs are pressured to smile at those they serve, to speak in honeyed tones, to be sexually attractive and to put up with sexual overtures at work, in order to sell the company product or to keep offices running smoothly. Women in part-time, low-paid, and insecure jobs tend to acquire histories and attitudes that reflect this experience; these can readily be attributed back onto them as justification for their economic position. Women, not jobs,

become associated with high labour turnover and low ambition (Wilson 1986, 122–23).

The occupation that is most stereotypically defined as women's work is homemaking. Approximately half of all married women in Canada are full-time homemakers, and most of the others assume principal responsibility for it in addition to their paid jobs. As work, it involves multiple services for family members including the standard tasks of cooking, cleaning, and shopping, the less visible "expressive" work of emotional support and tension management, and the physical, emotional, and tutorial care of children. It is performed in relative isolation in private homes. A Statistics Canada Report, published in April of 1994, estimated that the dollar value of unpaid housework would amount to $319 billion annually if all services rendered had to be purchased on the open market. But this does not alter the fact that women who do housework fulltime are defined as outside the labour force and ineligible even for minimal Canada pension benefits. From the perspective of political economy theory, the defining characteristic of housework is that it is unpaid, and those who do such work are dependent on the income-earning labour of others. It is outside the capitalist market system, notwithstanding its importance in maintaining and reproducing the labour force. Many of the traits defined as typically feminine: putting the needs of others first, being emotional rather than task-oriented or rational, being followers rather than leaders, deferring to men in important decisions, and the like, can be seen as appropriate responses to the lifetime experience of being financially dependent and powerless.

In summary, what functionalist theory interprets as appropriate gender-role behaviour for males and females in different social classes, political economy theory interprets as the structural demands placed on male and female workers by corporate capitalism. It makes good economic sense that boys in school concentrate on training for jobs while girls in school concentrate on getting married. Girls who look around them are likely to see very few women earning incomes that make them financially independent of a male wage. Only girls who make top marks in school can reasonably aspire to professional careers with large salaries. The "cult of feminity" among working-class girls—their preoccupation with makeup, clothes, and getting a boyfriend—is not based on a romanticized view of love and marriage so much as fear of being a "maiden-aunt" struggling to get by in a low-paying job and dependent on the generosity and pity of their parents (McRobbie 1991). Efforts by teachers toward a new kind of socialization that discourages gender stereotyping and promotes feminist consciousness-raising have little impact in the face of what girls and their parents see as the realistic options open to them (Gaskell 1988, 166; Gaskell, McLaren, and Novogrodsky 1989).

The Limitations of Political Economy Theory

Political economy theory describes the gendered character of class relations and draws attention to its importance in structuring gender relations. But the framework does not adequately account for how or why this gendered class structure exists. Why is it that male workers earn substantially higher average incomes than female workers, even when obvious factors linked to labour productivity, such as level of education, years on the job, and working full- or part-time are controlled? Why are women ghettoized in such a limited range of jobs? How did the economy come to be organized so that women rather than men assume principal responsibility for unpaid, domestic work?

The classic explanation offered within political economy theory for such patterns takes a functionalist form. The dual labour market exists because it is functional for the capitalist system. Business people need the cheap labour of women to increase profits. They also need the reserve army of women who can be hired and fired easily in order to ride out fluctuations in the market. Capitalism needs the unpaid domestic labour done by women to maintain current workers and reproduce the next generation of workers. But there are a number of logical and practical flaws with such arguments. Relations of subordination of women to men long pre-date the rise of capitalism. Capitalism was shaped by and also took advantage of pre-existing patriarchal relations, but did not produce them. Women's labour may have been essential to the preindustrial patterns of production organized around large family households. But this did not afford them equal status with men. Legally and politically, women had few rights. Household authority rested squarely with men. The rise of capitalism made life generally easier for women by reducing domestic drudgery and providing at least some opportunities for financial independence.

The argument that capitalism needs and therefore perpetuates the status of women as secondary, marginal, and cheap workers contradicts the logic of a profit-driven economy. In principle, if women in general are a cheap labour pool, and if they are as productive as men, then it would make good business sense to hire *only* women. If women are discriminated against by other, irrational employers, then their labour would be cheap. It makes good business sense to hire the people that others discriminate against to reduce one's own labour costs. Either way, demand for women's labour should rise, which would increase their wage-bargaining power and the differential price of male and female labour should decrease (Wilson 1986, 114). This generally does not happen, suggesting that the roots of the dual labour market do not rest solely in the play of business interests in the market.

Marxist analysis, with its focus on class and wage labour, provides a powerful explanation of the development of class society, and the reproduction of class domination, but its categories are fundamentally gender-blind. The theory does not address the question of why particular people fill particular jobs, or specifically why women are systematically subordinated in the labour market relative to men (Hartmann 1984). What remains to be analysed is why and how women are available to be exploited as cheap labour by capitalists, and the complicity of trade unions and male co-workers in these practices.

Political economy theory similarly fails to treat as problematic the division of labour that places principal responsibility for homemaking on women. Marx himself regarded how men and women organize to reproduce children within families as natural or biologically determined and hence as not warranting the kind of critical analysis that he directed to how people organize to produce commodities. Current feminist theory challenges this naturalness as ideology that obscures complex relations of power between men and women. Engels argued that patriarchal family relations arose when men gained control of means of production ([1884] 1978). But the theory fails to explain how and why it was men and not women who took such control, particularly when women supposedly held power in the communal, matriarchal households, and commonly did much of the work of cultivation and caring for domesticated animals. The theory pre-supposes male dominance in the process of trying to explain it.

Political economy theory suggests that the alienating conditions of work under capitalism and the aggressive, competitive behaviour that the system promotes, may be important in generating the frustrations and aggression that are manifest in domestic violence. But it is a large intellectual jump to assert that class oppression and alienation produce rapists, gay bashers, and child molesters (Brittan 1989, 69). The incidence of wife battering may well increase with unemployment, but it is not confined to such conditions. The predispositions that facilitate wife battering or attacks on gays and lesbians exist prior to the unemployment or to the job frustration, constructing particular categories of people, and marking them as acceptable targets.

The prevalence of sexual harassment against women in the workplace, and similar patterns of hostility and violence directed against gay men and lesbians, also cannot readily be accounted for within the framework of political economy theory. Discrimination in employment on the grounds of sexual orientation has been explicitly declared illegal under the Human Rights Code of Ontario since 1986, yet lesbian teachers still fear to identify themselves, under the very real expectation of harassment (Khayatt 1990). One school board voted to drop all reference to nondiscrimination clauses in their hiring policy rather than acknowledge that they might possibly hire lesbians as teachers. Gay men similarly face discrimination and harassment in employment. It is very difficult to be openly gay and hold an executive position. If they cannot be fired directly for sexual orientation, other excuses are likely to be used (Kinsman 1987b, ch. 8).

In summary, while political economy theory seems to offer important insights into the organization of gender relations, there is much that remains outside its focus. Sexual politics have brought to light patterns of power, interests, and conflicts that cannot readily be understood in terms of conventional class analysis. Gender inequality is clearly linked to class inequality, but cannot be simply subsumed under it. We need an expanded theoretical framework to understand the interrelationship between patriarchal and capitalist relations.

Sex and Gender as Social Constructions

The social constructionist perspective challenges much of what we generally take for granted as factual characteristics of people and society. All aspects of social life are regarded as processes that people accomplish rather than entities that can be described. Sex and gender are no exception. In our common-sense thinking, we tend to view a person's sex as given, as a biological fact of life.

Someone is either a male or a female; males display the gender characteristics of masculinity and females display feminity. Social constructionist theory pressures us to set these common-sense assumptions aside. It continually translates nouns into verbs, entities into practices. Instead of taking the two sex categories male and female as obvious, it asks "How do people do categorizing work such that they end up with two unambiguous groupings?"

Similarly, rather than treating male or female as nouns, constructionists ask "How are maleness and femaleness accomplished? How do people, in their practical, everyday interactions, accomplish themselves as male or female?" The study of what we customarily think of as gender attributes of masculinity and femininity also shifts the focus from describing characteristics to describing what people do to accomplish for themselves and for others the sense of being masculine or being feminine. How do we come to know, and know in common, what is recognizably being masculine or being feminine, and how do we accomplish such categorizing work for practical purposes?

Terminology becomes confusing at this point. Earlier we defined *sex* as biological attributes and *gender* as associated behavioural expectations that are socially learned. But this distinction no longer works. Some theorists use the term *gender* exclusively to convey the meaning that everything is socially accomplished, including what we usually think of as biologically determined. But this tends to obscure what aspect of common-sense thinking is being challenged at any particular point. We will use the term *sex* when the discussion focusses specifically on challenges to what are commonly thought of as biological states or attributes. However, this usage is not followed with any consistency in the literature being cited.

Sex as Social Construction

We opened this chapter with a discussion of biological theories about the foundations of male and female roles in society, where at least the notion that there are males and females could be taken as given, and that it is obvious which category an individual fits into. Probably most of you read this section without the thought even crossing your mind that there might be anything problematic about it. However, the ethnomethodological study by Kessler and McKenna (1978) makes precisely such obviousness problematic. Ethnomethodology involves the study of members' methods of making sense of what seems to be going on. This includes how people draw on background understandings and practical reasoning in a continual process of formulating and reformulating accounts of what is happening that seem to make sense for the purposes at hand. Kessler and McKenna apply this approach to the question of how people, in their everyday reasoning, come to decide whether someone is male or female. They first tried a simple experiment with stick drawings to see what features a sample of 950 people would use to label the figure as male or female, and how many features had to change before people changed their label. What they found was that once people had categorized the sex of the figure, almost any surface features could be changed without affecting the label. Once people labelled a particular figure male, for example, the addition of a series of typically female characteristics, including breasts, narrow waist, broad hips, long hair, low muscle mass, and absence of facial hair, were not sufficient to prompt people to change their labels.

Common-sense suggests that we see surface features and then form a decision about a person's sex, but in practice reasoning seems to work the other way around. People decide what sex someone is, and then interpret surface features to be consistent with that categorization. For example, suppose we were told that person X has a female gender identity, prefers male sex partners, wears skirts and dresses, has some facial hair, and has feminine interests. Would this be sufficient to determine conclusively whether the person is male or female? The answer is no. We need to have attributed the category male or female to the person *before* we could evaluate the information. If we were told that this person is a female, we would see all the information as consistent with a typical woman who perhaps has a cosmetic problem with facial hair. However, if we were told that this person is a male, we would see the same information as consistent with a male transvestite, perhaps with a different kind of hormone imbalance.

Kessler and McKenna's experiments with stick drawings indicated that the presence of a penis was often decisive in people's reasoning. If the stick figure had a penis it was generally labelled male no matter what other features were added, even a vagina. This reasoning that gender attribution is genital attribution, and specifically that having a penis determines maleness, was put into medical practice in 1984 when conjoined twins were surgically separated at the pelvis in a Toronto hospital. The twin boys had only one penis between them. From the moment of separation, the twin without the penis was called a girl, her testicle was removed, and

a "vagina" constructed from a piece of colon. "She" was thereafter shown in pictures with a ribbon or barrettes in her hair and wearing a dress. In terms of this practical reasoning, being female does not seem to have any positive status. It is defined by the lack of a penis, notwithstanding that the child had male chromosomes and a testicle and lacked any female genitalia or reproductive capabilities.

The irony in everyday life is that classification of people by sex is almost always made without seeing a person's genitals. The surface features that people so readily discounted when looking at stick figures are all we have to go on. This leaves open the question of how do we accomplish gender attribution. You might try an experiment for yourselves. Instead of assuming you

Conjoined boy twins became a girl and a boy after surgical separation in a Toronto hospital, despite the fact that the "girl" lacked female genitals.

know what sex someone is, put this in doubt. Go to a shopping mall, particularly during a winter noon hour when high-school students tend to congregate there. Now suppose you are told that at least one teenager is a transvestite, claiming a sex category incongruent with genitals. Concentrate on how you do the work of categorizing the teenagers by sex, and trying to find the anomalies. How often are you not quite certain? How would you test your conclusions—knowing that transvestites would angrily deny your insinuation that they might be other than they appear, and that nontransvestites would be equally angry if you made such a suggestion to them?

A famous description of cross-sex passing is Garfinkel's study of Agnes (1967, ch. 5). Agnes was apparently born and raised as a male, but decided at puberty that she wished to be female. So she forged her mother's prescriptions for estrogen to promote growth of breasts, copied all the behaviour patterns that she thought were "typically feminine," and was successful in getting all her acquaintances, including her boyfriend, to think of her as female. As a young adult she underwent a sex-change operation to have her penis converted into a vagina.

Kessler and McKenna suggest that transsexuals and transvestites can manage to "pass" relatively easily in our society because we so readily assume that individuals have to be either one sex or the other, and that they are what they appear to be. The Olympic games is one context in which concerns have been raised that men might try to pass as women in order to gain an unfair advantage. It was even considered possible that some countries might be so set on winning medals that they would surgically alter male athletes to look like females. In the early 1960s a chromosome test was developed, using cells from an athlete's mouth. Evidence of a Y chromosome is taken as proof that an athlete is not female and cannot compete as a woman. One woman who competed in the 1964 Olympic games, winning several medals, was banned in 1967 when Y chromosomes were detected in her cells. However, she continued to live, in her own and other's eyes, as a female.

Three or More Sexes? Opening up Options

The above discussion has been based on the assumption that there are only two sex categories and they are mutually exclusive, however tricky it might be in practice to slot everybody exclusively into one of them. But why be so certain that there can be only two? We have some evidence that people in other societies have not taken it for granted that sex is dichotomous, or determined solely by presence or absence of male genitals. Prior to colonization, some North American Indian tribes, including the Zuni, the Navajo, and the Mojave, accepted and revered individuals who were thought of as having a third sex that incorporated aspects of both male and female (Midnight Sun 1988; Roscoe 1988). In anthropological literature this third sex is often referred to as the **berdache**. The term cannot be translated into contemporary Western notions such as "homosexual." The berdache were thought of in very different ways. They had culturally defined, multidimensional social roles, and were accorded status and prestige in terms of their religious, economic, kinship, and political roles, not the single dimension of sexual orientation. Among the Mojave, such third-sex individuals often attained high prestige as shamans, or as the partners of shamans or chiefs. Biologically female berdache who adopted the male sex observed the menstruation taboos of their female partners rather than of themselves, and at social gatherings they sat with the men. Biologically male berdache would feign pregnancy and stillbirth, and scratch their legs to draw blood to imitate menstruation. The sexual partners of these individuals retained the gender identity associated with their own biological sex.

Enforcing Two Sexes: Closing Options

If it is possible in principle to categorize people in terms of three or perhaps more sexes, and far from straightforward to categorize them exclusively into either male or female, then how is it that we take for granted the rigid categorization of male or female? How do we accomplish and sustain the social construction of our world as made up of two distinct sexes, despite the failure of human reality on almost any count to be strictly dimorphic (Connell 1987, 75)? Connell's answer is that this definitely does not come naturally. It has to be worked at. Sustained effort to exaggerate differences between people categorized as male and female is needed precisely because biological logic cannot sustain the gender categories (1987, 83). Similarities far outweigh differences. Children have their sex categorization vehemently imposed upon them long before this has any relevance for purposes of sexual reproduction. Obsessive efforts go into the sex-typing of clothes and adornment, and the production of body images that exaggerate muscular physique for males and physical slimness and beauty for females. Frank (1992, 275–76) describes how teenaged boys actively worked on their bodies to produce desired effects, especially through involvement in sports and weight training. Until relatively recently in Western societies, girls were actively discouraged from involvement in muscle-building programs. When women did become involved in intensive sports training, the magnitude of supposed biological differences in the strength, endurance, and speed of male and female athletes dwindled to a fraction of their former size. Women who currently participate in Olympic sports can beat all but a small minority of men. They routinely shatter world records set by men at the turn of the century.

In summary, in social constructionist theory, bodies are not "givens." We are not simply born with our bodies. They are sites of action that men and women work on by a multitude of practices including sports, training, diet, and clothing. Surgical intervention is an extreme form of action on a continuum that has included such instruments of torture as whale-bone corsets, spike-heeled shoes, and other forms of clothing that restrict, twist, and shape bodies into the moulds considered naturally male or naturally female.

Gender as Social Construction

Members' methods for establishing the categorization of individuals into male and female are directly implicated in members' methods for accomplishing the recognition of masculinity and femininity as distinctive behavioural patterns. Much social science literature in the functionalist tradition is preoccupied with identifying sex-based differences in behaviour. Typically, such work begins with sex dimorphism as given, describes sets of traits associated with the two categories, conceptualizes these as typically male and typically female normative patterns, and defines these as the cultural norms for the group or groups with which the individuals are identified.

From the perspective of social constructionist theory, there are serious problems with this approach. The research process appears to be circular in two respects. Firstly, behavioural traits are commonly used in practical reasoning to decide the sex category in which to place the individuals being studied. Secondly, the methods used to discover typical traits actively work to create the realities of masculinity and feminity that such research is intended to describe. Psychological scales designed to measure masculinity and feminity, such as those developed by Bem (1974), provide valuable illustrations of such circularity. Social constructionist analysis focusses not on the accuracy of such scales for

describing reality, but on the detailed methods used by scientists to produce the scales themselves (Connell 1987, 171–74; Eichler 1980, 62). A common approach is to develop long lists of adjectives describing behavioural traits and then ask a large sample of people to classify each adjective as more typical for a male, or more typical for a female. Bem used a checklist of 400 adjectives. The final scale includes only those adjectives that are consistently identified by judges as typical for one sex with a high level of statistical accuracy. Further trials are used to eliminate adjectives or "items" that seem inconsistent with the others on the scale, in how people respond to them. Finally, when used to measure the supposed masculinity or feminity of particular people, responses to all items are added together and averaged, since any one item alone might be unreliable as a measure of the underlying gender trait.

The systematic deconstruction of these scales reveals the practices that produce the "reality" of gender traits that they supposedly describe. In the first stage, the selection of adjectives deemed to constitute gender-specific traits depends heavily on the view of the panel of judges. Typically, these comprise undergraduate psychology students. Eichler suggests that what poor, black women from American inner cities might recognize as "typical for a male" or "typical for a female" are likely to be very different from what psychology students pick out. But their opinions are not normally asked. Hypothetically, a wide enough variety of judges might result in no consistent list of gender-linked adjectives. The next step in scale formation accomplishes the construction of masculine and feminine as opposing categories. The vast majority of adjectives were seen by judges as commonly applying to both males and females, from which we might reasonably conclude that there is no gender dimorphism. But all these adjectives are eliminated. The scale devised by Bem, for example, includes only 40 of the original 400 adjectives, 20 for the masculinity measure and 20 for femininity. These practices construct gender traits as residual terms. Gender is what is left over when all the characteristics that men and women share are eliminated. "Masculine" thus necessarily constitutes what "femininity" is not, and vice versa. Final confirmation of sex-linked "gender" traits is achieved when researchers routinely discard as faulty those studies that do not find expected gender dimorphism.

These scales carry the aura of scientific objectivity backed by precise statistical data, which gives them considerable influence. Individual men and women who do not score higher or lower on the appropriate masculinity or femininity scale, may appear in the eyes of themselves and others to be gender deviants. But such apparent **deviance** or conformity to supposed gender traits are entirely an artifact of the scale's construction. The core of the constructionist critique of such measures is that they are inherently flawed because the underlying conceptualization of gender is false. Gender is not an essence or entity that can be abstracted and measured, but rather an ongoing accomplishment in social interaction. With this shift in focus, the central research question becomes how do people accomplish gender. What are the practices that individuals use to accomplish themselves as recognizably, accountably masculine or feminine for practical purposes in particular social situations?

Accomplishing Masculinity

Conversations with fourteen young men about what it means to be a man, revealed a high level of anxiety and doubt (Frank 1992). Most were not at all sure of their own masculinity, and went to considerable lengths to try to assert it, to themselves as much as to others. The boys talked of the strategies they adopted to accomplish themselves as recognizably, accountably masculine in everyday interaction. Most of them worked on their bodies, trying to build up muscle. Frank describes them as "using their bodies like suits of armour that they carry with them for protection" (1992, 275–76). Those who could usually did some sports, or otherwise they made a point of hanging around with bigger boys who did. They generally avoided friendships with girls lest they might compromise their appearance of being masculine, but at

Participation on sports teams is one way that young men work at accomplishing masculinity.

the same time they tried to get a girlfriend to establish themselves as heterosexual. They were well aware that there was no clear way to establish themselves conclusively as heterosexual, and felt continually under pressure to display their claims to "proper" masculinity. Typically, they engaged in "dirty talk" about girls and exaggerated heterosexist posturing with other boys. Another study of boys in Little League baseball teams revealed that they constantly taunted each other with comments like "You're a faggot," "What a queer," and "Kiss my ass" (Fine 1992). Most of the boys had only the vaguest notion of gay sexual behaviour and had never met anyone they knew to be gay. The taunts were mostly directed at boys who did not display the body-work, sports, and sex talk associated with masculinity claims. The main intent of such taunts, Fine suggests, is to reinforce the generally shaky sense of what proper masculinity should look like. The most insecure boys used such taunting the most to assert to themselves and to other boys their own accomplished masculinity.

Many of the boys who talked to Frank (1992) spoke of the gap they sensed between their public facade of exaggerated masculinity claims and the private practices and fantasies that they kept to themselves, or shared with only close confidants. Some were heterosexual in both practice and fantasies, while others had homosexual fantasies; others engaged in homosexual practices while maintaining a surface of heterosexuality. For those boys who do recognize homosexual desires in themselves, the exaggerated heterosexist taunting can be painful and even frightening (G. Smith 1992). The term *heterosexism* generally refers to the practices and the patterns of discourse, or ways of thinking and talking, that enforce heterosexual masculinity as "normal" and all other forms of sexual desire as aberrant. Heterosexism organizes the relations within which homophobic attitudes emerge as hostile personal attitudes toward gays, often by people who have never met any. Such an attitude set often co-exists with a rigid demarcation of male versus female tasks and activities, and a view of girls and women as inferior to boys and men (Fine 1992; Lehne 1976). Racism, or rigid notions about racial distinctions and relative superiority and inferiority of such groupings, is also a common corollary of homophobia.

Accomplishing Femininity

For young women, the practical accomplishment of themselves as recognizably feminine is complicated by the particularly amorphous and contradictory character of the concept. Scientific models of femininity in gender-trait scales generally portray it in passive or indirect forms as less aggressive and assertive, and less associated with initiative or risk-taking than masculinity. The women's movement has openly challenged traditional models of appropriate roles for women, to the point that being considered feminine is not necessarily complimentary. Smith (1990a) suggests that the fashion industry may play a pivotal role in organizing ways of thinking and talking about femininity, supported by an array of mass media that include women's magazines, television, advertising, retail displays of cosmetics and fashion, and romantic novels. The ubiquitous presence of the media makes it possible for total strangers to strike up conversations about fashions and the fashion industry's conception of femininity, and understand each other. They are likely also to understand how the fashion industry codes particular clothing styles and body shapes to convey certain messages about femininity. Preoccupation with clothes and cosmetics arguably plays a similar part in accomplishing femininity for young women as sports do for young men. But the relationship does not appear to be one of straightforwardly copying fashion images. We have some evidence of how girls actively manipulate fashion images and even consciously choose to get fat to create oppositional versions of femininity (Orbach 1979; Findlay 1975, 59). A group of working-class girls in Britain saw fashion and cosmetics as a way of asserting their independence from school and their superiority over middle-class girls who wore "horrible" school uniforms (McRobbie 1978). Conversely, working-class girls on the Yonge Street strip in Toronto flaunted the standard fashion by cross-dressing in black leather (Smith 1990a). The problem is that the meanings attached to such behaviour are continually in flux. It is also unclear whether women follow fashions or fashions follow women. The fashion industry is fine-tuned to pick up cues about innovations in clothing and to reproduce them in new styles, in an endless effort to keep women as fashion consumers. No sooner do teenagers take to ripping holes in their jeans and patching them with coloured rags, than the fashion industry produces jeans with holes and patches already made.

In summary, the view of masculinity and femininity that emerges from constructionist theory is very different from the traditional functionalist approach of socialization theory. There is no predefined set of cultural norms that individuals internalize and express in behaviour. Rather, the notions of what being a male and being a female might mean are actively constituted by the participants in ongoing interaction. Any subsequent description of behaviour as conforming to subcultural norms is an after-the-fact accounting. In effect, the ethnographers in the functionalist tradition create the reality of norms in the process of observing, categorizing, and assigning normative labels to the behaviour they describe. This is a circular process in that whatever people do becomes what the cultural norms are. This descriptive labelling of patterns as cultural norms, however, misses the processes involved in their constitution.

Currently, we lack a body of research that explores in intimate ways how young men and women accomplish what it means to be a man or a woman. Frank's study is limited to a small number of boys and we do not have information on their class background or social situation. Strategies adopted by other groups of boys may differ widely from the pattern of bodywork, sports, and girlfriend that these boys describe. We also have very little understanding of the strategies by which girls accomplish being female, with or without the contradictory image of being feminine and fashion-conscious.

Sexuality as Social Construction

In common-sense accounting, sexuality is a biological fact of life. The experience of erotic desires, the intensity of attendant emotions, and the preoccupation with attracting members of the opposite sex, are thought to reflect the surge of sex hormones at the onset of puberty. But conflicting and contradictory accounts of what has been understood to be natural sexuality in different historical periods and societies cannot be easily reconciled with the notion of biological determination. During the Victorian era in Europe and North America, the official view of what constitutes natural sexuality defined people as procreators rather than erotic beings (Katz 1990). Prevailing notions of true love, true womanhood, and true manhood stressed purity and freedom from sexuality. In the medical discourse of the Victorian era, erotic impulses and desires to masturbate, especially when displayed by women, were defined as physiological disorders of such seriousness as to warrant surgical intervention to cure them. In 1906 a gynaecological surgeon estimated that some 150 000 American women had undergone ovariotomy—removal of the ovaries—to control female personality disorders (Carby 1982, 222). The last recorded clitoridectomy—removal of a woman's clitoris—was performed in the United States in 1948 on a five-year-old child as a cure for masturbation.

Such views stand in stark contrast to those prevailing in contemporary North America where the absence of erotic desire is considered abnormal. Far from being a diseased state, eroticism is heralded. Advertisers routinely exploit it to sell commodities, striving to identify their products with sex appeal. Media idols and pop stars who can incite erotic passions in mass audiences stand to reap huge profits.

Social constructionist theory does not address the issue of which version of sexuality is "natural," or which version might best describe subcultural views of appropriate sexuality. It raises questions about how prevailing notions of sexuality come to be constituted in particular historical periods, and especially the role of experts in the construction of common-sense reasoning. The objective is to deconstruct discourses about sexuality, to reveal how they sustain the appearance of truth. **Discourses** are the prevailing ways of thinking and talking about an issue such as sexuality. Expert discourses within medicine and the social sciences have a powerful impact on common-sense reasoning. They appear to have scientific credibility as factual descriptions of the way things are. People draw on them in constructing accounts of their own experiences, both for themselves and for others. Discourses do not provide descriptions of normal or typical behaviour, but rather conceptualizations that serve to "normalize" and legitimate certain behaviour patterns and to subordinate others. Relations of power are embedded in the authoritative interpretations of experts. When these interpretations gain ascendancy, they mandate courses of action to bring people in conformity with them. As noted above, Victorian medical discourse about sexuality justified actions that would now be considered grievous bodily mutilation. Successful normalization sustains the uniformity that functionalist research can describe as "norms" for the society or the subgroups being studied.

The work of Michel Foucault on *The History of Sexuality* (1978) is a formative study in this field. Foucault traces broad historical shifts in discourses around sexuality, linking them to changing economic relations, and the state's increasing concern to control the behaviour of the emergent working-class masses who flooded the cities in the late nineteenth-century. With the rise of capitalism, families changed from centres of production to privatized units of consumption. Individuals worked for wages outside the home, creating the possibility for young men, and occasionally young women, to become financially independent. They had more opportunities than ever before to live alone and to experiment with sex for pleasure, outside of procreation. New forms of authority emerged to control this freedom.

Foucault argues that experts within medicine and the social sciences took over the traditional authority of churches and family elders in the management of sexuality. A virtual obsession with sexuality emerged in these disciplines behind the mask of Victorian prudery and repression, with sex increasingly proposed as the cause of any and everything. This, in turn, justified extensive inquisition into it. Sex was conceptualized as a **taboo** topic, a powerful psychic force that was hidden from people or repressed into their unconscious. Hence experts were justified in extracting hidden sexual drives and preoccupations through forced confession. Confession, in turn, came to be treated as therapy, required for diagnosis and "normalization."

Within medical discourse, erotic heterosexual desire became defined as normal with all other forms of sexuality as illnesses or perversions that should be subject to treatment. Categories of sexual "types" proliferated in medical and psychiatric discourses: types of women included the indifferent or obsessive mother, the frigid wife, or the nervous and neurotic woman: types of men included the impotent, the perverse, and the sadistic husband; children were categorized as the masturbating child, or the precocious and already-exhausted child. In 1869, the term *homosexual* was introduced as a category within the discourses of psychology, psychiatry, medicine, and law. Formerly sodomy was considered just a form of nonprocreative sexual practice proscribed by the church. It became transformed in medical discourse from an activity to a particular type of person. Such persons thereby became subject to the power and control of experts in the professions.

These professional discourses were not simply objective or detached scientific theorizing. They mandated courses of action that subjected people to intensive surveillance and control, justified by the powerful ideology of scientific rationality. Foucault maintains that the goal behind the professional fixation on sex was to attain deeper power and control over the body. Norms of sexual development were defined from childhood to old age, with all possible deviations described and labelled as forms of illness to be treated. Children were conceptualized as latent sexual beings who must be continually controlled and repressed through perpetual surveillance, discipline, precautions, and punishments.

Educators, doctors, school administrators, and parents were all implicated in this discourse. Parents were used to spread new notions of sexuality, and then for monitoring it under the guidance of experts. Masturbation by children was constituted as a secret and forced into hiding as a form of abnormality. Then it became possible to justify compelling children to admit to practicing it so that they could be subjected to correction and treatment. This, in turn, multiplied the power exerted by experts in medicine, law, and education. Foucault suggests that this fixation on childhood sexuality and its repression, monitored by segregation and surveillance in the family, created the very environment that would promote incest. The family thus became constituted as the focus of still more intensive monitoring, confession, and therapy. Donzelot (1979) documents two centuries of government intervention in families justified through the discourses of medical and social work experts. The status of women's work as homemakers was improved, but at the same time that work was subordinated to directives from experts as to how it should be performed (Ehrenreich and English 1979).

The practice of confession is embedded in relations of power. The person who confesses is seen as ignorant of his own psychic processes, or at best as having only incomplete knowledge. It is the listener—the priest, doctor, psychologist, social worker, or educator—who is seen as having the knowledge to interpret what is said, and to treat the person with the aim of normalizing their behaviour. Techniques of knowledge and strategies for power are thus tightly interrelated.

People who engaged in forms of same-gender sex were subjected to a combination of legal punishments and forced therapy that amounted to psychological and social terrorism (Kinsman 1987a, 106). They were portrayed as types of people who threatened social order. Military elites saw intense friendships between men as undermining discipline; gay men were hounded from government jobs as potential national security risks. It was not until 1969 that homosexual acts conducted in private between consenting adults aged twenty-one and over became decriminalized in Canada, two years after a similar legal amendment was passed in Britain. Since then the struggle over policing has centred around the definition of *private*. Any living spaces within the armed forces, gay bath houses, even closed toilet cubicles, could be declared "public" areas for purposes of policing. Even a photograph could constitute evidence of public sex, in that a third person, the photographer, must have been present. During the four years after homosexual acts were decriminalized in Britain, the conviction rate for homosexual offences increased by 160 percent (Kinsman 1987b, 143).

Power and Resistance

Power is always an ongoing accomplishment, never absolute, or attained once and for all. For Foucault, any exercise of power inevitably generates resistance because people never can be reduced to the socialized, normative role-players envisioned in functionalist theory.

The power of scientific expertise is no exception. But it is unique in that it is generally not experienced as force imposed from above, but rather as normal, rational activity generated in ordinary, everyday interaction. Parents and educators turn to experts to learn how to do a better job of parenting and teaching children. Psychologists and social workers study their disciplines in order to help people overcome their problems and feel "normal." Resistance seems irrational. It is difficult even to be sure what one is rebelling against when the mechanisms of power—confession, exposure, and therapy—are themselves often presented as rebellion against Victorian prudery and repression.

Nonetheless, people do resist the force of scientific rationality. The medical and scientific discourses that defined homosexual activity in terms of aberrant personality types also provided a focus for self-identity, and for resistance to forced therapy and to the deviantizing practices of policing. People involved in same-gender sex adopted the label *homosexual* as a basis for claiming a distinct identity and therefore grounds for some recognition, and human rights protection (Foucault 1978, 101; Kinsman 1987a, 111). Demands for "gay liberation" challenged the assumed naturalness of heterosexuality. Gay networks slowly transformed into ghetto communities in cities such as Toronto and Montreal, organized around gay commerce and markets. They fostered the emergence of distinctive cultural values and claims to respectability as a quasi-ethnic group, with a new stratum of "experts" who act as spokespersons for the "gay community" (Kinsman 1987b, ch. 10). Lesbians have not emerged to the same extent as gay men, in part reflecting their more limited access to economic resources.

The rise of gay culture and attendant claims to quasi-ethnic status have brought important gains in the form of greater public acceptance, but not without costs. Pressures to establish respectability by emphasizing masculinity or macho-style gay behaviour marginalizes those who do not fit the ascendant gay-cultural definitions. The political dilemma is that in accepting the categorizing of homosexuality as a personality type, people who engage in same-gender sex adopt the hegemonic heterosexual discourse that defines them as a deviant minority. On the other hand, in deconstructing the category to challenge the notion of "types of people" they undermine the basis for political activism in naming their own sexual experiences and resisting oppression. Activists argue that the deconstruction of the category "homosexual" must await the deconstruction of the category "heterosexual."

The Limitations of Social Constructionism

The social constructionist perspective avoids the deterministic implications of the functionalist theory of socialization into gender roles, and also simplified versions of economic relations determining gender. The conceptualization of sex and gender relations as ongoing accomplishments allows for enormous variation in their expression and for rapid, dynamic change. Discourse analysis holds up for inspection whatever is taken to be factual statements about human nature as socially constructed and subject to negotiation.

The main criticism launched against this perspective is that it does not go far enough in its own investigation of the dynamics of power that structure discourse. The central feature of sexuality and gender relations is inequality—the privileging of a particular expression of male sexuality and the generalized dominance of males over females. Social constructionist analysis exposes the power of such myths to structure the practices that constitute gender relations. But such analysis does not by itself explain why it is male sexuality, and a particular form of masculinity, that becomes privileged in this discourse. We have to look outside the discourse itself to explore the relations of male domination that the talk reflects. Male sexuality, gender inequality, and the privileging of male sexuality in discourse is not itself the effect of discourse, although this is a potent mechanism through which such patterns are maintained. What needs further investigation is the institutionalized and systemic character of gender inequality. This is the central focus of feminist theories of gender relations.

Feminist Theories of Gender Relations

When **feminist theory** is viewed in its broadest sense as an approach that asks questions about women in society and makes their presence visible in the theory and practices of sociology, then everything discussed in this chapter can be classified under the rubric of *feminist*. The sociology of gender relations, including the study of masculinity and men's roles, had its origins in the **feminist movement**.

In this section, however, we will go beyond the inclusion of women as a topic, to concentrate on the second stage in development of feminist theory that seeks to explore the social world from the standpoint of women. In particular, we will explore the thesis specific to feminist theory, namely that the social world can be meaningfully understood as organized in terms of **patriarchy**. The patriarchy thesis asserts that there is a systematic and institutionalized complex of relations and practices that organize and perpetuate the subordination of women to men. This pattern cannot be reduced to the voluntary behaviour or attitudes of individuals. It is systemic to how social relations are organized.

There is much diversity within feminist thought. The liberal, Marxist, socialist, and radical feminist perspectives approach the study of women's subordination in different ways and are associated with different political strategies for transforming patriarchal structures. These labels, however, are not precise and they tend to be used inconsistently in feminist literature. As conceptual divisions, they are useful for ordering the overview of feminist literature on gender relations, but as we will see the approaches overlap considerably in practice.

Liberal Feminism: The Struggle for Equal Opportunity

Liberal feminist thought focusses on the issue of equal rights for women and men in the public arena, with a special emphasis on legal reforms. Historically, it was a long and bitter struggle to win recognition for any independent legal status and political rights for women. Prior to 1929, women in Canada were not fully recognized as "persons" under the British North America Act. Even thereafter, the inclusion of women under "persons" was only selectively applied by the courts. With few exceptions, Canadian women were systematically and universally disenfranchised. It was 1918 before women were granted the right to vote in federal elections. Most of the provinces extended the franchise to women over the six-year period 1916 to 1922, but Quebec did not do so until 1940.

For the majority of women, the most important legislation defining their status was probably the marriage contract. In British and Canadian marital law until the latter half of the nineteenth century, married women were subsumed under the legal personhood of their husband. They were barred from owning or disposing of property in their own names. Their husband's authorization in writing was required before they signed any legal contracts. All children born to a married woman were the legal heirs of her husband. If the marriage broke down for whatever reason, and the woman separated from her husband, he retained absolute legal custody of any children (Smart 1984).

Piecemeal changes in these laws were won only very slowly, and often in forms that made it difficult for the majority of women to benefit. In the 1890s, married women gained the right to own and dispose of their own property. For women from wealthier families who inherited property, this was a significant change. It meant that they did not automatically relinquish control of it to their husband on marriage. But few women had any means to earn money or amass property in their own name. Any property that the husband brought with him into the marriage belonged legally only to him. So also did all the property that the couple amassed during the marriage. In the infamous Murdoch case, in 1975, the Supreme Court of Canada decided that a wife who had worked alongside her husband to run the family ranch for more than twenty years, had done "just about what the ordinary rancher's wife does" and had "no right to share in it" upon dissolution of her twenty-five-year marriage to an abusive husband (Bissett-Johnson 1988). Only in the 1980s were marital property laws in Canada amended to state that the work of homemakers in nurturing the family entitled them to an equal share in family property.

Changes in legislation governing divorce and custody of children came equally slowly. By the late 1880s in Canada, mothers were granted the right to petition for a custody order, but to be successful they had to prove their exemplary character. Desire to leave a marriage was in itself evidence of being a bad mother, unless extreme abuse could be demonstrated. Also, any suggestion of adultery on the mother's part was considered suf-

ficient to disqualify her, although no such strictures were applied to adulterous fathers (Backhouse 1991, ch. 7).

A feminist review of Canadian legal history provides ample evidence of institutionalized patriarchy, but by the 1980s most of the obvious examples of discriminatory laws had been repealed. The enactment of the Canadian Charter of Rights and Freedoms in 1981 seemed to epitomize the triumph of liberal feminism. It enshrines absolute legal equality for male and female persons, together with endorsement of affirmative action to ameliorate social inequalities. Section 15 of the Charter states:

(1) Every individual is equal before and under the law and has the right to equal protection and equal benefit of the law, without discrimination and, in particular, without discrimination based on race, national or ethnic origin, colour, religion, sex, age, or mental or physical disability.

(2) Subsection (1) does not preclude any law, program or activity that has as its object the amelioration of conditions of disadvantaged individuals or groups including those that are disadvantaged because of race, national or ethnic origin, colour, religion, sex, age, or mental or physical disability.

Section 28 of the Charter further states:

Notwithstanding anything in this Charter, the rights and freedoms referred to in it are guaranteed equally to male and female persons.

The aftermath of the Charter, as with many of the legal reforms that preceded it, has been disappointment and disillusionment with the power of law to radically change gender inequalities. In practice, the rights of women are always subject to interpretation and to counterclaims from other interests. Gender bias still appears to be pervasive within the Canadian justice system (Brockman and Chunn 1993). In addition, hard-won rights are not necessarily permanent. The National Action Committee on the Status of Women (NAC) came out strongly against the proposed Charlottetown Accord in 1992 that would have amended the Canadian Constitution. Among other serious reservations, NAC specifically feared that the Canada Clause included in this Accord would have permitted Section 28 of the Charter to be overridden in the interests of language and culture. Native women would also have had their Charter protection removed under the new proposals for aboriginal self-government.

The central problem for liberal feminist analysis is that guarantees of legal equality have not been sufficient to overcome pervasive economic and social inequalities between women and men. Women vote, but they are not voted for as often as men. Women are entitled to an equal share in marital property and have the right to sue for divorce and custody of children equally with men, but this does not solve the financial problems facing women who are single parents. As we have seen, women typically earn incomes almost 40 percent below the average incomes for men. Commonly, divorced women find they cannot afford the mortgage payments on the half of a house they might receive. Broad estimates suggest that divorce typically results in a 73 percent decline in the living standards for women with young children in the first year after divorce, and a 43 percent rise in men's incomes in the same period (Eichler 1988a, 249). The strict application of gender neutrality in custody disputes can also readily result in fathers looking like the better parent; they are more likely to have a stable job, a higher income, and to remarry and so to have a new wife to act as caregiver for the children (Boyd 1993, 172–75). True gender equality in society seems to be much more complex than legal equality.

Marxist Feminism: Challenging Exploitation in the Economy

Marxist feminist thought focusses particularly on the exploitative character of capitalist relations and the superexploitation of women as cheap, part-time, and temporary labour power. This perspective tries to redress the gender blindness of traditional Marxist theory, and the inadequacy of mainstream or "malestream" attempts to add women as a topic without rethinking the theoretical frameworks. Hartmann laments that "The 'marriage' of marxism and feminism has been like the marriage of husband and wife depicted in English common law: marxism and feminism are one, and that one is marxism" (Hartmann 1984, 172).

Feminist research into the history of women's labour-force participation has documented the systematic practices by male-dominated unions and by employers that have contributed to the subordination of women workers. Male workers had good reason to fear that the availability of women as cheap labour would undermine their own ability to command high wages. They responded by restricting the access of women to apprenticeships, and by promoting protective legislation to limit the hours that women and children could work (White 1980, 12–18; Hartmann 1984, 182). Such legislation did help women who had little bargaining power to protect themselves but it simultaneously made them less attractive to employers relative to men. Historically, it was also common practice for male-dominated unions to bargain for lower wages and lower increases for women workers within their own ranks. The justification was that men needed a family wage, whereas women should be supported by men.

By the 1970s, such practices had largely disappeared in Canada. The Canadian Labour Congress (CLC) endorsed principles of equal opportunity for women, equal pay for work of equal value, paid maternity leave without loss of seniority or benefits, and affirmative action policies for women (White 1980, 65–73). By the mid-1980s, the CLC also endorsed free choice on abortion. The problems, however, remain. A relatively small proportion of employed women are union members, provision for maternity and parenting responsibility are very limited, and there are wide discrepancies in the average pay of women and men.

Women are typically employed in sectors of the labour market that have always been hard to unionize, namely services, retail trades, and finance, especially banks, and they are isolated and fragmented in a myriad of small offices. From such locations it is extremely difficult even to communicate with fellow workers, let alone to organize collectively. Where women have tried to unionize they have often met ferocious resistance from employers fearful of losing their pool of cheap labour. Banks have a particularly notorious reputation for breaking unions. In 1980 there were 7600 bank branches in Canada and only 65 were unionized. Unions that had formed had frequently been broken by intimidation and penalties, including the proliferation of expensive and long-drawn-out grievances, contracts that were worse than agreements in nonunionized branches, and the transfer of union members to other branches (Warskett 1988). Contract clauses of particular interest to women, such as maternity leave and flexible hours, are very hard to win even by established unions, because employers often cut back on pay raises when improved benefits are demanded. Few union members, women included, want to accept such conditions.

The gender-segregated character of the labour force makes it possible for large discrepancies in average pay for women and men to continue despite tough equal pay legislation. Discrimination is hard to demonstrate when there are no comparison groups of identically situated men to measure against women. Female-dominated professions like nursing, kindergarten teaching, and secretarial work thus continue to be among the lowest paid relative to the levels of education and job skills required. To counter the problem of job segregation, feminists have fought for legislation to guarantee "equal pay for work of equal value." Such legislation is now law in the Canadian federal government and the Ontario provincial government. In principle, jobs are compared on a points system that quantifies such characteristics as skill level, experience, responsibilities, hazards, and the like. In practice, such schemes are very difficult to operationalize because so much subjective judgment goes into assessments (Armstrong and Armstrong 1992). The private sector has so far largely resisted such evaluations. The prevailing cry is that any enforcement of such policies would bankrupt employers (Breckenridge 1985). The cheap labour of women seems to be a requirement for capitalists to be competitive.

Marxist feminist analysis of patriarchy has served to highlight many of the practices that constitute the subordination of women within the labour force. But like liberal feminism, the strategies for transforming these practices are still far from achieving the goal of substantive equality for women and men. The systemic nature of patriarchal relations goes deeper than a reorganization of opportunities within the labour force can resolve.

Socialist Feminism: The Double System of Social Production

Socialist feminism explores the complex ways in which **relations of reproduction** within the family are interlinked with **relations of production** within the economy. Relations of reproduction refers to how people organize to produce children and raise them to maturity. Relations of production refers to how people organize to produce goods. The core argument is that transformation of relations in both fields of human practices are needed to substantially alleviate the subordination of women. Patriarchy, in other words, is multifaceted and not confined to the public arena.

The organization of reproduction within the home forms part of the explanation for women's disadvantaged position within the wage-labour market. Studies suggest that even when women are employed full-time in paid jobs they still do the bulk of domestic, child-care, and people-servicing work at home (Armstrong and Armstrong 1990, 72–74). In effect, men take advantage

of the labour power of women so that they can return to their jobs relaxed and refreshed while women return exhausted from their double day. Legislation to prevent discrimination against women employees does nothing to resolve the built-in discriminatory practices that assume that "normal" employees are not responsible for child care. Hence when particular employees—usually female—ask for child-care leave or flexible working hours, it sounds like an appeal for special treatment (Mackinnon 1989, 219). Similarly, potential employees who have a combination of undesirable traits, such as being older, lacking in current work experience, having large gaps in their employment careers, and who seem likely to quit the job after a few years, are less likely to be selected than applicants with few or none of these negative traits. Strictly gender-neutral hiring practices will do nothing to resolve the fact that typically it is women rather than men who manifest all of these negative traits. These patterns are rooted in the domestic division of labour, and their transformation would require systemic changes that are much more complex than law reform. Eisenstein (1984) argues that the women's movement has precipitated a crisis in liberal thought precisely because the principles of individual freedom and equality do not work when applied to women and men.

The elimination of systemic disadvantages that women face in employment would entail a reorganization both of domestic labour and paid employment so as to make childbirth and caring for children inconsequential for education and career opportunities of women and men. Some of the changes in the social relations of child care that feminists have proposed include provision of extended parenting leave for both mothers and fathers with full incomes and guaranteed job security, child-sick-leave days, flexible working hours, universally accessible, quality day-care facilities, and guaranteed income support for children and homemakers. But such proposals are contrary to the traditional discourses of mothering that idealize full-time caring for children in the home. They have been strongly resisted by the powerful "New Right" or moral conservative movement as undermining a man's responsibility to support mothers and children, and hence threatening family life and social order itself (Eichler 1985b). In a sense, the New Right is correct. Socialist feminist theory exposes the extent to which traditional patterns of organizing domestic relations work to perpetuate a social order in which the majority of women are socially marginalized in private homes and economically dependent. This patriarchal social order is precisely what is being challenged.

Radical Feminism: The Struggle Against Exploitative Sexuality

Radical feminist theory carries the exploration of domestic relations more deeply than socialist feminist concerns with division of labour, to highlight the sphere of private and intimate relations between women and men. The core argument is that the root of patriarchy lies in sexuality—specifically in the systemic institutionalization and legitimation of male sexual dominance. In a multiplicity of ways, laws and social practices can be shown as organized to protect and defend male ownership, control, and use of female sexuality and reproductive power. Sexual oppression of women parallels and perhaps even surpasses in importance the exploitation of women's labour power, with women's economic dependence being a critical strategy used by men to secure women's sexual subordination (O'Brien 1981).

Historically, the marriage contract did not merely give the husband effective control over material property. It defined wives explicitly as the sexual property of their husband. Until as recently as the 1980s, rape in marriage was a legal impossibility in British and Canadian law. A husband had the legal right to the sexual services of his wife as and when he chose. But there was no reciprocal responsibility on the husband's part to meet his wife's sexual needs (Smart 1984, 94–95). A wife's refusal to have sexual intercourse constituted grounds for divorce as an act of cruelty, but a husband's refusal to have intercourse with his wife constituted only "natural disinclination" and not cruelty. Not until 1966 did the Courts of Appeal in Britain begin to apply the principle of sexual frustration equally to wives in considering divorce. Adultery was always considered a more serious offence for a wife than a husband.

Historically also, both the authority of the Catholic Church and British common law recognized the right of a husband to beat his wife for her moral betterment, or in effect to enforce his right to her obedience. This is the origin of the "rule of thumb" that refers to the convention that such beatings were proper so long as the stick used was no thicker than a man's thumb. Fathers had the same acknowledged right to thrash children into obedience. Wives have never been accorded the religious or legal right to beat their husbands, no matter what their behaviour. Canadian law no longer condones the thrashing of wives and children but domestic violence is still endemic in many families. It was the early 1970s, thanks in large measure to the women's movement, that wife

battery received public attention. It is exceptionally difficult to measure the incidence with any accuracy, but the physical evidence of battered women in transition houses, and the results of many surveys, suggest that some 10 percent of women have been beaten at least once by their male partner. An important effect, and arguably the main intent behind wife battery is the woman's subservience to the man's will.

The crime of rape is regarded in feminist jurisprudence as the most extreme expression of male power to subordinate and exploit women as sexual objects for their use. But historically, it was not regarded as a crime against women at all, but a violation of a man's property right over his chaste wife or virginal daughter. Theoretically, the sexual violation of women who had transgressed the norms of chastity was unimportant, because such women had no value to lose (Clark and Lewis 1977, ch. 7). Subsequently, under the impact of more liberal sexual mores and the women's movement, legislation was changed to focus on a woman's right to consent to sexual intercourse. This shift in thinking, however, did not significantly alter courtroom practices. The onus of proof was placed on women to demonstrate to the court that she did not consent to intercourse. Judges and jurors were predisposed to believe that any woman who was not a chaste wife or virgin probably did consent to have sex, or that the alleged rapist could reasonably have assumed that she was consenting, and hence that he was not guilty. In 1983 in Canada, the crime of rape was redefined as "sexual assault" shifting the focus from penetration by a penis to unwanted sexual touching. The new law removes the legal exemption against a victim's husband being charged with rape and also incorporates sexual assaults against males (DeKeseredy and Hinch 1991, 62–65). The term *rape,* however, is still widely used and defended as a stronger and descriptively more accurate term to describe most of the offences.

Radical feminist studies of courtroom practices suggest that while the laws may have changed, the old notions that a virgin or chaste married woman is valuable, whereas other women are "open territory," still prevail in the minds of police, jurors, and judges. A woman's sexual history remains critical in a defendant's claim that he had an honest-if-mistaken belief that the woman consented to sexual intercourse with him because she had consented with other men in the past. Feminists denounce such arguments as ludicrous, and contend that sexual history has no bearing on the critical question of whether the woman might be lying about having consented to sex with the man on trial. Arguably, it is women with chaste reputations rather than sexually active women who would be more likely to misrepresent consensual sex as rape (Boyle and Rowley 1987). But this is not typically how judges and jurors reason. Many studies suggest that in rape trials the woman's character is on trial more than the defendant's. The publicity surrounding such trials helps to constitute the discourse around acceptable feminine behaviour. Women who do not abide by the rules can expect little protection from courts if they are sexually violated. In principle, prostitutes are entitled to the same legal protection from sexual assault as other women, but in practice they have little hope of winning their case.

Prostitution is condemned within radical feminist theory as a trade in women's bodies that expresses and reinforces their status as objects for male use. A double standard has always prevailed in the laws that govern its management and prosecution to target the women who sell their sex, not their male customers. Historically, the major concern behind vigilance and control over prostitutes was fear that they would spread diseases to young men—particularly to soldiers (Bland 1985). Few worried that soldiers might spread diseases to women. Efforts by feminist groups in the nineteenth century to protect women from false entrapment and forced vaginal inspections under the Contagious Diseases Act only seemed to strengthen patriarchal relations, providing justification for increased custodial control over women (Walkowitz 1983, 423–24).

Current legislation in Canada makes prostitution semi-legal. It is not illegal to sell sex, but it is illegal to solicit customers in a public place, to communicate for the purposes of prostitution, to create a public nuisance, or to keep a bawdy house. The net result of such legislation is to give police broad powers to arrest and prosecute women while customers are left alone. These laws significantly increase the risks to women from sometimes deranged or violent male customers. To avoid a charge of soliciting in a public place, the women must get into a customer's car before negotiating a deal or being able to check him out. Similarly, to avoid a charge of keeping a bawdy house, the woman must go to a customer's room rather than bringing different customers back to the same room in which the woman might arrange some protection for herself. Even having a boyfriend is risky because he can be charged with living on the avails of her work. The semilegal status of prostitution means that the women who do this work have no legal recourse for crimes committed against them (Scott 1987).

In radical feminist theory, pornography ranks alongside prostitution as trade in women's bodies, a multibillion-dollar industry that sells women as sexual objects for men. The extreme position is that any erotica can be seen as problematic in that by packaging women as objects it serves to normalize and naturalize sexism (Mackinnon 1989, ch. 11; Dworkin 1980). It is morally easier to rape an object than a person, and easier to see women who complain as unnaturally frigid, manipulative, or lying. Others, however, see no problem with non-exploitative erotica depicting sex between consenting adults, and argue against any policing of sexuality for pleasure (Valverde 1987).

There is greater consensus among feminists on the evils of that segment of hard core pornography that depicts the violent penetration, bondage, and dismemberment of women's bodies as a sexual release for men. But there remains a sharp division of opinion about strategies for dealing with it. Activists such as Mackinnon and Dworkin argue strongly in favour of censorship and prosecution on the grounds that it constitutes hate literature. But many others argue against censorship on practical grounds. Violent pornography is a symptom, not a cause, of sexism and in a deeply sexist society censorship rarely works as feminist advocates intend. On the one hand, illicit materials only increase in value. They do not disappear. On the other hand, experience indicates that censors often ban materials that women themselves want, like information on contraceptives and sex education. The main targets of censorship by the Canadian customs have been bookstores that carry lesbian and gay erotica. Ironically, even Dworkin's book opposing violent pornography has been banned because it discusses violent sex (*Globe and Mail,* 12 Feb. 1994, D1, D5).

Men's Liberation or Antisexism

Feminist analysis of gender relations as patriarchy raises difficult questions for the relationship of men generally to the women's movement. Responses within the men's movement have varied from active hostility and backlash against feminism (Faludi 1991) to challenges to hegemonic forms of masculinity, and to attempts to deal with issues of male privilege and power in relations with women. From the feminist perspective, any approach to men's liberation that does not directly address this power imbalance constitutes antifeminism. Much of the literature on **men's liberation** has focussed on the oppressive character of male socialization. Men are

Drawing by Cheney; © 1992 The New Yorker Magazine, Inc.

invited to learn how to become more nurturing and emotionally expressive, and more involved with children. The problem with this focus is that it rarely incorporates an analysis of sexism as political action (Lyttleton 1990). In its extreme form, oppression disappears altogether; it is men who are oppressed while women are conceptualized as having power of motherhood, or the power to engulf and humiliate men behind the scenes. Men's liberation becomes part of the discourse of sexism that challenges women's struggle towards social equality. From the feminist perspective, an antisexist men's movement has to begin with the recognition of power and incorporate the intention to counteract it. The power of hegemonic heterosexist masculinity to marginalize and subordinate other expressions of masculinity is part of this antisexist struggle.

Limitations of Feminist Theory

Taking the standpoint of women has illuminated aspects of the social world that were invisible to mainstream social theories. The concept of patriarchy has proven a powerful analytical tool in challenging the taken-for-grantedness of gender relations and turning the spotlight on practices of gender inequality. The problem with this spotlight approach, however, is that many of the subtleties and inconsistencies of social life disappear from view.

Feminist theorizing is prone to categoricalism, the tendency to view social relations in terms of two internally undifferentiated categories of male and female, related by power and conflicts of interest. This singular view of a woman's standpoint is being challenged by women from many different minority group backgrounds as itself an oppressive form of theorizing that reflects white, middle-class, heterosexist bias. Women of colour have argued that systemic racism—the inequalities organized along lines of racial and ethnic differences—has as profound an impact as gender inequalities upon their lives and those of their family members (Kline 1989). They cannot simply align themselves politically with women and against men. Other women cite classism and the social organization of poverty as more central to their lives than gender. Women who never excelled in school find little to interest them in the preoccupation of academic feminists with gender equality in professional careers. Lesbian women describe their sense of oppression and ostracism as they struggle against the heterosexism within the mainstream feminist movement (Bunch 1975; Kinsman 1991, 93). A typical response within feminist analysis has been to try to incorporate diversity by adding categories to the theory of gender. But as the "isms" proliferate, the analytical utility of division into categories itself comes into question. A more dynamic analysis of practical politics seems needed.

An implicit functionalism underlies much feminist theorizing, particularly radical feminism. Analysis tends to be framed in terms of how the social system is organized for a purpose, and that purpose is male control of women's sexuality. The function of elements within the system are understood through the contribution they make to the maintenance of this pattern. The conceptualization of the state as a patriarchal system organized to protect and defend male dominance is an extreme statement of this position (Mackinnon 1989). This approach, however, has all the limitations and the rigidities of systems theory. It posits a level of systematization and singularity of purpose that do not reflect experience. It is by no means evident that state repression is directed principally at women. When the state is repressive, young men are much more likely to be the targets than are women (Connell 1987, 128). In Canadian prisons, for example, men outnumber women by a ratio of more than nine to one. Although it may be true that women are more likely to be attacked by men than men are to be attacked by women, it is also true that other males are far more likely to be targets of male violence than are women. The notion of patriarchy offers little to the understanding of men's experience of other men (Frank 1992, 297).

The relationship between state institutions and the women's movement is full of inconsistencies. Universal franchise, affirmative action policies in employment, and Charter protection are only some examples of state support for cherished goals of the women's movement and these coexist with policies to reduce child support or daycare programs. The legal system is similarly full of inconsistencies and contradictory practices. Like the state, it is more usefully understood as the site of multiple practices and struggles than as the unified and purposive agent of sexist policy (Smart 1989, ch. 1). Women's experiences within nuclear families are similarly so diverse and multifaceted that they cannot be captured solely by the notion of family as a patriarchal institution.

The active agency of women themselves is curiously understated in some feminist writings. They are sometimes portrayed as the passive victims of male aggression and dominance than as actively constructing their own lives. This has been especially true with respect to the analysis of sexuality. Some of the women who work as prostitutes describe their ambivalent relationship to feminism, rejecting the patronizing image of themselves as victims (Scott 1987; Kinsman 1986). Underneath the radical feminist critique of prostitution and pornography they suggest is a puritanical conception of female's passionlessness and male sexual control.

These disagreements seem to stem less from the intent of feminist analysis than the effect of an overly simplistic conceptualization of power. While power is recognized in feminist theory, the practical politics of choice, doubt, strategy, planning, error and transformation are often not adequately developed (Connell 1987, 61). The current trend in feminist sociology within Canada is toward a merging of social constructionist and feminist analysis that seeks to retain the insights into gender inequality that the concept of patriarchy provides, while avoiding the rigidities of systems theory analysis.

Suggested Reading

Elaine Morgan's book *The Descent of Women* (1972) gives a very entertaining and insightful critique of sociobiological explanations of gender differences and human evolution. She speculates on a woman-centred sociobiology and in the process reveals the biases inherent in much of this literature. Esther Greenglass's article on "Socialization of Girls and Boys" (1992) provides many illustrations of how mothers and fathers interact differently with sons and daughters and how these experiences may be linked to distinctive gender traits.

Susannah Wilson's book *Women, The Family and the Economy* (1986), especially part 3 on women's work, gives a powerful historical analysis of how women have been exploited in the Canadian labour force, and what the impact is on other aspects of women's lives. Meg Luxton's study of the lives of women in the small mining town of Flin Flon, *More than A Labour of Love* (1980), is a deeply moving account of the impact of virtual lifelong economic dependency on relationships between husbands and wives in the town.

Harold Garfinkel's study of Agnes in *Studies in Ethnomethodology* (1967, ch. 5) is an unusual and fascinating account of the social construction of an alternative gender. Agnes describes how she accomplished "being normally and naturally a female all along" for years before her sex-change operation.

Jonathan Katz's article on "The Invention of Heterosexuality" (1990) pushes us to recognize how what we currently assume to be "natural" heterosexual desires and feelings are quite recent inventions that reflect specific historical and cultural conditions. Gary Kinsman's article "Men Loving Men: The Challenge of Gay Liberation" (1987) pushes us to recognize and to question heterosexist assumptions concerning what is "normal." Didi Khayatt's study of "Legalized Invisibility: The Effect of Bill 7 on Lesbian Teachers" (1990) reveals how vulnerable and secretive are the lives of lesbian teachers, notwithstanding legislation that formally prohibits discrimination on the basis of sexual orientation.

Heidi Hartmann's article on "The Unhappy Marriage of Marxism and Feminism" (1984) provides a detailed historical account of the organized discrimination practiced by male workers against women co-workers. Mackinnon's text *Toward a Feminist Theory of the State* (1989) offers a series of essays from a stridently radical feminist perspective that document the power and the violence associated with patriarchy.

Questions

1. Distinguish between *sex role* and *gender role*. What is problematic about this distinction?

2. What key observation is used to support the theory of biological determinism in role behaviour?

3. In functionalist theory, what key process is held to account both for variation and for stability in gender-role behaviour?

4. How do sociobiology and functionalism differentially explain the apparent predisposition for females to do domestic work?

5. In feminist psychoanalysis, what single factor is seen as explaining the ambivalence and hostility of many men towards women?

6. What problem challenges the prediction that gender equality would follow women's entry into the paid labour force?

7. Contrast functionalist and Marxist explanation for evidence that girls appear less motivated than boys to do advanced school work.

8. What is the goal of ethnomethodological analysis with respect to gender?

9. List three mechanisms by which Eichler feels the Bem scale produces a distorted view of gender behaviour.

10. List two ways in which Foucault sees the "knowledge" of experts as a power mechanism.

CHAPTER 6

Cohesion and Morality: A Critical Look at Durkheim

Sociological theory in the eighteenth and nineteenth centuries was powerfully influenced by belief in progress and evolution of social and biological forms from simpler to more advanced states. The industrial and political revolutions occurring in Europe and North America were viewed not as a threat to social order but as the emergence of a new and potentially better order. The new order, based on science and reason, promised to liberate individuals from the constraints of superstition and feudalism. A central question for sociological theory was how individuals, freed from traditional constraints, could nonetheless cohere into a greater whole called society.

The Emergence of the Scientific Study of Society

Early theorists of society struggled to account for the spectacular advance of science and the Industrial Revolution in European societies. Prevailing theories of progress conceptualized societies as developing through a series of stages, with nonindustrial societies viewed as being at earlier stages of development than Western European cities. Comparative studies of supposedly more primitive societies promised to yield insights into the origins and course of development of technologically advanced societies. Such theories gathered momentum under the impact of colonialism. Following the European conquest of Africa and Asia, and the Americas, the colonizers and missionaries began to study these subjugated societies. They tended to take for granted the superiority of European societies and the more "primitive" or "uncivilized" status of the peoples they conquered.

Auguste Comte and Positive Society

Auguste Comte (1798–1857) developed one of the earliest and most famous theories of societal progress. Comte wrote during the restoration of Bourbon monarchy in France, following the turbulent period of the French Revolution and the defeat of Napoleon in 1815. Comte sought to understand the basis of the new order in which the old powers of absolute monarchy, military, and church had been swept away. Comte argued that changes at the level of society reflect fundamental changes in prevailing ways of thinking and reasoning. He proposed a law of three stages in which the emergence of distinct types of knowledge and belief is associated with distinct forms of organization of society and social institutions.

The **theological stage** is a form of society dominated by primitive religious thought. People seek to explain events and phenomena in terms of supernatural forces such as gods or spirits. Such a society is based on intuition, sentiment, and feelings. It is ruled by priests and by military personnel, and its moral structure is centred around blood ties.

The **metaphysical stage** of society is associated with a limited development of critical thought. It is marked by a transition to belief in a single deity and some kind of unified reality. People try to explain phenomena in terms of abstract forces rather than irrational spirits. Such forms of thought foster a concept of society as unified around a centralized state.

The third stage is **positive society** based on scientific **empiricism**. Science seeks to explain phenomena through factual knowledge derived from observation, experiment, comparison, and prediction. It rejects religious explanations as unobservable and untestable. Scientists rather than priests become the intellectual and spiritual leaders of emerging rational, industrial society.

Changes in patterns of thought are thus mirrored in changing social structures. In military states progress is

based on conquest and plunder, but in industrial states wealth is generated by the rational, scientific organization of work. Comte reasoned that war would have little place in industrial societies since plunder was no longer the basis of wealth. Comte saw scientific reasoning as the decisive feature of societal progress. The application of science to the large-scale organization of labour in factories fosters the unparalleled development of wealth and resources in Western European societies.

What was needed to complete the transition to a positive society was a science of society itself—*sociology*. Sociology, Comte reasoned, would complete the study of natural laws, which had begun with the physical world. The scientific study of the laws of society promised to provide a factual basis on which to reorganize society in more rational ways. Comte is one of the first philosophers to advocate the study of society in essentially the same way as the physical sciences, using methods of controlled observation and experiment to search for law-like or invariant relations between observable social phenomena. Such methods would have vast practical applications for engineering controlled social change.

Problems with Comte

The direct influence of Comte's ideas on modern sociology is small. Comte's theory of intellectual and social progress through theological, metaphysical and positive stages lacks any clear statement of the mechanisms that might drive such changes, or why either the prevailing forms of thought or forms of societal organization should develop in the directions he proposed. Comte also failed to develop clear ideas on how to link observed empirical regularities with unobservable 'laws' that he proposed as explanations. The main value of his thought in the history of sociology lies in his insistence that all questions about change and variation in human nature and social organization can in principle be settled by scientific investigation. In this sense he is the father of the discipline of sociology.

Herbert Spencer and Social Evolution

The British philosopher Herbert Spencer (1820–1903) was strongly influenced by Comte's classification of stages in the development of societies and his scientific approach to the study of social organization. Spencer's goal was to develop a grand theory of evolution that would explain the mechanisms underlying social progress. These evolutionary mechanisms, he reasoned, were essentially the same for the physical, biological, and social phenomena (Keat and Urry 1982, 80). All matter, he argues, tends to move from a state of relatively disorganized flux towards increasing order and stability. In the course of this movement, simple forms and structures give rise to more complex ones by means of two simultaneous processes: differentiation and integration. Differentiation refers to the breakdown of simple, unspecialized structures into many separate specialized parts. Integration means the development of a specialized function that preserves unity among the differentiated parts. Societies evolve toward even greater institutional complexity based on greater specialization of tasks or division of labour. This complexity is integrated through the development of some central co-ordinating agency, such as the modern state.

Spencer saw competitive struggle as the fundamental mechanism governing evolutionary change in both organic and social systems. Competition encourages more complex and specialized forms to emerge out of simpler ones. Organisms that develop the flexibility to adapt to a specialized niche or to develop specialized ways of obtaining food or other scarce resources gain a competitive edge. Competitive struggle between social groups similarly promotes flexible adaptation that gives rise to differentiation and specialization, and in turn the need for centralized regulation and integration. Groups that cannot make the necessary adaptations will be eliminated in favour of those that can. It was Spencer, not Darwin, who first coined the phrase "survival of the fittest" to describe this process.

For adaptations to be successful in promoting the survival of social systems, Spencer reasoned, they must meet three critical conditions or functions. There must be a *sustaining system*, which comprises economic arrangements, such as agricultural and industrial production, that provide a means of livelihood for members of society; a *distribution system*, which allocates products and services between members; and a *regulation system*, which manages and co-ordinates these separate activities. More advanced societies are those with more flexible systems of regulation, namely those based on voluntary rather than forced compliance.

Spencer's ideas had enormous impact on the society of his time. Leading industrialists such as the Carnegies and the Rockefellers welcomed him when he traveled through the United States in 1882. His model of competitive advantage meshed perfectly with their view of themselves as the fittest competitors to survive in economic markets. Competitive struggle in economic markets maximizes economic progress by favouring the most flexible and adaptive competitors while the weaker ones fail.

Problems with Spencer

Spencer's view of societies as all evolving at different rates on a single evolutionary path from essentially the same 'primitive' origins to more 'advanced' states has been widely challenged. Critics argue that different societies have developed in very different ways, and there is no reason to assume that all will converge into one societal form. Moreover, some of the societies that Spencer viewed as 'primitive' may have regressed into that state due to impact of Western colonial conquest, rather than as a result of inherently weak adaptive mechanisms. Spencer's main contribution to the development of sociology is seen in his conception of society as a functioning system comparable to biological organisms. Spencer pioneered the comparative study of whole societies as functioning systems that develop and change through processes of differentiation and specialization, giving rise to social forms with specialized functions. His ideas had a major influence on the development of structural functionalist theory.

Durkheim's Theory of Morality and Cohesion

Emile Durkheim (1858–1917) shared with Comte and Spencer a concern with the comparative evolution of societal forms and a commitment to a positivist or natural-science methodology that seeks to identify cause and effect relations shaping social behaviour (Keat and Urry 1982, 81–82). He rejected the idea that deities or metaphysical forces could explain the observable social world. At the same time, however, he stressed the importance of internal mental states or consciousness of individuals, their moral beliefs and values, and their motives for actions in structuring social order. Durkheim's influence upon the subsequent development of sociology far exceeds that of Comte and Spencer.

Details of Durkheim's personal life give valuable insights into his sociology. He knew both the horrors of civil war, and the marginal status of being a displaced person, an immigrant, and a member of a minority group subject to systemic discrimination. His central concern with the moral foundations of social cohesion and order make sense in the face of these experiences. Durkhiem was born a Jew in the Rhineland province of Alsace, a territory that was the focus of prolonged disputes between France and Prussia during the nineteenth century. His family moved to France and became French citizens but, as a Jewish immigrant, he always felt himself to be a somewhat marginal member of French society. France at that time was just emerging from a long period of political instability that had begun with the French Revolution of 1789. This was followed by the rise of Napoleon and the Napoleonic wars, the restoration of the Bourbon monarchy, further revolutions in 1830 and 1848, followed by the coup d'état of Napoleon's nephew Louis Napoleon. Two events of 1870 ended this period: a crushing military defeat by Prussia and the last brief flowering of the Parisian insurrection known as the Paris Commune, which Marx regarded as a true proletarian uprising. The Third Republic, inaugurated in 1871, was to last until the German invasion of 1940. Durkheim strongly supported the Third Republic and the promise of stability that it brought. He saw himself as a socialist but rejected revolutionary politics in favour of a more administrative form of socialism.

As a Jew in predominantly Catholic France, Durkheim experienced prejudice and oppression at first hand. Although an atheist himself, he understood the intense commitment of Jews to their community and the power of the religion of Judaism as a social force. He was very concerned with religious tolerance, and he insisted that in a highly diversified, multiracial, and multiethnic society, such tolerance for individual differences was essential. This belief motivated his political involvement in the Dreyfus case in 1894. Dreyfus, an Alsatian Jew like Durkheim, was a French army officer. He was falsely accused of selling information to the Germans and was convicted on the basis of minimal evidence. After a counter-intelligence review concluded he was innocent, it was a full two years before his case was re-opened and he was pardoned. All France took sides in what came to be seen as a blatant case of anti-Semitism. Durkheim's argument was that anti-Semitism threatened the cohesion of modern multiethnic society, directly undermining social solidarity.

The themes of intense commitment to community, and the religious character of this commitment, together with his insistence on the sanctity of the individual person and individual rights, and the necessity of tolerance for diversity, are central to all of Durkheim's sociological writings. Each of his major works addresses the question of the origins and nature of morality as the expression of the relationship between individuals and society. In his first major work, *The Division of Labour in Society* ([1893] 1964), Durkheim develops his theory of the evolution of society from relatively simple, undifferentiated, small-scale communities to complex and heterogeneous industrial societies. His central theme traces the evolution of a new form of social cohesion. His most significant contributions to contemporary sociology are his pioneering work in the application of scientific methods to the study of society, his focus on macrosocietal structures as the basis for understanding individual happiness, his explication of the foundations of social order in industrial society, and his seminal concept of *anomie* or moral breakdown. These contributions are examined in detail below.

The Scientific Study of Morality

The first premise of Durkheim's sociology is that social forces exist as a distinct level of reality. "Social facts', he argues, should be studied using scientific methods in the same way as though they were things ([1895] 1964, 14). By this rule, Durkheim does not mean that aspects of social life can simply be observed like physical objects, but that they share the characteristics of things in two respects: they are external to individuals, and they exercise constraint over individual behaviour. Social facts comprise anything that people experience as external constraints on their behaviour. The sense of being constrained provides a sign of the presence of social facts. These facts, or external constraints, cannot be understood in terms of individual personality and circumstances alone, nor will wishful thinking make them disappear.

In the preface to *The Division of Labour in Society* ([1893] 1964, 32), Durkheim defines his goal as using scientific methods to explore the regularities or 'laws' that explain moral life. His central argument is that the conditions under which people live give rise to moral rules, and these rules change when society changes. The nature of social order and cohesion underlying complex industrial society are necessarily very different from simpler societies, but they nonetheless do have a moral base.

The moral order, for Durkheim, refers to two central aspects of society. The first is integration, or the achievement of a sense of solidarity and cohesiveness with others. The second is regulation, which involves restraint—including self-restraint or altruism—upon the pursuit of self-interest. Durkheim's basic thesis in *The Division of Labour in Society* is that there are two fundamentally different kinds of solidarity and therefore of morality. First, there is **mechanical solidarity**, which is based on sameness and shared conditions. This idea is captured in the saying that "birds of a feather flock together." People feel closer to others with whom they share very similar backgrounds and experiences than with those who seem very different. The other form of solidarity is **organic solidarity**. This is based on recognition of differences that complement and complete us and that are experienced in exchange and mutual dependence. Durkheim gives the example of the bonding between a woman and a man in marriage, where their differences and resulting dependence unites them. Durkheim argues that organic solidarity based on complementary differences is ultimately stronger than the simpler mechanical solidarity based on sameness.

Law and Morality

The moral order of a society can be studied objectively through the ways in which members of the society intervene to regulate each other's behaviour. Durkheim argues that any form of behaviour that threatens the solidarity of a community will be experienced as immoral and will be subject to sanctions. Law constitutes the codified morality of a society. Hence the study of law provides an objective basis for the scientific study of the underlying moral life of the society.

Durkheim argues that the two kinds of solidarity are reflected in two very different kinds of law. Mechanical solidarity based on sameness promotes penal or **repressive law**. Such law is concerned with the punishment of offenders who have transgressed the shared values of the community. He then uses the French words *conscience collective* to refer to this sense of collective moral awareness and mutual obligation. He defines **conscience collective** as "the totality of beliefs and sentiments common to the average citizens of the same society" (Durkheim [1893] 1964, 79). There is some dispute as to whether *conscience collective* should be translated into English as "collective conscience"—referring to people's sense of what is right or wrong—or as "collec-

tive consciousness"—referring to people's sense of involvement in a community. The French term implies both meanings. Many sociologists who write about Durkheim's work prefer to use the French form to alert readers that the term has this dual meaning.

Durkheim emphasizes that the totality of beliefs and sentiments associated with the *conscience collective* forms a system that has its own life and that exists independently of individual members of society. Any one member encounters these beliefs and sentiments as social facts, as constraints upon behaviour above and beyond individual whims or feelings. Repressive laws control behaviour that violates the collective conscience of the community of people. The societal function of punishment is not primarily to take revenge against the perpetrator of crime, but to publicly reaffirm collective values and thus to strengthen the collective conscience itself. Organic solidarity, based on differences and mutual dependence, promotes **restitutive law** or contract law. This is exemplified by civil law, encompassing commercial, contractual, constitutional, and administrative regulations. Restitutive law is less concerned with punishment than with the return of things as they were, or with re-establishing reciprocal obligations between members of a society. As such, civil law presupposes a division of labour among people who have specialized functions and who therefore depend upon each other to perform these functions in definite, reciprocal ways.

Durkheim uses these two models—mechanical solidarity and repressive law versus organic solidarity and restitutive law—to develop a theory of the evolution of society from simple agricultural to complex industrial patterns.

Societies Based on Mechanical Solidarity

Durkheim argues that simpler, preindustrial societies are characterized by mechanical solidarity, the form of cohesion that is based fundamentally on sameness. Most of the members of such societies live very similar lives, with little specialization or division of labour beyond that associated with age and sex. Members feel bound together by their shared beliefs and sentiments. The stronger the uniformity of beliefs and practices in such communities, the stronger the social solidarity—hence the intensity with which these beliefs and practices are defended against diversity.

For Durkheim, any strong convictions that are shared by members of a community take on a religious character because they inspire reverence. Violation of these convictions is viewed as sin. The system of law associated with such intensely-felt values is essentially repressive. Repressive or penal law is thus, at root, religious law. Religion is critically important and tends to regulate all details of social life. Nonconformity in such communities constitutes a threat precisely because uniformity of beliefs is the basis of solidarity. If such beliefs are allowed to weaken through tolerance for nonconformity, then the very cohesion of the community itself is threatened.

Transition in Forms of Society

Mechanical solidarity can be very powerful in relatively isolated and homogeneous communities, but it cannot retain its hold over individual consciousness in the face of rapid social change, or in the context of heterogeneous, multiethnic, and multi-religious societies such as the France of Durkheim's time. The erosion of mechanical solidarity as a unifying force is the inevitable result of the cultural, demographic, and economic changes that occur with industrialization.

Durkheim proposes three factors as critical in generating the transition form mechanical to organic solidarity. The first is the expansion of communication over vast areas, which allows information to reach previously isolated segments. The second factor is demographic: an increase in population size. As population pressure increases, people are forced to diversify in order to survive. This diversity allows them to co-operate rather than compete. Arising from diversity is the third major factor—division of labour. Durkheim likens this process to biological evolution where plants and animals adapt so as to occupy different niches.

The combined effects of these three factors upon the moral basis of social order are far-reaching. The common consciousness of shared beliefs and sentiments necessarily becomes more abstract as it encompasses local diversities. As Durkheim expresses it, "the gods take leave of space." The God of humanity is necessarily less concrete than the god of an individual clan. This process makes possible individual emancipation, because there is more room for variation and for diversity of beliefs and sentiments. Durkheim argues that once people experience diversity and freedom of thought, those liberties become increasingly more necessary and inevitable. There can be no turning back. The social basis of individual emancipation is division of labour. As people develop specialized functions, they have different life experiences, and so develop different perspectives on life.

Societies Based on Organic Solidarity

Durkheim argues that complex, industrialized societies are characterized by organic solidarity, the form of social cohesion that is based on division of labour and interdependence. As people become more specialized, they also become more dependent upon each other. A homesteading family engaged in subsistence farming, for example, may survive with little or no help from similar homesteaders, but specialized workers in a garment factory cannot survive without a host of other specialized workers supplying their other basic needs. Members of a society characterized by advanced division of labour are united by mutual obligations, and not merely by sentiments of sameness. Co-operation is essential. It cannot be neglected.

Some of the theories of urbanism that we explored in chapter 4 suggest that increasing size, density, and heterogeneity in populations inevitably weaken social cohesion. Durkheim rejects this view, arguing instead that homogeneous societies, made up of relatively undifferentiated family groupings, were actually more fragile. The parts, or family groupings, that made up such societies, could break away from each other and remain relatively independent on their homesteads, or in their small villages or kin communities. This is impossible in societies characterized by advanced division of labour. Heterogeneous, urban societies may foster a far greater degree of individualism, but these individuals are also more interdependent. Specialized parts need each other and cannot break away. Diversity gives rise to ties of mutual obligation and co-operation that grow progressively stronger as specialization increases.

In heterogenous societies, repressive or religious law necessarily declines because the core of common beliefs and sentiments declines. Restitutive or contract law expands in its place. Restitutive law regulates the rules of justice that cannot be violated by individual contracts. Respect for the individual and for individual rights constitutes the fundamental ground of justice, or what Durkheim calls the "precontractual basis of contract", that expresses morality in highly specialized societies. Respect for the individual and for individual rights is not merely "good." It is essential for social order and cohesion in modern society. The grip of religious dogma on everyday life declines, and the *conscience collective*—the shared beliefs and sentiments—becomes more abstract. What replaces it is the religion of individualism, or humanism. Moral individualism entails not selfish self-interest, but reciprocal obligations and mutual respect.

Durkheim's recognition of the fundamental moral role of the division of labour in society is his most important theoretical contribution to sociology. Durhkeim totally rejects the arguments of Spencer and utilitarian economists who suggest that a stable society could be based upon unbridled self-interest. He argues that "there is nothing less constant than interest. Today it unites me to you; tomorrow it will make me your enemy. Such a cause can only give rise to transient relations and passing associations" ([1893] 1964, 204). Even purely economic contracts presuppose a precontractual basis of moral standards that underlies and regulates the agreements between people and determines standards of justice.

Problems with Durkheim

Critics challenge Durkheim's model of a unilinear process of change from mechanical to organic solidarity as seriously oversimplified. Division of labour and contractual obligation occur within and between nonspecialized, simpler societies, and likewise, mechanical solidarity is evident in industrial societies, manifest in strong identification with religious and ethnic groups. Repressive, penal law has by no means disappeared in modern societies. Authoritarian regimes abound in the twenty-first century, demanding conformity to dominant religious and political doctrines.

In defense of Durkheim, it can be more reasonably argued that the transition from mechanical to organic solidarity is one of relative shifts in the importance of shared culture over interdependence of labour, rather than an absolute shift from one form of solidarity to another. As a member of the Jewish community in France, Durkheim was certainly well aware of strong religious and ethnic affiliations, and he probably never intended his formulation to be interpreted rigidly. Specialization and differentiation certainly exist in non-industrialized societies, but not to the same extent as in industrial societies. In Canada in the twenty-first century, even rural areas are totally tied to specialized mono-crop production, and farmers are as dependent as industrial workers upon the market economy for their subsistence needs.

The criticism, that repressive religious law has not disappeared, is harder to deal with. Division of labour has the potential for sustaining organic solidarity based on mutual obligation and duty, with humanism

as the supreme religion. Yet this state is far from being realized. The struggle to establish a universal commitment to human rights is one of the most pressing international moral issues of our time. Respect for basic human rights is an important requirement for political stability in our interdependent world community, but it has not yet been achieved. Like the Marxist vision of a socialist utopia, Durkheim's vision of a cohesive, co-operative world community has nowhere been realized.

Anomic Division of Labour

Durkheim's concept of 'anomie' remains a lasting contribution to sociological understanding of the moral ills of contemporary industrial society. Anomie is a complex concept, referring to a relative absence or confusion of values and to a corresponding lack of clear regulations or norms for behaviour. In a state of anomie, people feel lost and disorganized, unsure of how to behave or what to believe in, so that their lives come to feel meaningless or purposeless.

Durkheim's analysis of anomic division of labour anticipates much modern writing on the meaninglessness of much industrial work and the breakdown of moral order in the face of injustice and inequality. Durkheim argued that conflicts are not a necessary result of industrialized society, and they cannot be resolved by a retreat to the mechanical solidarity of nationalism or religion. Moral uniformity cannot be forced in the face of functional diversity. The key problem, he argues, is lack of regulation. Parts of the social order are insufficiently co-ordinated, leaving individual workers with a sense of isolation and meaninglessness. The laissez-faire economic system, with its powerful inducements to selfish behaviour, hurts people. Workers feel separated and alone, without a sense of how their work is important for others.

Unjust or forced division of labour, Durkheim argues, is a major cause of anomie. To be just, division of labour or specialization must fit natural talents. People must be able to choose their occupations freely. A sense of natural co-operation is destroyed when rules constrain people by force. Fair contracts, moreover, require that parties to the contract be equal, so that each may freely enter the contract. This basis for justice is violated by inherited wealth; hence hereditary privilege should be abolished. There cannot be rich and poor at birth, says

Durkheim, without there being unjust contracts (Durkheim [1893] 1964, 384).

Fractionalized work is a further cause of anomie. This is precisely the kind of work pattern produced by the system of workplace rule known as 'scientific management'. Scientific management aims to maximize labour productivity and control by breaking work tasks down into tiny components. Workers specialize in a small repetitive task rather than following the operation through. Their jobs become fragmented, lacking unity, co-ordination, and coherence. As a result, workers cannot sustain a feeling of solidarity and continuity of work essential to the sense of organic community. They cannot sustain any sense of pride in their own contribution to the labour process. Work becomes meaningless when individual workers are reduced to machines, subjected to monotonous routines without intrinsic interest. Normal specialization does not require this forced level of fragmentation. Durkheim insists that ensuring justice in the treatment of workers in industrial society is a critical task facing technologically advanced societies. Liberty for individuals can only be attained through just regulations. It is not enough that there be rules governing contracts; the rules must be just.

Durkheimian and Marxist analyses are largely in agreement this far. Where they diverge is on the question whether just regulation will ever be possible within a capitalist economic order. While Durkheim describes factors that give rise to "abnormal forms" of division of labour, Marxists seek to examine the origins of these abnormal forms within the exploitative structures of capitalism. The Marxist thesis is that justice is impossible within a profit-motivated system where a small class of people controls the means of production upon which others depend. From this perspective, capitalism itself creates the lack of regulation, the egoism, and the immorality in collective life that Durkheim identifies as abnormal. Alienation rather than anomie is the central concept in Marxist theory.

The next two chapters explore at more length the concepts of anomie and alienation in the study of law and crime in industrial society, and the continuing significance of religion. The remainder of this chapter focuses on Durhkeim's seminal study of *Suicide* ([1879] 1951).

Suicide: A Scientific Study of Happiness and Social Cohesion

Durkheim designed his study of suicide as a scientific test of his central theory that individual happiness depends upon two central conditions of the moral order of society: integration and regulation. When the moral order of a society is disturbed or undermined, he reasoned, the level of unhappiness among members of that society will rise. The challenge Durkheim faced was to find some objective scientific method that draws on observable, empirical evidence or 'social facts' to study such essentially intangible and subjective states as social integration and unhappiness. Durkheim's brilliantly innovative proposal was to use data on suicide rates to measure the level of unhappiness within a society. He defines suicide as "intentional self-death by any action known to have that effect" (Durkheim [1897] 1951, 44)—a definition that focuses on intent to die rather than on the outcome of action.

The act of committing suicide is a supremely individual and private act, but suicide *rates* are social facts. The suicide rate is the actual number of people per 100,000 population recorded as having intentionally killed themselves. It is a statistic that is regularly published by government agencies. Suicide, thankfully, occurs relatively rarely, and it is almost impossible to observe directly. When statistics are kept for large populations and over long periods of time, however, it becomes possible to study patterns and to compare differences in rates among nations and among subgroups. For Durkheim, therefore, officially recorded suicide rates provide objective facts that can stand as indicators of the general level of happiness of members of different communities.

Durkheim was not trying to predict any one individual's suicide, but rather the conditions that increase the general level of unhappiness in a society, and thus the proportion of people unhappy enough to consider killing themselves. He carefully examines bio-medical factors such as mental illnesses, but concludes that such illnesses tend to occur randomly across populations and do not account for differences in rates of suicide between social groups. Durkheim's theory is that specific kinds of social conditions generate increasing unhappiness and higher suicide rates.

Durkheim's Model of Social Order and Suicide Rates

Durkheim theorized that social order comprises two central features: integration and regulation. Integration refers to people's sense of closeness and bonding between themselves and others, while regulation refers to peoples' sense of stability and clarity in normative expectations. Abnormal states of either integration or regulation in society, he reasoned, whether too weak or too excessive, would threaten the general level of happiness of members. Logically, his model predicts four abnormal states, each associated with a particular form or type of suicide.

Weak integration is associated with *egoistic suicide*, when people lack a sense of strong bonds linking them with others. Weak regulation fosters *anomic suicide* when people lack a sense of their place in society and what is expected of them. At the other extreme, excessive integration fosters *altruistic suicide* when people submerge their individuality into the group and sacrifice themselves for the group. Lastly, excessive regulation fosters *fatalistic suicide* when people's lives are entirely regimented by group norms.

In order to test this theoretical model using scientific methods, Durkheim needed to find objective, empirically observable measures of each of his four key types of societal conditions so that they could be compared with suicide rates. The statistical techniques to which Durkheim had access were crude by contemporary standards but he nonetheless provides an impressive array of comparative evidence to support his model.

To test the proposed association between weak integration and *egoistic* suicide, Durkheim used a series of comparisons based on religious affiliation and marital status as indicators of relative weakness or strength of social bonds. His first comparison was drawn between Protestant and Catholic regions of Europe. Protestants, he reasoned, emphasised free inquiry by individuals while Catholics have a ready-made faith and relative certainty of beliefs. Thus, Protestants would have weaker social cohesion than Catholics. Durkheim predicted that Protestants should have higher suicide rates than Catholics. Official suicide rates kept for Protestant and Catholic administrative areas over many decades confirmed this prediction. In Protestant areas the recorded suicide rates were significantly higher than in Catholic areas.

Durkheim's Model of Social Order and Happiness

Weak Integration		Excessive Integration
Egoism		**Altruism**
paired comparisons:		Army—officers; enlisted v conscript
Prot-cath		Islam—suicide bombers; martyrs
Married-single		Inuit: old leave when food scarce
Children or not	*1) Integration* Bonds = happiness	Japan—honour suicides
Widowed with kids or not		
Rural-urban		
Ethnic minority		
Level of education/free thinking		
	2) regulation Normative order = happiness	
Weak Regulation		Excessive Regulation
Anomie		**Fatalism**
Sudden wealth—boom, lottery		Slaves
Sudden poverty, loss of social position		Older childless married women
Divorce		Very young husbands
		[Women in China, Japan, India]

Secondly, Durkheim argues that people who remain single and without children experience significantly weaker social bonds than people who marry and have children, and hence would predictably have higher rates of suicide. Almost all the comparative data on rates of suicide confirmed these predictions. Single men committed suicide more often than married men, and childless married men more than husbands with children, and childless widowers more than widowers with children. Similarly, Durkheim reasoned that urban areas are less cohesive than rural because people are less likely to know each other. Again his prediction was supported: urban communities did have higher rates of suicide than rural ones. Durkheim further reasoned that highly educated people would experience lower social cohesion than less educated people because education promotes critical thinking and hence reduced acceptance of traditional norms and practices.

A particularly significant comparison is between Jews and gentiles. Jews are predominantly urban dwellers and are highly educated, both factors associated with higher suicide rates in general. As a persecuted religious minority, however, they tend to be intensely cohesive. Durkheim hypothesizes that the internal cohesion would counteract the divisive forces of urbanism and education. The data confirm his prediction that Jews would have lower suicide rates than non-Jews.

There is only one statistic that goes against Durkheim's predictions. Women had higher suicide rates when married than when never married, although the rates were lower when they had children than when they were without children. Durkheim concludes that marriage benefits men more than women. Men, he suggests, need restraints more than women, an argument developed further below in the discussion of anomic suicide. In general, however, the recorded suicide rates were strongly consistent with Durkheim's theoretical prediction that, under conditions where bonds of social cohesion are relatively weak, suicide rates are relatively high.

Durkheim's second broad theoretical prediction is that rates of *anomic* suicide will be higher under social conditions when people experience a sense of loss of meaningful regulations ordering their lives. When people have a clear sense of their position in life, have meaningful goals and realistic expectations as to what they should be and should become, then they are contented and happy. But when these constraints are vague, and the limits unclear, people tend to become dissatisfied with their lot, unhappy, and frustrated. Durkheim predicts that the suicide rate, reflecting the proportion of

people too unhappy to live, will increase as social regulation declines.

The main data with which he tests this prediction are periods of economic boom or bust compared with periods of relative stability. One might expect that people may become depressed during periods of economic collapse, but Durkheim shows that boom times are similarly associated with higher suicide rates. When people suddenly become rich, he reasoned, the regulations that shaped their former lives may lose all meaning, and their lives lose direction. Most people expect to work hard all their lives to provide and care for themselves and their family members, but if they suddenly win a fortune, then much of the point of working or doing anything may be lost. Regulations are lacking. Goals appear without limit and consequently without value or meaning. Under such conditions of anomie, Durkheim reasoned, suicide rates go up. Sudden poverty may also plunge people into despair, not simply because of privation, but because all the standards and expectations of their former position in life no longer apply.

Similar feelings of anomie may follow divorce, when the regulations and sexual constraints of marriage are suddenly lifted. The relationship holds at the aggregate level of societies as a whole and not only at individual level. Durkheim reasoned that during periods when the institution of marriage itself weakened, evident in rising divorce rates, the marriage tie would offer weaker protection from social disorganization (Besnard 2000, 134). He found a close relation between high divorce rates and high suicide rates, again with men suffering more than women. As noted above, Durkheim reasoned that men need the constraints of marriage more than women, because general social controls on men's sexual freedom are so much weaker than for women. Divorced men are more prone to go on drunken sprees, consort with many different women, and then fall into despair and suicide. The explanation is only guesswork on Durkheim's part, as he had no direct data on motives, but the gender difference in suicide rates by marital status in Western societies has stood the test of time. Divorced people have a four to five times higher rate of suicide than do married people, with divorced men being significantly more vulnerable than women.

Excessive Integration and Regulation

Durkheim theorized that excessive levels of integration or regulation also disrupt social balance, giving rise to *altruistic* and *fatalistic* suicide respectively. A*ltruistic* *suicide* occurs when social bonds are so strong that people submerge their individuality into the group and become willing to sacrifice themselves for the honour or wellbeing of the group. Durkheim identifies suicides by military officers or samurai in traditional Japan as this type. Samurai would rather die by falling upon their own swords than dishonour the Emperor. During the Second World War, Japanese kamikaze pilots flew their planes directly into their target, knowing that they would die, but willing to do so for the success of their country in war. During times of famine, old or sick Inuit people would walk away from their camp to die so that others could travel more swiftly in search of food.

Durkheim suggests that altruistic suicide is comparatively rare in modern society because individualism is valued more intensely than religion—egoistic or anomic suicide is more likely. The only context where he finds rates of altruistic suicide to be quite high is in the army. He found that army personnel have higher suicide rates than civilians, volunteers more than conscripts, officers more than privates, and re-enlisted men more than newcomers. If the main explanation were merely the hard life of the army, Durkheim reasoned, one would expect all these rates to be reversed. Durkheim concludes that higher rates for volunteers, officers, and re-enlisted men reflect the greater subordination of their individuality to the group. They are willing to die for their unit and their country. More recent examples of altruistic suicide have included members of the Irish Republican Army imprisoned by the British government, who starved themselves to death to protest their classification as 'common criminals' rather than prisoners of war. In contemporary global society, altruistic suicide has sadly become commonplace, with scores of people willing to offer their lives as suicide bombers to attack targets they identify as enemies of Islam.

The state of excessive regulation in society, Durkheim theorized, would lead to an increase in *fatalism,* a despair arising when society offers minimal room for individuality. Durkheim found few conditions of excessive regulation in his data from European societies but suggests that higher suicide rates among very young husbands, and older childless married women might fit this category.

Methodological Challenges to Durkheim's Study

Over a hundred years after it was first published in 1897, Durhiem's study of suicide rates is still famous as a clas-sic application of scientific methods to social issues. Durkheim hoped his analysis would revolutionize social science approaches to the phenomenon of suicide, but this recognition was not to come for another 60 years (Besnard 2000, 97–105). Early critics reasoned that notwithstanding obvious social patterning, suicidal behaviour had to be understood primarily in psychological terms. Durkheim did associate his four types of suicide with certain psychological states, such as loneliness, meaninglessness, submission, and despair. But critics point out that he has no evidence to support these claims. Contemporary research into suicide motivation typically relies on analysis of suicide notes, or interviews and surveys with individuals who attempt but do not complete suicidal acts. However, in defence of Durkheim's methodology, statistical patterns differ markedly between attempts and completed suicides, suggesting that they may well reflect different psychological states (Lester 1997, ch. 1).

Other critics note that Durkheim lacked the advanced statistical techniques like correlation coefficients, and the computer technology that facilitate multiple and partial correlations and path analysis, all used by contemporary statisticians. Re-analysis of his original data using these techniques have raised questions about some of Durkheim's findings. His famous generalization that Protestants have higher suicide rates than Catholics has become the focus of particularly sharp debate. In Durkheim's data being 'Protestant' was highly correlated with living in urban areas and being involved in business or entrepreneurial capitalism (Tomasi 2000, 15; Pickering 2000, 66). Since all these states are associated with heightened individualism it was not possible for Durkheim to separate their individual effects. Others challenge the circular way in which Durkheim reasoned from data to theory (Gane 2000). Ideally, to test a theory one must define categories in advance of checking against available evidence. But at times Durkheim also reasoned in the other direction, finding statistical patterns and then working up his theory to fit them. Such observations offer valuable insights, but the data from which they arise cannot work to test the accuracy of the reasoning.

A more serious methodological problem that arises with respect to all forms of aggregate data, is the risk of **'ecological fallacy'**—the fallacy of arguing from grouped data to individual behaviour. In his discussion of anomic suicide, Durkheim shows that economic booms are associated with increased suicide rates. However, it is not possible to argue directly from such data that individuals who suddenly become wealthy are more prone to commit suicide. It might be impoverished individuals who feel left out of the rising wealth they see around them that push up the suicide rates. Durkheim did have some individual-level cause-of-death data to support his generalizations (Besard 2000, 119) but it remains difficult to determine whether suicide data reflect the tip of an iceberg of widespread unhappiness, or islands of misery in a wider sea of relative contentment with life.

A final area of methodological concern focusses on the questionable quality of national statistics on suicide rates themselves (Varty 2000). It is never easy to distinguish true suicides from homicides or accidental deaths, and coroners with differing religious convictions or institutional pressures to disguise problematic rates, may well sway the classification of cases. Durkheim concluded that the data were good enough for his purposes, but as we discuss further below, social constructionist analysis casts some doubt on whether theories about motives for suicide can ever be clearly separated from classification of deaths. (Douglas 1967).

Theoretical Challenges to Durkheim's Analysis

Durhkeim's theoretical focus on structural factors at societal level as causal explanations for suicide rates has been repeated challenged by theorists who find individual-level psychological explanations like stress and personal sense of loneliness more appropriate (Halbwachs 1930; Travis 1990). Others argue that macro-level societal structures may impact on local relations and these in turn impact on individuals (Berkman et. al., 2000).

Durkheim's four-part model of weak or excessive integration or regulation giving rise to four different types of suicide has been widely challenged. Durkheim himself could find only weak support for his model of excessive social constraints. As evidence of fatalism, he offers only the high suicide rates among young husbands and elderly childless wives. Similarly for altruism he cites only the high suicide rates within the armed forces. Other critics argue further that the distinction between anomie and egoism is weak, and might usefully be collapsed into a single category with 'low integration' as the decisive societal condition explaining all suicides (Pope 1976).

More recent research, however, is coming out in favour of Durkheim's more complex four-part model

(Davies and Neal 2000). Fatalism resulting from excessive regulation did not show up strongly in Durkheim's Eurocentric data, but it has proven useful to account for higher suicide rates among women in the strongly traditionalistic and closed rural societies of China, Japan, and India. Role expectations were so rigidly defined that people had no means to escape their excessively regulated lives. Evidence that suicide rates *fell* in Japan as the society became more individualistic cannot be explained by egoism (ibid. 45). The concept of altruism also best accounts for obligatory suicides practised among the more privileged strata particularly military elites in these hierarchical, collectivist societies.

In summary, Durkhiem's *Suicide* is acclaimed as a masterpiece of sociological investigation, notwithstanding its flaws. It has inspired a host of later studies that explore the multiple questions it raises. His study shows irrefutably that suicide is socially patterned, a patterning that purely bio-medical and psychological explanations cannot account for. His theoretical model remains dominant in suicide research and his four types are widely accepted and applied (Lester 1997a, 133). The remainder of this chapter explores how contemporary theoretical perspectives in sociology have absorbed and responded to Durkheim's approach.

Suicide Rates—Statistics Canada

Sociological theories that address suicide rates must try to account for the following patterns: Canada as a whole enjoys exceptional advantages of political and economic stability, yet has suicide rates that approximate the global average. Within Canada, suicide rates are higher among young adults than older people, markedly higher among men of all ages, and especially young men, than among women. Rates among Inuit and First Nations peoples of all ages are some six times higher than Canadian averages, ranking among the highest of any communities in the world.

In detail, international statistics cited by Lester (2003, 1157–8) rank Canada 34th out of 69 countries with an overall suicide rate of 12.7 per 100 000, similar to the USA but higher than Britain with 8.1, and lower than France, Germany and Sweden with rates between 17 to 20 per 100 000. Canada ranks far lower than countries recently separated from the former Soviet Block, and the Russian federation with a rate of 26.5 per 100 000. The Canadian average, however, glosses over marked variation in rates by gender and race. Canada, along with other European societies, has a long established pattern of significantly higher rates for males than females. Among the age group 15–24, for example, suicide rates for men were 24.7 per 100 000 compared with 4.9 for women (ibid. 1159–1160). Expressed another way, young men are five times more likely to die from suicide than young women in Canada.

When suicide rates are separated out for First Nations communities within Canada there are striking differences. Between 1979–1991 the rates for the total population of Canada fluctuated between 13–15 per 100 000. For First Nations the rates fluctuated between a low of 28 and a high of 45 per 100 000—a rate that exceeds any nation state included in the World Health Organization list. Suicide rates for Aboriginal youth cited by Tester and McNicoll (2004) far exceed those for non-Aboriginal Canadians. In the age range 10–19 Aboriginal males approaches 60 per 100 000 compared with 10 for non-Aboriginal males. In the most vulnerable age-rage 20–29 the comparative rates are 108 and 30. For young females the rates are lower, but the gap between Aboriginal and non-Aboriginal remain striking. For the age range 10–15 the rates are 21 per 100 000 for Aboriginal females and 2.5 for non-Aboriginal females. In the most vulnerable 20–29 age cohort the rates are 28 and 6 respectively. Tester and McNicoll note further that not only are suicide rates among Aboriginal peoples of Canada several orders of magnitude higher than for other Canadians; these rates are continuing to rise. Rates in Nunavut Territory were recorded as 48.7 per 100 000 on 1985–7. By 1988–90 the rate was 66.7. Then it rose again to 75.1 by 1991–3 and 85.5 by 1994–6. Similar dramatic increases are recorded for Inuit communities in Alaska, Greenland, Arctic Quebec, and Labrador.

Functionalist Perspectives on Suicide

Functionalist analysis of suicide draws extensively on Durkheim's model, focusing on theories of social disorganization and weak integration and regulation, as local institutions, social networks, and systems of values lose their influence over individuals during periods of rapid social change. Social turbulence resulting from the rapid economic and political shift from communism to free market capitalism in former Soviet block countries provides a ready explanation for the higher than average national suicide rates in these countries.

In Canada, the rapid social and economic changes associated with the "Quiet Revolution" within Quebec in the 1970s was associated with a very rapid rise in suicide rates (Boyer et. al., 1998; Sakinowsky 1998, 43). Quebec shifted from being ninth out of ten Canadian provinces for male suicide rates in 1950 to top by 1990, and from being seventh to third for female rates. The strains of modernization and secularisation, associated with a radical change in values and a steep decline in church attendance, are seen as responsible for widespread anomie. The numbers of people getting legally married declined while divorce rates rose sharply—factors noted by Durkheim as indicators of weakened social integration and regulation. Patterns in Quebec are consistent with national statistics from 53 modern nations (Lester 1989 and 1997, 126). Lester concludes that societies that are moderate on measures such as marriage rates and religious freedom have the lowest comparative suicide rates, while societies scoring high on both or low on both had higher suicide rates. The Quiet Revolution in Quebec seems to have shifted the society from moderate to low levels of social integration, with increasing suicide rates as the result.

Most functionalist research focuses on integration at the level of families and local communities. Surveys that measure suicidal thoughts and attempts typically show that family problems are important predictors of suicidal thoughts and behaviour. Adolescents most at risk of suicidal thoughts are those with a history of family disruption, a sense of not feeling loved within the family (Wild et. al., 2004), having parents who are divorced or who have died, parents who have drug and alcohol problems, family violence, and especially when combined with experience of sexual abuse (Graham et. al., 2004; Rossow and Lauritzen 2001; Lester 1997, ch. 5). Victims of bullying and marginalisation at school are also more prone to suicidal thoughts although the correlation is less strong (Baldry and Winkel 2003). Other plausible relationships between patterns of psychological or physical punishment by parents and suicidal thoughts as possibly the expression of aggression turned inwards show inconclusive results.

Studies using cause-of-death statistics confirm Durkheim's finding that marriage and children offer protection from completed suicide, and particularly so for men. The weakening of the institution of marriage, evident in higher divorce rates, continues to favour women more than men, but there have been significant changes in patterns for young men since Durkheim's time. Single men are noticeably less at risk of suicide than formerly. Membership in other social networks continues to be associated with measures of mental health. Typically surveys measure numbers of close friends and relatives, and affiliation or membership in religious and voluntary associations. High levels of integration are usually inferred from evidence of membership. More detailed measures include variation in frequency, intensity and extent of social supports—emotional, practical, and normative guidance. The evidence supports the theory that having multiple social roles promotes personal sense of well-being and positive coping strategies, and these in turn influence mental and physical health (Berkman et. al., 2000).

Measures of religious affiliation have had mixed results. Level of commitment to spiritual values seems more important than distinctions between Protestant or Catholic (Garroutte et. al., 2003). Conformity to prevailing cultural values for men and women may also be more significant than what these values are in protecting adolescents from suicidal thoughts (Lam et. al., 2004). Among adolescents in Hong Kong, commitment to values of self direction and independence reduced the risk for boys but was irrelevant for girls, while conversely endorsement of values of obedience and respect for elders reduced risk for girls but was irrelevant for boys. Acceptance of traditional sex-typical cultural role expectations seems to have been the important factor in risk reduction.

Rural Urban Differences

The question whether rural or urban communities offer better protection from suicidal thoughts has become contentious in recent research. In Durkheim's time it could be safely assumed that rural communities were relatively cohesive, while urban areas suffered social dislocation from the rapid influx of migrants seeking factory work. Current research suggests there has been a significant decline in the protective features of rural life. Suicide rates in rural areas in many parts of the world have been rising rapidly, in some places exceeding rates for urban areas. A study in England and Wales recorded a ten-fold increase in suicides for rural males and a four-fold increase for rural females between 1981 and 1998 (Middleton et. al., 2003). Similar patterns have been reported in Australia (Bourke 2003; Dudley et. al., 1997;

Cantor et. al., 1995), Japan (Otsu et. al., 2004; Charlton 1995) and Sweden (Ferrada-Noli 1997). Explanations for the rise in suicide rates in rural areas are varied. The study in England and Wales found no association between changes in suicide rates and changes in measures of socio-economic status or unemployment rates. In contrast, Bourke's Australian study did find heightened rates of unemployment, low education levels and a dearth of social and youth services. She also describes rigid cultural expectations for young men and women in rural Australian society, centred around exaggerated masculine images of hard-drinking, football-playing men who accept violence, and images of passive women focused on domestic duties. Those who do not fit in, she suggests, feel shamed and marginalised. Any admission of feeling depressed is further stigmatized as weakness, thus discouraging troubled youth from seeking the help of professional mental health-care workers.

Expanding agribusiness practices in Canada and other countries are also contributing to the destabilization of rural communities. Corporate farming requires both heavy capital investments and fewer workers. The results are widespread bankruptcies, economic stress, declining communities as young people move away in search of alternative work, and working lives for those who remain that are more akin to urban factory work than traditional family farms. A Canadian study further suggests that exposure to pesticides in forestry and agriculture may be contributing factor in rising rates of mental illness and suicide (Green 1987, 1991). Rural gentrification is simultaneously taking place in rural areas close to large urban population centres, as wealthy urban families buy up rural homes and estates that local residents cannot afford. They may also help to spread urban individualistic consumer values in rural areas. While explanations vary, the emerging consensus remains that rural communities no longer seem to offer the protection they once did from risk of suicide.

Functionalist Analysis of Aboriginal Suicide Rates

Cultural genocide, and associated social dislocation, and family breakdown are the main themes in functionalist analysis of the exceptionally high suicide rates among indigenous peoples in Canada and abroad. Indigenous peoples the world over have suffered the social trauma of forced and rapid social and economic change. Societies that subsisted for centuries by means of communal hunting and gathering have been forced to abandon their traditional lifestyles as they were pushed from traditional homelands by western colonizers. Most have not adapted well to sedentary life, often on reservations, and to the demands of formal education required to find employment in modern industrial economies (Sinclair 1998; Kirmayer et. al., 1996, 1998 a, b; Balikci 1970). Successive colonial governments in Canada deliberately suppressed the cultures of First Nations peoples by policies that outlawed what colonizers saw as primitive and barbaric religious rituals and practices. Governments further ordered that First Nations children be removed from their parents and sent to residential schools across Canada, where they were instructed only in English or French, and taught only the Christian religion. The expectation was that children would quickly assimilate the now dominant western culture. However, this rarely happened. Children commonly resisted the imposed and alien culture, but after ten years of such schooling they returned to their own communities largely ignorant of their own cultural traditions and unable to speak their native languages. Often too, they absorbed the attitudes of their colonial teachers who saw native traditions as primitive and inferior to western culture.

The pervasive experience of being raised in residential schools left many of these young adults ill-equipped to raise their own families, thus contributing to widespread family breakdown within First Nations communities. Mental health surveys show strong correlations between high rates family breakdown and high rates of suicidal thoughts and attempts among Indian and Inuit peoples. Measures of family breakdown include having parents with drinking and/or drug problems, having parents separated or dead, having relatives with psychiatric problems or who have themselves attempted or committed suicide, family violence and sexual abuse (Tester and McNicoll 2004, 2632). A study of Inuit families by Jean Briggs (1985, 1995) suggest that many Inuit parents lack adequate parenting skills. Parents, she argues, vacillate between intense attachment, bonding and nurturing relations with children and the need to treat children in controlling, aggressive, and even rejecting ways, both to protect themselves from the loss of their children and to push the children into independence. Inuit children in return experience great difficulties when they have to leave home to go to high schools. In effect, Briggs suggests, traditional Inuit family culture has failed to adapt to modern demands.

Interventions to deal with these many risk factors precipitating high suicide rates include school and commu-

nity programs designed to foster positive Aboriginal identities and cultural heritage, activities that bring Elders and youth together in cultural centres and school activities. The government also pays for mental health professionals to work in the indigenous communities to provide counselling and parenting skills workshops (The Report of the Advisory Group on Suicide Prevention 2003). Available evidence suggests, however, that these programs are having little success in reducing suicide rates (Leenaars and Lester 2004).

The Political Economy Perspective on Suicide

The political economy perspective focuses on structural inequalities rooted in relations of production to understand variation in suicide rates. While Durkheim's analysis stresses the breakdown of moral order in society, Marxist analysis explore the economic forces that cause such moral breakdown. Unrelenting competition and pursuit of profits over community obligations and loyalties are required to succeed in capitalist economies. They foster the egoism that Durkheim associates with weakened social integration. Capitalists cannot afford to be too committed to their workers. Workers displaced by technological advances are expected to uproot and move to wherever employment options are better, regardless of family ties. The crass consumerism promoted by advertising teaches individuals to value themselves and others by their possessions. These values, combined with ever-growing income gaps between the poor and the wealthy, foster the anomie of meaningless striving for empty goals that Durkheim associates with loss of regulation. Both Durkheimian and Marxist perspectives incorporate a sense of fatalism, although understood in very different ways. Durkheim's model points to despair that arises when people feel their lives totally controlled by inflexible cultural rules from which they cannot break free. Despair also arises when people experience their lives as ruled by impersonal market forces that seem to work like some inexorable machine, grinding the 'inefficient', the 'unproductive', and the 'obsolete' in its path. Unprofitable enterprises close down no matter how dependent communities may be on the lost jobs. Undercapitalised farms go bankrupt no matter how strongly farm families may love their way of life. People find themselves unemployable when technological developments render their skills and talents obsolete. Individuals, entire communities, and even nation states across the globe feel powerless to influence these market forces within which their lives are embedded. Marxist analysis suggests that only the collective consciousness of workers uniting in their struggle to overthrow the capitalist system might foster the moral force of self sacrifice for the communal good that Durkheim associates with altruistic suicide.

Research into the effects of capitalist relations on suicide rates is complicated by the pervasiveness of the global capitalist system. There are no societies remaining outside the system that can function as comparison groups. A further complication, is that evidence of an association between economic booms or slumps and suicide rates does not tell us which individuals become more suicide prone. We do not know whether it is the newly rich in economic boom times who lose a sense of meaning in their lives, or the poor people who are left behind in the sea of rising prosperity. Likewise, rising suicide rates when economies contract might reflect the despair of the newly poor, or the anguish of the guilt-ridden rich living in a sea of poverty who find their lives meaningless. We need data at the level of individuals to explore such questions. However, when researchers do collect data at the individual level, they tend to analyse the results in terms of individual misfortune or failings and lose sight of the structural forces that shape these data. This is easy to do when, on an aggregate level, economic conditions look good.

A study of variation in suicide rates and economic inequalities among Canadian provinces between 1969–71 and 1979–81, shows just how tricky such analysis can be. Provinces with relatively higher male suicide rates were those with more rapidly expanding job opportunities for males. Yet ironically, these provinces simultaneously had higher male unemployment rates (Sakinofsky and Roberts 1987; Sakinofsky 1998, 41). So many new workers migrated into these provinces in search of work that they outstripped the positions available. Women also started looking for work in far higher numbers, resulting in a sharp rise in both employment and unemployment rates for women in the relatively higher-suicide provinces. The authors conclude that the misery of unemployment was intensified by living in the midst of communities experiencing unprecedented prosperity. Higher suicide rates during the era of the Quiet Revolution in Quebec may reflect the same crushing impact of rising expectations followed by failure. Other studies suggest that there is a time lag of some nine months between becoming unemployed and experiencing suicidal thoughts and that people may slowly become adjusted to it after two years (ibid. 42).

A similarly complicated mix of prosperity and poverty seems to underlie the rising suicide rates in rural England studied by Middleton et.al. (2003). The index of social deprivation that they developed, using measures like unemployment rates, overcrowded living conditions, households that are renting rather than owning, and the like, was not statistically associated with suicide rates. But the practice of wealthy city families buying up rural property may have obscured the reality of widespread rural poverty. Studies of rising suicide rates in rural Australian communities do suggest that increasing poverty, relative to larger towns, was a significant factor (Bourke 2003; Cantor et. al., 1995). Rural unemployment rates were particularly high among young people, especially males in the 15–24 age range. People in these small towns were reluctant to discuss suicides, although most knew someone who had done it. When they talked, they used terms like 'waste', 'shame' and 'poor mental health' that carried the implication of personal failure. Suicides are committed by sick individuals who fail to contribute productively to their society. The pervasive sense of shame inhibited people who were experiencing suicidal thoughts and feelings from seeking professional help, thus contributing to the problem. Whatever conclusions we draw from these complex data, there is little doubt that unemployment is an extremely stressful experience for workers and their families. Unemployment is associated with high levels of anxiety, depression, fear, loneliness, insomnia, headaches and stomach problems (Horwitz 1984).

Suicide and Alienation in Aboriginal Communities

Marxist analysis of suicide rates among aboriginal peoples focuses attention on the colonial destruction of indigenous economies. Few Canadian studies have explicitly employed a Marxist framework to address suicide rates, but all reports document the extremes of poverty and unemployment that characterize most aboriginal reservation communities in Canada. It is important to recognize that Marxist theoretical analysis involves more than a simplistic assertion that poverty leads to misery and suicide. The concept of alienation refers explicitly to the loss of human relationships, justice and meaning in work. Giving Aboriginal people larger welfare cheques does not resolve alienation at this deeper level. Some reservations in Canada have benefited from lucrative oil revenues but measures of social breakdown, including suicide rates, remain high. Welfare payments do not provide any sense of meaningful participation in interdependent networks of human production.

Marxist analysis suggests that the functionalist-inspired solution of promoting aboriginal cultural revival is likely to fail for the same reasons. Marxist theory views culture as emerging from practical lived experience. Culture cannot float free from economic realities. Indigenous hunting and gathering economies fostered a communal and egalitarian spirituality that values the intimate connection between humanity and the natural world. A reservation economy based on welfare payments or individual wage-work cannot sustain these cultural values. Nothing short of a total reorganization of indigenous economies, ideally along communal lines, and based on sustainable economic resources, seems likely to achieve a lasting solution.

Suicide Rates as Social Constructions

The social constructionist approach to the study of suicide explores the active practices of people in particular local settings that produce the phenomenon of 'suicide rates', and particularly the practices used by professionals to gather evidence, categorize it, and interpret it to produce our understanding of risk factors and causes that we associate with 'suicidal behaviour'. This approach reminds us that knowledge inherently involves potential relations of power and control. What we know about suicidal behaviour, and more importantly, what we think we know and *how* we know it, are not simply matters of academic debate. Statistics and reports about suicide rates have immediate practical relevance for government policies and the practices of social services workers rely on such studies and reports to decide how best to intervene in peoples' lives to reduce the incidence of suicidal behaviour.

Durkheim's classic study, like many others inspired by it, relied on cause-of-death statistics kept by government agencies to test his theory of how weak or excessive integration and regulation influence suicidal behaviour. Constructionist analysis suggests that the patterns that Durkheim found in these statistics are not necessarily accurate as descriptions of causes of death. Rather, they reflect the decision-making practices of innumerable coroners working in a multitude of differ-

ent jurisdictions (Douglas 1967). Douglas suggests that when coroners decide how to classify cause-of-death in ambiguous cases, they routinely rely on many of the very same common-sense theoretical assumptions that Durkheim himself was looking for.

It may seem simple and unambiguous enough at first glance to make decisions about how someone died. But consider some of the following situations. A man dies when his car crashes at high speed into a tree; or dies from carbon-monoxide poisoning when his car engine is running in a closed garage; a women dies from an overdose of sleeping pills; or is found dead in her room with the doors and windows stuffed shut and the gas coming from an unlit heater. A coroner who assigns the label *suicide* to such cases, in effect, assigns responsibility for the death to the individual who has died. But how does one make such decisions? Was the car crash just an accident, or did the man intentionally drive full speed into a stationary object in the realistic expectation that this would end it all, while still permitting the family to claim his life insurance? Did the woman intentionally take an overdose of pills in order to die, or did she simply wake up in the night confused and half drugged and take some more pills without being conscious of what she was doing? Or again, did she intend only to take a nonlethal dose as a cry for attention or help? Did the old woman intend to gas herself, or had she simply stuffed the cracks to keep out the cold and become a victim when the gas fire did not ignite properly or blew out? Suicide, by definition, means intentional self-death, but did these people intend to die? We cannot know for certain because we cannot ask the dead.

The label *suicide* imputes motives after the fact, and coroners can only do this by guesswork, by looking for suicide notes, or by asking witnesses or close family members, and then deciding whether it was likely this person intended to die. This line of reasoning leads to other questions. How many witnesses were consulted with respect to assumed motives? One might get different answers from an estranged wife or from a Catholic priest. Suicide rates are the outcome of decisions such as these. Their "factual" character is much more problematic than the neat tables in Statistics Canada reports would have us believe.

Douglas challenges all the patterns that Durkheim claims to have found. As a first step, Douglas shows that huge changes in suicide rates occurred when the method of counting changes. In Prussia in 1868, for example, Catholic priests kept the records of suicides. The rate jumped 50 percent in one year when the methods were reformed and civilian officials began keeping the rates. Similar jumps occurred in the official statistics in Austria, Hungary, and Italy when recording methods changed. Douglas concludes that changes of between 10 and 50 percent can be attributed to methods of collection alone. Durkheim's tests of his theories of suicide causation often rely on smaller differences than these. Hence, the possibility arises that the patterns Durkheim describes might reflect more how different coroners did their work than how different social factors influenced suicidal behaviour.

Douglas further suggests that all the reasons hypothesized by Durkheim as causes of low social cohesion, and hence higher suicide rates, are the same reasons that influence coroners to make their decisions one way rather than the other. During the period in which Durkheim did his study, suicide was considered a mortal sin for Catholics and was sufficient grounds for denying them a Christian burial. One can realistically expect that when Catholic priests kept the rates, they would go to great lengths to give the benefit of the doubt to the deceased and list the death as accidental, and that Catholic family members would do likewise. Protestant record keepers and witnesses would not be under such pressure. Douglas shows that Catholic cantons in Switzerland recorded fewer suicides than did Protestant cantons, but more accidents. Douglas concludes that different rates may reflect different concealment and not real differences in the propensity of Catholics and Protestants to kill themselves.

Douglas suggests, similarly, that all the conditions of higher social integration listed by Durkheim are associated with a higher propensity, and ability, to cover up a suicide. When a person is married and has children, these family members are likely to want to influence a coroner to see the death as accidental, while a divorced person living alone has no one to speak for him or her. Members of a small rural community might be more likely to close ranks and cover up damning evidence of a suicide in their midst than neighbours in a loosely integrated city area. Durkheim was correct in claiming that the number of deaths officially classified as suicides is lower among Catholics, married people, and villagers, but differences in rates may be solely an artifact of how coroners were influenced to make their decisions. Smith (1983a) goes further than Douglas in demonstrating the essential circularity of theory and data in studies of suicide. She cites cases showing that witnesses and family members, as well as coroners, rely upon theories about motives for committing suicide when they produce accounts of what happened.

Consider the man who crashes his car into a tree. People generally believe that a married man with children is unlikely to commit suicide, but that a divorced man who keeps to himself might well be miserable and potentially suicidal. Thus, if the victim were a married man, friends might well comment, when questioned by a coroner, that he was a happy man, a bit reckless with the car, perhaps, and so assure themselves and the coroner that it was an accident. If the victim were divorced, friends would be much more likely to comment that they had always feared that he would do something terrible to himself, poor man, how miserable he must have been, and thus convince themselves and the coroner that his death was probably a suicide. All that is needed for people to become convinced of the truth of their speculation is for like-minded people to reinforce their interpretation. People tend retrospectively to pick out the incidents that support their emerging theory, and they downplay evidence to the contrary. Experts who analyse such accounts for features of suicidal behaviour are likely to discover in them the theories that people use when they put their accounts together.

In defence of Durkheim's study, Durkheim was aware that available statistics were shaky but judged them good enough for his purpose. More recent studies routinely do check for obvious shifts and inconsistencies in how officials compile statistics. Douglas himself was more interested in researching how coroners do their work than testing the validity of official statistics. While he speculates that coroners and witnesses might engage in systematic bias and cover-up in reporting suicides, he does not offer evidence that this actually happens.

Ideological Practices in Suicide Research

Constructionist analysis focuses attention on how evidence is structured by the methods people use to gather it, and the standpoint or interpretive frame that guides what people pay attention to. Most of the what we know about suicide rates among Canadian aboriginal peoples is gathered under the direction of federal and provincial government agencies, and structured to be useful to the various professionals—social workers, mental-health workers, and teachers, employed by the governments to work with aboriginal communities. How these professionals understand the causes of suicide influence what researchers pay attention to, the kinds of evidence highlighted or ignored, the connections found within the evidence, and by extension, the policies recommended to address the extremely high suicide rates found within aboriginal communities.

Constructionist analysis prompts us to think about this diverse body of research as forms of discourse, or ways of talking about experiences, rather than as sets of factual knowledge. To get a sense of how significant this shift in perspective can be, we look at Tester and McNicholl's (2004) critique of research on high suicide rates among the Inuit of Northern Canada.

Research from the Standpoint of Government: Problems that Inuit Have

The methodology most frequently used by sociologists is quantitative survey research that asks large samples of people about socio-psychological risk factors associated with suicidal attempts and feelings (Kirchmayer et. al., 1996; 1998). Family problems are strongly associated with suicide attempts. High risk factors include having been adopted, having parents who are separated or dead, having alcoholic or drug-addicted parents, experience of being sexually abused, especially by close relatives, and having friends or relatives who have attempted or committed suicide. Individual factors associated with suicidal behaviour include drug and alcohol abuse, self perception of poor health and having a personal mental health problem in the previous year. Qualitative case-study research complements survey data in exploring in greater depth the mal-adaptive parenting strategies that contribute to family disorganization. Briggs (1995) draws attention to what she sees as bonding problems between Inuit parents and children. These are manifest in contradictory practices like intense attachment to and over-protection of children combined with aggressive and rejecting behaviour as parents try to compensate by pushing adolescents out of the home. A high death rate in Inuit communities from epidemics of smallpox, measles, and influenza contribute to such dysfunctional child-rearing practices, as do memories of residential schools, and the necessity of adolescents leaving isolated communities to attend high school.

Extensive mental-health diagnostic research within aboriginal communities has also unearthed evidence of widespread diagnosable mental illness, including high levels of anxiety-neurosis, psychosis, and schizophrenia (Sampath 1976; Travis 1990). Possible causes include the effects of extreme isolation and genetic inbreeding in small communities, particularly among very isolated northern communities. Yet other research focuses on cultural factors associated with social disorganization at community level (Balikci 1970; Kral 1998; Kirmayer et.

al., 1996,1998). On the one hand the loss of traditional religious and social values are associated with a loss of identity and low self esteem at the individual level. On the other hand, traditional cultural patterns that were once appropriate for life in small-scale, nomadic hunter-gatherer communities are identified as dysfunctional for adaptation to modern industrial societies.

This extensive and diverse body of research guides comprehensive intervention strategies by social workers, health professionals, law-enforcement officers and teachers (*Royal Commission on Aboriginal Peoples* 1995). Family social workers use survey data on high risk factors to help identify individuals at risk of committing suicide, and to intervene in pathological family units. When felt necessary, children can be removed from dysfunctional families and placed in foster homes or hostels. Case-study research by Briggs, guides professionals in implementing parenting-skills classes, counselling services, and programs for early intervention in problem families. Evidence of extensive mental illness has been used to pressure the Canadian government to commit high levels of funding to increase the numbers of mental-health professionals in these communities. Policing has expanded in an effort to stem the tide of drug trafficking and curb alcoholism. Educational programs have been developed for schools that attempt to re-socialize children to help them bridge the immense gap between traditional Inuit culture and the culture of modern Western societies. These programs typically incorporate traditional stories, arts and crafts, and where possible, courses in native languages, with the goal of fostering a positive self identity among children. At the same time schools promote exposure to television, computers, and the internet, that teach the norms and values more appropriate for modern Western industrial society.

Intensive suicide-prevention programs along these lines have been widely instituted in Inuit and other aboriginal communities over the last twenty years. New studies repeat the calls on the Canadian government to expand these programs still further and to ensure that all professionals work together to integrate their services. Yet, despite this mountain of research and well-intentioned professional commitment to bring suicide rates down, the results have been dismal. Suicide rates continue to rise, and evidence from program-evaluation research indicates that suicide levels in communities with comprehensive prevention programs are no lower than in communities without them (Leenaars and Lester 2004: Breton et. al., 1998).

Research from the Standpoint of the Inuit: Problems Caused by Colonial Rule

Research from the Inuit standpoint reverses the direction of the gaze. Rather than focussing on problems within their communities, the gaze turns outwards to focus on the practices that colonial governments have imposed on them. Consider how you and members of your own family might feel if you endured the following experiences: Imagine that everyone you know is rounded up, without any consultation or explanation, and confined to a small settlement far from where you once lived. Strangers take over the lands you once lived on and flood them for hydro development, so you cannot ever go back. Meanwhile, all your family members lose whatever means of livelihood they once had. Now you live on welfare. In your new settlement area you experience a litany of acts of great cruelty. Your family dogs are shot dead by police, meaning that you lose both your pets and your primary means of transportation (dog-sleds), and you also lose any hope of hunting for food. Your new settlement area is constantly monitored and controlled by foreign police; your community affairs administered by foreign agents; your religious beliefs and practices are criminalized; and your traditions openly denigrated by these foreign agents, who refer to your family members as stupid, ignorant, and primitive. In effect, everyone you know is confined to an open prison. Then the greatest act of cruelty of all. Every child between the ages of 6 and 16, in every family you know, is forcibly removed from home and placed in prisons a thousand miles away. Parents and children have no means to communicate with each other for the ten years that children are confined. When your children are finally released you barely recognize each other, and you cannot talk easily because you no longer speak a common language. You can find nothing to do. Young people can marry and have children of their own, but you know that these children in turn will be taken away by foreign government agents when they reach six years of age. Would it be surprising if you and people you loved became suicidal under such conditions, or that you turned to alcohol and drugs to deaden your sense of helplessness and shame? All these conditions and worse have been experienced by indigenous peoples in Canada.

Within this reversed gaze, the evidence of suicidal behaviour amassed by colonial researchers takes on new meanings. The multitude of 'risk factors' identified in survey research as causes of suicide appear as merely spurious. Alcoholism, addictions, suicides, psychoses, and family dysfunctions all become visible as symptoms of the same underlying experience of colonisation. These symptoms are endlessly reinforced in vicious cycles that cannot be broken so long as the underlying condition of colonization remains. People who feel helpless either to provide for themselves or to protect or even hold on to their own children are likely to exhibit the pathologies found in these studies. Elders too traumatized and ashamed to talk about their experiences with young people cannot make strong leaders.

The conditions of overt colonial oppression described above have thankfully retreated but their legacy remains. White social workers may do the best they know how to intervene in at-risk families to try to protect another generation of children from harm. But from the standpoint of the colonized, these social workers retain their awful powers to take children away. One of the greatest fears of families on welfare, as we shall see in the chapter on 'Family' is the power of social workers to remove children from parents who are considered failures. White police officers, along with Native colleagues, may do their best to stem the scourge of drug trafficking and alcohol. But they represent the same law-enforcement officers who, in earlier times, forced families to move, shot the dogs, enforced child removals, and legalized the pillage of traditional lands by foreign corporations. White teachers may do their utmost to teach the skills needed to adjust to Western society. But in the colonizer's gaze these represent the same authority figures who crushed already traumatized children in residential schools.

Mainstream sociologists may also do their best to research the conditions underlying suicide rates as objectively as possible but their theoretical discourse for the most part continues to blame the colonized for their own victimization (Tester and McNicholl 2004). The discourse of "social disorganization" faults traditional cultures for failure to adapt to change, or failure to adjust to the demands of modernization. But the discourse omits the horrific details about what changed, and how changes were brought about, and by whom such changes were enforced. The discourse of "loosely-integrated societies" borrows from Durkheim's theories but ignores the outside controls and forces that produce and perpetuate such weak integration in aboriginal communities. The discourse of "risk factors" incorporates moral judgements about blame. Mothers whose own lives are filled with misery are blamed for the foetal alcohol syndrome that renders their children exceptionally hard to care for. The hopeful discourse of "narratives" that encourages elders to talk and to recreate lost traditional cultures ignores the history of colonialism that undermines their capacity to talk. The discourse of "social isolation" ignores the systemic marginalization and racism that perpetuates this isolation. The discourse of "mental health professionals" ignores the long history of shame and distrust of whites, and the continuing politics of power that trigger the symptoms of psychosis that psychiatrists diagnose as illness.

From the standpoint of the colonized, solutions to the problem of escalating suicide rates lie not in ameliorative programs traditionally proposed, but in the end of colonialism itself. This entails the settlement of land claims, the return of sufficient resources for economic self sufficiency as communities, and compensation for exploited resources on traditional lands. It also requires structures that return political autonomy to communities, and ensure political power for First Nations communities in the heart of colonial Canadian government. It further requires an end to the ongoing colonizing practices within the centres of Canadian cities, manifest in the continuing displacement of First Nations peoples.

In summary, this shift in standpoint from the gaze of the colonizers to the gaze of the colonized does not invalidate the evidence gathered by survey research, mental health studies, case studies, and cultural studies describe above. But it does profoundly alter how we understand this evidence, the causal connections we infer among facets of evidence, and the conclusions we draw. The shift in standpoint also affects the direction of future research, focussing attention on the legal structures and institutional practices that perpetuate the colonial experience. Objectivity in social science research thus depends less on the methods we use to gather evidence than on the deliberate adoption of different standpoints. Aboriginal researchers have called explicitly for more 'decolonizing methodologies' (Smith 1999) that take as their starting point the issues and questions crucial to indigenous peoples around the world.

Feminist Theory: Suicide as Gendered Practice

Suicide is cleared gendered behaviour. Rates for committed suicides and for attempted suicides differ markedly for women and men. But they differ in opposite directions. In Canada, as in most Western societies, men kill themselves far more often that women, but women attempt suicide far more often than men. Theoretical explanations differ markedly, depending on which statistic is given primacy.

Firstly with respect to completed suicide rates, official statistics across Western societies from Durkheim's time to the present show that suicide rates for men are significantly higher than for women. Statistics Canada Health Reports for 2004 (Volume 15, 2) cites the male suicide rate as 21.8 per 100 000 compared with 5.4 for women—a ratio of 4:1. Among Canadian youth in the age range 15–24 the ratio is as high as 5.2:1. Comparable World Health Organization data reports suicide rates for the United States as 17.1 per 100 000 for males and 4.0 for females. For the United Kingdom 11.8 for males and 3.3 for females; and for France 26.1 for males and 9.4 for females (www.who.int/mental_health/prevention/suicide/) These gaps are so consistent and so large that suicide is widely described as "a masculine behaviour" (Neuringer and Lettieri 1982, 14, 15).

On the other hand, reported suicide *attempts* have consistently show higher rates for women. Statistics Canada health Reports (Volume 13, 2) shows the hospitalization rate for females as 108 per 100 000 and 70 for males. For the most vulnerable age group 15–19 the comparative rates were 221 for females to 87 for males, a ratio of over 2.5:1. Since the number of attempts is several times greater than the number of completed suicides, the combined figures suggest that women may have a higher overall rate of suicidal behaviour.

Feminist research generally gives more weight to the high frequency of attempted over completed suicides, suggesting that the combined numbers for completed and attempted suicide give a more valid measure of suicidal behaviour generally. Counted in this way, it is women who are more depressed and suicidal than men, by a ratio of 2.5:1, notwithstanding their lower death rates. This view is supported by separate medical evidence that shows twice as many women as men in Canada diagnosed with depressive illnesses and prescribed anti-depressant medication (Stoppard and McMullen 2003, 1; McMullen 2003, 18).

The explanations offered for higher rates of depression among women parallel those described above with respect to Inuit suicide rates. A straightforward explanation is physiology—depressed people are thought to have lower brain-serotonin levels, a condition that can be remedied with drugs. But physiology alone will not account for wide variation in rates of depressive illness across communities. Changes in brain chemistry may themselves be triggered by socio-psychological factors that promote feelings of depression. Sociological explanations focus attention on contradictory cultural pressures and demands placed on women in contemporary western societies. Women are pushed to fulfil the roles of youthful sexual idols, wives and mothers, and career women, often simultaneously. Women readily absorb cultural values that admire autonomous individuals with freedom, responsibility and achievement, and then blame themselves for failing to live up to the image (McMullen 2003, 32). Mothers of young children often find themselves juggling the multiple demands and stresses of paid job, caring for husband, caring for children, and running a home, managing on limited sleep and without time to care for themselves. They may pressure husbands to help, but the majority do not (Hochschild 1989). Alternatively, Women may find themselves outside the social loop, isolated and undervalued as full-time homemakers, dependent on husband or welfare for the survival of themselves and their children. Such dependence makes these women especially vulnerable to domestic abuse. Gendered economic inequalities, as we will see in later chapters, are reflected in the feminization of poverty. Women in the labour force are concentrated in a much narrower range of occupations than men, and typically earn less money. Patriarchal social structures result in women having unequal access to positions of power and influence in most sectors of society.

Women may feel much anger about their situation but be culturally inhibited from outwardly expressing it. Anger turned inwards may promote both depression and suicidal feelings (Jack 2003).

Suicide Rates Among Men

When the focus shifts from suicidal attempts to committed suicides, men are clearly the primary victims in Western societies. In Canada, the ratio is between 4 an 5 male deaths to 1 female death from suicide in all age cohorts from 15 to 75 and older. Men are less frequently diagnosed with depression than women. Yet they seem to be less protected from falling into the depth of despair that leads to suicide.

The classic explanation posed for the higher rates of completed suicides for men invokes a mixture of biology and socialization (Lester 1997, ch. 12). The argument suggests that males are naturally more aggressive, especially young men with high testosterone levels. Males are also socialized to be more physically violent than females, and to externalize their anger. Males who kill themselves are more likely to use violent means like

guns and knives. Women are more likely to use passive means like drug overdoses, or cutting their wrists—means that are less likely to result in quick death. This line of reasoning further implies that women may be more suicidal than men but less effective at carrying out the act.

An alternative argument is that suicide attempts in general may be a distinctively different form of behaviour from completed suicides, and reflect different motives. Attempts may be more a cry for help or attention, rather than a failed attempt to kill oneself. However, this may be true also for some of the committed suicides. There is no way to be sure. There is some evidence to suggest that men and women may have different motives for killing themselves—based on a small study of 264 suicide notes in Australia, of which 198 were left by men. Notes left by women suggested a theme of wanting to die or wanting to escape. Notes left by men more often expressed anger towards others and a desire to make them suffer, especially with respect to thwarted love affairs (Lester et. al, 2004).

Research into social conditions that may differentially protect women and men from committing suicide continues to draw heavily on Durkheim's classic theory of levels of societal integration and regulation. Durkheim reasoned that strong social bonds between people, and especially the bonds of marriage and family, offered the best protection from egoistic suicide. He predicted that married people would have lower suicide rates than never married or divorced and widowed people. The presence of children, he predicted, would strengthen this protection. These predictions worked in all cases for men. But there was one significant exception for women. Married women without children were *not* protected more than unmarried women. The presence of children offered protection, but not the state of marriage itself.

To account for this anomaly, Durkheim reasoned that men needed the constraints of marriage more than women. Single and divorced men, without the constraints of marriage, were likely to engage in sexually loose behaviour with many different women, be unable to find any satisfaction or regulation in their lives, and fall into despair. Women, in contrast, are more strongly constrained by societal norms—perhaps even overly constrained. The state of marriage thus did not offer significantly more protection from loss of regulation.

Durkheim's theory is difficult to test with government statistics because data on suicides by marital status rarely indicate whether or not the victims had children. Suicide rates are lower for married than single women, as they are for men, but married women are also far more likely to have children than single women. An interesting test situation that Besnard exploits for research occurred in France between 1973–1975 (Besnard 2000). A combination of legal and social changes resulted in a sharp increase in divorce rates and a decline in rate of first marriages. Besnard reasons that during this period the state of marriage as a social institution was weakened. If Durkheim's theory is correct, a weakening of the marital institution would lower the protection against suicide that marriage affords men, relative to single men. Conversely, the weakening of the institution of marriage would improve the situation for married women because of the greater option of getting out. Besnard found the data consistent with these predictions, thus supporting Durkheim's theory. Strong marital institutions protect men, he argues, but may produce an excess of restraint for women, hence slightly increasing the risk of fatalistic suicide.

Marital Institutions and Suicide Rates Cross-culturally

Comparative evidence from non-European societies provides opportunities to test these generalizations further. The evidence Durkheim used to develop his model was confined to European states, but national statistics are now available virtually worldwide. Comparative data challenge the assumption that suicide rates for men are universally higher than for women. Lester (1997) found that death rates from suicide continue to be significantly higher for men than women across all Western societies. However male/female ratios are more even in Asian nations. In the special case of China, suicide rates are higher for women. These data contradict the argument noted above that biological characteristics like testosterone levels make men innately more violent and prone to suicide than women. They also contradict the argument that women are innately less capable of killing themselves than men. However, they support Durkheim's argument that an excess of regulation in collectivist societies like Japan and China increases the risk of fatalistic suicide.

A case study of suicide in rural China (Meng 2002) offers a particularly vivid illustration of fatalistic suicide. The article recounts a harrowing story of the life and death by suicide of a woman who challenged cultural norms by marrying for love against the wishes of her parents and mother-in-law. She then faced rejection and unrelenting harassment from her in-laws who branded her a troublemaker. Her husband sided with his parents in beating her for showing disrespect to his mother. Her efforts to get away failed as she would have had to abandon her children. Only after her death did she gain some revenge. Her suicide publicly shamed her in-laws, and her natal family demanded extensive compensation and an elaborate funeral. Behind this one story is a backdrop of rigid controls over women's lives, enforced by powerful vested interests.

One of the implications of this international evidence is that suicide rates are likely to differ for ethnic minorities living in the West. The Statistics Canada Health Report (Volume 15, 2) on committed suicides show lower rates for immigrants overall than for the Canadian born. The Report's authors suggest that these differences may reflect the greater social integration of immigrant communities, especially in large cities like Toronto, Montreal, and Vancouver. The gap between suicide rates for women and men is smaller than among the Canadian born—a ratio of 2.7 men for 1 woman among immigrants compared with 4 to 1 for Canadian born. Immigrant males thus have significantly lower rates of suicide than Canadian-born males, while the pattern for immigrant and Canadian-born women is closer.

An important qualification in the interpretation of these data is the distinction drawn above between completed suicides and suicide attempts or self harm. The Statistics Canada Report on hospitalization for suicide attempts does not show this breakdown. However, a study in Britain (Bhardwaj 2001) reports that among Asian females in the age range 15–35, incidents of suicide and self-harm combined are 2–3 times higher than for white, African and Caribbean female counterparts. Self-harm is defined as overdosing on drugs, slashing or burning themselves, and eating disorders. Bhardwaj describes women in these communities as subject to increasingly rigid social controls. They are held responsible for maintaining community and family honour. Any deviation from rigidly defined family and marital roles are severely punished. Speaking out about domestic violence is defined as bringing public shame on a family, and itself heavily sanctioned, as is any attempt by women to leave their family. When a woman feels she has no control over anything else, Bhardwaj suggests, the last remaining site for control is her own body. Refusing to eat, slashing herself, burning herself, and swallowing pills offer small acts of defiance. Women talked about the sense of temporary release they felt from self harm, and also their hope that such acts might draw attention from family members and bring about some positive changes in their lives.

The code of silence imposed on women by the wider community, however, makes any intervention or treatment difficult. Culturally sensitive mental-health staff are important but not sufficient. A critical problem is that social workers and family physicians within the Asian communities commonly see themselves as 'self-appointed community caretakers'. They are known to side with their community rather than with individual female clients, and report confidences back to family members. Women who expose their problems risk further revenge and punishment.

From the standpoint of the host society looking into minority communities, it is easy to locate the source of the problem in traditional Asian cultures that clash with more progressive or liberal Western culture of the host society. But when we gaze outwards from the standpoint of minority communities, other pressures come into view. Bhardwaj views the increasingly rigid practices of conformity and closure within Asian immigrant communities in Britain as themselves a form of reaction to racist and exclusionary practices in white British society. In Canada, Bannerji (2000) similarly sees the inward-looking closure of Asian communities as a response to practices that 'minoritize' non-white immigrants. National politics are in turn located in the wider framework of global struggles, particularly since the September 11th 2001 bombing of the World Trade Centre in New York, and the Pentagon. In Canada, and globally, claims to distinctive culture and religion are powerful levers for exerting political influence. The enhanced status of male elites as spokespersons for their communities with host-society officials, in turn depends upon maintaining strong internal cohesion, a central compo-

nent of which is control over women's behaviour as symbols of minority cultural integrity. This package of practices that constitute 'relations of ruling' from the standpoint of Asian women are explored in greater depth in the chapter on Race and Ethnic Relations.

Conclusion

Durkheim's analysis of the social foundations of suicidal behaviour has stood the test of one hundred years of further research, notwithstanding flaws in data collection and statistics. His theoretical model of weak and excessive integration and regulation leading to four distinctive kinds of suicide egoistic, anomic, altrustic and fatalistic, are still widely applied. His emphasis on the structural foundations of individual motivation is closer to Marxist thought than much contemporary research on individual risk factors. For Durkheim, as for Marx, modernization as such is not the cause of rising suicide rates, but rather how modernization is instituted. In Marxist analysis, egoism and anomie are symptoms of selfish individualism and cutthroat competition at the heart of capitalist economic relations. These values are in turn reflected in the individualistic focus on much contemporary research into 'risk-factors'. The other side of Durkheim's theoretical model, which focuses on conditions of excessive integration and regulation, and their reflection in altruistic and fatalistic suicides, becomes more significant when we move beyond a Eurocentric focus. The rise in altruistic suicide bombers in the Middle East, and fatalistic suicides among aboriginal peoples, and women in some Asian societies can both be seen as rooted in global practices of colonialism and racism.

CHAPTER 7

Sociology of Law and Deviance

 Functionalist Perspectives: Law and Social Order.

The Functionalist perspective views systems of law and criminal justice as central institutions that function to maintain social order and manage deviant behaviour that threatens this order. Law is seen as a formal statement of the moral rules of society, with the content of particular laws representing agreed codes of conduct that safeguard the well-being of the society as a whole. Crime constitutes the violation of normative rules of society, as codified in current standards of law. The criminal justice system functions to deter and punish crime. The system endeavours to reform offenders or to remove them from mainstream society.

Functionalism draws extensively on Durkheim's classical theoretical work, and particularly his concept of the *conscience collective* or common conscience, the body of shared norms, beliefs and sentiments that form the foundations of social cohesion. Durkheim used law as an objective, empirical basis for studying changes in the nature of social cohesion. In his seminal study *The Division of Labour in Society*, he traces the increasing prevalence of contract over penal law as societies change from relatively homogenous communities to highly differentiated industrial societies. He argues that this reflects a decline in the importance of shared culture or *conscience collective* relative to contractual obligations in maintaining social cohesion. The moral foundations of contract law, he concludes, are respect for justice and for individual human rights.

Early Canadian Law and Societal Values

The laws that settlers established in Canada were modelled initially on British and French common law. This body of law has evolved over time, with a major shift occurring in 1982, with the patriation of the constitution and the promulgation of the Canadian Charter of Rights and Freedoms. The history of laws governing immigration to Canada from the nineteenth century to the present are briefly highlighted below because they are particularly insightful in revealing shifts in normative values from those of white settler society to contemporary multiculturalism. These laws explicitly defined the kinds of people who were welcomed into Canada in various periods and those who were not.

Nineteenth century laws make it very clear that cultural homogeneity was far more strongly and centrally valued than individual justice or human rights. People from Britain and France were favoured while people from China, Japan and other parts of Asia were opposed. Section 38(c) of the Immigration Act of 1910 states clearly the concern of the time that newcomers share the customs and normative values that prevailed in societies of Britain and France, or be sufficiently similar that they could be expected to assimilate quickly into mainstream culture. Others were to be systematically excluded. Specifically to be denied entry were "any *nationality* or *race* of immigrants . . . *deemed unsuitable* having regard to the climatic, industrial, social, educational, labour [conditions] . . . or because such immigrants are deemed *undesirable* owing to their peculiar customs, habits, modes of life, methods of holding property and because of their probable inability to become readily assimilated or to assume the duties and responsibilities of Canadian citizenship within a reasonable time after their entry" (Jakubowski 1999, 104; emphasis in original). Chinese males were welcomed as labourers for mines and railroads, but a head tax and other restrictions blocked them from bringing wives and families. Continuous passage laws were designed to curtail immigrants from Asia. A "Gentleman's Agreement" with Japan permitted trade but minimized immigration. Jewish refugees from Nazi Germany were denied entry in 1939. All these actions, which now look blatantly discriminatory, conformed to the laws of the time. They were publically defended by political leaders as appropriate to ensure cultural cohesion and social order within the Dominion. The Indian Act of 1876, reflecting earlier provincial laws, was similarly designed to foster the rapid assimilation of indigenous peoples to Canadian European culture, or to pressure them onto separate reservations. Few people among mainstream white Canadians of the time saw reason to protest any of these laws.

The values of cultural conformity and Victorian morality that underlay restrictive immigration laws were further reflected in legislation designed to manage those immigrants who were approved. Middle-class women who organized the recruitment of women from Britain for domestic service explicitly wanted young, virtuous

"girls" who would be future mothers of the nation (Arat-Koc 1999, 129–132). People who conformed to values of middle-class decorum were sought. Not just anyone from Britain would do. Recruiters feared that lower class women would bring vices such as sexual license, drinking and gambling with them. Recruiters arranged for migrant women to be closely supervised to guard against sexual misconduct. Laws empowered Canadian authorities to deport anyone deemed "unsuitable", with the definition of "unsuitable" left sufficiently vague as to give maximum leeway to law enforcers. Further laws required that migrant women sign contracts before they left Britain to commit themselves to working for one year in a domestic service placement assigned to them—in effect binding them to indentured labour. These contracts had to be signed again immediately on arrival in Canada to ensure they were legally binding within Canadian provinces.

A host of other morality laws governing pornography, prostitution and homosexuality, dating back to before Confederation, were enforced with punitive religious justification in the name of ensuring social order. The same class of elite women who sponsored and chaperoned the new "mothers of the nation" had campaigned for the temperance movement, succeeding briefly in banning the manufacture, importation and sale of alcohol.

The Charter of Rights and Freedoms promulgated in 1982 followed the pattern Durkheim predicted in stressing individual human rights rather than cultural assimilation. Multicultural policies enacted in the 1970s and in the subsequent Canadian Multiculturalism Act of 1987 reinforced this shift in legal practice. The Charter formalized important principles to which all current and future laws must comply. The equality guarantees in Section 15(1) of the Charter means that any law that can be shown to be discriminatory is null and void. As a specific exception to this rule, Section 25 asserts that nothing in the Charter shall be construed as infringing or denying Aboriginal treaty rights, or other rights that they have acquired over the years. Section 27 of the Charter further defines Canada as officially bilingual and multicultural, with people having the right to preserve and enhance their multicultural heritage.

The Charter also provides that every individual within Canada has the right to life, liberty and security of the person, the right not to be arbitrarily detained or imprisoned, the right to a fair trial, to be presumed innocent until proven guilty, among other protections. Respect for justice and individual human rights, rather than cultural conformity, is now officially recognized in law as the foundation of social cohesion. The official symbol of law is a blindfolded maiden, untouched and uncorrupted and blind to differences of race and social status, carrying the scales of justice (Comack 1999, 21). The judiciary that administers law is formally separate from the legislature that makes law. The practice of law is also bound by the principle of precedent, intended to ensure that the law treats every case in legally comparable ways.

Individual Rights or Social Cohesion? A Clash of Concerns.

From the functionalist perspective, the major question surrounding the Charter is how to reconcile the need for cultural consensus to ensure social cohesion and order with the divisive potential inherent in respect for individual diversity and rights. Political leaders in the province of Quebec refused to endorse the Charter of Rights and Freedoms in 1982 because of their concerns that the Charter provided insufficient protection for the distinctive francophone culture of Quebec. Virtually all references to Durkheim's theoretical writings in sociological studies on law, focus on his concept of *conscience collective*. His model of organic solidarity between specialized and interdependent people, based on respect for individual diversity and human rights, is generally ignored. Many Charter challenges that have come before the Supreme Court have pitted guarantees of individual rights against the restriction in the opening clause that such rights and freedoms are subject to "reasonable limits" that can be "justified in a free and democratic society".

Laws that govern immigration, or the types of people welcomed or discouraged from entering Canada, have changed markedly since the early 1960s to eliminate any explicit reference to racial and cultural characteristics. Laws like those once enacted against Chinese and other Asian workers are now unconstitutional. What the functionalist perspective sensitizes us to, however, is how the practical implementation of immigration law is still slanted in favour of immigrants who share mainstream western cultural backgrounds, notwithstanding the far larger numbers of non-Western and non-white immigrants. The points system, with its emphasis on fluency in English or French and higher educational qualifications that fit exactly with Canadian models, the discretionary powers given to administrators, and the physical location of the maximum number of visa offices, all work to favour cultural conformity (Jakubowski 1999).

Laws that create a special status of "guest workers" for "underqualified" domestic workers, continue to make it very difficult for women from the Caribbean to obtain landed immigrant status (Arat-Koc 1999). People who are rejected as immigrants have little opportunity to challenge their exclusion.

The foundational Charter principle of individual human rights is itself being challenged in the climate of heightened fear of terrorism after the attacks on the World Trade Centre in New York and the Pentagon on September 11, 2001. Canadian governments in the past have claimed that suspension of human rights is justifiable in exceptional circumstances in the interests of protecting the security and order of the society as a whole. In October 1970 the Trudeau Government called on the War Measures Act, first passed in 1914, to suspend civil liberties in response to the kidnapping of two politicians by the terrorist *Front de Libération du Québec* (FLQ). One of the two hostages was murdered. During the 3 months in which War Measures were in force some 450 people were detained in Quebec, most of whom were eventually freed without being charged with any criminal offence. It remains contentious whether these measures were justified. Some believe they were useful in controlling terrorism in Quebec, while others argue that terrorism was averted by the growth of a democratic separatist movement in the 1970s, leading to the election of the *Parti Québécois* government in 1976 (Smith 1988, 1558). The War Measures Act itself was not nullified by the Charter of Rights, although it has not been used since 1970.

The Charter in principle guarantees to everyone the right of habeas corpus—the right not to be arbitrarily detained or imprisoned, the right to a prompt trial with legal representation, and to be presumed innocent until proven guilty. But since the September 11 attacks, the Canadian government has suspended these rights for at least five individuals suspected of possible involvement in planning terrorist activities, in the higher interest of protecting society as a whole. Security Certificates issued by the Solicitor General hold these individuals in long-term detention although they have not been explicitly charged or convicted of any offence. The government lacks sufficient evidence to convict them in open court, but claims sufficient covert information to fear that they might conspire to commit acts of terrorism if released. Three years after the September 11th attacks, no Charter challenge had been launched in their defence. In the United States far larger numbers of people are being held as security risks under similar exceptional legislation. Rights of habeas corpus have been totally denied to several thousand people detained on suspicion that they might be aiding or planning terrorist activities. It has also become common practice for refugees admitted to the USA to be detained in prison for months, and in some cases for years, pending administrative investigation of their cases (Detention Watch Network News Issues 14–18 2000–2001). These individuals are presumed to be a potential threat to social order and security until they can prove themselves to be harmless. In Canada small numbers of refugees take sanctuary in church basements for months, and sometimes years at a time to avoid deportation while pleading for reviews of their cases. The argument that lax immigration or refugee laws threaten the security of Canada as a whole is hard to counter. However, it is also clear that concern to protect the security of Canada from possible terrorist activity has compromised Charter principles in exceptional cases, and members of ethnic minority groups are the people most affected. Individuals have been picked up, interrogated, deported, and tortured in the name of possibly extracting information on potential terrorism. These issues will be considered in more depth in later chapters.

Law and Moral Order

An important assumption within the functionalist perspective is that commitment to a shared cultural system of normative beliefs, values and sentiments is a necessary foundation for social order. This does not mean that cultural beliefs can never change. Current standards of sexual behaviour have clearly changed significantly from Victorian standards of the nineteenth century. What functionalism does assume is that some recognized and widely respected normative system is necessary. The legal system functions to specify the boundaries of acceptable behaviour. As soon as the Charter of Rights and Freedoms was promulgated, challenges were raised as to how much personal freedom individuals could or would be granted to transgress mainstream norms before they would be subject to "reasonable limits prescribed by law".

In the influential Butler decision on pornography in 1992, the Supreme Court came down strongly on the side of community standards rather than individual freedom (Johnson 1999). The Butler case began in 1987 when Winnipeg police seized the entire inventory of a pornographic video store owned by Donald Butler, and charged him with 250 violations of section 163(8) of the

Criminal Code concerning possession of obscene materials. Butler appealed to the Supreme Court on the grounds that this law contravened his rights under section 2 of the Charter guaranteeing "freedom of thought, belief, opinion, and expression". The court upheld the reasoning that community standards of tolerance for obscenity should legitimately limit public access to obscene material in the interest of the proper functioning of society. The Court did not explicitly define these community standards, but argued that they should properly be determined by jurors for individual cases, with due sensitivity to local community standards. Following this decision, the Butler case went back to trial and Butler was convicted on most of the original charges. Subsequently, customs officers responsible for controlling the flow of pornographic materials across Canadian borders seized quantities of material destined for bookstores catering to gay and lesbian customers, as well as pornography that uses children. Customs officers judged homosexual erotica as potentially more threatening to Canadian values than traditional erotica destined for heterosexual males.

Crime Rates and Weakening Civil Order

The functionalist perspective views some level of crime as normal. Any behaviour that transgresses legally defined boundaries of acceptable behaviour constitutes crime. The concept of deviance encompasses a broader range of non-conformist behaviours that transgress normative expectations of society without necessarily breaking specific laws. The criminal justice system punishes law-breakers, and in so doing, functions to clarify and uphold the legally permissible limits of behaviour for the majority of conforming members of society.

What counts from the functionalist perspective is not the fact that some crime occurs, but the rate of criminal behaviour in the population, and particularly the high crime rates among certain sectors of the population. Increases in rates of criminal behaviour are viewed as symptoms of a weakening of community life. Most functionalist research into criminal behaviour focuses on conditions of failed socialization, where community standards and values are not adequately transmitted, efforts to identify types of people most prone to commit crimes, and techniques of deterrence. Various theories within this broad perspective include anomie, differential opportunity, differential association, and deviant subculture.

The Anomie Theory of Crime

The concept of anomie, as developed by Durkheim, refers to a relative absence or confusion of values and a corresponding lack of clear regulations or norms for behaviour. People feel lost and unsure of what to believe in or how to behave. Robert Merton (1968) systematized this concept into a general model, **the anomie theory of crime**, sometimes referred to as **strain theory**, to classify types of deviant behaviour and conditions in which high rates might be expected. Merton argues that deviance is a symptom of dissociation between culturally valued goals and socially approved means to achieve them. Strains develop because not everyone has the means needed to attain goals they have learned to value. Merton's model defines the five logically possible ways to respond to this situation (see table 7-1). **Conformists** accept both culturally valued goals and socially acceptable means to achieve them. Such people must constitute a majority of the population in any given society for that society to be stable or orderly. **Innovators** accept cultural goals such as material success but use illicit means such as theft, prostitution, or drug trafficking to achieve them. Merton suggests that this category accounts for the relatively high crime rates found among lower-class people. **Ritualists** give up on culturally valued goals, no longer even trying to attain them. They ritualistically obey the rules and conform to outward behaviour patterns but have no motivation to succeed. **Retreatists** reject both goals and means, withdrawing into various forms of apathy. Merton suggests that hobos, dropouts, skid-road alcoholics and drug addicts fit into this category. Drugs provide a retreat for those who have failed in society. Finally, **rebels** are people who generate new goals and means. One example would be political activists who reject the values of money, individualism and competition associated with capitalist consumer culture and favour alternative forms of social organization like communes.

Merton's typology is valuable for drawing attention to unequal opportunities and the strains generated by inequality. It accounts for the high rates of crime among poor people and disadvantaged minority groups in terms of the greater obstacles they face in achieving the success goals of the dominant culture.

Control theory, developed by Travis Hirschi (1969) focusses attention on the first category in Merton's model. Hirschi predicts that conformity to mainstream behavioural norms is most likely when individuals build strong attachments to conventional others, and are committed to and frequently involved in conventional activities through family, school, and church. A rise in rates of deviance are caused by erosion of ties to family and church, and reduced involvement in community activities.

The **differential opportunity theory** of delinquency developed by Cloward and Ohlin (1960) complements Merton's model by suggesting that access to criminal opportunities may explain why some nonconformists become deviant innovators while others remain ritualists or retreatists. Deviant careers are fostered in contexts where getting away with crime is relatively easy, or illicit means are readily accessible.

Subcultural theories of crime modify Merton's approach by questioning his assumption that there is only one set of cultural norms in complex societies such as Canada. They focus attention on distinctive subcultural socialization through which people learn unusual behaviour patterns. These people appear to engage in deviant behaviour from the perspective of mainstream society, but are normal conformists rather than innovators or rebels. The only difference is that they are conforming to unusual subcultural values learned from their neighbourhood or peer groups. To use Merton's terminology they have learned both deviant goals and means. Sutherland and Cressey (1960) proposed the theory of **differential association** to account for the behaviour of professional thieves and children from neighbourhoods where crime rates are high. Business people, Sutherland suggests, may learn attitudes of contempt for legal regulations that restrict sharp business practices like misleading advertising, infringing patents, unfair labour practices, and the like ([1949] 1961). Hence, they engage in such activities without feeling like deviants. More commonly, the theory is used to account for high rates of deviance among youths who 'hang out with the wrong crowd' (Peace et. al.,

Table 7-1

Merton's Typology of Modes of Adaptation (1968, 194)		
Mode of Adaptation	Culturally valued goals	Socially approved means
Conformist	accept	accept
Innovator	accept	reject
Ritualist	reject	accept
Retreatist	reject	reject
Rebel	replace	replace

2000, 4–5). Associations vary in frequency, duration, priority, and intensity, influencing the likelihood that individuals will internalize particular group values. As individuals begin to become publicly associated with deviant subgroups the vicious cycle of reaction and counter action described by **labelling theory** begins to happen. Others who disapprove of their deviant friends and activities begin to avoid them, driving them further to the margins of society.

Merton first applied his model to cultural strains associated with unequal means to achieve individual economic success, but as a generic model, it can be applied to any culturally desirable goals that are not easily achieved. In contemporary society, for example, achieving fame and celebrity may parallel economic achievement as a goal, generating new forms deviant adaptation to structural constraints (Parnaby and Sacco 2004). *Conformity* involves achieving public recognition in the media, celebrity status in the entertainment industry, winning the lottery, and the like. But few of us can hope to win such fame legitimately. *Innovators* seek notoriety through attention-grabbing acts of vandalism or deviance that the media then channel into millions of homes; *ritualists* scale down the 'celebrity' goals to a mundane level like waving at a television camera during public events or putting risqué pictures on a personal website and imagining others looking at them; *retreatists* give up on both goals and means, developing social phobias against appearing in any situation where others may look at them; *rebels* challenge the legitimacy of the cultural and economic structures that push celebrity status and consumer goods by defacing advertisements and exposing global systems of exploitation that underlie mass consumer society.

Gang Subculture: Rebels, Innovators or Retreatists?

Subcultural theories of deviance have been applied particularly in studies of youth gangs found in many large urban centres in North America, and particularly associated with lower-class and ethnic minority neighbourhoods (Cohen 1955; Thrasher 1963; Miller 1958; Totten 2000). Descriptions of gang cultures often read like studies of exotic tribes with their own internal social organization, moral codes, and sanctions. Typically, gang culture grants prestige to those who rebel, get into

trouble, outsmart others, take risks, and are tough and autonomous. Violation of legal norms for its own sake is a respected part of the culture. In the eyes of gang members, fighting, vandalism, sexual conquests, joy-riding in stolen cars, heavy use of alcohol, illicit drugs, and smoking, represent conformity to gang expectations rather than rebellion. Hirschi's concept of control theory can be readily applied as gang members commonly show limited respect for or involvement in mainstream institutions like school or religion. They associate primarily among themselves. In Willis's classic study of working-class boys in school in Britain (1981), the "lads" openly ridiculed school work, challenged the authority of teachers, and kept their involvement in class-work to the minimum.

Alternative views of gang behaviour, however, question the usefulness of explanations in terms of subcultural conformity to account for what motivates gang members. Claimed gang values are not just different from prevailing societal values; they are an exaggerated reversal of them. This complicates the application of Merton's typology because it is unclear whether gang members are truly conforming to an alternative cultural system, or rebels wishing to replace the dominant cultural system, or merely retreatists whose exaggerated talk covers fear of failure. Greenberg (1981b) notes that interest in gang membership among lower-class boys drops off sharply as they reach school-leaving age and begin to find jobs and earn money. Much delinquent behaviour among juveniles, he suggests, reflects status frustration. As teenagers, they want brand-name clothes, cigarettes, cars and motorbikes, and access to pubs and other adult entertainment. But as underage 'children' in school they have few opportunities to earn money. With adult status and a job, gang values lose their appeal. Willis's "lads", similarly, do not include all working-class boys in school, but rather those who are not succeeding by school standards. They have little hope of achieving more than factory jobs, even if they do conform to school norms.

For Totten also, experiences of frustration and failure seem to account better for gang behaviour than conformity to subcultural norms. Interviews with boys in gangs around Ottawa revealed very traditional views of what makes an "ideal man"—someone who is the family bread-winner, with a good job, material possessions, and a devoted homemaker-wife who defers to him (2000, 76). But few of the adult men in their lives had achieved these ideals. The more common experience was chronic unemployment, and even the humiliation of dependence on employed wives. The boys sometimes spoke of their own raging anger and frustration that they did not have jobs while girls they knew had money to pay for dates. This anger was often expressed in violence against their girlfriends, much as they describe seeing their mothers beaten up by their fathers.

Theories that focus on **family breakdown** and **inadequate socialization** as the root causes of deviant behaviour complement this analysis of status frustration because such experiences so commonly occur together. A subsequent study of young offenders convicted of murder and manslaughter (Kelly and Totten 2002) reveals how deeply most of them were harmed by difficult, impoverished lives. Overwhelmingly, they come from families unable to cope—mired in addictions, alcoholism and mental illness, and neglectful of their children (ibid. 8).

Social Disorganization theory suggests that periods of rapid social change, associated with accelerated urbanization, immigration, and technological advances, increase the likelihood of communities and families breaking down (Peace et. al., 2000, 7). Proportions of youth at risk of becoming deviant rise as the inevitable result.

Anomie theory, along with these complementary theories of family breakdown, inadequate socialization and social disorganization, forms a syndrome of experience that helps to account for the exceptionally high crime rates among aboriginal peoples (Gill 2002, 178–9). Gill cites 1999 data from the Elizabeth Fry society, estimating that Aboriginal people nationwide were nine times more likely to go to prison than non-Aboriginal Canadians. Aboriginal people represent 2 percent of the adult population of Canada, but accounted for 11 percent of admissions to federal prisons at the beginning of the 1990s and fully 17 percent by 1998 (Statistics Canada 1991, 1, cited in Gill 2002, 179). Proportional incarceration rates for Aboriginal youth are, if anything, worse. Functionalist theory traces the roots of these troubles in the breakdown of cultural norms and family life within aboriginal communities. Primary socialization into traditional native cultural values were undermined in many communities as children between the ages of 6 to 16 were removed from reservations to be educated in residential schools. Misery and loneliness, and vulnerability to physical and sometimes sexual abuses marred these schools as centres for secondary socialization. Young adults graduating from these schools were frequently ill-equipped psychologically to establish functional families of their own, resulting in trans-generational family break-

down (Braun 2002; Cote and Schissel 2002). Chronic poverty, alcoholism and child abuse, and conflict with the law, are pervasive features of life on reservations and among aboriginal peoples living in urban areas. The gradual re-socialization of people into traditional aboriginal cultures, both in native communities, and among aboriginal people in prisons is widely described as a critical process helping to change these patterns to bring about emotional healing and family stability, which in turn are reflected in reduced incidence of anti-social behaviour (Anderson and Lawrence 2003).

In summary, these varied theories outlined above offer complementary rather than competing explanations for deviant behaviour. What they all have in common is the concept of **anomie**—a confusion of values and lack of clear regulations or norms for behaviour. The theories highlight different aspects of the same underlying experience of family breakdown and loss of community, of people who lack strong ties to institutions of family, school or religion, who reject others and feel rejected in turn. Young people, and particularly young men, find themselves adrift, rejecting and often inverting the values and expectations of the dominant society that they feel unable to live up to, but without any satisfying alternative.

Gender Socialization and Crime

Traditional research in criminology largely avoided the question of gender differences by focussing only on males. As Adelberg and Currie (1987) expressed it, women are "too few to count" in criminology. Overall, only about 12 percent of all criminal code violations are attributed to women, and these tend to be less serious offences. Women make up fewer than 10 percent of inmates in Canada's prisons. Only with respect to the one offence of prostitution, do convictions of women outnumber men. Theorists who have tried to account for these gender differences have generally found anomie theory difficult to apply to women (Leonard 1982; Morris 1987). Anomie theories that focus on family breakdown, deviant neighbourhood subcultures, and frustrated economic success goals, would not predict such differences. After all, girls and boys grow up in the same families and neighbourhoods. Women also typically face greater barriers to economic achievement than men, and are more likely to live in poverty. Yet women as a whole are responsible for only about one-fifth of all property offences, and these are mostly for petty theft like shoplifting rather than large heists. Even in extremely anomic circumstances of divorced, single parenthood, crime rates among women remain far below averages for men.

Differential socialization of girls and boys is still the dominant explanation for lower crime rates among girls, along with implicit notions that girls may naturally be less aggressive than boys. Role theorists point out that, even though girls and boys grow up together, they are socialized differently and have different success goals. Girls tend to be protected and supervised more at home and encouraged to seek help in difficult situations, rather than to fight. They are given dolls to play with and expected to help with housework and care of younger children. They grow up to see being a wife and mother as their primary adult role, with economic success secondary. Wife-mothers are expected to defer to husband-fathers within the family. Boys, in contrast, are socialized to be tough and independent, to participate in physical contact sports, to fight back when hit, and to take risks. They are also freer to move around the neighbourhood without adults chaperoning them. They grow up to see getting a job and earning money as their primary role, with nurturing and care-giving roles as secondary. Such differences predispose boys to get into more trouble than girls, to be more physically violent. As adults they are more centrally affected by status frustrations that focus on money and power, and hence more prone to crime.

These theories predict that as the socialization of girls and boys becomes more similar their crime rates would tend to converge. Differential opportunity theory similarly predicts that as the women's liberation movement increased women's opportunities to commit crimes, more girls would get into trouble (Adler 1975; Faith and Jiwani 2002). Hypothetically, the converse might also happen. If boys are brought up to be more nurturing and home centred, and see their fathers sharing more of the nurturing and child-care responsibilities within the family, crime rates for boys and young men should decline.

Currently, there is more evidence to show rising crime rates and greater violence among girls, than declining rates for boys. Official statistics for youth crimes in Canada during the 1990s suggest that convictions for violent offences rose 127 percent for girls during the decade, while rates for boys rose only 67 percent (Bell 2002, 132–5). Bell notes, however, that much of this change can be accounted for by changes in policing practices, and a greater tendency to lay charges for common assaults than in the past. Percentages also vary wildly depending on the base year from which they are counted. A rise from one homicide to two, for example, can be described as an impressive 100 percent increase. Gender differences in actual rates of assault and robbery convictions remain large, with 90% of violent crimes still attributed to men.

A study of six adolescent girls who have been convicted of assaulting their peers supports the theory that such violence is a learned response to family environments in which conflict is "frequent, vehement, and ugly," with physical punishment designed to hurt and degrade (Artz 1998, cited in Bell 2002, 140). Artz argues further that these homes are strongly hierarchical and male-dominated. Girls learn early that men are more important and powerful than women, and that power resides in physical force. All the girls convicted of assaulting other girls had themselves been victimized. In effect they come from the same kind of families as the boys described in Totten's study of male gangs, described above. Boys learn to dominate by physical force, while girls learn to expect such abuse from boyfriends and to defer to them, while fighting girls who threaten to win the attention of boys. A survey of 1500 high-school students (Artz and Riecken 1994) found that girls who hit others were far more likely than non-violent girls to have experienced sexual and physical assault. Growing up in homes marred by violence is a common feature in multiple studies of women serving time in prison (Bell 2002:143).

Policing and Community Controls.

Punishment and incarceration are common responses to criminal behaviour. In principle, punishment functions to make offenders pay for harm to others and to deter future potential deviants from copying such behaviour. Punishment also serves to remind people of the legally-defined boundaries of acceptable behaviour, and thus to reinforce conformity among the general population. Punitive law enforcement, however, risks exacerbating the causes of deviance identified in functionalist analysis. Imprisonment may worsen deviance by bringing younger or first-time offenders into close and extended association with more hardened criminals, thus increasing the likelihood of deviant socialization. Criminal convictions carry strong negative labels that further contribute to the social marginalization that fosters deviant behaviour (Dick et. al., 2004). Punishment also does little to improve the conditions of community breakdown that are the foundational cause of anomie.

These concerns have led sociologists to propose more community-based strategies for reducing crime rates and for dealing with offenders. The core of Giddens' (1998, 87–8) proposals to the British government of Tony Blair is that police and the government need to work together with citizens to improve community standards, and to support all institutions involved in socialization of young people. Sponsoring parenting programs at community level was recommended, with the goal of teaching effective parenting skills, and especially programs targeted at parent of children at risk. The previous conservative British Prime Minister, Margaret Thatcher even suggested the possibility that parents be held legally responsible, and subject to heavy fines, for crimes committed by their underage children. Giddens and others further propose policies to keep families intact wherever possible, to promote mediation to resolve disputes between parents over children, and to insist on joint and continuing parenting responsibilities after divorce. In addition, police experimented with curfews for children under ten years of age to prevent them from being on the streets between 9 P.M. and 6 A.M. while not under the supervision of a 'responsible adult' (James and James 2001, 220–223). Police were also given increased powers to stop children outside school during school hours and return them to school (ibid. 217). In Canada in 2004, some municipalities proposed curfews after 11 P.M. for juveniles under age 16, to cut down on vandalism. While the proposal met with much popular support, opponents warned that it might violate the age-discrimination proscription in the Charter of Rights and Freedoms. The more general principle underlying all these proposals is that parents need to be pressured to assume greater responsibility for supervising their children's behaviour and teaching more respect for societal values.

Schools and education also feature centrally in Giddens' recommendations for strengthening community values and preventing crime among youth (James and James 2001, 215–219; Giddens 1998, 125). Schools are enjoined to teach the values of self discipline and control, reinforced by increased supervision and monitoring of children's behaviour while in school. School councils were instituted to involve children directly in arbitrating student complaints and managing disruptive behaviour. Frequent standardized testing and the ranking of schools and teachers are designed to increase discipline as well as standards. The British government also sponsored programs that place increased pressure on parents to give children more help with their homework,

with a view to increasing the effective involvement of parents and local communities in the education of their children (James and James 2001, 217).

Community policing programs provides a third avenue designed to strengthen community involvement in the management and reduction of crime. These range from informal "neighbourhood watch" programs and street patrols by officers, to state-sponsored joint programs between citizens and police (Klinenberg 2001). In Chicago, where police have organized monthly citizens' meetings in every neighbourhood since 1995, some 6000 citizens participate monthly and over a quarter of a million participated at least once during the first four years. A staff of roughly 50 workers regularly visit churches and schools in the neighbourhoods to encourage citizens to attend beet meetings. Attendees are further encouraged to go to court when neighbourhood "thugs" are on trial, to show that they care about crime prevention, and to participate in neighbourhood watch, and informal monitoring of delinquent activities in the local streets. The city government supports these police-citizen meetings by expediting responses to all complaints voiced through the meetings, from graffiti to broken street lights. Klinenberg suggests that community policing is providing avenues for previously isolated citizens to become involved in community life. Greater involvement promises to strengthen commitment to shared normative consensus.

A variety of community-based "restorative justice" programs are also being developed to manage the sentencing and sanctioning of offenders as an alternative to the prison system. These include approaches like peer courts or juvenile conferencing for first-time offenders, community sentencing circles, and the involvement of victims and family members in deciding appropriate punishment and community service work through which offenders can make reparation to individuals and communities for the harms they have caused (White 2002; Dick et. al., 2001). Programs specifically for Aboriginal inmates try to draw them into a greater awareness of their cultural and religious heritage and build a sense of belonging to a their ancestral communities. After years of struggle to gain recognition for Aboriginal spirituality as a 'religion' within the definition used by the Canadian criminal justice system (Waldram 1997) many of Canadian prisons now offer special services, offering pipe ceremonies, healing circles, sweatlodge and other sacred ceremonies, with community elders as religious leaders and counsellors. Evaluation studies suggest these programs have had significant success, notably with men formerly segregated in prisons as dangerous offenders (Braun 2002).

Manifest and Latent Functions: The Unintended Consequences of Crime Control

An important assumption within the functionalist perspective is that all social institutions are inter-linked in an overall system. Changes in one arena of activity have implications for multiple other sites of action that are not easily foreseen or controlled. The **manifest functions** or intents of a new policy may be to strengthen social order and community values, and so protect citizens from crime. However the **latent functions** of the policy may include disrupting balance in other areas of society, which generate new problems or dysfunctions for social order. Labelling theory, described above, points to a classic example of dysfunctional consequences of well-intentioned policies. Imprisonment and punishment deter offenders, but incarceration promotes deviant socialization and negative labelling that increase the risk of recidivism. The primary deviance that prompted the initial punishment may be relatively minor, compared with the long-term consequences of secondary deviance, especially for juveniles (Dick et. al., 2004).

Recognition of these negative consequences promoted many of the community-based programs described above. Critics warn, however, that these programs too may have unintended consequences that serve to reinforce rather than replace dominant forms of processing offenders through prisons (White 2002). When implemented as cheap and marginal programs appropriate only for trivial and first-time offences, they reinforce the view that hard-line criminal justice and prison terms are appropriate for all others. They also reinforce view of crime as individual failure rather than a symptom of problems at community level. Dick et. al similarly warn that more research is needed into the latent consequences of peer courts for juvenile offenders. We still do not know how effective they are in avoiding negative labelling or shaming, or how to strike a balance between too strict and too lenient punishment, or how readily juveniles internalize the idea that they have been treated fairly by peers or treated badly (2004, 1454–6). James and James (2001) lament that parent-education programs, school councils and standardized monitoring of school performance introduced in Britain will work to reduce children's agency and human rights rather than enhancing participatory democracy.

Articles in the July 2004 volume of *American Behavioral Scientist* provide a litany of other examples of unintended policy consequences. Aggressive policing of illicit drugs raises their street value and thus profitability for organized crime, and so increases drug trafficking. All interventions in problem gambling functioned to make problem gambling worse (Bernard and Preston 2004) Displaying losses to discourage players promotes 'chasing behaviour'—a desperate urge to win back lost money; slowing the rate of play promotes longer playing time; mandatory closing periods promote frenzied binge gambling, and so on. Medicaid funding intended to provide long-term nursing-home care for the poor is rapidly exhausted as wealthier families develop asset-transfer schemes so as to qualify for the aid (Wegner and Yuan 2004). Heightened airline security after the September 11th 2001 terrorist attacks served mostly to heighten public awareness of the impossibility of total security and hence increased insecurity (Russell and Preston 2004). Gun-free zones, intended to increase safety around schools, day-cares and hospitals in the USA, function to attract criminals who feel safer in such zones (Roots 2004). These authors all warn sociologists of the need to study the unintended consequences of policies they promote. Roots carries the functionalist notion of system equilibrium to its logical extreme by arguing that even well-meaning policies necessarily disturb the natural system equilibrium. All laws intended to block certain behaviours encourage counter-actions to get around them, and hence stimulate their own violation (Roots 2004, 1386).

Few researchers are as pessimistic as Roots in dismissing virtually all policy intervention as doomed to failure. But there is copious evidence that many decades of criminal justice intervention have failed to rid societies of crime, or even to stabilize crime rates. The number of violent crimes has declined somewhat in recent years, a fact usually attributed to an aging population. But overall incarceration rates are rising, drug abuse is rising exponentially notwithstanding decades of 'war on drugs', child pornography and gambling are spreading exponentially through the internet, organized crime has become global in size, prostitution rings operate globally through sex-tourism, and fear of crime remains pervasive (Reiman 2001, ch. 1). Reiman concludes that "nothing succeeds like failure," in that the solution most favoured by political leaders amounts to expanding the very criminal justice system that has failed in the past.

From the functionalist perspective, the main conclusion drawn is that maintaining systemic equilibrium is very difficult. This is particularly so during periods of rapid social change, both within individual societies and in the surrounding global environment. The task facing leaders working within existing institutions of socialization and criminal justice is to achieve a reasonable balance between individual autonomy and social control. Some of the critics cited above, however, argue that what we need is new ways of thinking about crime that offer the potential for very different and hopefully more effective modes of social response. Alternative sociological perspectives explore these ideas more closely.

Political Economy Perspective: Law and Criminal Justice under Capitalism

The political economy or Marxist perspective places the structures of capitalism at the centre of analysis of crime, rather than socialization of individuals into the moral order of society. The needs of the capitalist economic system are seen as driving changes in all other institutions of society, including law. Law functions to facilitate the accumulation of profits and to legitimate the resulting concentration of wealth (Comack 1999, 36–44; Quinney 1975; Chambliss 1975). Accumulation of wealth requires laws to enforce contracts and to safeguard property ownership and profits. Legitimacy of that wealth requires laws to manage relations between capital (employers) and labour (employees) in ways that reduce the potential for class conflict. In effect, Quinney argues, law functions at every stage, from enactment to enforcement, to protect and enhance the interests of the propertied ruling class.

As Durkheim recognized, restitutive or contract law increased exponentially with the rise of industrialization and capitalism in Europe. Currently within Canada an estimated 80 percent of all law is concerned with boundaries of property, transaction, and contract (MacDonald 2002, 26). Law reduces the risk of class conflict by giving a semblance of legitimacy or justice to contractual relations between capital and labour. Law protects the personal property and well-being of workers, so that they too develop a stake in the system. Marxist theorists are quick to point out that this does not mean that law is designed to *resolve* the basic contradiction between property owners and wage labourers: rather, law is a *symptom-solving* mechanism (Chambliss 1986; Comack 1999, 41). The official version of law as dispensing blind justice, promises equal treatment to all individuals under law, regardless of

poverty or wealth. Detractors comment that this amounts merely to prohibiting rich and poor equally from sleeping under bridges or panhandling on public transit. Defenders argue, however, that if legitimation is to work, equality under the law cannot be merely a sham (Comack 1999, 43; Thompson 1975). To maintain its appearance as fair, and therefore to function effectively in providing the social stability that capitalism needs, law must truly dispense justice at least some of the time. Hence law can function sometimes in the interests of workers against employers, and citizens against corporate capital.

Reiman (2001, 1–9) argues the extreme position that the capitalist system *needs* to criminalize the poor—the lumpenproletariat of the underemployed, jobless, and marginal workers. Criminalization facilitates the control of this class of people most likely to support insurrection against the inegalitarian economic system. It justifies the state's use of police, courts, and prisons to manage this population. The maintenance of a stable, visible class of criminals who are portrayed as pathological individuals further functions to win support of the mass of useful workers for institutionalized suppression, and diverts attention from the systemic contradictions of capitalism. The negative labelling of ex-convicts can be seen as useful from this viewpoint. Not all Marxist theorists agree with Quinney and Reiman that law is an instrument directly controlled by capitalists. What they do generally agree on is that law enforces social order in inherently exploitative, inegalitarian, and conflict-ridden capitalist societies. Capitalists do not always win struggles to control laws, but they do have a commanding advantage. Law upholds a moral order that endorses property-ownership, competitive individualism and consumerism.

Alienation, rather than anomie is the central concept through which anti-social behaviour is understood. Alienation refers to a syndrome or interrelated pattern of lived experiences shared in varying degrees by people across different class-sectors of society. These experiences include being powerless to secure one's own future in economies dominated by corporate giants and volatile job markets, trapped in a cycle of meaningless jobs rewarded with shoddy consumer goods, estranged from one's own sense of self respect in a culture that values only wealth and glamour. Above all, alienation refers to isolation from others in a moral order that promotes competitive individualism. Even those who succeed in this capitalist system, capitalists themselves, experience alienation. They too are isolated from meaningful social relations with others, trapped as they are in relentless competitive struggle for profits.

Law for the Propertied Class: Legalizing Colonization

We begin this analysis with the origins of capitalism itself as an economic system in the conversion of feudal estates to private property during seventeenth and eighteenth centuries in England. The rolling farmlands of southern England may look the picture of tranquil gentility but two centuries ago these lands were scarred with the blood and horror of what Marx terms "reckless terrorism" (Blomley 2004, xvii; citing Marx [1867] 1976, 713–733). Rural peasant families who had lived on and worked the lands for many generations were ruthlessly dispossessed and evicted by nobility who wanted to privatize the lands for commercial crops. In some particularly horrendous instances, peasants who refused to move were burned alive in their homes as villages were torched (Clegg and Dunkerley 1980, 48). Landless and destitute, these ex-peasants were forced to move into the cities to seek wage-work in factories that expanded rapidly with the invention of steam engines.

It is particularly significant that these mass evictions took place under the rule of law. The nobility were recognized in law as the rightful property owners of the former feudal estates, and had the legal right to evict peasants as they chose. A series of legal decisions emphasized the absolute property rights vested in the big estate owners over the coincident use-rights of villagers established over centuries of practice (Thompson 1975). Thompson describes one such law, called *The Black Act,* passed in 1723. It imposed the death sentence for any peasant caught with a blackened face, a disguise widely used by peasants while hunting on privatized lands. The death sentence was also imposed for such acts as poaching, hurting cattle, cutting trees and burning haystacks or barns on the estates. The wording of the laws appears neutral and impartial, merely protecting property held by one individual against damage or theft by another. But what such terminology obscured was class warfare. The laws simultaneously created and defended two classes of people—those who owned the means of production, and those who did not.

A similar body of laws legalized the colonization of Canada by merchant companies and settlers from Britain and France. Under the doctrine of *terra nullis* lands that were not developed for agricultural or commercial use and not inhabited by Christians, were legally deemed to be uninhabited (Razack 2002, 2–3; Blomley 2004, 3; Martin 2002, 229). Such lands were therefore deemed to be legally available for settlement by European settlers. *Terra populi*, in contrast, were lands to which merchant companies or individuals had legally documented private ownership, registered by the state. The discipline of cartography mapped and named 'space' in ways that meant it could be legally divided up, bounded, and sold in plots. These laws made it possible for Europeans to think of themselves as 'pioneers', the first people to tame and settle the wilderness—as if colonization never happened. The presence of indigenous peoples and their ancestral practices that recognized multiple use-rights to lands were rendered invisible. Western law, argues Blomley, was thus an instrument of civilization and of empire, facilitating the violent dispossession of indigenous peoples and simultaneously legitimating and depoliticizing their colonization. Cities across Canada were routinely settled by force of law. Maps laid out boundaries for new towns and parcelled out plots for sale. Indigenous residents were deemed to have no legal ownership or rights to residence, and were driven outside the town boundaries (Blomley 2004, 107; Razack 2002, 128–136). Constructed legally as 'wards of the state', indigenous peoples were "given" reservations, held in trust for them by the state. Police brutality and settler violence were routinely practised to enforce their spatial containment, and their exclusion from city boundaries.

More recently, the development of hydro-electric projects in Northern Canada were carried out with essentially the same view of land as "empty space", or more specifically as crown-owned land, with few individuals having clear property rights (Martin 2002). The Canadian legal system has found it almost impossible to determine appropriate compensation for Indians who lost their means of subsistence as lands on which they hunted were flooded, and migration paths for big game disrupted. Commercially the lands have no value. Individual Indians have no clear property rights based on formal purchase agreements. Yet these lands provided for the subsistence needs of entire communities. Depending on the standpoint taken, financial compensation should be minimal or should be sufficient to sustain entire communities for generations. Typically, compensation claims drag through the courts for years. Twenty-five years after their lands were flooded in 1977 by the Manitoba Hydro project, the Cree had still not received compensation (Gill 2002, 172). Meanwhile,

Manitoba Hydro had become the fourth largest electrical utility in Canada with net revenues well over $1 billion annually.

A similar struggle continues over the federal government's appropriation of Indian reservation lands at Ipperwash in 1942 for a wartime military base, and later for a training base (Bressette 2003). Displaced people crowded onto a neighbouring reserve, impoverishing both groups. An interim settlement of $2.2 million, intended as compensation for the wartime take-over of land, was finally agreed upon almost 40 years later. Half this amount was held in trust for future generations, leaving only $1000 per capita for the displaced people who qualified legally as status Indians. Local people are still struggling to get the land back. During one such confrontation in September 1995, Anthony 'Dudley' George died from a police bullet.

Colonizing the Inner-city.

The central assertion of Blomley's study of the politics of property, is that colonization is an ongoing process in cities across Canada, not something that happened a century or more ago. His study of conflicts over property rights in downtown eastside Vancouver draws close parallels between the legalized dispossession of indigenous peoples and the contemporary eviction of low-income residents from districts undergoing gentrification or corporate development. As with indigenous peoples, the multiple users of contested sites become invisible in law against the legally legitimated rights of property owners.

Community policing meetings become sites for class struggle between the rights of middle-class property owners to unimpeded enjoyment of their newly gentrified homes and small bed-and-breakfast businesses, pitted against the rights of residents of nearby homeless shelters and rooming houses, prostitutes, and other users of space. Typically, police side with property-owning residents' associations against the poor, regardless of who are the newcomers and who the long-term residents, and regardless also of their relative numbers. Police routinely pressure homeless people and shelter residents to keep moving until they are forced out of targeted streets. By-laws are enacted to prohibit 'loitering' or 'sleeping ' on park benches, and to lock public parks and toilets in the evenings so that homeless residents cannot stay in them. These laws function to preserve

these 'public' spaces for propertied residents (Kawash 1998).

In some instances, people have been denied the right to be within city limits at all. Saskatoon police stand accused in the 1990s of routinely arresting Aboriginal men who appeared drunk on the streets, and dumping them miles outside town, forcing them to walk home. Sometimes this was done on winter nights with temperatures approaching –30C. The frozen body of 17-year-old Neil Stonechild was found outside of town in late November 1990. Credible witnesses swear that on the night when he disappeared they saw him handcuffed and screaming in the back of a police cruiser (*Globe and Mail Oct 28, 04, A1*). The bodies of three Aboriginal men were found frozen in similar circumstances. A fourth man testified that he too had been dumped by police outside of town on a freezing night, but managed to survive. The public inquiry held in 2004 found that police at the time made minimal effort to investigate these allegations, and indeed actively threatened and intimidated witnesses who tried to speak out.

In law, Blomley argues, it is the propertyless who appear as 'transient', and whose claims to use rights appear unfounded. Rights to private ownership of property trump all other rights of residency and community rights to use and enjoy the space. Similarly, a rooming-house owner seeking to renovate property to attract upscale customers can use the force of law to evict tenants from his property, even if those tenants have lived in the same room for thirty years (Blomley 2004, ch. 1). There is nothing inevitable or obvious about such property rights, Blomley insists. They are a particular way of seeing moral relationships, and a way of not seeing other possible forms of communal claims to entitlement. Rights in property are not absolute. Home-owners, for example, do not have unencumbered rights to make as much noise as they wish, to rent rooms to any number of tenants, to chop down all the trees, to leave garbage in the front yard, to cover the roof with advertising signs, and so on. These legal restrictions, however, are designed primarily to protect the property values of the neighbourhood. There are no laws that protect the space-usage rights of the homeless from their propertied neighbours.

Social activists and long-term homeless residents of downtown eastside Vancouver joined forces in 1995 in an attempt to reclaim "community" usage rights to an abandoned department store, based on its years as public space for shopping and entertainment in the neighbourhood (Blomley 2004, 39–46). Squatters moved into the building, urging the government to turn it into a low-income public housing. The city, however, sided with developers who proposed to demolish the building and build upscale condominiums. Police were called in to evict the squatters on grounds of "public safety". In a related struggle, local activists argued that a public park and beach area in Vancouver extensively used by homeless people was threatened by the plans of corporate developers to build a casino complex for tourists (Blomley 2004, 46–50). From the perspective of law, however, the park appeared merely as derelict space, to which none of the regular users had proprietary rights. Within the maps produced by developers, the contested community space was merely empty space. The area was effectively terra nullis,—devoid of prior property owners whose interests needed to be considered in development plans.

Even when individuals do have some legal title to property this does not necessarily protect them from legal expropriation of land for other purposes supported by the state. This is especially so for slum-clearance projects when the properties in question are of low taxable or real-estate value and proposed developments are of greater economic value. The expropriation and subsequent obliteration of the black settlement area known as Africville by the city of Halifax in the 1960s was all carried out legally. This is notwithstanding the fact that the site of the settlement was legally purchased by the settlement's founders in 1840. Shabby properties, not serviced by either piped water or sewage, were classified as slums and hence legally of little value for purposes of financial compensation. Many current residents were unable to produce legal documentation of home ownership, because homes had often been shared and handed down among extended family members. Hence residents had the legal status only of squatters—not entitled to any financial compensation when their homes were expropriated, beyond small gifts of $500 from a benevolent city (Nelson 2002, 216). For Nelson, it was "precisely the legality of the process" that appeared so strikingly violent (ibid. 223). Every avenue through which former residents might pursue legal redress and compensation were closed to them. The final irony for Nelson is that after the settlement was destroyed, the proposed commercial development never materialized. The area was turned into a public park. When two prior residents subsequently set up a tent in the park in an effort to pressure the city for better compensation, the city passed by-laws to lock the only park toilet, and to ban sleeping in public parks overnight. The presence of campers was thus declared illegal, and they were evicted.

Treaty Rights and Legal Practice

Aboriginal peoples have a special legal status within Canada that is recognized in the Charter of Rights and Freedoms. Section 35 of the Charter states that "The existing aboriginal and treaty rights of the aboriginal peoples of Canada are hereby recognized and affirmed." Section 25 further affirms that nothing in the Charter shall be construed in any way that detracts from treaty or other rights that pertain to aboriginal peoples. In the ensuing two decades since the Charter was proclaimed, land claims and other treaty issues have been continually going through the courts. While there have been some successes, particularly in negotiating the implications that individual treaties have for subsistence and commercial access of Indians to natural resources, few major issues have been resolved.

Major problems result from the poor fit between the formal structure and functioning of the Canadian legal system and the structures needed to establish the meaning of treaties (Martin 2002; Monture-Angus 1999; Lawrence and Anderson 2002). A significant assertion by aboriginal peoples themselves is that treaties pertain to international law, signed between First Nations and the British colonial government, subsequently replaced by the Canadian federal government. Hence, treaties have different legal status from other Canadian laws. Even the jurisdiction of Canadian colonial courts to decide treaty issues has been challenged. The interpretation of treaties is made more complex by language barriers, and particularly by the very different ways in which agreements are understood and remembered in the oral traditions of First Nations communities at the time and the formal, legal and written language in which treaties are preserved by colonial governments. It is not always clear that individuals whose names appear as signatories to treaties had the legal status or moral right to represent the First Nations communities at the time. The land claims of First Nations communities that did not enter into treaties and hence never formally ceded lands to colonial authorities, are also in dispute. These claims drag interminably through the courts. The Indian Act that establishes the legal definition of an Indian is itself is a colonial document that is hotly contested. First Nations communities argue that they, and not a colonial government document, should define who their members are. Nonetheless, the distinction between status and non-status Indian remains centrally important in claims relating to treaty rights.

Even when these problems are set aside, it is questionable whether prevailing legal methods of reasoning are appropriate for deliberations on treaty rights. The rule of law in capitalist societies asserts both that everyone is subject to the law, and secondly that the law treats everyone as legal equals. What is presumed in this official version of law is the norm of a legal person as "able-bodied, autonomous, rational, educated, monied, competitive and essentially self-interested"(Comack 1999, 23, citing Naffine 1990; 52). Marxist theory views this notion of autonomous individuals, detached from community, as itself a product of capitalist relations of production. This means that legal reasoning routinely functions in ways that make it very difficult for communities to pressure their rights specifically as communities, rather than as individuals. Residents of Africville were treated in law as legal individuals within family units as spouses and dependent children. Whatever claims they may have had as a community, wanting to retain their residential and extended kinship networks in a new location, were not heard in court. Lawyers and judges trained in prevailing methods of legal reasoning are ill-equipped to consider claims that pertain to communities rather than individuals.

Aboriginal treaty rights pertain essentially to communities, compounding all the problems noted above in pressuring claims through Canadian courts. Everything that was done to indigenous peoples over three centuries of colonial wars was done through legal statutes. Now the onus rests entirely on First Nations themselves to establish, interpret, and enforce treaty rights and land claims. Monture-Angus, herself a qualified lawyer, concludes that the legal system, by the very way that it functions, cannot bring about transformative change—and indeed is not designed to do so. Each small success at Supreme Court level, won at enormous cost in money and energy, only seems to generate more court cases. In a supposedly landmark decision in the *Delgamuukw* case in 1997 the Supreme Court of Canada modified evidentiary rules to accommodate oral histories on an equal footing with written historical documents in determining historical facts. The result, however, was merely that the case returned to court for retrial. This case, which concerned Aboriginal title of hereditary chiefs, had already taken 374 days at trial and 141 days taking evidence out of court (ibid. 81).

Another landmark Supreme Court ruling in 1999 determined that Donald Marshall, a Mi'kmaq Indian, had the right, under a 1761 treaty to fish for eels without a licence and out of season. By 2004 the same treaty was back in court with the New Brunswick government contesting a lower-court interpretation that this reasoning implied a right to cut and sell timber from crown land (*The Daily Gleaner* Sept. 23, 2004, A2). The Supreme Court ruled earlier that treaty rights need to be interpreted to fit contemporary situations rather than being frozen in the pre-industrial context in which they were first concluded. However, the difficult legal issue remains of how standard reasoning for contract law can be applied to treaties more than 200 years old. In yet another case, agreement was reached on restricted fishing rights for the Mi'kmaq in Quebec. But this too collapsed into violent confrontations with police over whether their agreed 72 hours of fishing were to be on three consecutive days or six half-days (Martin 2002, 236). As Monture-Angus observes, every legal success seems to lead only to another legal challenge.

Property Laws and Class Struggle

In summary, property laws, by their very existence, support the interests of the propertied classes against those who do not own property. These laws are structured to recognize as legal rights, those that are based on the commercial purchase of real-estate as a commodity. The moral order that is sustained by property laws is that of individual competitive rights to purchase real estate. Property laws appear neutral and objective, but from the beginnings of the capitalist system to the present, they embody class war. Other forms of spatialized rights to use and inhabit space are not visible within the justice system. Occasionally the rights of people without commercial property are sustained in law. Treaty rights are interpreted as rights to restricted subsistence and commercial access to crown resources. Shelters for the homeless and subsidized housing for the poor, do sometimes win rights to space, along with limited rights for renters against arbitrary powers of owners. But these exceptions are visible within the capitalist system only as "special favours" or gifts. Indigenous peoples and others who assert rights to inhabit space that are not based on purchased property appear as nuisances, disturbing the more legitimate rights of purchasers of real estate to the unimpeded enjoyment of their property. Protection of plants and animals in the way of commercial exploitation of primary resources is similarly a nuisance that is occasionally accommodated but rarely highly valued. Any gains that non-propertied 'outsiders' make are won at high price in terms of time, efforts and money, and negative labelling. They have not achieved transformative visions of the validity of multiple and shared use rights to space that fall outside the capitalist model. At worst, small gains by outsiders may function to legitimate the fairness of the justice system, and thus reinforce the class structures that it represents.

The Political Economy of Crime and Criminology

A central assumption of political economy theory is that the capitalist system is criminogenic. Alienation in its varied forms is endemic in a social system that generates great inequalities in wealth and poverty and promotes a moral order that privileges the values of competitive individualism and ownership of consumer goods as the primary measure of self worth.

There is significant overlap between functionalist and political economy theories in analysis of how poverty contributes to criminal behaviour. Both approaches make visible the crimes of desperation as people steal food and necessities that they cannot afford to purchase. Both approaches also see the crimes of frustrations generated by the gap between socially valued goals and access to legitimate means to achieve them. Advertising incites impoverished people to want expensive consumer goods that they cannot afford, leaving them open to the lure of "innovative" criminal means to satisfy their desires. Desperation and relative deprivation combine to account for higher rates of petty crime among poor people, particularly break-and-enter and theft. Political economy theory differs from functionalism in placing this awareness in the context of a capitalist system that functions continually to reproduce an economically insecure class of underemployed and unwanted workers, and to exacerbate the gap between rich and poor.

Both functionalism and political economy theory see the desperation and deprivation that underlying high crime rates among Aboriginal peoples. But while functionalism stresses anomie, the loss of community values and religion, family breakdown and personal misery, political economy theory highlights the long and continuing history of colonialism. The systematic and brutal separation of Indians from means of production in lands and resources, and their marginalization on colonial postage-stamp reservations must bear much of the responsibility for the ensuing collapse of Aboriginal communities. Economic marginalization was made immeasurably worse by the colonial politics of the Indian Act that vested political power to manage reservation governance and resources in the hands of the Indian Affairs bureaucrats rather than First Nations themselves (Dyck 1992). The forced placement of children in residential schools is but one example of the state-enforced powerlessness of First Nations peoples.

The approach known as 'left realism' combines a sensitivity to social injustice as the root of crime, with a recognition that crimes committed out of desperation or deprivation threaten the well-being of community life. All too commonly the victims of these crimes come from the same deprived communities as the victimizers. Predatory crimes of burglary, theft, and mugging, and violence of all kinds occur far more commonly in poor neighbourhoods than in better-off areas. Left realists argue that punitive law-and-order approaches to crime control do little to deter anti-social behaviour among people already punished by deprived social lives. Restorative justice and peacemaking approaches that strive to bring perpetrators and victims together as members of the same communities, offer more hope of reducing destructive behaviour at neighbourhood level (Morris 2000). Where left realism differs most from mainstream functionalist approaches is in the kinds of structural changes advocated at societal level to reduce crime rates. Functionalists stress socialization, family responsibility, parenting classes, and stronger ties to school and religion as solutions to individual pathology. Left realists insist that lasting reduction in crime rates requires a reduction in economic injustices that incite people to crime. Few theorists on the left see a total transformation from capitalist to communal economies as a realistic or even a desirable option. But policies that promote progressive taxation, a strong social safety net, investment in social housing, and commitment to job protection and full employment would help. For First Nations communities, an economic resource base sufficient to establish communal self-sufficiency and political autonomy are essential (Boldt 1993).

Drug Wars as Class Wars

Drug use as a social problem is most visible in inner cities among the poor, the destitute and marginalized people. In a vicious interaction between cause and effect, people seek a drug-induced euphoria when their current lives are miserable and they see no hope for the future. In Black and Chicano ghettoes in American cities in particular, there are no decent jobs, no health care, poor education and infant mortality rates approaching

Third World levels (Ransom 1991, 6). In such contexts drug use is rampant. Drug addiction generates a desperate need for money to buy more drugs promoting predatory criminal behaviour like burglary, theft, and drug trafficking. These people create the most nuisance for law-abiding society, especially for their lower-class neighbours. Of all the people involved in the drug trade, these are the most likely to end up in prison (Seigel and McCormick 2003, 378). Individual pathology is the mainstream explanation. These people tend to come from impoverished families, with parents who also have criminal records; they do poorly in school and end up as young adults with little hope of succeeding in competitive job markets. They sink into a life of crime and chronic drug use, with frequent periods in prison (Saner, MacCoun and Reuter 1995, 362–73). Recreational drug users among better-off people who can afford to pay for their drugs without resorting to crime, may be far larger in number, but they do not attract the attention of either police or neighbours.

Largely invisible to this scenario are the organized business networks where the real profits are made. Profits are staggering. The markup from coca leaf purchase price to street value for cocaine is about 75 times, with $4 worth of leaves fetching $300 as finished cocaine (Seigel and McCormick 2003, 85). It is the illegality of the product that sustains both these incredible profits and the street crimes needed to pay for them. The criminal-justice solution to drug trafficking is itself a major contributor to the problem. Efforts to control the manufacture of drugs at source and their trading by international cartels have proven futile. Even the much hyped capture in 1993 of the billionaire Colombian drug lord Pablo Escobar, whose Medellin drug empire once controlled 80 percent of all cocaine imported into North America, barely created a dent in the flow of drugs. Competitive cartels across Latin America and elsewhere immediately filled the gap (ibid. 384). Efforts to rein in drug traffickers within Canada and the USA have proven equally futile for the same reasons. The demand is insatiable and the profits immense. Occasional major drug busts only help the trade by temporarily removing some competitors and raising drug prices.

Given the obvious failure of the criminal justice system to stem the drug trade the question arises why does the "war on drugs" continue? The moral argument that controlling drugs works to protect vulnerable populations from dangerous substances has been widely discredited. Marijuana has proven relatively harmless and non-addictive, but it is still illegal in Canada. Other illegal

drugs have not been shown to be markedly more addictive than legal ones like alcohol and nicotine (Reiman 2001, 37–8; Alexander 1990). The death rate among users of cigarettes is, if anything, higher than death rates among cocaine users. Risks of HIV-AIDS infections arise from sharing dirty needles, not from drug-use as such. Reports of drug-crazed behaviour are largely exaggerated. The main danger and nuisance arises from crimes committed to get drugs rather than from crazed behaviour while on them. Cocaine derivatives are reputed to be widely used as recreational drugs of choice among middle-class people. But middle-class people are largely ignored by the criminal justice system.

It is in relation to 'victimless' crimes like illicit drug use, that the instrumentalist Marxist argument is most convincing—that the criminal justice system functions in capitalist societies primarily to control the economically marginal populations. While efforts to stamp out drug use and drug trafficking have largely been futile, the criminalization of drugs works very well in providing legitimation for regular surveillance and control over poor people. Opium laws were first introduced in Canada in 1908 primarily to control the Chinese migrant-worker population in cities like Vancouver. The Chinese were left alone when their labour was needed during the height of railroad construction, but by the 1900s they were unwanted, and their cheap-labour posed a competitive threat to other workers. Laws were passed to restrict their immigration and settlement, and white workers turned against them. A particularly bad riot in 1907 that targeted Chinese workers caused extensive property damage. It was during the investigation of this damage that officials discovered opium dens. They used this information against the Chinese. The Opium Narcotic Act of 1908 and the wider Opium and Drug Act of 1911 gave police expanded powers of search and seizure that were directed against Asian minorities (Siegel and McCormick 2003, 374; Comack 1985).

Currently, drug laws legitimate mass surveillance, directed overwhelmingly at lower-class people who are marginalized from the capitalist system. The policy of zero tolerance for drugs, initiated in the early 1990s in the USA, provides a rationale for extensive police powers to suspend civil liberties, enter homes and vehicles and search occupants. Blacks are the prime targets of such searches. By the early 1990s an estimated one-quarter of all young black males in New York City have criminal records for drug-related offences. Whites make up 30 percent of arrests for sale and possession of drugs but less than 10 percent of all commitments to state prison for drug-related crime. Blacks make up 10 percent of the population of new York State but 50 percent of prison inmates (Cockburn and Cohen 1991). In many US states, individuals with a criminal record are prohibited from voting in elections, thus marginalizing them even further.

In Canada the Charter of Rights in principle protects people from arbitrary search and seizure. If police happen to find drugs in a private home or vehicle that they had no prior warrant to search, the find may not be accepted as evidence in court. Police need a search warrant, signed by a judge, to enter private homes. However, these are relatively easy to get when drug-use is commonplace among targeted populations, and the powers they confer are extensive. In one case in Halifax in 2001, police had a warrant to search a dance hall on a tip that a bottle of ecstasy pills was hidden there. They proceeded to strip search everyone present (Seigel and McCormick 2003, 246). In principle, citizens do not have to submit to being searched if they have not been arrested, but a police spokesperson suggested that anyone refusing to be searched under such circumstances likely would be placed under arrest.

The international "war on drugs" can similarly be analysed as a war on the powerless and impoverished peasant farmers in South American countries such as Peru, Bolivia, and Colombia. Wracked by debt and collapsing commodity prices since the 1980s, and unable to compete with multinational agribusiness corporations who have taken over prime agricultural lands, peasants on marginal hill farms have turned to growing coca as the one crop for which they can get a good price (Ransom 1991; Rance 1991). Americans have responded by spraying crops with harmful defoliants, and also by providing military funding to co-operating Latin American governments. These interventions were futile from the perspective of drug control, but effective politically, Rance suggests, in facilitating extensive American government controls in the internal politics of Latin American countries. The main beneficiaries have been military governments, bank-rolled on the promise of repressing coca farming among peasants, and simultaneously repressing potential communist uprisings among peasants. American multinational corporations find it safe to do business in these co-operating countries. In 1989 the American government sent 20 000 troops into Panama to arrest General Noriega on drug-trafficking charges. A puppet ruler, beholden to the USA, replaced him. Accusations surfaced at the time that the American Central Intelligence Agency (CIA) had itself been heavily involved in drug trafficking as a means to fund the Contra rebels in their bid to overthrow the elected socialist government in Nicaragua (Ransom 1991).

Meanwhile, the immense profits made from international drug-trafficking have to be disguised. Canadian banks are required to report any suspiciously large deposits, but privacy laws protect deposits in banks in Switzerland and Luxembourg, and the Bahamas, Cayman and Virgin Islands. Profits are routinely laundered through investments in legitimate businesses and real estate, and international arms deals. Political economists criticize the blinkered focus on traditional criminology on individuals who end up in prison, and drug offences at street level. The workings of vast international networks of drug-related business, and the complicity of governments in these networks cannot be understood in terms of pathological individual socialization.

Corporate Crime as Conformist Behaviour

The two central assertions in the political economy perspective—that capitalist systems are criminogenic, and that the criminal justice system is an instrument of class control, make their strongest case in relation to corporate crime. Classic anomie-related theories of individual pathology do not apply at this level. In terms of Merton's typology, the people involved in corporate crime are conformists. They suffer no gap between desirable goals and legitimate means to achieve them, no background of frustration, deprivation, low self-esteem or negative labelling. They have not been socialized into deviant subcultures. They are, for the most part, good, moral people, good parents and upstanding citizens (Bakan 2004, 50). They conform directly to the prevailing normative values of capitalist society—autonomous, rational, competitive, individualism oriented to economic achievement. Business corporations are the defining feature of any capitalist society. The argument that Bakan forcefully makes, both in his book and film called *The Corporation* (2004) is that business corporations are criminogenic in their most basic structure. Corporations are legal entities, run by managers in the interests of millions of shareholders. Managers are required by law to put the interest of making money for shareholders above all others, or they can be sued. Social responsibility is acceptable *only* in so far as it is demonstrably of benefit to corporate standing and profitability. Corporations seek to commercialize every aspect of life, particularly schools and entertainment centres, with the goal of winning customers and enhancing product sales. Even a catastrophe like the September 11, 2001 terrorist attack was immediately translated into an opportunity by commodities brokers to secure profits for their clients in gold markets that would be affected by the crisis (ibid. 111).

Since the 1980s governments in North America have progressively favoured policies of deregulation. They have left trans-national corporations, many of them economically more powerful than the nation states in which they do business, largely free to govern themselves. A century of struggle to develop laws protecting the interests of employees and customers, and the environment, have been systematically repealed, under pressure from the World Trade Organization to liberalize international trade. Laws and regulatory agencies governing corporate crime have become more lenient, or been abolished altogether (Sneider 1999; 2002). In 1997, the Canadian government closed down its research laboratories responsible for testing the safety of food and drugs. This was at a time when escalating numbers of companies were being caught putting untested and harmful products on the market. The budget for Environment Canada was cut by 30 percent in 1993–4 and the environment demoted from a senior to a junior ministry in 1997, despite a litany of environmental disasters. Fines for unlawful pollution declined by two-thirds in Ontario between 1995 and 1997. Annual workplace deaths in Canada are four times higher than the homicide rate yet agencies charged with protecting the health and safety of employees have been weakened. A particularly tragic example of weak protection of workers' health and safety is the Westray mine in Nova Scotia. A series of inspection reports between 1991–2 warned of safety violations and hazardous working conditions at the mine, but no charges were laid (Siegel and McCormick 2003, 350). On May 19, 1992 a methane gas explosion ignited coal dust in the mine, killing 26 miners. Criminal charges were laid alleging 52 violations of the Occupational Health and Safety Act, and two underground managers were charged with manslaughter and criminal negligence. Later, however, all charges were dropped as too vague. A long list of other corporate crimes causing injury and death can be added to the Westray saga, for which there has been minimal retribution or punishment (Sneider 1999, 186–196). Sneider estimates that the average amount stolen annually by bank robbers is less than 4 percent of the total stolen by corporate fraud. Typical fraud includes selling mislabelled products, tampering with evidence of harmful working conditions, conspiracy to restrict trade, false advertising, falsifying records, insider trading, hot deals

and fast stock flips by mutual fund operators, and the like. Fraudulent auditing that made companies appear financially sound and attractive to investors lay beneath the recent collapse of Enron and WorldCom, in which many thousands of families lost their life savings.

Sneider's central point is that such pervasive corporate misconduct falls largely outside the criminal justice system. Nation states, she argues, have virtually given up the struggle to control corporate criminals through law. Without independent regulatory agencies to check on corporate behaviour, corporate crime effectively disappears from public view. High publicity to a handful of cases, like Martha Stewart going to prison in 2004 for lying to investigators, gives the impression of justice being served, obscuring the reality of minimal investigation of corporate practices. The application of terms like 'fraud', 'crime' and 'criminal' to these corporate practices are really misnomers because they are rarely criminalized. They are viewed more as sharp business practices that are occasionally taken to excess, rather than crimes that should be prosecuted. Corporations are legally requried to maximize profits for investors and they tend to be faulted only when they fail.

The criminogenic character of contemporary corporate capitalism is revealed as much in currently legitimate practices as in the semi-legal grey areas listed above. The race to the bottom to find the cheapest 'sweatshop' labour for assembly work; ecological damage in the race to maximize the cheapest resource inputs; gambling trillions of dollars daily on currency exchanges regardless of impact on economies; contracts to exchange weapons for oil in countries facing civil war; lobbying to defeat legislation that might control fuel efficiency and pollution; using patent laws to prohibit development of alternative vehicle designs that threaten profits of gasoline-based models, saturation advertising and restrictive contracts to sell junk food and pop to school children . . . the list goes on. Many corporate employees who do this work protect their own self-esteem by an alienated consciousness, living morally compartmentalized lives (Bakan 2004, 54–5). Bakan, himself a law professor, argues that legal regulation of corporations is possible. But capitalist governments lack the political will to pass or enforce the legislation.

Political economy theory advocates a shift in the sociological definition of 'crime' itself from "breaking the law" to social harm. When laws can be shown to be implicated in class wars, blind obedience to law is not always morally defensible. Similarly, when legal corporate practices can be shown to cause more widespread social harm than much of what is now classified as criminal behaviour, the question of what kinds of acts deserve penal sanctions is revealed as strongly politicized. Economically marginalized lower-class people are vastly over-represented in prisons in part because they are targeted by the criminal justice system, while the social harms committed by better-off people who work in the heart of the corporate capitalist system are ignored.

Social Constructionist Perspective: Struggles over Meaning

The social constructionist perspective shifts the focus of inquiry from the behaviour of criminals to the study of the criminal justice system itself as the site of struggles over the meaning. It highlights the active practices of people who work within criminal justice agencies that together produce a working understanding of normalcy, deviance, and criminality for the practical purposes of social control.

Marked historical shifts in how discipline and punishment have been meted out in European societies reflect fundamental changes in the nature of social order (Foucault 1977; Ramp 2000). In the eighteenth century it was customary to hold public executions, as highly dramatized rituals designed to instill fear in onlookers. For the crime of treason against the king, a criminal might be hung, drawn, and quartered, and the body parts thrown to dogs. By the twentieth century in Europe, however, executions and other punishments were hidden from view behind prison walls. Foucault argues that these changes reflect the transition from the rule of king and nobility over subjects, to a democratic order based on self-sovereign citizens. In the former, kings ruled by fear, controlling their subjects by power over death. Violent and public punishments are still common in contemporary societies governed by military dictatorships. In democracies, in contrast, states exercise power over life rather than death. Citizens are controlled through a variety of techniques designed to produce 'normalized' and productive populations. In nineteenth-century Europe, penitentiaries, along with orphanages, workhouses, convents, and mental hospitals, were designed to correct abnormal behaviour. Surveillance and treatment administered by experts in social and physical sciences began to take precedence over raw punishment. Social science disciplines, as bodies of scientific knowledge, were increasingly used to discipline unruly bodies, especially the bodies of women, children, and marginalized populations. The 'psy' professions—psychoanalysis, psychology, and psychiatry became increasingly influential in many branches of social work, medicine, therapy, probation and education.

The central impetus for the rise of new forms of social control, Foucault argues, was class war. Social order of nineteenth-century Europe was profoundly shaken by the chaos and violence of the French Revolution of 1789, during which the feudal nobility were attacked by masses of destitute workers who were flooding into the cities. From then onwards, disciplining the lower classes in the cities became a central concern of the emerging capitalist states of Europe. Landless ex-peasants, freed from the controls of the feudal estates, had to be moulded into docile factory workers. Donzelot, a student of Foucault, explores how the notion of "juvenile delinquent" was invented around that time as part of a set of state practices for "policing families" (1979). Unruly juveniles, together with their mothers, were brought before justices and notables in special courts where they were subject to the 'psy' professions. Routinely, juveniles and their mothers were sentenced to continual surveillance or 'probation', with the threat of more punitive sanctions if they resisted. Conviction for some crime was not a requirement for these juvenile courts, only unruly behaviour or lack of respect for authority figures. Freudian psychoanalysis became an important conceptual tool in policing families. Freud reasoned that boys whose incestuous sexual fantasies were not adequately repressed by a strong father figure would fail to develop normal cultural controls for impulsive, ego-centric behaviour. Agents of the state were thus justified in imposing patriarchal controls within the family through the practices of social work, therapy and probation. Psychoanalytic theory is sufficiently vague, Donzelot suggests, that it justifies limitless therapy and surveillance, since parents could never know for certain whether they were parenting well, or being overly lax or overly controlling with their children. Either extreme leaves their children "at risk", with no clearly correct middle ground.

Foucault predicted that the importance of law and courts would decline relative to the 'psy' professions, but others suggest that the legal system has retained its power by incorporating these professions into itself.

Judges draw on professional expertise in court but retain their power to pass judgement and determine treatment (Smart 1989). We will see examples below of cases in which lawyers for the defence and the prosecution have called upon the 'expert' testimony of psychologists to bolster their arguments, but they still must convince a judge or jury.

Criminology as Ideology

Marx defined theories as *ideological* to the extent that they obscured structural causes of social problems, while blaming victims as the cause of their own disadvantage. Social constructionist analysis explores the active practices by which ideological work gets done, particularly in professions like criminology. They trace how prevailing explanations for problems are constructed and managed within professions and how they work to legitimate certain kinds of state policies while discrediting others.

During the 1960s, mainstream criminology stressed theories of delinquent personalities, linked to inadequate socialization and poor family upbringing as the primary explanations for crime. The preferred methodology of the time was longitudinal studies designed to profile and predict the life patterns of "chronic offenders". Then, for a brief period, more radical ideas held sway, including labelling theory, critical discourse analysis, Marxist class analysis, cultural Marxism and radical Feminism. All of these approaches were sharply critical of the focus on pathological individual psychology, shifting attention instead to inegalitarian and criminogenic social structures, and the role of the prison system itself in generating recidivism.

Yet when we look at mainstream criminology textbooks at the beginning of the twenty-first century, especially those published in the USA, the dominant theories and methodology have reverted back to those prevalent in the 1960s—favouring longitudinal surveys that focus on "risk factors", that prioritize early family life and inadequate mothering (Doran 2000). The only major shift Doran notes is an expanded focus from lower-class youth to youth in general as "at risk". Critical theories have been largely silenced or co-opted into socialization theory—included in mainstream texts as of historical interest for students, but not important for training future practitioners in the criminal justice system. The feminist emphasis on patriarchal victimization of women has been reduced to including women as objects in survey research.

The current resurgence of this faulty-parenting thesis, together with heavy emphasis on individual responsibility, seems to coincide with a marked decline in welfare state policies within corporate capitalist states in Europe and North America. Governments are withdrawing money from social services while increasing budgets for police and prisons. This shift from welfare state to penal state suggests that Foucault may have underestimated the continuing power of the state to punish (Wacquant 2001). The growth of the penal state and the unrestrained growth of big corporations appear to be occurring in tandem.

Potential resistance to a repressive economic order has been incorporated and silenced, Doran suggests (2000) within what he terms "new games of power sharing", including community policing and sentencing circles. Even the potentially critical Marxist approach of left realism has largely abandoned demands for transformative structural change, pressuring the more accommodating option of restorative justice at community level. A few Aboriginal leaders continue to pressure for more radical structural change, demanding compensation for the destructive effects of residential schools, and pressuring land claims as the only real solution to anomie within reservation societies (Monture-Angus 1999). Even as she voices these demands, however, Monture-Angus herself largely despairs of using law as a tool for transformative change. A legal system that reduces everything to individual responsibility cannot hear the struggles of colonized communities, or those of women crushed by patriarchal violence. Aboriginal mothers are still blamed as individuals for foetal alcohol syndrome (FAS) that ravages First Nations children, without recognition of the crushing structural factors that underlie these symptoms of despair.

How did this happen? Doran asks. What are the practices or *relations of ruling* within the criminal justice system in capitalist societies that silences social criticism, and shifts the blame back onto individual families? How is the academic discipline of criminology complicit in this process? How do governments within democratic societies persuade citizens to accept increasingly repressive policing? The following section explores the mundane practices that co-opt resistance into mechanisms of control.

Ruling Practices: Creating Fear

Fear of crime is a strong motivating force for citizens to push for more repressive policing, and these fears seem to be increasing regularly in communities across North America and Western Europe, and especially in the USA (Altheide 2002; Schissel 1997). Objectively, Altheide argues, citizens are safer and more secure and living longer lives than previous generations, but that is not how most people say they feel. The social constructionist perspective analyses levels of fear within communities as the outcome of active practices by opinion leaders that frame social meanings. Mass media of all forms, police and other formal agents of social control, politicians, businesses that sell security systems, and even social scientists, are linked in fear-generating networks that create and sustain a climate of panic in which citizens not merely tolerate, but actively demand aggressive policing, and ubiquitous electronic surveillance systems. Television, and the information-entertainment (infotainment) industry lie at the heart of the network, serving up an almost daily diet of shocking criminal violence, with an approach dubbed: "if it bleeds it leads". Altheide (2002, 21) cites 1998 data showing that the national murder rate in the USA had fallen 20 percent since 1990, but coverage of murders in network newscasts was up 600 percent in the same period. Multiple studies cite similar evidence of media preoccupation with stories of violent crimes committed by youths even though most youth crimes are non-violent (Faith and Jiwani 2002, 83–90). Feature stories of "Killer Girls" and violent girl gangs distort the reality that less than 1 percent of crimes by girls involve violence. Levels of fear, Altheide suggests, are self-perpetuating, as fearful people tend to stay home and watch more television, and become more fearful as they consume more infotainment. Mobile people with limited interpersonal connections with neighbours are particularly open to such influences. In this climate of fear people increasingly welcome all kinds of public surveillance, taking comfort in the electronic assurance that "You are being watched" (Pecora 2002, 347).

This does not mean that all fear is unrealistic or crime waves illusory, but rather that fear of crime can spiral way out of proportion to actual events. Given the right circumstances, media images of pervasive crime can trigger criminal behaviour itself, in a mutually reinforcing spiral (Sacco 2003). Extortion rackets associated with Italian immigrants in New York at the beginning of the Nineteenth century received dramatic coverage in newspapers, embellished with images of mysterious and foreign criminal conspiracies and secret societies, dubbed the "black hand crime wave". Such coverage in turn promoted a climate of fear in which petty criminals found it easy to frighten potential victims to hand over

money by even hinting in extortion notes that they might be part of the 'black hand' gang. More crime fuelled yet wilder newspaper coverage of black-hand extortion rackets that fuelled more fear, especially among new immigrants, and more victims ready to hand over money to extortionists while being too fearful to report them to police or to testify in court. The spiral burned out after some twenty years, Sacco suggests, as immigration rates dropped, and prohibition against the legal sale of alcohol offered more lucrative criminal opportunities.

Crime reporters get most of their material from institutional sources within the justice system, and particularly from the police. The result is that media coverage of crime tends to be framed from the perspective of law-and-order. The pervasive message is that police work is difficult and dangerous and requires more and more resources to be effective. Getting 'soft on crime' is not a rational option. Politicians use infotainment as a backdrop for popularizing tough policies that pinpoint antisocial or deviant individuals as the cause of social malaise, while businesses use it to sell a plethora of home security systems. Self-sustaining and mutually beneficial networks of motivations sustain the climate of fear.

Family life is at the core of the fear message, with fear *for* children and fear *of* children as recurring themes. Training in fear for the safety of children begins early in life, as parents, teachers, and social workers are warned to street-proof children to avoid all strangers, especially men, to reduce the risk of abduction and sexual assault. On October 22, 2004 a new computer game for children was released in Canada, designed explicitly to train children to distrust and avoid any adult they do not know. The CBC announcer noted that hundreds of children disappear annually. During the 1990s, local authorities in Britain placed signs in public washrooms warning parents to "Watch Your Child" because it only takes a minute for a child to be grabbed. In schools across Canada in 2004, children practised 'code red' drills to lock classroom doors and hide under desks in preparation for possible armed intruders (*Globe and Mail* Oct.18, 2004, A8). Spokespersons for the School Board acknowledge that there has been no recent increase in school violence, and that children are more at risk of being struck by lightening than being shot in school, but counter that children watch television and are well aware of the threat of terrorism and school attacks. A group of seniors putting on a puppet show for elementary school children in Fredericton in 2004 were warned in advance that school policy prohibits any interaction between the children and outside visitors, since visitors have not had police checks. Similar policies control who is permitted to work with children in church Sunday schools. All such practices are strongly defended as rational risk management.

The discourse of "stranger danger" in popular culture focuses on risk avoidance as the constant responsibility of adults in charge of children. Media coverage and official statistics on "missing children" convey the impression that the hundreds of thousands of children who go missing annually are abducted and violated by strangers (Best 1987; 1989). The evidence indicates that almost all of these cases are not newsworthy—they involve children who were quickly found to have been with friends, or were snatched by parents involved in custody disputes, or teenagers who run away from home. The small fraction of cases that truly involve abduction by strangers, however, attract infotainment attention. These cases then come to typify for citizens what happens when children go missing. These practices produce what functionalist analysis describes as typical cultural attitudes. Foucault further suggests that the constancy of media and professional interest in sexual abuse of children may be a significant factor inciting sexual interest in and abuse of children, especially inside families (Foucault 1978). Incest becomes a more thinkable or normalized option as individuals hear more about it.

A parallel discourse incites fear *of* children as often uncontrollable and prone to violent criminal behaviour (Schissel 1997; 2002). Crime-and-fear stories are featured in the media alongside images of girls as well as boys who are armed, on drugs, anti-social, and dangerous. Schissel cites extensive data showing that conviction and incarceration rates for youth in Canada more than doubled after 1985, following the passing of the *Young Offenders Act* in 1984. The statistics reflect, not a sudden explosion in criminal and violent behaviour, but a redirection into courts of petty offences that would formerly have been dealt with at the informal level of schools and neighbourhoods. The promotion of 'zero tolerance' policies for violence encourages teachers and others to report school-yard bullying and scuffles to police (Faith and Jiwani 2002, 89). Under new legislation, teachers themselves would risk an assault charge, should they try to physically restrain an angry child. The resulting surge in 'crime' rates is readily associated in infotainment with cases of newsworthy violence. Exceptional cases such as the murder of fourteen-year-old Reena Virk in Victoria BC in 1997, following a

severe beating by teenaged girls (Bell, 2002, 129), and the murder of two-year old James Bulger in England in 1993 by two ten-year-old boys (Siegel and McCormick 2003, 293), combined with evidence of soaring conviction rates, feed into a climate of fear. Masses of citizens lobby politicians to demand aggressive policing so that their families can feel safe. The prevailing functionalist explanation for such violence in terms of abusive, dysfunctional homes (ibid. 293) supports a wider discourse of moral and spiritual degeneration of youth.

Ruling Discourses, Theorizing Crime and Fear

Mainstream sociological and criminological theories of criminal behaviour are more likely to promote fears than to allay them. Anomie theories that focus on family and community breakdown frighten people who are themselves geographically mobile and disconnected from stable neighbourhood ties. Longitudinal studies use surveys to track cohorts of children through their school years, asking a series of questions about individual circumstances and behaviours that can be correlated with future deviance and criminal records. Such surveys are designed to pick out classic predictive factors like broken homes, single mothers, mothers on welfare, drug and alcohol use/abuse in homes, and abuse of physical discipline. Survey data then provide the scientific basis for identifying "youth at risk" of criminogenic behaviour, and in turn legitimate state intervention in families at risk.

Networks of social workers, psychologists, teachers, probation officers, child-protection workers, and others, are employed in current practices of policing families. Together they are engaged in the ideological work of "manufacturing 'bad' mothers" (Swift 1995). Both survey research design and social work practices function to turn the spotlight on parenting, or more specifically failed mothering, as the cause of criminogenic youth. The structured economic and social circumstances under which mothers do their work get factored out of the picture. When 'poverty' is statistically controlled, it is the mothers who fail to manage, rather than the miserable conditions they endure, that appear as the central predictor of children who fail. Since there is no viable alternative to mothers caring for children, especially when marriages break up, mothers must be 'policed to care' (Swift 1995, 113–5). The cycle theory of neglect blames poor mothering in one generation for poor mothering in the next, legitimating long-term state intervention at the level of families. Aboriginal families in Canada are statistically the most at risk of state intervention, with their children three times more likely to be taken into state care than non-native children. From the perspective of Aboriginal communities, child-welfare legislation functions as insidious continuing colonization, separating yet another generation of youth from their Aboriginal cultures (Swift 128–30). Other visible minorities in Canadian society, including gay and lesbian parents, are drawn into this same network of intensive surveillance under threat of the legalized removal of their children (Wachholz 2000). Shocking media coverage of neglected and abused children and neglecting and abusive parents readily legitimate these policing practices in the views of other citizens.

Critical Marxist theories point to high levels of structural unemployment and welfare rates set far below the levels that parents need to provide shelter, food and clothing for their children as the root of much family breakdown. But this critical discourse is largely silenced by more strongly articulated claims that there are jobs available for those who wish to work (Doherty 2000). Since 'normal' people have jobs, unemployed people appear as abnormal, lazy, or otherwise deficient. Low welfare rates are easily legitimated for normal citizens through discourses of deficit reduction, and fears that welfare handouts encourage dependency and laziness and undermine the will to find work. Hopelessness, drug and alcohol abuse, and petty crime form a vicious cycle that feeds into popular images of the poor as irresponsible and guilty.

In a social climate already charged with fear, Marxist-inspired analysis of criminal behaviour in terms of anger and desperation arising from poverty and relative deprivation, function to promote fear of the poor as dangerous. Panhandlers and squeegee kids come across as aggressive and threatening to nervous pedestrians and drivers in their locked-down vehicles. A few encounters with people begging for change and youths armed with damp sponges, prompt editorials and complaints to politicians from business people and tourists demanding legislation to clear such people from the streets (Schissel, 2002, 124). The enactment of the *Safe Streets Act* in Ontario January 2000, outlawed soliciting persons who are in vehicles or standing in queues to use bank machines, telephones, toilets, or transit. Soliciting includes trying to clean car windows for money (Moon 2002, 73–4; Hermer and Moser 2002).

The currently most popular explanation for crime in America is that crime is rational economic behaviour

governed by cost-benefit estimates. This view implies that most people will commit theft and fraud if they figure the risks of getting caught are small and expected punishment light, relative to the potential for high profits from crime (Zedner 2003, 29). Cost-benefit analysis views crime as expected, normative, rational everyday behaviour—a far cry from Durkheim's classic definition of crime as the violation of community values. Again, a vicious spiral of causality may be happening. As people are trained from childhood to expect others to steal from them, they are less likely to feel guilty and deviant when they themselves consider stealing from others. The growing dominance of economic analysis of crime, Zedner suggests, is driving the shift to a security-conscious society. Property owners expect to have to install security systems in their homes and offices, to drive in locked cars, and often also to carry weapons. Such defensive practices are not proportional to risk: the highest proportion of concealed weapons permits are issued for upscale, low-crime neighbourhoods while most break-ins happen in poor areas (Altheide 2002, 1). Police spokespersons routinely lecture seniors groups on the advisability of security systems, although objectively seniors as a group are least often victimized by crime.

Security alarms and locked cars function as daily reminders that people should be fearful of others. Trusting strangers is not rational behaviour. The argument that copycat vandalism will quickly escalate if even one house in a street is left with a broken window, further criminalizes trivial delinquency, inciting other residents to demand swift, punitive responses. As people grow more distrusting, social solidarity is further undermined, in yet another vicious spiral of interacting cause and effect. As more people are charged with offenses, crime rates rise, proving that more prisons are needed. The end result is that the very failure of the criminal justice system to reduce crime rates works to legitimate a penal state and to focus attention on anti-social individuals rather than economic structures (Reiman 2001).

In the aftermath of the September 11th 2001 terrorist attacks (9/11) in New York and Washington, the American government has issued almost permanent yellow and orange alerts warning citizens of the ever-present threat of another terrorist attack. As the state signals constant threats to national security, individuals respond by seeking greater private protection even as they demand heightened state regulations (Zedner 2003). Private security guards now outnumber state police in the USA, employed to patrol commercial buildings, shopping malls and public transit. Closed-circuit-television systems (CCTV) trawl continually for suspects. Youths, the poor and homeless, and members of marginalized ethnic minorities often find themselves excluded from supposedly public places like shopping malls as private guards evict them for loitering on private mall property. Heightened security promises reduced risk but at the price of eroding civil liberties, especially the liberties of marginalized groups. Under the Homeland Security Act of 2002, the U.S. government has the right to investigate every aspect of citizens' lives—including their e-mails, internet websites visited, and charge-card records, without requiring any prior evidence of criminal activity. In Canada, all but 18 of the 2544 applications by the Canadian Security Intelligence Service (CSIS) for intelligence-gathering warrants were approved between 1993–2003 (*Globe and Mail* Nov.15, 2004, A6). These warrants grant agents similarly invasive powers to search for information on suspected terrorists or foreign spies.

The paradox is that more security generates more insecurity as citizens are continually reminded of risk. Heightened air-line security only serves to expose the practical impossibility of achieving total security (Russell and Preston 2004). Media frequently carry exposés by reporters and others who manage to get forbidden items through checking systems, leaving passengers feeling less secure than before the scanners and armed guards were visibly in place. What is happening, suggests Zedner, is a significant shift in the nature of policing from 'criminal justice' that deals with people who have actually committed offences, to a 'security state' that polices suspect populations profiled in advance as at risk of having criminal intent.

Community policing and neighbourhood watch programs feed directly into the climate of fear, encouraging citizens to spy on their neighbours and report anything suspicious or unusual to the police. "Reality-TV" programs like *crime-stoppers* and *America's Most Wanted*, encourage individuals to regard spying on their neighbours and 'snitching' on them to authorities as the right thing to do (Pecora 2002, 347). People who rarely interact with their neighbours in any social events come together to monitor others whom they distrust (Klinenberg 2001). Anyone who looks different, who does not fit the profile of 'normal' attracts greater surveillance. The goal of neighbourhood security inevitably presumes that there are people who are unfit to belong in the area and who ought to be excluded. Distrust, suspicion, and fear, Klinenberg suggests, are

fast becoming central features of neighbourhood culture and local politics.

In summary, these prevailing discourses about crime show considerable variety at a surface level, focussing attention on family and community breakdown, poor parenting, unemployment and poverty, anger and desperation, rational greed and desire to get consumer goods without working for them. Yet they all feed into the same underlying cultural theme of fear. This underlying or "deep structure" cross-cuts class divisions to create a sense of consensus that all 'reasonable' citizens share (Doran 2002b; Hall 1974). This fear may be experienced differently by citizens at different social class levels. The better off have good reason to fear that their luxury homes, cars, and other possessions are coveted by others who do not have them, while the poor have even greater reason to fear that the anger and despair associated with poverty and broken families will explode into violence mostly in their own neighbourhoods. Liberals may blame environment while traditionalists blame moral breakdown, and others privately blame racialized minorities and immigrants, but all can agree on the need for stronger policing. Deeper questions about the criminogenic character of globalized corporate capitalist society rarely enter this public debate on crime, fear, terror, good-and-evil, and policing (Doran ibid. 165). Still more rarely is the reasonableness of fear itself opened to question.

Research with living in a high crime subsidized housing estate in Britain reminds us to be cautious in interpreting 'evidence' of fear of crime. Survey data did not fit with how people talked about their lived experience of life on the estate. While most people had indicated in response to an abstract survey question that they were fearful at the thought of muggings, break-ins, and the like, this did not mean that they were fearful in their everyday lives (Foster 1995). People knew that many residents in the two large apartment blocks where they lived had criminal records, and knew that some were actively involved in illicit activities. But nonetheless most people felt secure because they were familiar with their neighbours, and people kept an eye out for each other and constrained trouble-makers. As one local police officer put it, "a lot of them are sailing very close to the wind but they don't shit on their own doorstep. They have their own code" (571). Most people, including local police, felt that informal controls such as neighbours, or the well-known local beat police officer speaking to family members, worked better to keep deviance under control than formal arrests. During a period when inexperienced new officers and the local authority staff tried more heavy-handed threats, the common response was not to tell the police anything (579).

Policing Practices: Deviantizing Work

Police on street patrols and citizens who work with them in Community Policing and Neighbourhood Watch programs are engaged in practices of constituting normalcy, deviance, and criminality in the interests of maintaining security and order within the community. Police are mandated to apprehend people who violate laws, and to act preemptively to prevent crimes from being committed. Citizens are encouraged to call police whenever they notice suspicious activities in their neighbourhood. Foster's study of a subsidized housing estate in Britain, described above (1995), suggests that community policing works best as a back-up to informal sanctions rather than as heavy-handed presence. Neighbours spoke directly to trouble-makers or their parents, with the threat of calling in formal sanctions if all else failed. These sanctions worked across racial boundaries by white residents approaching Bengali neighbours they knew to ask them to speak to troublesome Bengali youth, and vice versa.

Social constructionist analysis explores the routine everyday reasoning methods that police and citizens on watch use to decide what looks sufficiently "suspicious for this time and place" to take action. Deviance and crime are not simply 'there' to be noticed by vigilant citizens; they are actively constituted through the ways in which police and their citizen assistants notice and categorize the flow of street life. Such decisions are also inherently associated with class war, constituting who is considered acceptable and who should be excluded from the neighbourhood. Enforcing the new *Safe Streets Act*, for example, requires multiple judgements: What constitutes "an aggressive manner" of begging or merely offering a window-washing service? When are pedestrians "a captive audience" with respect to whom begging is prohibited? Similarly with respect to policing prostitution, what constitutes "soliciting for the purposes of prostitution" or merely standing around, or responding to an invitation? What constitutes "loitering with intent" to commit a crime, or merely sitting on a bench? With

respect to youth on the streets, what constitutes criminal vandalism or merely excusable pranks? In shopping malls, what distinguishes a normal shopper from a vagrant or potential thief who should be ushered out?

The routine reasoning methods used in making these decisions produce statistics on arrest profiles, with their class-race-age-gender characteristics (James 2002). Young, Native and Black males dressed in cheap clothing attract the greatest attention, while conservatively-dressed, neat-looking, older white women and men pass unnoticed. Since 9/11, people of Arab and Muslim appearance also disproportionately attract suspicion. Only in the rare cases when victims caught in the net of suspicious gaze successfully challenge their labelling, do people pause to consider their reasoning. In the fall of 2004, as this chapter was being written, newspapers carried stories of a Canadian of Arab appearance being imprisoned and intensely interrogated for two weeks under suspicion of terrorist activity. His suspicious behaviour apparently consisted of photographing Toronto's landmark CN Tower from a city bus. Two black males made the news when judges agreed they had been wrongly arrested and roughed up by police, in one case for 'suspiciously' driving an expensive car, and another for merely looking vaguely like another suspect. These two are typical of a very long list of aggressive encounters between police and racialized citizens (James 2002; 1998; Comack 1999, 54–5). In each case police spokespersons expressed not remorse, but incredulity at the stupidity of judges for not understanding the realities of how police-work on the streets gets done. Police frequently allude to the inherent usefulness of racial profiling in their work even as they deny that racial profiling occurs.

The Power of Law: Defining "Truth"

Courts of law are accorded special authority to define truth through practices of legal reasoning, rules of inference, adversarial debate, and final judgement beyond reasonable doubt (Smart 1989, ch. 1). It is a criminal offence in law to challenge the conclusions of a judge or jury, except on grounds of technical procedures that are themselves determined by a higher-court judge. No other profession is accorded a similar level of deference.

Social constructionist analysis focuses attention on the routine reasoning practices used by lawyers, judges and jurors in determining the 'truth' of cases that come to court. Lawyers are trained to select specific evidence that has legal relevance for a case at hand, filtering out, and disqualifying much lived experience that participants themselves may consider relevant. Lawyers for the prosecution present the particulars of a case in a form that intends the conclusion that the police have indeed apprehended the guilty persons. Lawyers for the defence must respond to these particulars to try to construct them into an alternative account that suggests the defendant might be innocent (Smith 1990, ch. 4). Smith points out that when judges and jurors share similar notions about typical criminals as do the police, members of stigmatized minorities have greater than average difficulty in sustaining an alternative account of their behaviour. Native and Black defendants in Canada rarely face people like themselves on juries (Aylward 1999). People living on the street are even less likely to face any juror who has experienced everyday life the way they do. Poor people may also be unable to afford experienced lawyers, while drug lords can hire a battery of them.

These routine practices involved in "making a case" become visible mostly in the rare cases when judgements are overturned. In one intensely analysed case, Donald Marshall, a Micmac Indian, was found to have been wrongly convicted of murder after spending eleven years in prison. A public inquiry into the case in 1988 heard evidence that the police may have bullied witnesses into perjuring themselves in the original trial to secure the conviction, and covered up subsequent evidence pointing to an alternative culprit (Mannette 1992). More importantly, Mannette argues, the general climate of fear and hostility towards Indians in Sydney, NS at the time made it easy both for teenage witnesses and for jurors to convince themselves that the police account was correct, and extremely difficult for the seventeen-year-old Micmac defendant to present himself as innocent.

Investigations into other cases of wrongful conviction show that the Marshall case cannot be understood simply as an aberrant example of racism. Comparable accounts of bullied testimony and failure to disclose subsequent evidence surfaced in 1992 when the murder conviction of David Milgaard was overturned, after he had served twenty years in prison. Individual police officers associated with these cases commented on the routineness of the procedures used, their own certainty that they had apprehended a guilty person, and the necessity of working up evidence and witnesses to convince a jury. In 1994 Milgaard's mother, Joyce Milgaard helped to found an association of lawyers and other experts dedicated to the reinvestigation of murder convictions where plausible challenges to the original construction of evidence can be worked up. During the fall of 2004, as a

decision on the Stephen Truscott case being made, there were over 40 more plausible wrongful conviction cases under investigation.

"Not Making the Case"

The routine reasoning practices that sustain certain cases as credible also works to constitute other cases as not credible, or not founded. Legal reasoning that presumes a defendant innocent until proven guilty can make many cases difficult to process because they hinge on the relative believability of different people involved.

In Canada, investigation and judgement on cases of alleged discrimination are the exclusive responsibility of provincial and federal human rights commissions, subject to the overriding authority of the Charter. In principle, human rights legislation is designed to protect and to provide redress for people from all forms of unjustified discrimination, including but is not limited to grounds of race, gender, sexual orientation, religion, national or ethnic origin, colour, marital and family status, and disability. In practice, the system is plagued by such a litany of problems that it has been challenged as discriminatory in itself, and possibly in violation of Charter rights to equality of treatment (Aylward 1999, 165–174). Aylward cites evidence that the vast majority of human rights complaints are rejected at the investigation state—with discrimination on the basis of race rejected more than any other grounds (ibid. 166).

Overt discrimination, as when an employer bluntly states that he will not hire Indians, is easy to recognize, but the vast majority of cases involve covert and subtle unfairness. Human rights investigators begin with assumption that equality of treatment is the norm. It is the responsibility of a complainant to prove beyond reasonable doubt that alleged distressing experiences were explicitly caused by discrimination on the basis of some specified ground like 'race'. Defendants routinely raise counter claims like the alleged rejection of the complainant was either imaginary, or legitimately due to inadequate work, limited skills or experience, poorer quality schooling or other competences compared to some other preferred applicant, or to disagreeable personality, lack of collegiality, or a host of other negative characteristics. This leaves the complainant with the burden of proving that none of these other excuses apply. MacKinnon concludes that the one time a person of colour alleges discrimination is the one time that race will be deemed irrelevant (MacKinnon 1987, 65). *Critical race litigation* seeks to raise the consciousness of lawyers and jurors on how the lived experiences of racialized minorities are routinely disqualified in courts, and to promote alternative legal analysis.

The large majority of allegations of sexual assault are also dropped before they even reach a courtroom (Du Mont 2003). The presumption of the defendant's innocence works to place the full burden of proving the absence on consent onto the complainant. In multiple ways the experiences of rape victims are disqualified in court, with the social status of the complainant as a central determining factor in believability. Du Mont's survey of hospital, police, and prosecution records, as well as extensive reviews of other studies, concludes that women in low-income situations, with low levels of education, who are unemployed, and/or who have a higher risk of sexual assault but are significantly less likely to have their cases result in a charge. Judges generally tended to view sexual assault cases as less serious than physical assault cases and to minimize the impact of injury and harm to victims (ibid. 315). Du Mont's data is consistent with earlier research by Clark and Lewis (1977) showing that women who work in the sex trade, along with women on welfare, and Black and Native women are comparatively the least likely to be believed, while professional women are most likely to have their cases viewed as founded. Du Mont concludes that while the law on sexual assault was substantially changed in 1983, judicial discretion at all stages, from deciding to lay charges, to achieving convictions, and sentencing still reflect long-standing 'rape myths' that blame the victim.

Institutional Ethnography: Disqualification as Organizational Practice

The case studies summarized below use the technique of "institutional ethnography" to explore in detail how *relations of ruling* work at the level of routine everyday administrative practices in state agencies. Compensation for injured workers has long been a focus of class struggle, with workers blaming unsafe working conditions, while employers blamed worker negligence (Doran 2002). The arena of struggle changed in Canada in the early twentieth century with the enactment of workmen's compensation legislation based on the principle of no-fault-liability. Doran traces in meticulous detail how professional medico-legal discourses work to disqualify workers' lived experience of workplace-aggravated illness and death. Experts set "normative" health and illness levels, with statistical models to calculate the percentage of any given illness that might be attributable to the workplace, monitored by semi-annual medical examinations, and enforced by union contracts. How workers experience their own illnesses and their conditions of work become irrelevant.

Eligibility for legal aid for domestic-dispute litigation constitutes another highly gendered arena of class struggle. Court social workers have the authority to interpret eligibility rules governing access to legal aid for people, mostly women, for cases involving divorce, custody disputes and domestic violence (Beaman 2002). These workers decide such matters as whether there is sufficient evidence of domestic abuse to warrant a shift from custody mediation to a court case, or whether a woman will have sufficient access to disputed family assets to pay her own lawyer, or whether she is sufficiently recovered from mental illness to get back to work and earn money for a lawyer. Beaman supplies detailed evidence of how women's lived experiences are disqualified from the decision-making process. Their stories of threats, emotional abuse, depression, domestic assets being totally withheld from them or sold for less than the mortgage, and the like, are filtered out of legal relevance, as court workers deem them insufficient grounds to qualify them for legal aid. Without access to legal aid, such stories never reach the courts. Court workers in turn find themselves closely monitored to ensure that priority spending of scarce legal aid monies goes to criminal cases.

It is through such mundane reasoning practices at the levels of routine policing of streets, routine sorting of evidence to determine whether or not cases will proceed to court, or be heard as 'reasonable' by jurors, human rights commissioners, medical experts, court social workers, or employees at multiple locations within networks of formal administration that construct what we come to know as social justice and its gendered, ethnic, raced, and classed character.

The Feminist Perspective: Gendered Law

The feminist perspective explores how institutions of law and criminal justice sustain gendered social structures that disadvantage women, notwithstanding the formal commitment of contemporary legal systems to principles of objectivity, gender neutrality and equality under the Charter.

Law underpins the structure of family life—the institution viewed from the functionalist perspective as the foundation of society. Law defines who can or cannot be legally married, the legal age of consent to marriage, the responsibilities that spouses assume on marriage, property and inheritance rights, terms of divorce, custody of children, adoption, surrogacy, the rights and responsibilities that parents who are not married have towards their children, and the like. This body of family law has been the site of feminist struggles in Canada dating back over two centuries. The legal status of marriage as a binding contract becomes particularly evident at the point of divorce, where one or both parties consider breaking the contract. Hence, laws governing divorce are the main focus of the following section.

Historically, Canadian family law, rooted in British common law, reinforced a normative male-headed, patriarchal family form (Smart 1984; McBean 1987). Legally, a wife was subsumed under the civil status of her husband, meaning that only a husband could enter into a legally-binding contract. All marital property belonged exclusively to the husband, including any that a wife might have brought into the marriage, and any money that she might subsequently earn. Children were defined in law as belonging only to the father. On separation or divorce, for whatever reason, the children were legally bound to remain with their father, regardless of age. The explicit intent of these laws was to reinforce the marital union by making it punitively difficult for a wife-mother to leave.

These laws slowly began to change between the 1880s to 1920s under pressure of the argument that a morally sinful unmarried mother had more rights in law than respectable married women. However, these changes were slow, niggardly, and interpreted by judges in ways designed to minimize threats to the marital union. Property rights were changed to permit a married woman to retain property that she herself inherited or brought into the marriage, but gave her no right to any share in marital property. Mortgages and tenancies remained exclusively in the husband's name. A wife who could prove that she had been wilfully deserted by her husband was given the right to sue him for maintenance and custody of children. However, this right was subject to the stringent conditions that she be a morally deserving and deserted wife and mother. "Morally deserving" was interpreted in law to mean that she maintain strict sexual abstinence. Any evidence to suggest that she had

sex with another man was sufficient grounds for her ex-husband to stop paying maintenance and to have the children removed. This rule applied regardless of whether the husband was sexually involved with other women.

The right to seek a divorce was also slowly extended to women under the stringent condition that a wife prove herself the victim of adultery, desertion or cruelty. As late as the 1960s, some judges were still interpreting 'cruelty' in sexist ways (Smart 1984, 94), arguing that a wife could not fault her husband for the 'natural disinclination' to have sex with her, but she herself would be guilty of cruelty if she refused to fulfil her marital duty to have sex with her husband. Only if a wife were truly blameless and deserving in the eyes of a judge, did she have a right to maintenance after marital breakdown. If she were guilty of breaking up her children's home by leaving their father without good cause, or by committing adultery, she could be deemed a bad wife and mother and lose both maintenance and any right to appeal for custody of her children. Legal decisions controlling custody of children gradually shifted towards the "tender years doctrine" reasoning that infants needed to be with their mothers, until age seven, when legal guardianship of their father resumed.

Gender Equality, the Charter, and Family Law

Major shifts in family law towards the principle of gender equality in marriage eventually came about in North America and Western Europe under the impact of second-wave feminist struggles. They were endorsed in Canada in 1985 with the passage into law of the gender equality rights provision of the Canadian Charter. While a marked improvement over earlier laws, feminist research highlights the gendered inequalities still inherent in family law. These continuing inequalities are rooted in the substantially very different social and economic situations of wives and husbands that are obscured by the formal application of legal equality rules.

Marital property laws changed significantly in Canada in the 1980s, following the waves of political outrage that erupted after the 1975 Supreme Court decision on the Murdoch case. The Murdochs divorced after 25 years of marriage, during which they both developed the family ranch. Mrs Murdoch had regularly worked the ranch by herself for five to eight months of most years while her husband had employment elsewhere. Yet upon divorce, the Supreme Court determined that legally, the ranch and the house upon it belonged solely to her husband because the original down-payment and mortgage were in his name only. Her quarter-century of unpaid labour on the ranch counted for nothing (Machum 2002, 136-7; Atcheson et. al., 1984, 26). Machum notes further that Canadian tax laws from 1969 excluded wages to a farmer's wife as a business-expense deduction, although wages to a farmer's children and other hired hands were deductible. A farmer's wife was also explicitly not eligible for unemployment insurance or a Canada Pension.

Significant changes were made to family property laws from 1980 onwards, to explicitly recognize for the first time that domestic work and childcare counts equally with financial contributions in creating an interest in family property on marriage breakdown, including family businesses (Keet 1990). While laws governing division of marital property vary somewhat by province, the family home is recognized across Canada as belonging equally to both spouses, regardless of who paid for it.

The principle of formal legal equality between women and men is now entrenched in the Charter of Rights, sections 15(1) and 28. Earlier family laws that overtly subordinated wives to husbands are now unconstitutional. Substantial equality, however, has not been achieved in the actual lived experiences of women and men going through divorce. Critical feminist legal theory challenges the concept of formal equality as ideological in that it obscures the social and financial realities facing women and men that commonly result in very unequal outcomes from supposedly equal treatment in law (Razack 1991; Koggel, 1994; Jhappan 1998; L'Heureux-Dube 1997; Liu 2000). So long as wives generally take more time out from employment for pregnancy, childbirth and early childhood care, take primary responsibility for domestic work and child-rearing, and when employed, earn significantly lower incomes on average than their husbands, they do not face divorce on an equal financial footing (Cheal 1999, ch. 4). Wives who have been full-time homemakers for any length of time during a marriage may be left with half a house but no means to continue mortgage payments. Maintenance awards based on the principle that divorcing adults should become self supporting within a reasonable time typically result in women having a substantially lower standard of living after divorce while men typically are financially better off (Steel 1987; Richardson 1996, ch. 9).

Judges have considerable discretion in setting property and maintenance awards, weighing such factors as the likelihood that the ex-wife can become financially self-supporting, the ex-husband's financial situation and possible responsibilities towards a second family, how childcare is being shared, and the like. Judges also consider the viability of any commercial enterprise owned by an ex-spouse. It is not in the interest of the court or the partners to bankrupt a business by dividing assets. Concern for the viability of a farm commonly results in judicial decisions that give an ex-farm-wife no share in farm assets for many years, until the primary farmer retires or sells the farm (Keet 1990). Determining the interest that one spouse may have in career opportunities of the other can be very complex. In one case a wife had worked for years to support her husband and child while the husband studied dentistry. The marriage broke up as he graduated, a point when she had a low-wage job and no prospects while he had great earning potential but no assets (McCallum 1994). She had put her career development on hold to support him and their child, but on divorce the professional credentials and their income-earning potential were exclusively his. Critical feminist litigation struggles to make visible the structurally gendered inequality that underlies these stories that are obscured by objective, gender-blind application of equality.

Aboriginal Women's Rights

The Indian Act of 1876 was a piece of colonial legislation that imposed patriarchal family relations onto Aboriginal peoples. Under section 12(1)(b) of this Act, only Indian males could pass on their status as Indian to their spouse and offspring, and with it, the right to live on reservations. Indian women who married non-Indian men lost their status and had to leave their reserves. Property and housing on reserves was held only by men. This rule was justified initially by the argument that it would prevent white men from gaining possession of Indian lands and property through their Indian wives— an argument that itself presumed that husbands normally controlled the property of their wives. The Act was modified only in 1985 with the passing into law of Bill C-31, which enabled women who lost their status through marriage to regain it, along with the children of these marriages. The descendants of men who had lost status by becoming enfranchised, were also included.

Hailed by feminists as a major victory on behalf of Indian women, the changes still leave important inequalities between Indian women and men (Monture-Angus 1999). Men who marry a non-status woman continue to pass on status to their children and grandchildren. Women who marry out pass their status only to their children; both their sons and daughters lose status if they themselves marry a non-status person. Over time, Monture-Angus suggests, this means that the absolute number of status Indians is likely to decline. Other forms of discrimination against status-Indian women under the Indian Act remain unchanged. Certificates of possession, the system of property ownership on reserves, are normally only in the name of the male partner in a marriage. The Supreme Court determined that matrimonial property laws do not apply on reservations, so that on divorce, Indian women often find themselves with no property and no place to live. Monture-Angus concludes that while some 104 000 persons won the right to call themselves status Indians as a result of the 1985 Act, there has been little real change in the status of women on reserves.

Custody as Unequal Equality Rights

Following the Charter, the federal Divorce Law of 1985 replaced the old terminology of husband/wife and father/mother with gender neutral terms "spouse" and "parent", to be consistent with equality rights. The new law also substituted "best interests of the child" for earlier doctrines of paternal guardianship or maternal tender-years. Joint custody was declared the legally preferred option following divorce. This incorporated both the long-argued feminist position that both fathers and mothers should be equally responsible for the care of children, and psychology research highlighting the value to children of close contact with fathers. Fathers' Rights groups also challenged the prevalence of children remaining with mothers while fathers paid support as a violation of men's equality rights. The "friendly parent rule" incorporated into the Divorce Law enjoins judges to take into account the readiness of one parent to facilitate children's access to their other parent in deciding where best a child should live.

Critical feminist litigation has struggled to make visible the gendered inequalities that are obscured by the application of formal-legal equality rules to custody disputes. Custody of children is decided mostly by parents themselves without going to court, with children remaining with their mothers in the large majority of cases (Brophy 1989; McBean 1989; Graycar 1989). It is in the 10 to 15 percent of cases where custody is disputed, that

court-mandated divorce mediators or judges are called upon to balance equality rights of parents and best interests of children, in a context where parents themselves may be fighting, and using children as pawns to get at each other (Sandberg 1989). Gendered inequalities rooted in family structures carry over into these disputes.

The gender-neutral term 'parenting' obscures vastly different expectations for level of primary childcare from mothers and fathers, when the model of male breadwinner and female homemaker is considered normative (Boyd 1987; 1989a; 1989b; Fineman 1989a; 1989b). The principle of joint-legal custody does not necessarily or even usually entail equal co-parenting at the level of daily care of children. Mothers may find themselves doing the bulk of all child care while having their parenting decisions vetoed by their ex-husband (Gordon 1989). Traditionalist judges have also been known to conclude that it is more in children's best interests that they live with their father and a home-maker step-mother than with a biological mother who is employed full time, especially in demanding careers (Graycar 1989). Many judges have further concluded that it may not be in children's best interests to live with an overtly homosexual parent, and hence awarded disputed custody to the 'normal' parent (Arnup 1994; Boyd 1997; McCarthy and Radbord 1998; Wachholz 2002).

The presumption that divorce mediation is a cheaper and less-adversarial route than courts for settling property and custody disputes obscures the inequalities of power experienced by financially dependent spouses who may already have been victimized by years of emotional and physical abuse, be ignorant even of how much money or property their spouse might have, and be terrified of appearing an 'unfriendly parent' and losing their children if they fight too hard. Such lived inequalities in power may render people unable to represent their own interests or to negotiate their legally-recognized rights in mediation (Girdner 1989; Bottomley 1985). A history of violence in the family can be obscured in custody and access decisions both because some victims are afraid to speak up, and because some judges deem violence irrelevant if it were directed at the partner rather than the children (Rosnes 1997). Even when custody is awarded primarily to one parent, the principle of preserving a child's access to both parents sets up a situation where a vindictive non-custodial parent can repeatedly use the courts, in the name of Charter equality rights, to harass and control the lives of ex-spouse and children until the last child reaches legal adulthood (Gordon 1989; Graycar 1989; Delorey 1989; Holtrust et. al., 1989).

Such power relations can be established even when the parents were never married.

Neilson (2003) provides an extensive analysis of proposed amendments to the 1985 Divorce Act, introduced in Bill C-22 in 2003. Neilson suggests that the Bill does not go far enough in protecting the post-divorce interests of children from families where there was violence between parents. Good features, she argues, are that the Bill replaces concepts of 'parental rights' with responsibilities, and no longer presumes that shared parenting and maximum contact between children and both parents are priority concerns in families where there has been violence. Bad features include the absence of explicit direction to lawyers to fully document evidence of abuse and violence when parenting decisions are being made, lack of review for agreements reached in face-to-face mediation in family violence cases, a failure to recognize domination and control as forms of abuse, and the failure to include a reverse-onus provision requiring abusive parents to demonstrate that contact will be safe and beneficial for both children and the victimized parent. Without such changes, she argues, victimized parents will still face the daunting double onus of both proving that assault occurred and proving that children will be harmed by further contact. This may be all but impossible if they are denied legal aid.

What these many cases reflect are the inherent difficulties involved in trying to apply the principle of legal equality rights in family law in a social context of manifestly unequal power relations between spouses. In critical feminist litigation, even the use of the gender-neutral term 'spouse' in the above discussion is ideological in that it obscures the lived reality that the large majority of dependent, subordinated, and abused spouses are women, and the economic and socially dominant spouses are men.

Policing Domestic Violence

Violent homes breed more violence. An extensive body of research in sociology and psychology documents the harm suffered by children who witness violent conflicts between their parents, even when the children themselves are not directly targeted (See Neilson 2003, 13–14; also Jaffe, Wolfe & Wilson 1990). As we have seen earlier, girls charged with assaulting their peers are very likely to have grown up in homes characterized by exaggerated patriarchal dominance enforced by frequent physical violence (Artz 1998; Artz and Riecken 1994; Bell 2002). Boys who beat up their girlfriends have com-

monly seen their fathers use force to control women (Totten 2000). Children who kill have commonly grown up in worlds where violence is the normative way to handle conflict (Kelly and Totten 2002). Women and men in prison for crimes involving violence pervasively describe childhoods marred by physical and sexual assaults (Comack 1996: McKendy 1997). Homicides in Canada, and especially homicides committed by women, far more often involve family members than strangers. Yet domestic violence cases are among the most difficult arenas of policing work.

Police who respond to domestic disturbance calls know they may themselves be the target of rage from both the perpetrator and the complainant. Historically, wife-beating was seen largely as a private matter, legitimated as a means for men to discipline unruly wives (Smart 1992; Clark 1992). Until the 1980s, police routinely delayed responding to such calls or even ignored them in the hope that the altercation would die down without their intervention, or they tried to calm the situation and leave. Arrests were made typically only if weapons were visibly present, suggesting an immanent threat of grievous bodily harm or murder.

Feminists have struggled to change these police protocols, calling for mandatory arrests for domestic assaults, the same as if they occurred between individuals on public streets (Walker 1990; 1992). There are serious complications, however, with treating domestic fights in this way. The partner, typically a woman, who calls the police commonly has to continue living with the man she has charged, and may well face worse retaliation. Economically dependent women, especially those with children, may have few options beyond a short stay in a Transition House, followed by life on welfare. They are still tied to their abusive partner through their children and their economic dependence. They may also still love the man and call the police only to control the immediate situation of a drunken rage.

Domestic conflict is often mutual. Survey research using the *Conflict Tactics Scale* cite self report data suggesting that males and females are almost equally responsible for starting mild and serious physical and emotional attacks on partners (Straus and Gelles 1986; Straus 1993). Gay and lesbian partnerships are no exception. Feminists respond that statistics on domestic homicide, and on serious injuries requiring hospitalization, overwhelmingly involve female victims and male perpetrators (Kurz 1993; Dekeseredy 2000; Comack et. al., 2002). Many of the females who admit to fighting their partner are responding to long-term abuse and threats.

Females are also far more likely to be trapped in abusive relationships by economic dependence and cultural pressures that charge women with the primary responsibility for holding a family together for their children. They also face the realistic fear of retaliation against themselves and their children if they try to leave (Bowker 1993). Women who return to abusive relations have been found legally culpable in their own injuries (Hughes 1993). When police do not take domestic assaults seriously and courts give minimal sentences, women in seriously abusive partnerships may legitimately feel they have no place to turn.

Critical feminist litigation has struggled to make visible in courts the devastating psychological impact of long-term emotional and physical abuse on female partners as a mitigating factor in cases where women kill their partner (L'Heureux-Dubé 1997). In the landmark Lavallée case in 1990, the Supreme Court of Canada recognized *battered wife syndrome* as a legitimate defence of necessity in homicide. The defence recognizes that some female partners may become so humiliated, emotionally crushed, isolated and threatened by the long-term abusive and controlling behaviour of a male partner that killing him becomes a reasonable act of self defence. Such defence, however, is usually subject to rigorous challenge in court (Liu 2000; Boyle and Rowley 1989; Crocker 1985). Some judges have rejected the defence of battered woman syndrome for women who did not act in sufficiently submissive, dependent ways, and who fought back aggressively when a partner was beating them. These judges require the same self-defence rules that apply to men who kill during fights with other men. A 'reasonable man' is expected to walk away from a fight rather than return to the scene of conflict, and to use no more than 'sufficient' force to defend himself in a fight. Similar reasoning suggests that a once-battered wife who returns to the partnership is complicit in the violence. Also, since she was not killed during a previous beating, it seems unreasonable that she need to kill her partner in self-defence during a second beating. Trials often hang on competing expert testimonies from psychologists for the crown and the defence on why a 'battered woman' would not simply leave the relationship (Bowker 1993).

Aboriginal women living on reserves are far more likely than non-Aboriginal women to suffer long-term and extreme physical abuse from their male partners. They are also less likely to receive help from police (Dell 2002), or to have anywhere else to go except the streets when they leave their partner. Monture-Angus

(1999) describes violence towards women on reserves as an inseparable fact of life—a systemic and lifelong experience that is not individual, but part of a lived experience of colonialism suffered by entire communities of people. She describes her own experience of child sexual abuse, rape, and a battering partnership, as nothing unusual. Countless other Aboriginal women, many of them in prison, share stories of multifaceted violence— beginning with child abuse, rape, regular sexual abuse, witnessing of a murder, watching their mothers repeatedly beaten, and beatings at the hands of staff and other children in juvenile detention centres (Comack 1996). Women who flee the violence on the reserves commonly find themselves little better off in the cities, where they face repeated violence from men while working in the sex trade.

Monture-Angus and others see the alcoholic rages and violence of Aboriginal men as itself rooted in the humiliation, emotional destruction, sexual and physical violence that men themselves endured throughout a long history of broken homes, abusive residential schools, and juvenile detention centres, economic hopelessness and absence of coherent cultural identity—all symptoms of several hundred years of colonialism (Cote and Schissel 2002).

Policing Sexual Assault

Historically, women were viewed as the property of their fathers and husbands. These men could sue for damages if their daughter or wife were raped. Little damage was considered done if the woman raped was not either a virgin daughter or a chaste wife. Rape within marriage was legally impossible—marriage itself entailed a woman's agreement to have sex whenever and however her husband wished it. Feminist struggles over the years slowly challenged these assumptions to focus on the harm done to individual women themselves.

Rape trials (renamed 'sexual assault' in Canada in 1983) remain a hotly contested arena of struggle in law. Often, the question on trial is not whether sex occurred, but whether or not it was consensual. Critical feminist litigation struggles to make visible the ways in which legal processes in rape trials work to disqualify women's experience of their own sexuality (Smart 1989, ch. 2). The 'seduction scenario' that underlies most rape trials holds that males always want sex while women are often out of touch with their real sexual feelings and need to be pressured. When pressure is seen as part of normal sex, rape can be understood as merely 'undue' pressure—

a bit over the line but not a serious crime, unless there is evidence of bodily injury. Huge differences in estimates of the prevalence of date-rape on college campuses largely reflect such distinctions. It is quite possible for a woman to say she was raped and for a man to say they had consensual sex, with neither of them intentionally lying (Koss and Cook 1993; MacKinnon 1989, ch. 9). Jurors who are themselves familiar with the cultural scenario of seduction may have a hard time distinguishing normal sex from rape when a criminal conviction hangs on their judgement.

In rape trials, as in all other criminal trials, the defendant has a right to be presumed innocent until proven guilty. His past sexual behaviour is explicitly *not* relevant to the immediate question of whether he committed rape in the particular instance before the court. The complainant must prove to the court beyond reasonable doubt that she did not consent to sex, and the defence lawyer's job is to discredit her testimony in whatever way possible. Evidence concerning the woman's lifestyle and past sexual behaviour are directly relevant to challenging her claim of non-consent in court. Hence in many rape trials, it is the complainant's behaviour rather than the defendant's that is on trial.

Rape trials are widely described as resembling pornographic scenarios as lawyers for the defence push the complainant, as their primary witness, to give more and more details of the seduction process and the body-parts involved to convey the impression for jurors that the complainant was on some level a willing participant (Smart 1989, ch. 2). In the simplistic, binary logic of legal reasoning, Smart suggests, any evidence that a woman consented to some intimacy—by going out with him, drinking with him, inviting him home, listening to music, kissing—implies that she consented to sexual intercourse, and therefore that what happened was not rape. Also in legal logic, if she cannot prove she did not consent, it means that he is innocent and so she must have lied. This in turn feeds the view that women generally are prone to make up stories about rape to get men into trouble.

Feminist lawyers struggled for years to challenge these presumptions that discouraged all but the toughest of women from going to court. Significant changes in Canadian law were legislated in 1983 to address some of these problems, but with uneven results (Kelly 1997). Studies have repeatedly shown that sexual assaults reported to police are significantly less likely to be reported to the police, to have the report result in charges, and to have the charges result in a conviction, compared

with other physical assaults. A study of Toronto police reports from the 1970s, before revisions to sexual assault laws (Clarke and Lewis 1977) showed that the large majority of rape cases reported to police never come to trial. While reports made by professional women were all deemed "founded", only about half of those made by working-class women and students were accepted, a quarter of those made by housewives, and only a fifth of those by separated and divorced women. Only about 4 percent of impoverished women on welfare had their reports treated as "founded". Complainants who had been hitch-hiking or drinking, or who had even met their alleged assailant in a bar were turned away. Lawyers could undermine a complainant's credibility in court simply by asking a question like "are you on the pill?" even if the judge said she did not have to answer.

A follow up study of women seeking help from an urban sexual assault treatment centre in Ontario in 1994, a decade after the revisions, suggests little has changed in legal practice (Du Mont 2003). Of 284 women who sought help, 187 (66 percent) reported the sexual assault to the police. Of these 87 (47%) resulted in police laying charges, and 31 (17 percent) resulted in a conviction, or about 11 percent of all women who came to the treatment centre. Furthermore, a detailed analysis of police occurrence reports for those 31 cases that resulted in convictions suggests that even these were undercharged. All of them involved physical force, such as being pushed to the floor, choked, punched, slapped, grabbed, burned and/or bitten, and in 10 cases, or one-third, the assailant carried a weapon. Yet only one case was charged with level-three of sexual assault. Du Mont notes that sexual assaults by a current or previous partner were three times more likely to be under-charged than assault by a stranger. Assaults against a sexually active woman or a woman 'of poor reputation' were the least likely to result in convictions (ibid. 312).

The 1983 legislation replaced the term 'rape' with 'sexual assault', on the assumption that 'assault' carries no implication of consent by a victim. The prohibition against sexual assault charges being laid by a spouse was also removed. In accordance with Charter equality rights, gender-neutral terminology is used so that both alleged assailants and alleged victims can be either female or male. Anal and oral penetration are included along with vaginal penetration in the definition of sexual assault.

Other key changes involved the conduct of sexual assault trials. First, the doctrine of 'recent complaint' was repealed to permit adult victims of childhood assault to press charges. Formerly it was presumed that a true victim of rape would complain immediately the violation happened, and hence complaints about behaviour that supposedly occurred years earlier were probably vindictive lies. Lawyers countered by calling on the expert testimony of psychologists to debate theories of repressed or recovered memories, and to suggest that feminist therapists might generate false beliefs in the minds of emotionally troubled clients. A second change in legislation prohibited judges from counselling jurors not to convict a defendant on the word of a primary witness without corroboration. Formerly, judges could warn jurors not to convict unless medical evidence like torn clothing and bruises or semen were present. Now jurors decide such issues themselves, although defence lawyers can still argue that the absence of sufficient corroborating evidence invalidates a case.

The third and most contentious change involved restrictions on the use of past sexual history of the complainant. Formerly, a central strategy for defence lawyers was to try to discredit a complainant in the eyes of jurors as sexually promiscuous and hence a 'consenting type' of woman. Lawyers were now required to give notice to a judge that they wished to ask about past sexual activity of the complainant, and provide some evidence of its relevance before such questions could be asked in front of jurors. The qualifier was that now the complainant could be compelled to answer such questions, whereas formerly a judge could permit her not to answer. Defence lawyers responded by launching a Supreme Court challenge that any restrictions on their ability to probe into the sexual history of a complainant interfered with their clients' right to a fair trial and were therefore unconstitutional. Feminist lawyers countered that a woman's sexual behaviour logically has no relevance to a sexual assault trial (Boyle and Rowley 1987). The issue at trial is whether or not a woman is lying when she claims she did not consent to sexual intercourse with the defendant. Who is more likely to lie about consenting to sex—an openly sexually active woman or a former virgin or chaste wife with a reputation to protect? Why is it logical to assume that a woman who has several sexual partners probably said yes to the defendant, while a woman without another sexual partner would repel him? If a defendant can prove that a woman had just had sexual intercourse with another man at the scene, is it logical that she would promptly want sex again with the defendant? Even if a woman has had sexual intercourse with the defendant in the past, can she never say no in the future? The validity of defence

claims that the complainant's past sexual history is relevant at all depends on the cultural acceptance of the virile-male-grudging-woman seduction scenario described above. From the perspective of women's experience of their own sexuality, argue Boyle and Rowley, none of these arguments make sense.

In 1992 the Supreme Court partially upheld defence lawyers' right to probe sexual history, recasting restrictions in terms of "scope of permissible inquiry" (Kelly 1997). Defence lawyers countered with new techniques designed to undermine a complainant's credibility by presenting her as emotionally unstable and therefore prone to false memories and distorted understanding of sexual experiences, vulnerable to suggestions from therapists, and the like. A central strategy is to demand access to any and all possible records on the complainant's past. These include medical records from family doctors, gynaecologists, hospitals, any physician who prescribed medication, files from social workers, child protection services, therapists, school counsellors, other school records and personal letters. Any complainant who was a victim of abuse as a child, or who has had contact with child protection services, or who sought any kind of counselling, or whose family needed welfare, is vulnerable to such blanket searches. Refusal to divulge or to hand over any records can become grounds for dismissing the case. Lawyers for the defence can also try to generate records by asking that the complainant be assessed by a psychologist or gynaecologist of the defence counsel's choosing.

In summary, anyone who lays a charge of sexual assault, the vast majority being women, can expect to be cross-examined in court on all aspects of their emotional, psychological, behavioural and sexual histories, with information being presented in ways designed to discredit them. Virtually nothing will remain private.

Policing Child Sexual Abuse

Allegations of child sexual abuse are particularly hard to prosecute because primary witnesses are minors whose testimony may not stand up to the rigours of courtroom challenge. Historically, public panics around issues of child abuse have shifted focus from the sale of children into prostitution, sons in aristocratic families abusing working-class girls used as family servants, abuse by fathers and step-fathers, and perverted strangers (Smart 1989, ch. 3). By 1908 in England, incest with a daughter, granddaughter, sister, or mother was officially declared a crime, although prosecutions were rare. The most common response was not to prosecute the adult male suspect, but to remove the children into foster care. Victims of incest were viewed as morally damaged and possibly unfit to mix with other innocent children. The central concern, Smart suggests, was not to protect children but to protect families. By as late as the 1970s it was typical to blame the 'problem' on cramped living quarters, the lack of separate bedrooms for children, or frigid wives who drove frustrated male partners to look elsewhere. More recently in Canada the focus has shifted again to the homosexual rape of boys by priests and teachers in residential schools, and by other adults having close, unsupervised contact with children.

Since 1983 in Canada, the removal of time constraints on laying charges has made it easier for adults to lay charges against offending parents and other adults for abuse that happened during childhood. This avoids the problems involved in cross-examining minors in court, but the lapsed time exacerbates problems of faulty memory, and limited corroborating evidence. Conviction is still very difficult if the defendant flatly denies the charges and the complainant cannot cite supporting evidence that others knew about what was happening at the time. In 1994, for the first time in Canada, an adult daughter successfully sued both her parents—her stepfather for sexual abuse, and her mother for failing to protect her from that abuse (Grace and Vella 1994). The heavy financial damages awarded against the mother in this case effectively deemed the mother equally if not more responsible for the sexual abuse than her male partner. Feminist critics voice concerns that the decision did not take into full account the mother's circumstances as an abused, financially dependent woman herself, who feared that Children's Aid workers would take her child from her if she said anything, and who had no lawyer to defend her. When these conditions are ignored, mothers take the blame for whatever goes wrong.

Policing the Sex Trade

Prostitution is the one and only offence for which women are convicted more frequently than men. For all other criminal convictions in Canada, men outnumber women by ratios of 8 or 10 to 1; but for sex-trade convictions, women outnumber men by 6 to 4. The anomaly behind this statistic is that selling sex is not and never has been illegal in Canada. Consenting adults can legally buy and sell sex for money. It is the practices that facilitate the sex trade and make it publicly visible that are

criminalized—appearing to be a vagrant or loitering on the streets in a disorderly way, soliciting customers, having a house that is openly used for purposes of trading sex, inciting individuals to work in the trade, and living off the money that these individuals make.

The prosecution of people under sex-trade laws is gendered, classed and raced—that is, falling much more harshly on women than men, and especially on women at the bottom of the sex-trade hierarchy, and harshest of all on visible-minority women. Sellers, not customers, are assumed to cause all the problems. Male customers are rarely bothered by police. Pimps who organize much of the trade and live off the earnings of sex-trade workers are also rarely prosecuted. Women who work in higher-class massage parlours, escort services, and as call girls servicing wealthier clientele are also rarely bothered (Fedec 2002, 262). It is the women who walk the streets looking for customers, and especially the Aboriginal and other non-white women among them, who are most frequently prosecuted. They also bear more than their share of the pervasive violence suffered by sex-trade workers.

Normal Men, Deviant Women

The classic cultural assumptions of sexually virile males and reticent women that underlie the seduction scenario in rape trials, also underlie the social controls placed on prostitution. Male sexual needs are represented as naturally strong and easily aroused. Any man who has no steady sexual partner, and particularly married men whose wife permits sex only grudgingly, will naturally look for sex elsewhere. Hence, the reasoning goes, the customers of prostitutes are 'normal' and unproblematic males (McIntosh 1985). The question why are there still so many men who want to purchase sex in the sexually liberated context of contemporary western societies is rarely raised or considered of any interest. However, women who parade the streets looking for paying customers for sex are represented as deviant, sinful women who corrupt the morals of those around them, threaten families, and spread diseases, and hence need to be strictly and harshly controlled.

In pre-Confederation Canada vagrancy laws were used to control women (Shaver 1994; Larsen 2000). Any woman found loitering in a public place without a legitimate reason, could be arrested. The law only applied to women. After Confederation, some revisions were made to respond to concerns raised by feminists about 'white slavery'—girls from impoverished families being sold or procured into prostitution. In principle, the new laws targeted men who procured girls into prostitution and lived off their earnings. In practice, Shaver suggests, convictions of such men remained minimal. Policing focussed primarily on women working on the streets as causing a nuisance for other residents.

The sexual double standards through which prostitution is judged became particularly blatant during the First World War years in England, expressed as the state's concern to protect soldiers from 'investing, preying, haunting harpies' who hung around the army camps, infecting soldiers with venereal diseases (Bland 1985). The "Defence of the Realm Act" of 1914, banned women in towns where soldiers were stationed from being in taverns or on the streets between 7 pm to 8 am, with penalties of up to two months in prison. Another law made it a criminal offence for any woman, prostitute or not, to have sexual intercourse with a soldier if she were infected with a venereal disease. This gave police the right to arrest any woman found near army bases and hold them for up to a week pending a medical examination. Feminists dubbed this forced inspection 'rape by steel speculum' (Walkowitz 1982).

Some nineteenth-century feminists struggled against these double standards, and tried to shift the focus towards the protection of girls and women trapped into prostitution. But the social stigma against prostitution was such that most of the women active in the women's movements themselves feared being associated with them. The contemporary women's movement in Canada remains divided on how to think about prostitution (Shaver 1994). The dominant view is that women who engage in prostitution are young, poor, troubled individuals, who are running from abusive homes and often addicted to drugs, and who sink into prostitution as a means of survival. Prostitution degrades all women, not just those working in the trade because it reinforces the patriarchal view of women as objects for male use. From this perspective, rescuing women from the sex trade makes more sense than defending their legal rights.

The alternative liberal view is that the sex trade is best understood as work that women can choose to enter, and that offers better-than-average pay for women's work, particularly in the higher-status massage parlour and call-girl end of the trade. Even well educated women with other career options may be drawn to work as strippers or in peep shows because it feels fees exotic, wild, and rebellious (Mestemacher and Roberti 2004; Razack 1998) Arguably, the sex trade is not intrinsically more degrading work than what many other women do

who trade sex for entertainment, or the work of athletes who also trade their bodies for money (Shaver 1994). From this perspective legalizing the sex trade makes sense as a necessary basis for controlling working conditions, and protecting women from violence. It's semi-legal status, which justifies constant police harassment makes it almost impossible for women to organize collectively to protect themselves.

Gendered Policing of Gender-neutral Laws

Equality Rights provisions in the Canadian Charter prompted significant changes in the laws governing prostitution to make them explicitly gender neutral. Vagrancy laws that made it illegal just to be standing around on the streets, were replaced by regulations that criminalize all public communication for the purposes of prostitution, applying to sex-trade workers and customers alike. The definition of "public" includes automobiles and prohibits any attempt to stop automobiles or to impede pedestrians (Larsen 2000, 64). It also applies to any place open to public view, even if the actual conversations cannot be heard by other people.

Changes in terminology did not radically change policing practices. The view that street-walkers rather than their customers generated the 'nuisance' remained largely unchanged. Shaver (1994) cites data suggesting that 90 percent of arrests continued to be sex-trade workers rather than customers or pimps, and women rather than gay-male prostitutes. An important practical reason for this bias is that it is far easier for the police to get convictions for street walkers. They are easy to arrest, and rarely beat charges. They look like part of the criminal underclass to both judges and jurors, and can often be charged with additional offences like drug possession and theft (Fedec 2002, 261–2). In contrast, male customers charged with procuring offences look like law-abiding men. Courts commonly stay the charges or find them not guilty. Pimps, men who organize the trade and live off the avails of prostitution, are similarly difficult to convict. To win a case police need all the prostitutes working under a pimp to appear in court and testify against him. Few prostitutes are willing to do this, through a mixture of loyalty, dependency, and realistic fear of repercussions.

Women who work in massage parlours and as call girls are also less likely to be bothered by police. They are less visible and less of a nuisance at street level. This is also the sector of the trade in which pimps are concentrated because profits are easy. Fedec (2002, 260) cites one massage-parlour worker who paid $30 a day to the parlour, plus $10 for each client. She also kept only about 30 percent of the money she raised from calls while working in the phone-sex industry.

Detailed studies of the impact of the 1985 law on policing in Vancouver and Toronto confirm that the focus remains overwhelmingly on street nuisance and on women sex-trade workers (Larsen 2000, 57–60). The Vice Squad in Vancouver responded initially with large-scale sweeps in all the streets where prostitutes habitually worked, and prosecutors began to restrict the areas in which women could be seen, as a condition of probation. The long-term result was to concentrate more of the sex-trade in the Downtown Eastside region, but with no reduction in numbers of women on the streets. In Toronto, police had some initial success in reducing the trade by arresting customers, but this drove more workers into massage parlours and escort services, under the control of pimps. As police began to focus on these venues, the numbers in the streets increased again. The police practice of constantly pushing prostitutes from one area to another only spread the nuisance. Charter challenges also weakened somewhat the powers given to police to criminalize people for merely talking to each other on the street. Larsen concludes that the 1985 law was largely ineffective in reducing street prostitution.

Violence in the Sex Trade

The most disturbing effect of the new law, according to people who work for the rights of prostitutes is a marked increase in the levels of violence experienced by street prostitutes (Larsen 2000, 59). The extreme definition of "public communication" for the purpose of prostitution criminalizes talking in a parked car where others can see, even if they cannot hear, the exchange. As a result, prostitutes are pressured to jump into moving cars before they can check what the potential customer is like. Repeated police sweeps in residential areas have also driven workers into poorly-lit back lanes and more deserted industrial areas where they are in greater danger. Larsen cites a claim by a spokesperson for prostitutes' rights that while only one prostitute was murdered in Vancouver between 1978 and 1985, fully 40 were murdered between 1986 and 1992 (ibid. 59).

The combination of public apathy towards the plight of sex-trade workers and ineffective policing of violence against prostitutes further increases the propensity for violence. People who witness a prostitute being attacked routinely ignore it rather than coming to her aid (Fedec 2002,

254, 264). Men who are widely known to have beaten up a number of prostitutes are left free to victimize more girls. Such police inaction, Fedec suggests, sends a message that prostitutes are disposable objects that men can attack without repercussions. Increasingly, Razack argues (2002, 142) there are geographic spaces within Canadian cities where violence is permissible. These are the marginal zones—the spaces into which street walkers are pushed, along with the homeless and the vagrant.

The pervasiveness of violence in the lives of sex-trade workers on the streets challenges liberal assumption that street-prostitution is merely a job that some women choose. Such a view may hold for white women attracted to the thrill of the sex trade, who can choose to enter and to leave the marginal zones. It holds also for male customers who can engage in temporary slumming with impunity. What distinguishes them from the poor and racialized street walkers, Razack argues, is precisely their ability to enter temporarily and to leave with their respectability intact. Destitute and racialized women do not have the option of leaving. Colonizing practices that drove Aboriginal people from the settler cities continue to marginalize and exclude them. Aboriginal women, deprived of property and often of status rights on reservations by the Indian Act, and fleeing violence, disproportionately end up in urban slums. An estimated 60 percent of urban Aboriginal households live below the poverty line, and 80 to 90 percent of women-headed households (Razack 2002, 133). Prostitution offers survival, much as it does for other racialized migrant women fleeing destitution in third world countries. Homeless white women, trapped in these marginal zones by histories of abuse and addictions find themselves similarly racialized. These women's bodies are presumed to be sexually available. It is not an option they select, but a predefined category they must continually struggle against.

The pervasive violence enacted against the bodies of street walkers further challenges the cultural assumption that male customers who buy their bodies are simply average men seeking outlets for normal sexual urges. Violence is not an anomaly in the lives of street walkers, Razack insists, but a central feature. Violence functions to establish and confirm the dominance of white male colonizers, expressing their sense of entitlement to buy and to use the bodies of subjugated women. It is that unquestioned sense of entitlement that most horrifies Razack in her review of court records of the murder of Pamela George in 1995 by two young white males from Regina university. The young men felt comfortable bragging with their friends about beating up an Indian hooker. In this case as in others, being a hooker is treated in law as tacit consent to beatings, if not to murder (Hughes 1993).

The climate of indifference by public and police towards this endemic violence has made it possible for large numbers of women in Canada to go missing and presumed murdered with police barely bothering to look for them. Aboriginal women are disproportionately among the murdered. An *Amnesty International* Report released October 2004 (Jacobs 2004) lists 32 Aboriginal women missing from reserves in Northern BC and presumed murdered on the notorious Highway 16. The body parts of 22 women were found on a pig farm near to Vancouver in 2003. The farm owner, Robert Pickton, is currently awaiting trial for their murders. A police task force set up after this discovery is investigating the disappearance of 60 women from Vancouver over the last decade, 16 of them status Indians. The overall number of missing Aboriginal women in Canada over the last 50 years may be as high as 500. Status Indian women aged between 25–44 are five times more likely to die from violence than any other women in Canada of the same age. Official statistics do not separately categorize non-status and mixed-race women.

Child Prostitution

The legal age of consent to sexual intercourse is 16 when both sexual partners are under 18, and otherwise 18 years of age. Sex between adults and children under 18 is legally defined as a crime of sexual assault. This is routinely ignored for runaway teenagers who end up on the streets as prostitutes. Young women, and girls as young as 11–13 years are in high demand in the sex trade because they are physically attractive, more forbidden and therefore more exciting, and because they are believed less likely to carry venereal diseases (Fedec 2002, 258). The growth in the international sex tourism industry offers the bodies of children from impoverished developing countries for sex with wealthy westerners able to afford the trips. Local governments tacitly encourage the trade because it brings in coveted foreign currency. An attempt was made by lawyers in Canada in 2004 to charge men with sexual assault for buying sex with children in foreign countries, but this cross-national charge is unlikely to succeed.

Pornography

Pornography feeds into the sex-trade industry. MacKinnon (1989, chap. 11) identifies pornography as

the theory and rape as the practice of male power and domination over women. Pornography offers women's bodies as objects for male use. Feminist analysis of pornography, like prostitution, vacillates between viewing it as sexual freedom for women and sexual exploitation (Smart 1989, ch. 6). Feminists who oppose censorship of pornography point to the multiple ways it has been used against women's interests, to ban books on contraception and sex education, to challenge artistic representation of nude bodies, and to oppose sexual liberation. Feminists who call for censorship generally have violent, sadistic images in mind, but government bureaucrats who work on provincial boards of censors are rarely feminists (King 1985; Diamond 1985). Censor Boards have commonly found explicit sex and lesbian erotica more threatening to community standards than explicit violence. Concern with the exploitation of women who make pornography assumes a view of women as passive victims, rather than active agents who can make their own choices about involvement in the lucrative pornographic film industry.

Other feminists who favour criminalizing pornography counter that the extreme violence against women portrayed in hard-core pornography constitutes a hate crime. It endangers all women because it promotes the treatment of women's bodies as objects to be abused, and feeds the myth that women enjoy being raped. Radical feminists suggest that women who have been sexually assaulted by men who habitually watch hard-core pornography should be able to sue the industry for harm done to them (McKinnon 1989, ch. 11). Women who have fled battering relationships commonly report stories of male partners acting out violent and degrading scenes from pornographic videos (Busby 1994; MacKinnon 1987, 163–196) but such stories rarely carry sufficient evidence of direct causal connection to constitute proof in a court of law.

Feminist lawyers who sought intervener status with the Supreme Court of Canada in the 1992 Butler case discussed above, tried to walk a fine line between these two positions. The case hinged on whether possession and sale of pornography in Canada was protected under section 2 of the Charter guaranteeing "freedom of thought, belief, opinion, and expression." Feminist lawyers argued that depictions of erotica and explicit sex should be protected, but that hard-core pornographic materials that degrade, humiliate and subordinate women contravene the equality rights provision of the Charter and hence should not be protected (Busby 1994). The Supreme Court upheld the constitutionality of laws controlling pornography as a reasonable limit on freedom of expression, but not for the reasons advanced by feminist lawyers. The Court's reasoning stressed violation of community standards rather than women's equality rights. After the decision, police and Censor Boards continued to focus on materials depicting homosexual erotica rather than sexual violence.

There is far broader consensus favouring the criminalization of child pornography—materials depicting the rape of pre-pubescent children and infants, but enforcing workable laws to control such materials is far from easy. Child pornography is a global and multi-billion-dollar business. It is pervasively available over the Internet, where it is extremely hard to police. Profits from Internet pornography are so high that the industry is credited with largely sustaining the "free" global Internet. The debate that is emerging is whether a society's interest in controlling 'offensive' materials such as child pornography is sufficient to justify granting police and other agents of social control extensive powers to monitor private Internet use by citizens. As the technology for such monitoring advances, the arena of struggle around protection of citizens' right to privacy over the state's right to control objectionable practices will inevitably expand.

Conclusion

Debates around the role of law in policing prostitution and pornography provide a useful focus for pulling together the four broad theoretical perspectives on law and deviance that frame this chapter. The functionalist perspective focuses attention on the body of shared norms, beliefs and sentiments that form the foundations of society, and how these are shifting in contemporary society. Prevailing values of autonomous, rational, competitive individualism oriented to consumption help to legitimate the hedonism that normalizes buying sex for personal pleasure. Brand-name advertising industries and mass entertainment that sexualize the clothing and appearance of women and of younger and younger children help to make all aspects of the sex trade seem normative rather than deviant. The implicitly racist and colonial values of white settler society normalise the use of racialized minority bodies in marginalized city zones in ways that would be felt as more obviously deviant if performed in white middle-class communities.

Political economy draws attention to alienation fostered by relentless competitive struggle for profits. The lure of money, profits, and gross inequalities in wealth and poverty at global and local levels drive the sex-trade industry. Legalised class struggle works to evict impoverished, propertyless people to marginalized inner-city zones where prostitution and violence flourish. Desperation and poverty ensure no shortage of women and boys who turn to the sex trades.

Social constructionism explores struggles over meaning, highlighting the entertainment-for-advertising industry that sexualizes almost everything to titillate consumers to buy commodities. Policing practices and social controls at all levels of society work to deviantize prostitutes but not their customers, and to disqualify the lived realities of endemic violence as consensual trade.

The feminist perspective shows that none of these other explanations, either alone or in combination, can fully account for the sex-trade industry without understanding the patriarchal structures of law and society that pervasively subordinate women to men. Gender-neutral laws operating in highly gendered social contexts of domestic responsibilities, domestic violence and family breakdown, and inegalitarian job markets, all interact to foster the poverty of mother-headed households that fuels prostitution. Double standards paint sexually active men as normal but women as sluts. The virile-male-grudging-female seduction scenario that disqualifies women's experience of sexual assault works to normalize a predatory male sexuality that fuels the sex-trade industry. Patriarchal laws that structure tenuous rights to property and status on reservations, combine with domestic lives tortured by violence, to drive Aboriginal women in disproportionate numbers into the marginal zones of street prostitution. When these marginalized women are assaulted, they have no lawyers to defend them. When they go missing, police do not search for them.

All four theoretical perspectives contribute to our understanding of the sex trade. The challenge posed by this chapter is to use these perspectives systematically to explore all features of deviance, law and social control in our society.

CHAPTER 8

Karl Marx and the Analysis of Capitalism

Karl Marx (1818–1883) was a profound thinker whose work has had a phenomenal impact upon the twentieth century. His most famous treatise, the three-volume *Capital*, stands as a monumental study of Western industrial society. It is difficult to overstate Marx's importance. It is also very difficult to condense his prolific writings into one short chapter. Much controversy surrounds the interpretation of his ideas: some theorists see an important break, between his early philosophical and later economic works, while others stress the underlying continuity. Some see him as an **economic determinist**, others as the forerunner of the mode of analysis concerned with the **social construction of reality**. Analysis is made more difficult by the fact that Marx died before the last volume of *Capital*, particularly his section on class analysis, was complete. Much of this work was pulled together by his colleagues from his notes.

In 1844, Marx announced his intention to publish a critique of politics and political economy, dealing with the interconnection between political economy and the state, law, ethics, and civil life (Sayer 1985, 222–23). This vision was never completed, leaving *Capital* as his major work. Also, many of his early manuscripts were not published until the late 1920s and 1930s. The result, Sayer suggests, is that prevailing interpretations of Marx's writings may have given too much emphasis to the study of economic relations in *Capital*, in isolation from his broader critique of society.

Marxist thought also stirs up often intense political feelings for or against the communist world society that Marx advocated and predicted would come to pass with the collapse of capitalism. Such feelings tend to cloud the assessment of his work itself. It is not possible, therefore, to give a definitive summary statement of Marx's work. The presentation here is very much an introduction to his ideas. It is also slanted toward sociological theory. Economists and political scientists would place their emphasis differently.

Historical Materialism

Historical materialism is a theory of history in which the material conditions of life are seen as ultimately determining the course of human history. For Marx, the most fundamental aspect of human existence is the absolute necessity for people to produce the means for their own subsistence. In order to survive, people must produce food and process it to the point where it is edible. In all but the rarest conditions of an ideal climate, people need to produce clothing and shelter and heat for warmth and for cooking. They also need to produce the tools or technology required for such processes. Even the simplest hunting and gathering economies use surprisingly complex implements. People also organize themselves in complex ways to hunt and gather, to process and preserve food, to build shelters, and so on. As the means of providing for material needs become more complex–in herding economies, settled agriculture, trade and industry–so the ways in which people organize themselves around these activities change in both form and complexity.

Marx reasoned that the processes by which people meet their basic subsistence needs constitute the foundation of social organization. Any system of production entails a definite pattern of relations between people. Human production is by nature social. From simple economies to the most technologically complex industrial production, work is a co-operative activity. The way in which people co-operate varies with different modes of production, and this affects all other aspects of social life. **Relations of production** directly influence the prevailing family forms, political structures, religious ideas, and modes of thought. People experience social life as it is organized through relations of production. As they reflect on this experience, they generate the patterns of thought and ideas that come to prevail. For Marx, and theorists inspired by him, it makes sense to begin the analysis of economic and social life with the study of the prevailing mode of production and relations of production associated with it. All other aspects of social life can be understood as reflecting and responding to this underlying form of economic organization.

Modes of Production and Class Relations

Marx briefly traces historical changes in **modes of production**, or ways in which societies transform their material environment to meet subsistence needs. The simplest form is **primitive communism**, with production confined to hunting and gathering. Simple hand tools such as weapons, bowls, and digging sticks are easily made and shared. The key means of production–the flora and fauna in the surrounding territory–are accessible to all. No one has ownership rights to the terrain or its resources.

The second stage is ancient society or **slavery**, which already assumes a higher level of productivity within the society as a whole. There is sufficient surplus production that one class of people, the slave-owners, are supported by the labour of others without producing anything themselves. Slavery is associated with warfare: warring communities capture people from other societies and use them for drudgery and heavy manual labour.

The third stage, **feudalism**, is associated with settled agriculture. Here the predominant means of production are land and the draught animals, machinery, tools, seeds, and so on, required to work it. But this land is not shared equally as under primitive communism. An important division of labour emerges in which a certain stratum of people perform most of the work of cultivating the land while another stratum oversees and controls the land and extracts the surplus produced. The two great strata or classes under feudalism are serfs and nobles. The **serfs**, the people who actually work the land, inherit their position as labourers who are tied to the particular estate on which they are born. They are not free to leave or to work land elsewhere. A hereditary class of **nobles** exercise control over the estates, commonly held in trust under a superior military ruler or king. They extract surplus production from serfs in return for protecting them, maintaining law and order, and providing them with whatever is necessary to cultivate the land. Only land that is too poor to bear the double burden of labourers and landlord is likely to remain in the hands of small **peasant** producers.

Within the feudal mode of production no meaningful distinctions can be drawn between economy and polity or civil society. A person's economic, political, and community statuses—as serf, noble, vassal, or whatever, all coincide. The notion of property or ownership with respect to land also has no meaning. A multiplicity of obligations tie people and land together all the way up through the feudal hierarchy. No one has exclusive proprietary rights. The serfs or tenants who plough the land and gather the crops, their immediate lord to whom they pay dues, and the lord of the lords, can all claim that a particular plot is in a sense "my field." These rights also extend horizontally to the whole village community, without whose consent land cannot be leased or given away (Sayer 1985, 227).

Within feudalism the majority of people have direct access to the means of producing for their own subsistence needs. Serfs work plots of land and keep animals for themselves. But they are also required to work on the estates of the nobility. The extent of their exploitation is obvious, measured by the days on which they labour for the lord and the amount of produce that the lord appropriates.

Marx saw the transition from feudalism to **capitalism**, the fourth mode of production, as the most profoundly important change in the history of society. The emergence of private property, specifically the privatization of means of production, brought about the breakup of the unity of feudal social order. The separation of economic and political spheres of activity, the emergence of a *civil society* of isolated individuals, and the separation of the state as the sphere of public activity, were all interrelated aspects of the same process. Capitalism brought about the most extreme forms of alienation and exploitation, and at the same time mystified or disguised them beneath the institutions of property and wages.

The term *capitalism* refers to an economic system based on private ownership of **capital**, or the means of production, in the hands of a limited number of people. Capital comprises the funds and the stock of land, machinery, and materials used in production, together with the accumulated wealth that is invested to produce more capital.

The transition from feudalism to capitalism is a process that involves significant changes in people's relationship to land. Land becomes defined as the exclusive, private property of the former landlords. Estates are fenced off and used to produce cash crops such as wheat and wool for sale, with all the benefits going to the new landowners, rather than to meet the subsistence needs of the local community. Former serfs lose their hereditary rights to live and work on the land. In one sense they are "freed" from the shackles of feudal obligations that tied them to the land of their fathers, but by the same token they lose all their former rights and control over what the community produces. The families of serfs who had supported themselves for generations on the land are forcibly pushed off, losing all direct access to the means of producing their own subsistence. They are left with nothing but their capacity to work, their labour power. They can survive only by selling their labour power for wages to whomever will hire them, and by using the money they earn to purchase what they

need. The two great classes that emerge within capitalism comprise those who own the means of production and those who do not. As we say in chapter 2, people who sell their labour power are collectively referred to as the *proletariat* or working class, while those who own the means of production and purchase the labour power of others are referred to as the *bourgeoisie* or capitalists.

The concept of class has a historically specific meaning in the context of capitalism, referring to a person's status in purely economic terms. Under feudalism, there is no distinction between economic and political status. But in capitalism production is privatized. Strictly "economic" activities become independent of any community control. They begin to appear as a world apart, subject to the "laws of the market." The notion of labour also takes on a historical special meaning as *labour power*, involving the separation of one's capacity to work from the means to use it in production, and hence the necessity of selling that labour power to others for wages. As means of production become separated from community ties and obligations, so people become individualized. It becomes possible to think in terms of the eighteenth-century notion of autonomous subjects or isolated individuals who enter into social contracts with each other. The modern notion of the state also gradually emerges as the arena of general, public concerns, with individuals as citizens of the polity with legal rights (Sayer 1985, 223). This shifting of community interests to the separate sphere of the polity and the state is the practical expression of the depoliticization of the community. Concepts such as *class*, individual, economy, polity, state, civil society, contracts, are thus all very modern ideas that only make sense when the unity of the feudal order has been shattered.

This privatization of means of production, its freeing from former political and social obligations so that it can appear as the exclusive possession of individuals, was a very complex process that stretched over centuries. In England, on the eve of the **Industrial Revolution**, the **enclosure** movement spread as landlords claimed the right to fence off huge tracts of land for sheep pastures to produce wool for sale. Some of the former serfs were able to get work as wage-labourers on big farms, tending the cereal crops and the sheep. The rest found themselves destitute. They had no choice but to migrate to the cities and compete with each other for whatever jobs they could get, often working under wretched conditions in the factories that were slowly opening up. Over time, industrial technology and factories became the dominant means of production, with land becoming steadily less important. Marx saw the separation of town and country as a particularly significant division of mental and manual labour, marking the separation of capital and landed property (Sayer 1985, 230). The factories and the industrial technology, like the land, were privately owned by a relatively small class of wealthy people. The mass of people who own neither land nor other capital have to sell their labour power to the owners of factories.

Marx foresaw a fifth mode of production, which he called **advanced communism**, where all the important means of production in a society–farmland, factories, technology, and so on–would be communally controlled. Capitalism emancipated individuals from the servitude of feudalism but also led to their inability to control the productive relations that their activities create. **Communism**, as envisioned by Marx, is a mode of production that has the potential to overcome this alienation. Much more is involved than merely an equitable redistribution of wealth, or a changing of title deeds on property. The goal is to create the conditions within which people can directly control the processes of production and the social relations they entail, so that, ideally, all can develop their individual capacities to the full and mutual benefit of the collective enterprise. When all have access to the means of production, class differences will disappear. Also, when a community of people directly controls the productive forces that their activities create, economic and political activities will no longer be differentiated and a separate state as arbiter of public good would be redundant. Hence, in the sense in which these terms are understood within capitalist society, advanced communism would be both classless and stateless (Sayer 1985, 245–50).

Marx believed that this mode of organizing production would take advantage of all the benefits of technological advances made under capitalism without the devastating costs of inequality, exploitation, and alienation that capitalism entails. But we are getting ahead of ourselves. We need to go back and explore what is so important and distinctive about capitalism as a mode of production, and why it seems in Marxist analysis to be both the key to progress and, at the same time, an inherently destructive system.

Capitalism and Technological Progress

Capitalism, more than any other mode of production, is associated with an ever-accelerating pace of technological change. It is uniquely geared toward the continual reinvestment of profits in innovative technology to enhance labour productivity. All types of economies are oriented toward generating surpluses to make life easier or more comfortable for people. Only under capitalism is there a never-ending compulsion to invest the surplus or profit in accumulating productive forces, rather than to consume it in luxuries or leisure. It is this compulsion to invest, to accumulate capital, and to increase labour productivity that is the engine of economic development. But from where does this compulsion come? To answer this question, we draw upon the work of the contemporary Marxist, Robert Brenner (1977), who elaborates the unique relationship between capitalism and modernization.

Brenner begins with a critical look at Adam Smith's famous treatise, *The Wealth of Nations* ([1776] 1894). For Smith, the expansion of trade relations promotes division of labour, specialization, and rising productivity. Increasing food demands of large manufacturing centres stimulate rural production, which in turn induces the expansion of manufacturing to supply the countryside. These processes of self-sustaining growth are fuelled by the central values of capitalism: rational individuals in free competition in the marketplace, each striving to maximize profits.

The problem with this theory, suggests Brenner, is not that Adam Smith was wrong, but that he assumed too much. The core values of competition and profit maximization in the market presuppose structural conditions that Smith ignores. The principal condition is that producers are separated from the means of production; that is, from the ability to produce their own subsistence. Labour becomes a commodity that can be freely bought and sold. Subsistence has to be bought in the market. The means of production themselves, such as land and later factories and machines, have to be bought or rented in the market, for they are also commodities. It is only under these conditions—conditions specific to the capitalist mode of production—that people must trade in order to survive. Only then do money and transactions in the market become important. Concerns with competition and profit maximization follow from this. Brenner stresses that the use of money to buy commodities to make more money does not exist under other modes of production, such as slavery, feudalism, or small peasant landholdings.

In feudal economies, the direct producers are still tied to the land. On their own plots they produce crops that have use value for their own subsistence. The landlords can also provide their own means of subsistence through their command of the land and the labourers who work it for them. They market only what is left over after their own needs or wants are filled. The critical difference from capitalism is that neither serf nor lord depends upon markets for survival, and hence at a fundamental level it does not matter whether they beat the competition or maximize profits. There is no immediate pressure to innovate or to increase the productivity of labour.

Under this system, exploitation takes the form of squeezing serfs to extract more **absolute surplus**. In other words, the absolute amount that a particular labourer can produce in a particular period of time remains roughly constant, but more of what is produced is taken for sale in the market. This can be done by cutting the subsistence standards of the workers to have more left over for the market or by cutting the workers' leisure time to extend the length of the working day.

Under both slavery and feudalism, the direct producers themselves have no interest in the productive process. Slaves are maintained by the master; it is not in their interest to produce more for the owner to market. Serfs have their own plots for subsistence; it does not matter to them how much or how little landlords can sell. Under these conditions, when trade expands, it may result only in more intensive squeezing to extract more surplus. The long-term result may actually be a decline in production as serf's lack time to tend their own plots, and soils are exhausted.

Small peasant farmers who own their land are similarly independent of the market. Since they can produce their own means of subsistence, the pressures of competition and profit maximization are largely irrelevant. It is in their own interest to produce a variety of crops and animals to enhance their own subsistence standards of living. They may sell surplus produce in the market to buy luxuries, but they are not dependent upon the market.

Brenner argues that, in order to establish capitalism, it is necessary to break the ability of producers to produce their own means of subsistence. They must be separated from land, so that they have to rent it for cash or buy it in the real estate market. Then they must earn money in the market to survive. Once farmers must pay rent or mortgages, Brenner argues, they must be concerned with competition in the market and with profit maximization. They have to make the average rate of profit on what they produce, because otherwise they will be unable to pay the going rents and will be thrown off the land. Hence, they have to increase their labour productivity to keep up with competitors, which forces them to be concerned with technological innovations.

Large landowners, cultivating their lands with the aid of wage-labourers or rent-paying tenants, must also be concerned with labour productivity. They cannot, squeeze the workers indefinitely to extract a greater absolute surplus for themselves, because the workers will go elsewhere. They must focus on **relative surplus**; that is, upon increasing the productivity of workers through **labour-saving technology**. If they do not, they will be unable to pay the going wage rate, and workers will leave. It is actually in the interest of the landowners to invest in their lands so that the tenants or labourers can produce more and pay higher rents.

Brenner concludes that both labour power and means of production must become commodities in the market for market forces to have the impact upon people that they do under capitalism. The ideology of market forces and profit maximization taken for granted by Adam Smith is the *effect* of this capitalist mode of production and not the *cause* of it. Capitalism presupposes some form of class struggle that forcibly separates producers from means of production. The history of capitalism has been, in this sense, the history of class struggle, taking various forms in different times and regions.

Capitalism in Canada

In Canada, the emergence of capitalism and the class struggles associated with it took a very different form than in Europe. As we have seen, capitalism presupposes a large class of people who have no direct access to any means of production and who are thus forced to sell their labour power. But such a class of people did not exist in Canada before the 1850s. It took active government policies and a peculiarly Canadian version of the class struggle to produce it.

Indigenous peoples in Canada practised a hunting and gathering mode of production, supplemented by horticulture and trade, including the fur trade with Europeans. They could support themselves and had little interest in becoming permanent wage-labourers. They had to be forcibly driven from the land by settlers, the buffalo exterminated, and traditional northern hunting grounds disrupted by mining, exploration, and lumber companies, before they would begin to turn to wage-labour for their livelihood.

Attracting immigrants to Canada was not difficult. Masses of displaced and landless people were produced by the enclosure movement and the capitalization of agriculture in Europe, as land belonging to the great estates was fenced off for keeping sheep or growing cereal crops, and the serfs were driven off. These land-less people were willing, and indeed desperate, to seek a new life in North America. During the first half of the 1800s, tens of thousands of immigrants came to Canada every year from Ireland alone, fleeing the appalling conditions of enclosures, economic; collapse, and famine generated by economic domination from England (Pentland 1959, 459). They joined the multitudes of immigrants leaving similarly wretched conditions throughout Europe. Mass immigration from China and other parts of Asia began toward the end of the nineteenth century. Few European immigrants had any intention of remaining wage-labourers if they had any choice. What they found in Canada was a vast and sparsely populated land. So long as free or cheap land was available, the majority of immigrants preferred to acquire land and to work for themselves rather than for employers.

The problem, from the perspective of members of the business class, eager to develop capitalism in Canada, was how to staunch this outflow from the labour pool (Pentland 1959, 458–59). This was at the root of deliberate policies to make land so expensive that immigrants would be forced to labour for many years to earn even a down payment for a farm. Policies included monopolization of land for speculative purposes all across Canada and grants of huge tracts to absentee proprietors (Teeple 1972, 46). In one day in 1767, for example, the whole of Prince Edward Island was granted to a few dozen absentee landlords. Between 1760 and 1773, Nova Scotia had a population of about 13 000, but 5.4 million acres of the best land were given in grants to individuals and companies based in Britain and the United States. Similar policies were followed in central Canada, sparking riots against land monopolies in 1794 and 1796. On the Prairies there were vast tracts of virgin land, and the Homestead Act granted 160 acres per settler. Yet even here the enormity of land speculation was eventually to stifle settlement and drive land prices far beyond the reach of the average immigrant.

Such policies were far from accidental. The Land Act of 1841 clearly expresses the objective of "creating a labour pool" by the two-pronged approach of promoting massive immigration and making land prohibitively expensive. The land speculators and the class of merchant industrialists who wanted a cheap wage-labour force, to build canals and railways and to work in factories, were the same people, and so indeed were members of the government! The wretched conditions of poverty and unemployment within the developing industrial cities of Canada from the mid-nineteenth century

mirrored in many respects the conditions of early industrialization in Britain.

Alienation Under Capitalism

A central unifying theme in Marx's early philosophical writings is the concept of **alienation**. This refers to the dehumanizing character of social relations that emerge in their purest form under the capitalist mode of production. Marx saw people as, by nature, producers, engaged in a creative relationship with their physical environment to transform it to their needs. They are also, by nature, social beings, co-operating together in their creative, productive process.

People experience alienation from their human nature when the fundamental relationship to production is broken: when they are denied access to the basic means of producing for their own subsistence needs, when they are separated from the products of their labour so that what they create does not belong to them, and when their social relations with other producers are broken.

Life within hunting and gathering societies is often harsh, but it is not alienating. People relate to the natural world and to each other in a direct and immediate way in meeting their collective subsistence needs. Under feudalism, the tied labourers are exploited but are still not alienated in the same way as under capitalism. They work with the land directly and collectively to produce what they consume. They are exploited to the extent that what they produce as labourers on the estates belongs not to them but to those who control the estates. All the surplus, beyond what is needed for their immediate subsistence, is expropriated. Under harsh landlords, the labourers themselves may lie reduced to the meanest level of survival while the leisured, ruling class lives in luxury on what the workers produce. Yet, there is still a human relationship between the two great classes of those who work the land and those who control it. Feudal lords acknowledge a hereditary obligation to sustain the families attached to their estates in the bad years as well as the good, and the labouring families have a hereditary right to use that land for their own needs, generation after generation.

It is only under capitalism that alienation is experienced in its fullest and harshest form, pervading every aspect of human relations. The root cause of alienation is separation of the mass of people from the means of production, leaving them unable to provide for themselves. In order to survive, they must sell that labour power as a commodity to the owners of capital, who will use it for their own productive purposes in return for a cash wage. Almost everything that workers need to survive must be bought for cash in the marketplace. It is during times of high unemployment, or low demand for wage workers relative to supply, that the alienating character of capitalism is most immediately experienced. People can offer their labour power for sale, but there is nothing to oblige employers to buy it. Unwanted workers cannot use their labour power to meet their own subsistence needs because they have no access to any means of production, and they have no hereditary rights to share in what, the society as a whole produces.

Under the capitalist mode of production, alienation is experienced in multiple ways. Workers are alienated from the products of their labour. Feudal serfs had a right to a share of the harvest, but factory workers have no claims whatever to their products. They are paid a wage, but everything they produce belongs to the factory owner. In effect, the harder they work and the more they produce, the more impoverished they become, because more and more of their creative effort is taken from them. Workers in developing industrial capitalism are also alienated from the work task itself, which has no intrinsic meaning or sense of purpose. Under such alienating conditions, Marx suggests, people avoid work. They are often forced to work under miserable conditions. People are reduced to becoming appendages to machines; the work rhythms are set not by the changing seasons, or by the human body, but by the machines.

Bad as the conditions of work often were during early industrialization, and still are in many industries, they are a reflection rather than the cause of alienation experienced in social relations of production. The underlying problem is that, under capitalism, human relations of production are reduced to inhuman cash payments. Within the labour market, it is not a whole person who is bought and sold, as in slavery, but her or his labour power–the power to produce. Labour power is purchased by capitalists as needed, and laid off when not needed, with no further responsibilities to meet the subsistence needs of those who provide that labour power or of their dependants. The sole obligation of employers is to pay wages for labour power as and when they need it. People no longer co-operate with each other as full human beings in the production process. Marx suggests that in the capitalist exchange of labour power for wages, the employers are themselves as alienated as the workers, for they too are cut

off from human social relations. Private property and money dominate their existence.

It is precisely these inhuman relations of production that make possible the classical economics concepts of *economic men, profit maximization,* and *market forces.* In addition, these relations encourage the functionalist conception of human relations as emotionless, narrow, and calculated by market attributes. These concepts do not describe human nature or society in the abstract. They arise out of the historically specific conditions of capitalism.

The Model of Capitalism as an Economic System

So far in this chapter we have alluded to capitalism or to the capitalist system without describing this system itself in detail. But it is the actual workings of capitalism, its internal dynamics and its contradictions, that occupied Marx's central attention in all his later work. His three volumes on *Capital* comprise an extensive analysis of the capitalist system, and his model still forms the basis of the contemporary theory of political economy. A condensed version of his elaborate model is laid out below.

Certain key terms are useful in understanding Marx's model of a capitalist economy. A **commodity** is anything produced for exchange, and not for use by the producer. The production of commodities presupposes a division of labour. It is only as people become specialized in distinct occupations, and cease to produce everything that they need for themselves, that exchange becomes important. **Exchange value** refers to the amount of human labour time that went into the production of a commodity. It measures a social relation between producers. As people exchange what they have produced, they are exchanging the time and skill that each has contributed to the product. **Abstract labour time** refers to labour in general, to the average amount of time that it takes to produce a given commodity in a society with a given level of technology and knowledge.

The Theory of Exchange

The **theory of exchange** is fundamental to Marx's analysis. He begins from the observation that people in every society must labour to produce goods. Commodities exchange in definite proportions in the market. It is usually possible, for example, to calculate roughly how many pairs of shoes a cobbler would have to sell or barter in order to buy a wool coat or a given amount of firewood. Each such commodity also absorbs a definite amount of human labour time. From these basic propositions, Marx derives his **labour theory of value**. The theory posits that the exchange value or price of a commodity is determined not by the laws of supply and demand proposed by classical economists, but by the amount of labour that goes into the commodity.

For Marx, the exchange ratio between commodities is the labour-time ratio. In other words, in order to calculate the true exchange value of one commodity, such as shoes, for another commodity, such as firewood, one has to calculate how much total time went into raising the cow, getting the hide, tanning it into leather, and fashioning it into shoes, compared with the time it takes to care for trees to the appropriate age, cut the timber, saw it into logs, and take them to market. In using labour time as the fundamental measure of value, Marx is not suggesting that lazy people who take twice as long as others to do something will thereby be able to exchange their production for twice as much, or that people who make things quickly will get less. What counts, over the economy as a whole, is how long it takes, on average, to produce commodities, given the prevailing level of technology and skills. Marx refers to this as **socially necessary labour time**; it averages out lazy, unskilled, and unusually quick people. **Skilled labour time** includes teaching and learning in the calculation of socially necessary labour time.

Consider a simple example of exchange within a hunting society. Suppose, in a given community at a given time of year, it takes the average hunter one hour to catch a deer and two hours to trap a beaver. Fair exchange would then be two deer for one beaver. This exchange has nothing to do with the nature of the commodities themselves: the size of the animal, the amount of meat, the relative utility of deer skins over beaver pelts. It is based on the amount of human labour time it takes to catch them. If hunters could not get two deer for one beaver, they would pretty quickly stop "wasting time" catching beaver and start catching deer instead. People would start trapping beaver again when they were sufficiently scarce, or people wanted them enough, that the labour time spent would be compensated by what the beaver could be exchanged for. The classical relations of supply and demand are thus balanced by time. Individual producers decide how best to allocate

their labour time so that what they produce in the course of a day's labour will exchange for the equivalent of a day's labour by other people.

In the traditional exchange process money may be used, but only as a convenient mechanism for keeping tallies on exchanges between many different people, particularly when spread out over time. The fundamental exchange is still one useful commodity, for another.

Capitalist exchange entails a subtle but extremely important difference from this traditional exchange process. The basis of exchange is not one commodity for another, but some money for more money by means of a commodity. The objective is not to trade useful items, but to increase the amount of money one started with. Money as such has no use value. One cannot eat money or dress up in it. We want money because we can exchange it for something else. This fact itself makes the desire for money very different from desire for useful commodities. There is a limit to our desire for such commodities. We want only so much food, so much clothing, and so on, and we then lose interest in getting any more. Money is not like that. There is no intrinsic limit to how much we want. Desire for money is, in principle, insatiable. It is this desire that drives capitalist exchange.

Labour Commodity and Surplus Value

In capitalist exchange, labour itself is treated as a commodity. As we have already seen, the means of production are owned by a few people, while labour power is owned by others. As a commodity, labour has a value and, like every other commodity, that value is labour time needed to produce it. This is averaged out as the **subsistence wage**. This value includes not only the cost of maintaining the adult labourer at an acceptable standard of living, but the cost of replacing that labour through raising and educating children. Capitalists use money wages to purchase the commodity of labour power with the objective of using it to make more money.

In Marxist theory, profit comes from surplus value. The only way for the capitalist to make a profit is for labourers to produce goods of more value than the subsistence value of their labour time, for which they are paid in wages. Marx argues that profit does not normally arise through dishonest or underhanded practices. Nor does it come from simply charging more for given commodities. If all commodities, labour power included, were sold at double their previous price, nobody would benefit. The result would be inflation in which money would be worth half its former value.

The one place in the system where profit can routinely be made is in the use of labour power. Human labour can produce more than its own value. The exchange value of labour power, expressed in the subsistence wage, is the time it takes to produce and maintain the worker. Producing and maintaining a worker involves all the costs entailed in raising a child to maturity; training in work skills; feeding, clothing, and housing the worker and the worker's dependants. The exchange value of a commodity is the average time it takes a worker, with a given technology, to make that commodity. The goal of the capitalist is to maximize the productivity of labour power for a given subsistence wage; that is, to maximize the gap between the exchange value of the labour power and the exchange value of the commodities produced. This gap constitutes **surplus value**. For example, if in six hours a worker can produce a commodity with an exchange value equivalent to her or his daily wage, then any commodities produced outside of those six hours produce surplus value for the capitalist. The value of the time expended in producing the additional commodities accrues to the capitalist, not to the workers.

The gap between a day's wages and the resale value of all commodities produced by a worker in a day constitutes, in principle, an objective measure of the degree of exploitation of labour. The actual calculation of surplus value is more complicated than this. Capitalists have to spend money to buy or replace machines and materials, to rent the factory, and to satisfy their own subsistence needs. Surplus value arises over and above these socially necessary exchange values.

If the objective of production were solely to provide useful commodities for people, there would be no problem with hiring labour and then distributing everything produced. But this is not the objective of capitalist exchange. The objective is to make money, to maximize surplus value so that the largest possible amount of money comes back to the owner of capital.

Competition is crucial in the process of creating surplus value. Commodities exchange for the average time it takes to produce them in a given market, with a given level of technology. The goal of the capitalist is always to better this **average labour time**—to get more than the average amount of commodities for a given subsistence wage bill. Those who can better the average rate can make large profits by having more commodities for exchange at the going rate or by undercutting competitors and controlling the market. Those who only make the average rate may break even, but they will not make much profit. Those whose level of production falls

below the average rate will go bankrupt. They will have insufficient commodities to sell at the going price to cover their higher-than-average labour time costs.

How can individual capitalists maximize surplus value? Logically there are only three ways to do so. First, the capitalist can extend the working day, trying to harness more and more of the workers' energy. During the early stages of capitalism in Britain, workdays often extended to sixteen and eighteen hours, workweeks to six or seven days, even for children in factories and coal mines. Ultimately, however, this became self-defeating. Workers reach such a point of exhaustion that they can no longer produce anything. Pushed to the extreme, people die. Long before this point is reached, overworked people become markedly slower and less efficient so that overall production actually falls.

The second possibility is depressing real wages. This can be done either by raising prices while wages stay the same, by reducing actual wages while other commodity prices remain the same, or by some combination of lower wages and higher prices. This process also has natural limits. If wages drop so low relative to prices that workers cannot meet subsistence needs or feed and educate their children, people collapse and the labour power available drops both in quantity and quality. Workers are also not totally passive under such conditions, and employers can expect strikes and sabotage if they push these policies too far. As Marx acknowledged, there tends to be an acceptable minimum standard of living for a particular community of people, and employers cannot easily push workers below this level. Individual capitalists cannot indefinitely drive their workers harder than the average, or pay them less than the average wage, because workers will quit their jobs and go to work elsewhere. The exception to this rule occurs wherever workers have limited mobility, as in peripheral regions where unemployment is high or in Third World countries. In such locations, workers can be exploited more than the average. But there are still absolute limits on how far even these workers can be pushed.

There is a third option that is much more important than the other two because it is, in principle, limitless. That option is to strive to increase the productivity of labour power through labour-saving technology. Machines are important for their usefulness for increasing the productivity of labour power. For a given number of working hours, and at a given level of wages, the proportion of surplus value goes up. In principle, if the introduction of a new machine doubles a worker's output, it would be possible to cut working hours per week by 25 percent and give a 25 percent pay raise to the workers, and still increase profits by about 50 percent once the new machine is paid for.

This process can work in several ways. New technology may speed up production while using the same workers. Alternatively, the technology may simplify the production process so that the time required to train workers is reduced hence, reducing the exchange value or wage costs of the labour power needed. Innovations that improve the quality of commodities are another way of improving the average rate of production. Other producers would require far more time to create a product of the same quality without the technology.

At first glance, it looks as though everybody wins under this scenario. Workers get a better standard of living while capitalists make more profits. In the short run, this is correct. In the long run, however, there is a very serious problem: the process becomes self-defeating. In fact, Marx saw this process as the fundamental contradiction in capitalism and predicted that it would eventually bring about the collapse of the system.

Law of the Falling Rate of Profit

The problem begins from the fact that capitalists are competing among themselves for profits. The first ones to introduce new labour-saving technology can make large profits, since their commodities are cheaper to produce and they are able to undersell competitors in the marketplace. Other capitalists must rapidly introduce similar technology to keep their production costs down, or they will go bankrupt. Smaller or less efficient capitalist, who cannot afford to purchase the new technology, find themselves unable to compete in the marketplace. They have to drop their prices in order to sell their commodities, but they are unable to drop their costs of production. Eventually they become uncompetitive, go bankrupt, and drop out of the market. Those capitalists who remain can buy up the bankrupt person's machines and factories cheaply and can expand their market share with their high-volume, low-cost commodities.

Over time, however, profits start to drop. Eventually all the capitalists remaining in the market are using the new technology. They are all achieving the new rate of production. This becomes the standard or average labour time that sets the exchange value of the commodity. The average commodity price drops to this real exchange value, and nobody makes much profit. The economy will stagnate until some new technological breakthrough permits innovative capitalists, once again, to better the

average rate of production and raise profits. A further problem is that, as mechanization increases, capitalists must spend relatively more money on machines than on wages. Since profits are made on the latter, the actual rate of profit starts to fall. The new technology must increase productivity markedly over the older method of production for the capitalist to keep ahead.

Crisis of Overproduction

If this were the only problem with labour-saving technology, it might not be that serious, but there is a more serious problem associated with it. As the technological race increases, machines replace labour at an ever greater rate. The result is unemployment. Unemployed people are not the responsibility of the capitalist. The problem for capitalists is that unemployed people do not have the money needed to purchase the commodities that flood the market. Capitalists find themselves with surplus production that they cannot sell. In this situation, they are forced to operate more and more below capacity but, at the same time, they must make still greater efforts to develop technological innovations that will cut production costs so that they can sell more cheaply. They thus generate still more unemployment.

Labour-saving technology may increase productivity and so make possible an increase in wages in the short run. Expanding production will also give rise to increased demand for labour power, which will work to raise wages above the real subsistence value of labour power. Rising wages, however, reduce surplus value, and so generate a reaction. It becomes potentially more profitable to invest in more labour-saving technology to displace high-priced labour. As unemployment increases, the bargaining power of workers collapses. They start to undercut each other to get jobs, and wages start to fall, either in an absolute amount or relative to rising prices. People displaced by machines or bankrupted when they cannot keep up with competitors form a **lumpenproletariat**. Marx conceptualized the lumpenproletariat as a free-floating mass of people who are "declassed," separated from their class of origin and unable to find a place for themselves in the society. This disintegrated mass of ruined and impoverished people fall easy prey to reactionary or fascist ideologies and movements. Displaced workers struggling to regain a foothold in the working classes, form a **reserve army of labour**, their competition for jobs serving to depress wages still further. In the long run, Marx suggests, these processes work to force down the average wage across the market to subsistence value. Workers may make temporary gains in their standard of living, but these gains will always be insecure and threatened by the prospect of technological change that will make their work obsolete. Contradictions of capitalism look formidable. There is the tendency toward a falling rate of profit, as expensive technology replaces labour. Secondly, there is the tendency toward increasing concentration of capital and the resulting **polarization of classes** as members of the petite bourgeoisie are bankrupted and join the proletariat. Thirdly, there is the tendency toward the increasing poverty of the masses as unemployment forces wages down. Fourthly, there is the crisis of overproduction as unemployed and poorly paid people lack the money to purchase commodities. The remaining capitalists are driven to invent still more labour-saving technology to push down the costs of production in order to undercut competitors in an ever-tighter market. In the process, they produce yet more unemployment, tighter profit ratios, more bankruptcies, and a still bigger glut of commodities that people cannot afford to buy.

In these multiple ways, the competitive relations that develop between two great classes of workers and capitalists, and among capitalists themselves, in the marketplace, fetter the productive potential of new technology. Marx predicted that these internal contradictions within capitalism would generate an endless cycle of crises, of booms and slumps characterized by bankruptcies, unemployment, and overproduction. In the long run, the system would collapse due to its own internal problems. Marx expected, however, that social revolution would forcibly overthrow the system long before it reached this stage.

Marx foresaw the possibility of a new form of economic relations that would not be based on competition for profits and so would avoid all the internal contradictions of capitalism. New technology could be communally owned and worked to full capacity, with the products shared communally. As less and less labour time was needed to satisfy people's desire for useful products, relative to their desire for more free time, the portion of the day spent working could drop. In principle, people could work in the mornings, relax in the afternoons, and gather for intellectual, creative, or social activities in the evenings.

Counteracting Factors

An unavoidable question arises in relation to Marx's analysis of the capitalist system. If his theories were correct, why have his predictions not come to pass? How is

it that capitalism remains the dominant mode of production a century after he predicted its demise?

Critics of Marx's thesis have pointed to extensive empirical evidence that seems to contradict his predictions. Shareholder capitalism appears to have countered the tendency toward the concentration of capital foreseen by Marx. Twentieth-century workers are vastly better off than Marx ever foresaw, in some cases enjoying a standard of living that rivals that of the middle classes. The rise of the middle classes, in particular, appears to contradict Marx's law of the increasing polarization of classes. Democratic politics, the welfare state, and the organization of trade unions have also served to ameliorate the exploitative aspects of capitalism. From this perspective, capitalism appears to have weathered the crises.

Theorists within the Marxist tradition have countered these claims by pointing out that many of the crises that Marx foresaw do plague capitalist economies. The ultimate crisis, they argue, has been avoided so far by a series of counteracting factors. These serve to soften, but do not resolve, the internal contradictions of capitalism.

Central among such factors has been the accelerating rate of technological advance, which has staved off the falling rate of profits. Labour productivity has continued to rise with the aid of computers, robots, fossil fuels, and nuclear energy. An important effect of this accelerated innovation has been the cheapening of the costs of the machines themselves, as labour productivity has risen in heavy industry. Machines can be mass-produced in shorter periods of labour time. Some theorists suggest that bankruptcies and mergers have also significantly reduced the costs of heavy industry. Tax write-offs and other state benefits also help. Technological developments have also led to an explosion in the variety of cheap, mass-produced consumer goods available, which has helped to reduce the intensity of cut-throat competition to sell commodities. In addition, huge military expenditures in the centres of capitalist development have staved off the crisis of overproduction. Weapons constitute a staggering proportion of production. They are bought and blown up or thrown away as obsolete. Newer weapons are then purchased, and production in war industries is maintained.

The worldwide expansion of capitalism, through the economic domination that corporate interests in wealthy countries have been able to exert over underdeveloped countries, has meant that the worst contradictions of capitalism have been shifted from the centres of capitalism to the Third World. Here multinational corporations have been able to protect profits through cheap labour and long working hours. These countries are also sources of cheap raw materials and at the same time provide expanded markets for manufactured goods.

Within the developed centres, revolt has been held off by the lure of mass-produced consumer goods. Material comforts promote acceptance of the status quo, however inegalitarian it may be. Critical awareness is also dulled by processes of legitimation referred to as **ideological hegemony**. This is the capacity of the dominant class to rule not only by control over means of production, but also by control over ideas. When Marx dismissed religion as the opiate of the masses, he had in mind precisely the ways in which religion has been used to legitimate the social order and gross inequalities in wealth as manifestations of God's will. Conceptions of God and big business are still closely associated, as we have seen in the discussion of the Protestant ethic and the spirit of capitalism in chapter 6. Establishment religions generally legitimate the success of the wealthy, and at the same time enjoin the poor to endure misery on earth by the promise of rewards in the life after death. As religion has begun to lose its influence over everyday life for many people, other powerful ideological forces have taken its place, in particular the institution of the state and its administrative apparatuses.

The Bourgeois State in Marxist Theory

The **state** in bourgeois society plays a fundamental role in maintaining the social conditions necessary for capitalism to function. The state maintains social order and controls the potential for revolt through monopolizing the legitimate means of force in society. It sustains and legitimates the legal and administrative institutions that protect property rights, as well as contractual obligations essential for capitalist relations of production. It also serves to regulate divisions within the capitalist class, so as to ensure free competition in the market.

In Marxist theory, the state is in essence "nothing more than the form of organization which the bourgeoisie essentially adopts . . . for the mutual guarantee of their property and interests" (Marx and Engels [1846] 1970, 79). However, this relationship is far more com-

plex than one of control. As Sayer expresses it (1985, 241), the state is intrinsically a bourgeois form of social relationship in the sense that it emerges as a separate entity, beside and outside the community, with the privatization of property. This privatization makes it impossible for people as a community to control the material conditions of their collective existence. Social powers are taken from them and vested in a separate apparatus that operates over and above them. The apparatus of the state endeavours to secure communal interests when people are prevented from doing it themselves. The concept of *state* is thus a historically specific category, not a synonym for all forms of government.

Within the affairs of capitalism, the state occupies a paradoxical position that is both central and marginal. Its function is to preserve the conditions for capitalists to act freely as independent and competing individuals, while otherwise not interfering in the marketplace. The links between the state and members of the bourgeoisie are complex. As a class, the bourgeoisie is peculiarly divided. Its members relate to one another principally as competitors. Different sectors of the class, such as financiers and industrialists, have systematically divergent interests. They have a common interest only in maintaining the conditions within which they can freely compete, specifically in the protection of private property and contractual obligations. The role of the state is to maintain these conditions.

The Base-Superstructure Debate: Materialism Versus Idealism

Marx's analysis of the origins and functioning of the state in bourgeois society is part of his broader thesis that an adequate understanding of all the social institutions and cultures of any society must be grounded in analysis of relations of production.

Marx's early philosophical writings grew out of the philosophical traditions of his day, and yet profoundly transformed their meaning. He acknowledged a great intellectual debt to the eighteenth-century philosopher Hegel, and yet at the same time he claimed to have stood Hegel's work on its head. Hegel argues that the human spirit is the guiding force of history. The essence of what it is to be truly human is to strive constantly toward a better future, toward perfection, that would ultimately achieve the merging of humanity with God. It is this spirit that distinguishes people from other animals. In Hegel's view, the unified expression of the collective ideal, over and above individual selfishness is, at any particular stage in history, embodied by the state. For him, the state is the sphere of universal, rational, orderly life.

Marx also sees humanity as struggling toward perfection, but his is a materialist conception in which he reverses Hegel's idea of the causal relations between social structures and ideas. He argues that ideas develop out of and reflect material experience, and can only be understood by reference to this **base**. He sums this up in his famous statement that "it is not human consciousness that determines our existence, but our social existence that determines our consciousness" (Marx [1859] 1975, 452).

Marx praised the work of the philosopher Feuerbach for raising a similar criticism against traditional Christian theology (Marx and Engels [1846] 1970, 39–96). Feuerbach insisted that the starting point in philosophy had to be real people in their material, physical context. The concept of god he suggests is really the projection of human self-awareness. There is no pre-existing spiritual entity that creates humanity; rather humanity creates god. Feuerbach believed that people become alienated from themselves when their own projected ideal is held over them as if it were some external force, ordering and judging their actions.

Marx agreed, but he pushed the analysis further to question why people would conceive of god in such an alienating form, as set above and against them. Marx's answer is that people experience alienation in their everyday lives. Powerful forces are indeed set above them. They feel themselves utterly dependent for their existence on feudal lords, or capitalist market forces. It is little wonder that the mass of people would accept such an alienating feudal vision of the "lord god" or that the ruling intelligentsia among the aristocracy and the clergy would propound such doctrines. Marx further suggests that Feuerbach's efforts to criticize such alienating views of god would not be sufficient to make people change their ideas. So long as their material experience of life was alienating, so too would be their vision of god. One would have to change the material base before one could hope to change the thinking of the mass of people. So far, he argued, "philosophers have only interpreted the world in various ways. The point, however, is to change it" (Marx [1845] 1975, 5).

Ideology and False Consciousness

Marx's insistence that ideas reflect material experience raises serious questions about how false ideas can emerge. How can the mass of people be misled by ideological hegemony in capitalist society? How could Hegel have come up with the thesis of ideas determining history if his ideas are a reflection of his own material experience?

Ideology denotes falsity. If we accept Marx's argument that people's actions in, and consciousness of, the world are intrinsically related, then we imply that their consciousness, including ideology, must have some practical adequacy. Their ideas must make sense of their practical everyday activity (Sayer 1983, 8–9). Hence, we cannot explain ideology as merely a consequence of indoctrination or inadequate perception. If ideas are grounded in experience, then there must be something about the nature of experience that is capable of sustaining illusions.

Marx draws a critical distinction between phenomenal forms or appearance and essential relations or *essence*. He argues that the essential relations of capitalism are precisely those that produce illusory appearances. A critical example is the experience of exploitation. In feudalism the level of exploitation is obvious to all involved. Serfs know exactly how much time they labour on the big estates for the benefit of the lord, as distinct from working on their own plots to produce for themselves. In capitalism, however, exploitation is mystified in the relationships of wage-labour and private property (Gulalp 1990, 147). Workers appear to contract freely for wages that compensate them for the hours they work for an employer. Profits and interest appear to originate from capital, as legitimate compensation for using the privately owned property of the capitalist. The intrinsically exploitative character of the privatization of material resources of a community, and the appropriation of surplus value from labour power, are not immediately evident. To the extent that everyday conceptions of these relations are merely the conscious expression of the visible movements they will ordinarily be ideological in character (Sayer 1983, ix). Workers typically do not see that capitalism presupposes the violence of the class struggle described above by Brenner, in which the mass of people were forcibly separated from any means of production. What they see is their dependence on businesses to provide them with jobs, and what they commonly feel is gratitude for being given steady work and wages–what Marx termed **false consciousness**. They may see how money, investments, and technology are essential to making profits, but what they typically do not recognize is how processes of extracting surplus value work, so that their own labour power is the true basis of profits. In Marx's view it is a complex work of science to explore beyond immediately visible economic relationships to reveal the underlying relations of class struggle and exploitation that produce this visible experience of benevolent capitalists and grateful workers.

Classical Economics as Ideology

The most difficult aspect of this work is to get beyond the abstract logical models of classical economics that, in Marx's view, mystify relationships between people, including alienation, exploitation, and power, translating them into abstract market forces. Instead of people acting collectively in relation with each other to produce economic inequalities and dependence, the "economy" seems to be the causal agent, doing things to people. Human relations appear to be governed by the forces of competition, supply, demand, price, productivity, and the like, to which both capitalists and workers are subject.

In *The German Ideology,* Marx explains at some length the practices that create such distorted understanding. Three distortions or tricks are involved. The first trick is to separate the ruling ideas from the rulers. We lose sight of the connection between the dominant ideas of capitalism and the ruling class that propounds them. The second step is to order these ideas in terms of some mystical connections or abstract conceptual schemes. Complex mathematical models produced by economists are one example of such schemes. They seem to provide impressive models of how economies work, with all the messy details of what people are doing abstracted out of them. The models are based on concepts like *supply-demand curves, prices, wages, commodities,* and *markets.* The balance of supply and demand determines the price at which commodities exchange in the market, and governs the actions and decisions of "rational economic men." These abstract forces make up the **invisible hand of the market**. The third trick is to treat these abstract models as causal forces that explain behaviour. They appear to function in terms of laws of their own. Whatever people do in specific situations appears to be responses to economic

forces (Marx and Engels [1846] 1970, 64; Sayer 1983; Smith 1974a, 45–46). This is a powerful way of controlling people because the logical models do indeed seem to fit people's experience. Once people believe these models, they become obedient to them, and they can be more effectively controlled than if capitalists came right out and stated their class interests. People accept such practices as massive downsizing of business resulting in widespread unemployment as somehow inevitable, the effect of forces beyond anyone's control.

Marx himself did not contest whether these models of classical economics were adequate for describing market forces. The problem for him is that they remain at the level of appearances without exploring the essential processes that give rise to these appearances. Concepts are treated as abstract logical relations rather than historically specific social practices. The models assume precisely what needs to be explained.

Take the concept of *rational economic men,* for example. Marx argues that we cannot simply take for granted that it is human nature to be "profit-maximizers." People only begin to behave like this when they have lost all direct access to the means of providing for their own subsistence needs. When they have to buy and sell labour power for wages, and purchase everything they need in the commodity market, they become **intensely concerned with** making money. It is not abstract market forces that determine such behaviour, but very real relations of class struggle between people. All this gets covered up when we focus on market forces doing things to people. The classical economists' vision of abstract market forces is very similar to the theological vision of an abstract god that. Feuerbach criticized. Both are conceptualized as external to the lives of people, acting over them; doing things to them, punishing and rewarding their behaviour.

Marx dismisses these supposedly explanatory models of market forces and exchange of commodities as **commodity fetishism**. A **fetish** is an inanimate object that its worshipped for its magical powers. Commodities become fetishes in economics. Things appear to rule people instead of people producing things. Exchange appears to occur between things, rather than the exchange of labour power between people. Abstract typifications are treated as having active causal agency while people become objects, their lives determined by the properties of things.

Marx argues that capitalism, more than any other social form, create, illusory appearances, because its survival depends on it. Once it becomes obvious that all the suffering caused by abstract market forces is only a reflection of the concentration of private; ownership of the means of production, and the mass of people's forced separation from it, the entire edifice is likely to totter. Marx even goes so far as to suggest that once capitalism is overthrown and replaced by the openly visible, communal sharing of access to the means of production, social science itself will wither away. It would be unnecessary, since people could directly see for themselves what was going on (Cohen 1980).

Dialectical Method

Marx tried to develop a method of research that would help to expose the processes underlying human history and immediate experience. He borrowed the notion of **dialectical method** from Hegel and adapted it to his own purposes. In Hegel's philosophy, the dialectical method is a form of testing and developing logical arguments by first exploring the contradictions that may be present in a particular argument and then devising solutions. Hegel argues that the advancement of human knowledge reflects the recurrent cycles of thesis, antithesis, and synthesis. The **thesis** consists of any philosophical system or theory. Its **antithesis** comprises the logical inconsistencies, internal problems, and unexplained anomalies within the system of thought. These problems force philosophers to attempt to resolve them. **Synthesis** is achieved with the integration of a new system of ideas that resolves the old problems. This provides a new starting point or thesis, until new problems become obvious. The **dialectical** processes of antithesis and synthesis continue until perfection is reached.

Marx applied this dialectical method to material conditions to arrive at his theory of **dialectical materialism**. For him the thesis consists of the existing organization of production. The antithesis comprises the internal contradictions. These are the tensions and practical inconsistencies between productive potential of a given means and how people organize their productive relations. The synthesis breaks these contradictions by establishing new forms of organization capable of unleashing the full potential of the emerging means of production.

In relation to the historical processes of his own time. Marx identified feudalism as the original thesis. It is a mode of economic production that endured for centuries

and gave basic security of subsistence to all its members. But it was destined to give way under its own internal contradictions. The productive potential of feudalism was stifled by its social relations. Tied labourers, who were responsible for production, had no incentive to produce more than was necessary for their own subsistence, and those who controlled the estates had little incentive to invest in them. The system could only expand by squeezing the absolute surplus, to the point that production itself was threatened.

Capitalism seemed to resolve the contradictions inherent in feudalism. For all its faults, capitalism succeeded in breaking feudal restraints. Productive potential expanded exponentially under competitive capitalism, and labourers were freed from their hereditary bondage. It was because of this tremendous liberating potential of capitalism that Marx believed it was a necessary intermediate step between feudalism and communism.

When Lenin declared the communist revolution a fait accompli in Russia in 1917, a great many committed Marxist revolutionaries had their doubts. Most of what became the Soviet Union was trapped in a backward feudal mode of production, with only a tiny and mostly foreign bourgeoisie. Lenin argued that a centralized state-capitalist phase was required initially in the Soviet Union to promote development. He hoped that this would lead eventually to the next step of a truly socialist revolution (Resnick and Wolff 1993, 48–49).

Lenin's Marxist critics argued that it would be impossible to advance from feudalism to communism without the intermediate stage of capitalism. They were partially right. The struggle toward economic development in Eastern Europe was long and hard and involved severe internal repression that Marx had not foreseen. In part this reflects historical circumstances. Soviet society was surrounded by hostile capitalist states intent on its destruction, and this impelled the development of a coercive military apparatus (Panitch 1992, 143–44). But this coercive state capitalism itself generated exploitative class interests that blocked any easy route to socialism, while the inflexible collectivized socialist economy proved incapable of achieving the level of industrial and technological development of advanced capitalist societies. The theoretical analysis of this failure and the lessons to be learned from it are critical issues in contemporary Marxist scholarship.

In the West, the political rhetoric and euphoric claims of the triumph of democracy and capitalism that followed the collapse of communist states in Eastern Europe quickly faded as worldwide recession and government debt reached crisis proportions. These conditions are a stark reminder that, while capitalism may have broken the fetters of feudalism, it has its own internal problems and contradictions. Like feudalism, its productive potential is stifled by the relations of production. These relations generate the inherent tendencies toward concentration of capital, falling rate of profit, crises of overproduction, and increasing misery among the masses.

The new synthesis that Marx foresaw was advanced communism. When all members of a community could share in and exercise direct control over the means of advanced industrial production, this would finally remove the shackles on the productive potential of capitalism. There would no longer be a class of economically dependent labourers separated from the means of production and vulnerable to unemployment and poverty with every advance of labour-saving technology. Production could truly take off. There would be no crisis of overproduction until all the wants of all the people had been satiated. Then the system could settle down at this desired production level with the minimum input of labour, using the best labour-saving technology available. According to Marx, perfection would be reached. It is a utopian vision that is far removed from the reality of any of the so-called communist societies of Eastern Europe.

The Class Struggle

Marx did not expect the transition from capitalism to advanced communism to occur automatically as the inexorable workings of some grand evolutionary scheme. Rather, he saw a dynamic process in which class struggle would necessarily play a central role. As we have seen with respect to both, Europe and Canada, the development of capitalism was a violent process in which capitalists overthrew the existing relations of production and asserted their private property rights; this drove producers from the land and into the position where they had to sell their labour power for wages. It would take a similar struggle to break private ownership of the productive forces developed under capitalism.

A major problem that confronts Marxist politics, Sayer suggests, is the conflict between means and goals. Because the state is so central to bourgeois society, social struggle will have to take a political form (1985, 251–52). But at the same time, the state is part of what excludes people from directly controlling the circumstances of their lives. The focus on state politics promotes a hierarchical, oligarchic, or elitist, form of organization rather than an egalitarian, democratic form. In principle, socialist parties believed in giving power to the workers to control production, and abolishing the power of capitalists and their hierarchy of supervisors and bosses. But in practice, socialist parties found themselves compelled to work in **autocratic** and bureaucratic ways to function in a capitalist state system. The means they needed to confront the bourgeois state undermined the goals of democratic socialism itself.

Marx believed that the impetus for the struggle to overthrow capitalism would come from the mass of working people disadvantaged by the existing relations of production. But this would not be automatic. Before the struggle could begin, people would have to see through the ideology of rational market forces. They would have to understand the relations of production, and their own position within these relations, and see the potential for change. It would be the role of radical intellectuals to educate working people in these areas. But intellectual revelation alone would not be sufficient. Capitalist contradictions would first have to reach the point where they became part of the immediately experienced reality of the people so that experience and theory would connect. Then the class struggle might seriously begin.

Marx drew a clear distinction between the situation of people as a **class-in-itself** and their conscious realization of their situation as a **class-for-itself.** People who share the same relationship to the means of production constitute a class-in-itself. Only when such people become conscious of this shared class position, and act collectively in their class interests, do they come to form a class-for-itself. This *class consciousness* is a necessary starting point for revolutionary social action.

Contemporary Marxist Theory

Marx is such a complex theorist, and the implications of his work are so far-reaching, that it is simply not possible to sum his theory up in a way that would satisfy all contemporary Marxists. There is no single body of theory, even in the discipline of sociology, that now constitutes "Marxist theory." Marxist-inspired theoretical orientations have developed in several very different directions, especially in recent years, with much internal dissent and debate. Only the flavour of these alternative perspectives can be introduced here.

Marxist Structuralism and Political Economy Theory

The dominant perspective in Marxist theory in sociology is inspired by Marx's model of the capitalist system and its internal dynamics and contradictions. It takes from Marx his central observation that all social relations are determined, in the last instance, by the mode of production. The model of the capitalist system thus provides an explanatory framework that can account for specific characteristics of contemporary capitalist societies. This general orientation is widely referred to as **Marxist structuralism**. It forms the core of political economy theory. Its power as an approach for analysing contemporary Canadian society is explored in the next chapter.

The structuralist political economy perspective has come under increasing criticism in recent years from scholars working within the Marxist framework. Taken to its extreme, the application of Marx's model of the capitalist system as an explanatory scheme risks repeating the mistakes for which Marx himself castigated classical economists, namely, of giving causal force to abstract concepts. The structural contradictions of capitalism seem to produce their determined effects, while active human agency seems redundant. The Marxist historian E.P. Thompson (1978b) has come out strongly against economic-determinist versions of Marxist historicism. He insists that, in a Marxist approach, class does not constitute a *thing* but a *process*.

Classes do not exist as separate entities; look around, find an enemy class, and then start to struggle. On the contrary, people find themselves in a society structured in determined ways . . . they identify points of antagonistic interest, they commence to struggle around these issues and in the process of struggling they discover themselves as classes, they come to know this discovery as class-consciousness (Thompson 1978a, 149).

Marxism and Social Constructionist Theory

The social constructionist approach to Marxist analysis draws extensively on Marx's earlier philosophical writings, and the methods that he himself used in the development of his critique of classical economics (Smith 1990b; Sayer 1985; 1989). Marx insisted that an adequate understanding of bourgeois society could not stop at the descriptive models of classical economics. Sayer argues that Marx's seminal work of *Capital* can best be understood not as an economic theory of society and history, but as a historical sociology of economic forms (Sayer 1989, 49). Marx's methodological critique consisted in essence of tracing each of the supposedly abstract logical concepts of economics back to their historically specific roots in social relationships between people. Analysis is grounded in what, people actually do, in their immediate material situation of trying to make a living, and how they come to make sense of these experiences for practical purposes. From this perspective, concepts such as property, commodities, profit, and the like, are not merely abstract ideas, nor do they describe structural entities within the economy. Rather, they denote active practices and relationships between people. *Property* is the mystified form of privatizing the productive energies of members of a community embedded in active relationships of class struggle and exploitation of human energies. Profit is the visible manifestation of surplus labour power extracted from workers. *Commodities* embody the exchange of labour power between people. The abstract sphere of the economy itself is an expression of active processes that separate creative labour from community control, in turn producing the notion of "isolated individuals" in civil society who are condemned to compete incessantly as "rational economic men" These are all historically specific patterns of social relations.

Much of the contemporary work in sociology that adopts a social constructionist perspective is by theorists who define themselves as Marxists, but who avoid the more deterministic **structuralism** of dominant political economy theory. For this reason we have been careful to avoid treating the political economy perspective in sociology as synonymous with Marxist theory, even though it is based directly on Marx's analysis of capitalism, and is widely identified as "Marxist" theory.

Marxism Feminism and Radical Feminism

Marxist feminism constitutes a third theoretical approach developing out of the Marxist perspective. It uses the analytical tools of historical materialism, rather than Marx's actual writings, as inspiration. Marx himself said very little about women. Mitchell (1972, 24) suggests that if we actually start looking in Marx's work for material under the heading "women," we would probably conclude that Marx was a hopeless male chauvinist. There is little to suggest that Marx ever intended the generic term *mench* or *men* to include *women*. He conceives the proletariat to be, essentially, working *men*. Women enter the picture in so far as they themselves sell their labour power in the marketplace. But their work as women, as housewives, as domestic workers, and as mothers, had little place in Marx's analysis of capitalism and the class struggle in history.

Recent feminist theory takes two basic approaches to Marxist theory. The dominant one, represented in the domestic labour debate, which we examine in the next chapter, tends toward a structuralist approach. It seeks to explicate the position and role of women within the workings of the capitalist system. An alternative strategy is to try to rework the Marxist concept of class itself, not only to incorporate women as proletariat but also to give more central attention to the dimension of women's work as reproducers—both in the bearing and raising of children as the next generation of workers and the daily maintenance of workers themselves. The neglect of reproduction in Marxist theory is a very large omission in the scheme of things. A classical Marxist theorist would probably argue that the question of reproduction has been subsumed under the more general issue of means of subsistence for workers and their dependants. But this does not satisfy feminists. Classical Marxist structuralism. or political economy theory, is faulted for its unwarranted endorsement of the capitalist standpoint that defines the "main business" of ruling as capital accumulation, and marginalizes all other topics (Smith 1992a, 9–14).

Eisenstein (1984, 146) suggests that the Marxist version of class should be reworked to incorporate the notion of women as a **sexual class**. This does not mean that they are like the proletariat, defined in relation to the mode of production. Rather they are a sexual class in relation to the mode of reproduction. They are a class in that they perform the basic and necessary activities of society: reproduction, child-rearing, nurturing. consuming, domestic labouring, and wage earning. They are a sexual class because what they do as women, the activities for which they are responsible, and the labour they perform are essential and necessary to the operation of society, more important; even than the activities of the proletariat.

The feminist project of re-working Marxist theory to incorporate women's reproductive work draws inspiration from Marx's recognition that it is capitalism itself that breaks the integration of relationships of production and reproduction. The privatization of means of production within capitalism creates the abstraction known as "economic organization," an abstraction that makes no sense within earlier societies (Smith 1992a, 10). Feminist political economy tries to heal this rupture between production, producers, and reproduction by shifting the standpoint of women from periphery to centre stage.

Conclusion

It is not possible to draw any clear conclusions about the contribution of Marxism or Marxist theory to sociology because it is still very much in the process of formulation. Despite the fact that Marx died over a century ago, his ideas are only beginning to be established in mainstream sociology in North America. Marxism came to the fore during the 1960s as a critique of Parsonian functionalism. It is still considered rather avant garde in some sociological circles. The implications of Marxist thought for political economy, for the social construction of reality, and for feminist theory are very much still in the process of being worked out. There is no definitive interpretation of Marx. You should take the arguments presented here as a point of departure and raise questions for yourself.

The next chapter explores Marxist contributions to understanding contemporary Canadian political economy. The broader implications of Marxism, as they relate to the social relations of family, stratification, education, ethnicity, and modernization, are explored in more depth in later chapters as we present the value of Marxist theory as a critique of traditional functionalism in sociology.

The Political Economy of Canada

 This chapter juxtaposes the perspectives of Marxist political economy and liberal economics to explore their usefulness for understanding how the prevailing capitalist system of economic organization works within Canada. A later chapter explores capitalism as a global economic system.

As discussed in the previous chapter, Marx analysed nineteenth-century capitalism as a system of economic organization with immense creative potential, but plagued by inherent contradictions that he predicted would fracture societies into ever more extreme divisions of wealth and poverty, and ultimately bring about the system's collapse. Contemporary political economy theory draws extensively from Marxist analysis, not so much to make specific predictions about how twenty-first-century capitalism works, but as a frame for insight into what Carroll (2004, 2) refers to as a distinctively capitalist way of life, or capitalist ways of organizing economic and social class relations, and their social con-

sequences. We will be juxtaposing political economy with the alternative liberal-bourgeois perspective, particularly in its contemporary form that is widely referred to as 'neo-liberalism.' This alternative perspective holds that Marx was fundamentally wrong in his conception of capitalist relations. Rather than fomenting inequality and class conflict, neo-liberalism asserts that the free market principles and competitive individualism at the core of capitalist relations promise the best hope for individual freedom, economic well-being, and social and political democracy.

The chapter first summarise the main tenets of Marxist political-economy theory, and contrasts these with principles of liberalism and neo-liberalism. We then use these models to explore broad patterns in the structure of corporate capitalism in Canada, the distribution of ownership and control over capital, and structural shifts that are associated with free trade agreements between Canada and the United States and

Mexico. A key issue in the debates between political economy theory and liberalism concerns class analysis, particularly focused around how capitalist economic relations affect the distribution of income across the economy. Class analysis also addresses the relationship between political and economic institutions, exploring how divergent class interests of capitalists and organized labour are represented in democratic political institutions. The social constructionist perspective is interspersed at several stages in the debate between Marxist and liberal economics to explore how people actively manage economic models and concepts, and negotiate legal and political meanings, to continually bring about these economic relations. This perspective elaborates the Marxist concept of ideological hegemony to focus attention on how the worldviews of the dominant economic class come to gain widespread acceptance, and how they are embedded in policy initiatives, while other interests are discredited and subordinated.

Lastly, we explore the feminist perspective, which challenges both mainstream political economy and liberalism for their narrow focus, which assumes that "the main business" of the economy is to accumulate capital. Consequently, the work of women as homemakers, and the 'social economy' of caring for people, is ignored. When issues of concern to women are moved from the margins to the centre of discussion, the specifically gendered character of economic power and class oppression come into view, and with this a broader focus on family and community well-being as integral to economic activity. The chapter concludes with an extended exploration of primary production in farming in Canada, using this industry as a case study in the practical application of political-economy theories.

Marxist Theory: The Contradictions of Capitalism

Marx conceptualized capitalism as a system of economic production based on the private ownership of the means of production in the hands of a small class of capitalists referred to as the bourgeoisie. Others, who do not own any means of production, must sell their labour power in the marketplace to capitalists who use that labour power to run their enterprises and to make commodities. The term *capital* refers to productive resources—the stock of land, buildings, machinery, energy and raw materials used in the production of commodities. In capitalist exchange, money is used to purchase the productive resources and the labour power needed to convert these resources into commodities that can be sold to generate more money, or profit. The source of profit, Marx argues, is the surplus value created by the difference between the value of wages paid to workers and the value of the commodities that the workers make. Other resources constitute fixed costs for the capitalist, although they themselves incorporate human labour required in their own production. The rate of surplus value or profit to the capitalist provides an objective measure of the rate of exploitation of workers.

Marx argued that the contradictions of capitalism stem from competitive pressure to make profits. This pressure drives capitalists to maximize the exploitation of labourers through longer working hours, lower wages, and labour–saving technology to reduce costs. In the long run, this is self–defeating since, as the ratio of machines to labour increases, profits drop and unemployment rises, leading to crises of overproduction as people cannot afford to buy products. Capitalism thus seems prone to continual and ever–worsening cycles of booms and slumps. Falling profits, an insatiable drive for new technology, and bankruptcies among the smaller bourgeoisie lead to unemployment, the polarization of classes, and increasing poverty among workers. The system can be held together by a combination of global exploitation of cheap labour and cheap raw materials, insatiable drives to generate new consumer markets, with war as the ultimate consumer, or destroyer, of surplus production, and ideological control over prevailing political thought by the ruling capitalist class. This stability, however, is always tenuous. These ideas are listed below as a series of predictions that guide our analysis of contemporary Canadian experience:

1) *Increasing concentration of capital.* Marx predicts that giant corporations will control the economy as smaller businesses collapse or are bought out. These corporations will constantly increase in size and decrease in number as they merge or are bought out.

2) *Falling rate of profit.* As more and more money is needed for investment in technology, the returns on investment decline. Surplus value and profits come ultimately from labour power, not from machines.

3) *Polarization of classes.* Capitalists will get richer and richer with the concentration of control over markets. The middle class of small business people and

independent commodity producers will collapse into the working class.

4) *Increasing poverty of the masses.* Unemployment continually threatens to undermine wage levels. Labour–saving technology results in more and more people competing for fewer jobs. These workers will eventually be joined by bankrupted former members of the small business class. Basic wages will hover around subsistence levels. The gap between poor workers and rich capitalists will get larger.

5) *Recurrent crises of overproduction.* Due to unemployment and low wages, people lack the money to purchase the goods being produced. Productivity expands faster than markets can absorb the goods.

6 *A treadmill of technological innovation.* When capitalists cannot sell their products, they must drop their prices. They must increase productivity still further to undercut their competitors. Hence they are driven to develop better labour–saving technology, which will enable them to produce more goods with fewer workers.

7) *Recurrent cycles of booms and slumps.* Bankruptcies lead to unemployment and overproduction. Technological breakthroughs such as robotics and computers bring temporary affluence, but competitors catch up and the cycle repeats itself.

The advanced centres of capitalism may survive these contradictions, at least in the short run, by hyper-exploitation of cheap labour and cheap raw materials extracted from less developed countries, combined with expanding into their markets. The global conflicts generated by such inherent inequalities, promote constant military spending that in turn reduces crises of overproduction. Governments are predisposed to buy military equipment, use it up in fighting, or declare it obsolete, and buy more. In the longer term, however, the contradictions inherent in capitalism will only get worse.

The Liberal–Bourgeois Thesis

The liberal–bourgeois thesis, which has its roots in classical economics of Adam Smith, argues that Marx had a flawed understanding of the moderating and liberating potential of competition in the economic marketplace. Competition is viewed as the key mechanism controlling both profits and wages. If profits in any one industry are too high, other entrepreneurs will rush in to compete and prices will drop; if profits are too low, entrepreneurs will pull out and invest elsewhere. Overproduction of any one commodity is similarly regulated because as sales and profits drop, entrepreneurs will shift investments to new products for which there is more demand. The mechanism of free competition similarly keeps wages fair. Workers will leave those industries in which wage-rates are too low, to seek better–paying jobs, or if wage-rates are too high workers will rush into these areas until excess labour drives the rates down.

A strong advocate of this theory of competition was Milton Friedman (1978), a Nobel Prize winner in economics, and long a key advisor to the U.S. government and to its allies in Latin America. Friedman opposed in principle any state intervention in the economy because such interference upsets the delicate balance of supply and demand in the marketplace. Minimum wage legislation, for example, may be morally appealing, but its effects are regressive, he warned, hurting the very workers it is designed to help. Any artificial minimum wage functions to increase unemployment as jobs that might have been viable at lower rates of pay become uneconomical. Friedman argued further that the power of huge corporations would be limited by competition if they did not receive state aid and protection. Freedom of competition in a capitalist society is, in his view, the main guarantee of democracy and individual freedom.

Liberal-bourgeois theory argues further that advanced capitalism has the potential to avoid or overcome most of the inequalities foreseen by Marx. The expansion of shareholder capitalism fosters a democratization of ownership of capital, and a separation of ownership and control through the managerial revolution. Free competition has the potential to unleash virtually unlimited innovative and productive resources to sustain higher profits for capitalists and higher standards of living for the masses of workers. The demand within competitive capitalism for continual innovation promotes a professional middle class of highly paid knowledge workers and managers that counters the tendency towards polarization of wealth. Increasing affluence generated by capitalist enterprise promises to trickle down even to the unskilled working–class, sustaining a welfare state of social services, and a political democracy that gives expression to competing interest groups. Developing countries similarly stand to benefit from the demand for their labour and raw materials, and as they develop their own competitive markets and innovative potential.

The liberal-bourgeois thesis thus presents a far more optimistic view of advanced capitalism, at least for the foreseeable future. It predicts that technological innovation will outpace declining rates of profit. Productivity goes up exponentially with computers and robotics. Technology itself tends to get cheaper, so that absolute profit levels stay high, and wages can rise above subsistence levels. Shareholder capitalism will reduce the concentration of capital. The rise of the welfare state and trade unions will counter the tendency toward the increased poverty of the masses. Ultimately, the advanced capitalist societies will develop high levels of stability and consensus, because the system literally 'delivers the goods'. People's needs will be satisfied by consumer goods, and hence class conflict will be avoided. Free enterprise will foster democratic institutions that will balance and limit the power of capitalists.

Neoliberalism

Neoliberalism refers to an expanded and elaborated version of classical liberal bourgeois thesis that advocates extending competitive free-market principles to all aspects of society, particularly social services traditionally provided to citizens through the government. Neoliberalism extols the value of privatizing basic resources like water, electricity, sewage, garbage disposal, postal services, daycare, schools, universities, health services, correctional facilities, and virtually anything else that can be sold (Menashy 2007). Privatization involves converting services into businesses that charge fees, or sell services for profit. The basic reasoning of neoliberalism is that competition to provide services for profit in the marketplace best ensures efficiency. Efficiency is defined as the provision of maximum quality of services for minimum costs. For example, if all schools had to compete for fee-paying students, the best schools that offer high quality education for competitive fees would likely attract the most students. Those schools that offer substandard services, or have inflated costs, would likely fail to attract many students and be forced to improve their standards or close. In contrast, when services are provided through government monopolies and financed through taxes, there is no competition or profit motives to ensure quality services at low costs, and no inherent pressures promoting technological innovation. Neo-

liberal policies promote privatization as the solution to what they see as inherent problems of stagnation, inefficiency, and cost overruns that plague government services. Liberals further argue against high corporate taxes on the ground that such taxes lower competitiveness of Canadian businesses and ultimately lower revenues and jobs.

In summary, while Marxist political economy theory predicts that the capitalist system will spiral downwards into chaos, neoliberalism as economic theory and political philosophy asserts that market forces ensure an ever-expanding spiral of prosperity. Freedom to trade ensures equal opportunity for anyone with entrepreneurial spirit to offer goods and services for profit in the marketplace. The laws of supply and demand ensure fair exchange, with fair wages and profits. Individuals are rewarded on the basis of their effort and ability. Anyone who really wants to work can get a job, and by working hard can make their labour profitable and get ahead. Excessive government interference in free markets undermines prosperity. High corporate taxes stifle enterprise, and harm workers by reducing job opportunities. Money in workers' pockets promotes higher consumption, higher profits, and thus more business opportunities, more jobs, more profits and more shared wealth. Free market capitalism spreads democracy and peace.

These vastly different predictions guide the following exploration of Canadian experience as an advanced capitalist economy. Key research questions are whether capitalist institutions are tending towards corporate concentration of capital as predicted by Marxist theory or towards a dilution of ownership in shareholder capitalism foreseen by liberalism; whether structural inequality in Canada is tending towards a polarization of immense wealth and increasing poverty, or towards a more equitable sharing of affluence and social welfare; whether state policies work primarily in the interests of corporate monopoly capitalism, or to rein in the excesses of capitalism and ensure that fair market forces prevail; how competing political philosophies of Marxism and liberalism play out in the Canadian political arena; and the gendered class character of these politico-economic forces. These issues are explored below firstly on a broad national scale, and then specifically with respect to primary industries of farming, fishing and forestry. A focus on these industries opens up consideration of the critical issue of environmental degradation and its relation to advanced capitalism—an issue largely neglected by both Marxist theory and by classical liberalism until very recently.

Concentration of Capital in Canada

A central distinction between the Marxist and liberal predictions concerns the extent to which the concentration of capital in the hands of a small number of huge corporations will come to dominate and distort the market systems, so that the checks and balances of free competition no longer exist. Patterns of ownership in the contemporary Canadian economy suggests that such a concentration of power is far advanced. Out of more than a million firms operating in Canada in 1996, a mere twenty-five enterprises controlled 41 percent of all business assets (Carroll 2004, 201), up from one-third in 1983 (Veltmeyer 1987, 18–23). In 1996, the largest firms with assets of $25 million or annual revenues in excess of $100 million controlled almost 80 percent of all business assets in Canada (Statistics Canada 2001, 31, 44).

Corporate elites of presidents and chief executive officers who head these dominant enterprises, and major shareholders on their boards of directors wield immense power through control over how to invest vast pools of surplus capital. Beside them is a subordinate elite class of advisors—that Carroll terms 'organic intellectuals'— corporate lawyers, management and financial consultants, engineers and scientists, and policy advisors from academe and politics (Carroll 2004, 19–21).

Corporations grow chiefly by buying out or merging with existing corporations, with the express intent of dominating markets in their spheres of operation. Concentration takes variety of institutional forms. *Horizontal integration* involves the consolidation of firms in the same industry, giving dominant corporations enormous power to set labour contracts and fix prices. The Bertrand Report (1981) on *The State of Competition in the Canadian Petroleum Industry* estimated that, through price fixing, the then "big four'—Imperial, Texaco, Shell, and Gulf—Canadians were overcharged by about $12 billion for petroleum products between 1958 and 1978. Since then Imperial bought out Texaco. By the early 1980s, Canadian markets for tobacco, breweries and motor vehicles were already dominated by four firms controlling 90 percent of production. In a further twenty manufacturing industries, four firms controlled 75 percent of production. The rate at which mergers occur has accelerated since the free trade agreements of 1989 and 1994 have removed barriers to cross-national

investments and assured foreign-owned corporations the same property rights as national firms. The goal is increasingly not national, but global domination of markets. To give just one example, in May 2007 the Canadian newsprint giant Thomson Corporation announced a merger with Reuters of London to make the combined firm the world's largest provider of financial data and business news.

Vertical integration is another strategy followed by corporations to dominate their niche market, involving the takeover of firms that operate at different stages in the development of a product. The McCain potato company in New Brunswick consolidated its grip on potato processing in the province by incorporating seed, fertilizer, pesticide, farm machinery, storage, brokerage, wholesaling, and trucking lines into its group of companies, as well as purchasing major tracts of land.

Conglomerate mergers involve a strategy of diversifying holdings to increase stability of profits. The Thomson family empire referred to above controls an array of department stores, including Hudson's Bay, Simpsons, Zellers, and Fields, significant oil and gas interests, insurance companies and trucking lines, as well as its central interest in the newspaper market.

Holding Companies comprise corporate empires whose principle assets are shares in other companies. Prominent Canadian examples include Brookfield Asset Management (formerly Edper/Brascan) controlled by Peter and Edward Bronfman, Power Corporation controlled by Paul Desmarais, and Thomson Corporation, controlled by the Thomson family.

A cursory internet scan of these corporations gives some idea of size of the assets they control. Brookfield (Edper/Brascan) Corporation specializes in real estate, natural resources, energy and financial services, including Royal LePage, Noranda, and Great Lakes Power. In May 2007, the company controlled about US $70 billion in assets. Power Corporation is a group of companies specializing in financial services, including Great Western life Insurance, London Life, Canada Life, IGM Financial, Mackenzie Financial and Pargesa Holdings. In May 2007, the Company website quoted consolidated assets of $132.6 billion with additional assets under administration of $200 billion. Thomson Corporation is the world's largest information company, active in financial services, healthcare, law, and science and technology research, and tax accounting. Thomson was until recently a world leader in higher-education textbooks, until it sold Thomson learning Assets in 2006, using the funds to buy Reuters, the world's leading news agency.

In 2006 the company was valued at US $29 billion, with annual revenues of about US $6.6 billion.

It is very difficult to keep up with all the ramifications and threads of control exerted by such giant corporations because their contours can change so rapidly. Trillions of dollars flow daily at electronic speed through the Toronto stock market, itself a small market by world standards. To give just one example, Argus Corporation, founded by E.P. Taylor in 1945 was once a giant holding company with financial control over Canadian Breweries, Dominion Stores, Hollinger Mines, Crown Trust, Standard Broadcasting, Massey-Ferguson, and B.C. Forest products. It was so powerful in the 1970s that it became the focus of a 1975 Royal Commission on Corporate Concentration. In 1978 Conrad Black bought a controlling interest in Argus from Taylor's widow, and sold off most of the assets, leaving Argus retaining control only over Hollinger Inc, itself a subsidiary of Ravelston Corporation, controlled by Black and his colleague David Radler. In 1995 Argus assets were calculated to be a mere $440 million. In 2007 Black and Radler were found guilty of siphoning millions of dollars from Hollinger Corporation for their personal fortunes. Shareholders initiated a litany of civil suits to lay claim to his assets.

Holding companies gain financial control over other companies by purchasing a majority of voting shares, or the largest single block of shares, if share ownership is widely dispersed. For example, if a company were to have assets divided equally into bonds, non-voting preferred stock, and voting common stock, the purchase of half the voting common stock, or one-sixth of the total worth of the company, would give effective legal voting control. The holding company can further convert these assets into bonds, stock, and voting stock, sell the non-voting assets and still retain voting control over the original company or group of companies and subsidiaries (Veltmeyer 1987, 53). Primary capitalists require the services of a trusted elite class of financial, legal, and policy advisors—the 'organic intellectuals', to manage these vast pools of surplus capital. Between 1995 and 2005 American corporate elites expended over US $9 trillion in a huge takeover boom (Hutton 2007a, 46). Hutton argues that these takeovers are the principle mechanism driving job losses and downsizing. When the Thomson-Reuters merger occurred in 2007, shareholders were promised to deliver $500m in annual savings within 3 yrs, achievable mostly by merging operations and cutting staff. Business analysts in 2007 continued to describe North American markets as awash in surplus capital and to predict a period of unprecedented mergers and acquisitions.

Corporate Concentration, Competition, and Shareholder Capital

One important implication of this concentration of capital is that patterns of competition differ markedly from the classical liberal economics model of masses of small producers offering their wares in the same market. There still is competition between giant corporations, both nationally and globally, to maximize returns on their capital investments. There is also competition among subsidiary holdings, as sub-unit managers strive to outshine each other in returning profits to their parent holding company. But consistent with Marxist analysis, competition and business opportunities at this level are far from equal. Individual clients can shift their business from one life insurance company to another, but when all available sources of life insurance are controlled by the same corporate elite, the variation will be cosmetic. Customers can shop at Zellers or Sears, rather than Hudson Bay, but they cannot escape the reality that these are merely sub-departments of the same mega-store. Competition within sub-units of the same corporation does not work in the ways envisioned by the liberal bourgeois thesis. Moreover, when a few mega-corporations dominate the market in given industries, it is within their power and in their joint vested interests to mute competition to so as to shore up prices and to stabilise market share and profits. Such patterns of tacit cooperation are facilitated by interlocking networks of directorships among corporate elites that are explored further below. At the level of mega-corporations, competition is as likely to take the form of mergers and takeovers as heightened efficiency or undercutting prices. Small independent competitors can either be ignored or swiftly swamped with the power of the big corporations to undercut their markets—a strategy that Irving Oil is well known for in Eastern Canada and Maine. The result for consumers is often conformity of prices and product lines, with limited alternatives. Customers can drive to different shopping malls, but they are likely to find little variation in stores or goods available.

The liberal thesis predicts further that increasing affluence would result in ownership of capital becoming widely dispersed among masses of small investors, Consistent with this prediction, masses of ordinary

Canadians have become shareholders in corporate capital through investments in mutual funds and pension plans. Gross income from investments in Canada now compares closely with gross income from wages and salaries. But dispersal of shareholding has not translated into dispersal of control over capital. Investment companies that manage mutual funds and pensions are themselves major corporations specializing in finance capital. Their directors form an integral part of the corporate elite, managing immense pools of surplus capital. Individuals who own a few mutual-fund shares in a mega-corporation have minimal capacity to influence corporate board policies.

The distinction between 'finance' and 'industrial' capital has become increasingly blurred as pension and mutual fund directors shift from passive investing to active ownership of property (Carroll 2004, 204). The Ontario Teachers Pension Fund, for example, had assets of $106 billion in 2007. The Fund purchased Cadillac Fairview property development company in 2000, and through this company it owns controlling interests in an array of other subsidiaries, including Toronto Dominion Centre, Toronto Eaton Centre, Rideau Centre in Ottawa, Samsonite, Maple Leaf Sports Entertainment, Shoppers Drug Mart, and Worldspan. In July 2007 it bid successfully to takeover Bell Canada Enterprises, the telecommunications giant, for $34.8 billion, described in *The Globe and Mail* (July 2 2007, A1) as the biggest takeover in Canadian corporate history. The Ontario Municipal Employees Retirement Board similarly purchased Oxford Properties in 2001. In 2007 it had assets under management of $48 billion (*The Globe and Mail* 7 July 2007, B5). These funds are also major shareholders of banks. Fund directors commonly sit on the boards of other corporations, where they typically favour investment strategies that maximize short-term returns to shareholder over social responsibility. The question also widely debated in business news is whether this short-term shareholder return mentality will ultimately be good for businesses or undermine long-term development. The government Canada Pension Plan controlled assets under management of $116.6 billion in 2007, raising different business concerns about possible political interference.

In effect, Carroll suggests, pension funds have become virtually indistinguishable from other mega-corporations. Individuals who put their savings into these funds have minimal say in how the funds are managed, although some shareholders have made attempts to encourage ethical portfolios. In 2004, at the urging of Greenpeace, a group of concerned teachers pressured their union to pressure the Ontario Teachers Pension Fund to adopt ethical investment practices, and in particular to stop investing in tobacco companies (Vasil 2004). Pension Fund directors, however, countered that they were legally bound to invest funds in ways that maximize returns on investments. If they were to limit investment patterns as Greenpeace supporters advocated, they would risk being sued by other teachers for a shortfall in retirement pension assets. Further, even if the majority of the more than 250 000 active and retired Ontario teachers were to vote in favour of setting ethical investment limits, Pension Fund directors would further require that the provincial government grant them a special legal exemption from their 'fiduciary duty' to seek the highest returns on investments before they could legally comply. The stakes are high. A one-percent drop in rate of returns on $70 billion assets could mean a loss of $70 million in the plan's value. The teachers' experiences with their pension plan fund suggest that shareholders can work together to influence the boards of institutional investors, but it requires a collectively organized social movement supported by political will.

Corporate Structures: Stability and Change

A comparative study of intercorporate linkages between the top 250 Canadian firms in 1976 and 1996 (Carroll 2004) gives some insight into patterns of stability and change in the structure of corporate power in Canada. Carroll uses intercorporate linkages as a central measure of corporate integration. These linkages can be direct, as when a director or chief executive officer of one corporation sits on the board of another, or more often indirect, when the same outside director sits on the boards of two or more other corporations. These traditional linkages remained extensive in 1996, although noticeably less thick than in 1976.

One significant change has been the growing Canadianization of corporate networks compared to the 1970s. By 1996, Canada's top 250 firms, measured by size of assets, no longer included American branch plants, as they had in the 1970s. The continental market established by the 1989 Free Trade Deal made branch-plant production for the Canadian market largely obsolete. Also, the speed of electronic communications between sub-units of a corporation has reduced the need for on-site directors. Carroll found further that the boards of directors of foreign-based companies operating in Canada, both American and Japanese, were mostly insular, not sharing directors with other Canadian-based companies. The key players in intercorporate power networks in 1996 were almost exclusively Canadian, comprising family capitalists and institutional investors.

Significant structural reforms are also evident within the Canadian corporate boards to make the composition of boards of directors more meritocratic and democratic. By 1996, the average size of corporate boards had shrunk, with far fewer directors sitting on multiple corporate boards, fewer corporate insiders as board members, and more outsiders—people who are not themselves capitalists but who serve as expert advisors. Carroll suggests that pressures from greater global competition, and a few notable scandals and corporate failures in the early 1990s prompted these structural reforms. The traditional old-boy networks of directors, fostered by dinners at elite private clubs, became a liability.

The newer, slimmed-down boards, typically included far fewer bank directors than in 1976, reflecting a decline in the centrality of banks as controllers of investment capital. With deregulation of financial institutions, more corporations are themselves functioning as financial institutions. Institutional investors like mutual fund and pension fund directors are rivalling banks as sources of capital. Carroll emphasizes, however, that evidence of democratization within the corporate elite does not necessarily translate into greater societal control or influence. As noted above, institutional directors are driven by a single mandate to maximize short-term returns to shareholders—they are not social reformers. Family capitalists share their corporate boards with institutional investors and top echelons of organic intellectuals as chief executive officers. But the core of capitalist power—to extract surplus, to set business strategies, and to allocate surplus capital remain within the control of the owners of surplus capital.

The increasing influence of organic intellectuals on corporate boards reflects a managerial revolution on the lines foreseen by liberal economics, although not a dilution of corporate power. Former senior politicians are often sought out to serve as outside directors because of their insider knowledge of government regulations and geopolitical forces that affect business opportunities. In June 2007, former conservative prime minister Brian Mulroney joined the board of Blackstone Group Management (*Globe and Mail* 5 June 07, B10) a New York based company interested in takeovers of government-regulated telecommunications industries. Compensation was reported as $100 000 a year. Mulroney continued to be a partner in the corporate law

firm Ogilvy Renault, and to sit on eight other corporate boards. He only recently retired from a further five boards. Such thick interlocks across corporate boards and political parties work to sustain a corporate-political network of shared interests and worldview. They both reflect and foster an *organic conscience collective* that underlies competitive interests.

The Social Construction of Meaning: Achieving Political Will

A central interest in Carroll's network analysis of top Canadian firms was to track the capacity of the capitalist elite to act collectively. They clearly compete against each other in the marketplace for market share and profits, but they also clearly have common interests. These include maintaining the legal frameworks that manage market relations, protecting their profits or capital surplus from excessive taxation and wage demands, controlling labour unrest, limiting cyclical booms and slumps, and the like. By 1996 Canadian corporate directors were less likely to find themselves meeting fellow directors on overlapping boards, or on bank boards, or to plot strategies in exclusive club dining rooms.

The new location for intercorporate networking, Carroll suggests (2004, 157–171), has become the policy planning groups, colloquially referred to as 'think tanks'. Carroll identifies five major policy planning groups in Canada in 1996—The Conference Board of Canada, the C.D. Howe Institute, the Business Council on National Issues, the Fraser Institute, and the Atlantic Institute for Market Studies. All five policy groups are interlinked closely with each other, and with the Canadian corporate elite. By 1996 262 people sat on one or more of the five boards, and the majority of policy-group directors also directed one or more leading corporations. These Canadian policy groups are themselves linked to global policy planning groups like the Trilateral Commission, the World Business Council for Sustainable Development, the World Economic Forum, the Bilderberg Conference, and the International Chamber of Commerce. Carroll argues that these policy groups, nationally and globally, have become the principle cultural mechanisms that integrate the corporate elites and promote their interests as a class. American, European and Canadian corporate elites meet directly in these policy groups. Canadian prime ministers and finance ministers also routinely attend conferences organized by these policy groups.

A central objective of these organizations is to influence government policies in the interests of corporate capital. They promote transnational neoliberalism. Capitalists, however powerful they might be in the economic sphere, do not actually rule Canada. Capitalists as a class seek to exert their influence over how political leaders, legislators, media, and ultimately voters think about issues, in order to get support for, or at least acquiescence in, policies and institutions that advance the interests of corporate capitalism. When Canadian policy groups lobby the government on issues important to corporate elites, their credibility is enhanced by their apparent independence from any specific corporation. By the late 1990s, the C.D. Howe Institute was publishing 10 to 15 policy studies annually. The Business Council of Canada, comprising a select group of 150 invited chief executive officers from leading Canadian corporations, functioned as a virtual shadow cabinet, regularly sending task-force findings and recommendations on issues of international finance, trade, investment, environment and foreign affairs to relevant government committees. The Council also stages conferences to which media and government officials are invited. All the policy groups regularly publish books, reports, conference proceedings, and press releases with the broad objective of influencing prevailing attitudes and assumptions among the public at large towards a neoliberal worldview.

This work is generally not done by corporate elites themselves but by their delegates—lawyers, economists, former politicians, and academics who are employed directly by the policy groups, or whose research is funded through the groups. Using 1996 data, Carroll (2004, ch. 9) tracks thick interlocking networks linking the top 100 Canadian corporations with the top 18 Canadian universities, ranked by size, and the five bourgeois policy groups. These are two-way linkages, with universities inviting chief executive officers of corporations to sit on university boards of governors, and corporate elites inviting university presidents and senior officers to sit on corporate boards. Carroll argues that these linkages between organic intellectuals and corporate elites is critical for enabling the corporate elite as a class to realize its collective class interests—or in Marxist terms, to act as a class-for-itself in social and political arenas. To the

extent that neoliberalism as worldview becomes culturally accepted as common-sense, the corporate elites can effectively achieve their will without the appearance of force. The Marxist concept of "ideological hegemony" refers to this capacity to exert power through control over prevailing ideas.

The one group conspicuously excluded from this network is organized labour, or trade union leaders. Institutionally segregated left-wing policy groups like the Canadian Centre for Policy Alternatives (CCPA), the Council of Canadians, and the National Anti-Poverty Organization offer a counter-hegemonic working-class perspective on issues. However, they carry far weaker political clout. Business oriented policy groups are about ten times more likely to be cited in media or in government policy initiatives than the CCPA Monitor, not least because mass media outlets are themselves corporate capitalist enterprises. The CCPA Monitor also has to make do with vastly less investment money than business-supported policy groups.

Allocative Power: Shifting the Balance of Power between Business and Government

Classical Marxist analysis holds that ideological hegemony is critical in generating consent or acquiescence of the masses to the power of the corporate capitalist class. But, in the final analysis, Marxists argue, the root of this class power rests ultimately on control over fluid surplus capital. Corporate elites have the capacity to directly determine how and where surplus capital will be invested. To the extent that workers as a class, entire communities, and political parties, depend on these investments, the balance of power favours corporate elites. Neoliberalism, as ideology and practice works to promote the freedom of capital from social and political constraints.

Canadian corporate elites wield significant influence over Canadian politics through financial contributions to political parties. Historically, most of the leading corporations have hedged their political bets by funding both the Conservatives and the Liberals, although not always equally. Rarely have corporations funded the pro-labour New Democratic Party. In the 1988 elections when the proposed Free Trade Agreement between Canada and the United States was the central issue, with the Conservatives under Mulroney supporting it, and the Liberals under John Turner, and the NDP opposing, business elites made their bias clear. Corporate money poured into Conservative Party coffers (Carroll 2004,

176). Pro free-trade forces spent an estimated $6.5 million in the last three weeks of the campaign, compared to less than one million by those opposing free trade. By 1993 the Liberal Party had markedly shifted its political agenda in favour of free trade, endorsing the more extensive North Atlantic Free Trade Agreement, bringing the Party back into the favour with corporate donors. Both major parties now endorse neoliberal economic policies.

Revisions to the Canada Elections Act pushed through by the out-going Chretien Liberal government in 2003 restricts the size of direct corporate donations to party election expenses, although contributions can be made by corporate 'individuals' to individual candidates and ridings. These changes may limit the massive corporate intervention in elections on the scale of the 1988 federal election. But there remain many other ways that those who control surplus capital can influence policy, even when the party in power does not endorse neoliberal ideology.

The New Democratic Party won the BC provincial elections in 1991 and 1996, but lost decisively to the Liberals in 2001, retaining only two seats. The Party came in with an elaborate social-democratic agenda, that included improving the minimum wage, pay equity legislation, child-care programs, initiatives on public housing to combat homelessness, freezing utility rates and university tuition, promoting community participation in politics, environmental protection, tougher vehicle emission standards, just settlement with First Nations, and improved human rights legislation. After a decade in power, however, even party supporters concluded that it achieved almost no durable results (Carroll and Ratner 2005). Political leaders found themselves tightly constrained by constant threats from corporate interests to withhold or pull investment capital out of the province. Every NDP policy initiative—to bring in a new labour code, to impose environmental controls on industry, to increase tax revenues to support social services—were thwarted by threats that such policies would alienate business and imperil investment opportunity in the province. At the end of the decade BC did indeed lag behind other provinces in capital accumulation.

Negotiating Meanings: Screening Policy Options

How politicians came to think about policy alternatives, the people they turned to for advice and the interests that they tried to placate, were integrally part of processes that

undermined the New Democratic agenda. Personnel within the NDP's own Ministry of Finance came to adopt the neoliberal mantra of keeping costs down and saving tax-payers' money, to the point of cutting already meagre welfare rates. The government did manage to broker agreements with corporate business elites in private that favoured the interests of labour or other social services. But spokespersons for capital routinely criticized these same deals in public. They planed press releases that criticized the very same agreements that other company personnel had already endorsed. Commercial media also positioned themselves as the loyal business opposition bent on bringing down politicians. In effect, the NDP faced the combined power of the corporate capitalist class of British Columbia and lost.

A significant legal constraint on the power of the provincial government to take on the big resource extraction industries, was the federal government's signing of the free trade agreements, the FTA in 1989 and NAFTA in 1994. The pivotal *Chapter 11* of the NAFTA entrenches extensive corporate rights to control property and to manage investments to maximize profits without government interference, and guarantees these rights equally to domestic and foreign corporations. Teams of corporate lawyers acted as legal advisors to corporations in their efforts to manipulate judicial interpretations and establish legal precedents based on Chapter 11.

In 1995 the American-based company Sun Belt Water Inc, filed suit against the Canadian federal government for a moratorium that the BC provincial government imposed on bulk water exports (Oliver 2005). Sun Belt sought $220 million in damages, but was more interested in long term access to Canada's water. Corporate lawyers argued that the NDP's interest in protecting BC water resources should be interpreted under NAFTA rules as constituting the expropriation of corporate property, and thus that corporations interested in selling water should be compensated for potential loss of future revenues. Lawyers for the NDP won the first round of these legal challenges, but legal contests continue. Trilateral talks between government officials and business leaders from Canada, the United States and Mexico on bulk water exports were still ongoing in 2007 (Barlow 2007), and the stakes are getting higher as American states are facing increasingly severe water shortages. Barlow notes that under Chapter 11, as soon as any Canadian province permits the bulk export of water for profit, all corporations across continental North America will have rights of equal treatment, and the right to compensation for any efforts to restrict export of water.

In a similar dispute in 1996, Ethyl Corporation sued the Canadian government over its ban on the importation and trans-provincial transport of a fuel additive (MMT) judged by Canada to have potentially negative environmental and human health effects. Lawyers argued that Ethyl Corporation was not getting national treatment because some production of the fuel additive was still permitted within Canada. The lawyers argued further that the scientific data pertaining to the additive was contradictory and therefore did not constitute credible scientific proof required for banning the substance. Canada was therefore imposing 'unreasonable' performance requirements on the corporation, and this was tantamount to expropriation without just compensation. They asked for damages in excess of $250 million for loss of potential future profits. The Canadian government repealed the ban on transportation of the fuel additive, and paid $13 million in legal expenses to the corporation (Oliver 2005, 63–4). In a third case in 1999, the state government of California tried to phase out a different fuel additive (MTBA), based on evidence suggesting the additive was a 'possible' carcinogen that had the 'potential' for numerous harmful consequences, and that it was leaking into drinking water. Lawyers for Methanex corporation of Canada sued the United States government for $970 million, arguing that scientific evidence was 'contradictory' and therefore inconsistent with 'credible scientific evidence' required under Chapter 11 of NAFTA. The proposed ban on the additive therefore constituted a violation of NAFTA's fair treatment clause, an instance of expropriation of corporate property, and grounds for demanding compensation for all projected future loss of profits to the company. In all these cases the efforts of politicians and environmental activists to regulate local environmental and public health issues clash directly with the efforts of corporate lawyers to legal rights of corporate citizens are being encroached upon.

Neoliberal Policies and the Role of the State

A key assumption of neoliberalism that guides the relationship between corporate business and the state is that government interference in economic markets is inherently bad in that it distorts competition and creates inefficiencies. The second assumption is that the state should manage the social system in the interests of capital, and

specifically that it should promote policies that maximize conditions for global competitive capital. The two free trade deals, combined with deregulation of financial capital, have promoted the free flow of surplus capital investments across continental North America and globally.

These neoliberal assumptions fostered pressure on the Canadian federal government in the late 1980s to privatize the two major state transportation enterprises, Air Canada and Canadian National Railway. Those in favour of government-run transportation service stressed the public-service objectives of ensuring reliable national networks that would serve smaller communities and less profitable routes. Proponents of privatization argued that the state enterprises were inherently prone to waste money by running too many unprofitable routes and paying wages above industry norms, and using taxpayers' money in unfair competition with private businesses (Gillen et. al., 1988). Other state enterprises like the post office, hospitals, nursing homes, schools and universities are pressured to run as far as possible along the lines of a profitable commercial enterprise. Corporations that specialize in providing social services constantly lobby provincial and federal governments to open up sections of these services to private profit, again with the understanding that once such a change is made, there is no going back.

A key feature of the free trade agreements is that state enterprises that preceded the signing of the agreements would not have to be privatized, but once privatized they could not be re-privatized later without compensating all corporations conducting business in these fields for loss of potential future profits. No new state enterprises can be set up without compensation to business. Since Air Canada was privatized in 1988, no new state airline can be established without massive compensation to current and potential future private-sector airlines. The same broad ruling governs agricultural marketing boards. Boards already existing when the free trade agreements were signed did not have to be dismantled but new ones cannot be established without compensation.

The second neoliberal principle of fostering conditions that promote global competitive capital leads to pressures on the Canadian governments to scale down or demolish welfare state services. The chief argument is that the taxation levels required to pay for social services create an unfair trade disadvantage to Canadian corporations competing in the United States where corporate tax rates are lower. In 1993 Liberal finance minister Paul Martin faced heavy pressure from business interests to cut the federal deficit. He responded by imposing deep cuts across a wide range of social services. When the deficit was eliminated, the services were never replaced. Jim Stanford (2003) an economist with the Canadian Centre for Policy Alternatives calculates that increases in gross domestic product worked to eliminate similar deficits in other Western countries almost as quickly without cuts to welfare, and that the cuts had more to do with neoliberal ideology than with fiscal necessity.

With the deficit under control, neoliberal pressures shifted focus to push for financial incentives and tax concessions to corporations. It is in this area that contradictions become most evident between the two principles of neoliberalism—that governments should minimize interference in free market competition, but simultaneously maximize structural supports for capital. Structural supports often entail funnelling government funds into corporate coffers. Between 1982 and 2006 the Canadian government has channelled an estimated $18.4 billion to Canadian business in the form of government authorized grants, in the last decade averaging a billion dollars a year (CCPA Monitor 13(9) March 2007: page 2). The NDP politician Stephen Lewis (1972) first coined the phrase "corporate welfare bums" to highlight this contradiction that the very business voices that pressure for welfare reductions simultaneously pressure governments to promote subsidies to themselves. Conservative Party Leader Stephen Harper promised in 2004 that his government would go after "corporate welfare bums" by cutting government subsidies—but replacing them with lower corporate taxes.

Direct subsidies risk challenges of unfair competition under NAFTA while corporate tax breaks do not. However, such subsidies or 'bail-outs' remain extensive. When a large corporation is threatened with bankruptcy, the resulting job losses can threaten the livelihood of entire communities whose members depend on these jobs. Governments then face appeals from community leaders as well as businesses to provide subsidies. Primary resource industries in pulp and paper, fisheries and agriculture in Canada have often been the focus of such appeals. Corporations with surplus capital to invest also routinely pressure governments for incentives, loan guarantees, tax holidays, and infrastructure supports, as conditions to invest capital in one location rather than another. By far the largest government financial supports go to corporations involved in the armaments industry, these huge subsidies explicitly exempted from NAFTA on national security grounds.

Corporations further pressure governments to manage the education system in ways that meet business labour-force requirements, especially the expertise in science and technology needed for competitive edge in the 'knowledge economy.' Governments have responded by successive task forces in higher education oriented to pressuring schools and universities to prepare students to meet corporate needs. One feature of this broader policy has been that governments are increasing pressuring universities to seek public-private partnerships for research funding, thus promoting research that directly corresponds to corporate interests.

Structural Inequality Under Advanced Corporate Capital

Marxist and liberal economic models focus on very different features of structural inequality under conditions of advanced corporate capitalism, the former stressing extreme disparities in wealth and poverty, while the latter focuses on expanding affluence, with the expectation that wealth at the top will generally trickle down to make the poor better off. Evidence from different sectors within the Canadian economy provide support for both theoretical models.

There is ample evidence of extreme inequalities of wealth concentrated at the top of the corporate hierarchy, and poverty at the bottom. As noted above the top 25 corporations in Canada control 41 percent of investment capital. In sharp contrast among small businesses, fully two-thirds of those that start up, end in bankruptcy, while many others barely make minimum wage (Pinto, 2007). The income gap between the top and bottom 10 percent of Canadian families has tripled over the three decades between 1976 and 2004. The average earnings of the top 10 percent of Canadian families in 2004 was 82 times that earned by the poorest 10 percent of families, compared to a gap of 31 times in 1976 (Yainizyan 2007).

What principally seems to be driving the growing income gap is not the poor getting poorer but the rich getting immensely richer (Hutton 2007a, 2007b). In the United States, the income of the richest 0.01 percent of the population grew by almost 500 percent between 1972 and 2002. This happened, Hutton argues, because the social checks and balances on the incomes of corporate elites in the forms of government regulation, media scrutiny, competition rules, trade unions, or belief in the morality of social equity, have all progressively weakened. Chief executive officers virtually write their own pay deals.

A *Globe and Mail* annual report on executive compensation of the top 100 highest paid CEOs at Standard and Poor's Toronto Stock Exchange for 2006 (June 4, 2007, B4) Compensation comprises a mix of annual salary, annual bonus, and the cash value of other benefits which include insurance premiums, car and housing allowances, termination or retirement payments, and "other' income—shares, share units, trust units, long-term incentive plan payouts, gains from exercise of stock options and stock appreciation rights. At the top of the list the two CEOs of Research in Motion Ltd received total compensation of $54 million and $33 million. Paul Demarais of Power Corporation came in fourth with $24 million, CEO of Thomson Corporation 18th with $11.6 million. The CEOs of the banks of Montreal, Nova Scotia, Royal and National are in the top third with average compensation of $11 million. Even these annual figures are misleading because they are cited out of context of previous years. Galen Weston of George Weston Ltd. ranked only 77th in 2006 with total compensation of only $3.98 million, but in 2000 he topped the list with compensation of $32 million. James Buckee of Talisman Energy Inc came in 46th in 2006 with total compensation of $6.5 million, but in May 2007 he retired with $1.4m annual pension, cashed in stock options worth $24million, and continued to hold stock options worth $52m.

A comparable survey of the incomes of top American CEOs in 2005, cited on the AFL-CIO website, cites the average 'compensation of the Standard and Poor's 500 companies at $13.5 million. The CEOs of the top 100 American companies had a median compensation of $33.4 million, with the top one-third getting $50 million or more annually. Compensation is not necessarily closely tied to shareholder returns. The AFL-CIO website cites the case of IBM where share values dropped 36 percent in 2005, but the top CEO still received $4.5 million for management during difficult times.

Chief Executive Officer as Work Practice

CEOs are not paid these huge salaries for doing nothing. They operate at the core of the corporate capitalist system, responsible for managing strategic investments and productivity objectives to maximize profits to shareholders in highly competitive, global business environments. The CEO of newly merged corporation spearhead the work processes that accomplish what is referred to as 'economies of scale.' A central part of this process entails the management of complex personnel decisions required to downsize and amalgamate two formerly competing boards of directors into one integrated, cooperating board, and to oversee teams of subordinate managers as they carry out similar processes of departmental amalgamation to promote operational efficiencies at other levels of the enterprise, to eliminate duplication, handle expanded responsibilities, mange resistance that personnel changes and new organization generate, promote loyalty to the new enterprise, and the like. Most importantly, CEOs are primarily responsible for expanding a business, generating innovative technologies and operational efficiencies, promoting new product lines and new services, seeking new markets, and promoting brand loyalties that sustain market share. In Marxist terminology, they must beat the average rate of profit in the market. A CEO's own career advancement depends on achieving these objectives. Only the tough survive. The average term in office of the top CEOs of multinational corporations is about five years (Klein 2000, 255–6). Underneath this average are CEOs who stay with the same corporation for ten to fifteen years, or longer. Others quit or are forced out of office in one or two years. High performers are sought out by 'head-hunters' or retained with the incentive of huge stock options. Under-performers are pushed out.

New CEOs are often recruited specifically to improve profitability in a company with below-average shareholder returns, and this commonly involves a ruthless cutting of under-performing sectors of the corporation. Marxist analysis focuses on the devastating impact of such practices on the mass of employees whose livelihoods depend on these jobs. Klein characterises CEOs as 'SWAT teams' employing 'special weapons and tactics' to slash labour costs and push up shareholder returns. The most ruthless get the most pay. CEOs of the 30 companies with the largest layoffs got the biggest increases in their compensation packages. CEOs whose pay is directly linked to stock options are under even greater pressure to close plants, rollback wages and cut jobs. News that a company is downsizing typically prompts a surge in stock values, driven by the widespread assumption than 'economies of scale' generate profits. Larger companies are expected to out-perform smaller ones because they encompass more productive potential with a smaller ratio of labour.

Public Sector Management

CEOs who work in the 'public' sector of state-owned enterprises and government services have traditionally faced very different challenges, as the focus is on providing efficient services with taxpayers' money, rather than profits to shareholders. Public sector workers in Canada generally experience more secure jobs and stronger unions than comparable private-sector workers. The trend towards commercialization of government services, however, is reducing these differences. Corporate spokespersons and analysts associated with corporate-sponsored policy groups pressure governments relentlessly to cut corporate taxes to place Canadian businesses on a more level playing field with American corporations, and to make Canada more attractive for foreign investments. They endorse a neoliberal ideology that characterises government services as by definition 'uncompetitive' and therefore 'inefficient' and wasteful. A common demand is that government services should be accountable to taxpayers just as corporations are to shareholders, or preferably that such services become privatized as profit-driven enterprises. Increasingly private corporations specializing in management services are being hired by governments to run enterprises like hospitals and prisons, and to impose private-sector concepts of efficiency and accountability. Pressure towards public-private partnerships increases this trend. University presidents are now expected to combine the roles of academic leadership with chief executive of corporations that sell educational services in competitive markets to fee-paying students and research expertise for corporate clients seeking profitable innovations. Government ministries meanwhile demand accountability for tax-payers' contribution to higher education, with employability of graduates as a central indicator of returns on investment.

When abstract terms like 'efficiency' and 'accountability' are used it is important to inquire further into how the people using the terms mean them to be understood, and to recognize that how other people in different situations make sense of them may vary widely. As discussed in the chapter on bureaucracy, ' efficiency' as measured by comparative speed of management of specified categories of patients through hospitals, is very different from 'efficiency' as measured by nursing competence in the alleviation of suffering. Similarly in the private sector, the level of 'efficiency' of a corporation in generating profits over costs can vary greatly depending on which costs are included and excluded from the calculations. It can look very 'efficient' to transport goods thousands of miles by truck when the costs of road maintenance, polluted air, and climate change are paid for by tax-payers or put off for future generations (Norberg-Hodge et. al., 2002, 72).

Calculating the 'efficiencies' involved in university education also vary greatly with how primary goals of higher education are defined. Economic efficiencies are thus fundamentally and inextricably embedded in social and political interests and values—especially so when such interests and values are obscured behind conceptual abstractions like 'tax-payers' and 'shareholders'.

The Affluent Middle Classes

Liberal and Marxist economic theories agree that competition under advanced capitalism promotes a treadmill of technological development and innovation. However, they differ in their focus on long-term consequences of such structural pressures for class relations. While liberal economics focuses on the growing affluence of a well educated, middle-class workforce, Marxist analysis directs attention to how the corporate drive for higher profits and lower labour costs are undermining the same skilled workers that generate this affluence.

In the liberal thesis, businesses are driven to increase productivity and promote competitive advantage in global markets, and a highly educated labour force is an essential component of higher productivity. People with professional and managerial qualifications and technical skills merit the high salaries that they can command in competitive labour markets. As western economies have become increasingly knowledge-based, the presence of an expanding affluent middle class stimulates more affluence (Hutton 2007a, 46). Educated consumers with surplus income want new sophisticated services, and thus they promote markets for new forms of economic activity. Hutton argues that knowledge-based Western and North American economies are relatively protected from cheap labour competition in developing societies such as China. Unskilled, assembly-line manufacturing jobs have largely been sub-contracted out to low-wage economies, but not the more sophisticated, value-added jobs involving invention, design, financing, marketing, branding and advertising. Western economies continue to dominate exports in the fields of new technology, brands and patents, financial and managerial services. The export of knowledge-based services from Britain tripled in the decade between 1995–2005, with employment in these areas increasing from 30 to 41 percent of the labour force.

Hutton argues from this evidence that it is not true that western economies are being undermined by competition from ultra-cheap labour in developing economies. Nor is it true that global competition is driving profits down to levels than make welfare-state services unaffordable. Ideology and lack of political will have more to do with the dismantling of the welfare state, in his view, than lack of surplus capital to fund social services. Job losses occur more as a result of cutthroat mergers and downsizing than outsourcing of jobs to China. Here again what Hutton's analysis draws attention to the negotiated nature of the meaning of concepts in economic theory. What counts as causes from the liberal perspective counts as effects, or as altogether irrelevant in Hutton's re-working of Marxist analysis. Corporate spokespersons can draw on the rhetoric of 'economies of scale' and 'global competitiveness' to legitimate mergers, acquisitions, and employee lay-offs. They can also draw on the 'common-sense' explanation that job-losses at home are caused by cheap labour in developing societies. Such explanations serve to depoliticize and deflect attention from narrowly-defined economic costs and benefits that drive preoccupy influential economic decision-makers. Active practices appear as abstract operation of economic systems.

Outsourcing the 'Knowledge Economy'

The problem for the professional middle classes is that the cutthroat pressure for mergers and downsizing does not stop at the factory gates. Increasingly these pressures are engulfing the high-technology and managerial components of work. Microsoft offers a classic example of these restructuring processes. In earlier days, computer science experts working for Microsoft could look forward to secure jobs with high salaries inflated with stock options, but this market is being actively dismantled as the corporation has moved to limit full-time programmers (Klein 2000, 249–257). Microsoft still does need a central core of committed elite workers whose loyalty is bought with quarter-million dollar salaries and stock options. But about half of all the technicians, designers, and programmers who actually work on Microsoft products are officially not Microsoft employees. They are hired through contracts with outside "payroll agencies" who function as their official employer. As outsiders, they are not eligible for insider stock options, or for pensions or other benefits. Klein describes how Microsoft laid off 63 receptionists, rehiring them through an independent agency that specializes in providing temporary

workers. Those temporary workers who actually work for Microsoft for twelve months are required to be laid off for thirty days to ensure that they do not qualify for benefits as 'permanent' employees. By the late 1990s, the number of 'temporary workers' in 'Silicon Valley' was three times the national average, indicating that the strategies adopted by Microsoft were pervasive.

Other skilled workers are encouraged to set themselves up as individual entrepreneurs contracting out their services directly to corporations. Some enjoy the independence, and find they can negotiate for more money when jumping between contracts than being tied to one corporation at a fixed salary. In economic boom times entrepreneurs with sought-after skills can play the contract labour markets for high rewards. The problems come with recession, as in the late 1990s when the inflated value of technology stocks crashed. The risks of economic recession are born mostly by contract workers. Corporations can downsize rapidly simply by not renewing contracts for a year or two until markets turn around. Suddenly, masses of highly-skilled 'self-employed' contract workers can find themselves unemployed. The reality of contract work for the majority of workers, Klein suggests, is multiple temporary jobs with uneven income, no benefits or security, and little scheduling control. Universities similarly resort to limited-term contracts to hedge the risk of declines in fees as student enrollment fluctuates. The result is a cadre of permanently limited-term professors with fractured careers.

The Declining Working Class

Workers who are outside the high demand sectors of the 'knowledge-economy' bear the brunt of technological innovation driving unemployment and falling real wages. The post-war era of cheap mass production is often referred to as 'fordism' after Henry Ford's introduction of assembly-line technology catapulted Ford Motor Company to world leader in the production of affordable cars for mass markets. Henry Ford himself argued that it was in his company's interest to pay workers enough that they could afford to buy his cars. The very high productivity of assembly-line workers relative to other workers, made this possible. Manufacturing goods for mass markets provided monotonous, low-skill job for masses of workers, but they were well-paying, secure jobs, with good benefits packages, and with workers rights protected by strong unions.

Over the last quarter century, however, the trend across most advanced capitalist economies has been for these 'blue-collar' jobs to be replaced with low-paying, insecure and mostly part-time jobs in the retail service sector. Between 1980–2006, Britain experienced a 47 percent drop in manufacturing jobs, Sweden and France about 30 percent, and the United States a 25 percent drop (Socialist Bulletin No. 50, 31 May 2007, 2–3) Canada surprisingly bucked the trend with a 2 percent rise in manufacturing jobs over the same period, perhaps reflecting Canada's greater reliance on resource extraction industries than manufacturing. Manufacturing jobs comprised about 14.4 percent of all jobs in Canada in 2007, compared with 11.8 percent of jobs in the USA. But 2007 saw a major downturn in manufacturing in Canada as well with the loss of 52 000 jobs in the first five months. The losses sparked three mass workers' protests in Ontario in May, led by the auto-workers, steel-workers, and Communications, Energy and Paper workers unions.

Job losses in manufacturing are only partially accounted for by the export of jobs to low-wage developing world economies. The Socialist Bulletin notes that 85 percent of manufactured goods entering Canada still come from developed countries rather than developing ones (ibid. 3). The real value of goods manufactured in Canada (controlling for inflation) is about double what is was a century ago, but the number of workers needed to produce these goods has plummeted as a result of automated, labour-saving technology. Labour unions that won good contracts for workers in the post-war era of mass-production industries have lost ground. Union bargaining strength lies in their ability to shut down production, but this strategy cannot protect workers from corporate restructuring and plant shutdowns. The free trade agreements make it easier for corporations to relocate jobs, leaving workers competing to attract investors. Unions are under pressure to make concessions in wages and benefits and to cut jobs in an effort to keep at least some of their members employed, while governments are pressured to provide subsidies—often with no guarantees that the plant will stay open far into the future.

Absolute numbers of jobs also do not tell the whole story of what is happening in the blue-collar workforce. An equal number of jobs may be lost in Windsor, Ontario and created in Calgary but hundreds of workers cannot immediately move from Windsor to Calgary, uprooting families, and selling homes in a depressed area to buy new ones at three to five times higher mortgages. Job skills and qualifications suitable for one line of employment may well not fit with other available jobs. Nor can displaced workers in their late 40s and 50s

easily retrain for new careers. There can thus be severe mis-matches between available workers and available jobs, with high unemployment levels occurring alongside high job vacancies. Workers who lose jobs in manufacturing, are more likely to sink into lower-paid, non-union jobs in retail, clerical, tourism, and similar service sector jobs, than they are to rise into highly-paid 'knowledge economy' jobs.

The general pattern across the last 25 years has been for disparities in earnings from employment to widen, with well-paying jobs gaining, while earnings in low-end jobs have been static or declining (Maxwell 2002). Comparatively, Canada is relatively a low-wage country with 2 million workers, or almost one in four earning below the $10 threshold that defines the poverty line for single adults in urban areas of Canada (Rothman 2005; UNICEF 2005). Canada is second only to the USA in proportion of full-time workers earning wages below this poverty-level, compared with one worker in eight in Germany, and one in twenty in Sweden. The global retail giant Walmart sets the standard for minimizing retail-sector labour costs that competing corporations strive to emulate. Two thirds of the 1.3 million Walmart employees in the USA earn such low incomes that they cannot afford basic medical coverage premiums. In Canada in 2003, about one-quarter of all adult workers between ages of 24–54 were paid less than $10 per hour—below the Statistics Canada Poverty Line for a single person. These included about one-fifth of all adult women workers and one-tenth of adult male workers (Jackson 2006). In 2003 11.5 percent of all children in Canada lived below the poverty line, and about half of these children lived in families where at least one parent worked full time.

When the work available is low wage and part-time, it is very difficult to move from welfare to work. People lose medical and dental benefits, social housing benefits, and have to pay child-care costs. Maxwell (2002) cites examples of low-income workers paying a real tax rate of 70 percent on earned income as they crossed the rigid minimum income threshold of eligibility for child tax benefits and child-care subsidies. Many low wage workers are forced to work long hours at multiple jobs. Others supplement their income with crime. The United States federal government responded to this 'welfare trap' by setting a maximum lifetime limit of five years on welfare, thus forcing the poor to take work at whatever employers are willing to pay, with no statutory minimum. Canada, to date, has eschewed such harsh measures.

Jackson explores the debate within Marxist analysis whether the solution to the working poor is for the government to raise the minimum wage rate, or for the government to supplement low incomes with some kind of guaranteed minimum income for workers financed through taxes. The first option of a higher minimum wage risks job losses, especially for young workers as employers may find it unprofitable to hire them at the higher minimum. Option two of tax subsidies to workers risks subsidizing low-wage employers and thus pushing wage rates even lower than they would be on the 'free market'. Neither works well for the goal of reducing poverty, because they moderate but do not resolve the underlying causes.

Poverty and Policy

Liberal and Marxist economic analyses promote very different understanding of the underlying causes of poverty. The extreme neoliberal vision of inequality promoted by the pro-business Fraser Institute policy group (Rubenstein 2003) highlights merited effort and ability as the principle explanation for huge differences in wealth and assets between the top and bottom strata of Canadian. The billionaire elite class contribute the vision and entrepreneurial skills that generate the tens of thousands of wealth creating jobs in Canada and around the world on which the wellbeing of other workers depends. The richest Canadians pay the bulk of taxes that sustain the welfare state, and provide the 'free goods' for the non-tax-paying poor. The selflessness and philanthropy of the rich enhances the public good for generations to come.

Such a description may well fit the Toronto icon Edwin Mirvish who established *Honest Ed's* bargain discount store in Toronto in 1948 and turned it into a $ billion emporium. Over the next four decades he bought up surrounding houses and turned them into an artist's colony In 1960 he bought the *Royal Alexandra Theatre* and later revived the *Old Vic Theatre* in London England, build the new *Princess of Wales Theatre*. He became a major patron of the theatre arts in both countries. He even establishing the *Old Alex* in Toronto, a tiny theatre for avant garde and amateur productions. He became famous for lavish birthday parties in which he entertained tens of thousands of people in street parties, giving away pizza and pasta. Every Christmas he distributed thousands of frozen turkeys to people in need.

Rubenstein argues that business elites as a class create the surplus wealth that results in the poor being vastly better off than they would be without corporate capitalism. Large differences in wealth and assets of better-off and

impoverished families primarily reflects differences in education, work ethic, and lifestyle choices that people make. While some present-oriented young people drop out of school, max out their credit cards on easy living, other young people take out student loans and develop their 'human capital' qualifications, move to where the strong job markets are, get married and stay married, and defer their gratification while they build up their assets in housing, businesses, investments and the like.

The Marxist analysis that Rubenstein parodies (Kerstetter 2002) recognizes that corporate capitalism within Canada has generated wealth-creating jobs for some sectors of the working class, especially in the new knowledge economy. But the same capitalist elite has simultaneously destroyed tens of thousands of secure, well-paying unionized manufacturing jobs that were once the mainstay of the blue-collar workforce. Tens of thousands of more new jobs created by capitalism in Canada have not been 'wealth creating' but rather poverty-creating low-wage, temporary, and part-time jobs. Higher educational qualifications increase individual chances to compete for good jobs, but does not increase the number of such jobs available to be competed for. A glut of graduates can even make it easier for employers to shift such jobs from permanent to limited-term contract jobs and so reduce the supply of quality jobs available. Marxist analysis also points to the tremendous strains on family life that come with chronic poverty, low-waged, unstable and part-time jobs as the principle explanation for relationship between poverty, divorce and single parenthood (Edin and Kefalas 2005). It is not that anti-family cultural values lead to slothful work habits and thus poverty, but rather that young men without stable work cannot afford to support a family, and young women are reluctant to marry them. Corporate sponsored policy groups incessantly lobby governments to cut taxes for corporations and the rich. Their argument is that high corporate taxes in Canada impede competitiveness, while lower taxes would promote business enterprise, and thus result in more jobs and more tax revenues. Marxists challenge these arguments as self-serving corporate rhetoric that pushes the welfare burden increasingly onto middle income earners, while corporate welfare bums enjoy a major share of government subsidies and handouts. Clerical workers on limited-term contracts with Microsoft subsidize with their own lost medical and pension benefits the phenomenal wealth that billionaire Microsoft director and philanthropist Bill Gates gives to global charities. Corporate elites meanwhile limit their tax liability by moving their residence and corporate headquarters off-shore, and by transfer pricing practices between subsidiaries that shift paper profits to off-shore tax-havens, and paper losses to higher-tax locations in Canada.

In summary, Marxist analysis generally concedes the validity of liberal economics theory that advanced capitalist economies are generating new forms of wealth. The economic pie does not reduce to a simple zero-sum game, where the more A gets the less is left over for B (Hutton 2007a). As Hutton expresses it, the knowledge economy, and the worldwide explosion of trade have greatly enlarged the economic resources and options available for people to make a living. The problems of global and national inequality arise from the grossly unfair rules of the game that condemn masses of people to grinding poverty in the midst of plenty. It is little comfort to Canadian workers and their families who struggle to survive on minimum-wage jobs that they are better off than the estimated half the world or nearly 3 billion people globally who live on less than two dollars a day.

Feminist Political Economy

The gendered character of the capitalist economy receives limited attention from either classical liberal or Marxist political economy. Women are considered of marginal relevance to economic relations, conceptualized either as homemakers who are outside the labour market and dependents of male breadwinners, or as secondary workers whose primary responsibility is the home. Women's class location as housewives is defined through the male to whom they are most closely connected, or if employed, by their own occupational status, which is typically lower than the class location of their husband. Women are rarely located in centres of decision making or power associated with the generation of wealth, and hence easily overlooked in economic theory.

In 1980 when economist Susan Hewlett with the Economic Policy Council in the USA tried to set up a committee to study problems of women's work, family and child care, with a view to making recommendations to the US President and Congress, she reportedly found no takers (Smith 1992, 11–12) Virtually no one wanted to serve on the committee because the topics were not seen as relevant for the council. The challenge of feminist political economy has been to re-conceptualize the concept of economy itself, so that what women do becomes recognizable as productive economic work.

Women's Location in the Canadian Economy

The issue most widely addressed within male-stream liberal and Marxist perspectives has been women's location in the labour force, compared with men. Two broad generalizations can be made. Over the last quarter century, across all western economies, there has been a marked and persistent upward shift in women's labour force participation overall, especially among mothers with young children. Women now constitute about half the Canadian labour force. But notwithstanding significant gains, there remains a large gap between the average incomes of women and men. Between 1965 and 2005, women's average earnings rose from about 60 percent to 73 percent of male earnings (Rothman 2005). With this rate of change, feminists point out, it would take another hundred years for women to reach parity with men. Lower average earnings reflect women's disadvantaged location within the economy relative to men—their under-representation at the top of the economic hierarchy and over-representation at the bottom.

Women are rare exceptions among the elite of CEOs and top professional and managerial cadres. By the late 1990s all four women who were major shareholders of the Top 250 Corporations studied by Carroll (2004, 22) achieved that status through family connections. Among them is Belinda Stronach, daughter of the founder and chief executive of Magna International auto parts corporation, businesswoman and briefly federal politician and contender for the leadership of the Conservative Party of Canada. With the democratization of corporate boards, women have gained somewhat greater access to elite positions as corporate advisors or 'organic intellectuals' but usually at the lower strata and with smaller firms. In recent years, the proportion of women in undergraduate studies in Canada equals men, although they are concentrated in different fields. Women have made inroads into the professions, including law, sciences, engineering. But they remain heavily overrepresented in a small number of professions in education, health and social work, professions in which they are more likely working for governments than private corporations. In law schools, more women focus on family law while more men focus on corporate law—the specialization most in demand by corporate boards.

In the professions where women numerically outnumber men, they still lag behind men in high-end senior managerial roles. Employment equity Acts passed in 1986 and 1995 pressured Crown corporations and federally regulated agencies (including universities) with more than 100 employees to implement positive action plans to recruit more women into upper and middle management positions, along with visible minority and Aboriginal, and workers with disabilities (Leck 2002). Organizations subject to the Acts were required to analyse job categories in which women and other minorities are underrepresented, to review hiring policies and practices, identify barriers, and enact policies to promote more equitable representation of women relative to the available pool of qualified women. Leck reports that the number of women in middle management has risen by about 2 percent per year, although perhaps little more than would have occurred anyway with economic and demographic changes. The gap in the higher salary range of over $40 000 a year has actually been increasing, suggesting that women have been appointed to nominally higher level positions but not with pay increases. Women are also far more likely employed in less powerful 'staff' positions requiring technical skills and supervisory responsibilities, rather than 'line' management involving policy responsibilities. Hence they are blocked from further promotion into senior executive positions. In non-management occupations, women are concentrated in clerical and retail work. By 2000, fully 65% of employed women were classified as clerical workers, down only 5 percent from a high of over 70 percent (Leck 2002, S90).

Women frustrated by other options, have turned increasingly to opening their own businesses, or self employment. Fully 58 percent of new jobs created in Canada during the decade of the 1990s were self-employment. By 2003 one in six Canadians comprising 2.5 million workers, were classified as self-employed, and one third of them were women. A study of self-employed women in Alberta (Hughes 2003) describes them as drawing on professional qualifications to open businesses in accounting and consulting, health services, counselling and therapies, home-based services in dress-making, hairstyling, and small gift shops and food stores. The question much debated in the literature is whether this trend towards self employment reflects the 'pull' of independence and autonomy, individual agency and choice—the explanation favoured by neoliberal perspective, or 'push' factors like downsizing and job loss—the favoured Marxist explanation. Statistics Canada's *Survey of Work Arrangements* (1997, 35–6) supports the neoliberal perspective, suggesting that

strong pull factors like desire for challenging work, positive work environment, desire for independence and meaningful work, flexible schedule, work-family balance, and ability to work from home, all contributed to a positive choice of self employment.

Again, however, the social constructionist perspective raises questions concerning how survey questions derive their meaning. The standpoints from which respondents interpret the questions and how they intend their answers to carry meaning may be very different from the interpretations placed on them by Statisitcs Canada analysts and by readers of the resulting reports (Hughes 2003). Researchers working with Statistics Canada both structured their survey questions to explore the neoliberal assumptions about the positive values associated with self employment, and then interpreted the resulting answers in terms of these assumptions. This is an example of what the theorist Dorothy Smith refers to as 'ideological circles', where initial assumptions, methodology and interpretive conclusions reinforce each other in a closed circle of thought. The juxtaposition of survey answers with more detailed qualitative interviews with 61 self-employed women in Alberta, suggest the meanings these women intended to convey in their survey answers referred mostly desperation to escape miserable work environments generated by job restructuring in the public and private sectors. Women who formerly worked in health services described constant threats of downsizing and layoffs, incredible stress and erosion of working conditions as government services had been decimated over the past 12 years, and burnout from growing administrative and bureaucratic demands associated with 'total quality management' practices. Self-employment represented a relief from the toxic work environments generated by decade of deficit reduction and 'accountability' pressures. But for two-thirds of the women interviewed by Hughes, this relief was hedged by worry over low income from the business, fear of bankruptcy, and impossibility of saving for retirement. Among women who defined themselves as forced into self employment by lack of other options, fully 91 percent expressed frustration with earning less than their previous employment and with low returns on their education and work experience (ibid. 445). This compares with about half of those women who more freely chose to open a business. Self employment brought intrinsic satisfactions, but for the majority of women it did not bring income security.

It is at the bottom of the labour force that women are most heavily overrepresented. Women predominate in the low-waged, insecure and part-time, non-union jobs in retail sales and service, and their numbers are increasing. About 22 percent of women working full time in 2005 earned less than $10 per hour, compared with 12 percent of men (Rothman 2005). Ten dollars an hour is roughly the amount needed to reach the poverty line for a single person working full-time in a large urban centre. About a quarter of all lone mothers working full-time do not earn enough to raise their children above the poverty line. In 2004, 34 percent of children living below the poverty line lived in families where at least one parent worked full-time for the entire year, compared with 27 percent in 1993 (*Campaign 2000* Report Card on Child and Family Poverty in Canada 2006). The proportion of part-time jobs in the Canadian labour force grew from 11 to 17 percent between 1975–1995, and the proportion of workers who wanted a full-time job but could not find one increased from 11 to 35 percent (Schellenberg 1995). The vast majority of these involuntary part-time workers live in families below the poverty line.

Terms like 'flexible' and 'part-time', Klein suggests (2000, 242–3) cover a variety of actual work situations. A 'good' part-time job that working mothers may well appreciate, is one with less than full-time hours but otherwise with a good hourly wage and benefits, and a regular schedule with shift lengths sufficient to compensate for the time it takes to commute to and from work. But increasingly 'flexible' jobs in hotel chains and food-services corporations like Starbucks, has come to mean low wage jobs with random hours and no security or benefits. Workers are required to remain on call—available if and when management needs them, but not scheduled and not paid until called.

Explaining the Gender Gap

Classical liberal economics theory conceptualizes the gender gap in the labour market as rooted in social and cultural processes not connected with the economic system itself. Consistent with Parsonian functionalist theory in sociology, the values and orientations associated with family life are seen as clashing with those of market relations and thus as forcing some separation of spheres. Once women make the choice to become wives and mothers, the argument goes, their primary focus becomes family life, and they are thus only secondarily in the labour market. Mothers are expected to take years out of paid labour force to raise children, or to choose part-time or less responsible work that are more easily combined with domestic responsibilities.

Shaping the 'choices' women make is the pervasive assumption by employers and husbands that child-care is and ought to be primarily women's responsibility. The absence of a national, publicly-funded childcare program in Canada, is a further reflection of neoliberal policies that pressure governments to privatize services..

The underlying logic is that women who are motivated to advance in their careers on a par with men, must choose to avoid having children. The hard-driven, competitive corporate culture permits no 'slack' to accommodate child care or other family responsibilities. Feminine cultural values are also thought to limit women's effectiveness as workers. In principle, women can aspire to rise up the corporate ladder and break through the 'glass ceiling' into corporate executive suites, but they typically lack the necessary levels of competitive, aggressive, risk-taking attitudes. Women are seen as choosing careers in teaching, nursing and clerical work for similar reasons that they are more compatible with time out for child-rearing and with nurturing values than typically male professions. Women typically earn less than men because they choose less skilled, less responsible occupations. Closing the income gap would thus requires women to shift careers into currently male-dominated fields, or for men to choose lower-waged service careers attractive to women.

Marxist analysis shifts the explanations for the gender gap in average earnings from private choices by individual women to structural processes within advanced capitalist economies. The unrelenting pressure within corporate capitalist economies to deskill and cheapen labour costs produces the glut of substandard jobs that vulnerable workers compete for.

Married women make up a reserve army of cheap disposable labour. They even out fluctuating demands for labour because they can be hired when there is a shortage and pushed back into unpaid domestic work at other times, without becoming welfare burdens.

Only when there is an acute shortage of educated labour, as happened in postwar Sweden, has there been concerted pressure by capitalists to persuade governments to develop publicly funded maternity and child care leave. It is under conditions of labour shortages in the knowledge economy, when employers are anxious to retain experienced female labour, and also anxious to maintain a high birthrate, that the power relations and policy options that structure 'women's choices' become visible. In Sweden, 'parents', as distinct from 'mothers', are guaranteed paid 'parenting leave' for eighteen months, that is expected to be shared by both fathers and mothers, and that can be spread over a child's first eight years of life. Paid homecare services for sick and dependent people supported by taxes, further 'protect' corporate interests in maintaining stable female labour force participation.

Feminist Political Economy: Patriarchal Capitalism

Feminist political economy focuses attention on patriarchal practices that sustain the hyper-exploitation of women's labour at all levels of the capitalist economy. Patriarchal assumptions are embedded in the conception of what constitutes 'economy', of what counts as 'work' and what services ought or ought not to be compensated with money, and in grudging accommodations made by capital to enable workers to balance domestic and employment responsibilities. Patriarchal assumptions also foster discrimination in hiring practices, and job classifications and actively undermine policies designed to promote greater gender equity.

Challenging the "Main Business"

A feminist re-visioning of political economy articulated by Dorothy Smith (1992) challenges the flawed definition of 'economy' that is implied in both the liberal and Marxist perspectives. Smith argues that Marxist political economy is itself embedded in the ruling apparatus of capitalism in that it assumes the 'main business' of the economy is the accumulation of capital. It is this starting assumption, that Marxism shares with liberal economics, that results in the view of women's service work within the paid economy as marginal, and the homemaking work performed by the vast majority of women as outside the economy altogether.

In pre-capitalist economies there is no meaningful distinction between spheres production and reproduction. People produced what they and their children needed for their own subsistence. Capitalism rent asunder this unity between production and people's lives. Capitalism shifted the focus of production from goods that have use-value for their producers, to commodities that are intended to be sold for profit. The fundamental purpose of capitalist production is not use-value but profit or surplus value. When the focus of economics shift back from profits to use-value, then the work that women do within the paid economy and in the home appears, not as marginal activity, but as

central to the economic system. Within this re-visioned economic focus on use-value, it makes no sense to suggest that workers engaged in education, health, and social services are marginal workers who would be better employed in jobs that produce more shareholder profits.

Domestic Labour for Capital

A feminist reconceptualization of homemaking as work helps to make visible how it functions at the heart of the capitalist economic system. Far from being outside the economy, domestic work provides the foundation that keeps the entire capitalist system going. Pioneering feminist studies in the late 1970s and 1980s made visible the complex and demanding nature of work labelled 'housework (Luxton 1980). It encompasses all the activities involved in maintaining a home and servicing members, including the planning and preparing of meals, the financial work of consumption management, and all the complex rhythms of motherwork. Often it involves juggling several different schedules to accommodate the demands of a baby, preschoolers, school timetables, a husband's work timetable and the woman's own work

From the standpoint of the wider capitalist economy, domestic labour performs a variety of functions that are essential for the maintenance of labour power. Homemakers, who are mostly mothers, raise and care for children until they reach working age. Mothers are held primarily responsible for continually motivating children to regularly attend school, repairing whatever stress and damage occurs in school, so that children absorb the curricular skills and knowledge that future employers expect. In this respect mothers are centrally involved in the reproduction of the culture of corporate capitalism, eventually giving up their primary product— their children—to the corporate system. A case study of wives of Japanese corporate executives based in Toronto, documents how the work of preparing their sons for success in the series of examinations required for entry into elite Japanese universities that are the recruiting grounds for executive careers in Japanese corporations, itself became a full time career for these corporate wives (Ueda 1995). The success of mothers in raising their children properly is itself measured by their children's success in achieving corporate careers.

Homemakers also maintain and care for workers themselves on a daily basis, performing all the backstage work required to keep workers returning, rested and ready, for another day's work. Patterns of domestic work are very closely tied to and structured by the kinds of work that husbands do. Wives of men at the top of the labour hierarchy, work to sustain the pinstriped image of corporate executives and the lavish homes and stylized entertainment of business associates expected at this level. Their support work is sufficiently important that it is common practice for corporate boards to arrange to interview prospective senior executives and their partners together. Wives of low-income workers manage the very different demands of coping on inadequate incomes. They struggle to make ends meet, to buy what family members most need, and a little of what they most want, and to keep people happy in cramped and dingy living space. They also manage the stress of constantly motivating exploited and alienated workers to keep return to work, because their own domestic labour depends on the money these workers bring home (Luxton 1980). These are part of the work practices that make employers of blue-collar workers favour married men as employees. In these many ways families serve as subcontracted agents of corporations, working for corporations even though they are unpaid and may never even set foot in them. Much of this unpaid domestic work is done on top of women's paid work that often makes the difference between poverty and a reasonable standard of family living.

Other research has documented the complex and extensive contributions of homemaker wives to businesses that their husbands own and operate (Hamilton 2006). This can range from being centrally involved in all aspects of the business from the start-up planning, financing, and decision-making to keeping the books, running the home-office and typing and editing manuscripts, to being constantly on call, and raising children virtually as single parents while husbands are away at work. Women commonly worked in the business without pay for years to build up the enterprise. Yet in the ways in which family members represented the business to outsiders the image of the male as individual entrepreneur, owner/operator and CEO of the business prevailed. Only in the details did the contribution of wives to the enterprise become evident, and the struggles around authority.

Recession and Hyper-exploitation

The importance of domestic work for the stability of the capitalist system becomes most apparent during periods of recession when governments are under pressure from business interests to cut spending. "Savings" in the economy are made through loading more and more work onto women in the home without paying them anything for it and actually firing many who used to do such work for pay. Armstrong (1984) notes that when governments cut back on hospital services, women take up the slack by doing the nursing at home. They spend far more time in hospitals helping to care for relatives when adequate nursing services are not available. When patients are discharged early to "save" money, women take over their convalescent care at home. When governments cut back on senior citizens' homes and residential homes for the disabled, justifying the financial cuts by arguing that these people are better off within the community, it is women who take over this chronic care nursing for free. Free, that is, to the government. It may often be at great expense to the women themselves who forfeit hours of time, and often paid jobs, to do this care work. When the state cuts back on day-care services and kindergartens, women in the home do the work. When the state cuts back on teachers, homemakers take up the slack, giving their time to supervise lunches and after school activities, and doing the extra coaching and remedial work that teachers no longer have time to do. When youth employment opportunities are cut back, women at home take up the slack by providing homes and care for adolescents who would otherwise be independent. When wages are cut back, women make up the difference with their own labour, trying to substitute for purchases by making do, mending, sewing, knitting, managing with broken appliances. Above all, they double and treble their labour in stress management to absorb and contain the damage done to family members by such cutbacks.

All too often it is women who work in the social service sector who lose their paid jobs when the government cuts back. The government, in effect, defines their work as not in the marketplace, and thus saves all their salaries, while women continue to do the work without pay. Viewed from the standpoint of women in the home, government restraint programs appear as the most extreme example of total exploitation. Women are driven to perform services without any pay at all and are forced to depend upon others for subsistence. Yet this enormous hidden economy of housework, worth millions of dollars in government savings annually, is invisible to traditional political economy with its focus on capital accumulation. It is treated as non-productive, as not in the economy at all, and those who do such work are seen as nonentities or dependent consumers.

Doing the 'Second Shift'

There has been a revolution in the numbers of wives and mothers, including mothers of pre-school age children, taking up full-time, paid employment since the 1960s. But the revolution in numbers of husbands and fathers taking up the second shift of domestic work has been much weaker. In her pioneering research on the sharing of domestic labour in dual-career households Arlie Hochschild (1989) the most common pattern was 'transitional' with wives in full-time paid employment while continuing to do most or all domestic work as well. The 'modern' pattern in which husbands took equal responsibility for housework and childcare as their wives entered full-time employment was very rare. Husbands might 'help' if directly asked, particularly in the most enjoyable tasks like playing with children but still generally considered such work to be her primary responsibility.

All subsequent studies of the 'second shift' concur that employed women on average work far longer hours than employed men, because they bear the major responsibilities for housework—the planning, managing, shopping, cooking, cleaning, and child care—the nurturing, coaching, monitoring, motivating, nursing, and the general tension management of family life. This massive support work that women do frees up male workers not to do it, and thus contributes to this making male workers appear as more 'valuable' employees. Attributes like being 'more committed to their jobs', less distracted by other worries, more available to work overtime at the office, to do rush jobs, to travel at a moment's notice, and the like, appear as merit-worthy personality attributes of individual male workers. The work that women do to produce men as more valuable employees disappears from view.

Not only are women not rewarded for the unpaid support work that they do for corporations—they are financially penalized for doing it. Even women who are not married and or have no children, or who are utterly committed to their careers, appear suspect to potential employers because they potentially might later get married, or get pregnant, or take on responsibility for care of sick or elderly family members. Older women whose children are grown up avoid some of these problems— but then they are older. Male employees might take on such responsibilities as well, but statistically the risks of them doing so are lower. All these practices, and the cultural assumptions underlying them, converge to make white married male job applicants the preferred choice for fast-track, higher paying jobs.

Within the neoliberal world-view male workers appear as naturally superior. Neither corporations nor governments are seen as having any obligation to facilitate work-family balance or to provide quality child care arrangements that are needed to equalize employment opportunities for women. Any pressure for 'special arrangements' constitutes favouritism, and any efforts to counter resistance to women's advancement constitute discrimination against men. Truly gender-equity policies designed to encourage women to enter and to remain in full-time employment and in senior corporate careers and professions have been implemented only when they obviously suited corporate capitalist interests, that is where corporate employers faced labour shortages in the skilled and knowledge economy. Sweden currently has the most advanced equity policies of any western capitalist economy, guaranteeing state-supported maternity leave, parenting leave for mothers and fathers at close to full salary with job security protection, the option of reduced working hours during the first six years of children's lives, sick-leave for child-care, and a national child-care policy. The United States has the weakest policies, with Canada in between. Private market solutions to the domestic/child-care/paid work balance can be very effective for workers at the high end of the income range who can afford nannies, housekeepers, and quality day-care and kindergartens. But such services are prohibitively expensive for workers with average or below-average incomes.

Employment Equity Policy and Resistance

Employment Equity Acts passed in Canada in 1986 and 1995 were intended to address systemic barriers limiting career advancement for women, and unfairness in job classification and pay scales. These Acts explicitly focused on 'goals' for hiring women or other minorities proportional to available qualified applicants, rather than 'quotas' that might falsely imply that underqualified women had to be hired to make up the required numbers (Leck 2002). Twenty years later the proportions of women in senior managerial and professional ranks remains far below their availability in relevant labour pools. Leck concludes that the hegemonic liberal belief that all salary differentials in the 'free market' reflect individual choice and merited differences, combined with neoliberal aversion to government 'interference' in the labour market relations, have resulted in widespread resistance to employment equity policies. Women who gained employment in the context of equity programs typically found themselves pre-defined as incompetent or not meriting their jobs, boy-cotted by other female employees, denied adequate mentoring and training programs, overlooked for sub-sequent promotion, and generally undermined at work to the point that their work performance suffered and they lost confidence in their own abilities—thus sus-taining the self-fulfilling prophesy that employment equity undermines productivity. Fully 91 percent of 133 university students in a human resources management class viewed employment equity as discrimination against men (Leck 2002, S94). These students gave no thought to the cultural, social, structural barriers that limit women's access to better paying jobs, presuming simply that none exist.

Another aspect of Employment Equity Policy involves the development of objective job classification schemes designed to evaluate the skills and responsibil-ities associated with different job categories in the same industry or with the same employer, in order to imple-ment legally mandated 'equal pay for work of equal value'. The policies are intended to push employers and workers to question whether the skills and 'value-added' character of gender-typed jobs such as servicing cus-tomers or servicing machines warrant the markedly dif-ferent pay scales typically assigned to them. Feminist research struggles to make visible the complex skills and responsibilities involved in positions commonly filled by women, that are defined and paid at much lower rates than positions commonly filled by men. Reimer (1991–2) describes how the work of 'routine clerical workers' often entailed policy-related knowledge and managerial decision-making, but these skills were ren-dered invisible to the organization by reporting practices that attributed work completed by clerical workers to their department directors.

When employment equity challenges have suc-ceeded, particularly in the federal civil service, they have resulted in Human Rights Tribunal decisions awarding millions of dollars in back pay to women workers (Leck 2002, S92–3). In the prevailing neolib-eral discourse, however, such settlements are not char-acterised as corrections to rampant discrimination against female workers. Rather, they are attacked as unwarranted government interference in the free market, and unfair penalties on taxpayers and shareholder prof-its. For women who have won such awards the victory is mostly Pyrrhic. A lump-sum settlement does not make up for a decade of poverty, particularly when more than half of the windfall is deducted as income tax.

Conclusion: Patriarchal Capitalism

In summary, feminist political economy exposes patriar-chal processes operating at the heart of the capitalist sys-tem that work to systematically exclude and devalue women's labour. Support services that women typically provide for capital at all levels of the system are concep-tualized as 'outside' the economy, and 'free'; the women who do such work penalized as less than fully commit-ted workers; and their struggles to balance unpaid and paid work conceptualized as merely personal problems. Women are not equitably employed in comparison with men. The categories of paid employment in which women are concentrated are devalued and underpaid, and policies to promote equity in hiring practices and salaries are actively resisted and disparaged.

Political Economy of Farming in Canada

This section applies the theoretical debates around advanced capitalist economies to analyze restructuring processes in Canada's farming sector. Canada has a rela-tively high level of reliance on resource extraction indus-tries like agriculture, fishing, forestry and mining. In 2004 more than a quarter of population of rural Canada was employed in one of these resource industries (Stedman et.al. 2004, 223–4). Agriculture employed 14 percent of all Canadians, 6 percent in Atlantic region, 11 percent in central Canada—Ontario and Quebec, 28 per-cent in the Prairies, and 4 percent in British Columbia.

Patterns of change in the agricultural sector closely reflect the core predictions of Marxist political economy. The sector has long been described as in serious trouble with steadily declining profits and plummeting rates of employment. The broad pattern has been one of corpo-rate concentration in agribusiness, polarization of wealth with high agribusiness profits and declining farm incomes, increasing concentration of ownership in smaller numbers of larger farms, with fewer people directly employed in farming, and falling rates of profit as farms carry high debt loads to keep up with the tread-mill of technological innovation. These long-term trends are common across North America and Western Europe (Norberg-Hodge et. al., 2002, 5–10). These changes have had a devastating impact on rural communities in Canada, as elsewhere.

Potato Farming in the Maritimes

Farming in New Brunswick was being transformed by labour-saving technology as far back as the 1960s. In one generation between 1931–1961 farm capitalization—the amount of money that farmers invested in machinery, rose 450 percent while the number of workers employed in farming dropped by half and the output per worker doubled. Between 1951–1981 fully 80 percent of New Brunswick farms disappeared. In 1951 three million acres were being farmed by 26 000 farmers, but by 1981 only one million acres were being farmed by 4000 farmers. In Nova Scotia during roughly the same period 87 percent of farms failed, and 74 percent in PEI (Murphy 1987). By 1974 fully one-third of Maritime population were displaced farmers (Veltmeyer 1986, 49). In subsequent decades, the numbers of farms continued to fall. Between 1998–2007 New Brunswick lost another 600 farms. Across Canada the number of people employed in farming dropped by three-quarters in last half of the twentieth century.

These figures reflect a dramatic shift in the character of farming from primarily small family subsistence farms with mixed production to a capitalist mode of commodity production for corporate food processors. The establishment of McCain's potato processing plant in Florenceville in 1957 was a major catalyst in this process. The corporation specialized in the production of frozen french fries, thus creating a concentrated market for potatoes and encouraging a shift from mixed farming to monocrop production. McCain quickly grew from a start-up operation with 30 employees to over 6 600 within 25 years. By 2007, it was a multinational frozen food corporation, with 57 plants operating in 12 countries worldwide, over 20 000 employees, and annual revenues around $6 billion. In order to expand, the company needed to overcome the limitations of labour intensive manual harvesting, that restricted what one family could harvest to about five acres of potatoes. The introduction of mechanical harvesters in the in the late 1950s revolutionized potato farming. To justify the cost of a harvester, farms required a minimum of 70 acres of potatoes. Those farms that were too hilly to use the mechanical harvesters, or too small to invest in such expensive machinery, rapidly went out of business.

Over the next 25 years, McCain established a vertically integrated agribusiness processing system, controlling all elements in the production chain (Machum 2002, 141). This started with land. The McCain corporation purchased about 15 000 acres of land in Carleton and Victoria counties (Valley Farms Ltd) to supply its own potatoes and to gain a strong negotiating position with other farms. McCain also expanded into a series of subsidiary companies (Thomas Equipment Ltd)that sold farm machinery—the harvesters, sprayers, tractors and trucks that farmers needed, along with seeds (Foreston Seed Co. Ltd.), fertilizers (McCain Fertilizers Ltd.) and pesticides, and storage facilities (Carleton Cold Storage Co. Ltd.). McCain also established its own trucking company (Day and Ross Ltd and M&D Transfer Ltd.) to truck its produce to markets in central Canada and beyond (McCain International Ltd.).

Sub-contracting the Risks: Dependent Commodity Production

It is significant that the McCain Corporation did not expand in the direction of taking over vast tracts of land to establish corporate capitalist farms. The company's experiment with its own corporate farms in the 1980s proved less profitable than reliance on independent family farms. The main variable was exploitation of labour power. Independent farm owners and their family members were willing to work very long hours without extra pay to maintain their farms, and in bad years they would work for free. In contrast, hourly wage workers and salaried managers on corporate farms would not work extra hours without overtime pay. It was thus in McCain's corporate interests not to take over the bulk of farm production, but rather to maintain family farms in a dependent relation to the corporation. The result has been that family farms of varied sizes have survived alongside corporate farms. At one end are small low-mechanized, family farms that supply all their own labour and strive to minimize debts on machinery. At the other end are highly mechanized 'corporate family farms' (McLaughlin 1990), heavily invested in new technology and partially reliant on non-family labour. Corporate capitalist farms that use entirely waged labour are physically the largest in acreage but not the most numerous.

As the near monopoly purchaser of potatoes in the province, buying from 300 to 400 farms, the McCain company exerts enormous control over individual farmers selling potatoes. A typical contract between McCain and dependent producers specified the kind of seed potato to be planted, the amounts and kind of fertilizers and pesticides to be used, and the tonnage to be delivered to the company at the company's time and convenience. Interim storage costs and all production risks were born by individual farmers. In a bad year, farmers would have to make up any shortfall by purchasing potatoes elsewhere to deliver to McCain. In a good year farmers might have to store potatoes at their own expense for months before the company bought them, absorbing all losses from disease or rot themselves. Banks typically refused to give loans to farmers until they had a signed contract with McCain. All debts owing to the McCain group of companies for machinery or other inputs could be deducted before the farmer would be paid. One farmer, (Lecture by Darrell McLaughlin, St. Thomas University, Fredericton 1998) describes the experience of being forced to buy potatoes from a neighbour to make up a shortfall in the amount he had contracted to sell to McCain, expecting to repay the neighbour after the sale. But he received no money for his crop. McCain wrote off the entire crop value against farm debts to other subsidiary companies, forcing the farmer to borrow money from a finance company at 18 percent interest to repay his neighbour. The farm got out from under staggering debt only by family members seeking off-farm employment—a strategy discussed further below.

In effect, small farmers became dependent commodity producers. As sub-contractors, these small farmers take all the risks. Technically they own their own means of production, but they are not economically independent. They are tied to agribusiness, producing raw materials for corporate food processors in a tightly integrated system in which they purchase all farm inputs from the same vertically integrated group of companies. Upstream they purchase seeds, fertilizer, chemical sprays, machinery, fuel, and labour. Downstream they sell to processors and wholesalers, or sometimes to marketing boards. Typically farms sell little of what they produce directly to consumers, at the farm gate or through farmers' markets.

Efficiency or Exploitation?

Classical liberal economics uses concepts like 'efficiency' and 'economies of scale' to account for differential profitability of businesses in an industry. The market functions to regulate commodity prices by balancing supply and demand. Efficient farmers will make a fair return on their crops. Inefficient farmers whose labour productivity is too low, either because they have not invested in newer technology or their farms are too small to benefit from economies of scale, will fall below optimal productivity and should drop out of the market.

In the context of dependent commodity production, however, the concept of 'efficiency" is ambiguous. A corporate family farm that was inherited without a mortgage and with a low debt load is in a qualitatively different business situation than a family farm with high mortgage repayments and debts on a machinery. Once a farm has specialized in potatoes it is very difficult to change direction because of the high capital costs of specialized machinery. A farmer who is lucky, or who has close relations with McCain' may get to deliver potatoes early in the season without carrying the costs of storage and inevitable deterioration. In 1996 some farmers lost over half their crop to potato blight. Blight can cause enormous damage in storage. Contracts with McCain are generally so close to optimal costs of production that any problems can result in the forced sale of potatoes at below their cost of production.

Marxist analysis of contradictions of capitalism involving falling rates of profit and polarization of wealth better fits the realities of capitalist farming than simple efficiency models. Many farms are caught in a cost-price squeeze of very high debts and falling commodity prices. Farmers are pressured to invest in expensive machinery which requires expanded production to meet payments. Year after year the contract price for potatoes has fallen below the cost of production (Machum 2002, 145). In PEI between 1971 and 1986 potato farmers received the cost of production in only 4 of 15 years. During the same years potato dealers, shippers and processors made large profits. There are stories of PEI farmers who did not have a contract with a big island processor Humpty Dumpty keeping potatoes in storage for a full year and eventually composting them because they could not find buyers. Processors prefer to deal with bulk orders rather than bother with small farms (Wells, 2007, 62).

Farmers survive these impossible conditions only by government subsidies (Norberg-Hodge 2002, 8). Farming is heavily subsidized across North America and the European Union. Direct subsidies reached $27 billion in the USA in 2000. Overwhelmingly, governments direct their subsidies to large corporate farms, consistent with the advice of liberal economists that large enterprises practising 'economies of scale' are more 'efficient' and should be encouraged rather than 'inefficient' smaller, undercapitalized farms. Such subsidies look like they benefit farmers, but they work to push down the price of raw materials for corporate food processors, and so maintain the economic relations that result in high profits to processors. Processors like McCain and Cargill thus appear as highly efficient while farmers appear as inefficient and living on welfare handouts. Processors also benefit from indirect subsidies that pay for research into chemical and biotech agriculture, the costs of removing fertilizer and pesticide residues from drinking water, and the transportation infrastructure required for bulk transport of food over thousands of miles (Norberg-Hodge 2002, 72). Again, we are reminded that 'efficiency' is a slippery concept whose meaning is determined by how and what is being measured.

Farm debts in Canada have been rising sharply. In 1970 the total farm debt was $4.4 billion, by 1981 this had risen to $18.1 billion, and by 1991 $21.2 billion. These increases are despite the millions of dollars written off by creditors through farm foreclosures. A researcher with the left-wing *Canadian Council for Policy Alternatives* (Qualman 2004) estimates that when controlling for inflation, retail food prices have doubled or tripled since 1975 but actual farm incomes have been static. All the increase in prices have gone to processors. Farms have increased productivity by an average of 3.4 percent per year over this period, compared with the average productivity increase for all businesses in Canada of 1.2 percent. In other words, Qualman argues, farmers have been far more efficient than processors. Farmers have massively adopted new labour-saving and productivity-enhancing technologies, but they have not reaped the profits. Only between 5 to 10 percent of the purchase price of food in supermarkets actually goes to farmers, with over 90 percent going to corporations that control the rest of the supply chain.

Migrant Labour—Vulnerable Labour Power

Migrant farm labour, entering Canada mostly from the Caribbean and Mexico on temporary permits to pick fruits and vegetables, are the most vulnerable and dependent sub-class of workers in Canada. They come from impoverished areas with high unemployment, and need the seasonal employment to support families. But as temporary workers they are excluded from any of the benefits or protections of landed immigrants like unemployment insurance, welfare, or medical coverage. Nor are they covered by minimum wage legislation. Labour organizers in Canada have tried to organize them but against heavy odds.

The first ever group of 64 migrant agricultural workers became certified as a union on one farm in Canada on 27 June 2007. Problems emerged at the same moment the announcement was made on the CBC news, with the individual farmer declaring that he could not pay any more to the workers than he already does, and if any new contract enforced higher wages, he would sell the farm. Many of the migrant workers themselves, speaking through translators, said they had been tricked into signing union cards without fully understanding what they were, they did not want a union, and were fearful of losing their jobs. The root of the problem is that each farm in Canada is legally defined as an independent employer. Labour laws require separate employee unions for separate employers. Hence the more than 18,000 migrant farm workers in Canada cannot legally form one union to set terms and conditions of their labour across thousands of individual farm owners. Each small group of workers on each individual farm has to unionize separately. Workers face the immediate risks that this one farm will respond to unionization by closing down, with the workers laid off and blacklisted from employment on any other non-union farm. The individual farm-owner can also legitimately claim that he cannot afford his labour costs to be any higher than all other farms or he will be bankrupted. Yet without unions, migrant farm workers are subject to super-exploitation, legally exempted from minimum employment standards, and not eligible for unemployment insurance, social assistance, or pensions. They dare not complain about living conditions or health and safety violations, and they cannot even shift jobs within Canada, for fear that they will be sent home before their contract expires and barred by immigration authorities from entering Canada the following season (Sharma 2001, 426; Basok 2002, 126).

Negotiating Corporate Order: Agribusiness and the State

The Canadian government is a major player in the farming sector. The federal government provides farm credit programs and sets interest rates on these loans. It also carries out research into seeds, although increasingly this is being given over to private seed companies like Monsanto, which then collect royalties on the seeds. State policies in New Brunswick, as elsewhere, has been strongly slanted in favour of agribusiness. The New Brunswick government has to be mindful of the threat that a multinational corporation like McCain's can easily move operations out of province or over the border into Maine, if business conditions are more favourable elsewhere. Government policies towards small farmers in the province reflect classical liberal economic concepts of 'efficiency' and 'economies of scale.' Policy statements supports the rhetoric of 'preserving family farms' but only if they function as "efficient, mechanized family farm businesses' that provide low-cost inputs to agribusiness (Machum 2002, 142). Small family farms are disparaged as inefficient, obsolete and "welfare' operations. Farm bankruptcies are explained as the result of inefficient operations that are too small to make the necessary investments and scale economies to compete successfully in the market. Farm mergers and consolidation of holdings are praised.

Farmers responding to CBC discussion on farm closures in New Brunswick (22 May 2007, Information Morning, Fredericton) gave examples of this prevailing bias towards large investments and large farms. The New Brunswick Government offers farm loans at preferred low income rates. A farmer asking for $15,000 loan to renovate a dairy barn was denied while a neighbour who asked for $150,000 for a new barn was approved. This neighbouring farm later sold out, apparently because of excessive debt load. Other farmers explained how the absence of local produce in supermarkets was not an issue of price or quality, but quantity. Supermarkets purchase from wholesalers, not individual farms, and wholesalers demand sufficient quantity to provide all the stores that they supply. Small farms cannot meet these bulk-order demands. Hence they cannot market their produce in local supermarkets.

The Battle over Marketing Boards

Agricultural Marketing Boards are organizations legislated by the state to control the sale of specific products. Farmers are legally bound to sell their produce to the marketing board which then negotiates product sales with downstream processors. By 2007 Canada had marketing boards in dairy, wheat and 'feathers'(eggs and poultry) but not in potatoes or other vegetables. Marketing boards that existed prior to the signing of the free trade agreements are permitted to continue but no new ones can be established. The classical liberal economics view of marketing boards is that they represent a distortion or interference in the free market determination of optimal prices through relations of supply and demand. They function as a stop-gap measure to assist vulnerable and uninformed producers who are unable to compete in open markets or to negotiate fair market prices for themselves. Marxist political economy the-

ory views marketing boards as essential regulatory tools that protect the interests of thousands of small producers against the unbridled power of corporate capitalist processors that dominate markets for agricultural goods.

The Wheat Marketing Board in Saskatchewan is one whose existence is currently in dispute (Hugh and McLaughlin 2007). The Conservative Govt. of Stephen Harper came out strongly in 2006 in favour of abolishing the Wheat Board's monopoly or 'single-desk selling authority', arguing that it is outmoded, that farmers can use the internet to track global wheat prices and should be free to negotiate their own sales in global markets, rather than being forced to sell to the Wheat Board. The Wheat Board could continue as a voluntary agency for farmers who choose to sell to it. From the Marxist political economy perspective, wheat markets are already grossly distorted by an oligopoly of five corporations that together control 80 percent of global grain trade. (Pugh 2007, 9) . The largest of the five, the American company Cargill, controls 60 percent of global grain trade. Along with wheat, it also handles other grains, cotton, sugar, petroleum, and financial trading. In the food sector, Cargill has a very high level of vertical integration, owning subsidiaries in food processing, futures, brokering, feed and fertiliser, grain storage elevators, and even the bank from which American farmers apply for loans (Norberg-Hodge et. al., 2002, 9; Measner 2007.). In 2007 this company had an estimated worth of $73 billion. The other four companies sharing the market are similarly huge transnational conglomerates handling multiple goods. Individual farmers trying to sell their wheat have limited bargaining power with these giants, unless they form a united front in the marketing board. High volume corporate farm operators favour abolishing the Wheat Board monopoly because they anticipate negotiating lucrative deals for themselves with key buyers for top prices. Smaller farmers, however, fear that without the Wheat Board monopoly they will have no bargaining power and will be pushed to sell at a loss. In Ontario the provincial wheat board used to operate as a 'single desk selling authority for the softer Ontario wheat that is generally used in manufacturing cookies. In 2003 the Board created an open market system, removing all limits on the amounts of grain that farmers could sell privately. The Board now handles only about one fifth of the total crop and returns to farmers are reported to have dropped by about 20 percent (Wells, 2007, 60–61).

From Food to Biofuel

The market for grains, oilseeds, sugar and vegetable oils is currently being transformed by a sudden and massive increase in demand for renewable fuels or bio-fuels such as ethanol and biodiesel to dilute or reduce demand for gasoline. Farmland that once grew food and livestock feed can now be mined for fuel to drive cars. About one-fifth of the corn grown in Canada in 2006 or 55 million tonnes, was diverted from food grains to ethanol plants and this is expected to more than double in the next decade (*Globe and Mail* 6 July 2007, B3). This shift is being strongly promoted by subsidies from the United States and Canadian governments, anxious to claim that they are reducing dependence on gasoline and tackling global warming.

This shift is likely to have very uneven impacts on people at different locations in agricultural production. Vertically-integrated agri-business corporate farms supplying monocrop production to ethanol plants are likely to gain the most, with profits bolstered by the $1.5 billion biofuel subsidies over nine years promised by the Harper government in 2007 (ibid.). The same corporate lobbyists that deride marketing boards for distorting the free market price of grain accept government subsidies to corporations for ethanol production as valuable incentive for infrastructure development to promote the new industry. Other economists, however, warn that government subsidies distort the value of ethanol, promoting a fuel that is both less efficient and more costly to produce than gasoline. A possible hidden side effect of promoting ethanol production on agricultural land in North America may be a reduction in amounts of subsidized food in global markets that are blamed for undermining farm prices in developing countries. Small farmers may gain from projected higher food-crop prices. At worst, the diversion of vast acreage from food to fuel production may promote global famine. The longer-term costs of mining farmland for fuel may be soil depletion on a massive scale and global food shortages.

Hog Farming

Wheat farming in Manitoba was in decline by the 1990s as the result of falling grain prices and rising freight costs. Intensive hog farming began to replace it, driven by global demand for meat, especially from Asia. Shipping meat became more profitable than shipping grain. By 1990s hog farming was growing at 12 percent

per year, surpassing wheat and canola as the leading source of provincial revenue. Corporate capitalist investment in hog farming has resulted in the familiar pattern of falling numbers of farms and increasing farm size. Between 1986 and 2000 the number of hog farms dropped by 60 percent while the average number of hogs per farm quadrupled, and with the largest farms with 10 000 or more hogs making up half of all farms (Novek 2003a, 570).

Corporate farms dominate the industry with 40 percent of Manitoba hog farms, but as with potatoes vertical coordination is favoured over full vertical integration. Corporations can make higher profits by contracting out actual production to individual farmers. Farmers provide the site, the labour, and most importantly the land on which the liquid waste must be spread. Hog farms produce enormous volumes of manure, and currently the only way to dispose of it is by mixing it with water and spewing the slurry over fields. Novek describes private farms as reduced to little more than latrines for the hog industry. Corporations provide all the inputs, including hogs, feed, antibiotics, veterinary services, and climate-controlled barns, and they contract to purchase the fattened-up animals for processing. Maple Leaf Foods, an offshoot of McCain's agribusiness empire, dominates the industry. In 2000 the company constructed Canada's largest packing plant, with the capacity to slaughter 90 000 hogs per week. McCain competes with USA-based Smithfield, which bought out Schneiders meat packers. The industry expected to double production in a decade. Large producers lobbied successfully to dismantle the Manitoba Pork marketing board, arguing that it was blocking growth in the industry. Deregulation was heralded as a triumph by big producers and corporate investors and bitterly opposed by small producers and environmentalists.

Similar processes of intensive livestock production is happening in the beef cattle industry in neighbouring Alberta. Young cattle are concentrated in intensive feed-lots where they are force fed on high protein foods so that they mature for slaughter in 14 months instead of three years. The artificial feeding of herbivores with animal byproducts is held responsible for outbreaks of 'mad cow disease' (bovine spongiform encephalopathy) associated with the brain-wasting Creutzfeld-Jakob disease in humans. The discovery of a sick cow in Alberta in 2003 prompted the USA to close the border to Canadian cattle for three years with huge loss of revenues in the $2 billion annual export industry.

Corporate Hog Farming as Negotiated Order

In Liberal economics 'externalities' refer to costs of production that are not paid by the corporate producer, but suffered or paid for by surrounding communities. High-yield monocrop production requires heavy use of chemical fertilizers and pesticides which degrade the soil and pollute rivers and lakes. Intensive livestock operations produce concentrated volumes of animal wastes that pollute air, water and soil. The disaster in Walkerton, Ontario in spring 2000 in which 2 300 people became sick and 7 died when the municipal water supply was contaminated with e-coli from cattle manure, was a particularly dramatic example of a much wider problem.

Local communities and governments typically lack both the legal mechanisms and the political will to control these externalities or to regulate corporate responsibility for these externalities. Municipalities in Manitoba lacked even the by-laws to require public hearings for new hog-farm proposals (ibid. 575). The Manitoba government also stands to gain so much revenue from hog farms that it protects investors from environmentalists rather than protecting the environment. These intensive livestock operations are a major global investment opportunity, sustaining related industries in feed mill and trucking—all important revenue sources. In 2000, a record 52 proposals were submitted for new or expanded operations worth over $200 million, this beating the record of 40 new operations two years earlier. By 2003, not a single hog barn proposal had been turned down, even in a flood-prone inter-lake area. Under Chapter 11 of NAFTA it is not even clear that governments have the power to limit the number of hog barn licences. Corporate lawyers argue that any corporation denied a licence has the right to sue government for discrimination, and for potential loss of revenues. Under this interpretation, the only effective limit on the treadmill expansion of hog farming in the region is economic. The rate of new investment will stall only when unused land becomes sufficiently scarce and therefore expensive that it deters new investors, or when hog production outstrips demand, and prices drop. The expanding demand in Chinese markets for cheap pork shows no sign of levelling off.

Novek's research (2003a, b) describes how corporate hog farming became systemically 'disembedded' from municipal community and provincial government controls to the extent that there were no enforceable external controls over corporate practices and no corporate responsibility for the costs or 'diseconomies' associated with concentrated hog farming. A coalition of interest groups including community leaders, family farm operators, and animal welfare groups have actively opposed the expansion of hog production, but with limited effect. One Manitoba resident did win a civil suit in 1975 against a neighbouring hog farm for damages from strong odours. The Manitoba government, however, responded with the Nuisance Act and the Farm Practices Protection Act to protect farmers from nuisance litigation. Government and corporate spokespersons worked up discourses to legitimate the treadmill expansion in hog farming, and to exempt it from community regulation. Chapter 11 of NAFTA requires 'scientific proof' of harm as criterion for government regulation of industries. The Manitoba government used this Chapter 11 language to exempt livestock operations from environmental regulations, in citing lack of 'scientific knowledge' of harm from odours (Novek2003b, 8). Complaints are merely 'subjective', not 'scientific', and therefore not actionable. Legislation protecting hog producers from complaints about 'nuisance' uses the discourse of "right to farm" and right to carry out 'normal pursuits'. As critics developed the discourse of 'lack of balance with nature' to challenge the large amounts of animal waste on restricted areas, agribusiness proponents responded with the discourse of "managed scarcity synthesis" and "sustainable development" to legitimate continued growth. The government represented itself as 'defender of agriculture', promoting 'sustainable development' through hog farms, which provide 'organic fertilizers'. Provincial government coffers benefit from global investments, but rural communities mostly do not share in the profits. Small communities are decimated as small family farms are bankrupted and families move away.

Animal rights activists struggle to draw public attention to yet another cost of factory farming—the super-exploitation of animals that has become part of 'normal' farming practices in these intensive livestock operations. Animals live truncated lives under miserable living conditions, crammed into cages and restricted from walking about or even turning around in the cage, so that they will fatten up more quickly for slaughter. The resulting meats are tainted with growth hormones and the antibiotics required to keep animals alive under these conditions. Lack of political will, not the inevitable results of capitalist food production, must share the blame for these conditions. Sweden has long banned the inhumane farming practices that are still permitted in Canada. In 1988 Sweden passed the Animal Protection Act that requires that technology be adapted to animals, not the reverse. The act explicitly outlaws the use of battery cages for chickens, and requires that cattle be put out to graze, and that pigs are not to be tethered, have straw and litter in their stalls and boxes, and have sufficient room to move around. The problem, as Novek expresses it, is that corporate capitalist livestock production has become disembedded from social, political, and legal controls (2003a, 567). The industry is able to pursue the single-minded maximization of profits and shareholder returns on investments with no societal controls.

Bio-engineering: Money or Life?

Yet another arena of struggle over environmental and health costs of industrial agriculture involves genetic engineering of crops and livestock. Companies aim to produce disease and pesticide resistant plants, so that pesticides will kill other plants but leave the target crops unharmed. They also engineer fruits and vegetables to be slow ripening, harder, easier to transport and with longer shelf life. Livestock engineering aims to increase growth rates in cattle, sheep, pigs and chickens and promote disease resistance under factory farming conditions. A hormone additive for milk-producing cattle (rBST) promotes increased milk production. Five bio-technology companies currently control the markets for all transgenic seeds and 60 percent of the global pesticide market, and they gain high profits from patents in new bio-engineered life forms. Critics of biological engineering of crops highlight associated risks of allergic reactions from cross-species gene splicing, the spread of herbicide and viral resistance to wild plants with potentially serious consequences, genetic damage to wildlife, birds, and insects that feed on transgenic crops, heightened resistance to antibiotics in farm animals and people, and heightened cancer risks from growth hormones in meat and milk products. Genetic engineering of fruits and vegetables genetically engineered for easy transportation and long shelf life have resulted in food with significant loss of nutritional content (Landon and Wark 2004). Biotech industries consistently promote the benefits of genetic engineering while refusing to accept any risk liability. Governments collude in this limited liability by setting lax standards for food safety, that then shield companies from negligence claims (Norberg-Hodge et.al. 2002, 63).

Governments in North America and Europe are directly involved in bio-engineering, both through research funding and through regulations governing the patenting, testing and labelling of new products. The close interconnections between the American Food and Drug Administration (FDA) and the bio-tech industry means that monitoring and controls are relatively weak (Anderson 1999, 85–104). Corporations fund the research trials that test their own inventions, and interpret the results to support favourable evaluations. Brief trials of food fed to rats have been deemed sufficient to declare food additives safe for long-term human consumption, while negative test results are downplayed. The safety of new agribusiness chemicals are tested for safety one at a time, rather than in the multiple combinations that people may actually e exposed to (Norberg-Hodge 2002, 55–6). In 1998 the FDA even recommended that genetically engineered foods could be labelled 'organic'. While this proposal failed, the companies did win legal rulings that genetically engineered foods do not have to be labelled as such. Moreover, Monsanto filed lawsuits against other organizations that tried to label their produce as not genetically modified or not using milk from cattle treated with growth hormones. Lawyers for Monsanto also successfully threatened Fox News with reprisals if it aired a documentary on health risks to cattle and humans from the hormone to promote milk production (ibid. 105–114). Lawyers for bio-tech corporations like Monsanto draw on free trade regulations to challenge any government interference in their right to pursue profits in the absence of scientific proof of harm. Fears about risks from genetically modified cereals, or hormones in milk, are merely subjective attitudes or superstitions. The onus of proof is on the critics to provide scientific proof of harm beyond any legally arguable doubt in order to warrant impinging on corporate rights to do business. The particular irony in the case of hormones to promote milk production is that between 1980-1985 Monsanto was earning $500 million from sales of the hormone at the same time as the American government was spending about $2 billion per year to buy and destroy surplus milk to prevent prices from plummeting (ibid., 112). This is a classic example of Milton Friedman's argument that government interference distorts free markets and directly sustains excessive corporate profits.

Organic Farming: An Alternative to Agribusiness?

Organic farming made up only 1.5 percent of all farming in Canada in 2000 but it has been growing steadily at the rate of 15–20 percent per year. Statistics Canada figures for May 2007 indicated that 6.8 percent of farms across Canada were organic, and nearly one in six or 16.3 percent of farms in BC. Demand for organic produce is currently outstripping supply, making this a promising sector for new investment.

The liberal-economics argument in favour of industrial farming, involving land consolidation, specialization, mechanization, and chemical fertilizers and pesticides, is that these techniques create economies of scale that make possible the mass production of cheap food required to feed global human population. Critics argue that calculations of the relative productivity of industrial over organic farming look very different when different measures are used to define 'productivity' (Norberg-Hodge 2002, 74–78). When the measure is productivity-per-farm-worker, industrial farming wins. When the measure is productivity per unit of land, organic farms come out ahead. Organic farms employ more workers per acre because diversified crops cannot be easily mechanized, but the yields per acre are much higher. On indirect measures, like long-term sustainability of soil, protection of wildlife, quality of life of farm workers, and sustainability of rural communities, organic farming comes out way ahead.

Corporate-Organic or Small-Scale?

A question still debated is whether small scale organic family farming will remain viable in Canada, or will follow the pattern of conventional agribusiness, with farms getting bigger, more capital intensive, with higher debt loads, and a focus on monocrop production for exports? The trend seems to be going this way in California, but not in New Zealand and not in Ontario. Lobbyists for agribusiness in the United States cam very close in 1999 to persuading the Department of Agriculture to define 'organic' as including "genetically modified seed, fertilized with municipal waste and sterilized by irradiation" (Norberg-Hodge et. al., 2002, 43). Much produce sold in supermarkets under the label 'organic' come from monocrop farms that truck produce thousands of miles. Contrasting evidence from Canada, however, suggest that organic farming has not been pervasively hijacked by agribusiness. A survey of 259 Ontario farms in 1999 concluded that they have remained unspecialized, mixed-commodity, family farms that have avoided high mechanization and debt loads (Hall and Mogyorody 2001). On average the farms grew16 varieties of fruits and vegetables, or four-crop

rotations for field crops, mixing soybeans with pasture, barley, clover, peas, wheat and rye. These family farms survived with very little state support—although the Canadian federal government create national organic standards accreditation system in 1999 and a research centre (ibid. 403).

A major factor limiting the incursion of agribusiness into organic farming is that certification of produce as 'organic' precludes use of chemical fertilizers and pesticides. Monocrop production is so susceptible to diseases, pests, and soil depletion that it is incompatible with organic farming techniques. Conversely, mixed farming and crop rotation is incompatible with the use of specialized machinery, and so tends to remain labour intensive. Most organic farms in Ontario continued to rely on family labour, with only 5 percent of organic fruit and vegetable farms hiring migrant farm labour. About half hired some labour, but still continued to work as full-time farmers themselves.

A separate question is whether organic and conventional farmers support qualitatively different beliefs and values concerning the relationship between people and animals and the environment. The dominant worldview associated with capitalist farming includes belief in growth, progress and profits, faith in science and technology as a basis for social decision-making, a view of nature as separate from humans, as a resource to be exploited to meet human needs, and faith in free market economics. The alternative worldview places nurturing of the environment and sustainability above values of growth and profits, and views nature and other life forms as having intrinsic value that humans need to work with, rather than subdue (Abaidoo and Dickinson 2002). A survey of Saskatchewan farmers with exclusively conventional, mixed, and exclusively organic farming techniques showed considerable overlap in worldviews but with a clear shift in preponderance of values. Conventional farmers were more likely to favour the dominant worldview while organic farmers were more likely to accept alternative views. The authors conclude that about 60 percent of organic farmers had decided to go organic primarily for profits rather than philosophical conviction. This is particularly true for the mixed farms where farmers were beginning to experiment with organic crops. Forty percent of organic farmers were fully committed to ecologically friendly and nature-centred worldviews.

The large majority of farmers from all three groups believed that markets were more important than governments in promoting improved environmental practices.

Researchers were surprised that the highest proportion of 80 percent of respondents supporting markets were among organic farmers. Behind this apparent anomaly were very different interpretive understanding of what 'markets' refers to. Researchers and conventional farmers were thinking about global food processing corporations. Organic farmers were thinking about local farmers' markets and niche up-scale 'green markets' specializing in organic food, seeing the growth in these alternative markets as critical for the shift to organic farming. The green market caters to relatively affluent consumers who are prepared to pay more for foods that are certified free from artificial chemicals, pesticides, growth hormones and antibiotics.

Corporate capitalist interests are seeking to gain entry into this green market, offering marginally 'organic foods' on supermarket shelves, flown in from thousands of miles. But there remain intrinsic limits to the mass production of organic foods. For the time being, at least, organic farming provides a niche market in which small family farms can continue to survive, so long as relatively affluent consumers are willing to pay the premium for high quality food that is produced locally and with environmentally friendly farming practices. The caveat is that as markets for organic food grow and the sector becomes more profitable the drive to industrialize the sector also grows, with pressures to squeeze out small farmers and water down organic standards (Norberg-Hodge et. al., 2002,43; Worth 2007). Some communities are fighting back in small ways by promoting organic gardens in city lots (Werkerle 2004). Toronto food cooperatives are promoting buy-local campaigns and micro-enterprises that link farmers, consumers, and community kitchens. They support community gardens at public sites like libraries and in housing projects and open ground around high-rise apartments, and herb production on roof gardens. Werkerle describes it as a form of 'globalization from below' in which farmers and consumers try to bypass corporate-controlled global food systems.

Feminist Perspectives: Women in Farming

Women's contribution to farming has been largely invisible and ignored by research in both classical liberal economics and Marxist political economy. Yet there would be no family farming without women's work. As Machum expresses it (2002, 133–4) when a woman marries a farmer whose primary work is a family farm operation, she also marries the farm. She has a home and an income so long as the farm succeeds, but if it fails, she loses both. Conversely, the family farm is likely to fail if the marriage fails and the woman withdraws her labour. Few women own farms in their own right, reflecting pervasive patrilineal inheritance patterns, in which farms are handed down from fathers to sons.

Women sustain the family farm through their work in farm production, their domestic and reproductive work in the farm house, their income-substitution work, and often additional off-farm paid employment which subsidizes the farm. On New Brunswick potato farms, farm wives are routinely involved in all aspects of potato production from driving machinery, going for parts, harvesting potatoes, managing work crews and providing their meals, washing multiple loads of overalls for every farm worker after every truck-load of potatoes are handled, to minimize the spread of diseases between farms. Farm wives were also routinely involved in the daily care of livestock. Women tell stories of having closed-circuit television links between barns and bedroom so that they can monitor lambing and calving pens. Ranchers' wives like Irene Murdoch are routinely involved in 'haying, raking, swathing, moving, driving trucks and tractors and teams, quieting horses, taking cattle back and forth to the reserve, dehorning, vaccinating, branding, and doing anything else that was to be done."(Machum 2002, 136, citing Acheson et. al., 1984, 26). On more highly mechanized farms women typically work in management roles, answering the telephones, keeping accounts, handling finances and payroll, and the extensive paperwork associated with government farm programs. Cash-replacement work commonly involves canning and freezing garden produce, raising chickens and selling eggs, as well as knitting, sewing and selling crafts.

When farms are struggling financially, farm wives are the most likely farm members to seek off-farm employment (Bessant 2006; Shortall 2002; Heather et. al., 2005). Off-farm jobs offer some relief from the stress of farm work, and a source of status and recognition not received on farm. But as their income from off-farm jobs is increasingly used to pay farm debts women are in effect working for the farm and not for themselves. The farm still remains defined as the primary family business and her work as secondary. Women work themselves to the point of physical illness in their efforts to keep their farms operational and in the process to preserve their farm family way of life and their rural communities (Heather et. al., 2005, 93). But the farm is still defined as 'his' and themselves as merely junior partners.

Classical liberal economics characterises such off-farm supplementary incomes as a form of 'self-exploitation' that serves only to subsidize unprofitable inefficient enterprises that ought to go out of business (Bessant 2006). However, such pluriactivity appears increasingly common among family members for large as well as smaller farms. Heather et.al cite Statistics Canada data for 2001 indicating that income directly from farm operations made up merely 22.8 percent of total farm income, with 56.9 percent from off-farm employment income, and 28.3 percent from other sources, including pensions and farm subsidies. Such data indicate how severely primary producers are exploited in agribusiness chain of food production.

Farm wives who earn off-farm incomes in their rural communities are further exploited when these secondary occupations are themselves targeted for cutbacks. Half of the 34 farm wives interviewed in rural Alberta also worked as rural nurses (Heather et. al., 2005). When rural health services were regionalised and restructured in 1994, they found themselves more isolated and with heavier workloads as the number of Health Units were cut from 27 to 17, and nurses covered more of the work formerly done by community physicians. Nursing stations are chronically understaffed, to the extent that if one nurse is out sick or takes a day off, she is not replaced, and another nurse has to do the work of two people. The Alberta government in the mid-1990s had phenomenal revenues from oil, but chose to cut taxes rather than invest in rural health. Rural nurses absorb the extra work. Most of the wives interviewed did not identify themselves as 'feminists' because it seemed too selfish to focus on themselves when their farms, and their entire rural communities were at stake.

Patriarchal Rural Relations and the State

For all the work they do in sustaining family farms, farm wives receive minimal recognition or economic return. Departments of agriculture have recognized their value to the extent of promoting farm management and agricultural training programs for farm wives (Machum 2002, 138) but with the clear assumption that their services to their farms would be 'free'. Patriarchal class relations in Canadian farming have long been directly sustained by Canadian state policies and legislation.

Prior to 1980 farm wives had no ownership rights to the farm on death, separation or divorce. In the infamous Irene Murdoch case, she had undeniably made a substantial contribution to the ranch for 25 years, including running the ranch by herself for five to eight months of the year while he left to work for the Canadian Forestry Service. Yet when they divorced, the judge determined that her work was simply what any ranch wife would do, and it did not confer any financial interests or legal rights in the ranch.

The outrage generated by this case prompted changes in legislation to improve women's rights to share marital property. The Matrimonial Property Act on 1980 gave formal recognition of a wife's contribution in household management and child care created a right to an interest in property on marriage breakdown as well as financial contributions. In principle, wives are now entitled to half of the value of marital property on divorce. However, this rarely translates into half of the value of a farm (Keet 1990). Multiple legal exemptions, presumptions that the male farmer is the primary operator of the farm as a business, and policies to preserve viable farms, continue to ensure that property-owning farm husbands retain the major share of farm property on divorce.

Most farm wives do not receive income from their farm work. The 1969 income tax guide specified that wages to a wife could not be deducted from farm income as a tax expense, although wages paid to hired hands and to children could be deducted. Wives also could not pay into Canada Pension Plan. In 1993 the tax act was changed to permit spousal wages to be deducted from male farm incomes, but only if the wife was not a partner in the farm. Tax accountants encourage women to take wages and to pay into the Canada Pension Plan in their own names—but she must be legally defined as an employee, not a partner, to do this. Not surprisingly, most farm wives refuse to take this option (Machum 2002,138–9). Most farm organizations exclude women as members, or include them only in subordinate 'feminized' categories as farm-ettes (Shortall 2001). Within the organizations they typically work on all-women committees dealing with farm family issues. Organizations like the *Canadian Farm Women's Network* have struggled to highlight issues that affect women on farms. These include the importance of legalizing their stake in the farm business, getting women involved in farming organizations and government farming bodies and marketing boards, and lobbying the Canadian Census to change farm operator categories so that women's names can appear. However they remain marginalised as merely 'women's' issues. The state gives funding to the Farm Women's Network for 'farm women's issues' but refuses to fund educational courses for women on farming issues on the grounds that these are not of specific relevance to women. The state thus reinforces gender-role segregation in the industry. The exclusion of women from farming organizations beyond gendered family committees perpetuates the limited understanding of the enormous stress and work loads that farm women carry.

Conclusion

In conclusion, both the liberal economics and Marxist political economy perspectives contribute important insight into understanding the complexity of economic relations. The optimistic liberal view of capitalism highlights opportunities for business enterprise, wealth-generating activities and expanding job opportunities, especially in the 'knowledge economy'. The Marxist perspective focusses attention on the inherent tendencies towards concentration of wealth and power in the hands of a numerically small but extremely influential capitalist elite class, and escalating class divisions between a prosperous middle class of workers employed in the knowledge economy and an expanding sector of low-income contract and service jobs that absorbs the risks and slumps of post-industrial capitalism. The different possible directions in which these relationships work in practical situations and within particular industries like farming is not inexorably determined by impersonal market forces. Rather, these directions are promoted or restricted, sustained or changed by how people come to understand and interpret what is happening, and thereby exert their influence on laws and policies, and market choices.

Legal and political institutions actively collude in the dis-embedding of corporate capitalist enterprise from community controls and thereby sustain the conditions within which narrowly-defined corporate goals to maximize profits and shareholder returns trump competing interests.

It is the meticulous and mostly qualitative social-constructionist research that gives most insight into what people do to continually bring about these systemic patterns. The 'organic intellectuals'—the corporate lawyers, the physical and social scientists who conduct collaborative research with industry, the analysts who work within policy think-tanks and government committees to covert theoretical assumptions into practical initiatives, the academics and journalists who generate text books and mass media representations that influence how masses of people come to think about alternatives, that sustain or undermine these systemic 'market forces'. The pervasively patriarchal character of these ostensibly abstract and rational economic forces help further to remind us that these are fundamentally social constructions. They are embedded in cultural assumptions about gender and power.

The Family: The Site of Love, Exploitation, and Oppression

Functionalist theory views society as an integrated and self-maintaining system, analogous to a living organism. Like an organism, it is composed of numerous organs or institutions that are structured to meet the specialized needs or prerequisites of the social system as a whole. The system normally exists in a state of dynamic equilibrium. Built-in mechanisms balance change in one part of the system with complementary changes in other parts, so that the order of the whole is maintained despite major changes in structure. Within subsystems of action, or institutions, are individual roles, which comprise typical patterns of action. The entire system is held together by the mechanisms of **normative consensus** and shared role expectations. These values and expectations for behaviour are internalized by members of society through the complex process of socialization.

The family is an institution that plays a vital part within this functionalist model of society. Functionalists argue that the family is extremely important, indeed indispensable, for the survival of society. For many theorists, society itself can be conceptualized as made up of families linked together. The family is a universal institution; no known society has existed without it. The central integrative process of socialization—the internalization of behaviour patterns and values—occurs primarily within the family. Institutions such as school and church also play a part in the socialization process, but this is generally only after the newborn infant has developed into a socially functioning child. The few documented cases of feral children, or those who have survived in the wild or in extreme isolation without family contact, indicate that these children's behaviour is less than human. Even after they have been intensively trained in clinics, these children have not been able to learn to talk or to think in terms of the symbolic meaning systems that distinguish humans from other animals. Functionalists suggest that, without families, there would be no humanity and hence no society. Functionalists accord no other social institution such central importance. For this reason, the study of sociology of the family offers the strongest test of the contributions and the limitations of the functionalist perspective.

Functionalist Theories of the Family

Any institution can be studied from two related perspectives: the contribution of that institution to the functioning of society as a whole or the institution's internal functioning as a subsystem in its own right, with its own set of prerequisites for maintaining a dynamic equilibrium.

The four main functions that the family unit performs for society are: reproduction of society's members; socialization of new members, especially the newborn and young children; regulation of sexual relations; and economic co-operation to sustain adults and their offspring. The family constitutes the basic emotional or expressive social unit, providing nurturing, protection, and affection for members, controlling their behaviour, and channelling fundamental sexual and reproductive drives into socially acceptable forms. Although reproduction and sexual relations can and do take place outside of families, they are only socially legitimated within families. Reiss suggests that this is because the family context best ensures the nurturance of the newborn, with kinship groups on both the father's and the mother's side acknowledging a relationship with, and some responsibility for, the child (Reiss 1976, ch. 2).

The family occurs in a great variety of forms in different societies. There are **extended families**, in which several generations of kin live in the same dwelling usually under the authority of the most senior male or the most senior female in a matriarchal society, and **nuclear families** consisting of isolated couples with their dependent children. Legitimate sexual relations include **monogamy** (one man and one woman) or forms of **polygamy** (more than one spouse). The more common form of polygamy is **polygyny** (one man having two or

more wives), but some societies practise **polyandry** (one woman having more than one husband). Whatever the particular arrangement favoured in a given society, functionalists argue that there is an essential core that is universal. This core was defined by George Murdock (1949, 2):

> The family is a social group characterized by common residence, economic co-operation, and reproduction. It includes adults of both sexes, at least two of whom maintain a socially approved sexual relationship, and one or more children, own or adopted, of the sexually cohabiting adults.

Not all members of a society conform to this pattern of living at any one time, but most people spend a significant part of their lives in a family situation. In Canada, most people marry and have children, and most of these children will do the same when they are adults. Kinship ties remain extremely important to people throughout life, even for those individuals who do not form families of their own.

The nuclear family is seen by functionalists as having a biological base.

The nuclear family core of two sexually cohabiting adults of the opposite sex, together with their dependent children, is seen by functionalists as having an essential biological foundation (Goode 1982, 15–32). This thesis incorporates the core ideas of **sociobiology**, a branch of sociology closely associated with functionalism, which studies the biological bases of social behaviour. Functionalists argue that the vital institution of family is rooted in sexual drives and the imperative of reproduction and in the sociological imperative of transforming the biological organism of a newborn baby into a human or social being. Unlike many animals, the argument goes, human babies are born with relatively few instincts. They rely upon a complex brain to learn, through symbols and abstractions, the essentials of survival in society. This necessitates a long period of social dependency that lasts well into adolescence and beyond in industrial society. Because of this, there is a relatively long period during which the nurturing mother depends upon care and support of other adults, usually the husband/father, to meet her economic needs while she is engaged in child care.

Many biological drives predispose humans for male-female pair bonding. Goode suggests that, despite the fact that there is some homosexuality, people are pre-programmed for heterosexuality. The constancy of the human sex drive, far more intense than is needed for reproduction itself, promotes long-term, stable relations between men and women. The biologically based impulse of jealousy reinforces this pair bonding through the urge to regard one's mate as one's exclusive sexual property. Another very general biological drive is territoriality, the natural desire to settle in one location and defend it from others. This is combined with a biologically determined reproductive strategy of having few offspring and caring intensively for them, rather than producing many offspring at once and leaving them to fend for themselves. All these traits create strong impulses in humans to form families.

Functionalists argue that sexual differences promote heterosexual bonding. Only women undergo menstruation, pregnancy, and lactation, and hence they are biologically predisposed to perform the task of caring for children. Breastfeeding intensifies the bond between mother and child. Women are relatively weak during pregnancy and just after birth; hence natural choice as well as efficiency dictate that they will stay close to home and children. Males, on the other hand, have greater strength and aggressiveness, which gave them the edge in early hunting societies and hence provided a biological basis for early male dominance. Lionel Tiger (1977) argues that "man the hunter" was preprogrammed for aggression and dominance over females and also for strong male bonding in hunting packs. This predisposition for male bonding gives man an advantage in politics and in business. Tiger argues that women are preprogrammed to be submissive and to be oriented toward their children rather than to form bonds with other women. These biological predispositions favour the sex-role division of labour within families, with women concentrating on nurturing roles within the home while men concentrate on the role of economic provider.

Functionalists posit that sociological factors stemming from the nature of work in industrial societies strongly reinforce this biologically based tendency toward sex-role division of labour within families. Parsons argues that family and industry are based on diametrically opposed patterns of action orientation and hence must be separated if both are to function effectively. Family life is based on emotional ties between members; membership is dependent on ascriptive characteristics and not qualifications; individuals are judged by particularistic values as unique family members; and there are diffuse obligations to meet each others' needs in multiple ways. Industry necessarily operates in terms of totally different patterns. Relations among people in industry are emotionally neutral; membership is ideally determined by achievements; judgments are based upon universalistic criteria of standards of performance; and obligations are specific to the particular transaction. The specialization of sex roles, with women concentrating upon the internal affairs of the family while men concentrate upon occupational roles, best serves to minimize confusion of values across the two spheres.

In functionalist analysis, the family constitutes a social system with its own internal needs that must be met if the family is to maintain its equilibrium. Individual families, like society as a whole, must meet the four basic prerequisites of goal attainment, adaptation, integration, and latency or pattern maintenance. Parsons and Bales (1956, ch. 1) analyse how families function internally to divide up roles along sex-specific lines. Bales maintains that small groups typically develop two kinds of leaders: an **instrumental leader** who gets tasks done and an **expressive leader** who supports and encourages group members and smooths over tensions. Parsons proposes that, within families, one adult, typically the male, performs instrumental tasks, while the female performs the expressive roles. In terms of system prerequisites, instrumental roles include goal attainment and adaptation. The man typically represents the family to the external social system, making the key decisions that set family goals and earning the resources needed for the family to adapt to its surroundings and survive. Expressive roles are oriented toward the internal needs of the family, meeting the prerequisites of integration and latency by supporting and nurturing people, smoothing over tensions, and teaching the family values and patterns of behaviour to the children. Parsons argues that these functional imperatives reinforce, if they do not totally mandate, sex-role division of labour within families.

Spencer (1976, ch. 11) speculates on what might happen if a particular husband and wife decided to change this pattern. In order to challenge male control over goals and adaptation decisions, she argues, a couple must first acknowledge their present functions. Western societies generally mandate a certain pattern of sex-role specialization, such that the male is obliged to support and defend his wife and children. Thus society penalizes the male if both partners want to stay home. If men and women want equal work opportunities, both must take equal responsibility for support of the family. If the wife were to become the chief breadwinner, Spencer argues, then she would have to have authority within the household. If her job required her to move, then the rest of the family would have to move with good grace. If she pays the bills, she would have to decide the family budget. If she is to be fit and awake for her job, then her dependants would have to protect her health, her mood, her rest, and so on, by obeying her requests. Spencer notes that these are the prerogatives now enjoyed by men and resented by women. She concludes that traditional roles are designed to protect children and are functionally necessary, at least to some degree.

Functionalists also argue that the typical nuclear family pattern, consisting of a married couple with their children, is mandated by the requirements of industrial society. Industrialization is founded on free labour markets and a flexible, mobile work force. Workers and their families must be willing to move as and where the breadwinner's work demands. The nuclear group is much more mobile than the extended family group, which is commonly tied to landed property.

In summary, functionalism appears to offer a comprehensive theory that accounts for all the essential features of family as we know it in industrialized society. The heterosexual pair bonding at the core of any family system stems from biological imperatives—not merely the sex drive, but the need for long-term nurturing of newborn infants and children. The sex-role division of labour within families and the segregation of women's domestic nurturing work from male instrumental roles in the work force are rooted both in biological predispositions and in the very distinctive values and behaviour orientations of family life and occupational roles in industrial society. The authority of males in the home in terms of the allocation of money also reflects the imperatives of the breadwinner role that men normally hold. The demands for a mobile work force account for the predominantly isolated nuclear family residence pattern. The explanation seems complete. It suggests that efforts to change family life or sex roles in any significant way are impractical.

Critique of Functionalist Theory

The functionalist theory of the family has come under considerable attack, however, primarily for elevating a historically specific form of family into a universal principle. The theory ignores the wide diversity of family forms. Such diversity renders a rigidly defined notion of the family, such as that proposed by Murdock (1949), useless. Functionalist views of the family have been challenged, especially by Marxist and feminist theorists, as an ideology that seeks to justify the status quo while ignoring the ways in which family life is constrained by interests associated with capitalism and patriarchy. These are interests that benefit in multiple ways from exploiting the cheap labour of women in the home. Functionalism supports that exploitation by legitimating it as if it were unavoidable and universal. The traditional functionalist model of the family has been criticized particularly for a false universalism that implies that all the functions associated with family life are necessarily met by a single institution in which all functional elements are combined. In Eichler's view, such theorizing is flawed by four major biases: monolithic, conservative, sexist, and microstructural (Eichler 1988a, chs. 1–4). In this section we briefly examine each of these biases in turn.

Monolithic Bias

The **monolithic bias** is inherent in Murdock's definition of the family, which functionalists tend to treat as a given. A host of alternative family forms that have existed in other societies, and that are emerging in contemporary industrial societies such as Canada, are simply ignored or treated as problematic deviations. Anthropologists have long been familiar with examples of cultural patterns in other societies that violate some or all elements of Murdock's supposedly universal family form.

The Nayars of South India had, until the beginning of the twentieth century, a family form that incorporated none of the attributes considered essential by functionalists. Family life was not organized around sexually cohabiting pairs. There was no economic co-operation between women and their sexual partners, and the children of such liaisons had no socially recognized relationship with their biological fathers. They might not even know who their father was. Nayar families were organized around the female line. The joint family comprised the mother, her siblings, and her own and her sisters' children. A brief ceremony took place before girls reached puberty that linked each girl with a man from her own social rank. The ritual functioned only to establish female adult sexual status. From then on, women were free to have sexual relations with whomever they chose. Children lived in their mother's joint family home. Men did not live with the sexual partners; they continued to live in their own mother's household. All property belonging to the joint family was inherited through the mother's line. The mother's eldest brother commonly managed the property, but he did not own it and could not dispose of it. His principal relationship with children was as uncle to his sisters' offspring (Liddle and Joshi 1986, 28, 51–52).

Other studies suggest that in Jamaica, and in poor black communities in the United States, nuclear families are also not the norm. The stable relationship is between a woman and her children, while she has only temporary and sequential relations with male partners (Reiss 1976, 14–15).

Functionalists have responded to these challenges to the universality of the family by proposing various redefinitions around the mother-child dyad or, more commonly, by dismissing variations as rare aberrations that prove the general rule (Reiss 1976, ch. 2). The Nayar culture can be viewed as an anthropological anomaly that developed in the exceptional circumstances of extensive migration of males in search of work as soldiers. The fact that this type of family broke down in the early twentieth century during British rule in India indicates that it was not a viable form. Critics doubt whether such a system could work in any larger society. The female-headed households among poor blacks do not represent a cultural ideal so much as the collapse of normal family life in the face of the abject poverty and chronic unemployment of black males. The ideal remains permanent marriage and stable fatherhood.

But charges of monolithic bias cannot be avoided simply by dismissing these family forms as aberrations. Eichler challenges the monolithic bias squarely within the North American society that functionalist theory is designed to explain. She argues that the image of family as the monogamous nuclear group comprising husband, wife, and their biological children applies to only a minority of structures that participants themselves regard as family. The argument that most individuals may have lived in a nuclear family at some time in their lives does not alter the fact that the majority of people in Canada are not now living in such families. Functionalists arbitrarily exclude from their definition of family a multitude of other arrangements: common-law couples (see table 10-1); commuting couples where

Table 10-1

Number of Persons Living in Common-law Unions, by Age Group and Sex, Canada, 1981, 1986, and 1991						
Age Group	1981		1986		1991	
	Men	Women	Men	Women	Men	Women
Total	356 610	356 310	486 945	486 945	725 945	725 945
15–19	8 340	32 450	4 655	21 535	6 570	26 135
20–24	83 080	109 625	81 630	123 500	89 195	138 485
25–29	88 120	77 675	122 670	116 085	163 840	169 060
30–34	61 160	47 865	90 335	76 730	140 410	130 900
35–39	38 715	29 325	65 010	52 670	101 305	91 980
40–44	24 230	18 715	42 395	33 950	76 735	65 490
45–49	17 630	13 275	26 525	21 110	53 570	42 130
50–54	13 315	10 290	19 215	14 430	34 155	24 310
55–59	9 080	7 450	13 710	10 410	24 020	14 680
60–64	5 740	4 770	9 245	7 625	16 330	9 710
65+	7 200	5 170	11 555	8 895	19 815	13 065

Source: Reproduced by authority of the Ministry of Industry, 1994. Adapted from Statistics Canada (1994a), *Age, Sex, Marital Status, and Common-law Status*, Cat. 92-325E.

spouses have careers in different places and meet only on weekends or holidays; couples who do not have children; couples whose children live elsewhere; **reconstituted families** where one or both spouses may have children living elsewhere; single-parent families; homosexual couples; and so on.

Eichler suggests that, if functionalists insist on having one definition to cover all forms of family, it would have to look something like the following: A family is a social group that may or may not include adults of both sexes, may or may not have children born in wedlock, or originating in the marriage, may or may not be living in a common residence, may or may not be sexually cohabiting, and may or may not include love, attraction, economic support, and so on (Eichler 1988a, 4).

Eichler proposes that the attempt to define the family should be abandoned in favour of an alternative approach that empirically researches the dimensions of family life. The important dimensions that Eichler (1988a, 6) singles out are procreation, socialization of children, sexual relations, residence patterns, economic co-operation, and emotional support. Functionalists assume that members of a family will be high on all dimensions. A husband and wife will have children together, socialize them, have sexual relations with each other, live together, co-operate economically, and give

Gay rights activitists in Toronto lobby for social benefits for same-sex couples under the banner "We Are Family."

each other emotional support. This global assumption is false. Eichler addresses each dimension in turn, suggesting how it needs to be reconceptualized in terms of a range of behaviour options that vary widely, depending on circumstances.

The dimension of *procreation,* for example, has been radically affected by the number of couples choosing to remain childless and by the high rate of divorce and remarriage. Eichler (1988a, 243) cites evidence that, in Canada in 1985, one in three marriages ended in divorce. Statistics Canada data indicates that between 15 to 20 percent of brides or grooms in 1985 were previously married. We can estimate that between a quarter to a third of all Canadian children grow up in reconstituted families where one of the adults with whom they live is not their biological parent.

The dimension of *socialization* is likewise a variable. A child may be socialized by both biological parents together, or by one parent alone, or one parent with one step-parent, or one parent and step-parent in one house and another parent and step-parent in a second house, or some other combination of possible arrangements. It also cannot be assumed that simply because a parent lives in the same house as a child that that parent is involved in socialization. It is quite possible and probably common for one parent to do most of the socialization work while the other does very little. Similarly, we cannot assume that when parents are divorced, the absentee parent is necessarily not involved in socialization. It may well be that divorced fathers give more time and attention to children than do fathers in two-parent households who take it for granted that the mother will do all the child-rearing work. Even the assumption that socialization gets done by parents can be questioned in a society in which very large numbers of young children spend most of their waking time in child-care centres, or with nannies, and in the company of television.

The notion that *sexual relations* take place only between married or cohabiting partners can readily be challenged. Lifelong chastity in marriage may be the exception rather than the rule. This, in turn, has important implications for procreation. It cannot simply be assumed that all children are the biological offspring of the mother's spouse.

Residence patterns also vary widely. In divorced and reconstituted families, children may have two separate family homes and commute between them. It is possible, although rare in our society, for children to have one residence while the parents rotate. Many two-career families have two or even three separate homes, one near the husband's and/or the wife's work and another family home elsewhere. Many more couples may live in one place during the winter and another during the summer.

Economic co-operation cannot be treated as given within a family. Functionalists conceive of the husband-breadwinner providing economic resources for the homemaking wife and their children, but many other arrangements are common. A sole breadwinner may pool all income for joint family use, or may keep some or most of the money for private use and give only a housekeeping allowance to the spouse. In extreme cases, the nonemployed spouse may get no money at all: the breadwinner keeps everything and makes all decisions about what to buy. Two-income families have another set of possible arrangements; this is compounded when there are adult, income-earning children living at home.

The last dimension of family interaction, *emotional relations,* may vary all the way from close, loving, and mutually supportive ties to shallow and detached relations with little emotional involvement. In extreme though by no means uncommon situations, emotional relations may be characterized by abuse, violence, and hatred.

Traditional functionalist theory is not adequate to explore the dimensions of family life because the theoretical structure itself is too rigid. The monolithic bias is so pervasive that most sociology of the family textbooks, even in the 1980s, ignore the huge number of reconstituted families and all other forms of living arrangements not organized around heterosexually cohabiting pairs (see figure 10-1). All other family forms are predefined as "problem families" regardless of how participants feel about them. We know little or nothing about the internal economies of families, because functionalism does not go beyond treating families as economic units. Most textbooks ignore the issue of family violence entirely or at best treat it as an aberration. This is notwithstanding the evidence of extensive wife battering and the physical and sexual abuse of children. Eichler suggests that, far from being an aberration, emotional stress and violence may be normal occurrences in families. The situation of enforced intimacy between people of different sexes, different careers, different incomes, and markedly different ages would normally be seen as conducive to high stress in any context other than families. Why would we expect families to be immune?

Figure 10-1

Percentage Distribution of Census Families, by Family Structure, 1971 and 1986

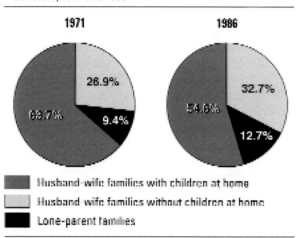

Source: Statistics Canada, 1971 and 1986 Censuses of Canada.

Conservative Bias

Other biases compound the distortions arising from a monolithic focus. Eichler criticizes traditional sociology of the family literature for its **conservative bias**, reflected in a pervasive failure to focus upon changes that are transforming family life. Demographic variables are high on the list of critical changes. People in Canada are having fewer children than in the past and are living much longer. Declining fertility rates mean that most women experience pregnancy only twice in their lives. A full-time mothering role is no longer a lifetime expectation. Over half the adult women in Canada are employed outside the home. Even for the stereotypical family, the period of "Mom, Dad, and the kids" may cover only a limited stage in the family life cycle. Couples who have one or two children in their early twenties can look forward to twenty to thirty years of working lives after their children have left home. They can also realistically expect ten or more years of life after retirement.

Changes in longevity have been dramatic and are having a profound impact on family life. Eichler (1988a, 42) notes that, in 1931, the average life expectancy for a male at birth was 60.0 years, but this had risen to 70.2 years by 1986. The rise in life expectancy for women was even larger: from 62.1 years in 1932 to 78.3 years in 1986. Thus, women, on average, outlive men by over eight years, and they also tend to marry men who are older than themselves.

The combined effect of women's longer life expectancy and men's older age of marriage leads to very different experiences for women and men (Eichler 1988a, 42–43). Figures for 1986 show that 74 percent of men aged 65 and over were married, compared with 42 percent of women aged 65 and older who were married, and 46 percent widowed. Roughly 12 percent of both groups were single, separated, or divorced (see figure 10-2). These differences mean that the majority of men can expect to be cared for in their old age by their younger wives, while women of the same age can rarely expect to be cared for by their husbands. It would take a dramatic change in marriage patterns to redress this imbalance, but there is no evidence that this is happening.

Eichler points out that the pattern of long widowhood for women is particularly problematic because of the uneven distribution of earnings and pensions between

women and men. Women who have worked as homemakers all their lives have no individual pension entitlements when their husbands die, other than the universal old age pensions paid by the government. Women generally spend more years outside the paid labour force than men to care for children. Even when they do work full-time, they earn significantly less money than men. Low earnings translate into low pensions. Poverty rates rise steeply for women in older age groups, where most are widowed. The 1992 poverty rates are shown in figure 10-3.

The rise in average life expectancies also means that a greater proportion of people are living into their eighties and nineties. What this means is that people who are themselves elderly and retired commonly have parents who require care. These responsibilities fall particularly heavily upon women, since it tends to be women rather than men who do the caring work within families. Many women around sixty-five years of age may find themselves caring for their own very elderly mother, and perhaps their father and in-laws, as well as for their older, retired husband. This is a great deal of work to do at an age when the woman herself might have expected to be able to retire from the obligations of looking after other people.

All of these are very dramatic changes from family life in Canada only a few generations earlier, yet they receive little attention in functionalist theory.

Sexist Bias

The **sexist bias** in family sociology is reflected in the pervasive stereotyping of female and male roles around images of the pregnant woman and man the hunter. Such images are largely irrelevant in an era when few women have more than two pregnancies, and the vast majority of men neither hunt nor have jobs that require hard physical labour. This stereotyping perpetuates the myth that women are only marginally involved in the work force and that men are marginally involved in homelife and child-rearing. Still worse, functionalist theory elevates such myths to the level of functional imperatives, conveying the impression that alternative lifestyles threaten the equilibrium of family and occupational subsystems, and hence threaten society itself.

Microstructural Bias

Lastly, the **microstructural bias** in functionalist theory is reflected in a primary focus on the internal workings of individual family units. Most sociology of the family textbooks give little consideration to the impact of the

Figure 10-2

Marital Status of Elderly Men and Women, Canada, 1986

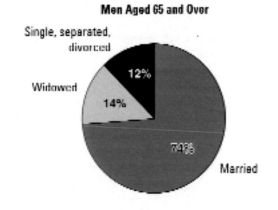

Men Aged 65 and Over

Single, separated, divorced 12%

Widowed 14%

74% Married

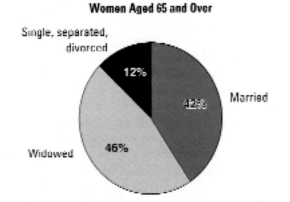

Women Aged 65 and Over

Single, separated, divorced 12%

42% Married

Widowed 46%

Source: Statistics Canada, 1986 Censuses of Canada.

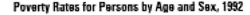

Figure 10-3

Poverty Rates, 1992

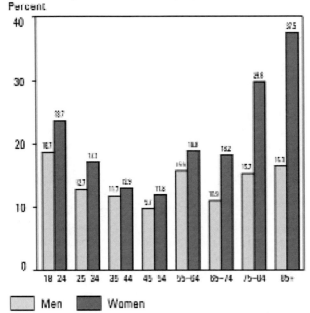

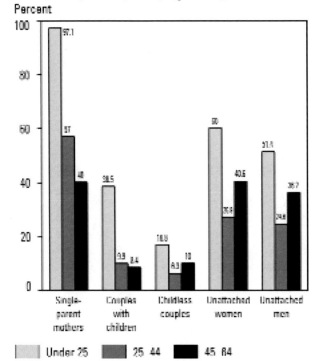

Source: National Council of Welfare (1994, 32).

wider political economy and the nature of government policies as they affect family life. Functionalists tend to discuss family problems as if they arose from inadequacies in the role of performance of individual members, rather than from external pressures on people. The microstructural bias is inherent in each of the other biases described above. We cannot understand what is happening to families apart from studying the political economy in relation to which people organize their personal lives.

Marxist Theories of the Family

The Marxist approach to sociology of the family challenges the microstructural bias of traditional functionalist theory. Marxists argue that both the organization of economic production in the wider society and the way people earn their living critically influence the organization of family life. The family form that functionalists assert as universal represents only one historically specific form, prevalent only at a certain stage in the development of capitalism and only for members of a certain social class. Marxist feminists accept this broad analysis of the relationship between modes of production and family forms but give special attention to the impact of the economy on women's roles within the family. They challenge Parsons' notion of a separation between the **private realm** of family life and the **public realm** of industry. They claim that the demands of capitalism intrude into the most intimate personal relations of family life. Homemakers work for the corporations as much as employees do. The only difference is that the homemakers' work is not acknowledged and is not paid for.

The Marxist Theory of Patriarchy

The Marxist perspective draws its initial inspiration from an early essay by Engels ([1884] 1978), a long-time colleague of Marx. Engels speculates that the earliest form of family was probably communal, based on relatively free sexual relations and organized around matriarchal households, reflecting the known biological relation between mother and child. The family form among the Nayars, described earlier, closely resembles the model that Engels had in mind.

Engels argues that this original matriarchal family

form was probably undermined by two factors: the knowledge of paternity and male control over private property. Awareness of the male role in conception represented a profound leap of knowledge, Engels suggests, with important implications for power within the family, especially when combined with control over property. As the means of subsistence changed from hunting and gathering to more settled herding and agriculture, men gained control over land and domestic herds and thus over the economic surplus. As men gained wealth, they wanted to control inheritance through the male line. This necessitated control over women's sexuality and over their offspring. Monogamy and patriarchy emerged together, Engels suggests. Monogamy was strictly required for women; men could still enjoy relative sexual freedom. This inequality gave rise to prostitution. Engels comments that "the overthrow of mother right was the world historic defeat of the female sex. The man seized the reins of the house also, the woman was degraded, enthralled, the slave of man's lust, a mere instrument for breeding children" (Engels [1884] 1978, 736).

Engels suggests that inegalitarian family forms would disappear only under two possible situations. The first was where people were so poor that men would have no property to inherit or pass on. The second was under a system of communal ownership of the means of production and equal employment of women in a socialist society. This would remove forever the basis of male power over women.

Engels' essay, and particularly his theory of the transition from matriarchy to patriarchy, is speculative, based on little anthropological evidence. But his argument concerning the importance of control over property as a determinant of male dominance in the household is widely accepted.

Capitalism and Family Forms in Canada

In a series of essays, Dorothy Smith (1977, 1979b, 1983b) traces changing forms of property ownership associated with the development of capitalism in Canada. She examines how these changes transformed relations between women and men in the home. During the early homesteading period, she argues, a husband and wife shared all property. They depended on each other and worked together to produce everything they needed to survive. There was no separation between domestic and productive work. Men cleared and ploughed land for crops while women maintained gardens, kept chickens, pigs, and cows, helped in the harvest, and preserved the food. Women owned not only what they produced, but also whatever money they could make by selling surplus vegetables, eggs, and butter in the market. Thus, a basic economic and social equality existed between wife and husband.

This equality changed in a subtle but significant way with the transition from subsistence homesteading to cash production. Land speculation led to escalating prices, and settlers required heavy mortgages to buy land and equipment. This meant that they were no longer merely producing food for the subsistence needs of their families. Their survival depended on producing cash crops like wheat from which to earn the money to pay bank loans. Laws of property, debt, and credit endowed only the husband with full economic status in a marriage. Land was held as collateral for loans and mortgages made to him. The result, suggests Smith, was drudgery and tyranny for farm wives, who were totally subordinated to their husbands. They laboured on the homesteads, but all their labour went to pay off bank loans. When the mortgage was finally paid off, the farm belonged legally only to the husband. Women owned nothing. All the results of their labour were appropriated by their husbands.

The powerlessness of farm wives was underlined by the Supreme Court of Canada decision in 1975 concerning Irene Murdoch. She had worked on the family farm for twenty-five years with her husband but, after their divorce, the court decreed that she had no legal right to any of the farm property. Women who worked with their husbands in other kinds of small business enterprises found themselves in essentially the same situation. They had no assurance of a share in the assets of a business to which they had contributed. It took a national outcry from women's organizations after the Murdoch decision to change the law to give women a share in marital property and family business.

As capitalism had advanced, the petite bourgeoisie—people who earn their living by means of family farms and family-run businesses—had declined. In the current era of corporate monopoly capitalism, the vast majority of Canadian families depend upon employment in large corporations and state bureaucracies. This dependence on wages and salaries from work done outside the home and beyond the control of family members has critical implications for the working lives of those adults who still remain within the home. Typically, men were the first to leave the home to work for wages. Women continued to do domestic work and care for children, but they were cut off from the productive enterprise. Production was no longer centred around the home but took place in factories to which they did not have access. Marxists argue that this historically specific change in the development of housewife and the model of the private family segregated from the occupational world. This is the same model that Parsons treats as a universal principle.

Marxist feminist theorists argue that women's work in the home remains crucial to the productive enterprise. The ties that bind homemakers to the corporations are less immediately visible than those binding employees but, nonetheless, almost all aspects of their working days are dictated by corporate demands. Women's labour within the home is appropriated by corporations in multiple ways, but this relation tends to be covered up by the misleading notion of the homemaker's work as a private service to her breadwinner husband. Smith argues that this "private service" by homemakers for their husbands and children may ultimately be responsible for holding together the entire system of capitalist relations of production. Smith rejects the simplistic version of Marxist theory that claims that class structure determines family structure. She insists that we must examine what people do in their everyday lives to produce the relations that we subsequently come to see as the class structure. Women's work in the home is an integral part of the processes through which class relations are produced and maintained on a daily basis. It is these work processes that we briefly explore below.

The Social Construction of Class Relations in the Home

Whether or not women work outside the home, they maintain the responsibility for homework. This responsibility and the ways in which women's homework is appropriated by capitalism vary with the social class or occupation of employed family members, which may include the women themselves. A working-class wife has to put a home together, often under conditions of poverty and inadequate housing. Her labour is vital in the struggle for some measure of comfort on a limited income. Her efforts make it possible for people to survive on incomes that may barely meet subsistence needs. Her fundamental work for the corporation is to keep her husband working under these conditions. Corporations

know well that married men make more stable workers than single men because of their responsibility to support their families. It is less easy for married men to leave if they do not like the working conditions. The working-class wife supports the capitalist system against her husband because she depends so heavily upon his wages to provide for herself and her children. She cannot let him quit. An unemployed man may commonly be punished by his wife, through nagging, criticism, and humiliation, to pressure him back into the work force.

Luxton (1980, ch. 3) describes with stark realism the harsh lives of women married to miners in the single-industry town of Flin Flon in northern Manitoba. The working lives of these housewives remain totally tied to the rhythms of their husbands' work. A housewife must get up long before the mine whistle goes, to get her husband up, fed, and ready for work, and she must be there to greet him with his dinner when he returns. When he is working shifts, she must alter her entire schedule to meet his and yet still maintain the school schedules of their children. She must keep the children quiet and out of the way when he is sleeping, do her housework only when it will not disturb him, provide meals when he wants them, and in effect manage the family so that he turns up regularly for work. In a sense, she is as much an employee of the mine as he is, but she does not get paid.

The appropriation of the labour of middle-class women by capitalism takes a different form. In material terms, their lives may be more comfortable and their homemaking responsibilities easier to meet than those of working-class housewives because they do not have to struggle against poverty. But the wives of men who hold managerial and executive positions within corporations may have less personal autonomy as they find themselves more trapped by the demands of the corporation. Smith (1977) argues that, while a working-class man has a job within a corporation, a man in a more senior rank plays a role for the corporation. He must meet the image of a corporation man, and it is his wife's duty to maintain this image and to mould their children to fit it. The family home becomes something of a subcontracted agency of the corporation. The housewife works to produce the image that the corporation wants. The image that is on display is largely set by the media and disseminated in glossy magazines and television advertising; the housewife herself has little control over it. It is subtly but rigidly enforced within the corporate hierarchy. An executive whose personal and family appearance does not conform to the corporate mould tends to be viewed with suspicion and overlooked for promotion.

Middle-class women routinely support the careers of their husbands by relieving them of household and child-care responsibilities. The corporate man is then free to display his undivided loyalty to the corporation by spending long hours of overtime at the office on evenings and weekends and travelling on business whenever requested. In the highly competitive corporate world, such behaviour is often essential for mobility up the corporate hierarchy. The support work that wives do often begins very early in men's corporate careers. A wife may work to support her husband through college. Subsequently, she may help his career by entertaining his business associates and doing unpaid secretarial work. The wife of a professor often helps with the research, sorting, and editing involved in writing, although the resulting work bears only his name. Corporations thus appropriate the labour time of the wives of their executives and professional staff through the support services that wives are routinely expected to provide for their husbands. The competence of wives, especially wives of executives, to perform these support roles can be so important that some corporations have insisted on interviewing not only the male applicants for senior positions, but their wives as well (Kanter 1977).

A middle-class homemaker further serves the corporation through absorbing the tensions generated by the career demands made on her husband. In this there is a catch-22; when she supports and repairs him and sends him back refreshed, she is in fact supporting the external system that oppresses him. But, like her working-class counterpart, she has little choice. To be a good homemaker, she must make her husband's success visible. She cannot afford to let him fail.

Corporations also appropriate the mothering work of middle-class women. Middle-class status is inherited not through property, but through careers, and mothering work is essential to this process. The academic streaming of children begins very early in the education process, and a mother who wants her children to succeed in future corporate careers must groom them even in infancy so that they will perform well from the first days of kindergarten. Her children's failure in school will be seen as evidence that she does not love them enough.

In times of economic recession, women's unpaid labour in the home absorbs the resulting social problems. As unemployment rises, women are disproportionately affected, laid off more frequently, and pushed into part-time work. They bear the increased burden of the emotional stress felt by workers who risk being unemployed or who may be squeezed out in corporate mergers. Women in the home must absorb the extra work no longer being done by professionals when social services are cut back for the elderly, the handicapped, and the sick. (Armstrong 1984, ch. 7).

In these multiple ways, homemakers work for the corporate capitalist system—work for which they receive no pay and rarely any acknowledgment. The enormity of their exploitation is hidden under the myth of private family life. Until the women's movement began to have some impact, all the work that women did in the home was not even identified as work. It was considered merely "a labour of love" (Luxton 1980).

Research in the Marxist feminist tradition has documented the processes through which relations of political economy intrude into the most intimate relations of love and marriage. Luxton's study of Flin Flon shows how courtship and marriage are affected by the economy of this single-industry mining town, in which there are few well-paying jobs for women. Marriage is the only viable option for adult women in the town. This reality pervades the dating game and sexual activities. Boys have the chance to earn good money working in the mine while girls do not. Girls therefore trade sexual favours for a good time and economic rewards. Boys pay for the date and expect, sooner rather than later, that the girl will "come across." This same dependency continues after marriage and is made all the more evident if pregnancy has forced a quick wedding. Both the woman and the man feel trapped by her dependence on his wages.

Luxton (1980, ch. 6) suggests that this economic reality is at the root of much domestic violence. She describes the explosive tensions that revolve around the fact that he earns the money and she spends it. Men who come home drained and exhausted from a day's work at the mine often feel they have a right to control the household because they are responsible for its subsistence. Many of the women whom Luxton interviewed described how they took the brunt of their husband's resentment against his job. One woman summed it up this way: "He puts up with shit every day at work and he only works because he has to support me and the kids. Weren't for us he'd be off trapping on his own—no boss" (Luxton 980, 70). Women blame themselves, feeling guilty for having induced male hostility and aggression by being a burden. Women absorb the tensions. In extreme cases they absorb violence and beatings. More commonly, they deny themselves even basic needs because they cannot escape the sense of guilt that they are spending "his" money on themselves. This is the reality that is glossed over in the abstract functionalist category of "tension management."

Such dependent relationships may only be marginally improved for most women who take up employment outside the home. Having their own income allows women some independence, but the reality is that few women can hope to earn enough to support themselves and their children above the poverty line. With the exception of a minority of professional women, a male wage is still essential to support an average middle-class family lifestyle.

In summary, Marxist feminists argue that family relations and domestic work are embedded in the political economy of corporate capitalism. Homemakers are agents of tension management and pattern maintenance for corporations, but their work is not acknowledged and not paid for. They remain outside the corporations and so cannot influence any of the decisions that direct their lives. Smith (1977) sees this as the root of depression and mental illness among women. Women are oppressed in a nameless way by a system from which they appear to be entirely separated and yet which comes to rule the most intimate aspects of their lives. This thesis avoids the monolithic and conservative biases evident in functionalist theory by analyzing family structures in their historical and class contexts. Family forms in Canada changed markedly with transformations in capitalism from early homesteading, through cash cropping and small business, to the current form of monopoly capitalism. The thesis also incorporates an analysis of the processes through which people socially construct the realities of family life in the situation in which they find themselves.

The Radical Feminist Critique: Capitalism or Patriarchy?

The **radical feminist** perspective shares with Marxism an appreciation of the impact of capitalism on family life, but challenges the narrow, deterministic focus on political economy as the cause of family structures. These theorists argue that this tunnel vision of traditional Marxists gives inadequate attention to relations of

patriarchy or gender hierarchy that cannot be subsumed under capitalism. In particular, they challenge the more deterministic version of Marxist theory, sometimes referred to as Marxist structuralism, that explains family structures by reference to their functions for the capitalist system.

Marxists would argue, for example, that the privatization of women in the home occurs because it is functional for capitalism (Armstrong and Armstrong 1985). Capitalism is based on free wage-labour that requires the separation of a public, commodity-production unit from a private subsistence unit in which free labourers are reproduced and maintained. Hence the subordination of women appears to be a necessary condition for the capitalist system. Structuralist Marxists also describe the position of women as a reserve army of labour, which can be stored cheaply within the home, as necessary for the capitalist system. The implications of this thesis are that the **privatization** of women was not evident in the precapitalist era. It arose with capitalism and will decline with the transition to socialism.

Radical feminists argue that the evidence does not support this thesis. In precapitalist Europe, the economy may have centred around domestic production in which women were involved, but this did not ensure gender equality, either in family practice or in religious and social ideologies. In many parts of contemporary Asia, in both Hindu and Muslim cultures, the traditions of **purdah**, which include an emphasis on the extreme subjugation and segregation of women within the home, still persist. The origins of the purdah system long predate the emergence of capitalism. If anything, this extreme privatization of women has begun to break down under capitalism, as more women gain access to education and professional employment outside the home.

The Marxist thesis shows how capitalism accommodates and uses existing inequalities between women and men in the household, but this is not sufficient to explain why such inequalities developed in the first place or why they persist (Miles 1985). We still need to explain why capitalism developed in such a way as to bolster men's power over women. We need to explain why the sexual division of labour appears as it does. Why is it, almost invariably, women and not men who are engaged in unpaid domestic labour? Marx tends to treat this as the biological nature of things, but it is by no means biologically determined that women must do the domestic work beyond the actual physical acts of giving birth and breast-feeding. Why is it mostly women who bear the double burden of domestic work and a paid job? Why do husbands continue to do so little domestic work in comparison with their wives, even when wives are employed full-time? Why is it that the issue of whether a wife should be employed takes on the connotations of a threat to male power and status? Reference to the needs of capitalism does not seem to explain this. Marxist theory would actually predict the opposite response, that men would generally welcome any reduction in the economic burden of a dependent wife.

The prevalence of domestic violence is also not adequately explained within the Marxist thesis. Economic dependence helps to explain the vulnerability of women to male power, but it does not explain why so many wives are battered in the first place (Miles 1985, 47). Nor does economic dependence account for other forms of male violence against women and children, such as rape, incest, and sexual harassment. It cannot explain practices such as burning widows alive on the funeral pyres of their husband, foot-binding, genital mutilation, and **dowry murders**, which are prevalent in some non-Western societies.

Radical feminists assert that Marxist theory describes but does not explain male supremacy inside and outside the home. The exploitation of workers under capitalism and the oppression of women by men are not equivalent concepts (Eisenstein 1979, 22). Relations of patriarchy have to be addressed directly. In trying to subsume issues of patriarchy under the blanket explanation of capitalism, Marxist theory functions as an ideology. It can serve to legitimate male domination over women by displacing responsibility onto the economy.

This misuse of Marxist theory was powerfully illustrated at a meeting of the Canadian Asian Studies Association in response to a paper describing women's oppression in Pakistan under President Zia's "Islamization" program (Rafiq 1988; Hale 1988b). Part of the paper referred to Islamic law concerning rape. A woman who claims she has been raped requires no less than four male witnesses, all of impeccable character, before she can press charges in court. Otherwise, her case will be dismissed, and she herself can be sentenced to public flogging for having engaged in unlawful sex. Men in the audience reinterpreted this paper in terms of the capitalist mode of production, debating how it was in the interests of the capitalist class to keep women at home as cheap labour. In this determinist, structuralist version of Marxism, the men who commit the violence disappear: it is the system that appears to do things. A woman's experience of being raped, with those who violate her not only immune to punishment, but able to have

her flogged for even mentioning what they had done to her, was excluded from the debate. It became trivialized as a form of false consciousness, while the concerns of men with their own class oppression took precedence. Radical feminist theory addresses this failure to analyse the oppression of women by placing the issue of patriarchy at the centre of sociology of the family.

The Roots of Male Power

O'Brien (1981) challenges the original thesis proposed by Engels that links male power and control over property. Engels argues that, with the development of settled agriculture and herding, men controlled the means of production and hence the wealth of society. Men sought control over women in order to ensure that their property would be inherited by their own biological children. Thus, the institution of monogamy for women became important. O'Brien suggests that this thesis has too many unquestioned assumptions. Why did men gain control over property in the first place? Why did it have to be inherited through the male line? Why did it have to be inherited individually rather than by the community as a whole? Among the **matrilineal** Nayar in South India, land and animals were communally owned by the mother's joint family and inherited by her children. Men did not have the right to own or to dispose of such property. Why and how did men come to wrest control from the original matriarchal communal families?

O'Brien proposes that the basic causal relationship between control over property and control over women's sexuality should be reversed. Men, she suggests, seek to control property in order to control women's sexual and reproductive powers, not the other way around. The material base of the gender hierarchy is the means of reproduction of children rather than production of material goods. When a woman has sexual freedom, a man has no way of knowing which, if any, of her children he fathered. Paternity is reduced to an abstract idea. O'Brien argues that male alienation from birth, and thus from human continuity through children, is profound. This alienation can only be partially overcome by the institution of monogamy, through which a man asserts an exclusive right of sexual access to a particular woman.

Male power over women is not automatic, but is the result of continual struggle, in which final victory is impossible. Men can struggle to control women, but it is women who control reproduction. Male control over a woman's reproductive powers, and hence male appropriation of her children as his own, is always uncertain.

It depends upon absolute faith in her chastity or upon the strictest possible control over her, including her seclusion from other men. It depends also on trust in other men. But such trust is tenuous, especially in the context of war, competition, and hierarchical divisions among men. Male dominance over other men in war is often expressed through sexual violation of the women "belonging" to the enemy.

O'Brien situates the origin of the private family, and the split between the private realm of women and the public realm of men, in this male struggle for exclusive sexual access to women, rather than in the development of capitalism. The economic dependence of women on men and the inability of women to support themselves and their children apart from a man are essential mechanisms for male control over women. The inheritance of property from father to son is also of paramount importance in the social assertion of the principle of paternity over biological maternity. Male control over property and inheritance thus remains central in O'Brien's thesis, but for different reasons than Engels proposes.

The major difference between the two formulations becomes evident in predicting the behaviour of males who own no property. Engels predicts that when men have no property to control or to transmit to children, they will have no interest in controlling women. O'Brien predicts that such men will still try to control women's sexual and reproductive powers through any other means at their disposal, including sexual violence.

The history of the mother-centred Nayar households gives insight into the nature of the struggle for control over family property and women's reproductive powers. The Nayar family organization did not disappear as an inevitable result of developments in agriculture industrialization. It was deliberately and systematically undermined by the British Imperial government in India.

The British passed a series of laws between 1868 and 1933 that broke up the matrilineal households and imposed a monogamous, maleheaded marriage system. The first law held that a man had to provide for his wife and children, a law that had no meaning in the Nayar situation. The next law declared that the wife and children had the right of maintenance by the husband. Again this had little effect because the Nayar did not register marriages. Then followed various Nayar Regulation Laws that decreed that the brief ceremony that took place when a girl reached puberty constituted a legal marriage that could only be dissolved through a legal divorce. The man gained the right to inherit the property of his wife rather than sharing in the communal property of his mother's household. Further laws declared that all property held in common in the matrilineal household could be broken up and inherited and that a man's heirs were no longer his sister's children but his wife's children. The laws were part of a long struggle for supremacy between men and women within the Nayar communities, and they are still bitterly resented and resisted by the Nayar women. Males gained the advantage under the British, both through the laws and through access to an English education, which enabled men but not women to obtain administrative posts in the British colonial service. Men thereby gained personal income and economic independence from the communal household, and they were granted the legal right to dispose of this private property as they wished (Liddle and Joshi 1986, 28–29).

In Canada, male power over women and property was similarly imposed through patriarchal laws. It was not the inevitable outcome of capitalist farming that dispossessed women homesteaders, but specific laws that required a man to have single, unencumbered title to real estate for it to stand as collateral for mortgages and loans. It was only after the Irene Murdoch case in 1975 that these laws were revised to permit and subsequently to require joint ownership by husband and wife of family property used as collateral. Native women were dispossessed by the British North America Act which decreed that any Native woman who married a non-Native forfeited all her rights to Native status and to band property. It was 1984 before this law was changed, and then only after it had been challenged before the World Court.

Given that ownership of property is such an important mechanism in male control over the sexual and reproductive powers of women, it follows that women's paid employment outside the home threatens that control. Radical feminist theory argues that men fear the expansion of income-earning opportunities for their wives, even though this relieves them of the economic burden of a dependent family. The theory predicts that men will strive to minimize the level of economic independence and also that they will strive to reassert control through other mechanisms including domestic violence and medical and legal control over reproduction.

Limits to Economic Freedom for Women

Liddle and Joshi (1986, part IV) argue that class hierarchy in the labour force is built upon and reinforces gender hierarchy. Women are employed but predominantly within low-paid job ghettos. Their incomes supplement their husbands' earnings but do not supercede them. Few women earn sufficient money to provide for themselves and their children at an average standard of living. They still depend on a male wage earner.

The unequal division of domestic labour within the home is cited by Liddle and Joshi as a primary mechanism ensuring the continued economic and familial dominance of men. Even when women are employed in full-time jobs outside the home, they commonly bear almost the entire responsibility for domestic work. Men, by and large, refuse to do this work, or at best contribute only in the least onerous areas. Men appropriate women's labour in the home to restore their own energies. They return to work relaxed and refreshed, while women return to work exhausted from doing three jobs: domestic work, child care, and the work for which they are paid. Then women are penalized in the labour market for having less strength and energy and making slower career progress than men.

Child care outside the home is limited and expensive, so that only women who earn above-average incomes can afford it. The majority of women are faced with the choice of taking long periods of time out of the paid

Few women earn enough money to support themselves and their children.

labour force to care for young children or of working themselves to exhaustion trying to do everything. Women who take such time out, or who begin to develop a career only in their late thirties or early forties, present no competition to men who are far advanced in their positions.

This inequality in the labour force stemming from women's responsibility for domestic work becomes apparent whenever marriages break down. Wives are legally entitled to an equitable share in family property, but husbands take their income-earning capacity with them. All too often, women find themselves left with half a house, but without the income to maintain it.

This artificial separation between the realms of public and private, the world of men and world of women and children, creates its own dynamic that tends to reinforce male efforts to control and possess women. The public realm is associated with rational and technical concerns of production, and the private family with meeting emotional needs. Men come to depend on women in the home to meet their ongoing need for nurturing or mothering, in addition to their need for women to procreate and to nurture their children. This may be especially so in societies where men are discouraged from being nurturing themselves and where they spend their working lives in a public realm, which is characterized by competitive, fragmented, impersonal, and emotionally neutral or nonaffective relationships. Long after children have been born and raised, men may still seek to possess women in order to ensure that their own nurturing needs are met. This need for personal nurturing may be so overwhelming for some men that they become jealous of their own children and the attention they are given by the nurturer-mother.

Domestic Violence

The threat and the reality of domestic violence, in all its forms, is another powerful mechanism for asserting male control over women and children. Until recently, wife beating had both religious and legal approval. The Roman Catholic law of chastisement enjoined a husband to beat his wife for her moral betterment. This injunction was carried over to British common law and Canadian and American law and only began to be challenged toward the end of the nineteenth century. Fathers were also endowed with the religious prescription and legal right to discipline their children using physical force.

In addition to physical battering, children are also victims of sexual abuse. Estimates of such abuse vary widely depending on the measurements used (Badgley

1984, 114). The rate most commonly cited is that one in five girls and one in ten boys have experienced unwanted sexual attention. Guessing rates by pitting the findings of different sources against each other is a largely futile exercise. But the fact that physical and sexual abuse of children occurs in a significant number of families is not in dispute. Why does such behaviour occur?

The Marxist thesis attributes the violence primarily to the frustration experienced by men who are employed or are trapped in low-paid, alienating jobs. Radical feminists dispute this explanation as inadequate to account for the extent of wife battery and incest. An American study (Shupe, Stacey, and Hazlewood 1987, 22–21) cites evidence that the social background of wife batterers in selected counseling sessions and police records mirrored the population at large with respect to age, education, race, ethnicity, religion, and occupation. The one exception was that the percentage of unemployed men among the batterers was double the national average. Unemployed men seem more likely to batter, perhaps because they have lost the economic basis of their control over their wives, but this does not alter the evidence that men from all strata of the population—including doctors, lawyers, politicians, ministers, and police officers—beat their wives. Similarly, many of the men who commit incest are "pillars of the community" in other respects.

Various psychological explanations have been put forward to account for wife battering. They include the common argument that it is a symptom of other emotional problems that can stem from trauma from abuse as a child, learned behaviour from watching an abusive father, lack of communication skills with the spouse, low self-esteem, lack of emotional controls, and the need to express repressed anger and frustration (Adams 1988). Radical feminists argue that such explanations only offer excuses for the batterer to continue the behaviour. They also do not account for why the batterer's behaviour is directed at his wife. Batterers rarely assault anyone other than their wives. They do not habitually lose emotional control or lack of communication skills in other contexts.

Radical feminists argue that one has to examine the practical gains that accrue to the batterer from his violence; that is, fear and submission in his victim and compliance with his wishes (Adams 1988; Ptacek 1988). Wife battering is essentially a controlling behaviour designed to create and maintain an imbalance of power in the household. Battery and sexual abuse of children are the extreme expressions of male assertion of property rights over women and children. Less extreme forms of such controlling behaviour include verbal and non-verbal intimidation and psychological abuse, pressure tactics like withholding financial support, accusations or threats of infidelity, ultimatums and deadlines that force a woman to comply with her husband's wishes (Adams 1988, 191–94). Such persistent humiliation can be pushed to the point where competent, professional women have their self-esteem destroyed (Forward and Torres 1987, 15–85).

Not all expressions of violence are by husbands

Government agencies provide some support for women who are the victims of abuse, but violence against women is deep-rooted in our society.

against wives. Some wives abuse their husbands, but it is currently impossible even to guess at the rate. It would appear that much of the violence directed by wives toward husbands is defensive or retaliatory. The relatively small number of unprovoked attacks on men by female partners seems often to involve jealous ex-wives and ex-girlfriends. Firestone (1971, ch. 6) suggests that many women are so intensely socialized to see their own self-worth in terms of being a sexual partner for a male that, when their relationship breaks down and the male begins to see another woman, their sense of self-worth and identity are shattered. Occasionally these feelings may turn to rage and hatred. Such responses, however, are not equivalent in form or intent to the systematic, repeated brutality that constitutes wife battering. While it may be true that much abuse experienced by husbands goes unreported, the same is true of abused wives. We do know that the overwhelming majority of people who are injured in domestic violence are female. There is a vast body of evidence of systematic, severe, intimidating force used by men against women, while there is no such evidence for women against husbands (Dobash and Dobash 1988, 60–62).

The problems of wife battering and sexual abuse of children are very deep-rooted in our society. They reflect both the identification of masculine sexuality with aggression and the pervasive socialization of males to be aggressive. They also reflect the patriarchal structures of family life that accord authority, power, and control to the father figure. Such power carries with it the inherent risk of corruption. Thirdly, they highlight the emotional shallowness of relations among men, which leaves the family as the only source of human warmth and sensuality. But this source is itself constrained and distorted by the emphasis on exclusivity, possession, authority, and control. Wives and children bear the emotional brunt of these distorted relations.

Custody Battles: Shared Parenting or Patriarchal Control?

Divorce is a fact of life in Canadian society (see table 10-2), but its frequency does not lessen the traumatic effect on the parties involved. Divorce invariably means a significant drop in the income of single-parent families headed by women. Divorced fathers who do not want to pay child support face no effective pressure to do so. The default rate on court-ordered support payments has been estimated to be between 80 and 90 percent (Crean 1989, 20). While the court generally awards custody of children to mothers, about half the fathers who contest custody win their case, often in the face of evidence of minimal previous involvement in nurturing and despite evidence of physical or sexual abuse (Chesler 1991). Sexual abuse of children is difficult to prove, and mothers who raise the issue not only risk hav-

Table 10-2

Number of Divorces, Canada, 1950–91			
Year	Number of Divorces	Year	Number of Divorces
1950	5 386	1971	29 685
1951	5 270	1972	32 389
1952	5 650	1973	36 704
1953	6 160	1974	45 019
1954	5 923	1975	50 611
1955	6 053	1976	54 207
1956	6 002	1977	55 370
1957	6 688	1978	57 155
1958	6 279	1979	59 474
1959	6 543	1980	62 019
1960	6 980	1981	67 671
1961	6 563	1982	70 436
1962	6 768	1983	68 567
1963	7 686	1984	65 172
1964	8 623	1985	61 980
1965	8 974	1986	78 160
1966	10 239	1987	90 872
1967	11 165	1988	79 872
1968	11 343	1989	81 009
1969	26 093	1990	78 488
1970	29 775	1991	77 031

Source: Reproduced by authority of the Minister of Industry, 1994. Adapted from Statistics Canada (1994h), *Marriage and Conjugal Life in Canada,* Cat. 91-534E, table 18, p. 47.

ing their credibility challenged in court, but jeopardize their own custody claims by being labelled as an unfriendly parent who is trying to block rightful access by the father.

Custody battles over children and the demand for mandatory joint legal custody following divorce are forming a new arena of struggle between principles of feminism and patriarchy. Of particular concern to feminists are the threatening implications of seemingly progressive legislation aimed at ensuring the rights of divorced fathers in relation to their children. Mandatory joint custody legislation was passed in thirty-six American states between 1980 and 1988.

Across Canada, joint custody is an option but not a presumption. The Ontario Divorce Act of 1985 closely parallels the Ontario Children's Law Reform Act which states that the courts may award custody or access to one or more persons, but without any policy legislation favouring joint or sole custody. In each case "the best interests of the child" are paramount. A private member's bill introduced in the Ontario legislature in January 1988 sought to commit the province to mandatory joint custody, but the bill was not passed. Opponents emphasized the distinction between shared parenting and joint legal custody.

Medical and Legal Control over Reproduction

The struggle for control over women's reproductive power continues in the public arenas of medicine and law. In Canada, the medical profession has almost entirely succeeded in wresting technical control over childbirth from women (Burtch 1988). Formerly, O'Brien suggests (1981, 10), childbirth was an affirmation of sisterhood, a rite shared by the mother-to-be, the midwife, and other women friends who attended the birth in the community. However, as a government-financed health-care system developed, and as the traditional healing arts were professionalized and institutionalized, midwives were shut out. It became normal for childbirth to take place in an antiseptic hospital delivery room under the control of predominantly male obstetricians. Until very recently, it was normal for the mother to be drugged into semiconsciousness, her feet tied up in stirrups, while the baby was pulled out with forceps. While some accuse feminists of romanticizing simpler childbirths, feminists insist that the issue is male supremacy or, specifically, the supremacy of male doctors over mothers and midwives. Available evidence indicates that the mortality rate for home births with a midwife is as low or lower than physician-attended births in hospitals. Yet medical control remained absolute. Midwifery did not die out in Canada but it had no legal status. Women who attended home births could face criminal charges, especially if the newborn died. By law, a doctor had to be in attendance at a birth. As recently as April 1989, a Montreal doctor was suspended for six months for letting a midwife deliver the baby of one of his patients, without him being in the room.

Only in the 1990s has this control over birth by the medical profession begun to weaken, partly in response to pressure from the women's movement, and partly to cut medical costs. The province of Ontario led the way in 1986 with a decision to establish midwifery as a self-regulated profession. Five years later, the Midwifery Act was proclaimed, permitting midwives to work on maternity wards. On January 1, 1994, midwives were granted the right to admit women to hospital, deliver babies, and send them home, without consulting a doctor (*Globe and Mail,* 14 May 1994). In 1994, Quebec passed legislation approving midwifery in eight free-standing birthing centres but they met fierce opposition from doctors because they are not based in hospitals. By 1994, only one centre was still operating.

Recent developments in reproductive technology, including test-tube babies, embryo transplants, surrogate motherhood, and assisted insemination, further this process of control over birth by predominantly male scientists. The medico-scientific takeover of birth is being

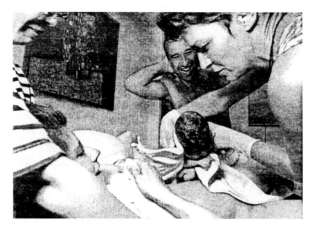

Midwives can now deliver babies in Ontario, allowing women to take back some medical control over childbirth.

combined with increasing legislative controls over the lives of pregnant women. Court-ordered stays in hospital and cesarean sections against the mother's will have already occurred in Canada (*Globe and Mail,* 1 Aug. 1986, D1–2). A Vancouver lawyer hired to fight one such case commented that one should not underestimate the male fixation on having the perfect son and heir, or what a man might do if a woman pregnant with his child was perceived to be disobeying orders that related to having that perfect baby. The desperation of some men to find a **surrogate mother** for artificial insemination with their sperm, and the amount they are prepared to pay for this service (around $15 000 U.S. plus expenses), underline how important biological reproduction is to many men.

The Canadian Royal Commission on New Reproductive Technologies, which issued its formal report in December of 1993, came out strongly against the commercialization of any aspect of human reproduction, including the sale of sperm or fetal tissue. The report also stressed the importance of a pregnant woman's autonomy and right to bodily integrity. It opposed any judicial intervention in pregnancy, favouring voluntary care and assistance to pregnant women instead (Canada, Royal Commission on New Reproductive Technologies 1993, 24). However, the Commission also favoured the establishment of a federal regulatory and licensing body for reproductive technology, and proposed strict limits on the availability of treatment that is still considered experimental. It recommended that in-vitro fertilization technology for preconception arrangements, for post-menopausal women, and for profit should be banned. Commercial fertilization clinics would also be banned. If such recommendations are adopted, women's choices would remain tightly controlled by professional decision-makers with all other commercial avenues for treatment blocked within Canada.

The Abortion Debate: Pro-life or Pro-patriarchy?

The abortion issue is at the centre of the political struggle surrounding reproductive rights in Canada and the United States. In January 1988 the Supreme Court of Canada struck down Canada's existing abortion law as unconstitutional because it was being applied in an arbitrary and discriminatory manner. There were huge geographic disparities in accessibility, and women experienced long and sometimes dangerous delays in having abortions approved. The Supreme Court decision added fuel to the political struggle between the opposing forces.

New legislation on abortion proposed by the Mulroney government in 1989 marginally passed a House of Commons vote but was defeated in the senate on 31 January 1991. Since then Canada has had no legislation governing abortions. The Medical Services Act of Nova Scotia, which prohibited the performance of abortions outside of hospitals, was also struck down in October of 1990. The Morgentaler abortion clinic in Halifax was thus declared lawful. In the summer of 1994, Morgentaler challenged a similar law in New Brunswick by opening a free-standing abortion clinic in Fredericton. Another clinic is planned for Prince Edward Island, the only province in which no abortions are available, even in hospitals. The struggle continues around whether Medicare will cover the cost of abortions performed in clinics.

The issue of a woman's right to an abortion never seems to be settled once and for all. Physicians who are known to perform abortions continue to have their careers and their lives threatened by anti-abortion activists. On the surface, the anti-abortion lobby speaks to a humanistic concern for the sanctity of human life and a reluctance to kill that potential life for motives of convenience. But opponents of the lobby fear that the "pro-life" label obscures a political agenda that is fiercely antifeminist (Eichler 1985b; Dubinsky 1985). In principle, Eichler argues, the pro-life stand should be consistent with supporting every effort to minimize unwanted pregnancies and to maximize all forms of social support that would encourage pregnant women to keep their babies. But, in practice, the lobby groups fighting hardest to have abortion declared illegal are publicly against most of the policies intended to help women with children.

The anti-abortion movement in the United States campaigned strenuously to bring about the defeat of the Equal Rights Amendment, which would have prohibited discrimination on the basis of sex (Eisenstein 1984). They actively opposed welfare payments to mothers, public day-care programs, and **affirmative action** policies to promote employment for women. A similar lobby group in Canada, REAL women (Realistic Equal Active for Life), is anti-abortion and is also against welfare and against enshrining equality provisions for women in the Charter of Rights and Freedoms. The REAL women platform opposes abortion under all circumstances; opposes the contraceptive pill as suppressing maternal instincts; opposes sex education in schools as inciting immorality; opposes welfare and public day-care as undermining family responsibilities; opposes affirmative action for women in employment because this creates competition with male breadwinners; opposes feminist counsellors in homes for battered women because they advocate the breakup of the family; opposes the National Action Committee on the Status of Women as antifamily and antihousewife; and favours the right of a woman to be a full-time homemaker and the obligation of her husband to support her.

This agenda is a clear example of the politics of the "New Right." At the root of the New Right political agenda is a concern with the preservation of the traditional patriarchal family form, centred around the private family home. Women perform the expressive roles of full-time homemaker, mother, and nurturer of the family members, while men are responsible for public instrumental roles as providers. Policies to promote women's employment, state welfare, and public day-care are all seen as threatening such families by relieving men of their primary provider role. To the extent that women's domestic work and men's family responsibilities ensure a cheaply maintained, rested, committed, and stable work force, such policies also threaten capitalist interests. The New Right fears that contraception and abortion rights trivialize the mother role, reduce male commitment or obligation to support mothers and children, and hence undercut the social foundations of a stable family and work force.

The clash between New Right politics and feminism essentially revolves around the different views of the ideal family. Conservatives frequently claim that feminism leads to the breakdown of the family. The family they have in mind is the traditional patriarchal form that ensures male authority and female domesticity and dependence. The feminist movement advocates a very different form based on a consensual and egalitarian union that maximizes freedom of choice in the division of roles and responsibilities between spouses.

The National Action Committee on the Status of Women (NAC) is an umbrella organization that represents a broad range of feminist concerns. Its policy platform challenges the economic exploitation of women in the home and in the labour force and challenges the mechanisms of male oppression of women through economic dependence, the domestic burden, family violence, and medico-legal controls over women's reproductive freedom. Specific policies favoured by NAC include affirmative action in employment, universal, affordable child care, transition houses for battered women, income support for women and children to escape the dependency that makes women vulnerable to domestic violence, and protection of women's reproductive choice through safer and more effective contraception, maximum support services for pregnant women, and abortion as a back-up. In this context, abortion rights symbolize the inviolable right of women to control their own reproductive power.

The vision of family at the root of the feminist political agenda is a consensual union between equal partners, free from relations of dependency and without any forced sex-role division of labour between private and public, expressive and instrumental tasks. This vision of family equality presupposes a transformation in the position of women in the labour force and in the ways in which work time is organized. The feminist platform shares with the nascent men's liberation movement a belief that the alienation of men from children can be overcome not through possession of women and children, but through participation as equals in the nurturing process. If men as parents are to assume equal responsibilities with women for domestic and child-care work,

then the ways in which men as workers are exploited by capitalism will also have to be transformed.

The abortion debate has become a focal point for struggle around these two very different conceptions of family. Both sides claim to be defending the true interests of women and children. Eisenstein (1984, ch. 7) suggests that the New Right political agenda appeals to many women because it addresses their real material conditions in a patriarchal and capitalist society. The reality is that the mass of women with children are dependent on male breadwinners for their survival. The women's movement, combined with developments in capitalism, has widened opportunities for women beyond traditional domestic roles, but this opportunity is largely illusory. Women predominate in low-paid job ghettos. Rising divorce rates mean that many women must struggle in abject poverty as single parents. The superwoman image of professionals who manage to combine careers and domestic and child-care responsibilities has limited appeal for women who already feel overburdened. Feminism threatens their security without being able to bring about the radical social and economic change needed to provide women with real alternatives.

The Limitations of Radical Feminism

The weakness of radical feminist analysis of family life stems from its overly narrow focus. The perspective has drawn attention to widespread and serious problems of violence and abuse within families, which have been overlooked or downplayed by other approaches. But radical feminist research also tends to overstate the case for patriarchy to the extent that the abnormal becomes the norm. Some sources speculate, for example, that as many as one girl in two and one boy in three are victims of incest, an estimate that encompasses virtually every family in Canada. When concepts are pushed to this extreme, it becomes impossible to make distinctions between different experiences of family life. Radical feminism runs the risk of generating its own form of monolithic bias.

We know that, however pervasive the hidden problems might be, not all people experience family life as abusive. Most people do get married, and most of those who get divorced subsequently remarry. The majority of women and men thus appear to find marriage worth the struggle, or at least feel that it is more rewarding than living alone.

There is evidence of widespread changes in family roles. Husbands and fathers are increasingly getting involved in domestic work and in the nurturing of children, albeit generally not at the same level of responsibility as women. The combination of shorter working hours, free weekends, and changing conceptions of fatherhood means that children and fathers are more closely involved with each other than in the past. The real suffering of many fathers who are separated from their children by divorce cannot be subsumed under the blanket explanations of desire for revenge and legal control over their ex-wives.

The problem for radical feminist theory is to account for these different experiences. The pioneering work of feminist research into family violence means that we can no longer discount the 10 to 20 percent of families characterized by wife battery and other forms of abuse. But neither can we discount the majority of families where couples manage to establish mutually supportive relations and where children can look to both fathers and mothers for nurturance and emotional support. We need more research into the processes that account for this variation.

We are still far from understanding the factors that encourage egalitarian marriages and shared parenting as opposed to patriarchy and rigid role differentiation. Such analysis will need to take into account the context of political economy and the processes that exploit people and help to perpetuate role differentiation and yet simultaneously provide opportunities for women to be financially independent. The analysis will also need to take into account the emotional stress generated by patriarchal family forms and the evidence that men who abuse wives and children were commonly abused themselves when young. Abuse may generate the emotional insecurity that finds expression in the drive for domination and possession in marriage. From this perspective, patriarchy appears less as the expression of male power than of chronic insecurity, powerlessness, and fear. This remains speculation. Feminist theory has opened up the debate by focusing attention on issues that have been ignored by mainstream theories. But the research needed to explain the conflicting patterns of egalitarian and patriarchal families, and nurturing and abusive family relations, is still in its infancy.

Conclusion

Family life may be the most difficult area of sociology to study. It is so familiar and so emotionally charged that it is hard for us to distance ourselves from it. Sociological analysis has moved a long way from the original functionalist view that sex-role divisions within the nuclear family were natural, rational, and efficient adaptations to industrial society. But functionalist formulations still dominate most sociological textbooks. Monolithic, conservative, sexist, and microstructural biases in functionalist analysis of the family are being eliminated only with difficulty. Research in Marxist tradition shows how different family forms are embedded in economic relations that exploit both women and men and set constraints on their lives. Feminist theory reveals other aspects of the family as the central arena for the struggle between competing principles of gender equality and patriarchy. The processes that influence the outcome of these struggles are still far from understood.

Suggested Reading

An excellent source of statistical information on families in Canada is Margrit Eichler, *Families in Canada Today: Recent Changes and their Policy Consequences,* 2nd ed. (1988a). Eichler takes a very critical approach to traditional sociology of the family and provides quantities of data to back her argument that family life in Canada is diverse and rapidly changing.

For the functionalist perspective, a particularly useful source is the short text by William J. Goode, *The Family,* 2nd ed. (1982). He presents an easily readable account of the functions that families perform for the society as a whole.

For the Marxist feminist approach, an excellent book is Meg Luxton, *More than a Labour of Love* (1980). Luxton presents an indepth description of the lives of three generations of women in a small mining town in northern Manitoba. She conveys through the words of the women themselves how deeply their family lives are influenced by the economic reality of their dependence on male wages.

For a radical feminist perspective, an excellent source book is the collection of articles edited by Yllö and Bograd, *Feminist Perspectives on Wife Abuse* (1988). Articles here by Dobash and Dobash, Adams, and Saunders give insight into the experience of wife battery and the difficult problems of doing research and analysis in this area.

Questions

1. List four critical functions of family according to functionalist theory.

2. a) List two respects in which Nayar family form deviates from the functionalist view of universal family form.

   b) How does functionalist theory typically discount this deviation?

   c) How does feminist theory challenge the functionalist account of the collapse of Nayar family form?

3. What procedure or methodology does Eichler recommend to avoid "monolithic" bias in research on family life?

4. Regarding conservative bias, what two critical factors are commonly cited as radically altering family structure?

5. What functionalist bias is particularly addressed by Marxist theory of family?

6. What single factor is seen by Engels as accounting for monogamy for women?

7. According to Engels, what two conditions are necessary to eliminate inequality within families?

8. In Smith's historical survey, why did women's farm labour change from equality to drudgery and tyranny under the capitalist mode of production?

9. List three ways in which the labour of middleclass homemakers can be seen as appropriated by corporations.

10. How is mothering-work implicated in ideological hegemony with respect to capitalism?

Stratification: Meritocracy as Ideology

Inequality is a pervasive feature of social life. It may be manifested in disparities in access to money and other material resources in the power to manipulate events in one's own interest, in the prestige enjoyed in relations with others, and in the overall quality of life. The extent of these disparities varies widely across societies. In an industrially advanced economy such as Canada's, very few people are so poor or disadvantaged that their physical survival is threatened by starvation or lack of rudimentary shelter and sanitation. Yet, as we have seen in earlier chapters, Canada does have a visible and growing underclass of homeless and destitute people who rely on food banks and hostels for a meagre survival. At the other extreme, Canada has a class of super-rich, comprising mostly members of the corporate elite, some of whom rank among the richest people in the world.

Various forms of inequality commonly go together, suggesting that there are important causal relationships between them. Powerful people are often rich, command high prestige, and enjoy pleasurable, even luxurious, lifestyles. The poor are often powerless, scorned, and live in misery. Yet there is no inevitable association between these elements. Winning a lottery, for example, may bring wealth and leisure but not necessarily influence or prestige. A large income may not improve the quality of life if it is earned at the expense of chronic anxiety in the high-pressure corporate rat race. In terms of influence, even poor people can exercise power, especially if they are politically united.

Societies vary greatly in the degree of opportunity for **mobility**; that is, the likelihood that people born poor may eventually become wealthy and influential or that people born rich may fall in status. Canadians tend to think of their society as relatively open, offering opportunities for mobility through individual effort and achievement. But we know that social position is very commonly inherited. Children tend to attain a similar social position to that of their parents or to move slightly upwards or downwards. Members of certain groups are disproportionately better or worse off than others. Children from white Anglo-Saxon Protestant (WASP) backgrounds have very different life chances on average than children of Native Indian or black parents. Why is this so?

Children of Native peoples have very different life chances than do children from WASP backgrounds.

The explanations for inequality offered by different sociological theories reveal core assumptions concerning the nature of social order. Traditional functionalism stresses individual merit. It posits that inequality reflects rewards for individual contributions to the functioning of society. Marxists stress the importance of control over critical means of production for accumulating wealth in industrial society. Variations in income among the mass of working people reflect the relative utility of different workers for the owners of capital. Interpretive theory looks within the grand schemes of functioning social systems, capitalism, and patriarchy to explore what people do in their everyday relations to produce the patterns of inequality that we subsequently perceive as merit, class, or gender hierarchies. Feminist theory focusses on disparities in wealth, power, prestige, and leisure between women and men, arguing that men, on average, are advantaged in all of these respects. These disparities reflect patriarchy, or the power of men over women, which is distinct from, although associated with, capitalism. These theoretical perspectives, and their relative strengths and limitations, are examined below.

Functionalist Theory: Stratification as Meritocracy

The traditional functionalist theory of **stratification** begins from the basic observation that no society is classless. There must be a universal necessity for such stratification. It must perform some function for the social system as a whole, a function so important that no society can do without it.

Davis and Moore (1945) provide one of the clearest functionalist explanations for why stratification occurs. Their central concern is with inequality of positions in society, not the characteristics of the individuals in those positions. The basic theoretical question is why roles themselves differ in prestige and rewards. They find the answer in the functional requirement of placing and motivating individuals in any social structure. A social system must distribute members into social positions and must instill in members the desire to perform the attached duties once in the position. This is a continuous challenge because people are constantly being born, aging, retiring, and dying. Competitive systems such as our own stress motives to achieve the positions; non-competitive systems, such as socialist societies, stress motives to perform the duties. Both systems, however, require motivation.

Roles differ enormously in the demands they place on people. If all roles were equally important, and everyone were able to do all of them, then placement would be no problem. However, some jobs are more agreeable, some serve more important social functions, some require more talent and training, and some require that duties be performed more diligently. Therefore, say Davis and Moore, a differential reward system is necessary. These differential inducements form part of the social order and produce stratification. Rewards may include sustenance and comfort provided by economic incentives; self-respect and ego development provided by prestige and power; and recreation and diversion made possible by more leisure time. These rewards are built into positions and constitute the rights that are related to the duties of the roles. Inequality is thus necessary, inevitable, and justifiable.

Two primary factors determine the relative rank of different positions: their importance for the society and the scarcity of personnel for the positions. Important jobs need sufficient rewards to ensure competent performance, but if such jobs are easily filled, great rewards will not be needed. Garbage collector and janitor, for example, are important jobs, but they are relatively easy to fill and so are not highly rewarded. On the other hand, important jobs that require both talent and long training must be well rewarded. No one would go through the training and do the work of a modern medical doctor, the argument goes, unless the position carried great material reward and prestige.

Variations among societies in the income received by the highest- and lowest-paid members are primarily explained by the degree of specialization of roles. Highly industrialized societies such as Canada have an immense variety of specialized occupations, each of them associated with small graduations in income and prestige. Simpler, less industrialized societies have a more limited range of occupations, which tend to require less specialized training. There are fewer gradations of income and prestige. The nature of functional emphasis—whether sacred or secular—also affects rewards. Industrialized societies place greater emphasis on science and technology than on religion, and so scientists and technicians get higher pay. In other societies where science is relatively undeveloped, religious leaders may have far greater influence, prestige, and material rewards than do scientists.

In summary, functionalists argue that stratification is justified on the basis of merit. The critical moral issue for functionalist theory is not equality of rewards, but rather equality of opportunity to compete for them. The true battle is over merit versus inherited advantage.

Critique of Functionalism

Equal Opportunity

Much of the research generated by the functionalist thesis of stratification has focussed on questions of social mobility and differential opportunities for access to positions that carry the highest rewards. Research in the sociology of education has cast doubts on the notion that rewards are based on merit. Tumin (1973) challenges the argument that only a limited amount of talent is available within a population to be trained in appropriate skills for important jobs. He maintains that stratification itself limits the talent pool. We can never know what talents are available among children born to impoverished and disprivileged homes when poverty so pervasively affects their relationship with the school system. Rich children have all the advantages and hence do better in school, get the credentials for better jobs, and in turn give advantages to their own children (see ch. 12).

Unequal distribution of motivation to succeed, so important to functionalist theory, is itself a direct product of stratification. Poverty breeds hopelessness. Imagination, curiosity, and aspiration are systematically blunted when children experience powerlessness and humiliation at first hand. It is hard to develop one's full potential under such conditions. The result is low credentials, poorly rewarded jobs, and another generation of children who are stunted and trapped in the poverty cycle.

The argument that conversion of talent into skills requires sacrifices during the training period, and hence merits rewards, again treats the effects of stratification as its cause. Poor families cannot afford to buy books and school supplies or to pay for dance or music lessons, and so on, without cutting back on food money. Poor families cannot afford to keep children in school after the minimum school-leaving age or to send them to university without great sacrifices. The expenses involved are not sacrifices for wealthy parents in the professions. Pay differentials between the unskilled work available at school-leaving age and the professional careers available to university graduates more than compensate students who defer the gratification of an early job. Tumin estimates that any loss of income is usually regained within seven to ten years of employment. After this, the lifetime earnings of graduates greatly surpass those of untrained people (see table 11-1).

Unequal Importance

The second pillar of the functionalist thesis on stratification is that the most important jobs in society must be the most rewarded, particularly when they require special skills. But, Tumin asks, how is importance to be

---

Table 11-1

Average Income of Full-year, Full-time Workers by Level of Education and Sex, 1991		
Education	Men	Women
Grade 0 to 8	$27 116	$18 138
Some secondary education	32 348	20 709
High-school graduation	33 583	23 265
Some postsecondary	35 845	24 891
Postsecondary diploma	37 887	26 951
University degree	56 522	40 537

Source: Reproduced by authority of the Minister of Industry, 1994. Statistics Canada (1994d), *Earnings of Men and Women*, Cat. 13-217, pp. 36–37.

measured? A typical answer is that importance is calculated in terms of a position's indispensability for society, but it is not difficult to find exceptions to this rule. Farming, for example, is important for survival in any society, and it requires skills that take a life-time to learn, but it is not well rewarded. In terms of industry, during wartime it proved easier to dispense with supervisors than to spare factory workers, but this relative indispensability is not translated into wages.

The real problem is conceptual. Relative importance is a value judgment that is inextricably tied to relative financial rewards. In other words, the argument is circular. Those jobs that are better paid tend to be regarded as more important, regardless of their actual contribution to society or the actual skill levels required for the work.

Women and Stratification

This kind of circularity is especially evident in relation to work habitually done by women. As a sex, women have lower social status than men, so that work identified as "women's work" tends to have low status. The skills and responsibilities involved in such work tend to be downplayed or ignored. Then the lower average earnings of women in the labour force are justified on the grounds that women are concentrated in low-status work. The circle is completed when women themselves internalize such evaluations of what they do, and the low pay associated with it, as justifying the lower status of women generally.

The most extreme example of these processes occurs in relation to homemaking. This is a critical, multi-dimensional job that, like farming, takes a lifetime to learn. But it goes unpaid and commands such low status that people habitually apologize for doing it. Up until recently, homemaking was not even defined as work.

Within the paid labour market generally, skills associated with women's work are undervalued and underpaid. Nursing, for example, is a high-stress, extremely important job that requires a great deal of responsibility. The survival and recovery time of patients often depend more upon the quality of nursing care than on intermittent doctors' visits. The job demands long hours, shift work, and advanced technical skills that require a university degree and years of practical experience. But one would never know this judging from the salary and status that nurses command.

On some university campuses, the starting salary for secretarial staff (virtually all women) is several dollars per hour below that for people who mow lawns (virtu-

ally all men). It would be very difficult to argue that lawn mowing is either more important or more highly skilled than the work that secretaries do. The skills of advanced clerical workers are commonly ignored by bureaucratic classification systems that characterize such work as routine delegated tasks.

Women and men might do virtually identical work, but the work done by women tends to be called by a different name and to command lower status and salaries than the work associated with men. Positions like seamstress versus tailor, or cook versus chef, readily come to mind. In Muslim countries, where the work of buying household supplies is habitually done by men, it is seen as requiring important decision-making authority. When the same work is habitually done by women, as in our society, it tends to be thought of as mundane routine.

Relative Scarcity of Personnel

The functionalist thesis claims that relative scarcity of personnel raises rewards. Jobs that are easily filled need not be paid well. Women who compete with each other for limited jobs in the traditional women's occupations know this well. Tumin (1973), however, points out that scarcity is often artificially constructed in order to protect incomes. For example, predominantly male unions have historically tried to bar women and immigrants from access to unionized jobs, arguing that these groups would lower wages. Women were also barred from entry

Historically, male unions took an active role to ensure that women were confined to low-paying, subordinate positions.

into universities and hence from any profession that required a university degree. Professions have commonly been in a position to restrict access through their control over accreditation.

First-year admissions into medical schools in Canada were sharply reduced in the early 1980s and again in 1993 to an overall cut of 14 percent (Ryten 1994). Also, in 1993 for the first time, the number of women enrolled in first-year medicine exceeded the number of men, reflecting a 29 percent drop in the number of men admitted since the early eighties. These limitations on enrolments have the approval both of provincial governments and physicians' lobby groups, but for different reasons. Provincial governments hope to reduce the "oversupply" of doctors suggested by some reports on medical personnel and thereby to save money on Medicare payments. Physicians, on the other hand, lobbied successfully for cuts in enrolments and for restrictions on the licensing of immigrant doctors in order to limit the number of physicians and thus ensure their continued high salaries. Medical associations can then pressure for a fee schedule increase on the grounds of doctors' stressful work and the long hours they put in. Women doctors are more willing to trade high incomes for shorter working hours in group practices, but the male-dominated profession seems unlikely to encourage this.

Another common practice in limiting access to positions is to raise the qualifications needed to get into a job, thus putting up hurdles to stifle competition from below. Jobs in business and management, for example, which even a decade ago only required high-school graduation, now increasingly require university degrees. This effectively blocks competition from those who have learned their skills from work experience but do not have paper credentials.

Motivation

The last pillar of the functionalist argument is that differential rewards, and hence stratification, are necessary in order to motivate people to fill the more demanding positions. These rewards include money or material goods, leisure, respect, and prestige. Tumin's challenge to this thesis is that there are other kinds of motivators that could achieve the same results. An important one is work satisfaction. Positions that require training are usually the most interesting and the least routine. Tumin questions whether such positions need high pay to attract candidates and to ensure competent job perform-

ance. Other motives for job performance include the sense of a job well done, prestige from a social duty performed well, or increased leisure hours if the work is particularly demanding or difficult. Women commonly flock to jobs that give them the same time off and holidays as the schools so that they can cope with the extra work and responsibility of having children at home and not have to face the major expense of day-care.

Another question is whether money is, in fact, entirely effective as an **extrinsic reward**. In capitalist society, money is emphasized but people attracted by high salaries are just as likely to peddle their services elsewhere to the highest bidder. High salaries do not command loyalty. Senior executives, on average, remain only about four years with any one firm. There is an old joke about people in politics: they are the best politicians money can buy. The question is whether people who can be bought with money actually do make good politicians or good anything else.

In summary, Tumin's critique points to the fallacies of unity, indispensability, and universal functionalism. Disparities in material rewards may be demonstrably valuable for certain sectors of society, but they can simultaneously be damaging for others. Large differences in income may be useful for motivating people, but they are not indispensable. People can and frequently do commit themselves to doing important work out of a sense of responsibility for others, or for the pleasure and excitement of the work, without demanding high incomes in return. Many persisting differences in prestige, wealth, and power do not serve useful functions for society at all. Functional importance of different positions is a value judgment. Stratification itself limits talent and restricts educational opportunities while other techniques restrict access and cause scarcity to drive up incomes. Training for skilled jobs either is not, or need not be, a sacrifice. People can be motivated to fill positions on the basis of intrinsic job satisfactions and the prestige of the office, without gross inequalities in standards of living.

Marxist Theory: Inequality as Class Exploitation

Marxists agree with traditional functionalists that stratification does perform very important societal functions, but they argue that these functions specifically help to perpetuate capitalism as an economic system. The central Marxist argument is that stratification functions to preserve a system of expropriation of wage labour from the mass of people. Profits from this expropriation accrue to an elite minority of owners of capital. Stratification is at the same time profoundly functional for capitalists and dysfunctional for the interests of the majority of people who must sell their labour. This perspective rejects the **meritocracy thesis** as an ideological distortion that, rather than questioning the structure of the system within which people are forced to compete, blames the individuals who do not get to the top of the reward system.

The Structure of Unequal Opportunities

Marxist analysis begins from the premise that because of the structured inequality of positions in society there is no possibility of equality of opportunity for the masses. A simplified model of a social system illustrates the problem (Himelfarb and Richardson 1979, 174). Assume a perfectly closed society in which there are 1000 positions, 10 percent of which are elite and the remaining 90 percent ordinary. Then assume that each of these 1000 role incumbents has one child. What will happen to these children as they come to take over from their parents? In a society based absolutely upon inherited advantage, the 100 elite children will take over from the 100 elite parents, with no elite positions left for anyone else. The 900 children of people in the ordinary jobs will remain at the same level.

What will happen in the opposite case, where there is no inherited advantage and everyone has an equal chance to get an elite job? Only 10 percent of all positions, or 100 jobs are elite. With perfect equality, 10 percent of elite children, or 10 children, will get elite positions and the rest will have ordinary jobs. Ten percent, or 90 of the 900 ordinary children will get remaining elite positions, with the other 810, or 90 percent, remaining where they are. It is clear that, when there are few really good or elite positions to be had, it makes little practical difference to the masses whether they are filled by inherited advantage or absolute equality. Most people will not get such positions in either case.

Any real change in opportunity for ordinary people will require a change in the structure of positions so that there are many more good jobs to be had. After World War II there were huge increases in the United States in middle-class technical, managerial, and white-collar jobs, as well as pink-collar jobs for women. This expansion is the root of the American Dream, the myth that anyone can achieve upward mobility if they have enough drive and talent. After the war, children whose parents had struggled through the Great Depression found that there were many more well-paying jobs to be had. Children from elite homes enjoyed their usual advantage, but there were still many good positions opening up for others. Subsequently the picture changed. With recession came widespread unemployment and cutbacks in the economy. Fewer jobs meant that more children would not get positions equal to those of their parents, no matter how hard they tried. The structure of the job market and the distribution of wealth have to change in order to turn this around.

How does capitalism as a system function to give rise to the structure of the job market? This structure is largely treated as a given within traditional functionalist theory, so that the only question of interest is why existing jobs are rewarded differently. But for Marxists, the changing pattern of the job market itself requires explanation. Bowles and Gintis (1976, 10) insist that capitalist production is not simply a technical process, but is also a social process in which the central problem for employers is to maintain a set of social relations and organizational forms that will enable them to exploit wage-labourers to extract a profit. The objective of the system is to get the most production for the least wages; that is, to get workers to produce commodities of greater market value than the wages that they receive. Extremes of wealth and poverty are necessarily built into how this system works, and individual differences in abilities or effort count for little.

The problem for capitalism as a system is how to prevent revolt. Marxists ask how it is possible to maintain an inegalitarian system in relative equilibrium. What are the mechanisms that minimize the risk of workers forming coalitions to drive up wages or to wrest direct control over the means of production for themselves? The stability of the capitalist system is by no means assured. It has to be actively worked at.

Credentialism as Ideology

An important component assuring the stability of capitalism is force. Capitalists have the power to hire and fire people, and they can also call upon coercive laws to keep labour in line and to weaken unions. But naked force is itself inherently unstable in that it generates hostility and revolt. What is essential to the long-term stability of the system is that workers themselves come to accept the inequalities as just, or at least as inevitable, and therefore become resigned to them, even if they do not actively support them. The system of stratification or differential prestige ranking among workers serves this function, particularly when it is bolstered by the meritocratic ideology of traditional functionalism.

The stratification system, suggests Bowles and Gintis (1976, 81–85), is a direct reflection of capitalist policies of **divide and rule**. Its function is to fragment workers. In its cruder form, ascriptive criteria of race, ethnicity, and sex are manipulated to justify differential rewards. In the United States, older white males, particularly WASPs, are favoured for supervisory positions while immigrants, blacks, and women are given low-paid subordinate jobs. Those in superior positions are encouraged to see themselves as coming from better stock, while subordinates internalize their relative inferiority. The risk of coalitions to form a united front against capitalist employers is thus minimized.

Now that such ascriptive criteria are becoming increasingly discredited as a basis for legitimating inequalities, **credentialism** has come to take their place. This is precisely the meritocratic thesis of functionalism. Marxists agree that motivating people to strive for higher credentials does indeed perform an important function for capitalist society, but it is that of justifying inequality. People with different credentials readily come to see themselves as meriting different rewards. This effectively fragments wage-labourers and lessens the possibility of revolt. Those with relatively low credentials come to see themselves as meriting only limited rewards. Bowles and Gintis (1976, 81) argue forcefully that this is not merely a side effect of stratification but is its primary and intended purpose. Capitalists, they argue, will accede to higher wages for certain groups only when this increases social distance between groups of workers and strengthens capitalist control. Capitalists need to cement the loyalty of supervisors to the organization rather than to workers. Hence managers receive higher pay and privileges, regardless of relative scarcity of personnel.

It is important to recognize that Marxism reverses the cause-and-effect relation between credentials and rewards accepted by traditional functionalists. Functionalists, as we saw above, argue that certain jobs need people with higher skills and credentials. Since these people are in relatively scarce supply, the function of higher pay is to attract them to these difficult and important jobs. Marxists argue the reverse. Capitalism requires that workers be fragmented and stratified in order to minimize the risk of coalitions to challenge the controlling position of the capitalist class. Therefore, largely irrelevant criteria, such as race, ethnicity, sex, and credentials, are used as excuses to reward people differently and so divide them from each other. The function of focussing on credentials is to divide and rule workers by artificially stratifying them.

This is such a turn-around from how we are accustomed to think about credentials and rewards that it deserves further scrutiny. Bowles and Gintis categorically deny that schooling and credentials are actually needed for most jobs that currently demand them. True, there has been an explosion in public education in North America in recent decades, with ever-greater proportions of young people completing high school and seeking postsecondary education. True, on average, there is a **linear relation** between years of formal schooling and economic rewards: the more schooling, the more pay. But, this is not due to any essential requirement that better-paid jobs be filled by people with higher abilities. If such were the case, one would expect a very high correlation between measured intelligence and economic success. We do not find this. When measured intelligence and academic ability are controlled, the relation between years of schooling and pay remains virtually unaltered. It seems to be the piece of paper that counts, not the ability level (Bowles and Gintis 1976, 107).

The history of the Ontario Public School system offers a classic illustration of the triumph of credentialism over work experience (Casin 1992). At the time when individual schools were consolidated into school districts, women predominated as both rural and primary school teachers. Most of them had graduated from high school and had two years of Normal School training. After consolidation, a new credential structure deemed that university studies in specific subjects were more important than experience for salary and promotion. Teachers with the most experience, predominantly women, were placed at the bottom of the teaching hierarchy. During times of retrenchment in the 1930s and 1970s, teachers with secondary school certification in specific subject areas, mostly men, were granted access to teaching positions in primary schools even though they had no experience or training in primary-level teaching. They coped in large measure because women teachers on the job taught them everything they knew. Conversely, primary school teachers were barred from applying for positions in secondary schools, no matter how experienced they were, if they lacked the formal subject-area credentials.

The Deskilling of Work

Further support for the argument that the function of the growing emphasis on credentials is to fragment workers rather than to meet essential job requirements is that there is little evidence of any major increase in the complexity of jobs in advanced capitalist societies. If anything, the process seems to be working in reverse. Once-skilled jobs are being systematically **deskilled**; that is, they are broken down into simple component operations that can be easily learned. This process has been going on for a long time, dating back at least to the era of **Taylorism**, or **scientific management**, in the last decades of the nineteenth century (Braverman 1974, ch. 4). The expressed goal of Taylor's time-and-motion studies was to break the power that skilled craftsmen wielded through their control over knowledge of the work process. Work was minutely analysed and broken down into component parts, each of which could be assigned to a different worker. Only the boss retained knowledge of the whole process. Taylorism served two functions for capitalism. It fragmented workers and cheapened labour costs. Employers thus deliberately created the mass of repetitive and unskilled jobs that traditional functionalists point to as deserving only low pay and low prestige.

Braverman argues that this deskilling process has continued unabated, with more and more skilled and even professional occupations being degraded into fragmented, repetitive tasks. Workers are continually being replaced by machines, their skills rendered obsolete. Assembly lines and automation have replaced proud crafts. The impetus for deskilling work was not that average workers were unable to learn the jobs. The problem for capitalists has been that skilled workers are harder to control. They can use their knowledge and skills as bargaining chips to get concessions. They also tend to think of themselves as more deserving of rewards. In effect, they threaten profits. People doing simple, fragmented tasks have minimal bargaining power and come cheaper.

INCO in Sudbury successfully broke the skills and power of mine workers by introducing new technology to automate work. Highly skilled people, who commanded high salaries and prestige among other workers, found their jobs disappearing (Clement 1981, ch. 10). Children of men who once had skilled jobs at the mine can no longer expect to get similar positions in Sudbury, no matter how motivated and well-educated they might be.

This deskilling, fragmenting, and routinizing of work is not an inevitable consequence of modern technology. It is the result of the kinds of technology that owners of capital opt to promote and how they use it. Teams of skilled workers can put together entire cars themselves as readily and efficiently as can be done on assembly lines. The president of Volvo in Sweden experimented with precisely such teamwork during a period of relatively full employment when he found he could not keep workers in fragmented assembly-line jobs (Gyllenhammer 1977). The function of job fragmentation is not to ensure greater technical efficiency but to break down workers' power, cheapen their labour, and so raise profits.

There is a serious problem for the capitalist system, however, with reducing all jobs to unskilled, repetitive, minimum-wage work: how to prevent coalitions of workers from forming to overthrow the system. The answer in the steel industry was to introduce artificial job ladders. In effect, the owners created a system of stratification to fragment the workers. Petty differences were exploited, linked to credentials such as years of experience and apprenticeship certificates, and used to justify small differences in prestige and piece-rate payments. Workers competed with each other to get the better jobs, and the unions cemented these different pay scales in formal contracts. This was exactly what management wanted. If such petty differences in the job ladder can be linked to race and ethnic differences, so much the better.

Skilled Labour Under Capitalism

Braverman's thesis on the systematic deskilling of work has recently come under criticism from other Marxist theorists for oversimplifying labour-market processes in advanced capitalism (Morgan and Sayer 1988; Sayer and Walker 1992). The strategy of deskilling and thus cheapening and controlling the work force may enhance profits in long-established mass production industries, but it may spell economic disaster in high-technology industries where rapid product innovation is occurring. Morgan and Sayer argue that in such industries competitive advantage and profit maximization depend not on producing a standard product more cheaply than competitors, but on high quality and product innovation. Traditional firms that opt for a cheap, deskilled labour force that is tightly controlled will not be able to keep up in the race for product innovation and so will likely face bankruptcy. Rapid innovation requires a work force that is highly educated in science and advanced technology, and a management team capable of directing rapid and complex organizational changes. Highly skilled, innovative workers cannot be controlled by the tactics of Taylorism (Morgan and Sayer 1988, 26).

From this viewpoint, it makes sense for capitalists to fund applied university research and graduate programs, especially in the sciences, engineering, and business management. More is at stake than empty credentialism, or a desire to divide and rule the work force. Business interests have promoted a series of public and private reports over the last decade debating whether North American high-school and college students are adequately prepared in mathematics and sciences (Darrah 1994, 64). A central concern is that Japanese capitalists may be outperforming Americans in high-technology industries because of better-educated workers.

Sayer and Walker's (1992) comparative study of the structure of American and Japanese corporations suggests that very different patterns of work-force stratification have been developed in the two countries. Major Japanese corporations have reduced or eliminated the hierarchical job ladders and the proliferation of small distinctions in tasks and pay scales described by Bowles and Gintis. These have been replaced with three broad classifications incorporating a variety of jobs. Individual workers are encouraged to learn wide-ranging skills so that they can switch easily between jobs and so maximize flexibility in production. Hence, these corporations place a high premium on worker loyalty, and they foster it with guarantees of job security and salaries linked to length of service rather than location on a job ladder. These firms also promote contact, information exchange, and co-operation among production workers on the shopfloors, engineers, and managers. The intent of such management styles is to maximize the speed and the quality of product innovation, with production workers better able to understand new product designs, and engineers better able to recognize and correct production flaws. This kind of production system is not compatible with the strategy of shipping components to cheap labour assembly plants in the Third World.

The core argument in Sayer and Walker's analysis is that more than one possible structure of labour relations is compatible with advanced capitalism. The seemingly inexorable process of deskilling and cheapening labour described by Braverman is not inevitable. It is a historically specific pattern associated with a certain period of American capitalism and a certain kind of production. It is profitable mainly in association with a highly standardized product and long, mass production runs.

One consequence of a mix of mass production and high-technology industries is that processes of deskilling jobs and upgrading skills may occur simultaneously in different sectors of an economy, resulting in very uneven patterns of high unemployment generally, combined with shortages of skilled labour. Declining real incomes may be the lot of the mass of workers who compete for deskilled jobs while an elite of university graduates in the sciences, engineering, and applied management may be in high demand and able to command high salaries.

Summary

Political economy theory sets out to debunk the **technocratic-meritocratic thesis** of stratification as an ideological smokescreen that legitimates and therefore helps to perpetuate inequality and exploitation. It challenges functionalist theory for ignoring the processes through which capitalism structures the job market, deskills many jobs, fragments workers, and breaks their bargaining power, and then justifies low pay on the grounds that they are doing unskilled work. Advanced capitalism, organized around multinational corporations, produces an extremely unequal structure of job opportunities beyond the control of individual workers. Explanations for stratification that focus on individual efforts and abilities obscure these larger structural processes that constrain individual life chances.

Traditional structural Marxist theory, exemplified in the work of Bowles and Gintis, and Braverman, has been challenged in recent Marxist work for an oversimplified economic determinism. It is giving way to a more dynamic class analysis that explores the diversity of ways in which labour can be managed and exploited for profits in advanced capitalism. But the core argument remains that social inequality is a product of profit-driven corporate interests. Only such effort and ability as directly feeds these profits are likely to be rewarded.

The Social Construction of Stratification

In both functionalist and political economy perspectives on stratification, such key concepts as *jobs, duties, responsibilities, skills,* and *credentials* are taken for granted as common-sense aspects of work. Social constructionist theory challenges each of these concepts and the pattern of reasoning that underlies them. These concepts are embedded in the professional discourse that has emerged around employment equity policies, and the ongoing political debates concerning whether North American workers are adequately prepared for work that is being transformed by technological and organizational innovations.

Central to this discourse is the notion of jobs. Jobs are conceptualized as separate from the persons hired to do them and the quality of individual performances. A job constitutes an identifiable set of duties or tasks, associated with a defined bundle of skills required to get the tasks done. Individual jobs make different contributions to the overall organization or enterprise of which they are a part. Jobs, the value of their contribution, and associated pay scales, are analysed as structural features of organizations. Within this discourse, workers are decomposed into job incumbents with typical profiles or bundles of skills. Skilled workers appear to move freely between workplaces, carrying their skills like baggage.

This way of thinking about jobs fits readily into the functionalist theory of meritocracy discussed above. The vision of equity in employment that emerges within this discourse focusses on the routine application of standard procedures. Tasks and skills are identified, and pay scales set, prior to anyone being hired. The aura of neutrality and objectivity is further assured by hiring external consultants to design an employment equity policy for a specific organization. Independent managements teams are assumed to be unbiased because they do not directly profit from the implementation of the schemes they design. So long as hiring practices also follow objective procedures, matching workers' skill bundles to task-requirement bundles, equity on the basis of merit seems assured. The problem for employers is to attract appropriately qualified individuals, while educational institutions are enjoined to equip students with the skills called for in a given work force.

Social constructionist analysis suggests that the appearance of neutrality and objectivity is illusory. Employment equity policies are an aspect of management oriented principally to the justification of pay differentials. Systemic, or structured, inequality in the treatment of employees is embedded within them. Workers appear to be, and indeed *are* treated the same in ways that are authorized, sanctioned, and accepted practices of organization, and yet that have the consequence of inequality (Cassin 1991, 4).

The central argument is that while the discourse of jobs appears to reflect common-sense understanding of work, it fundamentally misrepresents the nature of work. The distinction between work as what people do, and jobs as disembodied sets of tasks obscures what people actually have to do to accomplish completed tasks and the knowledge that goes into such accomplishment.

The assumption that jobs can be decomposed into bundles of separate skills that can be listed does not correspond to how people experience the simultaneity of their work. In practice, workers are commonly required to juggle many tasks simultaneously, and amid constant interruptions. In the computer assembly plants studied by Darrah (1994) workers were expected to work on several units at once, depending on the availability of parts, and to repair several units at different stages in diagnostic cycles, as well as responding to other workplace demands. Individually, simple tasks required complex memory work under such conditions, but memory work was not part of the job description. Secretarial work is also routinely carried on in the context of continual interruptions from a wide range of disparate sources, including supervisors, bosses, a host of people flowing in and out of the office exchanging information, asking questions, wanting services, raising complaints, and telephones ringing, that all need to be attended to in the same limited space of time available to do the word processing, filing, and other paperwork expected. Listing tasks individually and measuring the skill required to do each one in turn gives a seriously inadequate picture of the complexity of the work being accomplished.

The notion that specific skills can be clearly identified as required for specific tasks obscures the difficulty involved in making such connections, and the potentially disparate ways in which similar work may be accomplished by different people. In his study of computer assembly workers, Darrah (1994) found little consensus as to which individual tasks or which skills were central to getting the work done, beyond the most basic level of some manual dexterity. Production managers based their hiring requirements on standard job descriptions that they borrowed from other local firms. This explained why system repair technicians were called upon to display knowledge of electronic principles such as Ohm's Law. Once on the job, both technicians and managers concurred that such knowledge was irrelevant. Management stressed literacy skills as essential for workers to communicate clearly between shifts, but in practice few of them had such skills. Communications did sometimes get scrambled, but the plant kept running, so presumably literacy was not as essential a skill as managers implied. Troubleshooting was identified as a single skill by engineers, supervisors, and machine operators alike, but in practice operators dealt with trouble in a wide variety of ways, using memory, reasoning, co-operation, and random guesswork. There was no single skill that could be labelled *problem solving*.

Workers further described many other aspects of their work that they found essential to getting the work done, but that did not appear in any specified skills list. These included developing strategies for dealing with aging and frequently recalcitrant machinery, strategies for conveying acceptable impressions of work commitment in front of management, and ways of training new supervisors to provide appropriate support before they were transferred out of the plant. All the supervisors saw was their work in training the operators.

The Community of Practice

An important asset in problem solving and in getting the routine work done proved to be support networks among workers. Darrah found that computer assembly workers compensated for gaps in their own abilities by pooling their heterogeneous skills to help each other. The main challenge facing a newly hired operator was to develop a network of helpers who would assist when inevitable problems arose. The conceptualization of jobs as performed by individual workers with bundles of skills makes this "community of practice" invisible (Darrah 1994, 82; Lave and Wenger 1991). The shift in focus from job to work group raises the possibility that overall plant performance may depend less on attracting individually skilled workers than developing a cooperative work environment, in which workers can routinely help and learn from each other.

The focus on workplace also facilitates a shift in emphasis for skills that workers bring with them to opportunities for learning on the job. It was in this regard that Darrah found blatant contradictions between the management's overt demand for skilled workers and systemic, organizational barriers to skill development. Management claimed to want educated workers who could "see the big picture" and understand the overall system of production. Yet workers complained repeatedly of being blocked in their efforts to learn more. Supervisors routinely prohibited any documentation that would allow workers to learn more and possibly advance their careers. Repair technicians were barred from having schematic drawings of the computers they repaired on the grounds that it was their job merely to replace faulty circuit boards. It was someone else's job to repair

the boards. In one instance, production workers were granted a tour of the firm's customer service department in an adjacent building. They found that much of the work overlapped particularly with respect to faulty products that customers had returned. Both departments reported the exchange of ideas valuable, but the production manager banned further excursions because he feared workers might use them to transfer to another department. These routine practices of information control reflected in structure and intent the deskilling practices referred to by Braverman (1974). Only the rhetoric of senior management had changed. Supervisors still boasted of controlling workers through ignorance.

Job Description as Ideological Practice

The gaps between jobs as task bundles described in job evaluation schemes and work as experienced by people cannot be bridged merely by adding elements to the bundle. The process of description itself is flawed. Descriptions appear to arise directly out of job design as objective statements, but these descriptive practices are themselves embedded in a managerial discourse that takes for granted distinctions between mental and manual labour, or between design and execution of tasks, and that also assumes the gendered character of work. Cassin (1991, 31–32) compares the following typical description of clerical work with what an equivalent description of managerial work would look like. Firstly, with respect to clerical work:

> Typically, employees are engaged in preparing, transcribing, systematizing and maintaining records, reports and communications by manual processes, or by operating various machinery and equipment; conducting analytical and investigative duties; determining the nature of enquiries and dealing with callers and customers in a service capacity/ performing a variety of related admin support tasks under guidance and direction of Supervisory/Mgt personnel.

An equivalent description of management work might be as follows:

> Typically (mgt) employees are engaged in talking on telephones, attending formal and informal meetings (32), chairing formal and informal meetings, touring company facilities, presiding over honorary occasions, representing the company in a variety of capacities, reading, answering and writing reports,

correspondence and other documentation, responding to requests of various kinds from subordinates, colleagues, customers, superiors.

As Cassin remarks, the first description appears reasonable while the latter appears ludicrous. We are used to managerial work being described by terms like: plan, organize, co-ordinate, control, and decide. Such terms describe mental processes, not physical descriptions of what managers can be seen to be doing. Clerical work could also be described in terms of mental processes—the planning, organizing, co-ordinating, and decision-making work involved. But all this managerial work is obscured by descriptions framed in terms of manual performance of tasks. Clerical descriptions focus on essentially "empty" functions that give no indication of the knowledge involved in doing any of the work, the contexts in which such work gets done, or the organizational relevance of this work. It is such omission that accomplishes the view of clerical work as contributing only limited value to organizations and thus warranting limited pay. Conversely, the inclusion of organizational context and relevance is what creates the basis for designating managerial work.

Cassin's central point is that clerical work is inherently managerial and administrative work. The routine designations "managerial," "administrative," and "clerical" work and occupations, are by and large distinctions within the same domain of work (1991, 30). Job evaluation schemes are premised on the assumption that jobs are to be defined by their differences, rather than by their sameness to each other. But this premise obscures the essentially collaborative and overlapping character of work. The "sealing off" of clerical work from managerial work also contributes to the construction of a domain of gender-segregated jobs—women's work—before there are any incumbents in the positions.

The close co-operation between clerical and managerial work, and the fine line dividing them is reflected in the work of the *Conditional Sales and Rental Clerk Position* in a Consumer's Gas Company (Cassin 1991, 58–59). The woman holding this position was responsible for determining the credit worthiness of customers and authorizing sales up to a value of $1500. Considerable judgment, knowledge of credit practices and sales contracts, and interactional abilities were involved in this work. The clerk prepared a report on credit worthiness, formed a judgment, and then sought approval from her supervisor. She represented the company to the customers—finding out what they wanted, offering explanations, and dealing with people variously angry, frightened, threatened, and abusive. Her work was a very significant contribution to the company. Indeed, sales could not take place without her. Yet none of this was visible in her job description, which focussed on the routine completion of paperwork. The fine line separating clerical from managerial designation was drawn at the point where the supervisor approved or questioned the final judgment. Seen from this viewpoint, the separation of mental from manual labour did not result in the deskilling of clerical *work*, but a downgrading of the job.

Similar research by Reimer (1987) documents how clerical staff routinely organize the work of their superiors, collecting materials, setting priorities, arranging agendas, dealing with correspondence, and the like. Complex judgments are involved in this work, which presuppose comprehensive knowledge of an organization. Yet their work was conceptualized by both themselves and others as comprising routine, delegated tasks, variously referred to as answering mail, typing or word processing, filing, and finding things. Even the advanced computerized technology and software packages that secretaries now manage are more likely to be described as "making their work easier" than as enhancing it (Cassin 1991, 58).

Invisibility of Skills as Social Construction

The invisibility of managerial forms of work performed by subordinates does not arise from accidental oversight, and cannot be corrected merely by pointing it out.

"You're a man of the world, Miss Wallis.
Tell me, what are sexist remarks really like?"

Institutionalized invisilibity is accomplished through organized sets of relationships that also accomplish relations of class and gender. Documents are central to these processes of recording, recognizing, and attributing work within formal organizations. They provide a way of tracking how the division between mental and manual, design and execution is organizationally sustained.

The work of nursing is a stereotypically female occupation, which, although it is recognized as a profession, is accorded relatively low status within the medical hierarchy of hospitals, and significantly lower pay than other medical personnel. Nurses routinely perform aspects of managerial, administrative, educational, and diagnostic work as part of patient care, yet only a small part of such work is documented (Gregor 1994). The dividing line in the hospital hierarchy was graphically recorded in the hospital studied by Gregor in a pamphlet called "Your Medical Team." This pamphlet, which was given to each new patient as part of the process of admission, described the qualifications and responsibilities of medical personnel a patient might encounter. It included attending physician, resident physician, intern, clinical clerk, and head nurse. The qualifications, ranking, work organization, and responsibilities of nurses below the level of head nurse were not mentioned. In effect, the people most directly involved in the daily care of patients did not appear as members of the medical team.

Institutional recognition of the educative work performed by nurses was accorded specifically to pre-operative education provided to patients on the surgical ward. Nurses were required to document that such work had been done by entering it into their patients' charts on a form entitled "Pre-op Patient Education Check List." Its content was also documented in a teaching manual "Before and After Surgery" to be used by nurses in instructing patients.

The educative work actually done by nurses extended far beyond this required minimum, but it received no official recognition, and even the nurses themselves generally failed to name it. Gregor records talk between nurses and patients in which nurses explained aspects of diagnosis and treatment, informed patients about various tests, clarified the meaning of symptoms, advised patients how to aid recovery, and explained aspects of hospital administration. Patient care could hardly have proceeded without such talk, but all that nurses were doing officially was "administering medication" or "checking the intravenous." The omission has potentially far-reaching implications in a period when hospital administration is being contracted out to management consulting firms. The computerized calculation of nursing staff ratios and time needed for patient care routinely incorporates only the officially sanctioned tasks listed in job descriptions.

The invisibility of educative work performed by nurses was further obscured by the fact that much of it contravened the recognized medical hierarchy. Nurses routinely advised less experienced health-care workers and physicians on appropriate pieces of equipment, how various kinds of medical work processes could be initiated through use of requisition forms, where to find such forms, and how to fill them in. Nurses also became involved in aspects of the diagnosis and treatment of patients. This often took the form of a "problems list" by which nurses informed hospital physicians about medical work that needed their attention. Such lists were prepared daily, usually by night nurses, and modified during the day as old problems were solved and new ones identified. Examples included "patient vomited 500cc. leave I.V. in?" or "re-order senecot—no bowel movement." The critical difference between the problems list and the pre-operative, education check list described above, was that it was not officially sanctioned. The lists were written on plain paper and never found their way into hospital records. In other instances, nurses were observed contacting a physician to explain a patient's problem, then suggesting the appropriate drug treatment and the normal dosage. The resulting prescription, however, carried only the physician's name. The collaborative character of the work process is actively hidden from view. As with the example of the clerical worker discussed above, the knowledge and judgment used by the subordinate worker was rendered invisible. Only the superior was officially recognized as making the decision, while the subordinate appeared merely to carry out orders. The suppression of the active involvement of subordinates in forming decisions is part of the set of practices that sustains the organizational hierarchy.

The organization of work within the hospital limited the opportunities for nurses to learn more about diagnoses and treatment plans in ways that paralleled the experience of computer assembly workers described above. Physicians routinely scheduled their rounds at the same time of day as nurses changed their work shifts. Even when physicians did come during the day, it was also not their practice to invite nurses to come with them when they went to see a patient. Such organizational practices, Gregor suggests, had the function, and perhaps also the direct intent of maintaining the status of the physician as authoritative knower in matters of patient care.

Maintaining the Fictions

The view of work as hierarchically ordered sets of task bundles that merit differential rewards, does not come naturally. It has to be worked at. The incorporation of workers' representatives on committees charged with designing job evaluation systems constitutes an important mechanism in gaining commitment to the schemes and in training workers to think in the appropriate conceptual framework (Cassin 1992, 68–73). Participants in these committees learn the job evaluation system, learn about jobs from this perspective, and learn to make and to defend judgments and decisions made within the constraints of job evaluation. Cassin suggests that an intensive orientation process is required to "break in" new members to a thinking process that belies common-sense experience of work.

Job descriptions define who is authorized to know certain aspects of work and these relations of hierarchy are continually reproduced and reinforced through displays of superordination and subordination. Gregor describes how nurses maintained the fiction of "doctor's orders" in relations with patients when they were quite capable of giving advice directly, and in fact even when they had initiated the doctor's order in question. In one of many examples, a patient asked a nurse how long she should wait before taking the bandages off her leg. The nurse responded with "You will have to ask your doctor" followed by questions such as "When will he come to see you next?" and "When is your next appointment?" After it became clear that the doctor had visited the patient, omitted any mention of removing bandages, and would not be seeing the patient for another six weeks, the nurse said it would be okay to soak the bandages off after ten days. How much nurses told patients depended primarily on the personality of the attending physician and what he would allow, not on what the nurses knew. Experienced nurses quickly warned incoming nurses what to expect in this regard.

The costs of this socially constructed hierarchy on those in subordinate positions are high. The most obvious cost is financial. The fine line separating managerial from managed can mark large differences in income. More subtle, but equally destructive are the costs in terms of social wellbeing and mental health. Blue-collar workers located at the bottom of the job-status hierarchy are much more likely to experience feelings of power-lessness and self-depreciation that closely mirror the symptoms of reactive depression (Archibald 1978, 177–80).

Summary

Social constructionist theory complements in many respects the political economy analysis of stratification in the work force. Both critique the artificiality of job ladders, and the lost potential for co-operation and pooling of knowledge that such distinctions tend to create. But constructionist analysis focusses attention on the routine practices through which **doing hierarchy** comes to be accepted and legitimated in common-sense reasoning as merited. In challenging the discourse of jobs and job evaluation, it also calls into question the extent to which distinctions between mental and manual labour, design and execution of tasks, can be sustained in everyday experience of work.

Feminist Theory and Stratification

Women are subordinated to men in Canadian society on just about every measure of social status—the average incomes they earn, ownership of property, control over capital, participation in politics, representation in managerial, administrative, and decision-making bodies. Women's contributions to society in general and to the world of work in particular, are not accorded the same value of recognition as those associated with men. Feminist theory addresses this systemic gender inequity and the generalized inadequacy of mainstream theories to account for it.

Statistics on the gender composition of different occupations in Canada present extensive evidence of the lower status of women generally in the work force. The proportion of adult women in the labour force more than doubled between 1941 and 1981, and it continues to rise (see figure 11-1). But women are heavily overrepresented in the reserve army of part-time, seasonal, and cheap labour.

In labour-market theory, the market is generally understood as divided into two sectors. Jobs in the primary sector are characterized by relatively good wages and working conditions and opportunities for promotion, whereas jobs in the secondary sector are short-

Figure 11-1

Labour Force Participation Rates for Women and Men Over 15 Years of Age, Canada 1911–93*

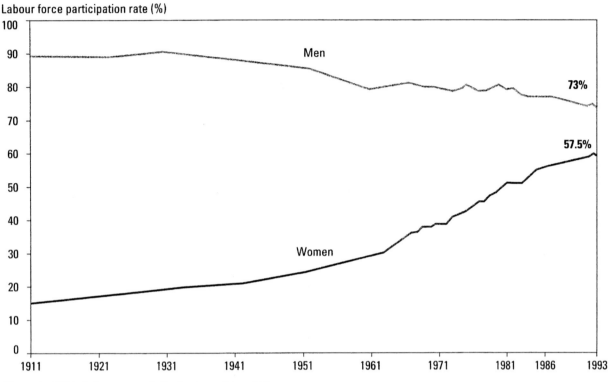

Labour force participation rate (%)

*Figures for 1941 include persons on Active Service on 2 June 1941.

Source: Eichler (1988a, 95). Adapted from Statistics Canada, 1961 Census of Canada, Vol. III (Part 1) Labour Force, table 1, for 1911–61; for 1966–79: Cat. 71-201 Historical Labour Force Statistics, pp. 151, 153, 158; for 1981–84; Historical Labour Force Statistics, 1984, Cat. 71-201, p. 220, D767895, p. 225, D768005; for 1985–86, Cat. 71-001; for 1986–93, Cat. 71-201.

term, low-paid, and dead end. White males hold the majority of jobs in the primary sector, while females form the large majority of workers in the secondary sector, along with many men from visible minorities (Armstrong and Armstrong 1990, 62).

Women are concentrated in a small number of occupations—clerical, service, sales, health and teaching—with three-quarters of employed women in the first three of these categories. When women enter professions they are overrepresented in low-status and low-paid categories. They are far more likely to be the dental hygienists, librarians, therapists, and dieticians, than the dentists, doctors, lawyers, engineers, or university professors (see table 11-2). These patterns are changing, but very slowly.

An important impetus for change has been the implementation of the equality rights section of the Canadian Charter of Rights and Freedoms in 1985, the federal Employment Equity Act passed in 1986, and particularly the section of the Act concerned with the Federal Contractors Program. The Act requires that all federally regulated companies (banks, transport, and communications companies) set up **employment equity** programs and file annual public reports on the demographic composition of their work force, including data on salaries and promotion for women and minorities.

The first reports filed in 1988 revealed major inequities in pay scales for women and men and restricted employment opportunities for disabled people and visible minorities. Women were concentrated in the

Table 11-2

Female Workers in Selected Professional and Technical Occupations, 1971 and 1981				
	Female % of Occupation		% of all Female Workers	
Occupation	1971	1981	1971	1981
Dental hygienists, assistants, and technicians	76.6	81.1	0.3	0.4
Social workers	53.4	62.6	0.2	0.4
Librarians and archivists	76.4	80.2	0.2	0.3
Physiotherapists, occupational and other therapists	81.6	84.6	0.2	0.2
University teachers	16.7	24.6	0.1	0.2
Physicians and surgeons	10.1	17.1	0.1	0.1
Pharmacists	23.1	41.3	0.1	0.1
Psychologists	47.2	52.0	0.1	0.1
Dieticians and nutritionists	95.3	94.0	0.1	0.1
Lawyers and notaries	4.8	15.1	—*	0.1
Industrial engineers	3.3	12.2	—	0.1
Dentists	4.7	7.9	—	—
Total	29.0	39.4	1.5	2.1

*— means less than 0.1 percent.

Source: Armstrong and Armstrong (1984). Adapted from 1971 *Census*, vol. 3.2, table 8; and from *1981 Census, Labour Force-Occupational Trends* (Cat. 92-920), table 1.

majority of jobs paying less than $25 000 while men predominated in jobs that paid more than $35 000. Women were rarely represented in the very high-paying jobs. Roughly 10 percent of the 13 800 male employees with Air Canada, for example, earned more than $70 000. Only 4 out of the 6300 women working for the corporation earned that much (*Globe and Mail*, 22 Oct. 1988).

The Act has come under heavy criticism from advocacy groups for not incorporating penalties for failure to practice employment equity. The Act leaves it up to individual members of disadvantaged groups to challenge these companies in court, using human rights legislation. But such action requires considerable time, money, effort, and legal expertise, as well as proof that failure to hire or to promote a particular individual was due to discrimination and not to some other factor.

The section dealing with federal contractors does have some teeth, in that every company that has 100 or more employees, and that wants to bid on a federal government contract of more than $200 000, must prove its commitment to gender and minority equity in terms of hiring, training, salary, and promotions. No equity plan, no federal contract (Kates 1988). These companies are under pressure to promote women and minorities into managerial positions, and also to keep them. Before the

Act, Kates suggests, a request for maternity leave was an instant ticket to a dead career, but companies are now more prepared to offer flexible policies in order to retain women in senior positions.

Employment equity policies and associated job evaluation schemes have had some successes in redressing overt discrimination in hiring practices, and in winning pay increases for categories of women workers found to be paid significantly less than men in closely comparable jobs. But the impact of such cases on the overall pattern of income differentials between women and men in the work force is small. As we have seen above in the social constructionist critique of job evaluation schemes, systemic discrimination remains largely invisible. Job descriptions are gendered at basic common-sense levels of practical reasoning. Hiring and promotion procedures that follow strict rules of gender neutrality and objectivity, still have gendered outcomes. Compensation for work done appears to be gender-neutral, based entirely on objective job characteristics, yet the pervasive outcome is that work primarily done by women is accorded less worth than work primarily done by men (Cassin 1991, 1–2).

The initial concentration of women and men in different entry-level job categories has cumulative implications for progression and career advancement. In order to appear qualified for promotion into managerial positions, junior personnel need to display knowledge and experience in policy areas, and decision-making capabilities. But, as we have seen above, clerical, sales, and service jobs are normally described in ways that obscure such experience. Personnel managers use job descriptions to structure performance appraisals, orienting questions around recognized task-related competences. Resulting evaluation procedures and interviews may give no scope for workers to display the managerial knowledge they might have. Jobs in which women are concentrated generally offer little scope for discretion, advancement, authority, or higher salaries. Clerical positions qualify women to compete for other clerical positions, but not for administrative or management

This woman's work is as valuable as a man's.

That's why Pay Equity is the law.

Get the facts! Call the hotline: Toll free in Ontario 1-800-387-8813

THE PAY EQUITY COMMISSION =

Pay equity programs have had some success, but systemic discrimination is largely invisible.

positions, even at entry level. Affirmative action programs designed to get more women into management appear to offer privileged and unfair competition to women. The structural barriers that make affirmative action necessary, remain invisible.

Feminist Challenge to Traditional Theory

Functionalist perspectives on stratification and effort, and socially learned differences in occupational choices by individual women and men serve to legitimate rather than challenge gendered inequality. Job evaluation schemes to date largely mirror functionalist assumptions. Traditional political economy theory, although much more critical of stratification, has mostly ignored its gendered character. The working class is generally conceptualized as an undifferentiated whole in labour-market theory, with marginal attention to women (Brittan and Maynard 1984, 56). Inequality between workers is broadly accounted for in terms of the interests of the capitalist class in fragmenting working-class solidarity so that some segments can be exploited for cheap labour while others control them.

This thesis, however, does not explain why women are so consistently singled out for super-exploitation at the bottom of the job and wage heap (Armstrong and Armstrong 1990, 66). Nor does it explain why male workers have for so long seen it as legitimate that fellow workers should be in subordinate, lower paid, and often insecure and temporary work, because they happen to be female (Beechey 1977). It is hard to blame capitalism for the pattern of women's economic subordination that long predates it. Capitalists can and do take advantage of this subordination, exploiting women as a pool of cheaper labour, controlling male workers by the threat that they can be replaced by cheaper women, and buying the compliance of men to the wage-labour hierarchy by appearing to favour them with differential rewards (Hartmann 1979). Such arguments, however, fall far short of claiming that capitalism causes gender inequality.

Historically, capitalism was associated with improvements in the relative social status of women by providing some opportunity for women to earn an income independently of men. Capitalists also stand to benefit from the increasing numbers of married women entering the labour force, in ways that go beyond exploitation of cheap labour. Wage-earning women expand the market for consumer goods of all kinds and open up market opportunities in the service sector to supplement domestic labour with day-care, take-out food, and domestic cleaning services.

A different order of explanation seems to be needed to explain the subordination of women in the labour force that goes beyond the structuralist argument that the pattern persists because it is in the interests of capital. Such an argument functions as ideological justification for patriarchy in that it obscures more fundamental relations of male power and oppression of women (Brittan and Maynard 1984, 52–55; Cockburn 1981, 54; Hartmann 1979). Hartmann focusses attention directly on how male workers, individually and collectively through unions, have acted to exclude women from well-paid jobs, preserving them as male strongholds. She traces what she sees as "centuries of patriarchal social relationships" in which men pushed women into subordinate economic roles. In Canada, women always worked alongside men in developing homesteads and family farms, yet patriarchal laws dispossessed them, vesting ownership rights in men. Men commonly kept that control even after death by willing the farms to their sons. During the early development of factories, men resisted factory labour, preferring their greater independence in agricultural work. Women and children were available as "more docile and malleable" labour, itself reflecting their long-term subordination to men in agriculture. As industrialization progressed, men dominated the skilled trades while women filled less important positions as casual labourers and assistants.

The potential problem with this arrangement was that the cheap labour of women might undercut men's jobs and wages, especially in a tight job market. Male-dominated unions took active steps to control this threat. Hartmann documents systematic actions by male unions to exclude women from membership and to prevent them from entering apprenticeships, and gaining the skills required for equal status jobs. Fear of job competition does not account for this pattern, since the same men who excluded women and girls from learning trades, offered such training to boys. In principle, both male and female workers could have joined together in unions to demand equal pay for women and men, and thus eliminate the threat of cheaper female labour. But this rarely happened. More commonly, male unionists used their organizational force to eliminate women from factories. In one example, male spinners even plotted to set fire to a factory in which girls were working at wages below those of male unionists.

Such overt discrimination against women in the work force has been virtually eliminated in Canada. Women and men who do the same work within the same organization are guaranteed equal pay. Women have been joining unions in steadily increasing numbers. The Canadian Labour Congress fully endorsed equality rights for women in employment, and unions have become active in pushing labour benefits for women workers, including improved maternity benefits. But there remains much overt and covert resistance to the acceptance of women as colleagues in traditionally male occupations. Companies that have actively instituted policies to hire more women managers to comply with the Employment Equity Act and qualify for government contracts, have also had to address the sexist attitudes of some male managers. In one report of an interview with a woman applicant for a management position with the Canadian Imperial Bank of Commerce, a male manager displayed such attitudes when he asked her if she were married or had any marital plans, and then commented later that she was not all that attractive. The senior manager at the bank commented "John's good, but he's got a problem with women. It will cost him" (Kates 1988).

In practice, however, it is women in management who more often bear the costs of male resistance to their presence on the team. This resistance undermines women's effectiveness as managers, which then becomes attributed to the women themselves as evidence of their relative incompetence, compared with men. The veiled hostility of male managers, especially younger ones who feel they are competing directly with women for promotion, may take such forms as withholding important information, sidelining women managers at meetings, creating behind-the-scenes barriers to co-operation, deliberately sabotaging projects, or transferring a bad worker to the woman's department to foul things up. Sexist comments betray male discomfort at having to work with women, even when this is denied. Token women managers are subjected to constant scrutiny, rating them lower than male colleagues regardless of their actual job records and blocking appointments and promotions that would give them authority over men.

The difficulties that many women managers experience in gaining informal acceptance among male members of management teams carry implications that go far beyond personal enjoyment of work. Darrah's (1994) research, described above, indicate the importance of newly hired workers developing a network of helpers who can assist when problems arise. It is this community of practice that makes it routinely possible for workers to compensate for individual weaknesses and enhance their overall competence. When women managers are not part of the informal social networks among male managers at the pub, the golf course, and elsewhere, they lose critically important opportunities for gaining insider knowledge of what is happening, how to present themselves and their work, how to discuss its policy relevance and not merely its technical adequacy, and so on. All these factors directly impact on their apparent potential for promotion (Cassin 1979; Kates 1988). On top of all this, women may find themselves pressured to underplay their abilities in front of male colleagues who feel threatened by competent women. Displays of subservience and deference to male views and male authority may be essential to gain a minimum of co-operation from such colleagues, and to avoid open harassment (Liddle and Joshi 1986, 178–80). Such compromises help to sustain the myth of women's relative incompetence, which further reduces the probability of their receiving recognition and promotion.

Domestic Division of Labour and Social Inequality

The most severe impediments to gender equality within the workplace may lie outside the workplace itself, in the very uneven distribution of domestic responsibilities between women and men. Most research in Canada and elsewhere concurs that even when married women are employed full-time, they still do the bulk of domestic work and child care. The class hierarchy presupposes the gender hierarchy in the sense that the organization of work and working hours assumes that workers are generally not involved in domestic labour or child care. Such work is presumed to be done by someone else. The class privileges of professional women similarly depend upon the gender subordination of other women who will perform domestic service work and child care so cheaply that they absorb only a portion of the money that professional women themselves earn (Liddle and Joshi 1986, 150–51).

The greatest impediment to women's success in corporate careers remains the very long, sixty-five-hour workweeks commonly expected of young executives on the fast track (Kates 1988). Men have traditionally been able to put in such long hours primarily because their wives have absorbed the bulk of their domestic responsibilities. But few women have spouses or other adults at home who can take up most of the domestic and mothering work. Men have a career advantage in this regard, but at a high price. Men who value home life and parenting lose out in their careers relative to traditional men in a corporate culture where being at the office during evenings and weekends, and willingness to uproot and to travel on corporate business, are taken as measures of career commitment.

Few women feel able or willing to pay such a high price for a career. An article in the *Globe and Mail* business magazine entitled "Thanks, But No Thanks" (Maynard and Brouse 1988) describes the lives of women who graduated with masters of business administration degrees from the University of Western Ontario. They got good, although not top, jobs as corporate business executives and were "keenly watched and courted [as] the standard bearers in women's drive for equality at work." They found themselves burned out

SALLY FORTH

Reprinted with special permission of King Features Syndicate.

and under extreme stress in the face of inhuman demands to give 110 percent to clients and 120 percent to children, to work from 7:30 A.M. to 6:30 P.M. and on weekends, and to travel for the company. Added to this was the desperate struggle to find and keep adequate day-care and the guilt that their children were victims of their relentless career demands. It was as if the companies were deliberately pushing women beyond human limits to prove they could not be equal to men and should give up and go home. According to the article, many of them did just that, or they started their own businesses. A few companies have moved some way towards reducing such strain, particularly under the pressure to make public their adherence to employment equity. But this has stopped at the level of maternity leave provisions and some flexibility in working hours. In August 1994, the Canadian Bar Association approved motions stating that time off for family responsibilities should not normally delay a lawyer's eligibility for partnership in a firm or affect the right to equitable pay (*Globe and Mail*, 22 Aug. 1994, B1–9). They also endorsed a motion that law firms should apply flexible treatment to men and women with children. They backed off, however, from making it a "legal duty" that firms accommodate such lawyers and from endorsing equal pay for women working shorter hours because of children. The lawyers prided themselves as "definitely leading all the other professions" on the issue.

Equality Rights as Ideology

The equality rights provisions in the Charter or in employment equity policies do nothing to redress such experiences. The principle of equality based on *sameness* in the treatment of women and men in the workplace ignores the additional demands of home and child care that are socially defined as women's responsibility. The strain of trying to do too much is readily attributed back to individual women as their personal inadequacy. It has prompted some feminist advocates like Betty Friedan (1981) to eschew earlier arguments that housewives were not living up to their potential, and to advocate motherhood as a valid career option.

Eisenstein (1984) rejects such "feminist revisionism" in favour of a conceptual shift in the meaning of equality. Feminism, she argues, shows up fundamental contradictions in the liberal philosophy of equal opportunity and merited hierarchy. The ideology of equal opportunity covers up an unequal system that privileges men by their ascribed sexual status. Affirmative action policies

that try in very minor and insignificant ways to redress this systemic privileging of men are attacked within liberalism as discrimination against men. The feminist movement threatens the foundations of liberal individualism by making visible women's situation as members of a sexual class. Women as child-bearers and child-rearers face major systemic disadvantages that cannot be alleviated by abstract notions of equal opportunity.

True gender equality, Eisenstein argues, will be achieved only when child-bearing and child-rearing become socially inconsequential; that is, when they do not restrict women's choices, and do not result in women being segregated in the institution of private, domesticated motherhood, or forced into economic dependence on men, or into secondary wage-earner status. Such equality implies far-reaching social and political changes that are not envisioned in current equality rights provisions within the Canadian Charter.

What would such a world look like? It might include, among other policies: reproductive freedom; new visions of child care and health care; statutory parenting leave that would acknowledge both the special needs of childbirth and the equal parenting responsibilities of mothers and fathers; flexible working hours; a fundamental rethinking of the notions of worker or employee to include the presumption of domestic and child-care responsibilities as intrinsic to the experience of work; economic independence for mothers that presupposes profound changes in the conceptualization of private family and social responsibility. These suggestions are only a beginning: the theory of true gender equality and what it would entail for society has scarcely begun to be developed. The absence, or gross inadequacy, of such policies in most industrial societies, attests to how patriarchal these societies are.

Conclusion

This exploration of stratification in capitalist society has taken us a long way from traditional functionalist analysis with its certainty of differential skill and requirements and merited differences in prestige and rewards. As the concepts used in analyses change, so also does the nature of the reality being talked about. Where traditional functionalists talk of "stratification," for example, Marxists talk of "class." *Class* essentially refers to power based on relationship to the means of production; stratification is essentially a prestige ranking. For traditional functionalists, stratification is based on innate individual differences in abilities and motivation but, seen from the political economy perspective, it refers primarily to the relative utility of different positions for the capitalist system at any one time (Boughey 1978, 130). Good jobs can quickly crumble into nothing once they cease to be useful to corporate employers. Members of the prestigious upper middle class of corporate executives have been finding this out to their cost during the 1980s and 1990s. Cutbacks in middle management positions have left many unemployed.

The dimension of power or powerlessness is central to the Marxist analysis, not the differences in income or lifestyle that occupy traditional functionalists. It certainly helps to have scarce skills that are high in demand, but it does not alter the fact that shifting labour-market demands, or new technologies, or just an overabundance of other people with similar skills can rapidly wipe out any advantage. Distinctions between professional, middle class, working class, and lower class begin to look unimportant under such conditions. What they have in common is insecurity and dependency in the labour market.

Marxist theories acknowledge the need for skills and professional training, and the need to attract particularly able, qualified, and dependable people to certain jobs. However, they use different criteria to answer the moral question of what differential rewards should be. Personal need and labour time, rather than importance and scarcity, are the key variables. The well-known Marxist motto is "To each according to need and from each according to ability." True justice requires equality in power, prestige, and property. People deserve equal power to influence government in their own society, equal dignity as human beings, and equal access to a good standard of living (Boughey 1978, 130). People do not automatically warrant a higher standard of living just because they happen to be born brighter, or with wealthy parents, or because they lucked into an elite job. In theory, people could be rewarded for the labour time they give to their jobs. The time taken to develop skills can be calculated into the amount. So can the extra time involved in doing quality work. Those who support more dependants should take home proportionately more money. These are the principles that underlie current state salary policies in China.

Social constructionist theory introduces a qualitatively different dimension into this analysis of stratification. It focusses attention on the practices through which people work up and accept notions of jobs and skills as common-sense features of work. Like Marxism, it draws

attention to the often arbitrary character of hierarchical divisions between jobs. It explores how such divisions are accomplished, particularly in the professional discourse of management experts in the field of job evaluation. It explore also how people adopt such accounts as "the way things are" and act accordingly.

Feminist theory, often in close association with social constructionism, makes visible how these practices are gendered. It explores, moreover, how a gender hierarchy, built on inegalitarian division of domestic labour, is presupposed in the organization of labour relations. Reform of institutionalized patriarchy requires fundamental changes in the organization of society, changes that go far beyond a shift in attitudes or procedures to establish formal equity in the evaluation of male and female job applicants.

Suggested Reading

An excellent source of statistical information on inequality in Canada is Henry Veltmeyer, *Canadian Class Structure* (1986). Veltmeyer takes a strong, structuralist Marxist approach to inequality, showing how capitalism works to create a class of super-rich at the top of the Canadian hierarchy and a class of poor and sometimes destitute people at the bottom.

For a clear presentation of functionalist theory of stratification, the article by Davis and Moore, "Some Principles of Stratification" (1945) is excellent. It is an older publication, but the main argument is very clear, without being hedged or qualified to avoid criticism. The rebuttal by Melvin Tumin, "Critical Analysis of 'Some Principles of Stratification'" (1953) is also very straightforward.

For the Marxist approach an excellent book is Harry Braverman, *Labour and Monopoly Capital* (1974). This descriptive and readable book presents a strong argument for the importance to capitalism of deskilling workers.

For the ethnomethodological perspective, any of the studies by Erving Goffman are valuable. They are all very readable descriptions of how everyday life is managed in ordinary interactions. One short book by Goffman is *Interaction Ritual* (1967).

Charles Darrah's article "Skill Requirements at Work" (1994) provides an insightful social constructionist analysis of work that challenges the adequacy of common-sense notions of skill, and also draws attention to the importance of interpersonal networks in generating and transmitting crucial work-related knowledge. The article also discusses how the deskilling practices of management seriously hamper the efforts of workers to learn more about their work.

It should have become apparent throughout this debate that education is related in critical, although contradictory, ways to stratification. Schools and colleges, with their technological-meritocratic principles, have become central arenas within which relations of stratifi-cation are worked out. It is to the analysis of the education system that we now turn.

From the perspective of radical feminism, Heidi Hartmann, "Capitalist Patriarchy and Job Segregation by Sex" (1979), presents a groundbreaking study of how male unions systematically limited the job opportunities open to women. A journalistic article by Rona Maynard and Cynthia Brouse, "Thanks, But No Thanks" (1988) documents the high stress experienced by women in corporate executive careers.

Questions

1. What do Davis and Moore see as the functional prerequisites that generate stratification in all known societies?

2. How can Tumin argue that, in a sense, equality and opportunity are inherently in conflict?

3. How does Tumin critique the argument that differential financial rewards are essential to motivate people to do important and difficult jobs?

4. What structural changes lie behind the American Dream that anyone can achieve upward mobility through talent and effort?

5. How does Marxist theory challenge the relationship between credentials and financial rewards?

6. In Braverman's classical Marxist theory, what is the functional importance of job ladders in industry? How might such structures be dysfunctional for competitive advantage in high-technology industries?

7. How does the notion of work as a community of practice undermine the notion that specific jobs require specific skills?

8. How do the job descriptions of clerical and managerial work function as ideological practices that distort understanding of what people are actually doing?

9. How can the incorporation of workers' representatives in job evaluation committees serve to further distort rather than enhance understanding of what workers actually do?

10. How is domestic division of labour directly implicated in gender inequality in paid work?

Education: Does It Moderate or Perpetuate Social Inequality?

Compulsory public schooling for children is a central feature of all industrialized societies. In Canada, the beginnings of a public school system can be traced back to the early 1840s in Ontario (MacDonald 1988, 102–3). In 1846, a general board of education was set up to examine the state of education in the province and to make recommendations for developing a common school system. In 1850 an Act was passed to regulate the classification of teachers and to establish boards of public instruction for each county to certify teachers and to select textbooks. In 1871, free, compulsory education was established. Children between the ages of seven and twelve had to attend school four months per year. In 1919, the school-leaving age was raised to sixteen. Secondary school

fees were abolished two years later. Other provinces slowly followed Ontario's lead.

In contemporary Canada, schooling is compulsory between the ages of six and sixteen, although many children are enrolled in formal educational institutions at an earlier age and remain in school past the legal school-leaving age. Statistics Canada data indicate that the numbers of children enrolled in pre-elementary education increased by 9 percent between 1977 and 1984, and a further 9 percent by 1991 to a total of 466123 children in 1991. During the same period the proportions of people aged 15 to 19 still in full-time education rose from 64.5 percent to 77.4 percent. Many people continue their formal education in a postsecondary institution. Full-time postsecondary enrolment grew by

1991–92 to a total of nearly 900 000, with 62 percent of these at university.

Why has compulsory and advanced education achieved such importance in industrial societies like Canada? What forms does education take? What are the explanations for inequalities among different social groups in access to and achievement in education? These are some of the central questions we examine in this chapter.

Theories of education are very closely linked to the theories of stratification explored in the previous chapter. In industrial society, careers have become more important than inherited wealth in determining the standard of living of the majority of people. These careers, in turn, depend on access to education. As in the previous chapter, we present the traditional functionalist perspective first, followed by the Marxist structuralist critique. Both of these approaches are challenged by contemporary efforts to reformulate theories of education in less deterministic ways. Such challenges give central attention to the social construction of schooling in daily interaction in classrooms and to feminist efforts to radically transform the curriculum and teaching methods.

Functionalism: The Liberal Theory of Education

Next to the family, education ranks as the most important institution within the traditional functionalist model of the social system. Education is responsible for developing moral or normative consensus, which is at the centre of social integration and pattern maintenance. It is also critical for giving young people the skills that will enable them to adapt to rapidly changing economic conditions.

The Ideal of Liberal Education

The nineteenth-century philosopher and reformer John Dewey advocated a free and universal school system as vitally important for democracy and for developing industrial society. He believed that schools have a central role to play in the psychic and moral development of the individual. By helping to develop the cognitive and psychomotor skills of students, schools also offer each individual the chance to compete openly for privileges in society (Bowles and Gintis 1976, 20–23). Dewey saw universal education as a powerful mecha-

nism for reducing extremes of wealth and poverty and for fostering equality. In his view, universal schooling was not only desirable in itself, but it was also an efficient way to train a skilled labour force. It would be, therefore, eminently compatible with capitalism.

This vision of the education system as democratic, just, and efficient stands at the heart of the functionalist view of stratification in industrial society. Functionalism focusses primarily on the objectives of socializing young people in the skills and moral commitment necessary for them to take over adult roles within the social system. The goal is to ensure the continuity of the system itself. Functionalists define equality of opportunity primarily in terms of meritocracy. The desired outcome of schooling, therefore, is that the more able and motivated students are allocated to the more difficult and important social roles.

The Functions of Schools

Parsons' essay, "The School Class as a Social System" (1961), provides a statement of the basic assumptions underlying the functionalist theory of education. In this essay, Parsons argues that families are not adequate to prepare children for adult roles in advanced industrial societies, primarily because the values and commitments appropriate for kinship roles conflict with those of the workplace. A primary function of schools is to help children to make the transition from the value orientations of family life to the affectively neutral, universalistic, and achievement-oriented values of the work world.

Parsons suggests that it is significant that close to nine out of ten elementary school teachers are women. The nurturing orientation that these teachers provide gives young children some continuity with the mother role and absorbs the strain of achievement and differential ranking. Children can relate to their female teacher and try to please her as they do their mothers. They have the same teacher for a whole year in all subjects. At the same time, the teacher is not a mother but is in an occupation. Each year children have a new teacher. This reinforces particularistic role identification. They also learn that the teacher judges them according to their achievements. Parsons further suggests that it is significant that traditionally a high proportion of American school teachers are unmarried. They thus avoid the contradictory demands of maternal and occupational roles for women.

Senior classes are differentiated into specialized subject areas, each taught by a different teacher. The majority of these teachers are men. Specialization by male teachers reduces attachment to any one teacher and promotes and reinforces the masculine image of affective neutrality and specificity. Hence children learn the pattern variables appropriate for adult sex roles.

At the same time, schools socialize children in required commitments and capabilities for adult roles. *Commitment* comprises two broad aspects: societal values and performance of specific roles. The two components of *capabilities* are skills to perform the task and role responsibility; that is, the ability to live up to the expectations of others. The school is thus crucial for the allocation of young people into future roles on the basis of achievement. At the elementary level, where cognitive skills appear relatively simple, the moral component of responsible citizenship takes precedence. Students are graded both for achievement and for "responsible good behaviour" such as respectfulness and co-operativeness in class. Parsons sees these as fundamental moral skills, important for future leadership and initiative. Stratification on the basis of cognitive skills is translated into college preparatory streaming at grade 9. Parsons admits that the ascriptive characteristics of class of origin influence this streaming, but he concludes that the main force is still achievement.

Parsons' essay is a masterpiece in displaying the working assumptions of the functionalist approach. The first assumption is *functional indispensability*. Parsons conveys the impression that all aspects of American schools in the 1950s had important functions within the education system and could not be easily replaced. He further accepts the basic assumption of *functional unity*. Any established patterns are regarded as good for the educational system, for society as a whole, and for individual members. There is no question in his model that practices such as the early streaming of children on the basis of behaviour rather than cognitive abilities might not be functional for all sectors of society. The third basic assumption, *universal functionalism*, is evident in Parsons' effort to find a valuable purpose for every detail that he notices. Nothing is dismissed as an irrelevant or useless habit left over from earlier times or from other life situations.

The main problem with this approach is that almost any change in the status quo is problematic. We are left with the impression that any change in the school system, such as using male teachers in elementary grades or married women specialists in later grades, or having mixed playground activities for girls and boys together, would be psychologically disturbing for the students.

Contemporary functionalist theories have largely discarded Parsons' assumptions concerning the importance of such details as spinsterhood for elementary teachers, but in other respects his essay still expresses the core ideas of functionalism.

The main functions of the school system, as highlighted by Parsons, can be summarized as follows:

1. to teach the values of achievement, universalistic standards of judgment, and emotional neutrality appropriate for specialized occupational roles;

2. to train in specific skills and knowledge appropriate for occupational roles;

3. to ensure the appropriate selection and allocation of young adults to occupational roles in accordance with merit, as measured by universal standards of achievement;

4. to legitimate inequalities in material rewards in democratic society through principles of merit established in the school grading system;

5. to develop stable social relations with age peers outside the family;

6. to inculcate appropriate sex-role identification.

The functionalist approach to the sociology of education has largely accepted this list of functions defining the roles that schooling plays in society, particularly in preparing children for the job market. The main focus of the debate has been on the extent to which schools are able to meet the moral goals set out by Dewey: to provide equality of opportunity to all children for personal and intellectual development and academic attainment across different social classes, races, and ethnic groups. More recently, the importance of sexual equality has also been recognized. The growing consensus is that, notwithstanding concerted efforts at educational reform, schools are failing miserably with respect to the goal of equality.

Equality and Educational Opportunity

The concept of *equality* in education has been understood in several contradictory ways. During the early era of the common school system, emphasis was placed on **equality of condition** or sameness. A common curriculum was planned for all children as a standardized, age-graded program of studies without reference to individual differences in interests or abilities. Later the interpretation of equality shifted to emphasize **equality of opportunity** for all children to develop their individual potential. A variety of curricula were planned to reflect the different needs, capacities, and interests of students, and their different occupational futures. Differential treatment is justified on the basis of merit. Specialized and advanced education would be open to all children who qualify on the basis of effort and ability.

The acknowledged difficulty with offering differentiated programs is that they can become a source of inequality of opportunity. Children risk becoming trapped in educational streams that limit their future options. A third approach shifted the focus to *equality of outcome.* A range of educational opportunities, resources, and different teaching methods were designed to meet the special needs of individual children, with the goal that all students would succeed in school to the best of their innate abilities.

Each of these approaches tries to grapple with the evidence of persistent and marked differences in the formal educational attainment of students from different backgrounds. These cannot be accounted for solely by variations in intellectual ability. Porter, Porter, and Blishen (1982) conducted an extensive survey of 2571 Ontario students in grades 8, 10, and 12 to explore the relationship between the backgrounds of students and their aspirations to attend university. The researchers found a direct and strong relation between the father's occupational status and the student's aspiration to graduate from grade 13 and to enter university (see figure 12-1). The higher the occupational status of the father, the more likely the student was to want to complete grade 13. Seventy-six percent of students whose fathers were in the higher professional category intended to go on to university, compared with 46 percent of students whose fathers had unskilled jobs. This gap could only be partially accounted for by the different ability levels of students. The researchers found that social class background was a more powerful indicator of aspiration to graduate from university than was measured mental ability (Porter, Porter, and Blishen 1982, 61).

Among the high-ability boys, 77 percent of those with upper-middle-class backgrounds aspired to graduate from university. The corresponding figure for lower-class boys was 47 percent. At the other extreme, among the low-ability boys, 46 percent of those with upper-class backgrounds aspired to university. By contrast, only 22 percent of low-ability boys with lower-class backgrounds wanted to graduate from university. Thus, there is a 24 to 30 percentage-point difference in proportions of boys aspiring to university that can be accounted for by the effect of social class background.

Figure 12-1

Percent Wanting to Graduate from University, by Socioeconomic Status, Mental Ability, and Sex, Grade 12

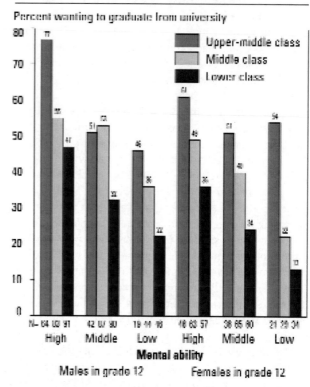

Source: Porter, Porter, and Blishen (1982, 61).

Grade 12 girls show similar differences in aspirations by social class. Among girls with high mental ability, 61 percent of the upper-middle-class girls aspired to university compared with only 36 percent of lower-class girls, a difference of 25 percentage points.

When grade 12 boys and girls are compared, boys have higher aspirations than girls across most categories of social class and mental ability. The exceptions occur among middle-ability and low-ability students within the upper-middle class where girls equal or exceed boys in aspirations.

These findings concerning the link between social class and aspirations for higher education closely mirror the results of research conducted in the 1950s in the United States by Tumin (1973, 46–54). This similarity suggests that the intervening twenty years of educational reforms had little effect on class bias in educational attainment. However, the differences between the sexes in the Ontario data are significantly less than in Tumin's data. Tumin found that, in every category of class and mental ability, boys had consistently higher educational aspirations than girls. The rise in aspirations among upper-middle-class girls in the Ontario data is striking.

A follow-up study of the Ontario grade 12 students confirmed the predicted relation between social class background and actual attendance at university, particularly among the high-ability students. In this group, 74 percent of the upper-middle-class students went to university compared with 62 percent of the middle-class and 59 percent of the lower-class students. Low-ability students showed similar differences in their rate of attendance by social class. Among the medium-ability group, however, there was an insignificant difference in attendance rates among the three classes.

In summary, the data suggest that the occupational class status of the father has significant effect on the likelihood of children aspiring to and attending university. The influence of social class exceeds that of mental ability, especially for boys. Students whose fathers are professionals are particularly likely to intend to go to university, even when their mental ability is low. Girls generally lag behind boys in their aspirations to attend university, although the differences seem to be decreasing, particularly within upper-middle-class families.

Functionalist Explanations for Class and Gender Bias in Educational Attainment

Functionalists view education as a system that provides for the appropriate allocation of young people into occupational roles on the basis of ability. How, then, do they explain the large numbers of high-ability students choosing not to attend university? Porter, Porter, and Blishen (1982, 25–29) draw upon the classical functionalist ideas of socialization and self-concept to explore the class and sex differences that are associated with the wasted talent. As we have seen in earlier chapters, socialization is the process through which children learn appropriate social roles and rules of behaviour for the groups in which they find themselves. These rules reflect those of the wider social settings of neighbourhood, social class, and religious group within which families are located. Through interacting with others, children learn to conform to the behaviour that others expect and learn to expect approval and esteem from others for such conformity. Of great importance to children is the approval of significant others. These people first consist of immediate family members and later the children's peers and teachers. Porter, Porter, and Blishen predict

that the roots of ambition lie in the early socialization process when the influence of parents is likely to be paramount.

Self-Concept

Self-concept, the image that we hold of ourselves, is closely related to socialization. Children develop a sense of who they are through coming to see themselves as they appear to others. Boys and girls growing up in different social classes come to develop different conceptions of themselves and their abilities. These self-concepts may not accurately reflect innate mental abilities, but they powerfully influence what children believe they can do, and therefore what they are willing to try.

Porter, Porter, and Blishen devised a series of questions to measure students' self-concepts and to determine who acted as their significant others. Their data suggest that parents seem to be more significant than either teachers or peers in influencing educational aspirations for the majority of children. In every social class, and for both sexes, a greater proportion of students aspired to university when parental influence was high, than when it was low. The high or low influence of peers made relatively little difference. Teachers appeared to have even less influence than peers on future educational plans.

The researchers found large differences between social classes in the amount of direct assistance that parents gave children with schoolwork. At the grade 10 level, they found a difference of 27 percentage points between upper-middle and lower-class boys, and 13 percentage points between upper-middle and lower-class girls in this regard. By grade 12 these differences rose to 34 and 41 percentage points respectively.

Self-concept of ability seems to be powerfully linked to parental influence and to school performance but minimally linked to measures of mental ability or to teacher's influence (Porter, Porter, and Blishen 1982, 125–29). Self-concept seems to account for the generally lower educational aspirations of girls relative to boys. The researchers found that girls had a lower self-concept of their own ability than boys for every measure used. Their striking finding was that girls achieved consistently better grade point averages in school than boys for every level of mental ability, and yet they had consistently lower self-concepts of their abilities than boys for every category of ability and performance. Girls, it seems, may be held back by their own low conceptions of themselves.

The researchers link the low self-concept of girls to a combination of socialization and realistic appraisal of the roles they see females perform, both of which are inconsistent with academic success and achievement. Girls, they suggest, are socialized to be overly dependent on the opinions of others and to be submissive. They are more likely to accede to the demands of female teachers and to perform well in school. But because they are not encouraged to be independent, they do not develop confidence in their ability to cope with their environment, and they receive less encouragement from parents to continue their education. They are taught to realize their ambitions through marriage and to passively accept the social status of their husbands.

Boys, on the other hand, are socialized to be independent and autonomous from their mothers, so they resist female teachers in early grades. But, as they near school-leaving age, they are under pressure to qualify for university, as this is linked to future male occupations. They encounter more male teachers in high school and new subjects associated with males in our culture. Thus, boys perform less well than girls throughout school but have higher self-concepts and are significantly more likely to go on to higher education.

If this analysis of the differential socialization and lower self-concepts of girls relative to boys accurately accounts for the 1971 data, it would appear that dramatic changes have occurred in gender socialization in one generation. In 1971, when Porter, Porter, and Blishen did their study, females comprised only 37.7 percent of full-time undergraduate enrolment. But by 1987–88, 50.3 percent of all full-time undergraduates were women, rising to over 53 percent by 1991–92 (see figure 12-2). The proportions in graduate programs remained stable between 1981 and 1991 with roughly three women to every four men enrolled. These figures suggest that the pattern found by Porter, Porter, and Blishen—that girls generally lack sufficient self-confidence in their abilities to develop high educational aspirations—no longer holds in the 1990s. We need new studies of family socialization to understand what changes have taken place and whether girls are attending university in numbers equal to boys because of, or in spite of, prevailing patterns of socialization.

The more general findings of Porter, Porter, and Blishen concerning differential educational aspirations and attainment by social class have not been challenged by any more recent data. The researchers conclude that different patterns of family socialization by

Figure 12-2

Full-time University Enrolment, by Level and Sex, Canada, 1981–82 and 1991–92

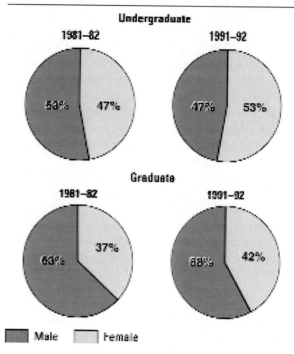

Source: Reproduced by authority of the Minister of Industry, 1994. Statistics Canada (1994e), *Education in Canada: A Statistical Review*, Cat. 81-229, p. 51.

social class constitute the primary cause of wasted talents in the education system. Parents are of central importance as significant others for children and are therefore significant in promoting or reducing educational aspirations. Upper-middle-class parents are more likely to take an interest in, and to help with, their children's schooling and to emphasize success in education as a factor in their approval and esteem. They promote higher aspirations in their children (see figure 12-3).

Schools may try to develop teaching methods to counter the negative influence of lower-class backgrounds on students, but the real solution seems to lie in changing the norms and values of lower- and lower-middle-class parents. Schools provide an avenue for upward social mobility, particularly in Canada. It is up to the students themselves to choose to take advantage of the opportunities provided.

Figure 12-3

Program by Socioeconomic Status, Grade 12

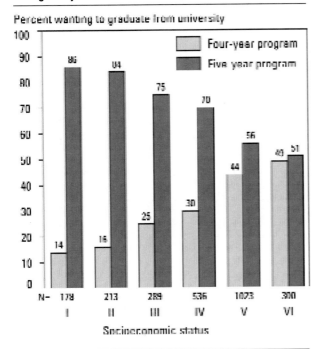

Source: Porter, Porter, and Blishen (1982, 193).

The Political Economy of Education: Schooling in Capitalist Society

The Marxist structuralist perspective is rooted in very different conceptions of stratification in capitalist society and of the associated role of education. It focusses primarily on the structure of the school system rather than on the aspirations of individual students. Differences in aspirations are regarded as the effects rather than the causes of inequality in education. Functionalists blame lower-class students for not wanting to take advantage of opportunities for higher education and social mobility. Marxists argue that the school system is structured in such a way as virtually to ensure their failure. In focussing on individual aspirations rather than underlying structures, functionalist theory acts as an ideology; that is, a means not to see what is really going on in the school system.

In this section we draw heavily on the work of Samuel Bowles and Herbert Gintis to illustrate the broad outlines of the Marxist structuralist perspective on education. Their study, *Schooling in Capitalist America* (1976), is widely cited as a seminal work that inspired a decade of Marxist-oriented research in education.

In a summary statement of their theory, Bowles and Gintis (1988) point to the contradictions between democracy and capitalism. Political democracy is based on rights invested in the person. The central problems for democracy concern how to maximize participation in decision-making, shield minorities against majority prejudice, and protect majorities against undue influence of an unrepresentative minority. The economic system is based on the principle of rights invested in property. The central problems are how to minimize participation of the majority (the workers), protect a specific minority (capitalists and managers) against the will of the majority, and subject the majority to the will of an unrepresentative minority.

Schools are caught in the middle. They are part of the democratic state system, but they are responsible for educating young people to fit into the economic system. Bowles and Gintis (1976, 54) argue that most of the problems in the school system stem from this contradiction between a democratic political system and a totalitarian economic system. The liberal conception of education, first put forward by Dewey, emphasizes three fundamental goals: (1) developing the full potential of individual students with respect to cognitive, physical, emotional, critical, and aesthetic powers; (2) promoting equality through common public schools that would overcome disadvantaged social backgrounds; and (3) ensuring social continuity through preparing young people for integration into adult social roles. Bowles and Gintis argue that these three goals are fundamentally incompatible. Schools cannot promote full personal development and social equality while integrating students into alienating and hierarchically ordered roles within the economy.

The problems are compounded by the compulsion within advanced capitalist economies to develop labour-saving technology that will either displace workers altogether or deskill them in order to cheapen their wage-labour and so raise profits. Bowles and Gintis accept the main theme of Braverman's *Labor and Monopoly Capital* (1974), which predicts that the vast majority of skilled craftworkers, clerical staff, and even professionals will be systematically deskilled and fragmented by technological advances. The resulting class structure will be characterized by a mass of low-skilled workers, controlled by a small class of supervisors and managers, with a very small elite class of highly skilled professionals and executives who run the huge corporations in the interests of the owners of capital. A principal function of schooling in relation to such a system is to prepare the mass of children to fit into a largely deskilled, fragmented, and hierarchical class system. Their natural abilities and desire for autonomy need to be suppressed rather than enhanced to make them comply.

Seen from this perspective, both the evidence of an apparent waste of talented lower-class children who drop out of school, and the lack of fit between mental ability and postsecondary education, take on new meanings (see table 12-1). Schools perpetuate class inequality because this is precisely what they are intended to do. Lower-class children are channelled into dead-end vocational streams, drop out of school early, and thus provide a ready supply of workers to fill the mass of unskilled jobs. Middle-class children, regardless of ability, stay in the education system long enough to get credentials that qualify them for better-paid positions. Bowles and Gintis argue that the main function of such credentials is to make distinctions between workers, and particularly to legitimate the higher pay and status of supervisors relative to workers. Very few of the people who achieve higher credentials actually find they need what they learned to do their jobs.

Bowles and Gintis (1976, 97–100) cite many examples to back up their argument that the relation between credentials and rewards is largely arbitrary. People who earn credentials, but who lack other attributes of superior status, tend not to get high economic rewards. For example, the economic returns on schooling—average increments in salary for each additional year of formal education—are twice as high for white males as for blacks and women in the United States. White males of upper-class background experience returns on education 66 percent higher than white males of lower-class background. Even when years of experience on the job are identical, white males are likely to have higher earnings than blacks and women. Body image is also important. Bowles and Gintis cite the results of one study that suggested that height was a more important determinant of earnings than either grade point average or a cum laude degree. Another survey of 15 000 executives found that those who were overweight were paid significantly less, the penalty being as much as $1000 a pound. People are much less likely to challenge the prestige, authority, and higher earnings of distinguished-looking older white males, regardless of their actual abilities, than they

would if younger, overweight, black women were promoted to supervisory positions.

From the perspective of traditional functionalism, such patterns are irrational—inexplicable holdovers of ascriptive criteria in what should be the impersonal and achievement-oriented bureaucratic world of business. But from the Marxist structuralist perspective these patterns serve to reinforce the status consciousness that fragments workers.

Structural Correspondence Theory

Structural correspondence theory argues that there is a close correspondence between how relationships are structured within schools and within the work force.

Table 12-1

Labour Force Participation and Unemployment Rate by Education and Sex, May 1994*

Level of Education	Unemployment Rate	
	Male	Female
0–8 years	16.4	16.3
Some secondary education	16.8	15.0
High-school graduate	9.9	9.8
Some postsecondary	12.7	13.2
Postsecondary diploma	9.2	8.6
University degree	5.5	5.7
Total	11.0	10.2

Level of Education	Participation Rate	
	Male	Female
0–8 years	41.7	19.3
Some secondary education	64.3	42.5
High-school graduate	81.6	63.9
Some postsecondary	80.9	70.6
Postsecondary diploma	84.8	70.9
University degree	86.3	80.5
Total	74.0	57.6

*The table shows relatively small differences in unemployment rates between males and females with comparable levels of education. Although there are large differences in official participation rates. The participation rate measures the proportions of people who are employed or actively seeking work at the time of the survey.

Source: Reproduced by authority of the Minister of Industry, 1994. Adapted from Statistics Canada (1994b), *Canada Year Book 1992*, table 5, p. B-16.

Common schools enforced military discipline and moral education well suited for training a docile and disciplined factory work force.

Schools reproduce the social relations required for production. Bowles and Gintis (1976, ch. 6) trace historical parallels between significant changes in the American capitalist economy and developments in the school system. The origin of the common schools in the mid-1830s in the United States coincided with the expansion of the factory system and the widespread labour unrest associated with it. What the factory owners desperately needed was not a skilled labour force, but a disciplined one. Common schools enforced military discipline and values of order, neatness, politeness, and punctuality that served to transform an ill-disciplined immigrant and farming populations into a docile and disciplined factory work force.

The subsequent progressive education movement, and greatly increased enrolment in public schools, coincided in the United States with the expansion of corporate capitalism between about 1890 and 1930 (Bowles and Gintis 1976, ch. 7). Corporate bosses needed a mass of middle-ranking employees who could be trusted to work without direct supervision in clerical, sales, bookkeeping, and junior supervisory roles. These employees also had to be divided socially from lower-level workers whom they supervised. More than obedience and punctuality was required. These employees had to internalize an identification with the employer and the corporation. It was this kind of stratified work force that the mass high schools produced. Schools expanded greatly in size and became bureaucratic, hierarchical, and competitive, ousting the once uniform curriculum of the common schools.

Social relations within vocational and college-track classes came to conform to different norms, consistent with the kinds of jobs for which children were being prepared. Vocational streams emphasized close supervision and obedience to rules, whereas college-track classes encouraged a more open atmosphere emphasizing internalization of norms, independent activities, and limited supervision. Near the top of the educational hierarchy, four-year colleges came to emphasize creative and critical thinking congruent with careers at senior levels of corporate hierarchies.

A classic in this research is the study by Jean Anyon (1980) into how social studies and language arts were taught in five elementary schools located in different communities in the eastern United States. The research describes marked variation in patterns of classroom interaction by the social class background of those attending school. Instruction in the elite school for the children of executives emphasized the development of analytical reasoning and leadership skills. Lessons were creative. Students made presentations to the class and criticized each other's work. In the middle-class school, lessons were very different. Language arts, for example, was reduced to grammar. Teachers checked for right answers rather than for critical understanding of the questions. In lower-class schools, children seemed to be taught primarily to follow rules set out by the teacher for completing the exercise. Their work was evaluated not by whether the answers were right, but whether the rules had been followed.

These differences reflect and reinforce the family backgrounds from which the different streams of children are drawn. Working-class parents favour stricter educational methods, directly reflecting their own knowledge that submission to authority is essential to getting and holding a steady job. Their children form the majority of pupils in vocational education streams. Professional and self-employed parents prefer a more open atmosphere with greater emphasis on motivational controls rewarding students for achievements rather than for obedience and good behaviour. Such an atmosphere is more consistent with their position in the labour force. Their children are mostly destined for college-track classes.

A third phase in the development of the education system, marked by the expansion of higher education in the 1960s, coincided with the effective domination of the capitalist economy by corporate and state sectors (Bowles and Gintis 1976, ch. 8). Self-employed entrepreneurs were relegated to increasingly peripheral roles. White-collar and professional employment expanded but became more fragmented and compartmentalized.

The expansion of community colleges and diploma courses came in response to this shifting job maket, producing what Bowles and Gintis refer to as skilled, sub-professional, white-collar workers. This category includes lower-level supervisors, secretaries, and para-professionals in dentistry, law, teaching, and medicine.

Liberal functionalists would largely agree with such an analysis, but Marxist structuralist theory goes further to draw attention to the changing social relations of higher education. Bowles and Gintis ask why the stress on free inquiry and liberal arts in higher education gave way to an emphasis on vocationalized and compartmentalized packages of credits. Why did the student politicization of the 1960s occur? Why has there been an overexpansion of graduates? The main answer they give is that free inquiry was appropriate for the entrepreneurial class, but not for corporate employees, except at the highest levels. Student radicals were drawn mostly from members of the declining entrepreneurial class who resented the loss of autonomy over their working lives. Mass higher education produced a surplus army of people with bachelors degrees and sub-profesional qualifications, and this served to break their bargaining power in the labour market. Corporations thus gained access to a highly skilled work force, while salaries and other concessions could be held to a minimum. Corporate profits were protected. The training of elites has now shifted further up into graduate and post-graduate education. Free inquiry tends to be stressed only at this heady level.

The pressure on universities to serve industry has now become more overt. It takes the form of cutbacks in public funding to force these institutions into greater direct co-operation with corporations. The result is that university autonomy is undermined, funding in less marketable liberal arts and humanities programs is threatened, and, even in the favoured science and engineering faculties, pure research is subordinated to short-term profit motives. Bowles and Gintis suggest that community colleges have already largely succumbed to pressure to produce the labour force that corporations want. They offer the veneer of higher education for lower-class students but, in reality, they may be little more than "high schools with ashtrays," channelling students into dead-end vocational programs (Bowles and Gintis 1976, 211).

Educational Reform: The Losing Battle?

Proposals for educational reform are compromised by the corporate context in which they are evaluated and implemented. Alternative, nonbureaucratic forms of schooling designed to promote the creative potential of children have operated in many pilot projects. They tend to be very successful in their own terms, and are described with great enthusiasm by teachers and students, but rarely do they expand beyond isolated schools for small numbers of privileged students. Bowles and Gintis blame reformers, not for their objectives, but for their narrow focus on schools while failing to target the wider economy that schools mirror.

The educational reformer Ivan Illich has long railed against the stultifying character of the North American public school system, which incarcerates students in classrooms, cuts them off from the real world, and teaches them to distrust their own knowledge and experience and to rely on experts (Illich 1971). "Knowledge" is treated as a packaged commodity that becomes the private property of those who attain credentials, while those who lack such paper credentials are predefined as incompetent. Illich proposes an alternative system of education in which students would recover responsibility for their own teaching and learning through watching people at work and learning alongside them. For Bowles and Gintis (1976, 255–62), the main problem with this vision of a deschooled society is that it treats the socialization agency of the school as the basic explanatory variable. But dismantling schools will not cure the effects of capitalism that cause schools to function as they do. Individuals cannot be held personally responsible for their own deschooling when schooling is obligatory for ten years and is the major means of access to a livelihood.

Schooling for Contemporary Capitalism

Critics of the structural **correspondence theory** suggest that Bowles and Gintis oversimplified the relationship between schools and capitalism. The rise of common schools in Upper Canada preceded the expansion of factories by some twenty-five years, discrediting the argument that their original purpose was to train workers for industrial capitalism (MacDonald 1988; Curtis 1987). The Ontario School Act of 1943 followed soon after the rebellions in Upper Canada in 1837–38 and seems to have been centrally concerned with promoting values of patriotism and citizenship in children. This was not incompatible with training a disciplined factory work force, but it did require a balancing of interests between democracy and capitalism.

The assertion that vocational schools were intended to prepare children for failure and entry into unskilled, dead-end jobs is also overstated. Automation and the systematic deskilling of the work force have played an important role in increasing profits to capitalists in mass-production industries. But the thesis that all capitalists want deskilled, cheap labour ignores the importance of rapid product innovation and a highly flexible, adaptive labour force in competitive global capitalism. The expansion of higher education since the 1960s, and the funds that capitalists have donated to certain university faculties, cannot be totally dismissed as credentialism. Authoritarian classrooms and standardized curriculum packages are not functional for the production of creative, innovative workers.

The signing of the North American Free Trade Agreement (NAFTA) in 1993 promises to usher in a new era of structural correspondence between the Canadian education system and global capitalism, characterized by the commercialization of society (Calvert and Kuehn 1993). Many aspects of education reflect a shift from a publicly funded social service to a private, profit-oriented system. Under NAFTA rules, once any aspect of the provision of educational services is opened to private contract, it cannot subsequently return to government control without all relevant United States firms being compensated for loss of market opportunity. Profit-making postsecondary training firms are expanding rapidly in Canada while funding for community colleges is being cut. Business colleges now routinely offer courses in keyboarding, computing skills, bookkeeping, and accounting. Any effort by governments to return such courses to the publicly funded community college system could be challenged under NAFTA regulations as unfair practices limiting markets for private firms.

The difference between public-service and private-profit educational institutions is, in any case, narrowing. In the language of administrators and new university presidents, education is increasingly being described as a product that managers market. Students are consumers and corporations are stakeholders. University administrators are corporate managers with objectives to run universities like a business, selling a product for which they must attract revenue or close down. Corporations are encouraged to rent university facilities for research in return for copyrights and patents. By 1993, fifteen universities and an estimated 800 researchers were linked with over 170 companies in joint research projects. Universities compete with each other to attract funding deals with corporations, as government revenues are frozen or reduced.

Provision of food services in schools is already being privatized with giant corporations like Burger King and McDonald's running school cafeterias. United States companies are also guaranteed **right of national treatment** in the publishing and distribution of textbooks. Intellectual property rights have been established over a wide range of educational materials including cable and satellite transmission of proprietary educational programs, courses, and learning aids that have patent protection. Educational television is fast becoming big business with companies providing equipment to schools in return for showing programs that carry commercials. The company Youth News Network incorporates a computer chip into its equipment to monitor how often a show is viewed, for how long, and at what volume, to be sure teachers don't "cheat" and spend time teaching instead of watching the show (Calvert and Kuehn 1993, 101).

The corporate agenda impacts on educational programs in multiple ways. Business groups are able to exert increasing pressure on high-school and university curriculum planning, arguing that Canada's global competitiveness depends on schools training children in business-oriented skills. In community colleges in particular, overt constraints are placed on teaching in the interest of serving business. Muller (1989) documents how any new programs introduced in community colleges in British Columbia are constrained to conform to local business interests. Standardized forms and procedures govern how new programs are to be presented to the provincial government. These forms require the signatures of relevant employers in the locality of the college—who might be expected to hire students graduating from such programs—to indicate that they have been consulted and have given their approval. Community college management standardizes the curriculum so it is no longer the prerogative of individual instructors. It is even possible for a student to take an instructor to court for breach of contract if the published course curriculum does not appear to have been strictly followed. Student services staff are explicitly directed to guide students toward training for which there are immediate jobs in the local market (Muller 1990). Instructors are also required by college management to keep up with any and all technological innovations, such as computer-designed instruction, that industry wants. Muller concludes that community college management, in effect, works for local industry, while being financed by the state.

Publishing companies exercise significant control over the context of the texts that are made available to teachers (Apple 1986, ch. 4). Acquisitions editors and decision makers in these companies are mostly males with a background in marketing. They focus principally on what they think will sell. The goal is to produce texts with standard content that will be used for years in multiple schools. Apple stresses the urgent need for detailed research into the routine daily work processes and the politics of publishing companies that produce textbooks.

Teachers are increasingly under pressure to use curriculum packages, with heavy emphasis on the preparation of worksheets and the standardized testing and evaluation of students. One effect of such packaged teaching, Apple suggests is to deskill teachers, reducing them to technicians rather than professionals who control their own activities (Apple 1986, ch. 2). Apple fears that the growing emphasis upon teaching computer literacy in schools will exacerbate the trend toward standardization and depersonalization of classrooms. Computer manufacturers foist machines onto schools, even offering a free machine for every classroom, in the hope that parents will be motivated to buy school-compatible models for their children to practise on at home. Computers come with standard software packages for classroom instruction. Rarely do these programs incorporate the richness of the professional experience of teachers. Nor do they include the "soft" curriculum of liberal arts. Humanities, ethnic studies, culture, history, politics are all likely to lose out to the mathematical and technical subjects that are readily adaptable to computers. Teachers may find themselves reduced to technicians running programs.

The influx of computers also seems likely to exacerbate class differences between schools. Rich schools can afford multiple machines for personal instruction, and wealthy parents are able to buy computers for home use. Poorly endowed schools and poorer students are not able to have these advantages. Apple argues, too, that elite children are more likely to learn the intellectually stimulating aspects of programming, while lower-class children are trained to use computers for drill and practice sessions.

Cutbacks in government funding for schools influence the social relations of schooling for teachers no less than for the children from poor families. Dorothy Smith and the Wollestonecraft Research Group (1979) document how cutbacks in school funding affect the everyday work of teachers and produce the classroom rigidities for which teachers are subsequently held responsible. When there is not enough science equipment for all pupils to conduct their own experiments, teachers have to demonstrate the experiments while pupils watch passively.

Larger classrooms mean that small-group work and seminars become less and less possible. Children who receive less hands-on experience and less attention get bored and distracted, discipline problems increase, and authoritarianism increases. Teachers do not have time to go through batches of essays or independent projects, so they assign fewer of them and rely more on uniform examinations. Teachers give more and more of their personal time to make up the shortfall in staffing until they burn out and leave the profession or become resigned to lower standards and autocratic methods. The schooling patterns criticized by Bowles and Gintis then take shape. The manifest function of budget cutbacks is to save taxpayers' money. The effect is increasingly authoritarian and rigid classrooms. The contrasts between the creative teaching in schools for elite children and the uninspired, autocratic styles of teaching in lower-class schools may well have more to do with teachers trying to cope with large classes and minimal teaching aids in lower-class schools than with any deliberate intention by such teachers to reproduce relations of class.

Standardized teaching practices are also becoming the norm in undergraduate university programs, although overt controls are less in evidence. Increasing enrolments in the face of limited budgets mean huge lecture halls, oppressive one-way teaching techniques, programmed assignments, and a reduction in individual projects. Students in lower-level sociology and psychology courses are more likely to be tested by multiple-choice examinations, marked by computers, which require rigid conformity to preprogrammed textbook answers. Fighting such trends requires tremendous effort on the part of professors who have to mark several hundred individual essays. Creative undergraduate research becomes progressively less possible as classes of a hundred or more students descend on libraries that can only afford one copy of each book and that have cut journal subscriptions to save money and space. These are the ways in which the social reality of undergraduate education for middle-level corporate conformity is socially constructed.

Schooling for Oppressive Social Relations

A central argument within the Marxist theory of education is that the school system within capitalist societies is designed to mould children to accept and submit to hierarchical and inegalitarian class relations within capitalist societies. Schools for children at the bottom of the social hierarchy exhibit these oppressive characteristics the most clearly. Bowles and Gintis claim that within

American public schools, relations between administrators and teachers, teachers and teachers, teachers and students, students and students, and also between students and their work, all replicate the hierarchical and fragmented division of labour within corporations (Bowles and Gintis 1976, 131). The content of the curriculum may be designed to teach the values of democratic citizenship, equality, freedom of speech, and so on. But the hierarchical relations within schools teach a very different lesson of submission to a rigid, rule-bound, and autocratic system. The usual liberal argument condoning such patterns is that students are children. They have not reached the stage of adult maturity when democratic rights of free choice would be appropriate.

Schools resemble factories in multiple ways. The architecture of the buildings, with separate rooms, offices, and recreation areas, arranged differently for staff, teachers, secretaries, and students, reproduces in concrete form the division of labour of the school. The seating arrangement in classrooms, with students in rows facing the front area controlled by the teacher, reinforces the hierarchy in which the teacher has authority and the students submit. The lessons of authority and submission are reported in the routines and rituals of the classroom that require students to speak only when spoken to and to leave and enter classrooms only when bells sound. Through such practices, children become inured to the discipline of the workplace. They develop the types of personal demeanor and self-image that fit them for future occupational roles in factories and bureaucracies. They learn to accept vertical lines of authority. They learn to accept the curriculum package offered. They learn to be motivated primarily through the extrinsic rewards of the grading system rather than the intrinsic pleasures of learning. Students are also fragmented through the insidious emphasis on competition and continual ranking and evaluation (Bowles and Gintis 1988, 2–3; 1976, 131).

The educational reformer, Paolo Freire, similarly decries the destructive impact of education on lower-class children, based on his observation of education in the slums of Brazil and ghetto schools in America (1970). He describes what he refers to as a banking concept of education. Students in classrooms are treated as objects rather than as acting subjects. They are containers to be filled by the teacher. The more meekly the receptacles permit themselves to be filled, the better students they are. In this system the teacher teaches and the students are taught; the teacher knows everything and the students know nothing; the teacher thinks and the students are thought about; the teacher talks and students

listen; the teacher chooses and enforces the choice and the students comply. In the process, schools perpetuate oppression by reinforcing subordination, passivity, and apathy among students. Teachers are created by and in turn reproduce the **culture of domination**. Students learn to respond with fatalism and docility towards authority and to direct their anger against comrades, rather than against their dominators. Their overwhelming aspiration is to take the place of the dominator and to boss others in their turn.

Education for Native Peoples

These descriptions of oppressive schooling may seem far removed from the everyday experience of Canadian university students who are used to the college-preparatory track of Canadian high schools. But for members of socially disadvantaged groups in ghetto classrooms in Canada, the parallels can be only too glaring. The following section, which focusses on an aspect of Canadian Native school experience, tries to bring this reality closer to home.

The traditional education of Native children took place through total involvement in community life. Children learned through sharing the lives of adults, through watching, listening, and learning by participation in the domestic, economic, political, and ceremonial life of the community. Formal schooling for Indian children in Canada was first provided by missionaries and later by government schools. Attendance at these schools became compulsory. Children from isolated bands were taken away from their communities and placed in residential schools. The explicit goal of residential schools was **assimilation**, or moulding Native children into whites. Native parents had no voice in what was taught. The language of instruction was English or French, and children were commonly punished for using their own language in school. This overtly imperialistic form of schooling was later replaced by smaller schools located within the band communities, particularly for the elementary grades. This shift toward educating Native students within their home communities was an important change, but much of the hidden curriculum of cultural domination remained intact. The description that follows is drawn from two anthropological studies of schools located within two Kwakiutl Indian villages situated along the northwest coast of British Columbia (Wolcott 1967; Rohner 1967). It is supplemented by an overview of formal education in an American Indian community (Wax, Wax, and Dumont 1964).

The hidden curriculum of the culture of domination was evident in both residential and reserve schools for Native children.

The hidden curriculum was manifest in the explicit assumption of many white educators in Native schools that only what the schools taught was worth knowing. Wax, Wax, and Dumont (1964, 67) refer to this attitude as the **vacuum ideology**. Teachers emphasized what they saw as the meager experience of Native children outside school and catalogued their multiple deficiencies relative to white children. The Native children's home experiences, the stories they heard from their parents, the skills of hunting, fishing, and trapping that they learned from parents were simple ignored because they fell outside the school curriculum. Teachers generally knew nothing of Native culture, values, or language, and had no respect for them either.

Teachers commonly lamented the overwhelming passivity of Native children, but this may well have been a symptom of the dehumanizing character of the schools and the breakdown in communication between teachers and pupils (Wax, Wax, and Dumont 1964, 98–99; Wolcott 1967, 92). The older the children grew, the shyer they seemed to become, so that by the eighth grade they were mute to all interrogation. Upper elementary grades were characterized by silent classrooms, the silence providing a shield behind which an unprepared, unwilling student could retreat. The teachers became ridiculous, futile figures, and they responded by condescension and dislike toward Native students. Students would arrive late for school and would drift home at midday, start some

task, and not return. They refused any active participation in classroom work. They expected boredom and even asked for highly repetitive work like copying. They had learned to equate the classroom with endless repetition, and they reacted against any variation in routines attempted by a new teacher. Their typical response was, "We didn't come to school for this, we came to do our schoolwork" (Wolcott 1967, 100).

This overt passivity within the classroom was combined with covert, horizontal violence against each other, which Freire observed among the oppressed people in Brazil (Wolcott 1967, 93). Younger children complained of being mercilessly teased, tortured, and bullied by classmates, behind the teacher's back. Some children absented themselves for days in fear. The only advice their mothers could give was to keep out of the way of the bigger children and not provoke them.

The school curriculum seemed irrelevant to the lives of adolescents on the reserves. Not only did it do nothing to prepare them for future jobs in their village, but it also actually conflicted with their informal education gained through participating in adult activities. Pupils resented attending school when they could otherwise be doing vital things like helping their fathers with fishing and clam digging.

The quality of academic performance in these reservation schools, measured in terms of universalistic grade standards, was abysmal (Wolcott 1967, 111; Rohner 1967, 110). The teachers, trained to respond to universalistic standards, found it almost impossible to adjust. When they administered normal intelligence tests, the Native students performed at near idiocy level. It was a hard shock for teachers, despite their knowledge that such tests are culturally biased. Teacher attitudes generally were highly unfavourable toward Native people. The village school studied by Rohner (1967, 105) had a turnover of eight teachers in fourteen years. Four of the eight had generated great hostility within the village. One had become so afraid of villagers that he had nailed up all the windows of his home and had refused to let his children play in the village. Another was so hated by the Native peoples that the superintendent had to remove him. Parents were equally intimidated by the teachers and were reduced to silence whenever they attended parent-teacher meetings. They asked only that the school open every day, start on time, and keep the pupils busy. Discipline problems were to be resolved by the teacher (Wolcott 1967, 86).

Given these kinds of school experiences, it would be miraculous if more than a small minority of Native pupils made it through to high-school graduation. Marxist structuralists would argue that they were being educated for failure. The oppressive school system defined all aspects of Native culture and traditional knowledge as irrelevant. It judged the students by white cultural standards and found them so ignorant that they were ranked as borderline mental defectives. Pupils learned to expect nothing but boredom and endless repetition in school, an expectation that exactly fits the menial, low-paying jobs that Native adults commonly attain in white capitalist society.

Since these studies were conducted there have been concerted efforts to address these problems. Many Native communities, in co-operation with the federal government, have begun to take control over their own education, and many universities in Canada and the United States have introduced Native Studies programs into their arts curriculum. The strategies seem to be working, evidenced in significantly higher numbers of

Figure 12-4

Postsecondary Participation Rate: A Comparison

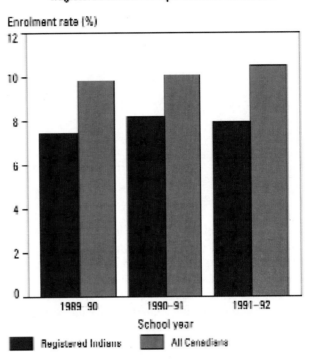

Full-time Postsecondary Enrolment Rates
Registered Indians Compared to All Canadians

Source: Indian and Northern Affairs Canada (1993), chart 17, p. 42.

Table 12-2

Enrolment in University and Postsecondary Institutions for the Registered Indian Population, Canada, 1960–61 to 1992–93		
School Year	University Enrolment	Postsecondary Enrolment[1]
1960–61	60	n/a
1965–66	131	n/a
1970–71	432	n/a
1975–76	2071	n/a
1980–81	4455	n/a
1985–86	5800	11 170
1986–87	n/a	13 196
1987–88	n/a	14 242
1988–89	n/a	15 572[2]
1989–90	n/a	18 535
1990–91	n/a	21 300
1991–92	n/a	21 442
1992–93	n/a	21 566

Notes:

[1]Includes Bill C-31 population. Total number of registered Indians funded by DIAND enrolled in postsecondary institutions also includes the number enrolled at university.

[2]Since 1988–89, numbers include students in the University and College Entry Program (UCEP).

Source: Indian and Northern Affairs Canada (1993), table 16, p. 41.

Native students pursuing some form of postsecondary education in recent years. Enrolment of Native students in all postsecondary institutions nearly doubled between 1985–86 and 1992–93 from 11 170 to 21 566 students (see table 12-2). Enrolment in university increased from a mere 60 Native students in 1960–61 to 5800 in 1985–86. The proportions, however, still remain well below those for Canadians as a whole (see figure 12-4).

Status Indians are eligible for financial assistance to attend university under the Postsecondary Student Assistance Program, but this funding was capped in 1989. This freeze on funding coincided with a significant increase in the numbers of Native students eligible under the program. The implementation of Bill C-31 granted recognition of aboriginal status to women who had formerly lost it by marrying men who were not status Indians. These women and their children now also qualify for financial assistance as defined within treaties. Band councils now have to make difficult decisions about how to allocate limited funds among a larger group of competing claimants.

Schooling and Poverty

Poverty exacerbates the problems of racism, language, and cultural divisions against which Native peoples struggle. Children in poverty, who comprised an estimated 18.2 percent of all children in Canada in 1992, face problems of ill health, malnutrition, and daily humiliation as a routine part of their educational experience (National Council of Welfare 1994). A study by the National Council of Welfare (1975) documents that poor children are more likely than others to be born premature and underweight, to contract childhood diseases, and to miss one to three months of school in a year because of illness.

The social effect of poverty on children, and their isolation from others in the classroom, may be less visible than inadequate clothing and ill health, but they are equally damaging to the children's educational aspirations and sense of well-being. Poor children face the humiliation of not being able to bring in money for special school events or excursions. They cannot afford to buy art supplies, sports equipment or uniforms, or instruments for the school band, and so they cannot join in many of the extracurricular activities open to other children. The list of barriers goes on and on (Gabriel 1986). Humiliation fosters withdrawal, defeat, and resentment. It drains them of the motivation to give their best efforts. Poor children lack money for school books and basic supplies, which makes it hard for them to keep up with homework. Cutbacks in school budgets often mean that teachers cannot provide books for all students and cannot permit them to take books home because they must be stored away and used in other classes. Poor children are also more likely to live in inadequate and overcrowded homes where they may have no quiet place to study. Teachers used to be able to supervise quiet study periods after school hours, but with budget and staff cutbacks, such "frills" are eliminated.

Poor children in senior classes may lack the time and energy for schoolwork because they take long hours of employment at minimum wage. If school counsellors suggest they would be better off quitting school to join the army or take a typing job, they are likely to agree. Realistically they see little possibility of mobility into professional occupations when all the people around them only have low-paying semiskilled jobs. **Headstart programs** for children in deprived areas may end up only making things worse because they raise unrealistic expectations, resulting in bitter disappointment for adolescents faced with limited opportunities.

The Limitations of Political Economy Theory

The major criticism of classical political economy theory of education concerns its reductionist and deterministic formulation. Ironically, an approach that began as a radical critique of traditional functionalism depends in practice on the same logic. The structure of parts are explained by their functions for the social system as a whole. The difference is that, in Marxist theory, the system is specifically capitalist. The explanation invokes rigid historical **reductionism**. All changes in the school system since its inception in the 1840s are explained as responses to the needs of capitalism (Aronowitz and Giroux 1985, 71, 117; Cole 1988, 7–37; Moore 1988, 58–61; Apple 1988, 124).

A significant problem with this form of explanation is that it presupposes a passive view of humanity. Human agency plays little part in analysis. Teachers and students are reduced to mere pawns of the capitalist system (Aronowitz and Giroux 1985, 71). According to Marxist structuralists, schools legitimate inequality and limit personal development to aid in the process whereby youths are resigned to their fate (Bowles and Gintis 1976, 266; Cole 1988, 35). From the perspective of social constructionist theory, Aronowitz and Giroux endorse the Marxist critique of capitalism, but challenge the oversimplified version that tries to reduce all explanations of human behaviour to position in the class structure. They argue (1985, ch. 2) that it is essential to recognize the role of teachers as professionals who are actively involved in the creation of what constitutes education. Teachers are not mere technicians who deliver standard curriculum packages and who function to preserve a hierarchical social order. For the best of them the opposite is closer to the truth, as teachers struggle to break the hold of inherited disadvantages, and push their students to develop enquiring minds and go on to academic careers. Historically, teachers have been active in professional associations that have fought for better working conditions, and for a greater say in what and how teachers teach and who evaluates them, and for control at the level of classroom practice (Apple 1986, 75). Students, too, are active in shaping the social relations of classrooms. The classic study by Willis (1981) documents how "the lads" in working-class schools in Britain actively resisted the efforts of teachers, imposing their own anti-school values on the classroom that mirrored the factory-floor culture of working-class men (see chapter 5). When Bowles and Gintis blame schools for reproducing class relations of capitalism, they may be attacking the wrong target, blaming schools for reproducing a culture that teachers are vainly trying to break.

Critics point out that, despite the Marxist commitment of Bowles and Gintis, the outcome of their theory is politically reactionary. It supports the status quo in that it leaves no space for individual or collective action to change the situation. The only viable option seems to be resignation or radical pessimism (Aronowitz and Giroux 1985, 79; Cole 1988, 35). More significantly, this ostensibly Marxist argument has been appropriated by spokespeople for the right wing in the United States. Conservatives are in full agreement with the view of Bowles and Gintis that schools are an adjunct to the labour market. They complain only that schools do not do this preparatory work well enough. The left wing seems to have no alternative to offer and to be constrained to silence (Aronowitz and Giroux 1985, 5–6). Aronowitz and Giroux (1985, 128) suggest that, despite their diametrically opposing political values, the philosophies of Marxist structuralism and capitalism share an uncritical acceptance of **scientism**: a reliance on simple cause and effect explanatory models that tend to reduce people to objects at the mercy of structural economic forces.

In this critique, we have referred to Marxist structuralism rather than Marxist theory in general, because there are important developments within contemporary Marxist theory that retain a radical critical perspective while rejecting the deterministic aspects of structuralism. This perspective shifts the focus of reearch from macro-studies of capitalism to the everyday interaction within the classroom of teachers and students.

How is it that capitalists are somehow able to dictate how people should relate to each other within classrooms? How do administrators, teachers, and students make sense of what is happening? How do they respond to such pressures? Why do they put up with them? When and how do they resist? These kinds of questions prompt a very different kind of research from that prevailing in either functionalist or Marxist structuralist approaches. Rather than mass surveys or sweeping historical overviews, **cultural Marxism** and the **social construction of reality** perspectives favour research into the intimate details of interpersonal relations within classrooms. It is these relations that we explore below.

The Social Construction of Schooling*

Proponents of the social construction of reality do not view classrooms as the effects of social structures. Classrooms are the location within which the **social structures** of class, gender, or race are produced. The causal processes involved are the meaningful interactions between people in intimate everyday activities. Many studies of classrooms are beginning to piece together the mechanisms that produce what Bowles and Gintis identify as the social relations of capitalism.

The Social Construction of "Academic Ability" and "Merit"

Research in both the functionalist and political economy traditions has demonstrated how children are streamed on the basis of apparent capabilities and commitments, beginning in kindergarten or first grade; how pervasively such streaming carries over into senior classes when children are directed into vocational and academic programs; and the close correlation between such streaming and the social class backgrounds of the children. But we still have little understanding of how this happens. We need to get beyond the circular reasoning that capitalist society needs to reproduce and to justify class divisions. Social constructionist research explores the practices that accomplish what teachers come to recognize as "bright middle-class children" and also the common-sense reasoning through which the behaviour of young children becomes coded into categories such as "academically gifted" or "not very bright."

Observations and analysis of conversations between mothers and children in Toronto playschools (Noble 1982; 1990) reveal the complex interactional practices through which these mothers produced the school readiness of their children. This mothering work involved training children in how to think in terms of abstract concepts and how to interact with other children and adult authority figures in ways that would fit them into the organization of school classrooms. Mothers continually prompted children into elaborating their sentences,

---

*The draft of this section on social constructionist approaches to education was prepared by Dr. Peter Weeks as an extension of his work on the microsociology of eveyday life for chapter 8 of this text.

introducing proper nouns and adjectives that were largely redundant in the immediate context. For example, one child displayed a small cut and explained, "I hit it here." Mother adds, "You hit your knee on the step."

Mothers also routinely took advantage of children's topics and activities to build mini-lesson structures into their interaction. A child playing with beads shows one to her mother and says, "Look what I got." Mother replies, "You've got beads. What colour are they?" More than a simple conversation is involved in such exchanges. The mother already knows the answer to the question and the child knows that the mother knows. The child is being encouraged and taught to display knowledge for adult evaluation (Noble 1982, 21).

Another mother playing alongside her child with a farm animals puzzle continually named and talked about each animal in turn, and also continually stressed the abstract category frame, "These are all <u>animals</u>, animals that live on the farm. Now let's put all the <u>animals</u> back in their place." When all the pieces were in place the mother asked, "How are all of these the same?" If the child failed to get the right answer, the mother might have prompted, "They are all _____." Another day the exercise will be run through again. Mothers showed by their intonational stress, and the energy directed to making it fun, just how favoured such games are.

Converations with kindergarten teachers revealed how important such mother-child interactions can be in the subsequent evaluation of children as precocious and "ready for academic work" or "not very bright." Children in kindergarten were encouraged to engage in "free play," but not all play was regarded equally. Children who chose "mere play," like slides and sand box, were seen by teachers as not ready to go on to academic work. Children who "spontaneously" chose the ostensibly more mentally demanding matching and categorizing equipment were seen as ready to move ahead (Noble 1982, 12).

Children whose mothers had convincingly presented puzzle-matching games as fun have a distinct advantage. It was important for teacher evaluations that children respond to the instructional "question-answer-evaluation" sequence. When a teacher asks a child, "That's a nice truck. How many wheels does it have?" the child who does not respond appears as "not very bright" or "not very verbal" compared with the child who immediately responds with the number. The interpretive framework used by the teacher takes for granted that the child has been test-broken into this instructional sequence, but this presupposes years of prior exposure to such question-answer "games" and the interactional awareness that they **must** respond.

In another kindergarten classroom, the teacher displayed a picture of rain coming out of a cloud and asked, "What other word do you think of when you think of the word *rain*?" (Noble 1982, 29). Children offered a range of experiential associations like "raincoat," "umbrella," and "boots," but they were all passed over until the answer "weather" was offered. Children who have been sensitized in advance to their mothers preferring category words like "These are all animals" have a distinct advantage. Similarly, children who fill their sentences with proper nouns and adjectives appear brighter and more verbally advanced than children who do not bother to state the obvious.

A requirement of the organization of kindergarten classrooms is that children know they must drop their own activities and attend to the relevances of the teacher, and with appropriate posture and facial displays. Noble gives the example of children dropping whatever else they are doing to sit in a circle when the teacher announces that it is circle time for reading (1982, 16–18). Years of prior work, of subordinating bodies so that instruction can take place, are required for children to appear to do this "naturally" and so to appear bright and interested in what the teacher is doing. Parents may carry out this intensive one-on-one work over years, first positioning infants in front of objects they want the infant to focus on, screening other objects from view, and even pinning down limbs to enforce appropriate looking and listening. If this bodily learning is not already in place when a child enters school, it is difficult for a teacher to remedy it, even in very small groups. Noble describes scenes of kindergarten teachers struggling to restrain children in circles so that storytime could begin, and forcibly holding one child's head so he would pay attention to instructions.

Noble suggests that mothers with conventional middle-class backgrounds are far more likely to be familiar with such child development work than parents with lower-class backgrounds, and to have more time and resources with which to accomplish it. This observation, however, begs the further questions of how mothers acquire these child-developing competences and the conditions under which motherwork gets done.

Intelligence as Interactional Competence

Differences in levels of **interactional competence** among kindergarten children are directly reflected in supposedly formal or objective tests of intelligence. Noble (1990) gives three examples of test questions in the Wechsler Preschool and Primary Scale of Intelligence

(WPPSI) (see table 12-3). An answer is assigned a score of 0 if unacceptable; 1 for a response that is appropriate but vague, experiential, or idiosyncratic; and 2 for a "better" answer that is more general, precise, and categorical.

According to Noble, what counts as intelligence includes:

1. being rule-governed, i.e., oriented to standard and conventional forms rather than personal and idiosyncratic ones;

2. being able to take a generalized position, external to yourself, and think in terms of the needs and interests of organizational entities beyond yourself;

3. being able to orient only to information given and solve questions asked only within the frame provided (Noble 1990, 55).

A child must know that general, categorical, and precise answers are preferred by adult testers over personal, experiential answers, in order to appear intelligent.

A similar study explores children's common-sense reasoning by asking them how they decided on their answers to a reading test (MacKay 1974a, 183–84). One stimulus sentence was about an animal that had been out in the rain. The "correct answer" was a picture of a room with dotted wallpaper walls and a floor imprinted with a

---

Table 12-3

Test Questions in the Wechsler Preschool and Primary Scale of Intelligence (WPPSI)

Example 1: Vocabulary Section

What is a knife?

Something to cut with . . . a weapon	2 points
Something to kill with	1 point
I have one . . . I play with it	0 points

Evidently, the 0 option is hopelessly experiential and does not treat *knife* as a general category. 1 is too restricted in terms of range of uses to count for the full 2 points.

Example 2: Similarities Section

Why shouldn't you play with matches?

So people won't get hurt . . . so your house won't burn down	2 points
You get burned . . . you can hurt yourself	1 point
You'll get a spanking	0 points

Though all these answers involve reasoning processes, some count more than others. While the 2 point answer is generalized in taking account of persons and property, the 0 option represents a refusal to take an adult view of morality.

Example 3: Comprehension Section

Why should children who are sick stay home?

So the class won't get the germs	2 points
So you don't get sicker	1 point
Their mommies get mad if they go out	0 points

To get the 2 points, the child again must take a generalized perspective, considering the interests of the organization (the school) rather than merely one's own.

Source: Adapted from Noble (1990, 54).

trail of animal tracks. One child misperceived the picture to be the outside of a house, with the dotted wallpaper being snowflakes. She consequently chose the "wrong" answer and scored zero. But her explanation clearly demonstrates interpretive skills in coming up with reasonable accounts of the world.

These interpretive studies reveal "brightness" as an interactional accomplishment rather than a measure of "real" intellectual capabilities. Teachers usually describe students in terms of cognitive attributes such as "bright" or "highly verbal" or else "nonverbal" or "not having a clue." But while these appear to be common-sense to teachers, Noble asserts that these are "ideological formulations" (1990, 45). In effect they are "class-defining practices."

Streaming as Practical Accomplishment

Teachers exercise a monopoly of professional competence to determine the academic ability and appropriate education stream of children in school. How these allocative decisions are made influences the future career opportunities of children. Interpretive approaches to education have tried to make visible the common-sense reasoning practices through which teachers accomplish streaming as visibly and accountably appropriate.

Studies that use a **labelling theory** approach show how teachers' practices in categorizing children as they enter kindergarten can shape the children's entire school careers. Labelling theory, was first developed in relation to studies of deviance. It explores the thesis that deviance is not inherent in any particular action, but in the judgments of witnesses. Those judgments determine how the person committing a "deviant" act comes to be treated thereafter.

Rist (1977) outlines a four-step process by which initial evaluations affect future options beginning with (1) the various evaluative mechanisms, both formal and informal, (2) how students react to them, (3) outcomes for personal interaction, particularly between teachers and students, and (4) the consequences of having a certain evaluative tag for the options available to students in the school (Rist 1977, 293). Rist argues that through such processes, failure in school becomes a self-fulfilling prophesy as teacher expectations are operationalized in the classroom to produce what the teacher had initially assumed.

Rist carried out a longitudinal study of an inner-city American urban ghetto school following the progress of children in kindergarten through to second grade. Within eight days of beginning kindergarten the teacher permanently assigned each child to a seat at one of the three tables for the remainder of the school year, based on her perception of their academic promise. Her judgments were based on immediate experience of interacting with the children in class for the first few days, together with knowledge of their older siblings, and information from admission forms and school social workers indicating which children were welfare recipients. The children assigned to Table 1, nearest the teacher, were generally more talkative to the teacher and more familiar with standard American English, and they participated well as group members.

One can speculate that children who had been coached in their prekindergarten years to use elaborate sentences with proper nouns and adjectives, who are cued in to the compulsory instructional form of question-answer-evaluation sequences, who know that abstract, category terms are preferred over personal associations in question-answer games, who choose matching and categorizing toys over the sandbox, and who have learned to subordinate their bodies and facial expressions to adult relevances, are far more likely to end up at Table 1. It was also clear in Rist's study that the children assigned to Table 1 were neat and clean in appearance and of higher average socioeconomic backgrounds than the children assigned to Table 3.

Once assigned to Table 1, these children were designated as "fast learners" and received more teaching time and attention while the "slow learners" at Table 3 were taught less frequently, subjected to more control, and received less support from the teacher. The gap in completion of academic material between the two groups widened during the course of the school year. Objective measures of past performance seemed to confirm the appropriateness of initial labelling on the eighth day of kindergarten. Two years later, the children from Table 1 in kindergarten were almost all together in Table 1 of grade 2, labelled as the "Tigers" or the winners, and they were still receiving more teaching time than other groups.

Another study of teachers' labelling practices (Becker 1977) confirms the high correlation between assessments of ability and socioeconomic backgrounds. He records a typical teacher's assessment of "slum" children:

> They don't have the right kind of study habits. They can't seem to apply themselves as well. Of course, it's not their fault; they aren't brought up right. After all, the parents in a neighbourhood like

that really aren't interested. . . . But as I say, those children don't learn very quickly. A great many of them don't seem to be really interested in getting an education. . . . It's hard to get anything done with children like that.

Children from upper-class neighbourhoods seemed to respond much more readily than slum children to ideas and suggestions from teachers and concentrated more on lessons. To get attention in a chemistry class in the slum area school, teachers felt they had to do flashy demonstrations with lots of noise and smoke.

Maintaining the Home-School Relation

Each of these studies, by Noble, Rist, and Becker, repeats the same observation that the behaviour of children in kindergarten is closely correlated with socioeconomic status. The children who fit most readily into the social organization of schools are "middle-class" children. But we still have limited understanding of how differences in parenting practices by social class are accomplished. We need more research into the organization of peoples' lives and the meanings that people bring to the situations they find themselves in—to the grinding effects of poverty and the dis-organizing practices that continually threaten to disrupt what poor people manage to put together. The teacher's comment that parents in poor neighbourhoods "really aren't interested" in the lives of their children is a summary term for ignorance rather than an explanation of differences in parenting work.

Intensive parenting work is also involved in accomplishing the appearance of being an "interested" parent (Noble 1982, 39–67). "Support" for school is not merely a matter of positive attitudes; it involves real resources of time, energy, and skills. Parents require tacit knowledge of what kind of support work and what kind of communication is appropriate. Managing parent-teacher interactions requires skills in picking up cues from teachers, knowing acceptable ways of asking questions about a child's progress or about what goes on in the classroom, and ways of expressing concern that will be interpreted by teachers as co-operative, responsible, and emotionally stable rather than hostile, unreasonable or overprotective. These are class-related skills. Middle-class mothers are likely to have far more experience of interacting as equals with people in professional careers than do working-class mothers.

The teaching profession generally claims expertise in the specific field of cognitive development with parents

A child's *mind* is an *open* book.

As a parent, it is your responsibility to fill the pages of a child's mind with wonder and joy. Reading together is a delightful way of accomplishing this and a means of ensuring that your child's future remains an open book.

Prepare a young mind for tomorrow. Open a book today.

ABC CANADA

Distribution of this message was made possible by the Canadian Advertising Foundation

Literacy support groups attempt to redress the imbalance of different parenting practices.

responsible for auxiliary work. Noble describes parent-teacher meetings as often providing a forum for teachers and principals to disseminate professional views on child-management to parents, with parents being held accountable for the socioemotional development. Parents can establish their presence as "interested" by asking about their child's "adjustment problems" in the classroom, and otherwise deferring to the teacher's professional expertise. Teachers, in turn, may be influenced to notice and to give more attention to a particular child in order to have something to talk to an "interested" parent about. But the parent-teacher relationship must be handled carefully if it is to result in protecting and improving children's chances at school.

Many working-class parents do not know how to play the parent-teacher game, do not feel at ease in contact with the school, and do not know how to raise topics with teachers. They withdraw under the weight of accumulated small intimidations and join the ranks of parents who appear "not interested" in their children. Parents who openly confront teachers and challenge their expertise may be regarded as "trouble-makers" with "personal problems," and they may well generate retaliation against their children in the classroom. Parents need to know how streaming works operationally. Objections to disadvantageous streaming decisions are more likely to be successful when parents do not attack test scores or teachers directly, but use the jargon of testing to focus on discrepancies.

In summary, the relationships between teachers as professionals and both children and parents from middle-class backgrounds work more smoothly than relationships with working-class families. Noble's work tries to make visible the interactional and discourse skills that accomplish this relation. Becker interprets his data as teacher reactions to cultural variations associated with social-class backgrounds, but much more than mere prejudice is involved.

Kindergarten teachers in Noble's study had to depend on children's willingness to sit quietly in a circle in order to read stories to them. On bad days, virtually one-on-one bodily monitoring was needed, with an adult blocking getaways and physically separating children from their toys before circle time could begin (Noble 1982, 16). A wide range of interactional competences, bodily subordi-

HERMAN

"I think you'll find my test results are a pretty good indication of your abilities as a teacher."

nation, and attending to adult relevances have to be assumed before lessons can happen.

Lessons as Social Accomplishments

Lessons do not happen naturally by themselves, either for students or for teachers. A branch of ethnomethodology known as **conversation analysis** researches detailed features of student-teacher interaction in lessons, using the technique of audio- and video-recordings. The questions explored include: the organization of turn-taking (McHoul 1978); teacher strategies to maximize participation of the class as a cohort (Payne and Hustler 1980); the detection and handling of deviance (Hester 1991); the overall organization of lessons from beginning to end (MacKay 1974a; Mehan 1979); and collaboration in students' writing stories employing computers (Heap 1986).

Weeks's study of primary-school oral reading lessons (1985) makes visible the error-correction sequences by which teachers alert a student that there is a problem and present an opportunity for the student to come up with the correct word. Complex interpretive practices or working assumptions are involved in both teacher and student getting the correction completed. The teacher may only hint at a problem with a brief "hm hm." The student has to have sufficient interpretive skills to pick up on the hint, figure out what the problem is, which word is wrong, and what to do about it. After a two-second pause the student enunciates another word, in a rising tone that indicates uncertainty or waiting for confirmation. The teacher's second "hm hm," with a different tone from before, means something quite different from the first utterance—a positive evaluation of the student's answer. Following this, the student resumes reading aloud from the text.

Highly complex but tacit interactional competences are assumed between teacher and student, and other members of the reading group, to get through this self-correction instructional sequence. Other correction techniques involve the teacher giving explicit directions like "Watch for the period!"—but even then the student has to know what to do with it. It is clearly not enough just to watch for a period; the reader has to manage proper intonation and to make a break at the right place. Students who are not attuned to such cues will not be able to follow the lesson.

Other studies explore the turn-taking organization of classrooms, and how teachers maintain authority by such practices as controlling the turn-taking, selecting specific students for next turns, who then have to return the "floor" to the teacher rather than hold onto it or select other students to speak (McHoul 1978). Teachers may organize lessons by posing a question that students lack the resources to answer at the beginning, but that they come to answer in the end through processes of hinting and filling in (Hammersley 1990). Teachers also commonly use "undirected questions" addressed to the class-as-a-whole, such as "Who knows the distance between Toronto and Montreal?" Such seemingly open invitations to respond are accompanied by the practice of students raising hands to bid for a turn, with the teacher as arbiter among competing bids.

It is through such practices that teachers organize the collectivity of students as a **cohort**—as one collective party to the talk with the teacher acting as the other party (Payne and Hustler 1980, 56). Students are thus led to take the teacher as their single focus of attention, with any one student being a potential target for the teacher's next question. Such practices also discourage students from talking to each other, except for prompting each other with candidate answers. Students who have not mastered the proper posture and facial expressions for conveying attention to the teacher are likely to be targeted.

Other research suggests that teachers tend to use positive evaluations like "That's right," "Okay," or "Well done" quite frequently, while avoiding negative ones by such tactics as offering cues to correct answers, and asking other members of the class if they agree or have other suggestions (McHoul 1990). This can be seen as another way of accomplishing "cohorting" by opening opportunities for wider student participation, and using each answer as an occasion for further instruction (Weeks 1994). When such tacit cohorting work and turn-taking practices fail to elicit appropriate responses from students, as in the slum schools described by Becker (1977), or the Native schools described in the previous section, teaching may be experienced as very difficult, if not impossible.

The Limitations of Social Constructionism

Interpretive perspectives open up the "black box" of schooling to show the complex interaction between background factors like social class and the routine practices of the school. We begin to see the practices that constitute what is traditionally understood as cultural deprivation, and how the social structural characteristics of inequality are accomplished through intimate everyday interaction in classrooms.

The potential strength of this approach can also become its weakness. Explanations that focus on the

intimate behaviour of individuals in classrooms risk losing sight of the structural contexts in which such interactions are embedded. Individual mothers, teachers, and students appear as blameworthy for failing to prepare students adequately for school, or for failing to adapt classroom instruction to compensate for different behavioural profiles. It remains important to recognize how structures of capitalism—the commercialization of education and the impact of corporate agendas on curriculum budget cutbacks, intensification of teachers' work, standardized curriculum and evaluation packages imposed on teachers, and the like—constrain teaching and learning in critical ways. The special contribution of the interpretive perspective is that it provides ways of seeing how these seemingly external structural factors work, through the activities of people at the level of everyday interaction.

Feminist Theory in Education

Until the beginning of the twentieth century women in Canada were largely excluded from all forms of higher education, and most had little formal schooling beyond learning to read and write. By the 1990s, the pattern was dramatically different. Women and men are equally likely to graduate from high school and enter undergraduate programs; however, they remain concentrated in different fields of study. Women are overrepresented in arts, nursing, and domestic science programs, and significantly underrepresented in mathematics, physical sciences, computer science, and technology (see figure 12-5 and table 12-4).

Feminist research in education has focussed attention on the different experiences of girls and boys in the school system. Much of this research has adopted the theoretical perspectives and methodology of social constructionism, recording detailed observation of classroom interaction to explore the practices through which gender differentiation is accomplished. Richer's (1979) study of an Ontario kindergarten class displays multiple ways in which the teacher emphasized gender distinctions. Gender was repeatedly used to organize classroom activities. Boys and girls were asked to line up separately before moving from one activity to another, to go to the library, the gymnasium, or the dining room, and to get ready to go home. Boys and girls hung their outdoor clothing in separate areas. Commonly they were pitted against each other by such comments as "Who can

Figure 12-5

Percentage Distribution of Full-time Fall Enrolment in Postsecondary Career Programs by Sex and Program Field, Canada, 1990–91

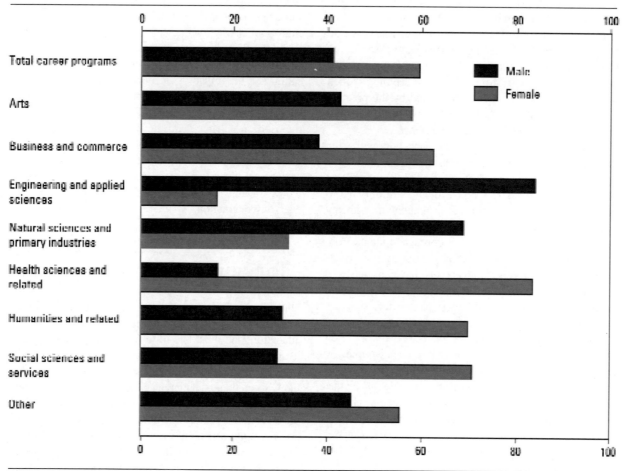

Source: Statistics Canada, Cat. 81-222, p. 17.

do this the fastest, boys or girls?" In co-ordination exercises commands were routinely given separately to boys and girls: "Boys, put your fingers on your nose; girls, put your hands in your laps; boys, touch your toes," etc. When any of the children responded to an activity intended for the other sex, the teacher commonly drew attention to it with a comment like "Are you a girl? I thought all along you were a boy" (Richer 1979, 201).

Observations of classroom interaction suggest that teachers may respond differently to girls and boys, and in ways that encourage boys to dominate classroom space while subtly devaluing the girls. Sadker and Sadker (1987, 144) found that teachers in the classes they observed tended to accept answers shouted out by boys who did not raise their hands and wait to be given a turn. When girls behaved similarly they were more likely to be reprimanded. Observations of elementary grades suggest that girls tend to be quieter and more obedient whereas boys are more likely to bounce around, ask questions, and be aggressive. One of the consequences seems to be that teachers generally find girls easier to deal with, so concentrate more attention on boys. Boys are likely to receive more disapproval, scolding, and other forms of negative attention than do girls, but they are also likely to receive more attention and praise (Huston 1983, 439; Basow 1986, 126). Teachers also admitted to finding boys more fun to teach (Schneider and Coutts 1979; Russell 1987, 240).

Table 12-4

Full-time Undergraduate Enrolment, by Field of Study and Sex, Canada 1983–84 and 1991–92						
	1983–84			1991–92		
Field of Study	Percent Male	Percent Female	Total	Percent Male	Percent Female	Total
Agricultural and biological sciences						
Agriculture	62.9	37.1	4 713	54.5	45.5	3 511
Biology	50.2	49.8	9 639	44.9	55.1	17 200
Household science	3.6	96.4	3 513	9.2	90.8	3 651
Veterinary medicine	45.9	54.1	1 053	35.7	64.3	1 187
Zoology	54.4	45.6	781	43.2	56.8	1 017
Education						
Education	25.6	74.4	27 431	25.3	74.7	37 777
Physical education	47.7	52.3	12 260	51.5	48.5	15 428
Engineering and applied sciences						
Architecture	70.0	30.0	2 220	64.0	36.0	2 344
Engineering	90.2	9.8	37 724	84.0	16.0	39 897
Forestry	88.4	11.6	1 335	80.9	19.1	1 325
Fine arts	39.7	60.3	13 872	38.3	61.7	16 459
Health professions						
Dental studies and research	73.8	26.2	1 982	59.7	40.3	1 749
Medical studies and research	58.2	41.8	8 411	54.8	45.2	8 389
Nursing	3.2	96.8	6 634	6.6	93.4	7 428
Pharmacy	32.8	67.2	2 696	38.5	61.5	3 183
Rehabilitation medicine	10.6	89.4	2 510	16.0	84.0	3 796
Humanities						
History	58.6	41.4	4 745	54.4	45.6	11 844
Languages	28.0	72.0	12 757	26.7	73.3	18 352
Other	51.7	48.2	9 858	46.9	53.1	13 401
Mathematics and physical sciences						
Chemistry	67.7	32.3	3 052	60.8	39.2	3 938
Geology	79.3	20.7	3 249	72.4	27.6	1 201
Mathematics	64.6	35.4	8 262	60.9	39.1	9 063
Computer science	72.7	27.3	12 250	79.8	20.2	9 039
Physics	88.2	11.8	2 407	83.0	17.0	2 753
Social sciences						
Business and commerce	58.8	41.2	48 835	54.1	45.9	57 382
Economics	68.8	31.2	10 009	67.8	32.2	12 278
Geography	64.1	35.9	4 466	60.0	40.0	7 680
Law	55.8	44.2	9 892	48.8	51.2	11 284
Political science	63.1	36.9	6 712	56.0	44.0	12 933
Psychology	27.4	72.6	13 187	23.9	76.1	23 184
Social work	18.3	81.7	4 227	16.9	83.1	5 587
Sociology	34.0	66.0	6 157	29.2	70.8	13 404
Grand Total*	52.6	47.4	397 351	49.8	56.2	485 418

*Individual totals will not add up to grand total because certain smaller fields, labelled "other," are omitted from this table.

Source: Reproduced by authority of the Minister of Industry, 1994. Adapted from Statistics Canada (1994e), *Education in Canada: A Statistical Review*, Cat. 81-229, table 13, pp. 84–87.

Russell's observations of grade 12 classes revealed that teachers were one-and-one-half to five times more likely to direct questions to boys than to girls. Girls dominated verbal interaction with the teacher in only 7 percent of the classes, while boys dominated in about 63 percent. In only about 30 percent of classes did teachers seem to select girls and boys equally in turn-taking interaction.

Observational studies also suggest that teachers tend to hold different expectations about the academic abilities of girls and boys. When girls outperformed boys in early grades, teachers explained their "overachievement" as a result of their docility and conscientiousness, subtly devaluing their work. (Russell 1987, 241). Conversely, when girls fell behind boys in high-school mathematics and science courses, teachers were inclined to treat this as "natural" and consistent with their lower expectations for girls in these subjects. Girls were more likely to be advised to drop such subjects than coached to improve their performance (Shapiro 1990, 57). High-school counsellors routinely encouraged high-achieving girls into "women's work" such as social work, teaching, and secretarial positions rather than into better-paid male-dominated business and professional positions (Russell 1987). Years of exposure to such classroom practices may accomplish what Porter, Porter, and Blishen (1982, 125–29) describe as the lower self-esteem of girls and lower self-assessment of their abilities than boys, even when they outperformed boys on school tests.

An explosion of feminist studies of classroom practices and school textbooks since the 1970s, combined with political lobbying, has produced significant changes in the Canadian school system (Mackie 1991, 162–65). Much effort has gone into changing the content of textbooks and school curricula to include nonsexist materials and present women in a wider variety of nonsex-typed activities (Gaskell and McLaren 1987, 8). Efforts are also being made by universities to encourage more girls in high school to consider careers in science and engineering (Armour 1988).

The question is whether such remedial actions will be sufficient to overcome wider social pressures beyond the schools. Richer (1988) carried out a comparative study of cohorts of students in an Ottawa elementary school before and after a seven-year consciousness-raising program in the school. The school established a "positive action committee" that provided films and reading materials for teachers on issues of gender and organized several seminars on teaching practices. In 1979, and again in 1986, children in grades 1 through 6 were asked to draw a picture of themselves engaged in their favourite activity. Comparison of the pictures showed virtually no drop in sex stereotyping. In 1986, fully 97 percent of boys' drawings and 87 percent of girls' drawings depicted sex-segregated activities. Richer concludes that influences outside the school have a greater impact on children than classroom teachers.

More detailed studies of classroom interaction are beginning to uncover ways in which students actively resist efforts by teachers to challenge gender and class stereotypes. Girls from a lower-class district in England collectively sabotaged lessons by tacitly and even blatantly withdrawing their attention (McRobbie 1978). When asked what they did during math lessons, they gave such answers as "carve boys' names on my desk," "comb my hair under the lid of the desk," "put makeup on, or look in my mirror." McRobbie suggests that while parents and teachers do try to encourage girls to study more to get a good job, the girls' own immediate experience of the types of jobs open to women like them does little to induce them to focus on schoolwork. They know that their chance for a decent home and money to support their children depends primarily upon the superior wages of a man. Hence, from as young as thirteen and fourteen years, their preoccupation is with boyfriends and going steady. Success in the classroom consists of asserting their "femaleness" and spending vast amounts of time discussing boyfriends in loud voices that disrupt the class.

This is irrational behaviour from the perspective of the teachers who, at least initially in their careers, are committed to trying to break this pattern and open new options for the girls. But it is fully rational from the perspective of the working-class girls themselves in the face of their expectations for their own future. Actually, it may be the teachers who are being unrealistic and irrational in assuming that they can somehow change the life chances for more than a minority of these girls. It is little wonder that many teachers become more realistic with experience and opt for a more class-biased curriculum to which the girls will respond. In a sense schools fail the girls, but in another sense girls fail the schools. The process of class and gender formation is thus mutually constructed within the everyday struggles of the classroom.

Feminism in the Universities

As noted above, women are entering Canadian universities in greater numbers than ever before, equalling the numbers of men at undergraduate level. Feminist research, however, suggests that women students generally experience university campuses as very much "male turf," with resentment, petty harassment, and depreciation of women commonplace.

A study by Hall and Sandler (1984) suggests that female students generally, and especially those who enroll in the traditional male bastions of physical sciences and engineering, face a "chilly campus climate" that is not conducive to learning. Women students tend to receive less attention and less feedback than male students from the predominantly male faculty. They are more likely to experience disparaging comments about their work or their commitment to studies, or comments that focus on their appearance rather than their performance. They are likely to be counselled into lower career goals than men. As graduates, they are less likely to be included as co-researchers with faculty in academic publications. Women who interrupt their studies, or attend part-time while raising children, are not taken seriously. A commentary written by a female geology student some ten years after this article was published suggests that little has changed (*Globe and Mail*, 13 July 1994). The student recounts being the butt of a series of more and more threatening practical "jokes" in the geology labs, combined with a constant barrage of insulting remarks about women in general. Repeated sexual comments and innuendos from one of her chemistry professors were directed at female students in the class.

Males dominate classroom and seminar discussions. Male styles of communication are highly assertive, combined with physical gestures that express ease, dominance, and control. They are more likely to interrupt other speakers and to control the topic of conversation. In laboratory classes, female students routinely complain that men take control over the equipment, relegating female students to note-takers. Females tend to be more personal in their communications, offering more self-disclosure rather than impersonal and abstract styles of speech. This style is disparaged as less intelligent. Women are more reticent in taking over conversations and tend to encourage other speakers. They often feel that they are imposing on advisers rather than that they have a right to ask questions.

Athletic activities by women get less support and attention than do male sports teams. Women are demeaned when campus organizations screen pornographic movies as fund-raisers and when student newspapers publish sexist articles and advertisements. Women who live in residences often face petty harassment from men in the guise of fun. In 1989, a rash of such actions and verbal assaults directed at female students, and feminists in particular, made headlines in Canadian newspapers. At Queen's University some male students mocked a campaign against date rape on campus by displaying posters bearing slogans such as "No Means Tie Her Up" and "No Means Kick Her in the Teeth" (*Globe and Mail*, 11 Nov. 1989, D1–2; 17 Nov. 1989). Engineering students' newspapers at Queen's and the University of Alberta, in particular, have been criticized for sexist content "that portrays women in a thoroughly demeaning and abusive manner" (*Globe and Mail*, 13 Dec. 1989, A5).

On 6 December 1989, a man armed with a semi-automatic rifle entered the engineering building at the University of Montreal. He massacred fourteen women engineering students before turning the gun on himself. In a three-page suicide note found on his body, the man

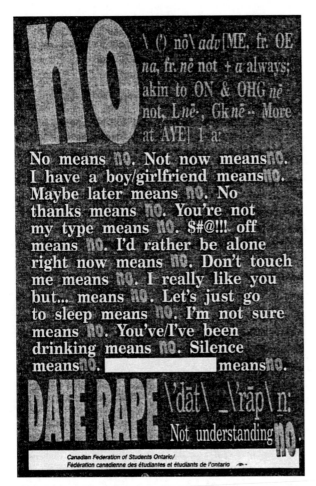

The "No Means No" campaign spells out sexual harassment in no uncertain terms.

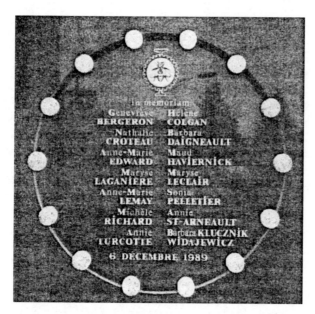

A plaque commemorates the women massacred at l'Ecole Polytechnique, the Université de Montréal's engineering school.

expressed his hatred of feminists, claiming that they had ruined his life. In the days that followed, seven male students at the University of Toronto set off firecrackers outside the women's residence, spreading panic. Following this experience, administrations on many campuses took steps to institute or strengthen policies against sexual harassment, to curtail the sexist content of engineering newspapers, and to set up programs to support and promote women in sciences and engineering. We have yet to see how effective these initiatives will be.

Feminist Pedagogy

Feminists also criticize traditional methods of teaching within universities as perpetuating a masculine orientation to learning that alienates women students. They echo the work of Paolo Freire in challenging oppressive and hierarchical approaches to knowledge as truths handed down from authority figures. Emphasis in lectures and seminars on competition, confrontation, and winning debates in a public forum, intimidate and silence many women, along with other students outside the dominant white middle-class male group, who lack a sense of social mastery, or lack the will to put others down. Belenky et. al., (1985) suggest that women generally respond better to "connected teaching" that emphasizes creative reflection on personal experience,

and that confirms not merely that women can learn, but that they already know something through personal experience.

The problem they highlight is that hierarchical methods of teaching are so closely associated with authority and professional competence that lecturers who are committed to involving students as equals in the classroom, and who affirm the value of knowledge based on personal experience, risk appearing weak and incompetent to their students (Bezucha 1985; Friedman 1985). Female professors can find themselves simultaneously challenged and resented by students, whichever approach they take. Students who accept authority, high standards, discipline, and toughness from male professors, often deeply resent the same demands from female professors. It violates their sense that females should not be in authority positions over them. Feminist pedagogy also clashes with the hierarchical structure of universities, and the necessity of grading students on classroom performance.

Feminist Theory and Resistance

As we noted in chapter 5, the introduction of women's courses into the curriculum of Canadian universities in the 1970s met with strong opposition, bordering on rage (Smith 1992d, 208). The women professors who were trying to develop the courses were subject to personal insults and their professional competence was called into question. Traditions of rational debate did not seem to extend to consideration of women's studies. By the mid-1990s, most Canadian universities have established some courses spread across the arts curriculum, but women's studies programs still tend to be seen as frills, given second-rate status and limited funds. Students aspiring to professional and corporate careers are discouraged from taking such courses. A common strategy for sidelining feminist courses, Bezucha suggests (1985, 90), is for established professors to support hiring a few women to teach designated women's studies courses, and then to use this to justify not including anything on women in the content of their own courses. Ignorance of feminist theory and research is studiously maintained. This studied ignorance is not emptiness or mere absence of knowledge. It is an active refusal to learn (Aronowitz and Giroux 1985, 159).

Students who are exposed to feminist theory develop their own forms of resistance, as their established frameworks of meaning are challenged. One response is to deny the validity of any evidence that goes against the dominant view of reality. Culley describes the common reactions of students, both female and male, when exposed for the first time to readily available statistics on education, employment categories, and income levels of women compared to men:

> "Who published those statistics?" (U.S. Department of Labor.) "When was that?" (Any time before yesterday is pre-history.) "Those figures must be based on women who work part time." Or, "A lot of women choose not to work, you know, are they in there?" Then soon after, "You can't get anywhere hating men, you can't blame them." And quietly to themselves or to each other, "I heard she's divorced, she's probably a lesbian or something" (1985, 212).

Culley suggests that it is important for teachers to let students express these defensive efforts to distance, discount, and deny. Only then can these responses be examined and questioned. Other professors who teach feminist theory describe instances of outright hostility from some students who actively try to disrupt classes by joking, chatting loudly, jeering, and attacking the credibility and professional competence of the professor (Bezucha 1985, 214; McIntyre 1986).

For all the difficulties encountered, feminist theory and research has made a significant impact across the arts curriculum. Traditional approaches may still be dominant but they have lost their taken-for-granted character. As radical pedagogy, feminism is potentially an agent of change through both the process and the content of teaching. Charlotte Bunch (1983) describes how she left university teaching to work full-time in the women's movement but later returned to university because she had become convinced that the development of feminist theory is essential to political action. Theory is not just a body of facts and opinions. It involves the development of explanations that can guide actions.

Bunch proposes a four-part model of theory. The first part is *description*. Changing people's perceptions of the world through new descriptions of reality is usually a prerequisite for changing that reality. In the 1960s, few people would have thought of American women as oppressed, but now the injustices and oppression experienced by women are widely recognized. Feminist work, which described that oppression in a number of different ways, played a critical role in making it visible. The second element of theory is *analysis*. Analysis involves trying to understand why the reality described in feminist work exists and what perpetuates it. The third element is *vision*. The work of envisioning what should

exist involves examining our basic assumptions about human nature and relationships. The fourth element of theory is *strategy*. Theoretical understanding of how social relations work is essential to planning ways of changing those relations. Teaching feminist theory thus involves teaching the basic skills of critical literacy—how to read, analyse, and think about ideas—and challenging students to develop their own ideas and to analyse the assumptions behind their actions.

Conclusion

Compulsory schooling has a profound effect on children's lives and upon their life chances after leaving school. This much is beyond dispute. It also seems clear that children with different class, gender, and ethnic characteristics experience schooling and higher education in very different ways, and end up with markedly unequal levels of educational attainment and formal credentials. Different perspectives in sociology struggle with the questions of how and why schooling affects children in these ways.

Functionalist and political economy perspectives agree that schools perform the function of selecting and allocating children for adult roles within the economy, but they focus on very different factors in their analysis of how this selection process works. Functionalists suggest that, by and large, schools do provide equal opportunities for all children to reach their full academic potential and to strive for social mobility. They locate the causes of unequal attainment by class and by sex primarily in socialization processes that occur within families, largely outside the influence of schools. Political economy theory, in contrast, locates the causes of low aspirations and unequal attainment in capitalism. This perspective takes for granted the argument that capitalists seek to standardize and deskill work in the interests of cheapening labour and increasing profits. Scope for creativity seems confined to the elite who direct the huge corporations. This political economy is held responsible for structuring schools in the corporate image.

The social constructionist perspective begins from the assumption that people, in their everyday interactions, create the social world and give it the patterns and the meanings that we come to see as the structures of capitalism. Research into intimate interaction within classrooms explores how students react to and against the pressures of school, in terms of how they themselves foresee the utility or irrelevance of education for their future lives. Teachers also struggle to retain some autonomy in their working lives, amid pressures to adopt packaged curricula, textbooks, and technical devices pushed by corporate interests, often acting in concert with school boards and college management.

The central debate within this perspective concerns how far it is possible for people to retain autonomy of thought and action in the face of the established ways of thinking within the prevailing culture. Teachers are criticized by radicals, and increasingly also by members of the business class, for not developing the capacity for creative and innovative thinking in their students. Yet, they themselves work in contexts that seem increasingly designed to minimize their own capacity for creative teaching. Feminist pedagogy is one form of teaching that takes seriously the possibility of challenging and changing established social relations by developing the power of critical reflection in students. The question for the future is whether this power will be neutralized and accommodated in the service of greater profits, or whether people will use it to push for more fundamental change.

Suggested Reading

An excellent study of education from the functionalist perspective is by John Porter, Marion Porter, and Bernard Blishen, *Stations and Callings: Making It Through the School System* (1982). The authors then incorporate these concepts into an elaborate explanatory model that guides their research into educational aspirations. The text includes many easily understandable statistical graphs and tables.

The main text that presents the structuralist Marxist perspective is by Samuel Bowles and Herbert Gintis, *Schooling in Capitalist America* (1976). A briefer introduction to the ideas debated at length in the text is provided in a collection of articles edited by Mike Cole, *Bowles and Gintis Revisited: Correspondence and Contradiction in Educational Theory* (1988).

A good introduction to the social construction of reality approach, and one that complements the work of Bowles and Gintis, is by Jean Anyon, "Social Class and the Hidden Curriculum of Work" (1980). She describes in detail the very different teaching techniques that she observed in elementary school classes in working-class, middle-class, and elite school districts. A class study in the rejection of school values by working-class children is P. Willis, *Learning to Labour: How Working Class Kids Get Working Class Jobs* (1981). Willis shows how boys have absorbed the shopfloor culture of their working-class fathers, including sexist and racist values, and utilize them to support their rejection of school. A similar study by Angela McRobbie, "Working-class Girls and the Culture of Femininity" (1978) describes how these girls reject the school culture in favour of their paramount concern with sexuality and attracting boyfriends.

Michael Apple's work, *Teachers and Texts: A Political Economy of Class and Gender Relations in Education* (1986), explores the contemporary work of teachers. Apple documents the pressures that threaten to reduce the role of teachers from autonomous professionals to deskilled technicians, constrained to use standardized curriculum packages.

A good overview of the feminist approach to education is provided by a collection of articles edited by Jane Gaskell and Arlene Tigar McLaren, *Women and Education: A Canadian Perspective* (1987). Among other useful updates, the collection includes a reprint of the classic article by Dorothy Smith, "An Analysis of Ideological Structures and How Women Are Excluded: Considerations for Academic Women" (1975).

Questions

1. What does Parsons see as the functional importance of women teachers in primary education?

2. Distinguish between *equality of condition, equality of opportunity,* and *equality of outcome.*

3. In what sense can the goals of liberal education—the development of individual potential, equality, and social continuity—be seen as internally contradictory?

4. How does structural correspondence theory account for the shift in higher education from broad liberal arts to packages of credits?

5. What principles does the educational reformer Ivan Illich advocate in his vision of a deschooled society, and why is this vision rejected as unrealistic by the Marxist theorists Bowles and Gintis?

6. How is the North American Free Trade Deal implicated in the structural correspondence between schooling and global capitalism?

7. What problems are highlighted by the notion of *a vacuum ideology* in reference to the policies of white educators towards Native peoples?

8. In what respects is intelligence an interactional accomplishment rather than a measure of intellectual capabilities?

9. What practices are involved in parents accomplishing themselves as "interested" in their children's education from the perspective of teachers?

10. What teaching practices are implicated in promoting the passivity of girls relative to boys in typical classroom interaction?

CHAPTER

Sociology of Race and Ethnic Relations

The analysis of racial and ethnic relations in society presents a major challenge to theories of social order, both functionalist and Marxist. The presence of diverse ethnic and racial groups within a society complicate traditional functionalist assumptions about social cohesion. The persistence of what Porter (1965) calls a **vertical mosaic**, with marked inequalities between different racial and ethnic groups on measures of class, status, and power, challenge our understanding of social hierarchy. In Canada, people of white Anglo-Saxon Protestant (WASP) origin are over-represented at the top of the economic hierarchy while aboriginal people are over-represented at the bottom. Various other European and non-white people range in between. Ethnic inequalities are also gendered—experienced very differently by women and men. Yet as soon as we try to pin down concepts like ethnicity and race they become elusive, their constantly shifting and contested meanings inseparable from the social practices of 'ethnicization' and 'racialization' that continually bring them into being. Traditional assumptions about the coincidence of racial and ethnic identity with geographic location and nation states are increasingly challenged by the realities of globalizing economic networks. These networks are associated with transnational flows of finance and personnel, cosmopolitan professional and managerial elites, and increasingly fluid labour migration. Instantaneous global communication networks have the potential to link migrants simultaneously to places of residence, places of origin, and to fragmented communities across the diaspora. The tools of sociological analysis are challenged to remain relevant in these new realities.

Traditional Functionalism: Consensus or Conflict?

The concept of shared culture is centrally important in functionalist theory of social order. Moral consensus is seen as internalized during early childhood socialization within the family, and reinforced through religion and education. Components of culture include language, history, religion, symbol systems, values, behavioural norms, expectations, and attitudes—in effect, the totality of what Durkheim refers to as the *conscience collective* of a community of people.

Functionalist theory views our sense of belonging to a cultural community or ethnic group as fundamental to our sense of personal identity. When asked who we are, we typically refer to some ethnic group as "our people" or "our community." Ethnic identity is understood in classical functionalist theory as 'primordial', deeply rooted in ties of kinship, blood, common territory, and shared language, and religious traditions that all invoke strong emotions (Shils 1957, 142; Horowitz 1985, 57; Geertz 1973, 259). It is extremely difficult to break ties with the ethnic group of one's birth, especially since it implies renouncing obligations to people closest to us. Children of ethnically mixed parentage are expected to experience some sense of marginality or partial belonging to two exclusive groups, unless mixed-blood people become an ethnic grouping in themselves, like the Métis of western Canada. In short, the definition of an 'ethnic group' in functionalist theory closely parallels that of a society as a whole, with a common culture functioning as the central institution maintaining social cohesion.

The concept of **race**, as distinct from **ethnicity,** refers to shared visible and inherited physical characteristics that are socially noticed, with skin colour as the most important. In principle, racial diversity should not give rise to the same societal problems as ethnic diversity, since race does not constitute any threat to cultural consensus. In practice, however, race tends to be confounded with ethnicity. Members of any given ethnic group tend to see themselves as racially homogeneous, and thus to regard people of visibly different racial stock as outsiders. Distinct racial characteristics commonly function as markers of ethnic difference.

The emphasis within functionalist theory on internalization of shared culture suggests that some level of ethnocentrism is normal. **Ethnocentrism** refers to an exaggerated view of the superior qualities and rightness of the culture of one's own group. **Stereotypes** refer to simplified versions or mental cartoons that we form of other ethnic groups by over-generalizing or exaggerating their distinctive characteristics. **Prejudice** is the logical mirror image of ethnocentrism. It involves prejudging in negative terms the characteristics that we assume are shared by members of other ethnic groups.

Racism applies such prejudices toward groups that we perceive to be different on the basis of inescapable genetic characteristics. In functionalist theory, these ethnocentric, stereotyped, prejudiced, and racist attitudes are understood as themselves part of the culturally learned attitudes that we internalize through socialization. Socialization also provides us with shared notions of the relative status of our own and other groups within the society.

Implications for Political Organization

Functionalist theory, which associates shared culture with social cohesion and order, has profound implications for the political organization of societies with diverse ethnic groups. It supports the view that the ideal society or state is one that is ethnically homogenous. Homogeneity implies stability and security, while ethnically and racially mixed societies, such as Canada, are seen as more prone to instability, divisions and conflict (Walling 2000). Theoretically, the presence of ethnic minorities within a society is problematic because minorities cannot be assumed to have internalized the expected values or behaviours common to the majority group. Interaction is thus likely to be strained and restricted, and social controls weak. Force, rather than desire for approval and acceptance, is assumed to play a greater role in the maintenance of order, which in turn presupposes domination by one cultural group. The only safe meeting ground for different ethnic groups is likely to be the impersonal marketplace. Classical theorists suggest that harmony is most readily sustained when distinct ethnic groups have both economic and legal autonomy, so that each group controls its own members' lives (Kuper 1969, 14–16; Van den Berghe 1969, 75–78).

Given the disruptive potential of ethnic differences, four viable options or models have been traditionally proposed for maintaining social order: **domination, separation**, or **assimilation** of ethnic minorities. The fourth option, **multiculturalism**, is proposed as viable for social harmony under the particular conditions of modern secular, rational societies.

The first two options are seen as mechanisms that may help states to manage or contain ethnic conflicts, but not ultimately to resolve them. In the long run, Walling suggests, either approach may work to escalate insecurities. Ethnic minorities that experience exclusion and repression may be more likely to identify intensely with their own subgroup and to struggle for some measure of political autonomy, which in turn threatens the integrity of the state and castes doubt on their political loyalties. Globally, such struggles have often erupted into civil wars, or politics of ethnic cleansing as states try to drive politically dangerous minorities out of the state's territorial boundaries, or as self-identified ethnic minorities struggle for autonomous statehood.

Walling cites a chilling history of ethnic cleansings from before the Middle Ages right through to the present. Historically, Canadian governments have employed policies of ethnic cleansing, to deport Acadians from the Maritimes in 1755, and to expel Canadians of Japanese origin from British Columbia in 1942. In Europe, during the inter-war period 1919–1938, policies intended to better fit ethnicity to national boundaries in the interests of increasing state security resulted in forced population movements of some 21 million refugees in Europe alone. More recently in 1992 the federation of Yugoslavia split apart amid brutal policies of ethnic cleansing. The deliberate orchestration of mass killing of civilians were condemned by outsiders as crimes against humanity, but excused by many insiders as no more than over-zealous acts of nation-building. Similar justifications are proposed for the Iraqi government's brutal suppression of ethnic Kurds.

The third option of assimilation is classically proposed as the ideal solution for the problems of ethnic diversity because it resolves the cultural threats to social cohesion and eliminates the need for control. The concept of assimilation refers to the process by which minority ethnic groups gradually adopt the lifestyles, language, values, and customs of the dominant group. Structural integration is expected to follow as minorities enter the social organization of the dominant group. Gordon (1964) suggests that groups tend to lose language and culture first, but to hold on to religion. Intermarriage is the last to go. The final stage is such total amalgamation that ethnic background is forgotten.

Classically, this is seen as being accomplished over three generations. New immigrants or first-generation settlers struggle to speak the host language, and are likely to retain strong emotional times to their home-country and to their own ethnic sub-group. Women who remain in the home may adjust more slowly than men exposed to the public sphere of work. Their children, or the second generation, are typically socialized into aspects of both cultures. Numerous ethnographic studies suggest these children experience culture conflict, being torn between the cultural values and religion that they learn within the family and new cultural values learned in school and the neighbourhood. Family val-

ues, focussed around sexuality, marriage and religion are likely to change more slowly than secular values. By the third generation, however, the children of children born or raised in the new country, are typically fully assimilated. This is the theory of the 'melting pot'. Waves of migrants come, settle, and then gradually intermarry and move out into and merge with the surrounding ethnic mainstream population.

The problem with this vision of assimilation is that it conflicts with the presumed strength of primordial ethnic attachments. Small numbers of voluntary migrants immersed in a new culture may make such adjustment, but in seems less likely to happen among groups subjected to forced or non-voluntary migration, or within larger ethnic minority groups and groups with significant cultural differences from the host society. Migrant resistance to assimilation is often compounded by resistance from the host society promoted by prevailing attitudes of ethnocentrism and racism. Under conditions where host societies feel threatened by the potentially divided loyalties of ethnic minorities, states have resorted to tactics for forced assimilation. These have typically taken the form of breaking up minority communities, banning minority ceremonial and religious practices, restricting use of minority languages, and intensive reeducation of minority children (Walling 2000). Sometimes such strategies work to disperse minorities, but more often, Walling suggests, they exacerbate problems of resentment, ethnic closure and resistance that promote struggles for greater self-determination.

The fourth option of **multiculturalism** constitutes a significant shift within functionalist theory from seeing culture as all-embracing to viewing it as a more partial and private component of societal integration. It draws implicitly on Durkheim's model of organic solidarity in advanced industrial societies characterised by specialization and differentiation. Ties based on interdependence and mutual obligations, Durkheim suggests, become more salient than shared cultural norms in maintaining social cohesion. This shift from mechanical to organic solidarity supports the view that cultural diversity can be successfully accommodated provided a foundation of core societal values are maintained—namely the values of mutual respect for diversity and for individual human rights.

The model of multiculturalism assumes that individuals live in society as members of culturally defined communities, that different communities can exist equitably within one society, and that individuals can participate actively in the society as a whole while maintaining their identity and membership within a minority cultural community. As subsystems within a wider societal system, ethnic communities are seen as serving many positive functions for members. These include providing material and emotional supports, aiding the adjustment of immigrants and refugees, overcoming isolation and reinforcing a sense of belonging, articulating group interests, and promoting economic and political involvement in society (Kelly 2003, 38). In Durkheim's terms such ethnic communities function to reduce anomie, providing an intermediate level of belonging between individuals and modern nation states. Ethnic community attachments are seen as functioning globally as well as within individual societies, to give comfort and security in an era of rapid and disruptive change and accelerated rates of migration (Giddens 2000, 62–3; Richmond 2002, 708; 1988,7–8). Giddens argues that in modern secular societies, ethnic traditions are necessarily no longer lived in traditional ways. They are maintained for rational, reflective reasons—because they are comforting, and not out of blind, unquestioning adherence. Hence, they are more flexible, open to continual adjustment or re-invention to fit changing circumstances. People can maintain their membership within distinctive ethnic, cultural and racial communities while at the same time interacting as equals with members of diverse other cultural communities within wider social and political institutions (Kelly 2003; Kim 2004). Differences are privatized—celebrated and protected as a sources of family values and emotional belonging, but at the same time depoliticized or separated from the public realm of secular, democratic political institutions and free-market economics. The challenge for modern societies is to manage diversity so as to preserve national unity, or in effect to make societies safe for diversity and safe from diversity (Fleras and Elliott 2003, 286). This is seen as best achieved by institutionalizing the two principles of difference and equality.

A brief overview of Canadian social and political history shows how all four of these different models of minority group relations have prevailed at different times, and with different ethnic groups.

Domination

The first model, where one ethnic group exercises institutional domination over another, characterizes the experience of Native peoples in Canada. Over more than two centuries of violent conflict, white settler society achieved decisive domination over Aboriginal tribal communities. As the fur trade declined and white settlers pushed westward onto the Prairies, aboriginal peoples were driven off their lands onto small reserves. Threats of war and starvation forced treaties onto captured populations (Lawrence 2004, 30). The Indian Act of 1869 established the legal, political, and economic dominance of the federal government over almost every aspect of reservation life. Successive modifications to the Indian Act subordinated aboriginal peoples as wards of state, treated much like minors. Elected Band Councils, with limited powers, replaced former indigenous governments and confederacies (ibid. 33). The Minister of Indian Affairs had the authority to attend all band council meetings, to veto any bylaws that the bands might pass, to control their finances, to approve all expenditures, and to dictate land sales. Similar practices of conquest and domination of aboriginal peoples occurred in what is now the United States, and in European colonies in Australia, New Zealand, and beyond. The Canadian system for governing reservations was adopted as a model by the white South African government for managing black residents in segregated 'homelands.'

Institutional Separation: a) First Nations

Contemporary relations between aboriginal peoples and the Canadian Federal government are slowly moving away from domination towards the model of institutional separation and partial self government, albeit under far from equal status. For aboriginal peoples the meaning of reserves has shifted from 'colonial tool' to territorial foundation for aboriginal identity and self government. Aboriginals increasingly insist on their tiny band communities being recognized and referred to as "First Nations" and their negotiations with the federal government, however unequal they might be, as nation-to-nation negotiations.

Progress towards the devolution of powers to First Nations has been painfully slow, reflected in interminable litigation and occasional violent confrontations. One of the worst was the Oka crisis in Quebec in 1988 during which the Mohawk Warriors of Kanesetake blocked the Mercier bridge into Montreal in an armed standoff that lasted 78 days. The struggle was focussed around blocking a proposal to build a golf course on traditional aboriginal land. Nonetheless, the principles of conditional autonomy, self government and self determination for First Nations peoples are slowly being worked out. Models of self determination vary with the size and resources of different bands but there are roughly between 60 to 80 recognized Nations within a thousand or so aboriginal communities. Two of the most significant accomplishments in self determination to date have been the establishment of the territory of Nunavut in 1999 and the Nisga'a agreement of 2000 in BC, a settlement described as "the first treaty since 1859" (Fleras and Elliott 2003, 168).

The debates, however, continue. Is the Nisga'a treaty a step backwards towards race-based apartheid under another name, or a step forward towards autonomous nationhood within the Canadian federation? A further problem with the model of autonomous First Nations is that relatively few of the more than one thousand reserve communities in Canada are large enough for this to be viable. First Nations also exclude the majority of people who claim aboriginal identity but who have lost their status or band membership, or moved to urban areas. We discuss these issues further below.

b) Institutional Separation: Quebec

The model of institutional separation also characterizes the relation between the predominantly francophone province of Quebec and the rest of predominantly anglophone Canada. The British North America Act of 1867 established Canada as a bilingual federal system to accommodate the French fact in Quebec. The British colonial government could subdue but not dominate Quebec as it had the aboriginal people, nor could it hope to assimilate French Catholics into English Protestants. Institutional separation appeared to be the only viable option in the British government's desire to unify the North against the rebellious American states.

From the beginning, however, this arrangement has been unstable. The relationship has been variously referred to as "two solitudes" or as "two scorpions in a bottle" (Fleras and Elliott 2002, 211). Canada seems to be in constant danger of either separating into two autonomous nations or reverting to the first option of quasi-colonial domination.

John Porter (1979a, 106) writes enthusiastically of the special relationship of "binationalism of French and English Canada as the founding principle of Confederation." This relationship only makes sense, he suggests, because of very specific historical conditions. The fact that 80 percent of French Canadians live in Quebec gives them a homeland that was conquered. This helps to make sense of, and to give impetus to, the notions of separation and eventual formation of a French state. In practice, the ideal of "separate but equal" status implied

in the separation model has never been a reality. The French ethnic group, even within Quebec, has until very recently formed a class with deprived status. French elites within the church and the state in Quebec collaborated with the federal government in return for protected status, but the mass of unilingual francophones occupied the low ranks in the class structure. Professional and business elites in Quebec have been predominantly English Canadians or Americans, and the language of business has clearly been English. The few Québécois who attained professional occupational status had to function in English.

The Royal Commission on Bilingualism and Biculturalism, established in 1963, concluded that either Canada would break up or there would have to be a new set of conditions for Quebec's future existence (Porter 1979a, 107). In 1969 the Official Languages Act moved toward providing special status for Quebec in Canada. It formalized bilingualism in the federal civil service, together with concessions, especially in social welfare legislation. But strife continued. During the 1960s a small group calling itself the Quebec Liberation Front (FLQ) used propaganda and terrorism against federalist targets to promote the goal of an independent socialist Quebec. This culminated in 1970 in the "October crisis" when FLQ cells kidnapped two political leaders. One of them was murdered. The Federal government, with Quebec's approval, invoked the War Measures Act to quell the 'apprehended insurrection'. The FLQ had largely fizzled by 1971, but separatist struggles have continued to the present.

The Parti Québécois first came to power in 1976, dedicated to achieving independent nationhood for Quebec by political means. In 1977 Quebec passed the French Language Charter (known as Bill 101) declaring Quebec officially a monolingual province, with French as the preferred language of work, education, commerce and service delivery. The Quebec government argued that the move was essential to preserve the French language and with it French culture from being swallowed up by English North America. The 1980 referendum on sovereignty association was only narrowly voted down. Subsequent efforts by the Canadian federal government to gain Quebec's support for constitutional reform in the proposed Meech Lake Accord in 1987 and the subsequent Charlottetown Accord in 1992 both failed. In September 1994, the Parti Québécois was again elected. In 1995 it held another referendum on sovereignty which failed by a margin of less than 1 percent. Quebec's history gives much supporting evidence for the functionalist thesis that ethnic pluralism in separate communities living side by side is inherently unstable and destined to be associated with continual conflict and stress.

Integration Through Assimilation

From the classical functionalist perspective, assimilation is by far the best option for achieving societal cohesion. It involves a process over time by which members of ethnic minorities absorb the cultural patterns and values of the dominant ethnic group until eventually they merge in with the majority. Successive Canadian governments have tried to force the assimilation of aboriginal peoples by a variety of means that together amount to a pattern that aboriginal people see as cultural genocide. Aboriginal religious traditions and practices were widely outlawed. Missions were established with the goal of converting these supposedly heathen peoples to Christianity. From the 1880s onward generations of aboriginal children were forcibly removed from their communities and sent great distances away to be taught in residential Christian schools, where children were routinely punished for speaking native languages (Davies and Guppy 1998, 131). The last of these schools were closed in the 1970s.

The Federal White Paper on aboriginals introduced by then Minister of Indian Affairs, Jean Chrétien in 1969 proposed a strategy that combined assimilation with legal extinction, under which the special status of aboriginal peoples would be terminated, and their land and assets divided on a per-capital basis to individuals. Aboriginal leaders rejected the legal proposals outright as 'callous expediency' and the vision of assimilation as 'cultural genocide' (Fleras and Elliott 2003, 183). Ensuing struggles converged in 1982 with the constitutional recognition of Aboriginal status and Treaty Rights under the Canadian Charter of Rights and Freedoms. Belatedly, the devastation caused to aboriginal communities by the destruction of their families and cultures a is slowly being recognized by the Canadian government. In 2006 the federal government is in the final stages of authorizing policies to compensate victims of residential schools—both for the physical and sexual abuses that some of them suffered, and for the pervasive loss of their cultures. Schools for aboriginal children in some of the larger reserves now teach heritage languages and traditions, actively assisted by Native Studies programmes in some Canadian universities. For most people of aboriginal descent, however, these changes come far too late. Their loss of traditional cultures is virtually complete,

although integration as equals in non-native society remains elusive.

Immigration and Potential for Assimilation

Immigration policies in Canada have historically been guided by assumptions about the perceived ease with which different kinds of migrants might be assimilated into white settler society. People from England were always preferred, although not without concerns that lower-class girls might be 'unsuitable' (Arat-Koc 1999, 129–132). The colony of Quebec similarly preferred migrants from France. Nineteenth-century Canadian politicians were dubious that non-French, non-British Europeans could be successfully assimilated into Canadian culture. Such people were recruited mostly to open up the prairies, in small settlements isolated from white settler society. There was outright scepticism that culturally and racially more distinct Asian and African people could ever fit in with white culture (Li 2003). Regulations such as a head tax, and continuous journey rules were implemented to block the immigration of people from China, Japan and India, even while European immigrants were being courted with incentive plans. Even when male migrants from Asia were accepted as labourers, women from these countries were banned, on the grounds that they and their children would not be assimilable (Thobani 2000, 36).

Racist attitudes that prevailed within the host society contributed significantly to the marginalization and segregation of aboriginal peoples and immigrants considered 'less assimilable'. Second generation Canadians of Japanese and other Asian origins were educated in Canadian schools, spoke fluent English, and often converted to Christianity, yet still found themselves discriminated against as outsiders. Such attitudes both facilitated and justified policies that fit the definition of ethnic cleansing. During the Second World War 20 881 Canadians of Japanese origin were expelled from coastal areas of British Columbia in 1942 and interned in work camps and ghost towns in the interior. After the war they were offered the option of deportation to Japan or indentured labour in prairie farms. All their property—homes, farms, fishing boats, and businesses, were confiscated and sold by the Canadian government to pay relocation costs (Adachi 1978; Sunahara 1981). National security concerns that Japanese in Canada might aid Japan during the war were cited as the official excuse for the expulsion, although no Japanese Canadians were ever charged for disloyalty to Canada. The charge that racist attitudes were centrally involved in these policies is supported by evidence that German Canadians in the Maritime provinces were not subjected to any such wartime controls.

Multiculturalism: Integration without Assimilation

The presence of francophone Quebec within Canada was an important impetus for the shift from the politics of assimilation to multiculturalism. By the mid-twentieth century it was obvious that francophone Québécois were fiercely resistant to assimilation into the dominant English Canadian culture. It was also an era of increasing migration of non-European and non-white peoples into Canada, as the supply of potential immigrants from Europe declined. The Immigration Act of 1967 abolished formal preference on the basis of race or ethnicity, instituting instead a points system that highlights skills and capacity to contribute to the Canadian economy. Critics have noted that immigration practices are still biased in favour of people from Europe through the geographic location of offices, points for proficiency in English or French, and leeway given to immigration officers in selection criteria (Simmons 1998). Nonetheless, by the 1990s immigrants from various parts of Asia comprise about half of all newcomers, one-fifth from the Caribbean or Africa, and one-fifth from Europe (Abu-Laban and Gabriel 2002, 14–15). By 1996, visible minorities, defined as non-Aboriginal and non-White, comprised 11 percent of the Canadian population.

Multiculturalism, within a bilingual framework, was first proclaimed by the Trudeau government in 1971 and entrenched as a fundamental principle of the Canadian Constitution in Section 27 of the Charter of Rights and Freedoms in 1982. The Charter also includes a very broad statement prohibiting discrimination. This is embedded in a particularly expansive definition of rights to equality *before* the law, and *under* the law, and equal *protection* and equal *benefit* of the law. These four qualifying definitions of rights have been interpreted by the Supreme Court of Canada as intended to protect minorities not only from deliberate or intended discrimination but also from rules that have the effect of disadvantaging minorities. A classic example of such a rule concerned height restrictions on eligibility for employment as police officers, which was found to have a discriminatory effect on Canadians from Asian origins, who are physically smaller on average than Europeans. Another

was the rule that men entering Canadian Legion premises remove head covering, which discriminated against Sikhs who wear turbans for religious observance. The ruling has also been interpreted as requiring employers to make 'reasonable accommodations' for cultural differences, such as scheduling hours of employment to permit Fridays or Saturdays to be holidays for religious observances and not exclusively Sundays.

The principles of multiculturalism have been further emphasised in subsequent policy amendments to the Multiculturalism Act in 1988 and 1997. In its most recent statement, under the Department of Canadian Heritage, multiculturalism is defined in terms of three goals of identity, civic participation and social justice (Abu-Laban and Gabriel 2002, 113–4). The primary goal of identity entails "fostering a society that recognizes, respects, and reflects a diversity of cultures such that people of all backgrounds feel a sense of belonging and attachment to Canada", and further that the state will develop among "Canada's diverse people, active citizens with both the opportunity and capacity to participate in shaping the future of their communities and their culture", and guarantees of "fair and equitable treatment that respects the dignity of and accommodates people of all origins".

The organization and leadership structures within ethnic communities in Canada vary widely in response to such factors as recency of large-scale migration, numbers and level of concentration in certain cities and regions, internal regional, language, and religious differences, and the like. A common pattern has been for leaders to be drawn initially from religious institutions, and gradually to be replaced by younger generations of educated and professional people (Jedwab 2001). These leaders often represent their community's interests in relations with the state.

Within Canada at the federal level, multicultural policies have involved state funding for ethnocultural groups for cultural maintenance and fostering cultural interchange and language training. Critics such as Trinidad-born novelist Neil Bissoondath (1994, 219) and Li (1994) argue that such programmes have marginalized minority artists as producing low-status folkloric art rather than high-status art that wins acclaim in galleries and museums. Judy Young (2001), however, argues in response that government grants under multicultural policies have functioned successfully to promote cultural and racial diversity in Canadian literature. She cites a host of minority-Canadian writers whose books have received national and international recognition as

Canadian literature, in part through the assistance of the programme.

Multicultural policies within schools are largely the responsibility of provinces in Canada, and they reflect the regional diversity in migrant settlement. The 1996 Census showed that fully 42 percent of Toronto residents were immigrants, 35 percent of Vancouver and 18 percent of Montreal (Abu-Laban and Gabriel 2002, 14–15). Relatively few immigrants settled in the Atlantic region. Migrants from Asia and the Pacific Rim are concentrated in British Columbia while migrants from the Caribbean and Africa are more numerous in Ontario.

Multicultural education required major changes in standard approaches to education that were designed to assimilate children into the mainstream dominant anglocultural norm. The avowed goal of multiculturalism is to be child-centred and inclusive, representing diversity as necessary, normal and beneficial for Canadian society (Fleras and Elliott 2002, 334–324). Early approaches that focussed on exposing children to a variety of cultures, were widely challenged for portraying overly static and romanticized views of cultures that risked trivializing or stereotyping differences. Emphasis has slowly shifted from descriptions of different cultures to a focus on relationships between cultural groups and problems of hierarchy and inequality. School curriculum has slowly shifted towards giving more time to exploring issues of racism, dispossession and imperialism, especially with respect to relations between white settler society and Aboriginal people. Efforts have been made to address the institutional features that act as barriers to successful inclusion and equal achievement of minority students, including the culture of the school, the hidden curriculum of white normative values in curriculum materials, and teacher attitudes and practices. This has gradually evolved into more explicitly anti-racist education designed to empower visible minorities.

The process of educational reform for multiculturalism has not been easy. Strong differences of opinion exist on how far 'reasonable accommodation' to cultural diversity can be made before it detracts from the wider goal of enhancing inclusive Canadian citizenship. One contentious issue has involved accommodation to religious prescriptions that conflict with the secular orientation of Canadian education, and gender equality. Fundamentalist Christian and Muslim parents have objected to Canadian schools being too inclusive of diversity in teachings on such matters as homosexuality, and not inclusive enough in teaching such matters as creationism, or accommodating religious prescriptions

around modesty of dress, appropriate separation of boys and girls, separate prayer rooms, prohibitions on depicting human figures, and the like. By 2002 there were 18 separate Islamic schools in Toronto with over 2000 students enrolled, and about 725 separate schools across Ontario, the vast majority Christian fundamentalist (Fleras and Elliott 2002, 338). The debate continues as to whether such separate schools reflect 'multiculturalism in action' or the failure of multicultural policies. Similar debates surrounded the proposal to legalize Islamic Sharia tribunals in Ontario to settle family disputes. The proposal was eventually abandoned as incompatible with Canadian Charter principles of equality rights for husbands and wives.

Challenges to Multiculturalism

Culturally-based attitudes and values that promote ethnocentrism and racism represent a continual threat to the goal of harmonious multicultural diversity. As noted above, functionalist theory sees primordial ethnic attachments as inherently conducive to beliefs about the superiority of one's own culture and the inferiority of others, and such views readily spill over into racism. The long cultural history of Euro-centrism and racism in white settler society is not easily overcome. Lawrence (1982) describes the roots of common sense racism in British culture, embedded in notions of 'white' as the colour of purity, and 'black' as dirty or soiled, and of white people generally as having a natural superiority of upbringing and breeding compared with more childlike dark-skinned people they encountered in the colonies. Discrimination and prejudice have been common experiences for visible minorities living in Canada, both from politicians who favour racist immigration policies and everyday treatment from neighbours (Reitz and Breton 1998; Chen 2004; Li 2003).

Three decades of official multiculturalism have not been sufficient to silence entirely the neo-conservative view that cultural differences threaten Canadian unity, and that 'newcomers' from 'non-traditional sources' may have irreconcilable values that threaten Canada's democracy. The view that mainstream Canadian cultural values need to change in order to better accommodate culturally diverse immigrants is rarely endorsed. As Li expresses it, racialized new immigrants are represented as multicultural objects, rather than subjects whose values, aspirations, and wishes need to be taken into account (2003, 10).

The picture, however, is mixed. Neo-conservative attitudes such as those Li describes may be widespread but they are not universal. In surveys, some two-thirds of Canadians indicate that they do *not* see multicultural-ism as threatening Canadian unity (Jedwab 2001), and three-quarters did not agree with the racist notion that Canada may be accepting "too many" visible minority immigrants (Galabuzi 2006, 72). In Chen's historical study of people from China living in Peterborough, Ontario prior to multicultural policies, widespread racism did not preclude the development of long-term friendships and respect between Chinese and White neighbours (2004, 86–7). Chen's description, however, implies strongly that the wholesale adoption of White Canadian culture with respect to dress, language, and even religion, was a precondition for improved relations. The message is one of assimilation rather than multicul-tural tolerance.

The 'War on Terror' and Limits to Multiculturalism.

Heightened fear of international terrorism in the after-math of the September 11th 2001 attack in the USA and subsequently in Madrid and London constitutes a signif-icant challenge to the ideal of multiculturalism. Canada, along with the USA and other western countries, has enacted far-reaching security legislation to protect the state against terrorism. A critical difference between security and regular policing, is that the focus is on watching and controlling people who might pose poten-tial risk of committing acts of violence in the future, rather than on apprehending criminals (Hornqvist 2005). In the pervasive climate of fear and suspicion, Muslim communities as a whole, and especially immigrant com-munities from Middle Eastern states, are finding them-selves under suspicion as potential 'aliens within'. The immense diversity of Islamic cultures across the world is obscured in popular discourse as the adjective 'Islamic' is readily linked in media shorthand and popu-lar talk with fundamentalism, extremism, and terrorism. In many of the member states within the European Union the shift from policies of multiculturalism towards assimilation or monoculturalism has become overt within regulations governing immigration (Fekete 2005). This shift is reflected in compulsory language and civics tests for citizenship applicants under threat of deportation, loss of residency rights and social security payments. Immigration regulations governing 'family reunification' have been modified to require that family members over the age of 12 must prove they have

accepted European values and norms as a precondition for immigration. Citizenship rights, even for the second and third generation children of immigrants have been subordinated to anti-terrorist legislation. In September 2004 the government of France moved to ban the wear-ing of hijab or headscarves in schools. German states likewise banned Muslim teachers from wearing hijab. In effect, Fekete argues, the war on terror has become inseparable from debates on the limits of cultural diver-sity in Western societies.

In Canada, official commitment to multiculturalism remains strong. Immediately after the September 11th attacks, all levels of government within Canada stressed the importance of not stigmatizing members of Canadian Muslim communities. Many municipalities adopted measures aimed at strengthening bonds between them and Muslim community leaders (Helly 2005, 41–4). Helly criticizes Canadian officials, however, for remain-ing largely silent since this initial outreach, failing to be proactive in dealing with waves of anti-Muslim 'hate crimes' that erupted during the months following the ter-rorist attacks. The Canadian Islamic Congress published figures indicating a 1600 percent increase in hate crimes against Muslim individuals or places of worship between September 2001 and September 2002, an increase in real numbers from 11 to 173 attacks (ibid. 26).

The picture, however, is mixed. As Helly notes, on the positive side, there were no calls by any Canadian politi-cal leaders for restrictions on the immigration of Muslims to Canada, or for internal controls. On the contrary, there has been widespread acknowledgement that there may be no viable option to multiculturalism given the reality of cultural diversity in Canada. A survey of Canadian Muslims in 2002 records a mix of prejudicial and sup-portive behaviour towards Muslims by White neighbours. Sixty percent of respondents are reported as saying that they had experienced bias or discrimination since the ter-rorist attacks. One-third agreed that their lives had changed for the worse, they felt disliked by fellow Canadians, and were concerned for their own safety and that of their families. But, on the other hand, 61 percent of these same respondents agreed that "they had experi-enced kindness or support from friends or colleagues of other faiths" (ibid. 42). Also, since 2002, the spate of hate crimes declined, due in part to the efforts of networks of local organizations to defuse conflicts (ibid. 28). Canada's commitment to multiculturalism has been credited for the absence of race riots like those in France in 2005.

In conclusion, the functionalist perspective focuses analysis on the continuing strength of primordial cultural and ethnic attachments. The general assumption that follows from traditional functionalist theory is that ethnically and racially mixed societies, such as Canada, are inherently unstable and prone to divisions and conflicts. The structural enforcement of multiculturalism in political and legal institutions, and its reinforcement in schools as secondary agents of socialization function to moderate but not to eliminate this potential for conflict. Consistent with this theoretical approach is the evidence that, since the end of the Cold War in the 1990s, the vast majority of conflicts across the world have involved civil wars, or ethnic conflicts within multicultural states.

The Political Economy Perspective: Racist Capitalism

The Political economy perspective focuses attention on how economies are organized—the structure of labour markets and struggles for material resources. These economic conditions are highlighted as the root cause of tensions between different racial and ethnic groups, rather than the clash of cultures. Prevailing attitudes, including ethnocentrism, prejudice, and racism, reflect societal organization of economic relations, and specifically class locations within capitalist economies, rather than supposedly primordial cultural attachments. Marxist analysis views culturally learned attitudes and practices not as irrelevant to the understanding of intergroup conflicts, but as responses to economic interests. Inequalities in access to economic rewards and opportunities, rather than multi-cultural intolerance, are highlighted as central concerns for political action. The classical or strong version of this theoretical approach, sometimes called 'structural Marxism' subsumes or reduces the understanding of race relations to class analysis, suggesting that ultimately only class interests and class conflicts explain group relations. The more nuanced contemporary political economy perspective explores how class interests influence and modify the mobilization of racial and ethnic group identification, in some contexts to promote hostilities and separation, and in other contexts to promote a coming together around shared interests. The increasingly global character of economic organization is heralded by theorists such as Hardt and Negri (2000, 43–4) as potentially generating cosmopolitan linkages between workers around the globe struggling together for economic jus-

tice, that may eventually overshadow fragmented allegiances to ethnic groups.

Colonialism: The Origin of 'Race' and 'Racism'

The concept of 'race', with attendant notions of innate biological differences between types of people has its roots in European imperialism and colonialism. Word usage shifted from the earlier reference to the distinction between blue-blooded aristocracy and commoners to that between 'white men' and the 'black', 'yellow' and 'red' peoples of Africa, Asia and the Americas (Solomos and Back 1994). Europeans, with their advanced military technology and gunboat diplomacy, found it appealing to think of themselves as innately superior to the peoples they conquered, and as destined to take on 'the white man's burden' of governing and civilizing the more 'primitive races' they encountered. Such thoughts assuaged the sense of guilt associated with the brutality of conquest and subsequent plunder of resources that fuelled industrialization in Europe. Different European powers carved up continents with scant regard for the tribal, ethnic and cultural identities of subordinated people, and they routinely promoted a subordinated elite class of local administrators to act as buffer groups between themselves and the masses, attributing an intermediate racialized status to them.

The social impact of these practices have had a very long reach into twentieth-century post-colonial nation building. Political-economy theory argues that the violence that has so often wracked post-colonial states is more usefully understood as class conflict than as ethnic cleansing. Intensified commitment to cultural values and practices disparaged under colonial rule provided emerging leaders with a tool for mobilizing people to assert themselves against European domination and arrogance. Resentment against racialized buffer groups who buttressed and mimicked colonial rulers readily exploded into violence as Europeans withdrew. In the ensuing power vacuum, local leaders and international corporate power brokers have conspired to manipulate ethnic subgroup loyalties in their bid to assert control over natural resources such as oil, minerals, diamonds, and lands suitable for agribusiness interests.

Drohan (2003) uses this kind of analysis to account for a range of violent conflicts still raging across Africa.

In South Africa, Zimbabwe, Congo, Mozambique, Angola, Nigeria, Sierra Leone, Sudan, Uganda and Rwanda, similar violent histories can be told. The worst yet has been the genocidal violence in Rwanda. Historically, Belgian colonial rulers delegated extensive power and privileges to a minority of Tutsi tribesmen that served them as a buffer group. The Belgians also racialized the Tutsi as supposedly more European in features than the majority Hutu. Then they left them to their fate as newly democratic elections brought the majority Hutu government to power with independence in the 1950s. As successive Hutu governments faltered amid severe recession in the monocrop coffee economy, they deflected growing unrest into attacks against prominent Tutsi, accusing them of treasonous plots to destabilize the government (Masire et. al. 2000; Verwimp 2003). Tensions exploded in April 1994 after the Hutu president was killed in a plane crash. An estimated 800 000 people, mostly Tutsi and moderate Hutu, were murdered over a period of three months. The Belgian government and the United Nations were warned repeatedly that such a massacre was immanent, but failed to take any preventive action. While it is clear that political leaders were able to mobilize ethnic subgroup hostilities and loyalties in this conflict, it is also clear that a clash of cultures was irrelevant. Peoples categorized as Tutsi and Hutu are indistinguishable from each other in terms of physical features, language, religion, or other cultural practices.

Across Latin America similar histories have unfolded of post-colonial civil wars between ethnic-class factions, often fuelled and financed by trans-national corporate interests intent on quick profits from resource extraction. Indigenous peoples, whose villages and homelands have come in the way of mining interests, have been indiscriminately eliminated. Again, these struggles have had little to do with clash of cultures, unless by cultural values, one means the clash of corporate capitalist shareholder values pitted against those of subsistence farmers seeking a different kind of living from the land.

Post-Colonial 'Race and Ethnic Relations'

By end of Second World War most of the former colonies had achieved political independence from European rulers. Expanding post-war capitalist manufacturing economies in Europe, along with the white settler societies of North America, were experiencing significant labour shortages. These changing political-economic realities fostered profound changes in the character of global migration and encounters between peoples from different continents. In the past, these encounters had been mostly confined to a relatively small class of European elites directly involved in the colonial service, and personnel in the armed forces and trading companies. White Americans and Black Africans encountered each other mostly through the infamous slave trade which brought captured Africans to work as slaves in Southern American plantations. But from the 1950s onwards people from Africa and Asia and Latin America began to migrate to Europe and North America in ever-increasing numbers. They were both pushed by poverty and wars at home, and pulled by the hope of greater economic opportunities. The general population of urban centres in Europe came into close contact with people from 'the colonies' for the first time. As the character of encounters changed, the concept of race and 'race relations' shifted from focus on biological differences to preoccupation with culture contact and assimilation. (Solomos and Back 1994). Sociological studies of race relations in Britain during the 1960s to the '80s focussed principally on descriptive ethnographies of ethnic communities, and boundary relations between ethnic groups.

The period of recession and economic restructuring during the 1980s resulted in high levels of structural unemployment that hit the immigrant workers and their families especially hard. Corporations increasingly opted to relocate unskilled mass production work to Asia to exploit vast supplies of ultra-cheap labour. Marxist analysis of crises of capitalism, plagued with cyclical booms and slumps, was increasingly applied to the study of race and ethnic relations. The central argument was that the quality of these relations would directly reflect the severity of competition for jobs, and for related material resources like affordable housing and social services (Rex and Moore 1967; Brittan and Maynard 1984, 35–6). Desperate migrant workers were willing to accept low-waged jobs, while local workers resented the competition and the threat their cheaper labour represented for wage-levels generally. At the same time, evidence of unemployed migrants drawing income assistance fosters more resentment and challenges that they are unfairly abusing social services intended for locals. Marxist ideology might foster the hope that workers would unite in a common struggle against exploitative capitalism. But the experience of Europe in the 1980s and 1990s found that the more common outcome was escalating conflict, as capitalist employers exploited the situation to pit subgroups of workers against each other, both to lower average wages and to deflect resentment against the slumps in the labour market.

The contemporary era of globalized capital and communications has promoted new and accelerated forms of labour migration. An elite cosmopolitan class of professionals and managers and experts in information technology move around freely across the globe in the service on transnational corporations. Also highly mobile are skilled workers in resource extraction industries, especially oil workers, along with skilled scientists, health-care workers, and teachers. Competing at the bottom of international labour markets are seasonal farm workers, and domestic service workers. Richmond (2002) estimates that by the beginning of the 21st century there were 120 million people working outside their country of birth, excluding 'permanent' emigrants. Political upheavals on a global scale are also producing reactive migration of refugees from conflict, famine and environmental degradation. Andersson (2005) recounts the desperate struggles of undocumented transmigrants from across Latin America trying to get into the United States to find work.

The result, Richmond concludes, is that almost all countries now have multiracial and multilingual populations that cut across class levels. The experiences of cosmopolitan elites who embrace hybrid cultures as creative and emancipating, are very different from those of destitute refugees, or unskilled migrant workers, and different again from disempowered local workers competing for increasingly precarious, temporary, contract and casual work (Galabuzi 2006, 10). Complicating the picture still further is evidence of population decline and demographic imbalance across western Europe and in Canada as the post-war 'baby boomers' near retirement, and birthrates decline. Political and economic leaders in these countries increasing extol higher immigration as necessary to provide the mass of service workers and tax-payers to support rapidly aging populations. Optimistic scenarios view these changes as potentially heralding a more integrated universal world system (Hardt and Negri 2000) while others foresee intensified nationalism and ethnocentrism as threatened populations fight to maintain their privileges or to carve out niches for themselves in competitive, exploitative and unstable labour markets. The cosmopolitan discourse and post-national loyalties of high-flying economic elites do not resonate easily with the experiences of the mass of non-mobile, middle and low-waged workers looking to the 'tate to protect basic services (Yeğenoğlu 2005).

'he next section explores in more depth how these

historical shifts in economy and migration have impacted on race and ethnic relations in Canada

Canada: Racialized Class Formation in White Settler Society

Processes of class formation in Canada have been inherently racialized from the earliest years of European incursion into the lands that are now Canada. Fur trading companies like Hudson's Bay were designed to profit European governments. They were never intended to enrich indigenous peoples. Indians supplied most of the furs, bartering them for European technology, clothes and trinkets, but they were not permitted to enter the forts as paid employees (Bourgeault 1983). White women were also banned from the forts, so that the Companies would not have to meet the costs of supporting families. Mixed-blood children born of liaisons between European men and Indian women were disowned in European law as the responsibility only of their Indian mothers. In the eastern territories, Mohawk traders were better able to exploit the arrival of Europeans by positioning themselves as autonomous middle-men traders between warring factions of English, French and Dutch merchants (Alfred 1995, ch. 2). But this economic base largely evaporated with peace settlements after the war of 1812. With the steep decline in the fur trade by the mid-1800s European merchant capitalists had little need for indigenous people. European settlers, intent on exploiting the 'empty wilderness' for ranching and agriculture, drove them out of their way, confining them to reservations on lands mostly unsuitable for European-style settlement. The vast herds of buffalo, along with deer, moose and caribou that had sustained countless generations of indigenous peoples were equally in the way of European settlers and their numbers rapidly decimated.

Economically, it may have been inevitable that indigenous hunting and gathering economies would decline with the influx of settlers (Stanley 1964, 3–5). But it was not inevitable that indigenous peoples would be forcibly excluded from alternative ranching and agricultural economies. It was not inevitable that European settlers would be allocated 160 acres of farmland per family while Native families received only 10 acres or less, and that of poor quality. The Indian Act of 1896 that established these reserves also gave extraordinary powers to the Minister of Indian Affairs to manage these reserves, and to expropriate lands for railways, mining, hydro-electricity, and other development interests in later years. The National Indian Brotherhood of Canada estimates that as much as half of all allocated reserve lands were lost through such expropriations between 1900 and 1930 alone (Kellough 1980, 348). Laws developed by and for White settler governments in the interests of capitalist development of resources made such appropriations easy, but made claims for compensation by indigenous inhabitants impossibly difficult to pursue, since the laws required claimants to hold clearly defined, individual property rights recognized under European law (Martin 2002; Gill 2003; Blomley 2004).

The visibly racialized class structure of the emerging White settler society of Canada was actively managed by Immigration Laws designed to mesh different cohorts of migrants with labour force requirements. Immigrants from England and France were actively recruited to meet capitalist labour needs in expanding urban centres. Capitalists facing a shortage of wage-labour for their factories pushed successive governments to promote land speculation designed to stem the leakage of labourers into independent farm-ownership (Pentland 1959, 458–9; Teeple 1972, 46). Land prices in eastern Canada were raised to such high levels that migrants were forced to work for many years as wage labourers in factories before they could think of becoming independent farmers. The Manitoba government under Clifford Sifton in the 1890s also aggressively recruited "stalwart peasants in sheep-skin coats" (Hall 1988, 2000) from other parts of Europe specifically on the understanding that they were willing to open up isolated tracts of wilderness for commercial farming. Under pressure from business and railway interests in the 1870s and 1880s the Canadian government instituted laws to permit Chinese and other Asian males to enter Western Canada primarily as cheap labour for heavy and dangerous work such as blasting track for the Canadian Pacific Railway. Companies advanced ticket money for the journey to Canada in return for signed bonds to work for periods of 5 to 10 years. They were not permitted to bring wives or children. Companies held all Chinese workers' earnings and were obliged to provide only the bare essentials for their workers. An estimated 600 Chinese labourers died during railway construction from accidents and appalling living conditions (Bolaria and Li 1988). Once the railway was completed they were exploited as cheap labour in mining, fishing and sawmills, as the supply of manual labour from Europe declined. They commonly worked for wages that were between a half to a quarter of wage rates paid to white workers. By the 1900s white workers who feared this ultra-cheap competitive labour began to agitate fiercely for restrictions on Asian immigration. White workers conceptualized Asians not as fellow workers who deserved protection from exploitation, but as aliens who should be driven out. Politicians campaigned for restrictive legislation that first imposed a head tax on all Chinese and Japanese immigrants, and then virtually blocked all immigration from Asia until after the second world war. Across Canada, Asian workers faced discrimination from employers that pushed them into the lowest-paid jobs in ethnic businesses such as laundries and restaurants (Chen 2005; Li 2003).

Slavery existed in Canada, but without the demand of plantation economies it never became widespread. But pervasive racist discrimination still pushed Black migrants into the lowest-paid marginal jobs. Blacks who entered Canada as Empire Loyalists after the American revolution of 1783 were promised land along with the White Loyalists, but the promises were never kept. Either they received no land at all or were given barren plots on the fringes of townships. Compelled to work at wage-rates of a quarter of White workers, they were both despised and feared by White workers as competition in the labour market.

In this sad history, race and class are inextricably tied together. Business elites supported racist immigration policies that ensured a supply of exceptionally cheap and compliant labour. Indentured Chinese immigrant workers, controlled by highly restrictive contracts and in virtual debt bondage to employers who paid their passage, had few resources to challenge appalling working conditions. Racially segregated employment patterns minimized the likelihood of migrants from Europe joining forces with migrants from Asia to struggle for shared interests. Black workers, similarly isolated in segregated settlements, and risking deportation to slave-owning states to the south, likewise had few social resources to mobilize for collective action.

At the same time, the visible presence of large numbers of super-exploited, non-white workers tamed the potential for collective strike action by somewhat better-paid white workers. Strikes for better working conditions did happen. The Winnipeg General Strike of 1919 is one of the largest and best known, when an estimated 30 000 workers left their jobs. However, this strike was quickly broken by a combination of police brutality, the discrediting of leaders as communist aliens from Eastern Europe, and a hastily-passed law permitting the government to deport British-born immigrants.

Canada's Labour Force in the 21st Century: A Multicultural Vertical Mosaic

As noted above, the Immigration Act of 1967 officially abolished any formal reference to race or ethnic background of immigrants, favouring instead a system of preferential ranking based on a combination of points for education, proficiency in English or French, and employment skills that match shortages in the Canadian labour market. The Charter of Rights 1982 explicitly forbids discrimination on the basis of race or ethnic origin, and the Employment Equity Act of 1995 goes beyond passive non-discrimination, to pressure federal government agencies and companies doing business with the government to actively recruit and promote qualified visible minorities, along with Aboriginals, disabled workers, and women, to achieve a workforce proportional to the size of these groups in the Canadian labour force as a whole. Business and political elites widely endorsed these policies on three major grounds. Canada can no longer afford to display overt racism against China or Japan now that they are major trading partners with Canada. Also, a multi-racial and multi-ethnic labour force gives Canadian businesses an advantage in language and cultural competence needed to promote international trade. Thirdly, the Canadian economy needs immigrants to compensate for a shrinking and rapidly aging population, migration from formerly favoured European and North American societies has fallen to very low levels. In total, 3.7 million immigrants came to Canada over the 25 years between 1968 and 1992. Almost half of them fitted the category of 'visible minorities', with 35.7 percent from Asia and 12.2 percent from Africa and the Caribbean (Galabuzi 2006, 2).

The central question Galabuzi explores is how these visible or racialized migrants and racialized Canadians generally have been integrated into the Canadian economy, measured by the variables of the kind of jobs they get, unemployment rates, and employment incomes when job skills and education are taken into account. He notes first that global economic restructuring has resulted in an expanding proportion of jobs in Canada fit the pattern of 'precarious work'—temporary, part-time, contract and casual work with low pay, no benefits, no job security and poor working conditions. Racialized persons are concentrated in such jobs in higher proportions than their numbers in the labour force (ch. 1). In 1995, only one-third of Canadian-born racialized earners were employed in full-time, full-year jobs compared with half of other Canadian-born earners (105). Visible minorities have higher levels of unemployment, at 12.6 percent, compared with 6.7 percent for the general population in 2001 (ibid. 16).They are more likely to be living below the poverty line at 35.6 percent, compared to 17.6 percent of the general population, not including Aboriginals (ibid.17), and their average incomes are 25 percent lower (ibid. 91). As a measure of the problem of racism in Canada, Galabuzi cites evidence that African Canadian university graduates in Toronto have the same rate of unemployment as White high-school dropouts (2006, 204).

Conventional explanations in terms of lower education or poorer quality of 'human capital' for visible minorities are not supported by the evidence that visible minorities, selectively approved for immigration according to the points system since 1968, have higher average levels of education than the general population. By 1990 40.7 percent of immigrants had university degrees and a further 20.2% had trade and college education, compared with Canadian averages of 22.2% and 31.7% respectively (111–113). Recent immigrants, half of whom are visible minorities, are highly educated and have advanced job skills. Yet they are not able to translate these educational advantages into professional careers. Even after 10 or more years of residence in Canada, visible minority immigrants are not catching up. When controlling for length of stay, the average income of racialized immigrants is lower than for non-racialized immigrants.

Galabuzi argues that this evidence of racialized inequality in the Canadian economy reflects extensive barriers to accreditation of immigrant qualifications that have not been resolved in the almost 40 years since the points system was introduced, and further, that this resistance itself reflects racist assumptions about human worth. Immigrant workers are being systematically excluded from higher segments of the Canadian labour market by a pervasive refusal to recognize foreign credentials or to value foreign work experience (Bauder 2003).

Migrants from Asia, Africa, and Latin America are being enticed into Canada with advanced degrees and professional practice in fields such as medicine, dentistry, nursing, veterinary science, law, social work, teaching, engineering, and trades such as plumbing, accounting, and mechanics (Galabuzi 2006, 52). Yet when they get here they find that Canadian licencing bodies will not accept their qualifications as adequate to practice in Canada. Individuals are told that they must virtually repeat their training in Canada before they can sit licencing examinations. Such demands are made without any provision to help immigrants meet the costs of such retraining and with limited places made available for them. Even doctors who have passed all their licencing examinations still find they cannot get essential residency positions because the number of such positions available is closely tied to numbers of Canadian medical-school admissions. Employers of non-professional labour cite different reasons, like risks associated with language and cultural barriers, for reluctance to hire immigrants before they have extensive Canadian employment experience. Immigrants are caught in the impossible situation of being required to have prior Canadian employment experience in their field before employers will hire them to work in Canada. Structural adjustment programs like intensive job-related language training, and job-shadowing that might fast-track immigrants into careers commensurate with their qualifications, are not offered.

Charter rights, multiculturalism, and employment equity policies all notwithstanding, there is still a racialized vertical mosaic in the Canadian economy. Critics of the government policies charge that they sound good in principle but have no teeth. The federal Employment Equity Policy has no mechanisms to enforce compliance and no sanctions for failure. Trudeau's Multiculturalism Policy stressed cultural equality for minorities, not economic or political equality (Ng 1995). As Bannerji scathingly expresses it visible minorities demanded the end of racist capitalism—and instead got "multiculturalism," (2000, 89). Business elites promote voluntary 'diversity management' as good for business (Wrench 2005) but in practice focus on the 'soft option' of sensitivity training for managers, rather than the 'hard option' of structural equality in hiring and promotion practices.

Ideological Hegemony: Preserving Privilege

A central prediction in Marxist analysis is that the prevailing cultural values of a society, continually reinforced by economic and political elites, will be those that support and justify the position of the economically privileged class. Such values predictably serve to mystify or obscure the exploitative features of capitalist economic organization in favour of rationalizations or ideologies that protect privilege as merited achievements. Commonly-accepted explanations for the evi-

dence of a racialized class structure in Canada, as in other western capitalist societies conform to this predicted pattern.

Structural barriers to the integration of visible minorities as equals in Canadian economy are all but ignored in prevailing explanations, in favour of a focus on presumed failings in the visible minorities themselves. Employers and licencing bodies assume from the start that foreign qualifications and experience are likely to be inferior to Canadian qualifications unless conclusively proven otherwise. Evidence that Canadian markets are full of cars and electronics manufactured in Asia is not taken as proof of the competence of Asian-trained scientists and mechanics who made them. Experimental research with matched White and visible-minority job applicants have demonstrated that employers routinely screen out minority applicants without even interviewing them, on the presumption that they would not have the abilities of White applicants (Galabuzi 2006,153). Evidence of excessively high unemployment among visible minorities in the 1990s was translated in government policies as evidencing the need to apply an even more rigorous points system to potential immigrants to ensure 'higher quality applicants, and to cut back on sponsored or family class immigration as imposing too much of a drain on social services. Canadian political parties became preoccupied with concerns about 'illegal' emigrants and 'bogus refugees' who 'abuse' social services who should be apprehended and deported. (Kirkham 1998, 248–253). When poverty and frustration among visible minority immigrants finds expression in criminal activities this has readily become translated in political and media debates as further evidence of the presumed low quality of visible minorities themselves, as culturally predisposed to criminal lifestyles.

Studies of the attitudes of White workers towards visible minorities commonly reflect a parallel set of assumptions that protect the interests of White workers against the potential claims of visible minorities to more of the economic pie. Such attitudes include the assumption that White workers generally are superior to visible minority workers; that the disadvantaged status of visible minorities, if true, is most likely their own fault; that the economy cannot absorb more immigrants without jeopardising the hard-earned and tenuous economic stability of middle-class workers and their families; and that employment equity or affirmative action policies constitute unwarranted discrimination against White workers. Rubin's (1994) study of struggling working-class White families in America suggests that people commonly believed in equal opportunity and white superiority at the same time. In their common-sense reasoning, Whites ought to get the better jobs because they are better workers, and hence if Blacks or other minority-group workers were hired ahead of themselves it was due to discriminatory affirmative action rather than merit. Members of Italian and Greek minorities who had themselves faced discrimination as immigrants to America, readily endorsed prejudices against other minorities, especially Black Americans, as inferior workers to themselves (Noivo 1998). Homeowners feared that the value of their properties would decline if visible minorities, and especially Black Americans started to buy houses in their neighbourhood (Massey 2005). When federal laws made it illegal to discriminate openly against Black buyers, real estate agents and mortgage lenders used more subtle means. Typically, they would withhold information about available properties in White neighbourhoods, and require Black home-buyers to make higher down-payments and meet more stringent repayment schedules to qualify for mortgages (Massey 2005).

Relatively privileged families in a middle-class town in England, actively resisted efforts to settle refugees in their community, even on a temporary basis. They signed petitions and organized demonstrations against a plan to use a local hotel as a refugee shelter on the grounds that the Saltdean economy could not cope with the influx (Grillo 2005). They argued that it was difficult enough for local people to care for their own elderly and needy people, without the added burden of caring for refugees who might also be a crime risk. Cutbacks to social services in the wake of recession made these arguments plausible. Shopkeepers in a London neighbourhood vented their resentment at Muslim immigrants for undermining the neighbourhood community (Wells and Watson 2005). With their businesses already threatened by large supermarkets, these shopkeepers felt further sidelined and unable to compete for business from these alien newcomers with their preference for halal meat and ethnic goods.

In all these studies, White respondents pervasively denied that they were racists, insisting that their views were factually realistic and legitimate. Any suggestion that affirmative action policies might be necessary or valid to ensure equal treatment for visible minorities was fiercely resisted. Affirmative Action was variously characterized by Whites as blatant discrimination against Whites, as itself racist, as a violation of fundamental

principles of equality, as giving underqualified visible minorities an undeserved easy ride, and actually making the situation worse for visible minorities who got jobs, scholarships, or other benefits, by confirming that they were not good enough to succeed without such discriminatory favours (Kleiner 1998; Augostinos, Tuffin and Every 2005; Donnelly, Cook, van Ausdale and Foley 2005). Even those who conceded that Aboriginals face more obstacles than Whites have disadvantages too but overcome them with determination and effort. White respondents referred to principles of equality, individual merit and achievement to discredit affirmative action and employment equity. They discussed racism but only to deny its relevance. They did not see or did not comment on the central requirement of these policies that minority applicants be appropriately qualified. Totally obscured in the commonsense understanding that White respondents displayed was any awareness of White privilege, the pervasive favouring of White applicants, the pervasive discrediting of foreign credentials and experiences as obviously inferior to Canadian credentials, the continuing colonialism that denies Aboriginal forms of title to lands and resources, the pervasive structural barriers that generations of racialized poverty place in the way of all but the strongest individuals to compete on the basis of standards solely defined by White educators and employers. When Rubin asked her Black American respondents for their thoughts on Affirmative Action, their views were surprisingly similar to those of White respondents. They too insisted that merit should count, and advocated a true meritocracy, in which Blacks would be hired equally with White workers. What they saw differently was that Black workers faced so much discrimination and so many barriers to equal opportunity that without affirmative action few of them would ever be hired (1994, ____).

From the political economy perspective, these commonsense forms of thinking, and the ethnocentrism and racism they displace, do not have their roots in primordial ethnic attachments, or in childhood socialization. They have their roots in the class relations of capitalism. They serve to protect White privilege, justify racialized inequalities as reflections only of individual merit or lack of merit, and obscure the structural workings of global corporate capitalism that continually throw up displaced and dispossessed refugees and asylum seekers on Europe's shores (Sivanandan 2001). White resentment against structural unemployment gets deflected into blaming people even more vulnerable than themselves for increasing competition for precarious jobs.

Resentment at the gutting of social programmes in the name of deficit reduction gets similarly deflected onto 'illegal aliens' or 'bogus refugees' or 'asylum seekers' who supposedly clog up the system and abuse tax-payers' money. Collectively these attitudes function as part of the ideological hegemony that shores up the capitalist system.

The Social Constructionist Perspective: Racialization and Ethnicization as Social Accomplishments

The social constructionist perspective focuses attention on processes of ethnicization and racialization—that is the processes through which people come to identify themselves and others or to feel themselves labelled by others as members of some particular ethnic or racial grouping.

Ethnic and racial identities are seen as negotiable features of social relationships rather than fixed, with the boundaries of exclusion and inclusion changing with specific historical and social situations and experiences. The salience given to ethnic or racial labelling relative to multiple other potential social relationships like age-grouping, occupation, religion, gender and sexual orientation, political affiliation, is also historically and socially specific. To the extent that people think of ethnic or racial identities as fixed by birth, or as centrally defining features of themselves or others, this sense of rigidity and centrality of boundary definitions itself has to be explained by reference to social processes that fix and enforce such identities. These boundary-defining processes work simultaneously at the level of shared group understandings of the kinds of people who are included in or excluded from membership categories, and individual choice of private and publically claimed membership. These processes fundamentally involve relations of power—the power to define oneself and others and to have those definitions recognized and acted upon, and conversely the power to exclude and to have those exclusions count.

Defining the 'Other': State Policy and Identity Formation

The British imperial government and later the federal state of Canada passed a series of laws and amendments to laws, including the Indian Act, various Immigration Acts and the Multiculturalism Act, that functioned to create boundaries of inclusion and exclusion around minority status.

The indigenous inhabitants of what is now Canada have struggled for centuries to define their individual and collective identities within the dominating frame of colonial legislation. During the fur-trade era, the children born of liaisons between men from Europe and indigenous women were considered "Indians". Their mothers and her kin were held responsible for these children, and explicitly not their white fathers. The intent was that mixed-blood offspring would have no legitimate claim to the wealth generated by the trading forts (Bourgeault 1983).

Later, as white settlers came in ever increasing numbers, settler governments pressured indigenous peoples to sign treaties restricting them to reserved lands, in return for various rights. The interests of successive colonial governments was now in minimizing the numbers of people who would be legally recognized as "Status Indians" with treaty entitlements to live on reserved land and to have access to education, medical and other benefits.

The first federal Indian Act of 1867 explicitly recognized *only* the descendants of Indian males as legally Status Indians, thereby excluding vast numbers of mixed-blood children of Indian women and white fathers from any legal claim to Indian ancestry. They became Canadians of aboriginal descent, but not socially recognized as either Indians or whites. Over time, the Indian Act, with its legalized discourse of classification and regulation, worked to create among regulated peoples and their descendants, the subjective identities of Status Indian and non-status or excluded people (Lawrence 2004). The act gave white bureaucrats, hired as Indian Agents, extensive powers to define the boundaries of legal residence on these reserves, and the right to evict 'squatters' and 'trespassers.' In one extreme case, a treaty signed in 1877 created the Pahpahstayo Reserve on 40 acres which are now part of South Edmonton, but a mere nine years later, all the residents were declared to be merely mixed-bloods and no longer Status Indians entitled to a reserve. They were forcibly removed and the reserve ceased to exist (ibid. 43).

The *Gradual Enfranchisement Act* of 1869 functioned to further restrict the numbers of Status Indians by enticing and forcing individual men, along with their wives and descendants, to give up their status in return for parcels of land, jobs with the military, the right to vote, and the like (ibid. 32–3). Successive government policies and practices, often of questionable legality, worked to further obscure and obliterate the Aboriginal status of thousands of people. Native children, rounded up and sent to Residential Schools, were stripped of their ancestral languages and cultures. School officials routinely changed the names of individuals or their families on residential school admission forms. Indian Agents removed the names of orphans sent to these schools from their band lists. Census takers refused to categorize individuals as 'Natives' on government forms, categorizing them as 'French' or 'Black'. Native wives were listed as 'French' on marriage registries. During the 1960s, as residential schools declined, federal social workers gained authority to remove children from difficult family situations on reservations, for off-reserve adoption. Many thousands of children lost their status as Indians, and their connections to family as tribe, through the bureaucratic erasure of their origins (ibid. 37).

The struggles of Aboriginal peoples to define their own identities still continue within Canadian courts, on terms set by White settler governments. Recent, and still on-going land-claims cases in Canada and the USA commonly revolve around legal definitions of Aboriginal status. In a case involving the Gitksan and Wet'suwet'en peoples of Northern British Columbia (ibid. 4), the Supreme Court of Canada determined that the claimants must not only prove that they have had unbroken governance of the land and land use for 12 000 years. They must also prove that they are essentially the same people as their ancestors were, in effect that they have retained intact and unchanged their blood-lines and primordial native cultural traditions. Evidence of cultural change or 'assimilation' is thus being defined legally as evidence of loss of Aboriginal status. In 1986 the Indian Act was revised yet again to grant limited status to Indian women who had lost their status on marriage to non-Status men, with the condition that Indian band councils gained the right to decide whether these new 'Status Indians' would gain band-membership status. Some bands have opted to use blood quantum of between 25 to 100 percent as the working definition of band membership, copying the racist criteria imposed by Canadian Courts in land-claims disputes (ibid. 68; Alfred 1995). Alfred argues that the rigid culture-based boundaries and ostensibly racist definitions of membership adopted by Kahnawake Mohawk near Montreal do not reflect ancestral values, which were actually far more fluid. Rather, they reflect the struggle of the Mohawk to define themselves in the context of ongoing Euro-Canadian efforts to destroy Aboriginal status and culture.

Multiculturalism as Policy: Creating Ethnics

The Canadian Multiculturalism Act, first proclaimed by the Trudeau government in 1971, is represented as recognizing and giving official status and protection to a wide variety of culturally distinct communities. These diverse communities became established in Canada as the new Immigration Act of 1967 facilitated the migration of non-white people from around the world. Social constructionist analysis, however, challenges this representation of pre-existing ethnic communities that arrive in Canada, exploring instead how the Act works to create and perpetuate the subject communities that it defines. Trudeau's policy speech in 1971 can be read as actively defining for members of parliament, and for Canadians generally, how to read the situation of worldwide migration into Canada as one of 'multiple cultures', and the policy issue as one of protecting 'multiple cultures' (Ng 1995). The situation could have been read very differently as one of global economic migrants who experience a vertical mosaic of unequal access to the Canadian economy. From this perspective, salient policies issues would focus on the need for flexible recognition of foreign qualifications and work experiences, expanded bridging training and job shadowing, and the need for anti-racist training and legislation governing employers and unions, all designed to promote greater equality in labour-force absorption. Instead, Trudeau's central focus is on 'cultures.' He proposed four policy initiatives designed to provide assistance to ethnic minority communities in their desire to contribute to Canada, to overcome cultural barriers to participation, to promote creative cultural encounters in the interests of Canadian national unity, and to provide basic language training in English or French. These initiatives were defined as the responsibility of the Citizenship Branch of the Department of the Secretary of State, with no responsibilities delegated to the Department of Employment and Immigration.

It has been widely argued that the true policy concern underlying the Multiculturalism Act was not to deal with ethnic minorities at all, but to manage heightened tensions between Francophone Quebec and the rest of Canada, especially following the FLQ kidnapping crisis in October of 1970. The Act established official bilingualism to appease Quebec while characterising Canada-outside-Quebec as multicultural in contrast to Quebec's supposedly narrow homogeneity (Ng 1995;

Fleras and Elliott 2003, Chap 8; Bannerji 2000, Chap 3). Whether in the interest of placating Quebec or other minorities, the focus of bureaucratic attention was centred squarely on the management of culturally distinct ethnic minority communities in Canada.

Policy initiatives developed through Multiculturalism envision encouraging leaders within various ethnic communities to consult with the state on matters of interest to their communities, to develop liaison with local members of parliament, and to apply for funds to promote cultural festivals and heritage language retention, as well as funds for training in Canada's two official languages. A central argument put forward by Ng and Bannerji is that these initiatives, and the forms they take, work to create or bring about the appearance of ethnic communities that the Act presupposes. In effect, government policies themselves form part of the boundary-defining processes that constitute ethnic difference.

Promoting 'Ethnic' Leaders

Ethnic communities are expected to have ethnic leaders who represent their communities in national politics. A plethora of arena for formal consultations have emerged at all levels of government in Canada, including for immigration hearings, social services, equity programmes, policing, government departments, crown corporations, hospitals and school boards, supported by a plethora of lectures and conferences sponsored by Ethnic Associations and universities across Canada (Amit-Talai 1996b). Self-identified ethnic leaders have come forward to fill these political roles as spokespersons, consultants, and advisors to the government. For every 'crisis' in ethnic relations that becomes identified, some new committee gets struck to consult with ethnic communities. The result, suggests Amit-Talai, is the emergence of an 'official ethnic minority circuit' from which the same names get put forward repeatedly for each new committee. Many such people make full-time careers out of the circuit, as equity officers, race-relations advisors, intercultural training consultants, committee appointees, and staff in ethnic minority and civil rights associations. While the political goal of extensive consultation with ethnic communities may sound impressive, it may be limited in practice to repeated conversations with the same small clique of individuals.

The elusive question is who do these individual 'leaders' represent, or for whom do they speak. A survey of studies of leadership in ethnic groups suggest that dis-

unity is the norm rather than the exception (Jedwab 2001). Categories like 'Muslim' or 'South Asian', for example, encompass a multiplicity of ethnic subgroups that cannot be represented by one spokesperson. Any one identifiable subgroup also commonly encompasses multiple factions along lines of gender, class, political orientation, traditional to secular outlook, and the like. But self-styled ethnic community leaders are under pressure to gloss over divisions and conflicting priorities. They need to project a sense of ethnic unity and consensus to non-members to bolster their own claims to be representatives of the 'community' with the government. In reality, Amit-Talai suggests, many of these minority circuit players may be marginal members of the ethnic communities they claim to represent, and viewed with suspicion by insiders.

Interrogating Ethnic 'Community'

The concept of ethnic community contains a double irony in that ethnic communities as lived experience at a local or neighbourhood level have often been ignored, the notion of 'ethnic community' as conceptual abstraction has become entrenched in the discourse and politics of multiculturalism.

City planners have routinely shown scant regard for community ties at the local level of small neighbourhoods, especially when they get in the way of building roads, or facilitating urban slum clearance for value-added commercial development. The black settlement of Africville in Halifax was bulldozed in 1964 to make way for a park, with no regard for the extended family ties and support networks that had sustained the settlement for over a century (Clairmont and Macgill [1974] 1999; Nelson 2002). The 400 black residents of Africville did feel a strong sense of community and attachment, albeit to an impoverished area of substandard housing. Forty years after the city forcibly removed the residents and bulldozed their homes, the 400 former residents, along with their descendants, were still organizing annual reunions at the site. The residents also created a permanent memorial to their community in the local library, preserving stories and photographs of their lives, their church congregations, ministers, schools, homes and creative arts (Clairmont and Magill 1997, 296). Blomley (2004, 47) tells similar stories of city planners in Vancouver demolishing areas full of cheap rental housing and homeless shelters, oblivious to the community ties and sense of belonging of long-term residents, including particularly urban Aboriginal people.

Residents of the Vancouver area of Downtown Eastside lobbied fruitlessly to preserve a small park for community use, while all the developers could see was 'weeds, rock and junk.'

The concept of 'ethnic communities' that pervades the political discourse of multiculturalism has little or nothing to do with lived experience of extended kin and support networks that people may develop with their friends and neighbours. It refers to an abstract categorization of people along lines of race and ethnicity, lines that are presumed to tie people together. Trudeau's speech on multiculturalism asserts as commonsense knowledge that people migrating to Canada come as members of ethnic communities, or form such communities once they arrive. Yet no such assumptions about community membership are made about Canadians who are considered mainstream. In classical sociological theory the notion of 'community' implies a sense of nostalgia for an earlier, more primitive form of folk society characteristic of isolated, homogenous rural lifestyles. People in industrialised urban societies are seen as more individualistic, forming loose-knit networks or associations around varieties of specialized interests. This perspective throws into question the commonsense assumption that mainstream Canadians form 'associations' while 'ethnic' Canadians form 'communities' (Alleyne 2002). Migrants typically arrive as individuals, or as members of nuclear families, Bannerji suggests (2000, 159). They may well look to close kin for help with getting settled, but whether they confine their primary interaction to ethnic enclaves depends more on a sense of external rejection from the host society than yearning for homogeneity.

Studies of migrants who came from the same geographic and ethnic backgrounds have commonly not supported the notion that they form close-knit folk societies, with shared cultural boundaries and mutual interests, envisioned in the discourse of ethnic community. Refugees from Bosnia, fleeing the civil wars that broke up Yugoslavia, expressed no clear sense of shared community in Britain. In their previous lives in Bosnia these refugees mostly had no prior experience of organizing or acting collectively, they were not politically conscious, and did not centrally identify themselves as Muslims. Most had lived in multi-religious and multi-ethnic cities, they had diverse economic and occupational backgrounds, and many were intermarried with Serbs and Croats (Kelly 2003). A Refugee Action Committee formed in Britain struggled to create a sense of community among the refugees, with the idea that this would be helpful for their adjustment to Britain. But in Kelly's view, such organizing produced at best a tenuous, contingent community, dependent on a few leaders who expected to benefit from assistance offered to 'refugee communities' from the host state. Otherwise the Bosnian association was internally faction-ridden, with few volunteer workers, and no sense of group obligation.

The so-called Iranian community in London, England appeared similarly tenuous (Sreberny 2000). The image of a primordial ethnic group, united by nostalgia for their ancestral home and working in solidarity with co-ethnics, that the concept of ethnic community brings to mind, turned out to be a myth. People living in London who came from Iran were divided by vast differences of political loyalties, class, and at least five different minority languages. Most described themselves as not particularly religious. A few individuals, mostly middle-aged men, who hoped eventually to return to Iran if the incumbent political regime were overthrown, used to read Iranian newspapers on the internet. But most respondents were not interested. There is no 'Iranian community' in London, Sreberny concludes—only a few local drop-in centres.

Negotiating Ethnic/Racial Communities

If we abandon the notion that ethnic or racial communities occur naturally, then the evidence that people do sometimes mobilize around ethnic/racial markers needs to be explained. How and why, and under what kinds of circumstances do people sometimes come to think of themselves as members of ethnic communities? Conditions within the host society, as much as conditions intrinsic to minorities themselves, seem to influence ethnic identity formation. A study of the emergence of Hindu self-identity among university students in Britain, suggests that it developed primarily as a response to multicultural politics, and the sense of being marginalized and not fully accepted as 'British' despite being born and raised in England. They described how they had begun to use the label 'Hindu' in response to incessant questioning from fellow British students about who they were. Their chosen label 'British' only prompted further questioning about where they were really, originally from. They also had to respond to constant questioning about whether they were like "this crap Asian programme on black families" shown in television documentaries and films. Hindu won out as the only positive label that seemed available.

Alternative geographic-origin labels like India or

East-Africa did not fit either as they had never seen these places. They were also 'not Pakistanis', 'not Muslims,' and 'not Blacks.' The label 'Hindu', Raj suggests, worked as an ethnic resource, an active response to the experience of being marked as racially and culturally different, and to increasing pressure from multicultural politics to assert some fixed religious-ethnic identity. The label Hindu was mostly without religious content, as these students had not been socialized into Hindu practices, and knew little about them. Once at university, the student Hindu Association gradually drew them in with explanatory talks on Hindu philosophy, and prominent Hindus politicians as guest lectures.

The emergence of 'Black' as actively negotiated, and hotly contested political label in contemporary Britain, reflects similar struggles to label a sense of shared issues (Sudbury 2001). Sudbury rejects the theoretical frame of 'ethnic resource mobilization' on the grounds that most of the women attracted to the Organization of Women Of African and Asian Descent (OWAAD) in 1978 did not come with ready-made identities to collective action, and they shared no common ethnic resource of language, religion, geographic origins or other elements of culture. Activists had a sense of community identification with local organizations set up to help Black families, but not with an abstract notion of a 'Black Community' across Britain (Reynolds 2002, 600). Early efforts by OWAAD organizers to generate shared political consciousness through notions of authentic blackness, expressed in Afro hairstyles, non-western dress and food choices, restrictions on appropriate sexual conduct and sexual orientations, resulted in such divisions that the organization imploded in conflict in 1982. It reemerged in the 1990s, Sudbury suggests, with a very different agenda expressed through a common rejection of colonial divide-and-rule legacy that pitted Africans against Asian buffer groups, derogated local cultural practices, and highlighted racial divisions. The emerging OWAAD political identity focuses on shared experiences of racism and marginalization as non-whites in Britain. The irony is that an important impetus for diverse people to come together under the umbrella label of 'Black' has been to challenge pervasive stereotypes that represents all non-whites as the same. Activist Black writers studied by Reynolds (2002) struggled against reductionist multicultural awareness that promotes 'Black literature' only when it fits the stereotype of black experience as centred on poverty, discrimination and/or abuse, and the writers' journeys of self-exploration and self-discovery.

Accounts that do not fit this genre tend to be rejected by publishers as not fitting what audiences would expect black authors to be writing about.

What these ethnicized and racialized people have most in common is not shared culture, but shared experience of 'othering', marking them as outsiders, as visible minorities, or as multi-cultured, different from the Whiteness and Europeanness that is taken for granted as mainstream culture. Highlighted in Bannerji's accounts of the lives of non-white immigrants in Canada are experiences that few 'invisible' or mainstream Canadians ever need to notice, but that few visibles can afford to ignore (2000, ch. 3). They include all-pervasive state regulations governing the lives of immigrants, the interrogation and suspicion they face when meeting requirements for visas and permits to enter, to travel, to study, or to bring family members. They include also a heightened awareness of public expressions of racism that those who are not targeted can more easily ignore—the anti-immigration stance of the Western Guard, the Heritage Front, the Reform Party, the neo-Nazi rock band Rahowa—its name an acronym for Racial Holy War (ibid. 110). There are also the stories of rejected migrants hiding for months in church basements in fear of deportation back to countries from which they have fled, of Black men shot by nervous and trigger-happy police, of skin-head attacks on Jewish property, of the frozen bodies of Aboriginal youth dumped by police miles outside of Prairie cities. Such stories intensify the sense of fear and exclusion felt by those who are othered in Canadian society. Visible minorities know themselves to be the primary targets of the heightened surveillance that comes with fear of terrorism. The ubiquitous closed-circuit television (CCTV) surveillance creates lines in public spaces "that Blacks cannot cross and Whites cannot see" (Fiske 2000, 53). Aboriginal and visible minority people are tracked and followed, stopped and searched, questioned and excluded, with the aid of technologies that are experienced by invisibles as unobtrusive, benign and helpful.

Contemporary global concerns around the 'war on terror', with associated involvement of the USA, Canada and Britain in wars in Iraq and Afghanistan, threats against Iran, also impact on the sense of identity migrants from these countries may feel with their homeland or kin still in these regions. So also does nightly news coverage of conflict and natural disasters around the globe. It seems likely that people from Iran who showed little sense of a sustained 'Iranian community' in London when studied by Sreberny in the late '90s, may respond differently in 2006 when Iran is being regularly portrayed in the media as under threat of sanctions or war for starting up its nuclear energy program.

In the era since the September 11th terrorist attacks in New York and Washington in 2001, Muslims living in the West have had to negotiate their sense of identity in the context of heavily stereotyped media coverage. They encompass a staggering diversity of socio-cultural backgrounds from Far East, Middle East and Palestine, different regions of Africa, the former Soviet Union, Eastern Europe and the Balkans, as well as Western Europe and North America, and they follow vastly differing religious practices, ranging from fundamentalist to reformist and secular. All this diversity tends to be homogenized into simplistic stereotypes of 'the Islamic mind' in Western mass media. People who have very little in common find themselves lumped together as if they formed a single 'Islamic community.'

Constructing the Vertical Mosaic: Insights from Institutional Ethnography

As described above, Statistics Canada data reveal a vertical mosaic of patterned inequalities in the Canadian labour force along racial and ethnic lines stretching back over many years (Porter 1965; Galabuzi 2006). Continuing reluctance by professional licencing bodies and employers to recognize foreign qualifications and work experiences account for some of the barriers facing professionals who migrate to Canada. But job qualifications alone are not sufficient to ensure equal employment opportunities for racialized and ethnicized people. The studies explored below give insights into the discriminatory effects of routine organizational practices through which decisions about hiring, retaining, and promoting people are made. These practices are often subtle and largely unacknowledged by those responsible for them or by those who benefit from the competitive advantages they sustain. They work at all levels of the class system.

A pioneer ethnographic study of a counselling agency designed to assist immigrant women with finding employment in Toronto describes in detail how bureaucratic accounting practices required by government regulators worked to ghettoise immigrant women in sweat-shop, garment-factory jobs from which counsellors had been trying to help them escape (Ng 1988). As a condition for receiving government funding to assist immigrants, the counselling agency had to supply detailed statistical information on a weekly, monthly and bi-annual basis on numbers of clients counselled from designated ethnic groups, numbers referred to job openings, and numbers of clients being hired. Continued funding depended upon both the numbers and proportions of clients counselled to clients hired. Ng describes how counsellors, desperate to retain the funding on which their own salaries depended, were driven to prioritize what regulators counted, namely the number of jobs filled. They routinely rejected clients who did not fit the four ethnic groups specified for government funding, they processed clients as quickly as possible by restricting their counselling to questions on forms that the regulators required, and they pressured them to accept any job the agency referred them to. A steady supply of job openings was a crucial requirement for meeting hiring quotas, and the bulk of these job openings were supplied by garment-factory bosses. Counsellors listed these job openings and bullied clients into taking them, even when they knew that working conditions were sub-standard, wages offered to immigrant 'trainees' and piece-rate workers were below the statutory minimum, and employers practised blatantly racist hiring restrictions. In effect, Ng concludes, once the counselling agency got government funding, it ceased to serve immigrant women. It became an agency of the state managing cheap immigrant labour on behalf of garment-factory bosses.

A personal narrative account by an Asian American sociology professor provides another point of entry for exploring discriminatory hiring practices, in her case with respect to professional university appointments at the elite end of the labour market (Glenn 1997, 94–99).

Officially, such appointments are governed by rigorous peer evaluation processes involving the presentation of scholarly publications, research talks, teaching evaluations, interviews and collegial decision making. Yet these procedures were routinely subverted when visible minority candidates were being considered. White male academics, disinterested in scholarship on gender, race or ethnicity, commonly did not bother to read the research papers presented by minority applicants, or dismissed their scholarly significance. They would then readily go along with any negative judgements offered by other faculty who opposed the candidate. Even faculty members who spoke in favour of diversifying the department and of hiring a visible minority applicant, were rarely sufficiently committed to employment equity to go against any colleague who strongly opposed such appointments. They valued avoiding conflict with colleagues more than fighting injustices against the excluded. Hence, it only took one or two prejudiced individuals in a large faculty to block minority appointments. Other common strategies that subverted appointments that were explicitly intended to attract visible minority applicants, was to leave the position vacant on the excuse that no minority applicant was good enough, or that only one famous minority scholar would do, and that person were unavailable, or that the position warranted a salary far below what qualified applicants were already earning. That many such applicants did eventually have successful careers at other universities, including Glenn herself who became a full professor of sociology at the prestigious University of California, Berkeley, is evidence that prejudice, rather than poor qualifications, played the central role in such exclusion. The result, suggests Glenn, is that visible minority professors remain underrepresented as a token presence at American universities and ghettoised in departments of Chicano, Native American or African American studies. Mainline departments remain 'white male bastions', ignoring scholarship that focuses on issues of race, ethnicity, and gender.

Since 1995, Canadian universities have been required by the Federal Employment Equity Act to work towards fair representation of visible minorities and Aboriginal peoples, along with women and people with disabilities. But these official policies offer little protection from the kinds of covert discriminatory practices described by Glenn, because they become visible only as evidence of underqualified applicants. The proportions of tenured professors and professors in senior ranks in Canadian universities from the four employment-equity categories still fall well below the proportions available in talent pool of graduates with doctorates from Canadian universities.

The potential talent pool of visible minority applicants is itself artificially restricted by familiar factors of poverty, restricted role models, low self esteem, low encouragement, and other barriers that visible-minority students typically experience at earlier stages in their education. An ethnographic study of Chinese students in a Canadian school (Jackson 1987) reveals how even well-meaning advice from sympathetic teachers and counsellors contributed to Chinese students opting for unchallenging vocational courses over courses that might qualify them for university entrance. The sense of alienation and marginalization that many Aboriginal students experience in Canadian universities likewise contributes to their dropping out in large numbers. As one student expressed it, "universities are as bad as residential schools except that we choose to come here."

Accomplishing Whiteness: The Invisible Norm

In classical sociology as well as in everyday talk, terms like 'ethnic' and 'multicultural' have been used to refer mostly to non-European, non-white people. Contemporary research in identity politics is shifting the focus of attention increasingly towards the invisible majority in Western societies—to those whose bodies escape attention. Warren's research (2003) gives detailed ethnographic attention to how students enrolled in theatre classes in New York routinely perform race. He tries to avoid preestablished racial categories to be open to how students themselves accomplish the representation of themselves and others as white or non-white, and to the multiple and repeated acts that socially construct whiteness as a central cultural signifier of normality and difference in American society (ibid. 14). He finds invisible normative whiteness pervasively constructed through literature and discourse that assumes the reader is white unless otherwise designated. To be white is to be human, to be human is to be white (ibid. 22). White bodies in films become noticeable as white only in contrast to black bodies. The unacknowledged, unnamed body is presumed white until signalled otherwise. There is no mention of bodies in the clean, quiet, normative school idealized in a conference paper, in contrast with the cacophony of noisy black bodies rushing about in the disparaged ghetto school. Staged performances of racism by theatre students focus on intent, and on extreme motives for harm, signified by violent black male predators, and by backlash against a white male who marries a black woman. Whiteness remains unsignified as protected identity, not responsible for the construction of inequality (55). Students enact cultural differences as unimportant, reiterating the discourse of colour blindness, while simultaneously signifying normative whiteness and erasing the central importance of racialized difference in the narratives performed by others. It is precisely this incessant repetition of colour-blind normative whiteness in student performances, Warren suggests, that constitutes white identity and gives whiteness such cultural power.

The power of normative whiteness to erase awareness of white privilege is reflected in studies of social work practice with mixed clientele. White social workers in a London borough with mostly black clientele largely rejected the idea that the professional skills or approach needed to work successfully with black families would be any different from white families (Stubbs 1985).

They strongly opposed the appointment of black social workers as inherently racist and even discriminatory in that it would subject black families to underqualified workers. If black social workers were to be hired, they argued, they should be trained and supervised by regular social workers to ensure that they performed their work in the same way. 'Good black social workers', in effect, were white social workers. Absent from their talk was any awareness that they were not serving black families well, that they were not sufficiently attuned to the racism that their clients endured, or how deeply it impacted on family lives. Only when there were sufficient black social workers to form a caucus were black social workers able to challenge the routine practice of removing children from black neighbourhoods to white foster families, and to propose collective politically radical action as potentially more constructive social work practice with families in racialized and impoverished black neighbourhoods than typical individual counselling.

Predominantly white social workers in an agency for abused women in southern USA expressed similar conviction that if they provided similar services for all their clients in a colour-blind way then the outcomes would be similarly effective for abused women from white and black families (Donnelly, Cook and van Ausdale 2005). They could readily suggest reasons why relatively few black women used their services, including that black women identify more strongly with abusive male partners as injured by racism, and view it as a form of race treason to turn them in to white male authorities, or to seek refuge in a shelter predominantly run by white women and located in white neighbourhoods. The white social workers also knew but discounted the greater vulnerability of visible minority women to heavy-handed social-work intervention, including a greater risk that social workers would take their children away. They failed to conceptualize these systemic differences as warranting different kinds of outreach and services for black women than the counselling they offered white women, counselling that typically favoured leaving abusive male partners and laying criminal charges. In effect, their colour-blind commitment to providing one normative standard service for all masked systemic privileging of white clients, a privileging that they had no interest in changing.

The charge that colour-blind normative whiteness in service provision is inherently racist in the context of critical systemic differences along racial and ethnic lines, typically promotes reactions of rage and incomprehension in white service providers. When black minority workers in a shelter for battered women in Toronto raised such accusations, predominantly white staff were so enraged and hurt that the centre closed down (Henry et. al. 1995, 162–165). The conflict erupted over the policy favoured by professional white social workers of allocating more funding for counselling, a policy that 'underqualified' black staff challenged as individualizing and de-politicizing the racism that was undermining the family lives of black clients.

Feminist commitment to democratic, egalitarian and consensus decision-making seems to have exacerbated the marginalization felt by women of colour in these organizations, because they felt under constant pressure to go along with what the majority white workers advocated (Scott 2005). Informal friendship networks closely reflected lines of class and race, with the more highly qualified and numerically dominant white workers able to exert their influence over others. Minority women of colour found they either had to argue constantly and appear racist and uncooperative in the process, or give up in silence, or leave. Scott argues that a significant transformation towards more racially inclusive politics occurred in one rape crisis centre only when consensus decision-making was abandoned, and a formal bureaucratic hierarchy established with two of the four paid directors being women of colour. Only then did they have the institutionalized power to change policies, and to promote outreach, recruitment and training programs more suited to the needs and situation of women of colour.

Affirmative Action: Equity or Reverse Racism?

Charges and counter-charges of racism reflect sharply differing understandings of processes of racialization and ethnicization. Those who support affirmative action policies and who challenge colour-blind normative whiteness, point to evidence of a pervasive and enduring patterns of systemic inequality and difference. From this perspective, some form of affirmative action for visible minorities seems necessary to counter entrenched advantages and the preferential treatment and opportunities that majority white decision-makers and authority figures afford to normative white applicants and colleagues. Aboriginal people see their access to welfare, health and educational benefits, not as 'affirmative action' at all, but as hard-won treaty rights, cruelly extracted in return for colonial domination that drove their ancestors from the land and destroyed their traditional livelihoods. From the perspective of colour-blind normative whiteness, however, all forms of affirmative action and employment equity policies appear as racist practices. Any form of 'special treatment' for Aboriginals or other visible minorities discriminates against merit-worthy individuals who happen to be white, many of whom themselves struggle against disadvantaged social and economic status.

A study of how white-American college students talk with each other about black students details how they routinely they collaborated in sustaining pseudo-arguments that discredited affirmative action policies (Kleiner 1998). By pseudo-arguments, Kleiner means one-sided arguments that are never challenged, and simulated straw-man arguments raised only to be discounted. Students repeatedly concurred in claiming that university entrance scholarships go overwhelmingly to undeserving black students who squander the money without ever having to work for it, who get a free ride in college, who have their college grades inflated, and when they graduate, manipulate affirmative action policies to get jobs for which they are not qualified. Most admitted that slavery and discrimination were bad in the past, but countered that blacks have already been compensated enough, yet they keep harping back on past wrongs and blaming whites who had nothing to do with them. Collaboratively such talk functions to discredit black claims, while defending the correctness of white students' beliefs against insinuations of racism, and asserting their own comparative victimization by policies that favour minorities against themselves. The arguments are pseudo, Kliener suggests, in that they are never tested against evidence: Objectively how hard was it/is it for the descendants of slaves to pull themselves into the American mainstream? What are the statistics on socio-economic status of black families with children in contemporary America? How hard have most black students had to work to qualify for college entrance? How hard do average black students work in comparison with average white students to pass college courses? How often, if ever, do faculty actually inflate the grades of visible minorities? How often, if ever, do patently incompetent black graduates actually get and hold down good jobs that they are incompetent to perform? Statistically, how do black graduates compare with white graduates in career paths? They also do not ask the reverse-onus questions: How were blacks and other visible minorities being treated in the past that warranted the implementation of affirmative action policies? How

commonly were merit-worthy black students denied the opportunity to attend university or to win scholarships because assessors scoffed at grades and references from low status ghetto schools? How commonly were merit-worth black graduates shut out from good career openings because assessors felt more secure hiring white graduates? What evidence is there that racial discrimination still routinely occurs in America? By never raising such questions and never researching for evidence that might answer them, students collaborate in protecting each other from charges that they themselves hold racist attitudes, and they collaborate in mutually reinforcing their own sense of resentment.

A study of talk by white students in Australia about affirmative action for Aboriginal students displays a similar pattern of pseudo argument (Augostinos, Tuffin and Every 2005). Students collectively defended the principles of individual merit and equal treatment as paramount, claiming that everyone can succeed if they try hard enough. Aboriginals do not succeed as well as whites because they have not learned the same values of individual hard work. Policies to assist Aboriginal students to attend university only make the situation worse by giving them an easy ride. Aboriginal students get university places and jobs which they do not have to work for and do not deserve. This in turn undermines their self esteem by confirming their inferiority and inability to compete as equals with whites. Again, such assertions are not questioned, nor tested with evidence. Statistically, what is the relationship between individual effort, qualifications, and financial rewards in labour force when race and ethnicity are taken into account? How systemically unequal are the family situations and school experiences of Aboriginal and white children? How hard is it for Aboriginal students to qualify for university entrance compared with white students? How hard do they work to graduate? What are the long-term, inter-generational effects of promoting university education for Aboriginal people?

These authors trace in the discourse of these students, the core elements of contemporary racism. The blatant and hostile racism of the past, which focused on biological superiority and inferiority of groups, has been widely discredited and is rarely openly expressed. What replaces it is a more subtle racism that attributes systemic inequalities to the intensity with which different cultural groups embrace values like self-reliance, discipline, hard work, achievement, initiative, and innovation. Inequalities, both global and local, thus appear as merited. In the ideology of contemporary racism, discrimination and disadvantages occurred only in the past. The current tactics and demands by visible minorities are thus undeserved and unfair, and serve to victimize the majority white people (Augostinos et. al. 2005, 316–7).

The special irony in this commonsense reasoning is that even as it denies the systemic validity of group differences, it encourages a racialized and ethnicized self-identification as 'white' people whose very 'invisibility' leaves them vulnerable to being ignored as others make claims on the system. The reverse-racism argument that white people generally are being disadvantaged by visible minorities who make unfair claims, sustains a politics of resentment by white people. A discourse of 'unfairness' permeates the complaints voiced by British locals in the suburb of 'Saltdean' to government plans to house asylum seekers in a local hotel (Grillo 2005). Organizers openly warned demonstrators to take care to avoid racist slants, mobilizing people around the slogan "We Are Not Racists, We Are Just Realists", citing fears for their safety from asylum seekers who might be criminals or terrorists, or carry diseases, and whose children would swamp local schools with their problems, to the detriment of the neighbourhood.

Small shopkeepers in a London neighbourhood voiced a similar discourse of feeling abandoned by politicians who direct economic resources to 'asylum seekers' demanding benefits like subsidized housing, free driving lessons and welfare, while 'if you are English, white English or black English' you get left out (Wells and Watson 2005, 270), and if you say anything, you will be called racists. Is their talk 'racist'? Yes and No, Grillo concludes. It is a multi-layered discourse full of coded references. It incorporates old racist fears of stigmatized, racialized 'others' who threaten house values, and new racism's questioning of cultural compatibility. It also incorporates a litany of negative pre-judgements and fears about asylum-seekers as likely to be cheating or lying to get into the country, abusing the welfare system, and possibly involved in criminal gangs or terrorist activities. Commonsense discourse offers few reasons for cheerfully welcoming asylum seekers or immigrants as new neighbours, although it concedes that individuals may be merit-worthy and deserving of compassion.

To understand how the local discourse of Saltdean protestors came to have these characteristics, one needs to look beyond the context of local talk between neighbours to explore the larger national talk on which it drew (Grillo 2005, 245). In a spiralling process of claims,

counter-claims, rejoinders and rebuttals, local people routinely echoed statements attributed to politicians that were repeated in television talk shows, and then picked up in 'letters to the editor of local newspapers', and repeated again when local people were asked by reporters to give comments. It is to this larger national talk that we now turn.

Constructing Public Opinion

Public opinion surveys have been widely criticized for how easily they can be manipulated by the way questions are worded and answers interpreted to fit the biases of those designing the surveys. But the question of how opinion surveys produce 'meaning' is more complex than clearing away distortions to get more accurate representations. The opinions people hold are themselves a reflection of what people know about a topic, or more precisely what people *think* they know and *how* they know it (Lewis 2001, 15). Few people can be blamed for wanting to distance themselves from criminals who defraud the government. The question is why so many Saltdean residents were predisposed to fear that 'asylum seekers' might be such people, especially when most of them had never met their prospective neighbours and knew nothing directly about them.

To understand how people come to know about racialized and ethnicized people we need to explore further the discourse of people in positions to manage the flow of information, including politicians and professional writers, and opinion leaders, how they are represented in mass media, and how audiences are attuned to respond to media reports (Cottle 2000, 1–30; van Dijk 2000, 33–49; van Dijk 1993).

Van Dijk argues that it makes sense to focus on the discourse of political and intellectual elites because they are particularly influential in producing commonsense understandings. These are the people whose opinions are sought and reproduced in the media, and who are most often asked to comment on claims made by others. It also makes sense to focus on respectable moderate parties rather than extreme fascist or white supremacist parties because the latter are more readily discredited. Further, he argues, we need to go beyond mere content analysis to focus on nuances in the text—*how* people say things, the metaphors and euphemisms they use, the disclaimers and qualifications they insert, that carry the emotional tones that audiences pick up. When political elites make disclaimers like "we have nothing against foreigners but . . ." Or "it is sad for refugees but . . ." the 'but' carries a powerful implicit message that the speaker is not racist, but realist, and that hearers should be suspicious and wary (Van Dijk 2000, 41). When political leaders and their media coverage define the topics as 'illegal immigrants, reception problems, social problems, resentment, deviance, illegal immigration, bogus refugees, 'floods of immigrants', crime-ridden minorities, and the like, they feed into the new racism. The message being repeated here is that everything about immigration is negative.

The extensive public consultations on immigration initiated by the Canadian federal government in 1994 slanted questions in ways that encouraged exclusionary, negative and problem-oriented responses. Canadians were asked how immigration should be managed to increase the benefits to the Canadian economy and reduce the costs, including specifically costs associated with excessive demands on social services and how to better detect and reduce abuses. Canadians were further invited to comment on how cultural diversity affects the social and cultural life of Canada, how much importance should be given to family reunification and whether there are special groups, institutions, and programs that need to be protected (Thobani 2000). Rather than trying to answer these questions, Thobani challenges the prejudiced assumptions behind them and the negative frame they gave to the consultations. Canada is a nation of immigrants, yet the consultations presumed that only non-immigrant Canadians would be consulted about the 'others'. The questions further presumed a homogenous 'social and cultural life' that might need to be protected from the diversity that immigrants cause, and that outside of economic benefits immigrants, and the family members they try to bring with them, produce costs and abuses that need to be better managed. It is not surprising, Thobani argues, that responses to the consultations fitted this frame, supporting subsequent policy changes to demand higher skills and job-readiness, to restrict family migration, and to make immigrants pay higher fees for processing and settlement. The consultation process might have had very different outcomes, had all Canadians—native born and foreign-born, been consulted, and questions focused around themes like how Canada could better assist immigrants to be economically successful, to bring family members more quickly, to have better access to social services they need, and to contribute their vibrant cultures more fully to the Canadian mosaic.

Academic writing, and particularly the content and tone of writing about race and ethnic relations included in introductory sociology texts, also warrants close scrutiny for how they frame students' understanding of issues, since students will make up the next generation of professionals (Van Dijk 1993, 164–177). Van Dijk criticises the texts he reviewed for pervasive use of the passive descriptive tense—as in phrases such as "Blacks were conquered and enslaved" because they elide the core question of exactly who was responsible for doing what to whom, and with what long-term consequences. Standard definitions of 'racism' and 'prejudice' that focus on irrational individual beliefs and attitudes about the biological superiority or inferiority of certain 'races' absolve people who use cultural explanations. Professors who assess white applicants as superior because they do research on more significant topics and publish in more prestigious journals are not challenged to think of themselves as racist or prejudiced. A definition of discrimination as disqualifying members of one group from opportunities open to others can be used to discredit affirmative action. Attacks on Aboriginal treaty rights can be represented as anti-racist activism. Such weak conceptualization, van Dijk argues, obscures systemic power and dominance relations between groups that fundamentally characterizes racism, and the systemic protection of privileges that perpetuate racialized and ethnicized inequality. Essentialized representations of cultural homogeneity both for 'Canada' and ethnic minority 'communities' are also commonplace. A detailed analysis of the portrayal of Aboriginal peoples in survey of 77 Canadian introductory sociology textbooks faults them for stereotyped images, historical inaccuracies, factual errors, and the prioritizing of outsider-anthropological accounts over Aboriginal voices (Steckley 2003). In so doing, Steckley concludes, sociological textbooks mostly perpetuate 'relations of ruling' rather than working to expose and undermine these relations.

Mass Media and Public Opinion

Mass media, including television, newspapers, magazines, and movies, exert a powerful influence of public opinion through the kinds of information that are covered or ignored, and the ways in which minority issues are framed. News and current affairs programs on television and in newspapers are particularly influential in that they are seen as presenting factual information. It is how Canadians learn much of what they feel they know about minorities, and also how minorities learn about themselves and each other, and develop a sense of their places as Canadians within the wider society.

Media are not monolithic. The framing of issues around minorities differs significantly across sources like the CBC or the Fox network, *The Globe and Mail* or a tabloid paper, in part because their producers know they are appealing to very different audiences. Journalists also draw on different explanatory theories to frame their current events stories, like the recent arrest of people suspected of planning a terrorist attack in Toronto—whether the psychology of angry disaffected youth, impressionistic kids egged on by a dangerous fanatic that moderate Muslims have been warning authorities about, the culture of Islamic extremism, the global war on terror and how Canada is next on Osama Bin Laden's hit list, recent history of Canadian military involvement in Afghanistan, or the need to protect 1000s of innocent and peaceful Canadian Muslims from attacks by fanatics of a different stripe.

The problem for media producers in the era of 'info-tainment' is that news and current affairs programming is required to be entertaining as well as informative, in order to provide a steady audience for advertisers. Hence they tend to be geared to providing excitement through dwelling on the bizarre and the bloody. Producers also work under pressure of tight deadlines and extremely short attention spans where stories have to be capsuled into two-minute sound bites, or one headline and an opening paragraph. Pressure to appeal to mass audiences constrains producers to slant stories to appeal to the presumed interests of mainstream audiences (read normative white invisible Anglo-Canadian), with the result that visible minorities tend to get noticed mostly when there is trouble. Media are widely criticized for both under-representing and misrepresenting minorities, featuring them disproportionately as involved in negative activities as drug pushers, gang members, violent criminals, pimps, dropouts and generally trouble-makers (Mahtani 2001). The normal humdrum everyday lives of the vast majority of people is not newsworthy.

The increased hiring of visible minority journalists in recent years has had mixed results. They are more in evidence in the CBC that is mandated to promote multiculturalism than in privately-owned television, the specialized minority channels excepted. It has proven difficult for visible minority journalists, particularly when they are low-status newcomers, to significantly alter the quantity or quality of coverage of minority issues because of entrenched professional and corporate structures of media production (Wilson 2000). Editors routinely cut stories that stray too far outside predefined news policy that advertisers and audiences expect. Black

journalists in any case learn the trade in the same schools of journalism, and are guided in their career development by more seasoned reporters. Their presence does make a difference in more nuanced and better-informed coverage of minority issues, access to alternative informants and alternative framing of events, but they operate within institutional constraints. Those who refuse to conform mostly leave the profession.

The 500-channel universe of specialty television offers some scope for programming designed for minority audiences. They significantly influence how individuals negotiate their sense of themselves as members of minority 'communities', being drawn together as audiences watching the same programmes. Aboriginal television channels, for example, encourage the retention of indigenous languages, and promote information exchange and networking. The global reach of instantaneous digital television coverage also influences the negotiation of diasporic identities among widely scattered migrant communities. The dramatization of Hindu sacred texts by the state television of India, serialized over a four-year period between 1988–92, was projected to Hindu audiences around the globe (Gillespie 2000). The series reached regular weekly audiences of an estimated 100 million people in India alone. It is credited by some analysts as powerfully contributing to the promotion of Hindu nationalism and anti-Muslim sentiments in India (Singh 1995; Rajagopal 2000). Controversy over a site of worship at Ayodhia, the mythical site of the birthplace of the Hindu God Rama, boiled over in January 1992 into communal violence during which hundreds died. The series was also watched by possibly another 20 million outside India. Audience members interviewed in England spoke of how powerfully the series impacted upon them, creating a sense of intimate connection with kin back in India. The also spoke of their disdain for a British version of the Mahabharata epic that, in their view, misrepresented the spiritual message of morality and honour as a simplified soap-opera story of a feisty Draupadi who calls on divine intervention to get back at her obnoxious relatives.

Studies of audiences reactions reveals that there is a complex and nuanced relationship between text and reception. One cannot simply read audience reactions directly from a content analysis of text. Nor is there a simple deterministic relationship between ethnic background of audience member and how a text will be interpreted. Meanings are negotiated by people who draw on existing interpretive frames and background understandings, including their sense of the credibility of sources, and conversations with others who watched the same programs to make sense of what they saw (Hooks 1992). Studies of audiences are further plagued by methodological problems around what constitutes a representative sample audience, with the risk of creating artificial groups of strangers who collectively produce situated responses in research settings to programs that they might not otherwise watch (Ross 2000).

Within these limitations, there is much evidence that different audiences interpret the same evidence in sharply different ways that reflect racialized and ethnicized background understandings of events. Black and White-Americans, both audience members and jurors, came to opposite conclusions concerning the probable innocence or guilt of O.J. Simpson, a famous black-American football player accused of the murder of his white wife and her friend in 1994 (Fiske 2000; Cottle 2000, 13–14). In a trial that was heavily televised, and covered in the press, Simpson was acquitted by a largely black Los Angeles jury in 1995, but subsequently found liable for their deaths in a largely white civil court in Santa Monica in 1997. Studies of public opinion around this trial suggest that black females were more likely to see Simpson as innocent than were white males. Black women's judgement drew on their situated local knowledge as powerless people that made it seem credible that police would tamper with evidence to get a conviction. They were also more likely to follow the trial in the tabloid press, and to watch Oprah Winfrey-style talk shows, both media sources that habitually challenge official versions of events. Similarly, Black audiences watching the amateur video of Rodney King being beaten by police in Los Angeles in 1992 (Gabriel 2000, 73) were more likely to see a defenceless black man on the ground being kicked by police, while whites were more likely to see in the same video a picture of a violent black male being appropriately subdued after being sexually abusive towards a white female police officer. A rare equivalent scepticism was triggered in Canada in 2006 when two white Canadian women were implicated by Mexican police in the murder of a couple on holiday in Cancun. Canadian media widely endorsed the argument that the Mexican police might plant incriminating evidence in the women's room in order to shift the spotlight from local people to protect their lucrative tourist trade.

Conclusion: Manipulating Public Opinion

How readily can public opinion be manipulated to whip up racialized and ethnicized hostilities, or conversely to

quieten them and promote multicultural tolerance? On the one hand there is evidence that the pronouncements of political leaders, academic elites, and mass media are influential in formulating public opinion. On the other hand there is evidence that audiences are selective in what they expose themselves to, and that they draw on local situated practical knowledge in assessing information. The example of ethnic violence in Yugoslavia in 1992 suggests that it was the combination of overlapping sources of information that framed events in the same way and simultaneously evoked locally situated knowledge to inflate fear and insecurity, that worked together to promote ethnic hatred (Oberschall 2000). While a small powerful group of extreme nationalist Serbs initiated the violent takeover of power in Prijedor district of North-West Bosnia, they were able to win the support of moderate Serbs by a campaign of propaganda. Serbian political elites saturated local media with wildly exaggerated stories of atrocities by Muslims, while a Serb professor claimed that Muslims intended to take over Yugoslavia, replace the population with Muslims, and cut Europe in half. A competitive spiral of patriotic or jingoistic journalism developed among reporters from different ethnic groups, with intentional and repetitive broadcasting of outright falsehoods. In normal times such jingoism would be challenged by other sources of information and readily discounted by sceptical audiences. But in the highly charged climate of fear and insecurity exacerbated by crumbling state authority, Oberschall suggests, people were predisposed to believe even wildly improbable horror stories. People stopped talking with anyone outside their own trusted group, so that they heard only the same fear-laden messages constantly repeated and embellished, and channelled into xenophobic ethnic nationalism.

Could such xenophobia ever develop in Canada? Historically, it did happen in 1942 when public opinion was whipped up against Japanese Canadians in the context of heightened wartime fear. By 1946 when the war was over and fears subsided, the propaganda lost force. The climate of public opinion changed and widespread protests against the injustice prevented the government from deporting more Japanese, and pushed for their re-enfranchisement (Sunahara 1981). At present there is some fear that public opinion in Canada might be whipped up against Muslims in the context of heightened fear of terrorism, but it seems very unlikely. Political and professional elites are officially committed to multiculturalism and to the protection of Muslim rights, the media framing of issues around the 'war on terror' and conflicts in Afghanistan, Iraq, and Palestine is diverse and frequently critical of international politics, and there is no generalized climate of fear in Canada.

In the USA, however, the dynamics governing public opinion are significantly different. There is a heightened climate of fear both abroad and within the country since the September 11, 2001 terrorist attack, with the federal government repeatedly issuing yellow and orange alerts prompting citizens and security forces to be hyper-alert. With America actively at war in Iraq and Afghanistan, and committed to the defence of Israel, there is strong pressure on political and academic leaders to be unanimous in their support for the war on terror in the abstract, and for the troops on the ground. American scholars of Middle-Eastern Studies report an active stifling of any real debate, reminiscent of the anti-communist frenzy of the cold war era (Bourne 2005; Beinin 2005). American mass media, with a few exceptions, police themselves in a form of literal or figurative embeddedness with the American military at war. There is a sense that Muslims in the USA are feeling increasingly isolated and viewed with suspicion by mainstream Americans. These conditions are conducive to the rise of ethnocentrism and racism.

In conclusion, from the social constructionist perspective there is no fixed reality that can be objectively described, no unbridgeable differences between pre-existing ethnic or racial groups to be documented. Rather, there are systemic practices engaged in by people in various positions of authority and influence, as well as ordinary people in their everyday interactions through which we negotiate, sustain or undermine our experiences and interpretations of the world as racialized and ethnicized.

Feminist Perspectives: Gendered Racialized, Ethnicized Relations.

Western feminist theory was rocked in the 1980s by charges that feminist concepts and perspectives were racist (Carby 1982, 1999). Critics raised three closely related issues. Feminist thought and activism, they argued, focusses almost exclusively on struggles central to the interests of middle-class, white, Western women. This theorising, however, is represented as applying universally to all women, while the voices of women of colour who try to articulate very different concerns, are either ignored or openly discounted. The sharpest criticism was that middle-class, white, western women are themselves complicit in the oppression of racialized women. This section explores the roots of this critique, and changes in contemporary feminist theorizing.

Patriarchy in European Colonial rule

European women were largely banned from Canada during the early fur-trade years. European men who were employed to develop and run the forts on behalf of trading companies presumed they could get sexual access to indigenous women who hung around the forts while men were working trap-lines. Sometimes these liaisons grew into long-term family relationships, but they were not accorded recognition by the churches or in law as marriages. Men owed no legal responsibilities to the women or their children. Eventually, as European wives became available, men routinely dissolved these informal 'country marriages' with Aboriginal women.

The historical situation of European women in the colonial settlement of Canada reflects the strongly patriarchal structures of nineteenth-century British society. Prior to reforms to marriage laws beginning in the 1880s in Britain, wives were legally subsumed under their husband's legal status. Any property or inheritance she might bring to the marriage became the legal property of her husband. He also had sole legal custody of the children (Smart 1984). Any woman who left her marriage, for whatever reason, had no right to maintenance, or even to see her children again. Women's subordination in marriage was widely defended as both sanctioned by the Bible and as functional for the preservation of stable family life. The Jesuit priest, Paul Lejeune, who tried to civilize and Christianize the Innu of Labrador, wrote of his astonishment and strong disapproval of the easy egalitarianism that he saw between Innu women and men. One of his goals for the Innu was to institute the ideal of patriarchal family relations, including the proper subordination of wives to husbands, and the corporal disciplining of children (Bear-Nicholas 1994).

According to the prevailing cultural discourse of the time, preached by political and religious elites, the proper role for the middle-class white women coming to Canada in increasing numbers by the nineteenth-century, was to promote civilized domestic life for the settlers. Women were to be exemplary moral reformers, responsible for the moral education of the supposedly socially dangerous or less civilized lower classes and racial inferiors (Henderson 2003). In effect, Henderson argues, the leaders of white settler society saw 'well-governed' women as the pillars of white rule, or 'race-making' in the colonies. Concepts of proper gender roles and normative sexuality were inherently part of the self-definition of white settler nationalism from the beginning. In the discourse of British colonial rulers, a self-disciplined society could claim rightful status as a self-governing colony, while societies considered less civilized, and incapable of self-discipline, should continue to be ruled as dominions. The merging of gender, sexuality, and nationalism evident in British colonial rule is reflected also in the subaltern nationalisms that emerged with independence struggles among colonized people, including Aboriginal people in Canada, as we will see further below. Women's bodies, their dress and decorum, functioned as powerful sites for symbolic representation of cultural reproduction (Kim-Puri 2005; Henderson 2003).

Henderson argues further that the writings of middle-class colonial women should not be considered authentic statements of how women themselves might have thought and felt at the time, because their status as moral educators or social reformers was the only acceptable public role available to them. Women argued that they should be given the right to vote because of their natural civilizing influence. Back in Britain, women argued for the right to become volunteer police officers on the grounds that they could better police their sexually fallen lower-class sisters than could men. In Canada, they set up Immigration Societies to monitor and control the working-class girls brought to Canada as suitable wives for white male settlers, and suitable 'mothers of the nation' (Arat-Koc 1999, 129–132). Not all white women qualified as civilized. There was much debate at the time as to whether 'Irish' qualified as 'white'. Their colonized status often trumped their skin colour. There are horrifying stories of destitute women from Ireland who worked, or rather slaved in bars and brothels in Britain and the colonies. Men are described as routinely urging these women to drink to insensibility, and then gang raping them on bar tables (Razack 1998, 343). Middle-class white women who ran the Immigration Societies took it upon themselves to supervise and police the women they recruited from Britain for domestic service in Canada, requiring them to sign contracts to work in assigned domestic-service placements for one year. Women deemed 'unsuitable' by reason of sexual or other misconduct were reported to the authorities for deportation (Arat-Koc 1999).

Within patriarchal role definitions thought appropriate for women at the time, women were classed into two broad categories—virginal daughters who would become respectable, domesticated wives and mothers—or in effect the property of white males. Otherwise they were classed as whores—women who were presumed to be sexually available outside marriage to service white male sexual appetites. Overwhelmingly it was non-white or 'racialized' women—Black, Asian, Aboriginal, and occasionally subaltern whites like the Irish, who were objectified as sexual targets (Razack 1999). It was their hyper-availability as sex objects, Razack argues, that served to define and support the hyper-respectability of white middle-class women. Aboriginal women were routinely labelled as prostitutes if found off their reserves, and they could be fined or thrown in prison for up to six months on suspicion of vagrancy (Lawrence 2004, 52). Indian agents also routinely withheld welfare rations to impoverished families on reserves as a bargaining chip for sexual favours. Enslaved black women and household servants were similarly vulnerable to the presumption of sexual availability.

The Indian Act: Constructing Patriarchal Aboriginal Status

The Indian Act, and its many revisions since it was first enacted in Canada in 1869, was inherently and intentionally patriarchal (Lawrence 2004). Legal status as Indian, with recognition for treaty rights and obligations, was only inherited through the male line. White women who married status-Indian men were defined as status Indians, and their offspring were similarly deemed full-blood status Indians. However, under Section 12(1)(b) of the Indian Act, status-Indian women who married a non-status male were deemed no longer Indian. They and their children lost all rights to live in their former communities, to inherit any property, or to be buried on the reserves. Illegitimate children of status-Indian mothers were likewise excluded, unless their father was known to be status Indian. Many thousands of Indian women who had formed liaisons with white men were cut out and often left destitute.

The Indian Act also imposed exogamy on Indian women—requiring them to move to their husband's community on marriage (ibid. 51) This requirement systematically broke up the matrilineal clan system of land control among the Iroquois Confederacy. Formerly while men organized the hunting, clan land available for hunting was inherited through women. The Indian Act abolished this. The legislation further divided reserves into individual lots inheritable only through the male line (ibid.). Wives were forced to live on their husband's reserve, but denied the right to inherit land on his reserve. Women thus lost all their former political roles in the governance of their own societies.

Bill C-31 and the Aftermath

The blatant discrimination against Indian women embedded in the Indian Act was first legally challenged in 1971 by Jeanette Lavell and Yvonne Bedard, two Indian women who had lost status through marriage (Lawrence 2004, 56–63). Lavell challenged the deletion of her name from her band list, while Bedard challenged her eviction from a house willed to her by her mother. Both argued that this treatment violated the Canadian Human Rights Act as discrimination on the basis of race and sex. In 1973 the Supreme Court of Canada ruled against them. The Court determined that the impugned clauses of the Indian Act applied only to women and not to all Indians, it did not constitute discrimination on the basis specifically of 'race'. Further, since Indian women who lost status, acquired the same status as all other non-Indian Canadian women, the clause was not 'sexist'. The Court further determined that the Human Rights Act in any case could not overrule the Indian Act.

Gender discrimination under the Indian Act was eventually successfully challenged by the Maliseet women of Tobique who challenged the rule that women could not own property on the reserve, which resulted in women and children being homeless when marriages broke down.

The Tobique women joined with Sandra Lovelace in an appeal to the United Nations Human Rights Committee on the grounds that loss of status on marriage under Section 12(1)(b) of the Indian Act constituted a violation of minority rights 'to enjoy their culture, practice their religion, and use their language in community with others from the group'. The U.N. Court ruled in their favour and put pressure on the Canadian government to change the Act. In expectation of these changes, the Canadian Government created an interim policy that allowed Indian bands to request suspension of Sections 12(1)(b) and 12(1) a(iv). The latter clause, known as the 'double mother' clause removed status from men as well as women whose mother *and* paternal grandmother were non-status. Lawrence records that 53 percent of all bands requested suspension of the double

mother clause—which directly affected men living on reserves. But only 19 percent chose to suspend the clause challenged by Lovelace that affected Indian women who married non-status men and so lived outside the reserves (Lawrence 2004, 61).

Gender discrimination under Section 12(1)(b) of the Indian Act was finally amended in 1985 to conform with Section 15(1) of the Canadian Charter of Rights and Freedoms. Indian women would no longer lose their status and rights on their reserves on marriage to non-status men. This seeming victory, however, was won for Indian women at high cost. The National Indian Brotherhood fought against the amendment on the grounds that it violated their rights as First Nations to determine their own citizenship. Further, it was argued, women have a stronger responsibility as 'mothers of the nation' to choose to marry within their communities and should not expect redress if they choose to marry out. Moreover, bands needed protection from white husbands. The outcome was a compromise in which some women regained their formal Indian status but male-dominated band councils gained the right to determine whether or not these women would be accorded band status, or the right to reside on the reserve.

Inheritance rights still discriminate against women. Women reinstated in 1985 only received partial status. They can pass their status on to their immediate children, but their grandchildren, males as well as females, cannot inherit Indian status. Status-Indian males confer status on both their children and grandchildren regardless of who they marry, although non-status wives cannot now gain status. Women who marry non-status men retain their status and confer status onto their children. However, their grandchildren permanently lose their status on marriage unless their spouse has status. Illegitimate children of status Indian mothers are also non-status, unless the father has status. In effect, within two generations from 1985 only descendants of status-Indian males will continue to have status. The 'bleeding off' of native band members is greater since the amendments than before.

Post-Colonial Gendered Ethnicity

Visible-minority immigrants entering Canada under the new Immigration Act of 1967 have mostly come from regions of the world that were formerly subject to European colonial rule. The politics of resistance and cultural nationalism that developed in these regions were profoundly influenced by the experience of foreign domination, and the inferiorizing cultural discourse of foreign rulers. British imperial rulers spread the same gendered cultural standards of white middle-class domestic respectability for their women in Africa and Asia as they did in Canada, with similar undercurrents of racialized denigration of 'other' women as exotic and sexually available. In formal political discourse and practices, behaviour that mimicked the European version of masculinity and domestic femininity were praised, while other practices were scorned as alien and culturally inferior.

Wherever they encountered matriarchal economic and political systems, they undermined them. British rulers systematically broke up the matriarchal system of landholding among the Nayar of Malabar in Kerala, South India in ways that parallel closely their destruction of female-centred forms of communal governance among the Iroquois. Traditionally, Nayar people held land communally within extended families, passing it down from mother to daughters (Liddle and Joshi 1986, 28–9). Men had access to land as brothers and sons but did not own or transfer land through marriage. Generally, adult men continued to live within their mother's household, while their female partners and her children remained in their own extended matriarchal households. British colonial rulers, however, insisted that communal lands be broken up and inherited only through the father's line to sons. They further insisted that men be made legally responsible for their 'wives' and children. They enforced this by the practice of employing exclusively men in the civil service bureaucracy, with this individual male-wage economy gradually replacing the former communal landholding economy. In political dealings, similarly, British rulers would only appoint, and negotiate with men. In Africa, for example, British rulers banned the practice they found common in Nigeria, of having women on local councils, insisting that such positions only be held by men.

At the same time as the British undermined matriarchal organization, they characterized non-Western forms of patriarchal organization as primitive and inferior. In India, British rulers expressed moral outrage at the practice among Hindus of *sati*—the burning of widows on the funeral pyre of their husband, female infanticide, child marriage, plural wives, arranged marriages, and extended family systems. They scorned dress codes favoured among wealthier women of wearing veils and Muslim women wearing full-length covering or burqa. Ironically, British courts worsened the situation for lower-class Indian women by interpreting practices followed mostly by Hindu elites as uniformly applicable to all women (Liddle and Joshi 1986, 26). They also denigrated the greater tolerance in some Islamic societies for gay and lesbian relations.

As pressure for self-rule intensified in India, British rulers used 'the women's issue' as a justification for foreign rule. They characterized the treatment of Hindu women as primitive and savage, and as evidence that Indians were not fit to rule themselves (ibid. 31). This strategy worked to divide the nationalist movement in India and to shackle the indigenous women's movement. On one hand British rulers seemed to be supporting feminist causes, but on the other, these same causes became discredited as foreign cultural domination, and the women who advocated them discredited as supporting colonial rule.

In the oppositional cultural discourse of independence struggles, women's bodies, their dress and decorum, became powerful signifiers of nationalist aspirations. Traditions that marked off Hindu and Muslim cultures from Western culture became intensified and often associated with militarized surveillance of women (Kim-Puri 2005). During the early years of post-colonial rule, it was common for pro-Western elites trained in colonial bureaucracies to mimic European rule. Representing themselves as modernizers and secularists, post-colonial rulers in Algeria, Egypt, Iran and Turkey, repeatedly attempted to force Muslim women to remove the veil. In the backlash against their often corrupt, inept, and Western-oriented rule, these modernizing elites were widely rejected as imposing cultural colonization. The practice of women wearing the veil became emblematic of Islamization and resistance to Western capitalist-dominated pressures for globalization (Franks 2000). Muslim women who did appear unveiled in public found themselves vulnerable to sexual harassment, especially those women not wealthy enough to travel in private cars. Nationalist leaders tried to purge their cultural narratives of references to what they saw as Western secular and libertine culture. The result was often that traditional religious practices and associated gender-role prescriptions became more rigidly enforced than in the past (Eid 2003).

Western militaristic discourse surrounding the 'war on terrorism' and 'Islamic fundamentalism' has added to this thick stew of gendered, religious nationalism. The characterization of the treatment of Afghan women under Taliban rule as 'barbaric' became part of the legitimation for war in 2002, along with the Taliban providing a safe haven for al-Qaeda terrorists (Thobani 2003). In Western discourse, the military invasion of Afghanistan is represented as liberating for Afghan women. Within Afghanistan itself, however, it casts supporters of indigenous women's resistance movements as traitors.

Gendered Ethnic Politics within Canada

Immigrants to Canada commonly bring memories of independence struggles with them. They are also inevitably exposed to ongoing nationalist struggles through global mass media and communication with relatives back in their home countries. In addition, the lived experience of being racialized and ethnicized as visible-minority refugees and immigrants within Canada resembles in some respects the experience of colonization (Bannerji 2000, 157–8). Multicultural politics encourage a sense of self-identification as members of distinct ethnic communities—an identification that is continually promoted by leaders whose own political influence is enhanced by claims to represent or speak on behalf of identifiable ethnic communities. These communities, Bannerji suggests, function like 'mini-cultural nationalities' subject once more to white rule. People tend to react to their sense of being subordinated outsiders by a defensive reinvention of tradition that can become even more rigid than in the countries they have left behind.

This reinvention of tradition profoundly impacts on the lives of migrant women—in the clothes that they feel encouraged or enjoined to wear, and more importantly in conformity to patriarchal expectations for behaviour within the family and beyond. Failure to conform can be read in multiple negative ways. It can be read as echoing the disrespect for their own ethnic group, that people already feel reflected in reactions of white Canadians. It can be read and resented by men as a challenge to their status within traditional patriarchal culture, when they are already feeling humiliated by their subordinated overall status in white society. It can also be read as a threat to the image of a unified ethnic community that enhances the influence that predominantly male political elites can wield in wider Canadian multicultural politics. For these and similar reasons women may personally internalize a desire to conform to traditional expectations as well as feeling socially pressured to do so. Family honour or shame is closely linked to women's decorum in traditional culture, to her remaining within the home or appropriately chaperoned by male relatives outside the home, acceptance of marriage to a partner who is approved of and chosen by her elders, and especially with respect to sexual chastity. Those who flaunt such expectations are likely to be judged harshly and avoided, or subject to more severe physical punishment (Bhardwaj 2001). In the context of strong community sanctions for non-compliance what women themselves say about traditional dress codes and other gendered expectations reflect a complex mix of inner conviction and outward conformity.

Muslim women who wear traditional Islamic clothing such as the headscarf (hijab) or full-body covering (burka or chador) within predominantly Islamic societies often speak of a sense of privacy and protection that such clothing affords them. They can gaze upon men without being themselves subject to male gaze, and they can go about in public with relative anonymity. Wearing the same clothing in Western societies, however, can provoke very different reactions from others (Franks 2000). Women commonly feel themselves the object of gazing by foreigners who range from just curious to hostile. They are also commonly labelled as primitive and backward, or as pitiable, subordinated women. Rather than feeling safe outside their homes, such reactions may discourage them from going out, or trying to mix with other women. Franks tells the story of a white-skinned British Muslim woman, the daughter of an Egyptian father and English mother, who opted to wear the hijab against her parents' wishes. Her parents feared, rightly, that she would be stared at. She wanted to show solidarity with and be recognizably Muslim to Bosnian refugees coming to England to escape the civil war in Yugoslavia. Blending in, by not following either Islamic dress codes or religious observances, she reasoned, had not prevented Bosnian Muslims from being attacked and murdered by Christian Serbs and Croats, so hiding her own Muslim identity would probably not protect her either. When she herself started wearing hijab in England, her middle-class English associates studiously avoided her, seeing her as making a spectacle of herself, and even as a traitor to her own white race.

Violence in the Lives of Racialized Women

Life for women who observe traditional lifestyles within South Asian enclave communities in Western societies can be experienced as extremely restricted, especially for those who do not speak the host society language (Bhardwaj 2001; Bannerji 2000, ch. 5). Bhardwaj notes that among Asian females in the age range 15–35, the rate of suicide, suicide attempts, and other forms of self harm are two to three times higher than among white and African and Caribbean female counterparts. Reflected in this misery is pervasive domestic violence and abuse against women, that is tacitly supported by the community leaders as a means to maintain traditional controls. Women themselves are constrained to silence, afraid of backlash against them if they speak out against abusive male kin, and afraid of how they will be heard by outsiders. Women have almost nowhere to turn. They cannot confide in physicians or social workers from their own Asian background because these professionals often see themselves as self-appointed guardians of the culture and may report women who seek help with depression back to their families. Injured women who seek hospital treatment may also find that the only people available to translate for them are maintenance and cleaning staff who likely will report back to family members.

Patriarchal attitudes and practices are certainly deep rooted in South Asian cultures, existing long before migration to Canada. But Bannerji suggests that while these practices are loosening up in India, in response to the women's movement and economic changes, they seem to be growing more rigid in South Asian ethnic enclaves in Canada (ibid. ch. 5). To understand the roots of this rigidity, Bannerji argues, we have to look beyond the cultural characteristics of the 'enclave communities' themselves to features of the wider host society in which such enclaves are embedded. Firstly, as noted above, ethnic enclaves are not primordial or 'given' features of peoples' lives. They are formed in response to lived experience of marginalization, which in turn reflects the structure of opportunities open for economic advancement and political influence.

The structure of opportunities are very differently experienced by immigrant women and men. Canada's patriarchal immigration laws are centrally implicated in women's marginalization and their structured subordination to men that promotes and sustains the heightened rigidity of culturally sanctioned controls over women's lives. These laws heighten the power of male household heads, and simultaneously silence women and close off avenues for support and help. Under contemporary immigration laws, primary independent-class economic migrants are overwhelmingly men. Their wives, regardless of levels of education or work experience, are admitted as legally dependent family-class migrants. Their male sponsors are required to support them financially for ten years. Sponsored wives are ineligible for social assistance, or for assisted language or job training. If they leave their marriage, for whatever reasons,

or their male sponsors refuse to support them, they are liable to deportation back to their country of origin. Women who are victimized in abusive marriages have few options or hope for redress.

Aboriginal women in Canada also endure significantly higher rates of domestic violence than do non-Aboriginal women (Monture-Agnus 1999). Monture-Agnus describes violence as an everyday fact of life for Aboriginal women of all ages. A hard legacy of colonialism, family breakdown following residential school experiences, destroyed economies, anger and frustration at limited future options, all contribute to this violence. But so also does the patriarchal Indian Act that establishes men as the carriers of Aboriginal status and property rights within reserves. Wives and children are especially vulnerable in situations of family breakdown since the husband has the presumptive right to live in the family home. In the past, women who lost status by marrying a non-status man lost all rights to return to live on their former reserve if their marriage should fail. Now, they retain their status, but band membership and access to band housing and resources are tenuous. The non-status wives of status-Indian males also have increased vulnerability since their right to live on reserves depends upon the marriage continuing. All these regulations result in Aboriginal women and children being more vulnerable when marriages fail than are non-Aboriginal Canadian women.

Racial and Ethnic Divisions Within Western Feminist Movements

The mainstream white feminist movement in Canada, as in Europe, was forged in the struggle to break out of the patriarchal nineteenth-century mould of women's proper place as domestic guardians of moral decorum. The movement focussed on bourgeois family life as the primary site of women's oppression, shored up by laws that subsumed the legal status of wives under that of their husbands, and vested all family property in the male 'household head'. Feminists struggled against the denial of basic rights of citizenship such as the right to vote, to hold public office, to become a member of parliament or the senate. They struggled for greater sexual freedom of expression, firstly for heterosexual women, and later for their lesbian sisters, challenging the pervasive double standards that penalized women harshly for extra-marital sex and conception while condoning or ignoring male transgressions. They fought against enforced domesticity, and the restrictive labelling of 'motherhood' as women's core defining identity. As women entered employment and public office in larger numbers they fought the pervasive discrimination against women in pay and promotion, justified on the grounds that women were dependant secondary family wage earners who do not 'need' the money, and who ought not to be taking good jobs from primary male workers. Women in positions of leadership struggled against hierarchical and bureaucratic modes of organization in favour of what they saw as more feminine egalitarian and collaborative organizational practices.

Women-of-colour who joined with Canadian feminist movements in greater numbers from the 1980s onward found themselves generally welcomed, but their voices and concerns subordinated and ignored wherever they differed from the mainstream feminist agenda. These differences have proven profound. What white feminists identified as universal features of feminist struggle, women-of-colour increasingly challenged as the limited concerns of specifically middle-class and white women (Carby 1982, 1999; Afshar and Maynard 2005). They challenged white women further to face up to their own complicity in the oppression of Asian, Black and Aboriginal women.

The white feminist focus on family as the site of oppression does not resonate with the experiences of Black feminists. Historically, slavery was the primary site of oppression for Black women, with family life fundamental for survival. Slaves had to fight to sustain any semblance of family life against slave-owners who would sell men and women separately for their own profit and convenience. Racialized economic inequality continues to undermine Black family life as such a high proportion of young Black men lack the financial means to support families. Black feminists struggle for greater recognition and respect for female-centred kinship systems that do not conform to standard north-American family forms. White feminist struggles to break from normative definitions of delicate feminine decorum and domesticity also do not resonate with Black women, and working-class women generally who were always expected to perform heavy physical labour. The centrality of the right to paid employment and independent income in white feminist liberation similarly means little to Black women who have commonly shouldered the burden of financially supporting their children, only to have their women-headed families decried by sociologists as pathological. Greater opportunity for Black men

to earn decent incomes is equally as important for Black women's liberation, as employment for themselves. Black women also mediate the contradictions experienced by white women between family and work demands through the domestic and child-care work that Black women perform for middle-class white families.

The treatment that Black women experience as domestic workers and nannies in white households is a central focus of Carby's characterization of white women as themselves oppressors of other women. In this arena, Carby argues, white women placed their class interests before sisterhood with subordinated and often racialized 'other' women. Canadian Immigration Law created the special category of "live-in caregiver program," to fill the demand from middle-class women desperate to find quality child-care and domestic help to enable them to be employed outside the home. Third-world women, mostly from the Philippines and the Caribbean are given temporary, two-year work permits to reside in Canada provided they work as live-in domestic servants (Arat-Koc 1989, 2001). These workers are tied to their employer's household as workplace and home, commonly called upon to work hours far in excess of other jobs, and to perform multiple tasks that are not contractually limited. Their income is not subject to minimum hourly wage regulations because they 'live-in', and they are not legally permitted to unionize. The Canadian government deducts taxes from their earnings for employment insurance and Canada Pension Plan, even though they are explicitly not eligible for these benefits. Should they leave their place of employment for whatever reason, they are reclassified as 'visitors' and given only two weeks to find another live-in domestic-worker position or be deported (Arat-Koc 2001, 364).

Changes to the legislation in 1991 now permit temporary care-workers to apply for landed-immigrant status after two years. However, there is no guarantee of approval. Domestic work is explicitly not counted as a work-skill under the points-system. Hence, in order to qualify, women must demonstrate that they have undertaken educational upgrading, at their own expense, while in Canada, to have a chance of being considered. While Black women solve the child-care crisis for wealthy, and usually white Canadian families, their own children are necessarily left behind with kin in their countries of origin.

Sexual Liberation

Racialized women's struggles for greater control over

their sexual lives, and for freedom from sexual oppression, also reflect very different lived experience. While nineteenth-century white middle-class women struggled for greater freedom of sexual expression against the stultifying asexual norms of bourgeois family life, their lower-class servants, and especially racialized Aboriginal and Black women struggled to defend themselves from the pervasive assumptions that they were sexually available outside marriage—to their employers, and to any man who offered money. Historically, Razack argues, (1998) the elevated sexual status of middle-class white women was protected at the cost of degraded sexual status of enslaved and colonized women. White men who fiercely guarded the chastity and virginity of women of their own kin, expected easy sexual access to racialized 'other' women. Even forced sex with these 'other' women was not considered in law to be rape, unless the encounter was particularly brutal.

Contemporary global patterns of sex trafficking in women and children for the sex trade reflects similarly racialized patterns of third-world women servicing affluent western male customers both in European brothels, and around military bases and sex-tourist destinations (Farr 2005). They are drawn mostly from Southeast Asia, South Asia, Latin America and the Caribbean, and Africa. Since the fall of the Soviet Union in 1991 women have come increasingly from Soviet Republics. Many of these trafficked women are abducted, sold into debt bondage by impoverished families, or lured by the promise of better-paying jobs in the west and then trapped in a vicious circle of debt bondage, violence and threat (ibid. 25–45). Others are driven into prostitution by destitution, with illegal migrants being especially vulnerable.

Liberal feminist activists have challenged societal and state prudery that stigmatizes sex-trade workers, and advocated legalizing the trade to empower workers and facilitate better regulation of the terms and conditions of work (Shaver 1994). But racialized women have counter-challenged this liberalizing approach as inherently racist (Razack 1998, 2000). The characterization of sex-trade work as an arena for women's choice does not fit with the lived experience of racialized poor women in Western societies. For racialized women who live in inner-city slum areas, the status of 'prostitute' is not a choice but a presumption. Within the sex-trade world, Razack argues, there are recognizably three kinds of women. White women on suburban streets who are rarely sexualized, black and Aboriginal women on the same streets who are routinely sexualized and proposi-

tioned by taxi-drives, and racialized women in inner-city slums who are presumed to be prostitutes. Liberal feminist discourse in the sex trade appears racist because it ignores the reality that *only* white women can talk like this, because only white women have a choice in whether they wish to be seen as sexually available. White women from the suburbs can choose to 'go slumming,' to enter prostitution zones like "The Stroll" in Regina, and to experiment with the sex-trade. To them it feels exotic and liberatory to make men pay money for sex, especially for women working in the high-end of the sex trade as escorts, strippers, dancers, or performers in peep shows. For urban poor Aboriginal women who routinely inhabit "the Stroll" there is no choice. Moving out to the suburbs is not an option.

The liberal feminist discourse is also racist in that it ignores the routine and racialized character of the violence that is enacted on women's bodies by the white men who visit The Stroll looking for sex. Razack describes these encounters as the contemporary site of enactment of colonial white male identity. Colonizing white males defined themselves as entitled to dominate space, entitled to the land they took over, and entitled to use violence to push other bodies from that space. They continue to define themselves as colonizing white males through their enactment of entitlement to buy and use the bodies of racialized others (Razack 2000). Razack describes in graphic detail the discourse and practices of the two white males eventually convicted of murdering Pamela George on Easter weekend in 1995. Razack describes the two university undergraduates repeatedly bragging to their friends that they "want to go find a hooker and beat and rape her" (ibid. 113) as part of their celebration of the end of examinations, and bragging later that they had "beat the shit out of an Indian hooker" and told her "if you don't give us head, we're going to kill you."(ibid. 111). They felt entitled to brag about such behaviour to their fellow male campus athletes, and to trust in their tacit acceptance, approval and even admiration for such acts, and their expectation that such information would not be used against them. Lawyers defending them at trial spoke of what they boys had done as "darn stupid things," but nonetheless commonplace behaviour in the locality—drinking heavily, picking up a prostitute, hitting her, and leaving her in the country to walk back by herself. What one sees in the trial, Razack argues, is how little the victim mattered. Her death was an inconvenience that got the boys into trouble.

Colour-blind discourse was studiously maintained

throughout the trial, with references made only to 'the Hungarians' and 'the prostitute'. The racist and colonial subtext of two dominant white men who raped and beat up an Indian woman was carefully silenced. Silenced also is the colonial history that accounts for so many women of Aboriginal descent in the inner-city slum zone, and for the violence that is normalized as part of contractual sex. For Razack, how little Pamela George mattered to her murderers or to the justice system is the measure of ongoing colonialism.

Conclusion

The critique of feminist theory by women-of-colour requires a more complex and nuanced response than colour-blind 'inclusion' or the politics of 'add women-of-colour and stir.' To achieve a racially and ethnically sensitive feminism, Bannerji argues (2000) analysis needs to be more historically situated and comparative. The point is not to advocate that white feminists begin to study black women, but rather that white feminists smash the myth that their story is the sole legitimate her-story, and become more aware of themselves historically and in the present as oppressors of subordinated 'other' women (Carby 1999). Institutional ethnographies of feminist organizations show that a philosophy of collaborative egalitarianism is not sufficient in itself to achieve egalitarian racial and ethnic integration in contexts of unequal social power (Scott 2005). Scott calls for more active and intentional listening to the voices and concerns of women who are differently situated, together with active practices that empower subordinated women to get their concerns acted upon at the centre of the feminist political agenda.

CHAPTER

14

Max Weber

◈ Max Weber and Rationality in Western Culture

Max Weber (1864–1920) is a monumental figure in the history of the social sciences. He was a historian, sociologist, and philosopher who left an indelible mark on the philosophy of history and on social science methodology. The scope of his scholarship is enormous. He wrote major books on comparative religions of Europe, India, and China, on the economy and political structures of democracy in western Europe, on music and musical forms, the rationality of law, and the structure and function of complex bureaucratic organization.

Background

Weber was born almost fifty years after Marx. Much of his work was a reaction to Marx or, more particularly, to the over-simplified versions of Marxist thought that focussed on economic determinism in social life. The two men wrote within very different cultural settings. Marx and his colleague Engels carried out much of their

research and writing in Britain during the early period of industrialization. By this time, the feudal estates had been broken up into grazing pastures. The peasants who formerly farmed these lands had been driven off. Masses of landless and desperately poor people flooded the cities seeking wage work as their only means of survival. They lived under appalling conditions in city slums and worked in the coal mines and expanding textile mills that fuelled the industrial revolution. The emerging merchant-capitalist class effectively challenged the political power and privileges of the declining aristocracy.

Weber lived in Germany during the period when the country was emerging from a collection of divided states into a unified and modernizing country under Otto von Bismarck. Germany's development was based upon centralized administration and the armaments industry rather than on private capitalism. It promoted a different view of the state and different theories of power and administration than those in Marx's work (Lee and Newby 1983, 169). Weber observed the outbreak of World War I and the concurrent collapse of the international socialist movement into nationalist blocs: the European proletariat supported their nation-states rather than the international working-class movement. Weber lived to see the Bolshevik Revolution in Russia in 1917, the collapse of the Spartacist Revolution in Berlin in 1919, and the rise of the Weimar Republic in Germany after the war.

In his personal life, Weber experienced long periods of severe depression. These are reflected in his profound pessimism concerning the future direction of Western civilization. He was intensely aware of the gap between the intended goals and ideals and the often unintended consequences of the means required to attain those goals. Weber himself long defended the ideal of a strong and unified Germany, only to feel contempt for the Kaiser and the policies that led Germany into World War I and eventual military defeat. In his work he argued strongly against any simplified analyses or unitary theories of social change, emphasizing instead the complex multicausality and inherently **probablistic** character of all theories of human action. Human action is the outcome of free will, he argued, and such freedom can never be described through fixed relations of cause and effect.

Weber's Scholarship

Weber struggled to synthesize the very different intellectual traditions that were prevalent in Europe at the time. Among them was **idealism** with its Hegelian emphasis on ideas and values as the distinctive moving force of human history. This was in contrast to Marxist theories of **historical materialism**, which contended that class conflict was the driving force of history and the primary determinant of human fate. The idealists emphasized human freedom and uniqueness, which could never be reduced to deterministic rules. Countering them were the **positivists** who sought to apply the methods of the natural sciences to the study of human behaviour, seeking predictive or deterministic laws of action.

Weber tried to reconcile the commitment to notions of individual freedom and religious values with the apparently contradictory commitment to scientific study of human behaviour and to an emphasis on economic materialism in history. He tried also to reconcile the obvious commitment of all researchers to political goals and values with the demand for objectivity in social science research. Lastly, he tried to reconcile the objectives of democracy, with its commitment to representative government based upon participation of an informed population, and the mechanism of **bureaucracy**, which seemed essential to democracy and yet at the same time

was its greatest threat. It is the mark of Weber's brilliance that he was largely able to achieve these syntheses in his work.

Weber's Methodological Contribution

Weber's study of methodology in the social sciences provides the foundations for contemporary ethnomethodology and interpretive sociology. Weber sought to synthesize the objective, empirical methods of the natural sciences with the intuitive aspects of the humanities. Positivism tries to explain events by reference to laws that describe cause-and-effect relations. It attempts to analyse the social system in terms of causes and effects in the same way that biological systems are analysed. Weber argues that this is impossible. Because people think about what they do, it is inappropriate to apply such law-like, or **nomothetic**, generalizations to human behaviour. People have purposes; their behaviour is meaningful to them. In biology we do not ask chemicals or microbes why they do things. We just account for what happens to reference to the laws of science. But with people, we do have to ask why. Our actions are determined not only by objective conditions and forces, but by the subjective meanings that we attach to our actions, in other words, by our own responses for doing something.

Weber also wanted to avoid the opposite trap of idealism or the view that all human behaviour entails unique spiritual events that can only be grasped by intuition or empathy. For idealists, the only explanation possible seems to be **ideographic**: unique, subjective, intuitive. The "science" in social science seems to be impossible. We seem to be forced to choose between the view that human action is predictable, which implies determinism, or the view that people have free will and hence that their actions are not determined by outside forces and so are not predictable.

Weber denies the validity of this apparent dilemma. He argues that meaningful behaviour, or behaviour guided by free will, is not unique and unpredictable or without any pattern or order. Unpredictable or random behaviour would not be meaningful; it would be mindless. Weber resolves the conflict between free will and determinism by arguing that there is no real contradiction between them. Action that is meaningful is, by its very nature, not haphazard, random, or patternless. The scientific study of meaningful behaviour is possible precisely because it is meaningful and therefore organized and predictable. It requires a different kind of explanation from that of the natural sciences, but it is nonetheless amenable to scientific study.

Weber defines sociology as "the science which attempts the interpretive understanding of social action in order thereby to arrive at a causal explanation of its cause and effects" (Ashley and Orenstein 1985, 213). For Weber, then, sociological analysis must do two things. First, it must explore the meaning of actions for the people involved. Secondly, it has to show how this meaning provides a causal explanation for the behaviour. **Social action** is, by definition, any human conduct that is meaningfully oriented to the past, present, or future expected behaviour of others. People relate to each other in meaningful ways, and it is these shared meanings that defined our expectations of others and ourselves.

The Study of Meaning

Weber draws heavily upon the work of his friend and colleague, Georg Simmel, who first developed the concept of *Verstehen*, or understanding, as crucial to sociological analysis. Sociologist have to become involved in the process of understanding because the actions that they are trying to explain are actions to which people themselves attach meanings. People do what they do because it is meaningful to them. Hence we can hardly ignore what these meanings are when we try to explain what they do. This does not mean that pure intuition is sufficient for analysis. We still need objective evidence. We need to develop techniques for interpreting meaning so that others can repeat the study and check the results.

The critical methodological question is how we do this. How can we develop an objective, verifiable, repeatable study of meaningful action? We need to remember that meaningful action is not random, but purposive and therefore organized by the people involved. *Verstehen* involves putting ourselves in the position of the people we are studying and trying to reconstruct the interpretations that they might give to their own action (Ashley and Orenstein 1985, 212).

Elliott Leyton neatly sums up this approach to explanation in sociology in a discussion of his study of serial killers and crimes of violence. The ideas for his book, *Hunting Humans* (1986), had one source. "When I can't

understand the reasons behind things, when I can't understand the behaviour. That's the genesis of everything I have written. In the act of writing and researching the book, I explain the behaviour to myself" (*Globe and Mail*, 12 Nov. 1987, A15). Explanations must be adequate at the level of meaning and at the level of causality. In other words, the explanation should make sense in terms of the intentions of the actor and should clarify the factors that would predispose someone to want to act in this way.

We feel we have explained the unusual behaviour of people in general, when we come to the point where we can say with some assurance that if we had similar life experiences and value orientations, and had found ourselves in similar circumstances, we could understand how we ourselves might have behaved in a similar way. This is a tall order, but we can do it precisely because we are studying fellow human beings. This is an advantage that we have over the physical scientists. They study objects from the outside, but in social science we study people as subjects engaged in meaningful behaviour, and we can approach an interpretive understanding of that behaviour from the inside.

Direct understanding or reconstruction of action is sometimes possible. It is relatively easy to arrive at a rational understanding of logical relations, such as as the reasoning involved in concluding that $2 \times 2 = 4$, or in concluding that certain facial expressions are a manifestation of anger (Giddens 1971, 148). At other times, in order to make behaviour intelligible, we need to understand people's underlying motives. It is relatively straightforward to understand rational means-end selection, as when people have a clearly stated objective with straightforward means to achieve it. In other contexts, the understanding of motives may require much deeper searching. Weber is well aware that human motives may require much deeper searching. Weber is well aware that human motives are complex. Similar actions may be done for a variety of underlying motives, while similar motives may be related to different forms of actual behaviour (Giddens 1971, 149). People also can waver between conflicting motives.

Given the complexity of human motivation, Weber argues that explanations in sociology must take the form of **probabilities** rather than the absolute predictions characteristic of the natural sciences. We have achieved an adequate explanation when the motive that we understand to be behind the behaviour in question would reasonably, or with some measure of probability, give rise to the kind of behaviour observed.

Such causal relationships or predictions are inevitably subject to qualifications and exceptions. They are not meant to be ahistorical and invariant. They reflect the particular historical situation in which people find themselves. For example, Weber argued that the Protestant religion was an important causal influence on the rise of capitalism in Europe. Capitalism also flourished in Japan but clearly not because of Protestantism, although there may have been a similar pattern of values in Japanese culture that triggered capitalistic behaviour (Ashley and Orenstein 1985, 214). Weber's model of typical characteristics of Calvinist values in contrast with typical Catholic values, makes possible broad generalizations about the relationship between religious ethics and business practices in Europe of that period. In the very different climate of the 1990s there may be no such relationship.

Marx recognized the historical character of explanations when he criticized the economists of his time for treating concepts such as supply, demand, commodities, labour power, and so on, as universal categories without realizing that they only exist within and because of the very particular and historically situated pattern of organization of economic relations of capitalism.

Human Agency

Weber's demand for adequacy at the level of meaning led him to challenge the utility of holistic or functionalist approaches to the study of human society. Functionalism, he argued, is useful and, in a sense, indispensable in providing a place from which to begin analysis. But the simple analogy between biological systems and social systems soon breaks down. Sociologists need to go beyond functional uniformities to arrive at an interpretive understand that takes account of the meanings that an action had for the people involved (Giddens 1971, 150).

It is easy for sociologists to be lured into explanations that refer to the social system as a whole, but one must never forget that the conceptual entity *society* is nothing more than the multiple interactions of individuals in a particular setting. Only individual people are agents who actually carry out subjectively understandable action. In functionalist and much Marxist writing, this collection called society tends to take on a reified identity of its own. The word is only a convenient descriptive summary. But it is converted into a thing and then used in explanations as if it were an acting unit with its own consciousness: society does such and such, or society has certain needs, and so on. This is similar to the complaint that Marx raised against the political

economy of his day and its tendency to refer to market forces as doing things to people, while losing sight of the fact that people, and only people, do things.

This is not to say that a sociologist should never use concepts that refer to collectives such as states or industrial corporations, but, Weber insists, we must remember that these collectivities are solely the result of organized actions of individual people. People may organize collectively to do something, and we may refer to this collective organization as, for example, a corporation, but corporations as such do nothing.

Weber's second demand, for adequacy at the level of causality, led him to reject the opposite extreme of **psychological reductionism** (Giddens 1971, 151). Psychology is certainly relevant to sociological understanding, as are several other disciplines. But we cannot understand how people are organized collectively or analyse these emergent institutions by examining only the psychological make-up of individuals. Psychology is likely to draw heavily upon sociology in understanding the socio-cultural influences that mould individuals.

Weber draws a careful distinction between the related disciplines of sociology and history. For Weber, history is concerned with the causal analysis of particular culturally significant events and personalities. Sociology, on the other hand, deals with the observation and explanation of general patterns of behaviour. History may well draw upon such general explanations to account for unique events. Weber saw himself primarily as a historian, but in his major work, *Economy and Society*, he was more concerned with uniformities of socio-economic organization, in effect with sociology.

Causal Pluralism

Weber's concern with adequacy at the level of causality also led him to insist on a strategy of **causal pluralism**; that is, on searching for multiple causes for social phenomena. He rejected as misguided and inadequate the efforts of some theorists, and particularly the approach of oversimplified Marxism, which attempt to explain social phenomena in terms of single factors such as economic determinism. Marx criticized Hegel for trying to analyse ideas without any regard for the social conditions in which they emerged. Weber agreed with Marx's criticism, but he also attacked the opposite fallacy committed by many of Marx's disciples who tried to analyse economic forces without regard for the subjectively meaningful response of individuals to their economic circumstances.

For Weber, sociological explanations have to encompass both objective conditions and subjective forces, for it is through subjective understanding and analysis that these objective conditions come to influence human actions as they do. Ideas and values cannot therefore be dismissed as mere by-products of class position, which can be ignored in explanations. Likewise, the economy is not an entity to which people adjust. It is the outcome of people's subjectively meaningful collective behaviour.

Ideal-Type Constructs

Weber advocated **ideal-type** constructs as a method of inquiry that would be adequate at the level of meaning or interpretive understanding of actions and would at the same time make possible objective and replicable analysis. As we saw in chapter 5, ideal-type constructs are theories that accentuate typical characteristics or elements of action. They are not intended to be literal or accurate descriptions of reality, but rather hypothetical models that can be compared with real situations.

Weber argues that this is not so much a new method as a clarification of what social scientists typically do when they try to isolate key elements in a situation. In chapter 5, we examined the model of *Gemeinschaft* and *Gesellschaft* developed by Tönnies to accentuate the distinctive characteristics of pre-industrial and urban societies. In chapter 6 we saw the models of mechanical and organic solidarity developed by Durkheim to accentuate typical forms of social cohesion in undifferentiated and specialized societies. Weber himself developed a series of ideal types of social action that he used as frameworks for exploring distinctive patterns of meaning and action among people in industrial capitalist societies. His ideal-type model of bureaucracy will be described at length later in this chapter.

Objectivity in Social Science

Weber demanded that the study of meaningful action be based upon objectively verifiable and repeatable research. This led to his deep concern with the place of values in research and how objectivity might be possible. Values necessarily enter research as aspects of the subject matter. They also enter as features of the researchers' orientation to the study. Researchers reveal their values by selecting from the infinity of possible subjects those that appear to them to be important or of interest. Nonetheless, Weber insists, the methodology and the outcome of research must be objective; that is, it must be independent of the values of the researcher.

Central to his concern with objectivity is Weber's insistence that science itself cannot pass judgment on values. It is impossible to establish values or ideals scientifically or to decide on a scientific basis what ought to be done. All that science can do is evaluate the adequacy of alternative practical means available for the attainment of given ends, the probable costs of selecting one means over another, and the additional or unforeseen consequences that may arise from particular means.

Weber frequently analysed the struggle for revolutionary socialism in these terms (Lee and Newby 1983, 200). He argued that the very goals of freedom that are part of the ideal of socialism are threatened by the use of force as a means to achieve socialism and by the political repression inevitably associated with the use of force. He also predicted that the consequences of trying to establish a socialist economy within a largely hostile capitalist world would result in multiple difficulties that would undermine the practice of socialism. Thirdly, and most importantly, he predicted that whatever means were used to bring about socialism, the ideals of socialism would be compromised by the organizational means needed to co-ordinate such a society, namely the bureaucratic state. Through his analysis, Weber could show the probably costs and long-term negative consequences of the struggle for socialism but, as he acknowledged himself, such analysis could never answer the ultimate question of whether the struggle would be worthwhile.

The free trade debate provides another example of the limitations of scientific analysis. Social science analysis can add to the debate by showing the probable consequences for various sectors of Canadian and American societies of measures incorporated within the agreement: threatened job losses in some sectors versus the promise of job gains in others; the probable impact upon Canada's cultural industries and social services; and so on. But what such analysis can never determine is whether the end justifies the means, or whether questions of culture or sovereignty should outweigh questions of economic gain, or whether losses to some people count more or less than gains to others. Science cannot answer these questions, which are based on values. At its best, science can only show what the probable costs will be of various means or actions that may be taken toward the attainment of desired goals.

Weber's powerful essays on "Politics as a Vocation" and "Science as a Vocation" address these ethical dilemmas. Weber distinguishes between two fundamental ethics: the **ethic of ultimate ends** and the **ethic of respon-**

sibility (Gerth and Mills 1946, 120). Neither ethic is in and of itself morally superior to the other. The ethic of ultimate ends is essentially religious. Those who pursue such an ethic are so totally committed to their objective that any means are acceptable if they will further this objective. Such people are not swayed by the consequences, however negative, of their means. When members of the Sons of Freedoms sect of the Doukhobours in British Columbia practise arson, they do so in the fervent belief that they are called by God to cleanse the world by fire of idolatry and evil. The immediate negative consequences for themselves or others may be of concern to them, but they do not effect their decision whether or not to commit such an act. The ultimate ethic of purification in the service of God has higher value.

Alternatively, those who accept the ethic of responsibility must take account of the consequences of their actions or means chosen to further their goals They must calculate at each step the probable consequences of and possible hardships and suffering caused by efforts to obtain their goal. This is particularly true in the face of the recognition that the decisive means for politics is violence. Political authority in any state implies a monopoly of the legitimate use of force. Science cannot answer the question whether, or to what extent, the end justifies the means. Those who imprison Doukhobour women for the crime of arson, and who considering paroling or pardoning them, must weigh the multiple consequences of these actions. They must take responsibility for the probable deaths of the imprisoned women on hunger strike and for the probable property damage in the further acts of arson that may result if the women are freed, and so on.

The recognition that science cannot pass judgement on questions of values led Weber to insist that professors should not teach political positions, any more than religious convictions, to students in the classroom (Gerth and Mills 1946, 145–47). Professors have the same opportunities as other people to air their views in the political arena. They should not use the lecture room for this. Weber was reacting against the practices of the German professors of his day who routinely used their lecterns as pulpits to impose a particular political view of the German state onto students.

Scientific objectivity has nothing to do with ethical neutrality or fence sitting, or taking some middle road. It has to do with commitment to the examination of facts, facts that are often inconvenient for our own or others' opinions. The ultimate questions of values and commitment lie beyond science, in the realms of faith and revelation.

▨ Weber's Substantive Contribution

Types of Action Orientation

Weber's model of types of action orientation outlines four basic kinds of meaningful action or typical orientations that individuals may adopt in relations with each other.

The simplest orientation is **traditional-rational behaviour**, which comprises action based on habit. It involves the least amount of conscious though. Neither the purpose of the actions nor the alternatives are consciously considered. Traditional-rational actions are done because they always have been done that way.

A second type of orientation, **affective-rationality**, is based on emotions. Actions are expressions of emotions, of passions, and they have an immediacy that involves neither calculated weighing of means or consequences nor commitment to values.

A third kind of orientation is **value-rational**. Here the primary focus is upon an overriding ideal, as in religion. Deeply committed people do not ask the consequences of their actions. They do what they believe is right, regardless of the outcome for themselves or others. This is the value orientation that underlies the ethic of ultimate ends.

The fourth and most important basis for authority is **purposive-rational action**. This involves the rational selection among alternative means of action that which is the most effective for a given end. It includes rational consideration of consequences in relation to other goals. This kind of rationality is easiest to understand and to analyse and is the basic assumption of theory in economics.

It is important to recognize that all four types of orientation are rational. Action in relation to religious values and emotions are equally rational and equally predictable, as are actions based on custom or habit, once the basic orientation itself is known.

This four-fold model of typical action orientations serves to guide research into the meaning of action from the perspective of the participants' own views of that action. The resulting causal explanation suggests the probability of responses of a certain kind, given the action orientation.

Model of Authority

Weber uses this typology as a basis for his subsequent model of legitimacy of political authority. He draws an important distinction between power that is based on authority and power based on brute force. Authority is legitimate in that the subordinates themselves accept that those in authority in practice as the probability that a given order will be obeyed by a specific group of people. He argues that there are three bases of authority: **traditional**, **charismatic**, and **rational-legal**.

The simplest and historically the most prevalent basis for authority is tradition. Orders are accepted as legitimate when they come from traditional incumbents of hereditary positions. The authority of an elder and patriarch and the divine right of kings rest on such legitimation. Parsons exercising power enjoy authority by virtue of their inherited status. Such authority is likely to have force only in relatively stable and unchanging societies.

Authority wielded by charismatic figures is very different. Here legitimation is based on the emotional response of followers to a leader who appears to have extraordinary gifts or supernatural virtue and powers. Great figures in history such as Jesus, Hitler, Gandhi, and Joan of Arc have had such charismatic authority and moved thousand and even millions of people to follow them. E.P. Thompson (1963, 421) described the charismatic power of prophets such as Joanna Southcott whose aura of spiritualism and extraordinary revelation drew a large cult following in England at the turn of the eighteenth century. Charisma means that people are so drawn by the dynamism of the particular person that they are willing to follow that individual without questioning the specifics of policies or direction. The inclusion of Hitler in the list of charismatic figures should be a warning that charisma is a force that can move people for evil as well as for good, or for fleeting goals as well as for critical social movements. It is a powerful force for change, but tells nothing about the direction that such change might take.

Weber saw charisma as the most dynamic and free expression of individual creativity, but also the most transitory of all forms of authority. The rise of charismatic figures is associated particularly with periods of trouble and emergency when people are already predisposed to respond to calls for change. A charismatic leader is always **radical** in challenging established practices and going beyond the rules of everyday life toward new visions.

The problem with authority based on charisma is that it is inherently unstable, lasting only so long as the leader survives and continues to manifest the extraordinary qualities that initially drew the followers. The inevitable death of the leader gives rise to the problem of succession since no successor can hope to command the same charisma. Weber suggests that succession since no successor can hope to command the same charisma. Weber suggests that succession can only take two basic forms. Either it can relapse into hereditary rule based on traditional authority or it can be formalized by elections and rules of organization that shift toward rational-legal authority.

Rational-legal authority is the most important basis for legitimation of power in Weber's model. He saw it as a precondition for the emergence of a modern state and the fundamental legitimation for bureaucratic administration. Rational-legal authority is based on acceptance of the utility of the rules themselves. Orders are obeyed without concern for the personality of the authority figure who set such rules, because the rules themselves are perceived as rational and purposeful.

The Sociology of Power

In his study of political power, Weber sought to elaborate the insights of Marx on the economic basis of class and class struggle. Weber advocated a wider focus on other bases of group identity and organized political action, and hence on alternatives bases of power, including the power vested in state administration. These relations, Weber argued, are too complex to be reducible to the single dimension of ownership of the means of production within a society. He developed an alternative model of power, which incorporates three distinct, although closely related, dimensions: class, status, and party.

Class

Weber shared with Marx the assumption that ownership or non-ownership of the means of production was a crucial determinant of class position. But he shifts the focus from one of relationships between people in the production process, to relative life-chances in the labour market. He defined **class** as the chance to use property, goods, and services for exchange in a competitive market. The most advantaged group in a capitalist economy is made up of the owners of land, factories, and financial capital, while the least advantaged class comprises people with no property and no skills. In between them are the middle classes. They comprise those who have some property—the petite bourgeoisie—and those like the intelligentsia, who have some skills. Weber recognized that the proletariat or working class is split by skill differentials. Those with privileged education or professions have very different life changes in the marketplace and very different access to political power than do blue-collar workers who own no property. Such divisions, he predicted, would limit the emergence of class consciousness, since these different life chances would give rise to different values and perspectives upon the world.

Status

Weber agreed with Marxist theorists that economic relations of class are central determinants of individual life chances. But he also insisted that actual life chances are too complex to be reducible to economics alone. **Status** also plays a critical role. Status, for Weber, refers to social prestige and honour and is reflected, above all, in styles of life (Gerth and Mill 1946, 186–94). Attributes ascribed by birth, such as nobility, race, ethnicity, and sex, and religious affiliation may be more immediately influential than objective class position in the development of group identity. The nouveau riche, people who make money in business or in a lottery, may well have the financial attributes of the upper class, such as expensive homes and possessions, but they may not have the status to gain acceptance from other members of the upper class. They may well be shunned by families with old wealth and breeding. With the passage of time, the offspring of the nouveau riche may gain acceptance within high status circles.

Political action is likely to reflect status group as class. Historical conflict between Catholics and Protestants in Northern Ireland, for example, cannot be reduced to class conflict. Similarly, in Canada, the struggle for a distinctive identity among the Québécois, native Indians, Doukhobours, and many other ethnic minorities cannot be reduced to relative economic advantage alone. Weber recognized that status is frequently a basis for exclusion or relative disadvantage in the market and that this may well foment group conflict and hostility. But he insisted that religious and ethnic identities exert an independent causal influence on group identity, styles of life, and life chances.

The relation between class and status in Weber's sociology is one of mutual influence. Shared class position within the economy may foster distinctive values and orientations toward life that can draw people together. In his study of comparative religions. Weber draws many parallels between economic experience and religious values. Disprivileged people, for example, are oriented toward other-wordly religions that promise salvation and just compensation for suffering on earth. Nobles are attracted to the view of a god of passion, wrath, and cunning who can be bribed with booty from war. Bureaucrats favour a comprehensive, sober religion such as Confucianism in China, which is expressed in terms of disciplined order and abstract values. Merchants are generally sceptical or indifferent to other-worldly religions that preach salvation, preferring worldly and non-prophetic theology. Shared religious orientation can in turn serve to reinforce separate group identities and loyalties, which may then be reflected in politics. For Marx, the economy has primacy, but for Weber, status is a related by distinct and powerful force in the political arena.

Party

The concept of **party** for Weber refers to actively organized relations in the political arena. Parties are oriented toward communal action designed to influence policy in favour of specified goals (Gerth and Mills 1946, 194–95). They may represent interests determined through class or through status, or through a combination of the two. Occasionally they represent neither. They differ widely in terms of both the means used to attain power and the kind of community interests that they represent. Above all, the structure and operation of parties reflect the structures of ruling, whether based on hereditary rule, democratic processes, or military coercion or other forms of violence.

A Culture of Rationality

Weber's study of the rise of rationality in western European culture, and its formal expression in capitalism and bureaucratic forms of state administration, stands as a major contribution to contemporary sociology. Weber returned again and again in his work to the theme of purposive-rational action and rational-legal authority as embodying the central features of modern industrial society.

Weber saw purposive rationality as the pervasive distinguishing characteristic of Western civilization. Other types of action orientation—toward tradition, emotions, or values—are identified by Weber as "rational" in the sense that they can be understood as organized and meaningful behaviour. But they are qualitatively very different forms of action from the distinctly calculated, goal-oriented strategies that constitute purposive-rational action. The differences are so striking that there is some debate whether the term "rational" should properly be applied only to purposive-rational behaviour. Weber clearly considered the latter to be a superior form of rationality, involving calculated orientation towards the efficient use of available means for attaining clearly thought-out goals.

Its predominance in Western culture accounts in large part for the spectacular progress of Western civilization. Weber found this calculated form of rationality to pervade all aspects of Western culture: religion, law, business, administration, politics, art, music, architecture, education, and formal organization, the ultimate expression of which is bureaucracy.

Weber highlighted worldly rationalism in many aspects of Western culture. Western music, for example, pioneered the development of chord patterns and arithmetical relations. Moreover, the formal writing and timing of music for orchestras developed only in the West. Western art moved toward an emphasis on realism and perspective; architecture was dominate by engineering principles, focussing on straight lines and prefabricated buildings rather than intricate designs. Science promoted emphasis on mastering the world.

Rationality also characterized the development of mass education. Weber suggests that this was intimately tied to the demand for trained experts for newly developing rational-legal administration. The education system was oriented to special examinations by means of which incumbents of official positions could be selected on the basis of merit rather than personal considerations. There was also a demand for regular curricula with standardized content. Rationality found formal expression at all levels of social organization. It was a central principle in the development of Western legal systems as traditional practices and arbitrary local regulations were replaced by a universal, impersonal legal system. Such a system spread over national and international markets and was essential for the development of capitalism. To do business with people across many different regions and societies, capitalists needed the assurance of a unified and calculable system of laws and regulations governing contracts.

The development of rationality in business was visible in several other areas. Rational bookkeeping was critical since it permitted the calculation of profits and losses in terms of money. Capitalism required wage labourers who were not tied to hereditary obligations to nobles but were free to dispose of their labour power in the market.

It also required the absence of restrictions on economic exchange in the market. Capitalism benefitted from the development of technology constructed on rational principles, free from religious or cultural sanctions. Weber suggests that Hinduism nay have retarded the development of technology in India be vesting it with religious significance and linking it with hereditary caste occupations. In contrast, the more rational religion of Protestantism was important in promoting the development of capitalism in western Europe.

In *The Protestant Ethic and the Spirit of Capitalism* ([1904] 1930), Weber argued that there was an affinity between the worldly ethic of Calvinism and the rise of capitalism. As we saw in chapter 8, Protestant doctrine held that it was morally proper and a sign of God's grace to amass wealth. But, at the same time, Calvinism discouraged spending money on idle consumption or to aid the poor, whose destitution was a sign of damnation. No other ethic, Weber suggests, could have been more exactly suited to the needs of capitalism. Calvinism provided the rational and emotional motivation for the calculated accumulation and reinvestment of profit.

Weber did not claim that Protestantism caused capitalism, although critics have accused him of this. Rather, he saw the affinity between the two: a mutually supportive relation in which the religious ethic encourages behaviour conducive to business rationality while, at the same time, the experience of capitalism generates a propensity to accept a supportive religious ethic. Above all, the development of capitalism required rational-legal administration. Bureaucracy, which embodies this principle to its fullest extent, was, for Weber, the most rational form of large-scale organization. An office within a bureaucracy is impersonal, separated from the private life and attachments of the incumbents, and obligations are due, not to the individual, but to the office itself.

Bureaucracy

Weber's ideal-type model of **bureaucracy** is the most famous and the most influential of all his typologies of social action. There are seven elements to this model.

1. Permanent offices guarantee continuous organization of functions, which are bounded by written rules.

2. The rules set out specialized tasks, with appropriate authority and sanctions, so that everyone knows precisely who has responsibility for what.

3. These specialized functions are organized in terms of the principle of hierarchy and levels of graded authority. Lower offices operate under the control and supervision of higher offices.

4. The principle of trained competence ensures that the incumbents of these offices have thorough and expert training, appropriate for their level within the hierarchy.

5. The resources of the organization are strictly separated from those of the individuals who occupy the different offices. This was a critical change from past practice when tax collectors, for example, were required to pay a certain amount from what they collected to the state and live on the surplus.

6. Administrative actions, decisions, and rules are recorded in writing. The combination of written documents and continuous organization of official functions constitutes the office.

7. These rules guarantee impersonality in the operations of the office, allowing neither favours nor patronage.

The Official

Weber elaborated a further model of the position of the official (Gerth and Mills 1946, 198–204). He stressed that the office is a **vocation**, with performance a duty not exploited for personal gain. Prescribed training and examinations are prerequisites for such employment. These promote the rationality in education noted above. Officers have specified obligations and fixed salaries. They are selected on the basis of their technical qualifications and not favouritism, nepotism, or ascribed characteristics. They are appointed rather than elected. Election, suggests Weber, would compromise the strictness of hierarchical subordination because incumbents would owe loyalties to those who elected them. As appointed officials, they are directly subordinate to the superior who appoints them. Work is a lifetime career, with a fixed salary and the right to a pension. This further serves to reduce susceptibility to bribery or to the temptation to use the office for personal profit. Independence from personal considerations in the discharge of official duties is legally guaranteed by tenure. The result of this form of organization is impartial performance of duties with maximum calculability and reliability.

It should be emphasized that Weber was constructing an ideal-type model of bureaucracy and bureaucratic officials. He was not claiming that any existing bureaucracy would exactly fit all these characteristics. The model is intended to function as a theoretical tool for practical research. It abstracts typical features and their typical interrelations. The extent to which any specific organization conforms to or deviates from this model is a matter for empirical research.

Advantages of Bureaucracy

Bureaucracies have major advantages over other forms of organization, such as honourific administration by courtiers, relatives of the ruler, or amateurs. Bureaucratic organizations have decisive technical superiority. They can operate with precision, speed, and with unambiguous and predictable performance based on rules. They ensure continuity, unity, and strict subordination, which reduces friction between officials. Personal and material costs of administration are reduced to a minimum.

Once fully established, bureaucracy is virtually indestructible. It is *the* means of carrying out community action. It can be made to work for anyone who can control it, because discipline and compliance are built into the structure. The system itself is able to ensure that the staff within the organization cannot squirm out of their responsibilities, for the specialized duties of each office are clearly spelled out. The consequences of bureaucratic power depend on the direction in which it is used. It is at the disposal of varied political and economic interests. As a technical means of organized action, it is vastly superior in effectiveness to any mass action that is not so organized.

Weber argued that bureaucracy was essential to many developments in the modern world. Capitalism needed the precise rules of bureaucracy to organize trade over long periods of time and in foreign countries. A centralized administration was critical for the development of a unified German state. In addition, bureaucracy is indispensable for democracy. As Weber expresses it, the fate of the masses depends on the steady, correct functioning of state administration. It is essential for the equality of treatment implied in democracy. All clients must be treated the same and be subject to the same uniform rules. Such equality presupposes impartial, regulated organization that operates without hatred or passion, without favouritism or prejudice. Weber argued that it is impossible to get rid of bureaucracies, for only such a system provides protection from undependable and amateur administration, favouritism, and corruption.

The Iron Cage

The negative side of bureaucracy lies in its power to compress all human diversity into conformity with its regulations. Bureaucracy threatens to become, in Weber's words, an **iron cage**, imprisoning the human spirit. For Weber, the bureaucratic mode of organization represents the purest expression of purposive-rational action. He never doubted its technical efficiency or its indispensability for rational capitalist enterprise and state administration. Yet he was deeply pessimistic regarding the negative impact of bureaucracy on the quality of modern life. No sphere of social action more completely exemplifies. Weber's warning that the means needed to achieve valued ends may have negative consequences that undermine or destroy the very ends themselves. Weber feared that bureaucratic organization threatened the most cherished political goals of the twentieth century: democracy and socialism.

Weber believed that bureaucracy, based on principles of technical expertise and professional secrecy of office, and swollen to millions of functionaries, would come to exercise virtually unassailable power. Democracy, with its goal of social levelling and equality of treatment, could not function without bureaucratic organization, yet this form of administration has the inherent effect of promoting and sustaining a closed group of officials, with the authority of officialdom, raised over public opinion. People would find themselves disempowered against the bureaucratic experts.

Not only ordinary people but their elected representatives would be effected. Efficient bureaucracy rests on technical superiority of knowledge. Inevitably, officials would welcome a poorly informed and hence powerless parliament. There are built-in incentives for officials to fight every attempt of parliament to gain knowledge of bureaucratic affairs. Elected ministers depend on bureaucrats for information on which to base policies.

The loyalty of officials lies not with the general public or the electorate, but with the bureaucracy itself. Their vocation is to serve their official duties. In Canada, as in other Western democracies, it is a criminal offence for civil servants within the state administration to divulge internal policy documents to the public. One official in the Department of Indian Affairs who leaked information about proposed cutbacks to native funding was summarily dismissed.

Socialism, no less than multi-party democracy, is threatened by bureaucratic administration. Socialism may abolish the power of the bourgeoisie through the socialization of the means of economic production, but is cannot abolish the power of the new class of officials. In all probability, Weber thought, officialdom might come to exert even more of a stranglehold on society under socialism because the countervailing forces of entrepreneurs and free enterprise under capitalism would be absent.

Weber argues that it would be illogical to try to control bureaucratic power by making the inner workings of officials subject to the scrutiny of laypeople. This would undermine the efficiency, speed, calculability, and impersonality of the bureaucratic machine itself, and thus undercut the very qualities that make for superior administration.

Weber saw that the inevitable consequence of the smoothly running bureaucratic machine would be the dehumanization of all who come into contact with it. The rigidly defined regulations and responsibilities of an office provide for calculated efficiency but, as a consequence, the individuality of people who must relate to it, either as employees or clients, cannot be admitted. Bureaucracies are oriented toward *formal* rationality: the purposively rational performance of standardized and routine functions. They are opposed in principle to the *substantive* rationality of individual circumstances. A system designed to treat everyone equally inevitably lacks the flexibility to treat individual cases as unique. Those who do not fit the patterns for which the rules are established cannot receive the specialized services they may need. For them the formally rational system becomes substantively irrational.

Those who work as employees within the bureaucracy are even more rigidly subject to its regulations. They operate as cogs in the machine. The major requirement for their position is unquestioning and strict adherence to written regulations within their narrowly defined areas of jurisdiction. Their individuality has no place within such a system, for it would disrupt the calculated order.

Weber believed that the iron cage spread beyond bureaucracy itself, for this mode of organization is only the extreme expression of the purposive rational orientation that dominates all aspects of Western civilization itself. Science brings with it the demythification of the universe. As Weber expresses it, "the fate of our times is characterized by rationalization and intellectualization, and above all, by the 'disenchantment of the world' " (Gerth and Mills 1946, 155). For Weber there is no escape. "To the person who cannot bear the fate of the retreat into silence and into the old religions. Weber feels that it is understandable that people should turn to religion in the hope of finding a refuge from scientific rationality and an alternative account of the meaning of life. Those who embrace religious doctrine are unable to face reality as it appears in the light of rational, scientific study. They may find comfort in the church, but only at the price of closing their minds to scientific knowledge, an intellectual sacrifice that Weber finds unacceptable. Such a retreat must inevitably fail to satisfy people because they are compelled to recognize their concomitant loss of intellectual integrity. As Weber sees it, "the arms of the old churches are opened widely and compassionately for [us]," but this emotional escape is only for those who cannot "meet the demands of the day." The iron cage of rationality is the fate of our time.

The Limitation of Weber's Thought

It is not easy to criticize Weber's thought on intellectual grounds for it seems that all the usual criticisms are synthesized or neutralized by Weber himself. The approach of functionalism, which locates people as socialized members of an overarching system, is subsumed and transcended in Weber's work. The Marxist thesis, which seeks to understand human alienation in the exploitative relations of capitalism, is also incorporated. Marxism offers no ultimate escape from the experience of alienation and dehumanization, for socialism is equally an iron cage, albeit of a different sort. Exploitation under capitalism is only replaced by a deeper dehumanization under centralized bureaucratic control. The interpretive focus on individuals as makers of their own social world is, or seems to be, incorporated as well, through Weber's emphasis on meaningful understanding. This understanding is subsumed in his ideal-type model of action orientation.

Weber is his own best critic. He acknowledges that the logical conclusions to his own arguments point to a world that he finds unbearable, dehumanized. For long periods of his life he was profoundly depressed and unable to work. This depression can only be partially accounted for in terms of his personal life and psychological make-up. In part it stemmed from the intellectual hell created by his own ideas.

Rational Action Re-examined

How can we challenge Weber's theory so that we are not condemned to the same disenchantment and despair? A basic problem in Weber's work seems to lie in its starting assumption, in the conceptualization of rationality itself. Weber divides rationality into four distinct types of orientation: traditional, affective, value, and purposive rationality. He claims that Western civilization is characterized by the triumph of the last form as reflected in science, in capitalism, in a worldly success ethic in religion, in rational-legal authority, and ultimately in bureaucratic organizations.

The question Weber does not raise is, how can a civilization, or a mode of organization, be rational if the result is the destruction of the human spirit itself? Weber is deeply aware that the rational choice of means may destroy the intended ends but he does not question the rationality of purposive action dissociated, as it is, from cultural traditions and emotional or spiritual foundations. He sees such separation as necessary for the modern world, whatever its emotional costs.

When Weber separates types of rationality, he is following a long intellectual tradition in Western thought. This tradition commonly draws a distinction between rational and emotional behaviour. Men tend to be thought of as more rational and intellectual while women are conceived of as more emotional and natural or physical. The masculine principle is thus rational. It is perhaps for this reason that Weber slips into the easy characterization of those who retreat into religion as people "who cannot bear the fate of the times like a *man*." The assumption seems to be that, in the modern world, retreat into emotions and religious values is inappropriate for men although perhaps acceptable and even normal for women.

Feminist theory, more clearly than other theoretical approaches in sociology, has challenged the separation of rational and emotional, of masculine and feminine, as an injustice to the nature of both women and men. Despite the enormous scope of his scholarship, and the depth of his insight, Weber nowhere explicitly considers the position of women or their role in the development of Western civilization. He does not seem to question their absence from intellectual debate. In his personal life, it is clear that his mother was a central figure in his own intellectual development and that his wife Marianne was the person who held him together during his years of depression and made it possible for him eventually to begin work again. Yet the role of women remains invisible in his intellectual work on the nature of man and civilization. How can this happen?

The feminist critique points to the crucial flaw in his starting assumptions of action orientation. He separates types of rationality such that purposive-rational-legal action—the masculine principle—is separated from the emotional and value-oriented dimensions—the feminine principle. Weber's characterization of Western civilization is, implicitly, a profoundly sexist characterization, although he did not perceive it as such.

The malaise in Weber's work is in essence the malaise of Western civilization itself. Weber sees only too clearly the nature of this disorder: the disenchantment inherent in a civilization that elevates purposive-rational action to the highest form. But he is unable to transcend this view. In Marcuse's terms, he remains trapped in one-dimensional thought, unable to conceive of viable alternatives that do not entail intellectual retreat.

It is the breakdown of the unity of cultural, emotional, and spiritual elements of purposive action that makes possible the colossal destruction wrought in the name of rational modernization in the pursuit of profit. The decision of a capitalist to exploit other people and the environment, to further the goal of short-term profit, is one that has emotional and moral components, whether these are recognized or not. It is also a decision embedded in a habitual or traditional mode of action in Western culture. Weber's artificial division into types of orientation, with only one dimension given recognition, does not hold up. The alternative view, which is reflected in feminist theory, albeit often in confused and half-understood ways, is that no individual, no action, no organization, no civilization can be truly rational if it does not integrate the "masculine" and the "feminine," such that tradition, emotion, and spiritually are integrated into purposive action.

The practical critiques of Weber's thesis on rationality, which we examine in the next chapter, usually have not gone this far, but they reflect the recognition that purposive-rational action, separated from other considerations, is often irrational, particularly in its practical embodiment in bureaucratic modes of organization. Weber's thesis that bureaucracy is the most efficient mode of organization has been challenged precisely because bureaucracy reduces employees to trained robots and clients to standardized cases where their substantively real circumstances cannot be taken into account.

The Marxist critique within organization theory rejects the notion of rationality as the root of bureaucratic structures. It raises the possibility that the very notion of rationality itself is a form of ideological hegemony to legitimate the exploitation of the mass of employees by those who direct the organization. Rationality is an ideology of the most invidious kind because it seems so neutral, so objective, that even to challenge it seems unreasonable.

As we shall see in the following chapter, theorists who have been most influenced by Weber's own methodological concern with interpretive understanding of human action have challenged his thesis as an unjustifiable reification of a system. From the perspective of the social construction of reality, and of ethnomethodology, Weber's model functions as ideology, or as a convenient way of accounting for what people seem to be doing, but not as a causal explanation for behaviour. The model of bureaucracy pays too little attention to the understanding that individuals themselves have of their relationships with each other. Nor does it pay enough attention to what people actually do, as distinct from what they are supposed to be doing according to the formal plan. The formal model is not a literal description of reality, but rather an accounting procedure, a way in which people have learned to talk about what they do to make sense of it.

Conclusion

The legacy of Weber in contemporary sociology is enormous. His concern with promoting a social science methodology that would have interpretive understanding as its central objective is only just coming to fruition with the development of ethnomethodology, which we discussed in chapter 4.

Weber's substantive and theoretical contribution to sociology was profoundly shaped by his lifelong dialogue with the ghost of Marx. Weber tried to build upon and go beyond the basic conception of the nature of capitalism and class in Marxist theory while rejecting the oversimplified versions of Marxist thought that reduce human behaviour to economic determinism. Weber insisted that emotional life, values, meaning, or culture must be taken into account as critical aspects of all human behaviour, including economic activities. His famous study of *The Protestant Ethic and the Spirit of Capitalism* explores the religious and moral basis of the drive to accumulate wealth, which helped to foster the development of capitalism in Europe. His other historical and comparative studies of religions and sects in Europe, India, and China focus upon the interrelationship between life experiences, base on class position and mode of production, and forms of religious thought. Some of these ideas are explored in the chapter on religion.

Weber shared with Marx an emphasis on the economic base of life chances in relation to modes of production, but he broadened this focus to explore the diversity of class experience. Weber recognized that, in complex industrial society, skills in themselves constitute a form of means of production. Those who have skills to sell in the marketplace are in a profoundly different class position from propertyless, unskilled labourers. Weber emphasized the importance of status in the formation of social groups. Status is based on ascriptive criteria of ethnicity, race, sex, age, and the like. For Marx, these were merely secondary reflections of economic class position, but for Weber they appeared as important determinants of life chance in their own right. The fact that these variables work at the level of meaning and emotion, rather than material need, makes them no less important as dimensions of human experience. Weber shared with Durkheim an awareness of the importance of social cohesion, which cannot be reduced to dimensions of class. Weber's contribution to the study of class and ethnicity are explored in later chapters.

Weber's distinctive contribution to sociology lies in his analysis of rationality in Western culture and its particular expression in the rise of bureaucratic modes of formal organization in business and government. This aspect of his work is the focus of the next chapter. Weber's model of bureaucracy has profoundly influenced the development of organization theory in sociology. Much of the work in the field is either an elaboration or test of his insights or a critical counterproposal to them. In contemporary postindustrial society, characterized by the corporate concentration of capital, multinational corporations the size of nation-states, and centralized state administrations, these bureaucratic organizations are not merely facts of life, but dominant features of human experience.

Glossary

There are many terms in sociology that do not have standard meanings. They are used differently depending on the theoretical perspective of the writer. The definitions suggested below provide a guide to the meaning of terms as they are used in this text. They are not definitive in the sense of specifying how such terms are utilized in all sociological writing. Many theoretical concepts require extensive explanation to capture their full meaning. The best way to understand terms in sociology is to see how they are used in context. There is little value in trying to memorize definitions.

Absolute surplus   For Marx, the amount of surplus production available when workers are driven to work as hard as possible and given the lowest possible standard of living.

Abstract labour time   Marx uses this term to refer to the average amount of time it takes to produce a given commodity in a society with a given level of technology and knowledge.

Accounting/Accountability   In ethnomethodology, these terms refer to the ways in which people use their common-sense knowledge and background understandings to make sense to themselves and to one another of what is going on.

Acculturation   The process through which newcomers learn and adopt the prevailing attitudes and values of the group or society that they are entering.

Achieved characteristics   Characteristics that one earns by learning skills or gaining credentials.

Actor   In functionalism, the conception of a person as a role player within a system of roles.

Adaptation   Parsons uses this term to refer to securing needed resources for an activity and distributing them among the people involved.

Adjacency pairs   This term is used in conversation analysis to refer to aspects of the structure of typical, orderly conversations. One expects that a certain kind of comment by a participant in a conversation will immediately be followed by a corresponding comment from another participant (i.e., that a question will be followed by an answer).

Advanced capitalism   For Marxist theorists, an economic order in which national and international markets are dominated by huge corporations rather than characterized by competition among entrepreneurs.

Advanced communism   An economic system where all the important means of production in a society— land, factories, technology—are communally owned. Everyone shares access to them and everyone labours collectively according to their ability to meet the collective needs of the community.

Affective-rational action   A term used by Weber to refer to action oriented to emotions.

Affectivity/Affective neutrality   Parsons uses these terms to refer to the amount of emotion that should properly be displayed in a given role.

Affirmative action   Action taken as part of a policy designed to increase the representation of members of specified groups deemed to be disadvantaged or underrepresented in certain positions relative to their numbers within the population as a whole.

Agency   The capacity of individual people to act in consciously chosen ways to influence social structures.

Agribusiness   The network of international corporations that controls production, processing, transport, storage, and financing of agriculture.

Alienation   Marx uses this term to refer to the dehumanizing character of social relations, particularly under capitalism. The term is used more generally to describe a syndrome or combination of characteristics including powerlessness, meaninglessness, isolation, and self-estrangement.

Altruism   Regard for others as a principle of action. Also, a readiness to put the interests of other members of society or those of society as a whole over personal interests.

Altruistic suicide   The form of suicide committed by people who are so intensely integrated into their social group or community that they are willing to sacrifice themselves for the good of that community.

Anomic division of labour   For Durkheim, a forced specialization that is experienced as unjust or as not regulated by reference to a clear and meaningful system of values.

Anomic suicide   The form of suicide committed by people who have lost any clear sense of values that regulate and give meaning to their lives.

Anomie   In general this refers to a breakdown in moral order. Durkheim uses the term to refer to the experience of a relative absence or confusion of values and a corresponding lack of meaningful regulations or a clear position and objectives in life.

Anomie theory of crime   A theory developed by Merton, which attributes variations in propensity for criminal behaviour to the discrepancy between culturally valued goals and access to socially approved means to achieve them.

Anti-Semitism   Prejudice against Jews.

Antithesis   See Dialectic; Dialectical materialism.

Apparatus of ruling   A term developed by Smith to refer to the organized activities that form part of the overall mechanisms for control in a society, including the activities of individual people who work in government offices and the forms and regulations that guide their behaviour.

Ascriptive characteristics/Ascription   Refers to the characteristics with which we are born, such as age, sex, height, and racial or ethnic background.

Assimilation   The process through which individuals or groups of people lose their distinctive ethnic or minority group patterns of behaviour and values and adopt the values and behavioural expectations of the dominant group.

Autocracy   Rule from above, without democratic participation.

Automation   Mechanical or electronic control of a process.

Average labour time   For Marx, the typical amount of time it takes a worker to produce a particular commodity with the technology that prevails in a given society.

Background understandings   In ethnomethodology, the knowledge that competent participants in an activity or conversation can be expected to have, which allows the activity or conversation to be understandable to them without any further explanation.

Base   A term used by Marx to refer to the social relations of production.

Behavioural organism   For Parsons, the human biological organism, which provides the fundamental energy and drive for activity and which also links the social system with the physical environment.

Berdache   A term used in anthropology to refer to people whose social identity is neither male nor female, but encompasses aspects of both.

Biological theory of race   The theory that people with different skin colours evolved from distinct subspecies of humans and that they have innately different levels of intelligence and other attributes.

Bourgeoisie   Those who own capital, or the means of production, and who hire wage-labourers to produce commodities for sale in order to make profits; capitalists.

Branch-plant economy   A society in which a significant proportion of all business enterprises are branch plants; that is, subsidiaries of multinational corporations with headquarters in another country.

Breaching experiments   A methodological approach in ethnomethodology that involves disturbing what the researcher thinks might be an unquestioned or taken-for-granted rule of normal behaviour in order to test the extent to which that normal behaviour is subsequently disturbed.

Bureaucracy   Generally, a formal organization characterized by a hierarchical chain of command and precisely delimited roles and responsibilities governed by written rules. For Foucault and Ferguson, bureaucracy constitutes the scientific organization of inequality through which people are dominated and oppressed. See Disciplinary society; Iron cage.

Bureaucratic discourse   Foucault uses the term to refer to a form of talk that translates all human concerns and human interaction into narrow technical language relevant for organizational purposes and for predefined classifications that relate to the specialized work of officials.

Bureaucratic language   Description of human interaction in terms of technical jargon referring to regulations defining responsibilities of role incumbents in organizations, often for the purpose of obfuscation.

Bureaucratic society   For Foucault, a society in which bureaucracy is the all-pervasive mode of social organization. See Disciplinary society.

Business-class immigrant   A category within the Immigration Act that refers to people who have capital to invest in Canadian industries and businesses and can provide guarantees that they will create employment opportunities in Canada.

Calvinism   Weber uses the term to refer to the religious doctrine of John Calvin, which advocates a sober, frugal lifestyle and a disciplined obligation to work as a means to serve God. It emphasizes the doctrine of predestination: that salvation is attainable by God's grace alone and that the identity of those who will be saved is known by God from the beginning of life.

Capital   The stock with which a company or person enters into business. The means of production. The accumulated wealth that is used in producing commodities.

Capitalism   A system of production in which capital, or the means of production, is privately owned by a small, elite class of people. The mass of people have no direct access to means of producing for their own needs. They depend on selling their capacity to labour to those who own the means of production.

Capitalists   Owners of capital or the means of production who hire wage-labourers to produce commodities for sale. The bourgeoisie.

Capitalization   The expansion in the amount of wealth invested in a business in order for it to remain competitive. Undercapitalized enterprises are those with insufficient investment in technology to remain competitive in the market.

Causal pluralism   For Weber, a research strategy that involves searching for multiple causes for social phenomena.

Causality   A relationship of cause and effect that is assumed to exist between two or more variables.

Census/Census data   Data obtained through comprehensive surveys of the entire population of a country, carried out with government funding and commonly with the force of law to compel people to answer the questions.

Charismatic authority   For Weber, authority legitimated by the extraordinary gifts or supernatural powers that the leader appears to have.

Chicago School (The)   A theoretical and methodological approach to urban sociology associated with the University of Chicago during the late 1920s and 1930s. An approach that emphasized the three variables of size, density, and cultural heterogeneity as critical determinants of the character of social life.

Circles of social control   The mechanisms by which conformity is produced, including guilt, desire for approval, economic sanctions, and force.

Class   Generally, the location in a hierarchically stratified work force, commonly divided into a set of ranked categories, on the basis of relative income and level of education or skill required. Alternatively, the location within a bureaucratic organization as defined by job classification schemes. Marx defined class as location in relation to the means of production, mostly as owners and nonowners, with some intermediate classes. Weber expanded Marx's definition to refer to differential life chances and the chance to use property, goods, and services for exchange in a competitive market.

Class-for-itself   In Marxist theory, the collectivity of members of a class who recognize their shared class position and come together to act in their class interests.

Class-in-itself   Marx uses the term as a theoretical concept referring to all people who share the same relationship to the means of production (i.e., capitalists as the class of all owners).

Class reductionism   The thesis that inequalities associated with gender, ethnicity, or race can be explained by class interests.

Class struggle   The conflict between those who own the means of production and those who do not. For Marx this is a dynamic process of struggle by which working people most disadvantaged by the existing relations of production struggle to change those relations.

Cohort   Persons banded together for the purposes of analysis, particularly on the basis of being born during the same period of time.

Colonialism   The process of establishing settlements in a conquered territory with the administration of such settlements fully or partially subject to control by the conquering state.

Commodity   Anything produced for exchange and not for use by the producer.

Commodity fetishism   The tendency to attribute causal agency to commodities exchanged in the marketplace, as if the commodities determined relations between people.

Common-sense understandings   Assumptions about how and why things work the way they do, based on immediate, personal experience.

Communism See Advanced communism; Primitive communism.

Community A body of people living in the same locality. Alternatively, a sense of identity and belonging shared among people living in the same locality. Also, the set of social relations found in a particular bounded area.

Competitive advantage Special conditions prevailing in certain areas that enable businesses to produce certain kinds of commodities more cheaply than they can be produced elsewhere.

Conflict theory The study of society, or specific elements of society, conceptualized as made up of parts held together by hierarchical relations of power and dependency. Conflict is seen as endemic.

Conformist A category in Merton's anomie theory of crime. One who accepts socially valued goals and socially approved means to achieve them.

Conglomerate mergers The consolidation of diverse industries within one corporation.

Conscience collective For Durkheim, the totality of beliefs and sentiments common to the average citizens of the same society. The French term is translated into English in two ways. *Collective conscience* refers to the collective sense of what is morally right and wrong. *Collective consciousness* refers to a sense of belonging and commitment to a collectivity or community of people.

Consensus In cultural Marxism, a kind of one-dimensional or group thinking manipulated by mass media and the professions to ensure that the values and behaviour expectations of the ruling class will prevail. See Ideological hegemony.

Conservative bias Generally, being disposed to maintain existing social institutions and to oppose efforts to change or reform them.

Conspicuous consumption A term referring to buying and displaying expensive items in order to demonstrate wealth and so enhance one's social status.

Consumerism The high value placed on the ownership or purchase of goods as a means of attaining personal happiness and as a measure of personal success and well-being.

Content analysis A methodological approach that involves the organized counting of content of written materials in relation to predefined categories that are determined by the theoretical hypothesis.

Contradictions of capitalism For Marx, the thesis that the capitalist system of production necessarily works in such a way that it generates problems that become steadily more disruptive for production as the system evolves. Eventually, capitalism is destined to collapse under its own internal problems.

Conversation analysis A theoretical approach within the broad perspective of ethnomethodology that explores the typical ways in which talk is structured by participants.

Corporate capitalism An economic system in which huge business enterprises are able to dominate the market and substantially influence or determine the supply and price of many commodities.

Correlation A statistical term referring to the degree to which change in one variable is associated with change in another variable.

Correspondence theory This theory, developed by Bowles and Gintis, posits that the pattern of social relations established in one institution (i.e., schools) parallels in critical respects the pattern of social relations established in another institution (i.e., industry).

Counterculture A system of norms and values held by members of a subgroup or class within a society that contradicts or opposes a significant number of the norms and values that prevail within the society as a whole.

Countervailing duties Import taxes that one country imposes on certain commodities from another country to compensate for subsidies that the exporting country has given to producers of the commodities.

Credentialism In Marxist theory, the thesis that formal qualifications are emphasized by capitalists to create artificial division and competition among workers rather than because such qualifications are essential for performance of particular jobs.

Critical literacy The capacity to reflect upon and to question the content of what one reads.

Critical theory Any sociological theory or research that challenges the legitimacy of the established social order and that seeks to understand the workings of that society as a basis for action to change it.

Cult of domesticity A set of attitudes and values that justifies the segregation of women in the private realm of the home.

Cult of rationality Justification of everything by reference to the supposedly objective principles of scientific and technical efficiency.

Cultural lag The failure or excessive slowness of prevailing values and norms in a society to adapt to economic changes associated with technological innovation.

Cultural Marxism Closely associated with the social construction of reality perspective, this is a variant of Marxist theory that emphasizes ideological hegemony rather than the determining force of capitalist structures in explaining social relations in capitalist societies.

Cultural system In functionalism, the system of beliefs, rituals, values, and symbols, including language as a symbol system, through which people confront ultimate questions about reality, the meaning of good and evil, suffering, and death.

Culturalism See Cultural Marxism.

Culture The set of shared ideas about what constitutes ideal behaviour within a given society.

Culture of domination A system of values and behavioural expectations that condones or legitimates subordination of the mass of people to autocratic rule.

Culture of poverty thesis The thesis that poverty is caused or perpetuated by the attitudes and values of poor people, which inhibit them from taking action to ameliorate their situation.

Cybernetic hierarchy For Parsons, a hierarchy of systems of control and communication in human action.

Deconstructionism The detailed investigation of how texts are organized or internally constructed so as to achieve their meaning.

Deferred gratification Foregoing immediate pleasures or rewards in order to work toward greater future rewards.

Defining the situation In symbolic interaction and ethnomethodology, the process of negotiating the meaning of what seems to be going on.

Demography/Demographic The study of vital statistics of a population, including such information as population size, births, marriages, deaths, migration, and so on.

Dependency theory A theory that the poverty evident in the Third World and in poorer regions of developed economies is generated and perpetuated through systematic exploitation by developed capitalist economies.

Dependent capitalism The experience of capitalist development in Third World countries caught in an already highly advanced corporate capitalist world system.

Dependent commodity producers A class of workers who own their own means of production of certain commodities but who are controlled by the corporate monopoly processors and distributors who dominate the market for what they produce. See also Petite bourgeoisie.

Dependent development The restricted pattern of development within a region or country where the economy is controlled externally by capitalist metropolises that develop the locality only as a resource hinterland. See Dependency theory.

Dependent variable The variable that is assumed to depend on or be caused by other variables included in research.

Deskilling The process of breaking down a complex operation or activity into simple component operations that can be easily learned.

Determinism Any thesis that sees human activity as caused or controlled by forces independent of human choice or will. See Economic determinism.

Deviance Behaviour that does not conform to behavioural expectations prevailing in a given group or community.

Deviant subculture See Subcultural theory of deviance.

Dialectic Recurrent cycles of thesis, antithesis, and synthesis. Thesis refers to the original idea, philosophy, or system of thought. Antithesis represents the logical inconsistencies, problems and anomalies within the thesis. The synthesis is a new system of ideas, thoughts, or philosophy that resolves these contradictions.

Dialectical materialism The application of dialectical reasoning to the organization of production. Thesis represents the existing organization of production. The antithesis refers to the tensions or problems that impede or shackle the full productive potential of this organization. The synthesis is a new form of organization of production that overcomes these problems and unleashes the full productive potential of the available means of production.

Dialectical method The application of dialectical thinking to a given problem, clarifying the original situation, explicating the contradictions inherent in it, and seeking a synthesis or new approach that will resolve these contradictions.

Differential association theory A theory that attributes variation in propensity for criminal behaviour to relative closeness of involvement with others whose subcultural values condone criminal behaviour.

Differential opportunity theory A theory that attributes variation in propensity for criminal behaviour to the relative availability of legitimate or illegitimate means to achieve valued goals. See Innovator.

Differentiation Generally, the process of becoming less alike as the result of performing more specialized social roles. Spencer used this term to refer to the breakdown of simple, unspecialized structures into many separate parts.

Diffuse obligations The perceived right of others, such as close family members, to expect a variety of services and support.

Disciplinary society The term is used by Foucault to refer to social order maintained through power based on intimate knowledge and regulation of individuals rather than on punitive sanctions.

Discipline Foucault uses this term to refer both to orderly conduct and to a branch of knowledge.

Discourse For Foucault, how we come to talk about our social world, which determines how it comes to be known to us and to have the form that it does.

Distributive justice The quality of fairness in the distribution of rewards or resources among participants in a situation or activity.

Divide and rule The policy of encouraging schisms within a mass of subordinate people to reduce the likelihood of concerted action by subordinates, making them easier to control.

Documentary construction of reality For Smith, a theoretical approach that focuses on how the seemingly neutral language of bureaucratic forms and categories actively structures social relations and what comes to be seen as factual information.

Documentary method of interpretation In ethnomethodology, the active search for patterns in the vague flux of everyday interaction, as a fundamental element of practical, everyday reasoning. This search is based on the premise that there is always an underlying pattern to everyday activity or conversation. Surface appearances are treated as evidence of, or as documenting, this presumed underlying pattern.

Dogmatism An assertion of opinion that is authoritarian.

Doing hierarchy In ethnomethodology, the actual practices of people in ongoing social interaction that produce and reproduce the experience of some individuals as inferior or superior to others.

Domestic labour debate A body of theory concerned with where and how homemakers fit into the capitalist economic system.

Dominant culture The set of values and behavioural expectations that prevails in a given society and that legitimates and supports the activities that directly benefit the dominant class. In capitalist society, the dominant culture is that which legitimates the activities of the capitalist class in the pursuit of profit.

Dominant values The values of the powerful class that tend to prevail within a society.

Domination In ethnic relations, the state of one ethnic group exerting regularized and institutionalized rule over other ethnic groups.

Double standard The standard for behaviour that is applied unevenly within a group or community such that given behaviour will be criticized and condemned if practiced by one sector of a community but considered acceptable when practiced by others.

Dowry murder A new bride murdered by her husband or his family because the amount of goods or money that the woman brought to the marriage is deemed inadequate. Dowry murder allows the husband to remarry to collect additional dowry.

Dramaturgical model Goffman's theoretical approach that studies how people creatively act out particular social roles in a manner analogous to how actors in a play creatively interpret their script.

Dynamic equilibrium In functionalist theory, the maintenance of balance and order between elements of a society by systematically adjusting for change in one element by complementary changes in other related elements.

Dysfunctions Effects or consequences of any given structure or pattern of behaviour that are damaging for some other element or for people in the wider social system.

Ecological fallacy A logically false or misleading argument that attempts to draw inferences about individuals from aggregate data.

Economic determinism A form of theorizing that reifies the abstract concept of an economic system, such that the system of production is held to cause or to determine all major aspects of social life, without reference to human agency.

Economies of scale A principle of economics that asserts that as the size of a business enterprise increases, the cost of producing any one unit of output decreases.

Ego In psychoanalytic theory, the conscious self that seeks to express and to realize fundamental drives and passions.

Egoism For Durkheim, a value system that places self-interest at the centre. Also, systematic selfishness, reflecting the absence of a sense of social bonds and commitment to other people.

Egoistic suicide The form of suicide committed by individuals who have lost any sense of social bonds linking them to other people.

Embourgeoisement thesis The thesis that, under capitalism, working-class people will become or are becoming steadily wealthier to the point that their lifestyles closely resemble those of professional middle-class people.

Emotional labour The work of managing facial expressions and manipulating the emotional responses of clients as part of one's job.

Empiricism A commitment to and quest for knowledge based on observation and experiment.

Employment equity Legislation and policies designed to ensure that women and men employed in jobs of equivalent levels of skill, responsibility, difficulty, etc., receive equivalent levels of pay.

Enclosure Feudal landlords' practice of fencing off huge tracts of arable land for sheep pastures thereby depriving serfs of access to land for subsistence crops.

Enumeration In survey research, the process of counting the total membership of a particular set of people from which a sample is to be drawn.

Equality of condition A policy that stresses sameness. In education, it means that a standardized age-graded curriculum be available for all students regardless of individual ability or interests.

Equality of opportunity A policy that, in principle, gives all individuals an equivalent chance to compete for social positions that carry relatively higher rewards. See Meritocracy thesis.

Equilibrium In functionalism, the maintenance of balance and order between elements of a society over long periods of time.

Ethic of responsibility For Weber, moral principles that take account of the probable consequences of actions.

Ethic of ultimate ends A term used by Weber to refer to morality based on obedience to religious doctrine or to what is perceived as the will of God, or some absolute value, regardless of the consequences.

Ethnic/Ethnicity Identity as a member of a distinctive cultural group associated with a particular country or region of origin. Social constructionists argue that ethnicity is used as an ideology that blames differences and inequalities caused by discriminatory treatment of certain people on intrinsic personal characteristics of the victims.

Ethnocentrism A belief that one's culture or way of life is superior to others. An exaggerated view of the quality and correctness of the culture of one's own groups. A self-centered view of social life lacking respect for the different perspectives or values of other people.

Ethnomethodology A theoretical approach that focusses on micro-interactions and explores the methods or practical reasoning that individuals use to make sense of what is going on around them. Ethnomethodologists argue that the process of formulating an account of what is happening produces reality for the practical purposes of participants.

Evolution A theory positing that societies developed from simple undifferentiated societies into highly complex industrial societies in a way analogous to evolution in the natural world where single-cell organisms evolved into complex advanced organisms.

Exchange value For Marx, the amount of human labour time that goes into the production of a commodity. The value of one commodity relative to another is measured by the labour time needed to make the commodities.

Experiment A methodological approach that, ideally, holds constant everything that might influence the phenomenon of interest and then allows one variable to change in a controlled manner. Any subsequent change observed in the phenomenon of interest is then attributed to the influence of the manipulated variable.

Expressive leader   One who is primarily responsible for relieving tensions and smoothing social relations in a group.

Extended family   A family in which several generations of kin live in the same home.

Extrinsic rewards   Payment or other benefits received for doing some activity. The opposite of intrinsic rewards.

Fact   Datum. That which is known as the result of empirical investigation conducted according to objective scientific methods of observation and experiment. Also, that which is attested to be correct by an appropriate official within a formal organization. See also Social facts.

False consciousness   The condition of some members of the working class who fail to understand their true or objective long-term class interests to the extent that they are predisposed to support a system of production that exploits them.

Familism   Particularly close attachment to kin, and high value placed on family membership, combined with generally shallow relations with nonkin.

Family-class immigrant   See Sponsored immigrant.

Family wage   The policy of paying male workers sufficient wages to support their wives and children.

Feedback mechanisms   The processes through which given structures or patterns of behaviour are selectively reinforced and perpetuated over time.

Feminist movement   Collective protest and political action to ameliorate the subordinate situation of women in society.

Feminist theory   A perspective that takes as its starting point the situation and experiences of women in questioning the adequacy of any analysis of human behaviour. See also Marxist feminism; Radical feminism.

Fetish   An inanimate object worshipped for its supposed magical powers. See Commodity fetishism.

Feudalism/Feudal system   An economic system in which land is the primary means of production. Land is owned by a hereditary elite of nobles or lords and is worked by a hereditary class of labourers or serfs who are tied to the land.

Folk society   An ideal-type model of isolated rural society.

Fragmentation   The subdivision of tasks or responsibilities among workers such that each worker performs highly repetitive and monotonous actions devoid of any intrinsic interest or sense of importance.

Frankfurt School (The)   See Critical theory.

Function   For functionalists, the basic needs or conditions that must be met by a social system in order to maintain itself in a state of equilibrium. Also, the particular contribution of parts of a social system to the maintenance of the whole system.

Functional indispensability   For Parsons, the assumption, borrowed from biology, that every element found within a social system is indispensable for the functioning of that system. Hence, no element can be removed or changed without some negative effect for the system as a whole.

Functional unity   For Parsons, the assumption, borrowed from biology, that every element found within a social system has effects or consequences that are good for the entire system.

Functionalism/Structural functionalism   The study of society as a functioning system comprising interdependent institutions or patterned relations that are stable over time, and that perform specialized functions for the whole. The central focus is on how order is maintained between elements of society. Any given pattern of relations or structures within society is explained by reference to the effects or functions that such patterns have for the wider whole.

GAIL model   See System prerequisites.

Gatekeepers   People who are in a strategic position to transmit or screen out information, especially in the media.

Gemeinschaft   A theoretical model of a society as a community of people united by relations of kinship, a strong sense of community identification, and shared values and norms. A community.

Gender   Culturally learned differences in behaviour of males and females.

Gender-class   Socially constructed location of women and men relative to the organization of the activities of production and reproduction. See also Sexual class, which is often used synonymously with gender-class.

Gender-ethnic-class   Location within the occupational hierarchy based on the combination of gender ethnic background and marketable job skills.

Gender-role socialization   The process by which children are taught and internalize behaviour deemed appropriate for their particular sex.

Gender roles   Markedly distinct and nonoverlapping roles for typical activities for women and men.

Generalized other   A group or class of people whose overall responses to us play an integral part in the development of our own sense of self-identity. Similarly, a class or team of people whose reactions we try to anticipate.

Gesellschaft   A theoretical model of an association of people related only by transitory and superficial contacts that are formal, contractual, and specified in character. An association.

Goal attainment   For Parsons, establishing priorities among competing goals and mobilizing members involved in a given activity to attain them.

Goal displacement   The tendency for groups or organizations set up to achieve some specific objective to shift priorities from this original objective to a concern with maintaining the group or organization itself.

Green revolution   A package of scientific developments in agriculture that promises to increase yields.

Headstart program   A policy of providing enriched learning experiences for young children from economically and culturally deprived families to help them keep up with the achievements of more advantaged children.

Hegemony   Relations of ruling through which the consent of subordinate classes to capitalism is achieved, particularly through control over how people think.

Heterosexism   The institutionalized organization of social relations that assumes that all women will be tied to men, usually in relations of sexual and economic interdependence.

Hidden curriculum   That which is taught by the form of teaching rather than by the explicit content of lessons.

Hidden diseconomies   The costs or negative consequences of economic activities that are not counted in corporate cost-benefit analyses, because members of the wider society, rather than the enterprise engaging in the activities, suffer from, and pay for, these consequences.

Hierarchy   Graded or ranked positions within a society or organization.

Hinterland   Underdeveloped areas that supply cheap labour and cheap raw materials or semiprocessed goods to developed centres.

Historical materialism   For Marx, the thesis that the processes by which people meet their basic subsistance needs constitute the foundation of social organization. Hence, the analysis of social life should begin with the study of prevailing modes of production and the relations that these generate between people.

Historical sociology   The study of how human actions generate social structures over time.

Holding company   A company that holds sufficient shares in multiple other companies to control their executive boards.

Horizontal integration   A corporation that owns or controls all or most stages in the production of a specific commodity, including production and supply of all raw materials, manufacturing, distribution, and retail sales.

Human relations school of management   A style of management that gives priority to generating a friendly and relaxed social atmosphere in the workplace, on the assumption that contented workers are more productive. The term can be used pejoratively to refer to management styles that manipulate a friendly social atmosphere among subordinates to divert attention from the deeper reality of exploitation.

Humanism   For Durkheim, a form of religion or spirituality in which the central value is devotion to humanity rather than to a divinity.

Hypothesis   A prediction made on the basis of a theory.

I and Me   Terms used by Mead to refer to two aspects of the individual. The I is the impulsive, spontaneous aspects of self. The Me is learned identity, incorporating the common attitudes and meanings of the group to which one belongs.

Id   In psychoanalytic theory, the vast reservoir of unconscious and semiconscious drives and passions, especially sexual drives, that underlie and energize our conscious activities.

Idealism   A philosophy that emphasizes ideas and values as the distinctive moving force of human history. The view that all human behaviour entails unique spiritual events that can only be grasped by intuition, not by objective scientific method.

Ideal-type model   A theoretical model that is designed to highlight the typical characteristics of the kind of social organization being studied.

Ideographic   Explanations based on unique, subjective, intuitive accounts.

Ideological hegemony   The capacity of the dominant class to rule through control over prevailing ideas or culture. It ensures that the mass of people accept as legitimate the activities that directly benefit the dominant class.

Ideology   Systems of values that justify certain kinds of action or ways of life, sometimes to the detriment of other people. Belief systems that strongly influence the way we see social reality. They tend to sensitize us in certain ways and blind us in others. Dorothy Smith uses the term to describe a method of inquiry about society that results in a systematic means not to see and not to know what is actually happening.

Imperfect competition   In economic theory this refers to a situation in which a few giant producers or purchasers of a commodity are able to dominate the market and to act in collusion rather than in competition.

Imperialism   The practice of one state extending its sovereignty over another by force, usually for the purpose of economic exploitation.

Imperialism of rationality   A form of control over, or manipulation of, people. It is exercised by presenting certain kinds of behaviour as consistent with reason or scientific knowledge, such that any disagreement or resistance seems irrational.

Inclusive language   Nonsexist language. Gender-neutral language that does not use masculine nouns and pronouns generally to include feminine forms.

Independent commodity producers   A class of workers who own their own means of production of certain commodities, generally referring to people engaged in farming, fishing, and the like. See also Petite bourgeoisie.

Independent immigrant   A category under the Immigration Act that refers to people whose entry into Canada is subject to economic requirements and criteria measured by a point system.

Independent variable   A factor included in research as a possible cause of some phenomenon of interest. It is treated as known or given for the purpose of the research and not as itself requiring explanation.

Indexicality   In ethnomethodology, the context-dependent character of the meaning of words or actions. The thesis that words or gestures always stand for or indicate a broader background and that this background understanding is essential for words to have meanings.

Indicator   An observable feature that is used in research to measure a particular concept.

Industrial Revolution   The period of transition associated with the eighteenth century in Europe when the primary means of production changed from land to machines located in factories.

Industrialization   Mechanization. The transition from dependence on human and animal energy to fossil fuels. Usually associated with a shift in primary means of production from land to machines located in factories.

Inner city   A general term referring to the central residential areas within large cities, usually characterized by high density housing.

Innovator   A component of Merton's anomie theory of crime. One who accepts socially valued goals but adopts socially disapproved means to achieve them.

Institutional ethnography   A theoretical and methodological approach that studies the active processes through which people construct their social reality through their everyday working activities in a local setting (ethnography). It then links these local dynamics to the wider institutional context that shapes them.

Institutionalization   The establishment of certain patterns of behaviour as typical and expected to the point that they are generally taken for granted as appropriate by most members of a society.

Institutions   Typical ways of structuring social relations around specific functions or needs of a society.

Instrumental leader   One who is concerned with and who directs task performance in a group.

Integration   Generally, to combine parts into a whole or to combine individuals into cohesive collectives. Spencer uses this term to refer to the evolutionary process of developing a central co-ordinating agency, such as state administration, to regulate relations between specialized elements of society. Parsons uses the term to refer to co-ordinating the behaviour of different members or role incumbents in a particular activity and maintaining orderly interrelations between role players.

Intelligence failure Loss of effective control in organizations resulting from distorted or inadequate information.

Interactional competence See Background understandings.

Interlocking directorships A situation where one person serves on the board of directors of two or more companies.

Internalization The process of learning group values and behavioural expectations and wanting to conform to them from an inner sense that they are morally right.

Interpretive theory A paradigm that focuses on micro-interactions and how people present themselves to each other and come to understand the surface and underlying meanings of their interaction. The perspective includes symbolic interaction and the dramaturgical model. Ethnomethodology is sometimes included with the interpretive perspective although it is distinct from traditional symbolic interaction. See Verstehen.

Intersubjectivity The capacity of knowing what another person actually intended.

Interviewer bias The interviewer's preconceived opinions or personal characteristics that influence the interaction with the respondent and influence in a measurable way the information being sought.

Invisible hand of the market The thesis that the competition between the mass of sellers, trying to get the best price for their commodities, and the mass of buyers, trying to buy commodities at the cheapest price, will produce the best outcome in the long run without external planning.

Iron cage Weber's vision of bureaucracy as an all-powerful system of organization that would regulate all aspects of individual life.

Iron law of oligarchy The process whereby power within any organization comes to be wielded by a tiny elite minority. A process hypothesized to occur regardless of democratic principles or procedures.

Isolation Absence of a sense of social bonds or belonging with other people. Particularly loss of a sense of loyalty or commitment to one's workplace. See Alienation.

Kin universe The average number of kin with whom an individual remains in regular contact.

Labelling theory An approach that focusses on how stereotypes or fixed mental images are applied to certain kinds of people, particularly by officials in positions of power, and the effects that this application has on the self-concepts and future behaviour of the people so labelled.

Labour-saving technology Machines designed to perform work previously done by people.

Labour theory of value For Marx, the theory that the average labour time that goes into the production of a commodity, with a given level of technology, determines the exchange value of that commodity.

Laissez-faire system An economic system that operates without any government control or regulation. Advocacy of such a system.

Latency See Pattern maintenance.

Latent functions Those effects or consequences of any given structure or pattern of behaviour that are important for maintaining social order but that are not directly recognized by people involved in the behaviour.

Leveraged buy-outs The practice of borrowing money to buy a controlling interest in a firm in the hope that assets so gained will generate sufficient profits to pay off the debt.

Liberalism Generally, a belief in the values of free enterprise and equality of opportunity for individuals to compete for social and economic rewards on the basis of merit. Used in a positive sense, it refers to a willingness to help individuals to overcome disadvantages or to open up opportunities for disadvantaged individuals. Critics use the term to refer to people who advocate piecemeal reform of the social system rather than radical or major changes to social structures. Critics also use the term to describe the tendency to blame inequality on personal merit or personal failings without acknowledging the structural constraints that disadvantage many groups.

Liberal-bourgeois thesis A theory that emphasizes the positive aspects of capitalism as an economic system. It is considered by Marxists to constitute the ideology of the bourgeoisie. Also, a thesis that associates capitalism with free enterprise and competitive markets that potentially provide opportunities for all people to improve their standard of living. See Liberalism.

Liberal feminism Feminist theory that focusses on establishing equal treatment for women and men as individuals in law, employment, and other public roles.

Liberation theology A religious doctrine that holds that the call to achieve social justice is central to the Christian message. See Social Gospel movement.

Linear relation An apparent relationship between two variables such that any change in the value of one variable is associated with an equivalent change in another variable.

Looking-glass self For Cooley, the way in which people reflect on how they appear to other people who are important to them, how their appearance is being judged by such people, and the effect of such reflection in feelings of pride or shame.

Lumpenproletariat In Marxist theory, unemployed workers who form a reserve army of cheap labour power to be used by capitalists as they require additional labour power.

Macrosociology The analysis of large-scale and long-term social processes, often treated as self-sufficient entities such as state, class, culture, and so on.

Macrovariable A variable that cannot be reduced to micro-elements.

Managerial mentality The thesis that organizations are rational and efficient entities and that people can be regarded as role incumbents and managed to maximize efficiency of co-operative activities. Generally, the endorsement of the viewpoint of managers.

Managerial revolution The thesis that ownership of corporations has become separated from control over them. The belief that managers rather than capitalists run corporations.

Manifest functions The consequences of any given structure or pattern of behaviour that are openly recognized and intended by the people involved in the behaviour.

Marginal workers A class of workers who are frequently unemployed or who can find work only in a succession of temporary and low-paid jobs.

Marxist feminism Feminist theory that focuses on the role of economy and private property in the subordination of women to men.

Marxist functionalism The modification of functionalist analysis to incorporate notions of power and unequal ability of different individuals and groups to selectively reinforce those social structures that they find beneficial.

Marxist structuralism The theory that utilizes the model of the capitalist system and its internal contradictions as an explanatory framework to account for specific characteristics of contemporary capitalist society.

Maternal deprivation theory The theory that young children require extensive physical and social contact with their mothers in order to become psychologically well adjusted and hence that all evidence for adult maladjustment, particularly delinquent behaviour, can be explained by inadequate maternal attention.

Matriarchy Social organization in which the mother is the head of the family.

Matrilineal Ancestry and inheritance through the mother's line.

Me See I and Me.

Meaninglessness Absence of a sense of involvement in a worthwhile activity. The term refers particularly to fragmented work where one individual's contribution is so small as to seem worthless. See Alienation.

Mechanical solidarity Durkheim used this term to describe a form of cohesion that is based fundamentally on sameness.

Members' competences See Background understandings.

Men's liberation A social and political movement concerned with challenging stereotypes of masculinity and the associated sex roles that confine men to the public occupational realm.

Mercantilism Trade, particularly referring to the historical period when European countries effectively dominated world trade and amassed great wealth at the expense of less developed countries.

Meritocracy Inequality in social rewards based on individual differences in ability and effort.

Meritocracy thesis In functionalist theory, the thesis that hierarchy and social inequality are accounted for by the need to motivate the more talented and competent individuals to occupy the more important and difficult roles in society.

Metaphysical stage A stage in Comte's model of the evolution of societies. Societies in the metaphysical stage are characterized by a prevailing belief in a single deity. Phenomena are explained by reference to abstract forces or ultimate reality rather than to a multiplicity of spirits.

Methodism A puritanical religious doctrine that stresses spiritual egalitarianism, grace through penitence, strictness in religious practice and moral behaviour, and submission to authority.

Methodological holism The principle that social experiences must be explained in terms of forces that operate at the level of the social system as a whole.

Methodological individualism The theory that social experiences can be reduced to the characteristics of individual people. See Psychological reductionism.

Metropolis The centre of capitalism, which dominates surrounding regions, extracting their economic resources.

Microhistory The study of how personal interaction is shaped over time.

Microsociology The detailed analysis of what people do, say, and think in the actual flow of momentary experience.

Microstructural bias A tendency to concentrate on the internal workings of organizations rather than to examine the effects of wider political and economic forces on them.

Microtranslation strategy The attempt to show how large-scale social structures can be understood as patterns of repetitive microinteractions.

Military-industrial complex The thesis that there is a close affinity between the interests of the elites within the military and industry.

Military-industrial-political complex The thesis that there is a close affinity between the personnel and the interests of elites within the military and industry and senior ranks of the civil service and government ministries.

Misogyny Hatred of women.

Mobility Geographic mobility refers to movement from one locality to another. Social mobility refers to a change in relative status, either up or down the social class hierarchy.

Mode of production Marx uses this term to refer to the prevailing way in which a society transforms the material environment to meet subsistence needs.

Monogamy Having only one mate. Marriage between one man and one woman.

Monolithic bias The assertion that a particular phenomenon is uniform throughout, allowing no variation.

Monopoly Exclusive possession of the trade in some commodity by one individual or one corporation.

Morality Durkheim uses the term to refer to the expression of the relationship between individuals and society.

Multinational corporations Business enterprises that operate in one or more countries in addition to the country housing the corporate headquarters.

Multivariate analysis An aspect of survey research in which statistical techniques are used to see how sets of variables interact in combination.

National Policy The policy instituted by John A. Macdonald in 1878 to establish high tariffs against American goods entering Canada in order to encourage industrialization in Canada. The effect was that American businesses invested in branch plants within Canada.

Natural attitude This term is used in ethnomethodology to refer to people's tendency to assume that social interaction is meaningful, without their reflecting on how such meaning comes to be perceived and sustained.

Natural laws Statement of a causal relationship between physical phenomena, held to be universally true under given conditions.

Need dispositions Parsons uses this term to refer to the way people tend to act in conformity with norms and feel dissatisfied when they cannot do so. Individual choices take the form of patterned behaviour because of the internalization of shared norms.

Neo-imperialism The practice of one country exerting effective control over the economy of another country and exploiting its resources even though it has formal independence.

Noble Under the feudal system, one who controls the estate on which serfs work.

Nomothetic Lawlike generalizations. Deterministic cause and effect relations.

Normalization Foucault uses this term to refer to a manipulated conformity managed by rational social science principles and legitimated by reference to models of healthy psychological and social adjustment. See Therapeutic intervention.

Normative consensus In functionalist theory, this refers to a social group's shared acceptance of a set of values and behavioural expectations as legitimate and appropriate. The establishment of normative consensus is considered critical in the maintenance of a stable social order to which members willingly conform.

Norms Typical expectations for behaviour in given situations that are seen as legitimate and appropriate.

Nuclear family A family unit comprising two sexually cohabiting adults of the opposite sex together with their dependent children.

Objectivity The attempt to present and to deal with facts, uncoloured by the feelings, opinions, and viewpoints of the person presenting them. Objective evidence is that which is accepted as factual and independent of the subjective opinions or theories of any observer.

Oligarchy Rule by a few people at the top without democratic participation.

Oligopoly Concentrated possession of the trade in some commodity by a few individuals or a few corporations.

One-dimensional thought The inability to conceive of viable alternative ways of organizing social relations. Acceptance of the status quo and of the prevailing ways of thinking as the only credible option.

Order theory Closely related to systems theory, a perspective in which the central focus is on how a stable balance is maintained between elements of a social system.

Organic solidarity Durkheim uses this term to refer to a form of cohesion based upon specialization and interdependence.

Other For Mead, those people whose responses to us play an integral part in the development of our own sense of self-identity.

Out-group A group of people considered sufficiently different as to be outside one's own cultural group.

Outsiders Nonconformists. People whose lifestyles or characteristics visibly violate at least some of the norms that define membership within a given community. See Symbolic brackets.

Paradigm A broad theoretical perspective that may encompass several more specific but related stories. A pattern.

Participant observation A methodological approach in which the researcher shares as fully as possible in the everyday activities of the people being studied in order to understand their lives through personal experience.

Participatory management A form of management in which workers are permitted some involvement in making decisions, usually as a way of winning their support for the implementation of such decisions.

Particularism/Particularistic standards For Parsons, evaluation based on the particular abilities, interests, and efforts of an individual.

Party Weber uses the term to refer to organized relations within the political arena, designed to influence policy in favour of a tribe or family.

Patriarch Father and ruler of a tribe or family.

Patriarchy A social system based on male dominance and female subordination.

Patrimony Property inherited from one's father. Also used to refer to a system of senior male mentors conferring rank or privileges onto specifically chosen junior males.

Pattern maintenance Parsons uses the term to refer to the mechanisms to manage tensions and ensure that individual role players in an activity have the skills and motivation needed to perform their given role(s) appropriately. Latency.

Pattern variables For Parsons, a patterned set of dichotomous options that systematize typical dilemmas of choice in any given role.

Pay equity Equal pay for equal work smeans that women and men who do identical work should receive identicall pay. Equal pay for work of equal value means that workers in different jobs should receive the same pay when their work involves the same level of skill, responsibility, or difficulty.

Peasant A person who works the land to produce food and other materials for immediate consumption rather than for sale or exchange. In discussions of feudalism, the term is often synonymous with serf. Generally, one who works the land.

Personal troubles Mills uses the term to refer to the private matters that lie within an individual's character and immediate relationships.

Personality system Parsons uses the term to refer to the learned component of individual behaviour. Socialization is a critical process in its formation.

Petite bourgeoisie Marx uses the term to describe the class of people who own their own means of production and work for themselves but who hire little or no additional wage-labour.

Phenomenology A theory of the methods or grounds of knowledge based on the premise that all knowledge constitutes interpretations of basic sense experience. The study of how sensory information becomes interpreted as meaningful.

Piece-rate payment A system of payment based on the number of items or units of work completed, rather than on the length of time worked.

Plutocracy A ruling class of wealthy persons. Rule by the wealthy.

Polarization of classes Marx's thesis that, under capitalism, wealth will become progressively more concentrated in the hands of a tiny elite class of capitalists as the mass of people become steadily more impoverished.

Political economy theory A theoretical perspective in which the central explanatory framework for analysing society is the Marxist model of capitalism. The dynamics of the capitalist economy are seen as the fundamental determinants of political structures and action.

Polyandry One woman having more than one husband at the same time. Wife sharing.

Polygamy Having more than one spouse at the same time.

Polygyny One man having more than one wife at the same time. Husband sharing.

Positive society The third stage of Comte's model of the evolution of societies. Positive society is characterized by a commitment to scientific rationality. Scientists rather than priests are the intellectual and spiritual leaders, and explanations take the form of regular lawlike connections between phenomena based on observation and experiment.

Positivism/Positivist A scientific approach to the study of society that seeks to emulate the methodology of the physical sciences. Emphasis is placed on quantitative, objective data rather than on subjective or impressionistic research. Conclusions are based upon observation and experiments that are assumed to provide factual, objective evidence, independent of the theories or opinions of any observer. Also, the search for deterministic or lawlike relations of cause and effect governing human behaviour. The philosophical assumption that observation and experimentation constitute the only valid human knowledge. In ethnomethodology the term refers to an ideology that accords the subjective interpretations of sense experience by other people.

Postmodernism A complex term that refers to architectural styles that incorporate a pastiche or merging of multiple styles in one building. In sociological theory, a perspective that rejects the search for grand theories or unifying explanations for society, conceptualizing social reality as heterogeneous, fluid, and contingent.

Poverty line A level of income below which people are defined as poor. Commonly calculated on the basis of the proportion of total income required to meet basic subsistence needs of food, shelter, and clothing in a particular society.

Powerlessness Lack of control over factors directly affecting one's life, particularly lack of control over one's work and fear of unemployment. See Alienation.

Practical reasoning In ethnomethodology, the methods by which ordinary people, in their everyday practical affairs, mutually create and sustain their common-sense notions of what is going on.

Precontractual basis of contract Durkheim uses the term to refer to a collective commitment to shared values that are a moral precondition for orderly contractual relations. It refers, in particular, to a commitment to respect for individual differences and human rights.

Predestination See Calvinism.

Prejudice Prejudging, usually in negative terms, the characteristics that are assumed to be shared by members of another group. Preconceived opinion or bias against or in favour of a person or thing. Commonly used to refer to negative opinions of people regarded as outside one's own cultural group.

Prerequisites Those needs or functions that must be met within any social system for that system to maintain a state of balance or equilibrium.

Presentation of self The image that we try to create for ourselves in the eyes of other people whose opinion we value.

Prescriptive norms Shared behavioural expectations concerning what one should do or how one ought to behave in a given situation.

Primitive communism An economic system characterized by a simple hunting and gathering technology where the means of production—the local plants and animals—are accessible to all, and no one has ownership rights to the terrain or to its resources.

Private realm In functionalism, the aspects of society perceived as oriented toward personal life, particularly family and leisure activities.

Privatization In the domestic labour debate, this refers to the process of separating domestic work, and the people—mostly women—who perform it, from other productive activities.

Probability The recognition that social phenomena have multiple causes and involve elements of free choice that cannot be predicted with certainty but can be explored with respect to the likelihood of their occurrence.

Procedural norms Rules that govern how a particular activity, such as contract negotiations, should proceed.

Profane Durkheim uses this term to describe that which does not belong to the sacred. Mundane, ordinary.

Proletariat Wage-labourers who survive by selling their labour power. Those who do not own any means to produce for themselves.

Proscriptive norms Shared behavioural expectations concerning what one should not do or what is unacceptable behaviour in a given situation.

Protectionism The situation where duties are applied to imported goods to raise their sale price relative to the price of equivalent local goods, usually to compensate for higher local production costs.

Protestant ethic Weber uses this term to refer to the moral value accorded to work as a spiritual duty and a sign of God's grace. This value system emphasizes accumulation of wealth as a sign of grace; poverty, laziness, and idle luxury are seen as signs of moral depravity and damnation.

Psychoanalysis A body of theory that focusses on infantile sexual drives and their repression within the nuclear family as the foundations of adult personality.

Psychological reductionism The attempt to explain collective social processes by reference only to the psychological processes within the individuals involved.

Psychologism See Psychological reductionism.

Public issues Mills uses this term to refer to the broad social forces that affect the life experiences of many people in similar circumstances.

Public realm In functionalism, aspects of society, particularly economic and political institutions, that are perceived to be oriented toward the society as a whole.

Purdah A cultural tradition among East Indians that emphasizes the seclusion of women in the home, as part of a pattern of restrictions on their behaviour. Literally, a curtain, especially one serving to screen women from the sight of strangers.

Puritanism A doctrine that emphasizes extreme strictness in moral behaviour such that frivolity, idleness, and luxury, and sex other than for procreation are condemned.

Purposive-rational action Weber uses this term to describe action based on calculation of the most effective means to achieve a particular desired outcome, balanced against probable costs.

Qualitative methods Methods that are not based on quantitative procedures. These methods are used to explore small settings in depth with the goal of gaining insight that may form the basis for generalizations.

Quantitative methods A methodological approach that counts instances of specified aspects of human behaviour in order to derive broad generalizations about patterns of experience.

Questionnaires A formulated series of questions used in survey research.

Race A concept that refers to people's visible and inherited physical differences that are socially noticed. It is commonly associated with differences in skin colour.

Racism Prejudicial attitudes toward groups perceived to be different on the basis of inescapable genetic characteristics. Feelings of antagonism, commonly associated with hostile and discriminatory behaviour toward people of a different race or visibly distinct descent group.

Radical One who advocates fundamental change that goes to the root of the existing social order as distinct from one advocating piecemeal changes.

Radical feminism Feminist theory that focusses on control over sexuality and relations of reproduction.

Radical microsociology The study of everyday life in second-by-second detail, using such techniques as audio- and video-recordings to permit the detailed analysis of conversations and nonverbal interaction.

Rationalization Cost-benefit analysis generally, with both costs and benefits defined primarily in narrow and technical terms rather than incorporating all social and emotional costs and benefits. Also, concentrating production in one or a few large enterprises with the objective of minimizing unit production costs. An aspect of the strategy of maximizing economies of scale.

Rational-legal authority Weber uses the term to describe authority legitimated by reference to the practical utility of the rules themselves.

Rebel A category in Merton's anomie theory of crime. One who replaces socially valued goals with alternative goals and who adopts alternative means to achieve these new goals.

Recipe knowledge Awareness of typical patterns of actions, learned through socialization, that provide a basis for interpreting the meaning of particular actions.

Reconstituted family A family produced by combining some members of two previously separate families, usually produced by the second marriage or one or both spouses who bring children from a previous marriage or partnership.

Reductionism The tendency to explain complex phenomena by reference to a single cause. The attempt to explain complex social processes by reference only to some lower level of analysis (i.e., to explain social phenomena by individual psychology). See Psychological reductionism.

Reflexive/Reflexivity In ethnomethodology, the assumption that there is a mutually determining relationship between appearances and underlying patterns. What one notices about an object or event is contingent upon what one assumes it to be. Similarly, what one assumes it to be is contingent upon the details that one notices.

Refugee status Status that can be accorded those fleeing to a foreign country to escape persecution.

Regulation Durkheim uses the term to refer to values and rules that restrain individual self-interest for the good of the social whole.

Reification The tendency to impute causal force or motives to abstract concepts such as society or markets instead of to the activities of people.

Relations of production Refers to how people organize to produce goods.

Relations of reproduction Refers to how people organize to produce children and raise them to maturity.

Relative deprivation The subjective experience of poverty or loss in comparison with other people rather than in terms of an absolute measure of penury.

Relative surplus Marx uses this term to refer to the amount of surplus production available after payment of wages, when the productivity of workers is increased through labour-saving technology.

Religion Durkheim describes religion as a unified system of beliefs and practices, relative to sacred things, which unite into a single moral community—a church—all adherents.

Repressive law Durkheim uses the term to refer to law that is essentially religious in character and that is concerned with punishing offenders who have transgressed the shared values of the community.

Reserve army of labour Marx uses the term to refer to those people who can be drawn into the labour market when needed by capitalists but let go, often to return to unpaid domestic work, when no longer needed.

Restitutive law Durkheim uses this term to refer to law that is concerned with the regulation of contracts and the re-establishment of reciprocal obligations between members of a society.

Retreatist A category in Merton's anomie theory of crime. One who rejects or gives up on socially approved goals and who fails to conform to behavioural expectations.

Right of national treatment Part of the free trade agreement between the American and Canadian governments. Any enterprise based in one country but doing business in the other would be subject to the same regulations as those that apply to local enterprise.

Ritualist A category in Merton's anomie theory of crime. One who rejects or gives up socially valued goals but conforms to behavioural expectations.

Role A typical pattern of behaviour in a predefined situation or status. In ethnomethodology, interpreting behaviour after the fact so as to render it meaningful or accountable, rather than random.

Role distancing Goffman uses the term to refer to a way of performing a social role so as to convey to onlookers the impression that this is not an activity to which one is wholeheartedly committed.

Role model A person whom others strive to emulate in the performance of a particular role.

Role segregation A separation of roles in time and space, which partly insulates one role from others.

Role set The set of all roles with which a person interacts in the process of playing a specific role. Alternatively, the set of all the different roles that any one person plays simultaneously.

Role strain The conflicting expectations and demands that the person playing a specific role experiences from other people in the wider set of related roles. Also, the conflicting expectations and demands that people experience when playing several different roles simultaneously.

Role-taking Mead uses the term to describe the way in which children develop an image of themselves through trying to see themselves as they appear to others.

Role theory In functionalism, the theory concerned with the patterns of interaction established in the performance of typical activities or functions in society.

Ruling apparatus The totality of processes through which the work of governing a society occurs, including the work of employees in local offices and the forms and documents around which their work is organized.

Sacred For Durkheim, that which is set apart by a community of people as the expression or symbol of highest spiritual value. Often, but not necessarily, that which is consecrated to a deity.

Sample A separated part of a population or type of situation being studied, which is used in research to illustrate the qualities of the population from which the part is drawn.

Science A search for knowledge that tries to test tentative assumptions or explanations through the systematic search for evidence.

Scientific management A principle of management of manual work based on the fragmentation of tasks into their smallest component actions, each of which can be precisely regulated through time and motion studies to achieve the maximum possible speed of performance. Sometimes referred to as Taylorism, after Frederick Taylor, the engineer who first developed the system.

Scientism A reliance on simple cause-and-effect explanatory models that imply that external forces rather than human agency determine human experience.

Secondary analysis Analysis that uses data collected in previous research for some other purpose.

Secondary deviance Used in labelling theory to refer to deviance caused or prompted by the sense of being considered a deviant person by other people.

Self The image of oneself comprising both spontaneous feelings and learned attributes.

Self-estrangement Absence of a sense of personal involvement or pride in what one does and hence a detachment from it. See Alienation.

Semiproletarianization The situation of people who were formerly self-sufficient producers but who have to take part-time wagework to survive.

Separation In the context of ethnic relations, this term refers to two or more distinct ethnic groups living within the same nation-state but maintaining separate political, economic, and cultural institutions and having minimal interaction.

Serf A tied labourer on a feudal estate. A person whose service is attached to the land and transferred with it.

Sets of roles See Role set.

Sex Biological differences in reproductive capacities of males and females.

Sex roles Activities that are defined within a particular culture as the typical responsibility only of women or only of men.

Sexism/Sexist bias Stereotyped and usually derogatory attitudes or discriminatory behaviour toward people of one sex, commonly but not necessarily toward people of the opposite sex.

Sexual class Location of women and men relative to the organization of the activities of reproduction involving conception, pregnancy, childbirth, nurturing, consuming, domestic labour, and wage earning.

Shareholder capitalism   The thesis that ownership of capital is becoming democratized through large numbers of people owning shares.

Shoptalk   The shorthand jargon that can be used in conversations between people who share specialized background understandings.

Significant others   People whose relationship to us and whose opinions of us are important.

Signified   The mental concept to which a signifier refers; e.g., a picture of a suitcase with an arrow (signifier) refers to the baggage claim area in an airport (signified).

Signifier   The physical form of a sign. In language, the sound or the word.

Skilled labour time   A concept developed by Marx to refer to the time it takes for a skilled person to produce a commodity. It includes the average time taken to learn the skill, including the teacher's time.

Slavery   Economic organization in which some persons are the legal property of another or others and are bound to labour for them.

Small groups laboratories   Rooms that, in order to facilitate experiments, are designed to permit a researcher to control a wide variety of factors that might influence interaction within a small group of people.

Social action   In functionalism, the structures and processes by which people form meaningful intentions and, more or less successfully, implement them in concrete situations. Weber used the term to refer to any human conduct that is meaningfully oriented to the past, present, or future expected behaviour of others.

Social construction of reality/Social constructionis   A theoretical perspective, loosely associated with Marxist theory, that explores how the immediate practical activities of people in their everyday working lives produce the patterns that we subsequently come to recognize as social structures.

Social facts   Durkheim uses this term to refer to social phenomena that are experienced as external to the individual and as constraints on the individual's behaviour.

Social Gospel movement   A movement that stresses the doctrine of collective social responsibility and the links between Christianity and socialism. Concepts of sin and salvation are interpreted in social rather than individual terms.

Social order   In ethnomethodology, the active processes of creating and sustaining notions of underlying patterns in the otherwise undefined flux of experience. It is accomplished through practical, everyday reasoning.

Social structures   A broad macrosociological term, referring to large-scale and long-term patterns of organization in society. Roughly equivalent to social institutions. In ethnomethodology, the outcome of practical reasoning processes engaged in by sociologists and others, to account for what seems to be going on. See Institutions.

Social system   In functionalism, the structures and processes that collectively organize action and manage the potential for conflict and disorganization to maintain order over time.

Socialism   A political and economic theory that advocates collective responsibility for the well-being of members of a society.

Social feminism   Feminist theory that focusses on the linkages between the economy and domestic division of labour.

Socialization   The lifelong process through which we learn the values and expected patterns of behaviour appropriate for particular social groups and specific roles. This learning process is particularly intense in infancy but continues throughout life as we change roles and group membership.

Socially necessary labour time   See Abstract labour time.

Society   Generally, the multiple interactions of individuals in a particular setting. A set of forces exerted by people over one another and over themselves. In functionalism, the term refers to a relatively self-sufficient, functioning social system comprising interdependent parts—polity, economy, family, administration, and so on—that each perform specialized functions for the whole. Parsons uses the term to refer to a large-scale social system that controls behaviour within a given territory, has relatively clear membership status, and is capable of meeting all the life needs of members from birth to death.

Sociobiology   The study of the biological bases of social behaviour.

Sociological imagination   The capacity to understand the relationships between elements of society and their impact on individual lives. The ability to use information in a critical way to achieve an understanding of what is going on in the world and what may be happening within one's own life experience.

Sociology   The scientific study of society. The study of relations of social life. Mills uses the term to refer to the study of the major parts or strctures of society (polity, economy, church, family, and so on), how these are interrelated, how they came to be as they appear, how they are changing, and the qualities or characteristics of the people involved. Weber uses this term to refer to the science that attempts the interpretive understanding of social action to arrive at an explanation of its cause and effects.

Solidarity   Durkheim uses the term to refer to the emotional experience of cohesion and bonding between individuals so that they feel integrated into a social whole.

Specific obligations   The perceived right of others to expect only a narrow range of services confined to the precise task at hand, such as in a business contract.

Sponsored immigrant   A category within the Immigration Act that refers to people who are permitted to enter Canada as the dependants of a resident of Canada who agrees to take financial responsibility for them.

State   Within the social construction of reality approach, the term is used to refer to the whole spectrum of government, including the behaviour of people at all levels of the civil service and related bureaucracies, agencies, departments, and offices.

Status   Generally, the position that one occupies in a society. Weber uses the term to refer to social prestige and honour accruing to a person or office.

Status degradation ceremonies   A term used by Garfinkel to refer to rites or actions that publicly signal a drop in social status of a person from a normal member of a group or community to a deviant or stigmatized person.

Stereotypes   Simplified versions of other groups of people. Such mental cartoons are formed by generalizing too much or exaggerating people's characteristics on the basis of too little information.

Stigma/Stigmatization   Disgrace attaching to some act or characteristic.

Stratification   The hierarchical organization of people in occupations that are differentially rewarded in terms of income, prestige, and authority. A general ranking or pattern of inequality in a society, commonly measured in terms of occupation, income, and education.

Structural correspondence theory   See Correspondence theory.

Structural functionalism   See Functionalism.

Structuralism   See Marxist structuralism.

Structure   See Social structures.

Structuring   The process in time through which actions at any one time set constraints upon subsequent actions.

Subcontracted agency   An organization that is used by another to supply goods or to perform work. The term is used figuratively to refer to domestic workers who provide a variety of goods and services for the benefit of corporations, even though not regulated by a specific contract.

Subcultural theory of deviance   Growing out of Merton's anomie theory of crime, this theory posits that deviance and crime reflect the values of the subculture of which the deviant is a member.

Subculture   A distinctive subset of values and behavioural expectations shared by a particular subgroup within a society.

Subjectivism   Any approach that explains human activity solely by reference to individual motivation without considering broader structural forces and constraints.

Subsidiary   A company controlled by another company that owns a majority of its shares.

Subsidy   Money contributed to an enterprise by the state.

Subsistence   Provision of the necessities of life but with little surplus for luxuries or profit.

Subsistence wage   The minimum wage required to cover the cost of sustaining workers and reproducing the next generation, given prevailing standards of living and education required by such workers.

Substantive norms   Rules that govern what activities should be done (i.e., the responsibilities of participants in a contract).

Suburbs   Residential areas in outlying districts of cities, usually characterized by relatively low-density housing.

Superego   In psychoanalysis, the veneer of learned values and behavioural expectations that control drives and passions.

Superstructure For Marx, all aspects of culture, ideas, religion, legal, and political institutions, and so on, that are seen as determined by the prevailing mode of production in that society.

Supply-curve demand The relationship between supply of a commodity in the market and the demand for it, mediated by the price.

Surplus value For Marx, the difference between the value of the wages paid and the value of the commodities produced by the worker.

Surrogate mother A woman who becomes pregnant in order to produce a child for someone else.

Survey research A methodological approach that utilizes questionnaires or structured interviews in which a series of questions are asked of a sample of people. Answers are then analysed with the aid of computers to provide broad comparative information.

Survival of the fittest The thesis that those biological organisms and societies that survive and prosper are the fittest or best adapted to their environment.

Symbolic brackets Erikson uses the term to refer to the culturally defined limits of acceptable behaviour that distinguish members of a community from nonmembers.

Symbolic interaction A theoretical approach within the interpretive perspective. It focusses on micro-interactions and how people use gestures and language to convey typical meanings in interaction with others who share a common cultural background.

Synthesis See Dialectic; Dialectical materialism.

System A complex whole. A set of connected parts.

System prerequisites For Parsons, the basic requirements of pattern maintenance, integration, goal attainment, and adaptation found in any ongoing social system and subsystem.

Systems theory The study of society as a whole or of specific elements of society as functionally interrelated elements, analogous to a biological organism or an organ within such an organism. The central focus is on how a stable balance is maintained between elements.

Taboo Sacred ban or prohibition.

Taylorism See Scientific management.

Technical civilization A vision of society as comprising a dense network of interlocking bureaucratic organizations penetrating all aspects of social life. See Bureaucratic society; Disciplinary society.

Technics/Language of technics The use of computer terminology to refer to human interaction (i.e., feedback, input, output instead of dialogue, debate, judgment).

Technocratic-meritocratic thesis The theory that hierarchy and social inequality in industrial societies reflect differential competence of individuals with respect to science and technology. See Meritocracy thesis.

Text See Textual analysis.

Textual analysis A methodological approach that involves the detailed study of particular pieces of writing to reveal how meaning is constructed by the text.

Theological stage A stage in Comte's model of the evolution of societies. In the theological stage, societies are dominated by primitive religious thought, and explanations for phenomena are expressed primarily in terms of supernatural forces.

Theory of exchange In Marxist analysis, the theory that the exchange value of a commodity is determined by the amount of labour that goes into a commodity. Under capitalism, the basis of exchange is money, rather than another commodity.

Theory of modernization A theory originating in Spencer's model of societal evolution. It sees societies evolving toward increased differentiation and specialization in political, cultural, economic, and social areas.

Therapeutic intervention For Foucault, the process of manipulating conformity and consensus in society through technical means developed in the social sciences and justified by reference to efficiency and healthy psychological and social adjustment.

Thesis See Dialectic; Dialectical materialism.

Third World The impoverished and technologically backward regions of Latin America, Africa, and Asia.

Totem Any natural object, especially a local animal or plant, that is recognized as the symbol or emblem of a clan or sometimes of an individual.

Traditional authority For Weber, authority legitimated by custom, such as that of hereditary rulers.

Traditional-rational action Weber uses the term to refer to action that is based on habit.

Transfer pricing   The prices charged when goods and services are exchanged between a parent corporation and one of its subsidiaries or between two subsidiaries of the same parent corporation.

Typify/Typifications   Sets of shared assumptions concerning what is normal behaviour for people in related roles or social positions. See Background understandings.

Typology   A theoretical model defining different categories or elements of a phenomenon.

Underdeveloped society   A society in which critical economic resources have been and still are being plundered and the internal economy undermined by processes within the world capitalist economic system.

Undeveloped society   A society in which the economy continues to function in an unchanged, traditional pattern without benefit of technological advance.

Universal functionalism   Parsons uses the term to refer to the assumption, borrowed from biology, that every element found within a social system must perform some function for the whole society.

Universalism/Universalistic standards   For Parsons, evaluation based on objective criteria that apply equally to any person performing a given activity.

Unobtrusive measures   Measures that avoid the possibility of influencing the phenomenon being measured.

Utterances   In ethnomethodology, sounds made by a person before they have been interpreted as having any meaning.

Vacuum ideology   An attitude that children from minority cultures learn virtually nothing worth knowing outside of school.

Value-rational action   Weber's term for action based on beliefs.

Values   The beliefs shared among members of a group or society concerning qualities thought to be desirable or esteemed.

Variable   Any phenomenon that has more than one value.

Verstehen   The interpretation of behaviour as involving meaningful intentions. A methodological approach that involves trying to reconstruct the interpretations that the people being studied might give to their own actions.

Vertical integration   Enterprises that operate at different stages in the production of a particular commodity and are consolidated into one corporation.

Vertical mosaic   A pattern of stratification in which members of different racial and ethnic groups are arranged vertically with respect to each other in terms of class position.

Victimless crimes   Transactional crimes where the persons involved participate willingly in exchanging goods and services and do not see themselves as either criminals or victims. Crimes against morality where there are no clear victims.

Vocation   For Weber, performance of the responsibilities of an office as a duty, not for personal gain.

Voluntarism   An explanation for action that refers to the rational and free choice of the actor.

Voluntaristic theory   For Parsons, a theory of social action that explains social order by reference to mutual agreement or consensus between actors.

Welfare state   A state that provides a range of social services for workers, including such benefits as health care, unemployment insurance, welfare payments, pensions, and the like. Such services ameliorate the effects of cyclical ups and downs in the economy as well as helping workers survive personal crises.

White-collar crime   Violations of the law committed by professional and business people.

Worked up   An expression used by Smith to describe the state of raw sense data having been categorized and organized in terms of an interpretive framework in the process of communicating it.

REFERENCES

Chapter 1

Berger, Peter L. 1963. *Invitation to Sociology: A Humanistic Perspective.* New York: Anchor Books.

Boughey, Harold. 1978. *The Insights of Sociology: An Introduction* Boston: Allyn and Bacon.

Carey, A. 1967. "The Hawthorne Studies: A Radical Critique." *American Sociological Review* 32:403–416.

Dandaneau, Steven. 2001. *Taking it Big: Developing Sociological Consciousness in Postmodern Times.* Thousand Oaks, California: Pine Forge Press.

Feyerabend, P.K. 1970. "How to Be a Good Empiricist: A Plea for Tolerance in Matters Epistemological." In *Readings in the Philosophy of Science.* Ed. B.A. Brody. Englewood Cliffs, NJ: Prentice Hall, Goffman, Erving. 1961. *Asylums.* Harmondsworth, Eng.: Penguin.

Hale, Sylvia M. 1992. "Facticity and Dogma in Introductory Sociology Texts: The Need for Alternative Methods." p. 135–153 in William K. Carroll, Linda Christiansen-Ruffman, Raymond F. Currie and Deborah Harrison (eds). *Fragile Truths: 25 years of Sociology and Anthropology in Canada.* Ottawa, ON: Carleton University Press.

Mayo, Elton. [1933] 1960. *The Human Problems of Industrial Civilization.* New York: Viking.

Mills, C. Wright. 1959. *The Sociological Imagination.* New York: Oxford University Press.

Mueller, Adele and Marilee Reimer. 2006. Stress and the transition from university to career: Career development supports for undergraduate women in Atlantic Canadian liberal arts. Paper presented at the Canadian Association for the Study of Women and Education 6th Bi-Annual Institute, May 30–June 1. York University.

Nicholson, J. 1984. *"Men and Women: How Different Are They?"* Oxford: Oxford University Press.

Smith, Dorothy E. 1990. *The Conceptual Practices of Power: A Feminist Sociology of Knowledge.* Toronto: University of Toronto Press.

Swift, Karen J. 1995. *Manufacturing 'Bad Mothers': A Critical Perspective On Child Neglect.* Toronto: University of Toronto Press.

Chapter 2

Aberle, D.F., A.K. Cohen, A.K. Davis, M.J. Levy Jr., and F.X. Sutton. 1950. "The Functional Prerequisites of a Society" *Ethics* 60(Jan.):100–11.

Acker, Joan. 1997. "My Life as a Feminist Sociologist; or, Getting the man out of My Head" in Ed. B. Laslett and B. Thorne *Feminist Sociology. Life Histories of a Movement* New Brunswick, NJ: Rutgers University Press 28–49.

Barker, C. 1999. *Television, Globalization and Cultural Identities* Buckingham, Philadelphia: Open University Press.

Barndt, Deborah. 2002. *Tangled Roots: Women, Work, and Globalization on the Tomato Trail.* Aurora, Ontario: Garamond Press.

Barthes. 1971. "The Rhetoric of the Image." *Cultural Studies* 1.

Bear-Nicholas, Andrea. 1994. "Colonialism and the Struggle for Liberation: The Experience of Maliseet Women" *University of New Brunswick Law Journal* 43:223–239.

Bear-Nicholas, Andrea. 2004. "Comments on final manuscript Changing Your World: Investigating Empowerment" Native Studies Department, St. Thomas University, Fredericton, NB Canada.

Bellah, Robert. 1990. "Civil Religion in America" pp 262–272 in Alexander, J.C. and S. Seidman (eds) *Culture and Society: Contemporary Debates* Cambridge & New York: Cambridge University Press.

Berg, Bruce. 2001. *Qualitative Research Methods for the Social Sciences.*

Berger, Peter L. 1963 *Invitation to Sociology: A Humanistic Perspective.* New York: Anchor Books.

Berger, Peter. 1967. *The Sacred Canopy. Elements of a Sociological Theory of Religion* New York: Doubleday.

Bernal, Victoria. 2004. "Eritrea Goes Global: Reflections on Nationalism in a Transnational Era" *Cultural Anthropology* 19(1):3–25.

Biddle, B.J. and E.J. Thomas, (eds). 1966. *Role Theory: Concepts and Research* New York: John Wiley and Sons.

Bibby, Reginald W. 1993. *Unknown Gods.*

Bibby, Reginald W. 2002. *Restless Gods. The Renaissance of Religion in Canada* Toronto: Stoddard.

Bonner, Kieran. 1994. "Hermeneutics and Symbolic Interactionism: The Problem of Solipsism". *Human Studies* 17:225–249.

Bonner, Kieran M. 2001. "Reflexivity and Interpretive Sociology: The Case of Analysis and the Problem of Nihilism." *Human Studies* 24:267–292.

Boughey, H. 1978. *The Insights of Sociology: An Introduction* Boston: Allyn & Bacon.

Brym, Robert J. with Bonnie Fox. 1989. *From Culture to Power. The Sociology of English Canada* Toronto: Oxford University Press.

Burnett, Jonathan. 2004. "Community, cohesion and the state" *Race and Class* 45(3):1–18.

Campbell, Marie and Ann Manicom (eds). 1995. *Knowledge, Experience, and Ruling Relations: Studies in the Social Organization of Knowledge* Toronto: University of Toronto Press.

Cassin, A.M. 1979. *Advancement Opportunities in the British Columbia Public Service.* British Columbia, Economic Analysis and Research Bureau. Ministry of Industry and Small Business Development.

Cassin, A.M. 1980. *"The Routine Production of Inequality: Implications for Affirmative Action".* Paper, Ontario Institute for Studies in Education.

Chodorow, N. 1989. *Feminism and psychoanalytic Theory.* Cambridge: Polity Press.

Chodorow, N. 1978. *The reproduction of Motherhood.* Berkeley, CA: University of California Press.

Clark, Samuel D. 1968. *The Developing Canadian Community* 2nd edition. Toronto: University of Toronto Press.

Clegg, S. and D. Dunkerley 1980. *Organization, Class, and Control.* London: Routledge and Kegan Paul.

Clow, M. with S. Machum 1993. *Stifling Debate: Canadian Newspapers and Nuclear Power.* Halofax: Fernwood.

Cohen, A.K. 1955. *Delinquent Boys: The Culture of the Gang* New York: Free Press.

Corrigan, P. *Schooling the Smash Street Kids* London: Macmillan.

Coser, L.A. 1956. *The functions of Social Conflict* Glencoe, IL: Free Press.

Connell, R. W. 1997. "Long and Winding Road" In Ed. Barbara Laslett and Barrie Thorne, *Feminist Sociology. Life Histories of a Movement* New Brunswick, New Jersey: Rutgers University Press 151–164.

Connell, R.W. 1987. *Gender & Power* Stanford, CA: Stanford University Press.

Cooley, C.H. 1964. *Human Nature and the Social Order.* New York: Schocken.

Curran, Laura. 2003. "The Culture of Race, Class, and Poverty: The Emergence of a Cultural Discourse in Early Cold War Social Work" (1946–1963) *Journal of Sociology and Social Welfare* 30(3):15–37.

Dandaneau, Steven 2001. *Taking it Big. Developing Sociological Consciousness in Postmodern Times.* Thousand Oaks, California: Pine Force Press.

Denzin, N.K. 1992. *Symbolic Interactionism and Cultural Studies: The Politics of Interpretation* Cambridge, MA: Blackwell.

DeVault, Marjorie L. and Lisa McCoy. 2002. "Institutional Ethnographies: Using interviews to Investigate Ruling Relations" pp 751–776 in Gubrium, Jaber E. and James A. Holstein (eds) *Handbook of Interview Research. Context and method.* Thousand Oaks: Sage.

Diamond, Jared 1999. *Guns, Germs, and Steel: The Fates of Human Societies.* New York: Norton.

Diamond, Sara. 1998. *Not By Politics Alone. The Enduring Influence of the Christian Right.* New York and London: The Guildford Press.

Douglas, M. 1979. *World of Goods: Toward an Anthropology of Consumption.* London: Allen Lane.

Douglas, M. 1966. *Purity and Danger: An Analysis of the Concepts of Pollution and Taboo* New York: Pantheon.

England, Paula 1999.

Fairclough, Norman. 2003. *Language in the new Capitalism* Language for new Capitalism website cddc.ve.edu/host/incarchive.html.

Fairclough, Norman. 2000. *New Language, New Labour* Routledge.

Fairclough, Norman. 2000. "Discourse, social Theory and Social Research: The Discourse of 'Welfare reform'" *Journal of Sociolinguistics* 4,(2).

Fairclough, Norman. 2000. "Global Capitalism and Critical Awareness of Language" *Language Awareness* 8(2).

Faludi, S. 1991. *Backlash: The Undeclared War Against American Women.* New York: Doubleday Anchor Books.

Foucault, M. 1980. *Power/Knowledge: Selected Interviews and Other Writings* 1972–1977. Ed. C. Gordon. New York: Pantheon.

Foucault, M. 1978. *The History of Sexuality. Vol. 1.* New York: Vintage.

Foucault, M. 1977. *Discipline and Punish: The Birth of the Prison* London: Allen Lane.

Frank, B. 1987. "Hegemonic heterosexual Masculinity" *Studies in Political Economy* 24 (Autumn):159–70.

Franklin, S., C. Lury, and J. Stacey, Eds. 1991. *Off-Centre: Feminism and Cultural Studies.* Cultural Studies, Birmingham Series. London: HarperCollins Academic

Freud, S. 1905. *The Standard Edition of the Complete Psychological Works of Sigmund Freud.* Vol 7. *The Three Essays on the Theory of Sexuality.* London: The Hogarth Press.

Freud, S. [1905]. 1976. "Three Essays on the Theory of Sexuality" In J. Strachey, trans. And ed. *The Complete Psychological Works.* Vol. 7. New York: Norton.

Fyvel, T.R. 1963. *The Insecure Offenders* London: Chatto & Windus.

Garfinkel, Harold. 1967. *Studies in Ethnomethodology* Englewood Cliffs, NJ: Prentice Hall.

Giddens, Anthony. 2000. *Runaway World. How globalization is Reshaping Our Lives* New York: Routledge.

Giddens, Anthony. 1984. *The Constitution of Society. Outline of the Theory of Structuration* Berkeley and Los Angeles: University of California Press.

Giddens, Anthony. 1983. "Four Theses on Ideology" *Canadian Journal of Political and Social Theory* 7.

Giddens, Anthony 1979. *Central Problems in Social Theory* London: Macmillan.

Goffman, E. 1959. *The Presentation of Self in Everyday Life* Garden City, N.J.: Doubleday.

Goffman, E. 1961a *Asylums* Harmondsworth: Penguin.

Goffman, E. 1961b "Role Distance." In *Encounters: Two Studies in the Sociology of Interaction* New York: Bobbs-Merrill.

Goffman, E. 1963. *Stigma: Notes on the Management of Spoiled Identity.* Englewood Cliffs, N.J.: Prentice Hall.

Gramsci, Antonio. 1971. *Selections from Prison Notebooks.* Ed and trans. Q. Hoare and G. Nowell-Smith. New York: International Publishers.

Grosz, E. 1990. *Jacques Lacan: A Feminist Introduction.* London: Routledge.

Hardt, Michael and Antonio Negri. 2000. *Empire* Cambridge, Massachusetts: Harvard University Press.

Hebdige, D. 1979. *Subculture: The Meaning of Style* London: Methuen.

Horowitz, D.L. 1985. *Ethnic Groups in Conflict.* Berkeley, CA: University of California Press.

Irigaray, L. 1985. *This Sex Which is Not One* trans. C. Porter and C. Burke. Ithaca, NY: Cornell University Press.

Jaggar, A.M., and P.S. Rothenberg. 1984. *Feminist Frameworks: Alternative Theoretical Accounts of the Relations Between Women and Men* 2nd ed. New York: McGraw-Hill.

Kalberg, Stephen. 2003. "The Influence of Political Culture upon Cross-Cultural Misperceptions and Foreign Policy. The United States and Germany." *German Politics and Society* 21(3):1–23.

Khayatt, M.D. 1992. *Lesbian Teachers: An Invisible Presence.* Albany, NY: State University of New York.

Kinsmen, G. 1987. *The Regulation of Desire: Sexuality in Canada.* Montreal: Black Rose Books.

Kintz, Linda and Julia Lessage (eds). 1998. *Media, Culture, and the Religious Right* Minnesota: University of Minnesota Press.

Klein, Naomi. 2000. *No Logo. Taking Aim At The Brand Bullies* Toronto: Vintage Canada.

Kreiger, Susan. 1997. "Lesbian in Academe" in Ed. B. Laslett and B. Thorne *Feminist Sociology. Life Histories of a Movement* New Brunswick, NJ: Rutgers University Press 194–208.

Kristeva, J. 1986. *The Kristeva Reader.* Ed T. Moi. *Oxford: Blackwell.*

Lacan, J. 1972. "The Insistence of the Letter in the Unconscious" In *The Structuralists: From Marx to Levi-Strauss* Ed. R. DeGeorge and F. DeGeorge. Garden City, NY: Anchor Books, 287–324.

Laframboise, Celia and Leigh West 1987–88 "The Case of All-Male Clubs: Freedom to Associate or Licence to Discriminate?" *Canadian Journal of Women and Law* 2:335–361.

Laslett, Barbara and Barrie Thorne, Eds. 1997. *Feminist Sociology. Life Histories of a Movement* New Brunswick, New Jersey: Rutgers University Press.

Lengermann, P.M. and J. Niebrugge-Brantley. 1990. "Feminist Sociological Theory: The Near Future Prospects" In *Frontiers of Social Theory: The New Synthesis* Ed. G. Ritzer. New York: Columbia University Press, 316–44.

Lewis, Justin. 2001. *Constructing Public Opinion: How Political Elites Do What They Like and Why We Seem to Go Along With It* New York: Columbia University Press.

Lipset, Seymour M. 1976. "Radicalism in North America: A Comparative View of the Party Systems in Canada and the United States" *Transactions of the Royal Society of Canada (Series IV)* vol.14:19–55.

Lipset, Seymour M. 1985. "Canada and the United States: The Cultural Dimension" pp 109–160 in C. Doran and J. Sigler eds. *Canada and the United States* Scarborough, Ont: Prentice Hall of Canada.

Lorde, A. 1984. *Sister Outsider.* New York: Crossing Press.

Loseke, D.R. 1987. "The Construction of Social Problems: The Case of Wife Abuse" *Symbolic interaction* 10,2:229–43.

Mannette, Joy A. 1992. "The social construction of ethnic containment: The Royal Commission on the Donald Marshall Jr. Prosecution" in *Elusive Justice. Beyond the Marshall Inquiry* Joy Mannette (ed) Halifax: Fernwood Poress.

Marshall, Barbara L. 2000. *Configuring Gender. Explorations in Theory and Politics* Peterborough, ON: Broadview Press.

McClung, Nellie. 1972. *In Times Like These* Toronto: University of Toronto Press.

McKendy, J. 1992. "Ideological Practices and the Management of Emotions: The Case of "Wife Abusers.'" *Critical Sociology* 19,2:61–80.

Mead, G.H. 1934. *Mind, Self, and Society.* Chicago: University of Chicago Press.

Merkel, UDO. 2003. "The Politics of Physical Culture and German Nationalism: Turnen versus English Sports and French Olympism" *German Politics & Society* 21(2):69–96.

Merton, Robert 1967 *On Theoretical Sociology: Five Essays, Old and New* New York: Free Press.

Miles, Robert and Rudy Torres. 1996. "Does 'Race' Matter? Transatlantic Perspectives on Racism after 'Race Relations'" in Amit-Talai, Vered and Caroline Knowles (eds) *Resituating Identities: The Politics of Race, Ethnicity, and Culture* Peterborough, Ontario: Broadview Press.

Mitchell, J. 1975. *Psychoanalysis and Feminism.* New York: Random House.

Nakano-Glenn, Evelyn. 1997. "Looking back in Anger? Remembering my Sociological Career" in Ed. B. Lazlett and B. Thorne *Feminist Sociology. Life Histories of a Movement* New Brunswick, NJ: Rutgers University Press 73–102.

Nesbitt-Larking, Paul. 2001. *Politics, Society, and the Media: Canadian Perspectives* Toronto: Broadview Press.

O'Brien, M. 1981. *The Politics of Reproduction* London: Routledge & Kegan Paul.

Pizzey, E. *1975 Scream Quietly or the Neighbours Will Hear.*

Porter, john. 1965. *The Vertical Mosaic. An Analysis of Social Class and Power in Canada.* Toronto: University of Toronto Press.

Porter, John 1979. *The measure of Canadian Society: Education, Equality and Opportunity.* Toronto: Gage.

Psathas, G. 1980. Early Goffman and the Analysis of Face-To-Face Interaction" in *Strategic Interaction. The View from Goffman.* Ed. J. Ditton. London: Macmillan, 52–79.

Rushton, J.P. 1988. "Race differences in behaviour: A review and evolutionary analysis". *Personality and Individual Differences* 9(6):1035–40.

Said, E. 1978. *Orientalism* London: Penguin.

Saussure, F. de [1916]1964. *Course in General Linguistics.* New York: McGraw-Hill.

Seidman, Steven. 1994. *Contested Knowledge. Social Theory in the Postmodern Era* Oxford UK and Cambridge USA: Blackwell.

Seidman, Steven. 1996. *Queer Theory/Sociology. Oxford: Basil Blackwell.*

Sharrock, W.W. 1987. "Individual and Society" in *Classic Disputes in Sociology.* Ed. R.J. Anderson, J.A. Hughes, and W.W. Sharrock. London: Allem & Unwin, 126–55.

Sklair, Leslie. 2002. *Globalization. Capitalism and its Alternatives.* Oxford: Oxford University Press.

Smith, D.E. 1975. "An Analysis of Ideological Structures and how Women Are Excluded: Considerations for Academic Women" *Canadian Review of Sociology and Anthropology* 12,4:353–69.

Smith, D. E. 1977. *Feminism and Marxism—A Place To Begin, A Way To Go* Vancouver: New Star Books.

Smith, D.E. 1979. "Using the Oppressor's Language" *Resources For Feminist Research* Special Publication no. 5 (Spring).

Smith, D.E. and G. Malnarich 1983. "Where Are The Women? A Critique of Socialist and Communist Political Organization" paper presented at the Conference on Marxism: The Next Two Decades: University of Manitoba.

Smith, D.E. 1992a "Sociology from Women's Experience: A Reaffirmation" *Sociological Theory* 10,1:88–98.

Smith, D.E. 1992b "Whistling Women: Reflections on Rage and Rationality." In Ed. W.K. Carroll (and others) *Fragile Truths: 25 Years of Sociology in Canada* Ottawa: Carleton University Press.

Smith, George W. 1998. The ideology of "Fag": The School Experience of Gay Students" *The Sociological Quarterly* 39,2:309–335.

Solomos, J. and L. Back. 1994. "Conceptualizing Racisms: Social Theory, Politics and Research" *Sociology* 28(1):143–161.

Stacey, Judith. 1997. "Disloyal to the Disciplines: A Feminist Trajectory in the Borderlands" In Ed. Barbara Laslett and Barrie Thorne, *Feminist Sociology. Life Histories of a Movement* New Brunswick, New Jersey: Rutgers University press 126–150.

Staggenborg, Suzanne. 2001. "Beyond Culture Versus Politics. A Case Study of a Local Women's Movement" *Gender and Society* 15(4):507–530.

Thorne, Barrie. 1997. "Brandeis as a Generative Institution: Critical Perspective, Marginality, and Feminism" 103–125 in Barbara Laslett and Barrie Thorne, Eds. 1997. *Feminist Sociology. Life Histories of a Movement* New Brunswick, New Jersey: Rutgers University Press.

Tong, R. 1989. *Feminist Thought: A Comprehensive Introduction* Boulder, CO: Westview Press.

Turner, G. 1990. *British Cultural Studies: An Introduction* Boston: Unwin Hyman.

Van Zoonen. 1994. *Feminist Media Studies.* London, Thousand Oaks, CA: Sage.

Walker, G. 1990a" The Conceptual Politics of Struggle: Wife Battering, the Women's Movement, and the State." *Studies in Political Economy* 33:63–90.

Walker, G. 1990b *Family Violence and the Women's Movement: The Conceptual Politics of Struggle.* Toronto: University of Toronto Press.

Weeks, P.A.D. 1988. "Musical Time as a Practical Accomplishment: A Change of Tempo" Paper presented to the Society for Phenomenology and the Human Sciences. Toronto.

Willis, P. 1981. *Learning to Labour: How Working Class Kids Get Working Class Jobs.* New York: Columbia University Press.

Wuthnow, R., J.D. Hunter, A. Bergesen, and E. Kurzweil. 1984. *Cultural Analysis: The Work of Peter L. Berger, Mary Douglas, Michel Foucault, and Jurgen Habermas.* London: Routledge & Kegan Paul.

Chapter 3

Allahar, Anton L. and James E. Cote. 1998. *Richer and Poorer. The Structure of inequality in Canada.* Toronto: Lorimer.

Ammerman, N. 1987. *Bible Believers: Fundamentalists in the Modern World.* New Brunswick, New Jersey: Rutgers.

Archibald, W.P. 1978. *Social Psychology as Political Economy.* Toronto: McGraw-Hill Ryerson.

Baruch, G. 1981. Moral Tales: Parents' stories of encounters with the health profession." *Sociology of Health and Illness* 3(3):275–296.

Bear-Nicholas, Andrea. 2006. Conference on Research and Research Ethics in First Nations Communities: Developing Research Ethics Protocols that Work. February 23, 2006. St. Thomas University, Fredericton, New Brunswick Canada.

Becker, H. S. 1963. *The Outsiders: Studies in the Sociology of Deviance.* New York: Free Press.

Briggs, J.L. 1973. *Never in Anger: Portrait of an Eskimo Family.* Cambridge, MA: Harvard University Press.

Campbell, Marie and Frances Gregor. 2002. *Mapping Social Relations. A primer in Doing Institutional Ethnography.* Aurora, ON: Garamond Press.

Chomski, N. 1988. *Manufacturing Consent: The Political Economy of the Mass Media.* New York: Pantheon.

Cicourel, A.V. 1974. *Theory and Method in a Study of Argentine Fertility.* New York: Wiley.

Comarow, M. 1993. "Are Sociologists above the law?" *The Chronicle of Higher Education.* 15 December, p.A44.

Dobash, R. Emerson and Russell P. Dobash. 2000. "Evaluating Criminal Justice Interventions for Domestic Violence." *Crime and Delinquency.* 46(2) April:252–270.

Dooley, D. 1984. S*ocial Research Methods.* Englewood Cliffs, NJ: Prentice Hall.

Doran, C. 2002. "Medico-legal Expertise and Industrial Disease Compensation" pp in Gayle MacDonald (ed) *Social Context and Social Location in the Sociology of Law* Peterborough, ON: Broadview Press.

Douglas, J. 1967. *The Social Meaning of Suicide.* Princeton: Princeton University Press.

Duelli Klein, R. 1980. "How To Do What We Want To Do: Thoughts About Feminist Methodology." In *Theories of Women's Studies.* Ed. G. Bowles and R. Duelli Klein. Berkeley, CA: University of California Press.

Eichler, M. 1988. *Families in Canada Today: Recent Changes and Their Policy Consequences.* 2nd ed. Toronto: Gage.

Eichler, M. 1985. "And the Work never Ends: Feminist Contributions" *Canadian Review of Sociology and Anthropology* 22 (5):619–44.

Freeman, D. 1983. *Margaret mead and Samoa: The Making and Unmaking of an Anthropological Myth.* Cambridge, MA: Harvard University Press.

Hiller, Harry H. And Linda DiLuzio. 2004. "The Interviewee and the Research Interview: Analyzing a Neglected Dimension in Research" *Canadian Review of Sociology and Anthropology.*

Hochschild, A. 1973. *The Unexpected Community.* Englewood Cliffs, NJ: Prentice-Hall.

Kirby, S. and K. Mckenna. 1989. *Experience, Research, Social Change: Methods from the Margins.* Toronto: Garamond.

Lewis, Justin. 2001. *Constructing Public Opinion: How Political Elites Do What They Like and Why We Seem To Go Along With It.* New York: Columbia University Press.

Lochhead, Clarence and Katherine Scott. 2000. *The Dynamics of Women's Poverty in Canada.* Status of Women Canada.

Mead, M. 1928. *Coming of Age in Samoa: A Psychological Study of Primitive Youth for Western Civilization.* New York: Blue Ribbon Books.

Muzychka, Martha and Carmen Poulin, with Barbara Cottrell, Baukje Miedema and Barbara Roberts. 1995. *Feminist Research Ethics: A Process.* Canadian Research Institute for the Advancement of Women (CRIAW).

Ng, Roxana. 1986. *The Politics of Community Services. Immigrant Women, Class, and the State.* Toronto: Garamond.

Ng, Roxana. 1995. "Multiculturalism as Ideology" pp 35–48 in Marie Campbell and Ann Manicom (eds) *Knowledge, Experience, and Ruling Relations: Studies in the Social Organization of Knowledge.* Toronto: University of Toronto Press.

Nuernberger, Kim. 2004. "Negotiations in Narrative: Exploring the Discursive Constructions of Childbirth in Internet-Based Birth Stories" Paper presented at Canadian Sociology and Anthropology Association meetings June 3, University of Winnipeg.

Oakley, Ann. 1981. "Interviewing Women: A Contradiction in Terms" pp 30–61 in Helen Roberts (ed) *Doing Feminist Research.* London and New York: Routledge.

O'Neill, P. 2000. "Good intentions and awkward outcomes: Ethical gatekeeping in fiend research." Paper presented at the 17th Qualitative Analysis Conference, Fredericton N.B. 18–21 May.

Opie, A. 1992. "Qualitative Research, Appropriation of the 'Other' and Empowerment." *Feminist Review* 40 (Sprint):52–69.

Pecora, Vincent P. 2002. "The Culture of Surveillance" *Qualitative Sociology* 25(3):345–358.

Pryor, Edward T., Gustave J. Goldman, Michael J. Sheridan and Pamela M. White. 1992. "Measuring Ethnicity in 'Canadian': an evolving indigenous category?" *Ethnic and Racial Studies* 15(2):214–235.

Richmond, A.H., M. Lyon, S. Hale, and R. King. 1973. *Migration and Race Relations in an English City.* London: Oxford University Press.

Schissel, Bernard. 1997. *Blaming Children. Youth Crime, Moral Panics, and the Politics of Hate.* Halifax: Fernwood.

Schutt, Russell K. 1996. *Investigating the Social World. The Process and Practice of Research.* Thousand Oaks CA: Pine Force Press.

Sherman, Lawrence W. 1992. *Policing Domestic Violence: Experiments and Dilemmas.* New York: Free Press.

Sherman, Lawrence W. and Richard A. Berk. 1984. "The Specific Deterrent Effects of Arrest for Domestic Assault" *American Sociological Review*, 49:261–272.

Sherman, Lawrence W. and Douglas A. Smith, with Hanell D. Schmidt and Dennis P. Rogan. 1992. "Crime, Punishment, and Stake in Conformity." *American Sociological Review*, 23:117–144.

Silverman, David. 1993. *Interpreting Qualitative Data: Methods for Analysing Talk, Text and Interaction.* London: Sage.

Smith, Dorothy E. 1974. "The Social Construction of Documentary Reality." *Sociological Inquiry* 44(4):257–68.

Smith, Dorothy E. 1999. *Writing the Social: Critique, Theory and Investigations.* Toronto: University of Toronto Press.

Smith, G. 1990. "Political Activist as Ethnographer." *Social Problems* 37(4)Nov:629–48.

Thomas, W.I. and F. Znaniecki. [1919]1971. *The Polish Peasant in Europe and America.* New York: Octagon Books.

Uhlmann, Allon J. 2004. "The sociology of subjectivity, and the subjectivity of sociologists: A critique of the sociology of gender in the Australian family". *The British Journal of Sociology* 55(1):79–97.

Van den Hoonaard, Will. 2001. "Is Research-Ethics Review a Moral Panic?" *The Canadian Review of Sociology and Anthropology.* 38(1):19–36).

Van den Hoonaard. 2004. "Giving Voice to the Spectrum: Is there a Way Out of the Ethics-review Mazeway?" Canadian Sociology and Anthropology Association meetings. Winnipeg June 4.

Van Dijk, Teun A. 1993. *Elite Discourse and Racism* London: Sage.

Warren, John T. 2003. *Performing Purity. Whiteness, Pedagogy, and the Reconstitution of Power.* NY: Peter Laing.

Whyte, W.F. 1943. *Street Corner Society.* Chicago: University of Chicago Press.

Chapter 4

Amit, Vered (ed). 2002. *Realizing Community. Concepts, Social Relationships and Sentiments.* London and New York: Routledge.

Amit, Vered 2002. "Reconceptualizing Community"In *Realizing Community. Concepts, Social Relationships and Sentiments.* Ed. V. Amit. London and New York: Routledge, 1–20.

Anderson, Benedict 1983/1991. *Imagined Communities: Reflections on the Origin and Spread of Nationalism.* London and New York: Verso.

Anderson, G. 1974. *Networks of Contact: The Portuguese and Toronto.* Waterloo, Ont: Wilfrid Laurier University Press.

Anderson, K. 1991. *Vancouver's Chinatown: Racial Discourses in Canada 1875–1980.* Montreal and Kingston: McGill-Queen's University Press.

Anderson, Kim and Bonita Lawrence (eds). 2003. *Strong Women Stories, Native Vision and Community Survival.* Toronto: Sumach Press.

Bannerji, Himani. 2000. *The Dark Side of the Nation: Essays on Multiculturalism, Nationalism and Gender* Toronto: Canadian Scholars Press.

Baskin, C. 2003. "From Victims to Leaders: Activism Against Violence Towards Women" In *Strong Women Stories, Native Vision and Community Survival.* In Ed. K. Anderson and B. Lawrence Toronto: Sumach Press, 213–227.

Bear-Nicholas, A. "St. John River Society and the Dispossession of the Maliseet People". Unpublished. St. Thomas University Dept. Of Native Studies.

Bear-Nicholas, A. 1994 "Colonialism and the Struggle for Liberation: The Experience of Maliseet Women" *University of New Brunswick Law Journal.* Vol. 43:223–239.

Bella, Leslie. 1992. *The Christmas Imperative. Leisure, Family, And Women's Work* Halifax: Fernwood.

Blaney, Fay. 2003. "Aboriginal Women's Action Network" In *Strong Women Stories, Native Vision and Community Survival.* In Ed. K. Anderson and B. Lawrence, Toronto: Sumach Press, 156–170.

Blomley, Nicholas. 2004. *Unsettling the City. Urban Land and the Politics of Property.* New York and London: Routledge.

Bonner, Kieran. 2002. "Understanding, Placemaning: Economics, Politics and Everyday Life in the Culture of Cities." *Canadian Journal of Urban Research* 11(1):1–16.

Bonner, Kieran. 1999. *A Great Place to Raise Kids: Interpretation, Science, and the urban-Rural Debate.* Montreal and Kingston: McGill-Queen's University Press.

Bonner, Kieran. 1998. "Reflexivity, Sociology, and the Rural-Urban Distinction in Marx, Tönnies, and Weber." *The Canadian Review of Sociology and Anthropology* 35(2) May:165–189.

Bressette, Shelly E. 2003. "The truth about us: Living in the aftermath of the Ipperwash crisis. In *Strong Women Stories, native Vision and Community Survival.* Ed.K. Anderson and B. Lawrence Toronto: Sumach Press, 228–241.

Burrill, G. and I. McKay, eds. 1978. *People, Resources, and Power: Critical Perspectives on Underdevelopment and Primary Industries in the Atlantic Region.* Fredericton: Acadiensis Press.

Calhoun, J.B. 1963. "Population Density and Social Pathology." in *The Urban condition.* Ed. L. Duhl. New York: Basic Books, 33–43.

Clairmont, D.H. and D. W. Macgill [1974]1999. *Africville: The life and death of a Canadian black community.3rd edition.* Toronto: Canadian Scholars Press.

Clark, S.D. 1978. *The New Urban Poor.* Toronto: McGraw-Hill Ryerson.

Cohen, Anthony P. 2002. "Epilogue" In *Realizing Community. Concepts, Social Relationships and Sentiments.* Ed. V. Amit. London and New York: Routledge, 165–170.

Cohen, Anthony P. 1985. *The Symbolic Construction of Community.* London and New York: Tavistock Publications.

Corcoran, Mary P. 2002. "Place Attachment and Community Sentiment in Marginalised Neighbourhoods: A European Case Study." *Canadian Journal of Urban Research* 11(1):47–67, 48).

Dawson, A. 2002. "The mining community and the ageing body: Towards a phenomenology of community?" in *Realizing Community. Concepts, social relationships and sentiments.* Ed. V. Amit. London and New York: Routledge 21–37.

Dowler, Kevin. 2004. "Planning the Culture of Cities: Cultural Policy in Dublin and Toronto." *Canadian Journal of Irish Studies* 30(2):21–29.

Driedger, Leo 2003. "Changing Boundaries: Sorting Space, Class, Ethnicity and Race in Ontario" *The Canadian Review of Sociology and Anthropology* 40(5):593–621.

Dyck, Noel. 2002. "'Have you been to Hayward Field?' Children's sport and the construction of community in suburban Canada" In *Realizing Community. Concepts, Social Relationships and Sentiments.* Ed. V. Amit. London and New York: Routledge, 105–123

Falardeau, J.C. 1964. "The Seventeenth-Century Parish in French Canada." In *French-Canadian Society*. Vol 1. Ed. M. Rioux and Y. Martin. Toronto: McClelland & Stewart, 19–32.

Foster, Janet. 1995. "Informal Social Control and Community Crime Prevention." *British Journal of Criminology* 35(4):563–583.

Garigue Philippe 1956. "French-Canadian Kinship and Urban Life." *American Anthropologist* 58:1090–101.

Garigue, Philippe 1964. "Change and Continuity in Rural French Canada." In *French-Canadian Society*. Vol 1. Ed. M. Rioux and Y. Martin. Toronto: McClelland & Stewart, 123–137.

Gans, H. 1962. *The Urban Villagers*. Glencoe, Il: Free Press.

Gérin L. 1964. "The French-Canadian Family: Its Strengths and Weaknesses." In *French-Canadian Society*. Vol 1. Ed. M. Rioux and Y. Martin. Toronto: McClelland & Stewart, 32–57.

Guindon, Herbert 1964. "The Social Evolution of Quebec Reconsidered." In *French-Canadian Society*. Vol 1. Ed. M. Rioux and Y. Martin. Toronto: McClelland & Stewart. 137–61.

Hall, E.T. 1966. *The Hidden Dimension*. Garden City, NY: Doubleday.

Harper, D. 1979. "Life on the Road." in *Images of Information*. Ed. J. Wagner, Beverly Hills:Sage, 25–42.

Henry, F. 1973. *Forgotten Canadians: The Blacks of Nova Scotia*. Toronto: Longman Canada.

Hodge, G. and M.A. Qadeer 1983. *Towns and Villages in Canada. The Importance of Being Unimportant*. Toronto: Butterworths.

Howell, Signe 2002. "Community beyond place: Adoptive families in Norway" In *Realizing Community. Concepts, Social Relationships and Sentiments*. Ed. V. Amit. London and New York: Routledge, 84–104.

Isin, Engin F. and Myer Siemiatycki. 2002. "Making Spaces for Mosques. Struggles for urban Citizenship in Diasporic Toronto." in Razack, Sherene H (ed.). 2002. *Race, Space, and the Law. Unmapping a White Settler Society*. Toronto: Between the Lines, 185–209.

Jacobs, Jane. 1961. *The Death and Life of Great American Cities* New York: Vintage.

James, C.E. 1990. *Making it: Black Youth, Racism and Career Aspirations in a Big City*. Oakville, Ont.: Mosaic Press.

Jencks, C. 1984. *The Language of Postmodern Architecture*. London: Academy Editions.

Kawash, Samira 1998. "The Homeless Body." *Public Culture* 10(2):319–339.

Lavine, Marie 1986. "Feminist Reflections on the Fertility of Women in Quebec." In *The Politics of Diversity: Feminism, Marxism, and Nationalism*. Ed. R. Hamilton and M. Barrett. Montreal: Book Centre, 303–21.

Lawrence, Bonita and Kim Anderson. 2003. "Introduction. For the Betterment of our Nations." In *Strong Women Stories, native Vision and Community Survival*. Ed. K. Anderson and B. Lawrence. Toronto: Sumach Press, 11–22.

Li, Peter. 1998. *The Chinese in Canada*. 2nd ed. Don Mills, Ont: Oxford University Press.

Lewis, Oscar 1949. *Life in a Mexican Village: Tepoztlan Restudied*. Urbana, Il: University of Illinois Press.

Lorimer, J. and M. Phillips. 1971. *Working People: Life in a Downtown City Neighbourhood*. Toronto: James Lewis and Samuel.

Machum, S. 1992. "The Impact of Agribusiness on Women's Work in the Household, On-the-farm and Off-the farm: A New Brunswick Case Study." Master's thesis, Department of Sociology and Social Anthropology, Dalhousie University.

Mackenzie, Suzanne. 1986a. "Feminist Geography." *The Canadian Geographer* 30,3:268–70.

Mackenzie, Suzanne. 1986b. "Women's Response to Economic Restructuring: Changing Gender Changing Space." in *"The Politics of Diversity: Feminism, Marxism, and Nationalism."* Ed. R. Hamilton and M. Barrett. Montreal: Book Centre, 81–100.

Mackenzie, Suzanne. 1987a. "Neglected Spaces in Peripheral Places: Homeworkers and the Creation of a new Economic Centre." *Cahiers de géographie du Québec* 31,83 (Sept.):247–60.

Mackenzie, Suzanne. 1987b. "The Politics of Restructuring: Gender and Economy in De-Industrialized Areas." Paper presented to the Canadian Association of Geographers, Hamilton, ON.

Maracle, Sylvia. 2003. "The Eagle has Landed: Native women, leadership and community development." In *Strong Women Stories, Native Vision and Community Survival*. Ed. K. Anderson and B. Lawrence. Toronto: Sumach Press, 70–80.

Marx, Karl and Frederiche Engels. [1845] 1965. *Manifesto of the Communist Party*. Peking: Foreign Languages Press.

Marx, Karl and Frederiche Engels. [1847] 1970. *The German Ideology* New York: International Publishers.

Martin, M. 2002. "The Crown Owns All the Land? The Mi'gmaq of Listugui Resist." In *Social Context & Social Location in the Sociology of Law*. Ed. G. MacDonald Peterborough, ON: Broadview Press, 229–246.

Martin-Hill, Dawn. 2003. "She No Speaks and other Colonial Constructs of "The Traditional Woman." In *Strong Women Stories, Native Vision and Community Survival*. Ed. K. Anderson and B. Lawrence. Toronto: Sumach Press, 106–120.

Mawani, Renisa. 2002. "In between and Out of Place. Mixed-race Identity, Liquor, and the law in British Columbia, 1850–1913" In *Race, Space, and the Law. Unmapping a White Settler Society*. Ed. S. Razack. Toronto: Between the Lines, 47–69.

McGahan, P. 1982. *Urban Sociology in Canada*. Toronto: Butterworths.

Michelson, W. 1970. *Man and His Urban Environment: A Sociological Approach*. Reading, MA:Addison-Wesley.

Michelson, W. 1988. "Divergent Convergence: The Daily Routines of Employed Spouses as a Public Affairs Agenda." In *Life Spaces: Gender, Household, Employment*. Ed. C. Andrew and B.M. Milroy. Vancouver: University of British Columbia Press, 81–102.

Miner, Horace 1939. *St. Denis: A French-Canadian Parish*. Chicago: University of Chicago Press.

Miner, Horace 1964. "Changes in Rural French-Canadian Culture." In *French-Canadian Society*. Vol 1. Ed. M. Rioux and Y. Martin. Toronto: McClelland & Stewart, 63–75.

Moore, Dene 2003. "Chief of Labrador Innu asks for help in treating gas-sniffing children." Canadian Press Oct. 27.

Muise, Gertie Mai 2003. "Where the spirits live: Women Rebuilding a Non-status Mi'kmaq community." In *Strong Women Stories, Native Vision and Community Survival*. Ed. K. Anderson and B. Lawrence. Toronto: Sumach Press, 25–36.

Nelson, Jennifer J. 2002. "The Space of Africville. Creating, Regulating, and Remembering the Urban "Slum"" In *Race, Space, and the Law. Unmapping a White Settler Society*. Ed. S. Razack. Toronto: Between the Lines, 211–232.

Nip, Joyce Y.M. 2004. "The Relationship Between Online and Offline Communities: The Case of the Queer Sisters" *Media, Culture & Society* 26(3):409–428.

Olwig, Karen F. 2002. "The ethnographic field revisited: Towards a study of common and not so common fields of belonging." In

Realizing Community. Concepts, social relationships and sentiments. Ed. V. Amit. London and New York: Routledge, 124–145.

Park, Robert E., Ernest W. Burgess, and Roderick D. McKenzie eds.[1925]. 1967. *The City.* Chicago: Chicago University Press.

Park, Robert E. [1932]1952. *Human Communities: The City and Human Ecology, Volume II; The Collected Papers of Robert Ezra Park.* Glencoe, Ill.: The Free Press.

Piddington, R. 1965. "The Kinship Network Among French-Canadians." *International Journal of Comparative Sociology* 6:145–65.

Ramp, William. 2001. " Book Reviews: Kieran Bonner, A Great Place to Raise Kids: Interpretation, Science and the Urban-Rural Debate. Montreal and Kingston: McGill-Queen's University Press, 1997, 241 p. *Canadian Review of Sociology and Anthropology* 38(1):349–355, 350).

Rapport, Nigel. 1993. *Diverse World-Views in an English Village.* Edinburgh:University of Edinburgh Press.

Razack, Sherene H. 2002. "Gendered Racial Violence and Spatialized Justice: The Murder of Pamela George." In *Race, Space, and the Law. Unmapping a White Settler Society.* Ed. S. Razack. Toronto: Between the Lines, 121–156.

Redfield, R. 1930. *Tepoztlan-A Mexican Village: A Study of Folk Life.* Chicago: University of Chicago Press.

Redfield, R. 1947. "The Folk Society." *American Journal of Sociology* 52(Jan.):293–303.

Redfield, R. 1964. "French-Canadian Culture in St-Denis." In *French-Canadian Society.* Vol. 1. Ed. M. Rioux and Y. Martin. Toronto: McClelland & Stewart, 57–62.

Rioux, Marcel 1964. "Remarks on the Socio-Cultural Development of French Canada." In *French-Canadian Society.* Vol. 1. Ed. M. Rioux and Y. Martin. Toronto: McClelland & Stewart.

Sacouman, R.J. 1980. "The Semi-proletarianization of the Domestic Mode of Production and the Underdevelopment of Rural Areas in Maritime Canada." Unpublished paper.

Sacouman, R.J. 1981. "The 'Peripheral' Maritimes and Canada-wide Marxist Political Economy." *Studies in Political Economy* 6 (Autumn):135–50.

Shaffir, W. 1974. *Life in a Religious Community: The Lubavitcher Chassidim in Montreal.* Toronto: Holt, Rinehart and Winston.

Shulman, N. 1976. "Role Differentiation in Urban Networks." *Sociological Focus.* 9:149–58.

Silver, Jim. 2006. *In Their Own Voices: Building Urban Aboriginal Communities.* Halifax: Fernwood.

Simich, Laura 2003. "Negotiating Boundaries of Refugee Resettlement: A Study of Settlement Patterns and Social Support." *The Canadian Review of Sociology and Anthropology* 40(5):575–592.

Simmel, George. 1950. "The Metropolis and Mental Life." in *The Sociology of George Simmel.* Glencoe, Il: Free press, 409–24.

Sprenger, Audrey. 2002. "Communities are Social: Locating Homeplace in the Sociology of Law" In *Social Context and Social Location in the Sociology of Law.* Ed. G. MacDonald. Peterborough, ON: Broadview Press, 209–228.

Statistics Canada 2003.*Aboriginal Peoples of Canada: A Demographic Profile.*

Stebbins, R.A. 1994. *The Franco-Calgarians: French Language, Leisure, and Linguistic Life-Style in an Anglophone City.* Toronto: University of Toronto Press.

Stevenson, Deborah. 2003. *Cities and Urban Culture.* Maidenhead, Philadelphia: Open University Press.

Strathern, Marilyn. 1982. "The Village as an Idea: Constructs of Village-ness in Elmdon, Essex." In *Belonging, Identity and Social Organization in British Rural Cultures.* Ed. A.P. Cohen. Manchester: University Press, 247–77.

Suttles, G.D. 1968. *The Social Order of the Slum.* Chicago: University of Chicago Press.

Tönnies, Ferdinand. [1887]1957. *Community and Society.* New York: Harper and Row.

Weber, Max. 1946. "Capitalism And Rural Society in Germany." Pp. 363–385 in Hans Gerth and C.W. Mills (eds) *From Max Weber: Essays in Sociology* New York: Oxford University Press.

Webster, C. and John Hood. 2001. "Surveillance in the community: Community development through the use of closed-circuit television." In. *Community Informatics. Shaping Computer-Mediated Social Relations.* Ed. L. Keeble and B.D. Loader. London & New York: Routledge, 220–239.

Wellman, Barry. 1978. "The Community Question: The Intimate networks of East Yorkers." University of Toronto Centre for Urban and Community Studies and Department of Sociology.

Wellman, Barry. 1992. "Which types of ties and networks give what kinds of social support?" *Advances in Group Processes.* Vol.9:207–35.

Wellman, Barry. 2001. "Physical place and cyberplace. The rise of networked individualism." In *Community Informatics. Shaping Computer-Mediated Social Relations.* Ed. L. Keeble and B.D. Loader. London & New York: Routledge, 17–42.

Wells, Karen and Sophie Watson. 2005. "A Politics of resentment: Shopkeepers in a London Neighbourhood." *Ethnic and Racial Studies* 28(2) March:261–277.

Winland, D.N. 1993. "The Quest for Mennonite Peoplehood: Ethno-religious Identity and the Dilemma of Definitions." *Canadian Review of Sociology and Anthropology* 30,1:110–138.

Wirth, L. 1938. "Urbanism as a Way of Life" *American Journal of Sociology.* 44,1:1–24.

Young, M. and P. Wilmott 1957. *Family and Kinship in East London.* London: Routledge & Kegan Paul.

Chapter 5

Armstrong, P., and H. Armstrong. 1992. "Lessons from Pay Equity." In *Feminism in Action.* Ed. M.P. Connelly and P. Armstrong. Toronto: Canadian Scholars Press, 295–316.

Backhouse, C. 1991. *Petticoats and Prejudice: Women and Law in Nineteenth-Century Canada.* Toronto: Women's Press.

Bem, S.L. 1974. "The Measurement of Psychological Androgyny." *Journal of Consulting and Clinical Psychology* 42, 2:155–62.

Bissett-Johnson, A. 1988. "Murdoch Case." In *The Canadian Encyclopedia.* 2nd ed. Vol 3. Edmonton: Hurtig, 1405.

Bland, L. 1985. "In the Name of Protection: The Policing of Women in the First World War." In *Women-In-Law: Explorations in Law, Family, and Sexuality.* Ed. J. Brophy and C. Smart. London: Routledge & Kegan Paul, 23–49.

Boyd, S.B. 1993. "Investigating Gender Bias in Canadian Child Custody Law: Reflections on Questions and Methods." In *Investigating Gender Bias: Law, Courts, and the Legal Profession.* Ed. J. Brockman and D. Chunn. Toronto: Thompson Educational, 169–90.

Boyle, C., and S.W. Rowley. 1987. "Sexual Assault and Family Violence: Reflections on Bias." In *Equality and Judicial Neutrality.* Ed. S. Martin and K. Mahoney. Toronto: Carswell, 312–26.

Breckenridge, J. 1985. "Equal Pay's Unequal Effect." *Report on Business Magazine* (Dec.).

Brittan, A. 1989. *Masculinity and Power.* Oxford: Basil Blackwell.

Brockman, J., and D. Chunn. 1993. *Investigating Gender Bias: Law, Courts, and the Legal Profession.* Toronto: Thompson Educational.

Bunch, C. 1975. "Not for Lesbians Only." *Quest* 11, 2 (Fall):245–48.

Carby, H.V. 1982. "White Woman Listen! Black Feminism and the Boundaries of Sisterhood." In *The Empire Strikes Back: Race and Racism in 70s Britain.* Centre for Contemporary Cultural Studies. London: Hutchinson, 212–35.

Chodorow, N. 1978. *The Reproduction of Mothering: Psychoanalysis and the Sociology of Gender.* Berkeley, CA: University of California Press.

Clark, L.M.G., and D.L. Lewis, 1977. *Rape: The Price of Coercive Sexuality.* Toronto: Women's Press.

Connell, R.W. 1987. *Gender and Power: Society, the Person and Sexual Politics.* Palo Alto, CA: Stanford University Press.

David, D.S., and R. Brannon, eds. 1976. *The Forty-Nine Percent Majority: The Male Sex Role.* New York: Random House.

Dawkins, R. 1976. *The Selfish Gene.* London: Oxford University Press.

DeKeseredy, W.S., and R. Hinch. 1991. *Woman Abuse: Sociological Perspectives.* Toronto: Thompson Educational.

Dinnerstein, D. 1976. *The Mermaid and the Minotaur: Sexual Arrangements and Human Malaise.* New York: Harper & Row.

Donzelot, J. 1979. *The Policing of Families.* New York: Pantheon.

Dworkin, A. 1980. "Pornography: A Hatred Without Bounds." *New Directions for Women* (Nov.-Dec.):20.

Eichler, M. 1980. *The Double Standard: A Feminist Critique of Feminist Social Science.* London: Croom Helm.

Eichler, M. 1985b. "The Pro-Family Movement: Are They for or Against Families?" *Feminist Perspectives Series.* Ottawa: Canadian Research Institute for the Advancement of Women.

Eisenstein, Z.R. 1984. *Feminism and Sexual Equality: Crisis in Liberal America.* New York: Monthly Review Press.

Engels, F. [1884] 1978. "The Origins of the Family, Private Property, and the State." In *The Marx-Engels Reader.* 2nd ed. Ed. R.C. Tucker. New York: W.W. Norton, 734–59.

Faludi, S. 1991. *Backlash: The Undeclared War Against American Women.* New York: Doubleday Anchor Books.

Fenn, M. 1980. *In the Spotlight: Women Executives in a Changing Environment.* Englewood Cliffs, NJ: Prentice-Hall.

Findlay, B. 1975. "Shrink! Shrank! Shriek!" In *Women Look at Psychiatry.* Ed. D.E. Smith and S.J. David. Vancouver: Press Gang.

Fine, G.A. 1992. "The Dirty Play of Little Boys." In *Men's Lives.* Ed. M.S. Kimmel and M.A. Messner. 2nd ed. New York: Macmillan, 135–43.

Foucault, M. 1978. *The History of Sexuality.* Vol. 1. New York: Vintage.

Frank, B. 1992. "Hegemonic Heterosexual Masculinity: Sports, Looks and a Woman, That's What Every Guy Needs to be Masculine." Paper presented at 26th Annual Meeting of Atlantic Association of Sociologists and Anthropologists. Session on Violence and Social Control in the Home, Workplace, Community and Institutions. ISER Conference Paper #3, ISER, Memorial University of Newfoundland.

Freud, S. 1905. *The Standard Edition of the Complete Psychological Works of Sigmund Freud.* Vol. 7. *The Three Essays on the Theory of Sexuality.* London: The Hogarth Press.

Freud, S. [1905] 1976. "Three Essays on the Theory of Sexuality." In J. Strachey, trans. and ed. *The Complete Psychological Works.* Vol. 7. New York: Norton.

Garfinkel, H. 1967. *Studies in Ethnomethodology.* Englewood Cliffs, NJ: Prentice-Hall.

Gaskell, J. 1988. "The Reproduction of Family Life: Perspectives of Male and Female Adolescents." In *Gender and Society: Creating a Canadian Women's Sociology.* Ed. A.T. McLaren. Toronto: Copp Clark Pitman, 146–68.

Gaskell, J., A. McLaren, and M. Novogrodsky. 1989. *Claiming an Education: Feminism and Canadian Schools.* Toronto: Our Schools/Our Selves Education Foundation.

Goldberg, S. 1973. *The Inevitability of Patriarchy.* New York: William Morrow.

Goode, W.J. 1982. *The Family.* 2nd ed. Englewood Cliffs, NJ: Prentice-Hall.

Gray, S. 1987. "Sharing the Shop Floor." In *Women and Men: Interdisciplinary Readings on Gender.* Ed. G. Hofmann Nemiroff. Toronto: Fitzhenry & Whiteside, 377–402.

Greenglass, E. 1992. "Socialization of Girls and Boys: How Gender Roles Are Acquired." In *Sociology for Canadians: A Reader.* 2nd ed. Ed. A. Himelfarb and C.J. Richardson. Toronto: McGraw-Hill Ryerson, 203–12.

Hale, S.M. 1987a. "The Documentary Construction of Female Mismanagement." *Canadian Review of Sociology and Anthropology* 24, 4 (Nov.):489–513.

Harlow, H.F. 1962. "The Heterosexual Affectional System in Monkeys." *American Psychologist* 17:1–9.

Harlow, H.F. 1965. "Sexual Behavior in the Rhesus Monkey." In *Sex and Behavior.* Ed. F.A. Beach. New York: Wiley.

Hartmann, H.I. 1984. "The Unhappy Marriage of Marxism and Feminism: Towards a More Progressive Union." In *Feminist Frameworks: Alterative Theoretical Accounts of the Relations Between Women and Men.* 2nd ed. Ed. A.M. Jaggar and P.S. Rothenberg. New York: McGraw-Hill, 171–89.

Hennig, M., and A. Jardim. 1981. *The Managerial Woman,* New York: Anchor Books.

Hoffman, L.W. 1977. "Changes in Family Roles, Socialization and Sex Differences." *American Psychologist* 32:644–67.

Kessler, S.J., and W. McKenna. 1978. *Gender: An Ethnomethodological Approach.* Chicago: University of Chicago Press.

Khayatt, M.D. 1990. "Legalized Invisibility: The Effect of Bill 7 on Lesbian Teachers." *Women's Studies International Forum* 13, 3:185–93.

Kinsman, G. 1987a. "Men Loving Men: The Challenge of Gay Liberation." In *Beyond Patriarchy: Essays by Men on Pleasure, Power, and Change.* Ed. M. Kaufman. Toronto: Oxford University Press, 103–19.

Kinsman, G. 1987b. *The Regulation of Desire: Sexuality in Canada.* Montreal: Black Rose Books.

Kinsman, G. 1991. "'Homosexuality' Historically Reconsidered Challenges Heterosexual Hegemony." *The Journal of Historical Sociology* 4, 2 (June):91–111.

Kline, M. 1989. "Women's Oppression and Racism: A Critique of the 'Feminist Standpoint.'" In *Race, Class, Gender: Bonds and Barriers.* Ed. J. Vorst et al. Toronto: Between the Lines (for the Society for Socialist Studies, Winnipeg).

Larwood, L., and M.M. Wood. 1977. *Women in Management.* Lexington, MA: Lexington Books.

Lehne, G.K. 1976. "Homophobia Among Men." In *The Forty-Nine Percent Majority: The Male Sex Role*. Ed. D.S. David and R. Brannon. New York: Random House, 66–92.

Luxton, M. 1980. *More than a Labour of Love: Three Generations of Women's Work in the Home*. Toronto: Women's Press.

Lynn, D.B. 1974. *The Father: His Role in Child Development*. Monterey, CA: Wadsworth.

Lyttleton, N. 1990. "Men's Liberation, Men Against Sexism and Major Dividing Lines." In *Women and Men*. Ed. G. Hofmann Nemiroff. Fitzhenry & Whiteside, 472–77.

Maccoby, E., and C.N. Jacklin. 1974. *The Psychology of Sex Differences*. Palo Alto, CA: Stanford University Press.

Mackie, M. 1991. *Gender Relations in Canada: Further Explorations*. Toronto: Butterworths.

Mackinnon, C.A. 1989. *Toward a Feminist Theory of the State*. Cambridge, MA: Harvard University Press.

Maynard, R., with C. Brouse. 1988. "Thanks, But No Thanks." *Report on Business Magazine* (Feb.):26–34.

McRobbie, A. 1978. "Working-Class Girls and the Culture of Femininity." In *Women Take Issue: Aspects of Women's Subordination*. London: Hutchinson, 96–108.

McRobbie, A. 1991. *Feminism and Youth Culture*. Houndsmills: MacMillan Education.

Mead, M. 1935. *Sex and Temperament in Three Primitive Societies*. New York: William Morrow.

Messner, M. 1992. "Boyhood, Organized Sports, and the Construction of Masculinities." In *Men's Lives*. Ed. M.S. Kimmel and M.A. Messner. 2nd ed. New York: Macmillan, 161–73.

Midnight Sun. 1988. "Sex/Gender Systems in Native North America." In *Living the Spirit: A Gay American Indian Anthology*. Ed. W. Roscoe and comp. Gay American Indians. New York: St. Martin's Press, 32–47.

Morgan, E. 1972. *The Descent of Woman*. New York: Stein & Day.

O'Brien, M. 1981. *The Politics of Reproduction*. London: Routledge & Kegan Paul.

Orbach, S. 1979. *Fat is a Feminist Issue: A Self-Help Guide for Compulsive Eaters*. New York: Berkley Books.

Prentice, A., et. al., 1988. *Canadian Women: A History*. Toronto: Harcourt Brace Jovanovich.

Rheingold, H., and K. Cook. 1975. "The Content of Boys' and Girls' Rooms as an Index of Parent Behavior." *Child Development* 46:459–63.

Roscoe, W. 1988. "The Zuni Man-Woman." *Outlook* 1, 2 (Summer):56–67.

Scott, V. 1987. "C-49: A New Wave of Oppression." In *Good Girls/Bad Girls: Sex Trade Workers and Feminists Face to Face*. Ed. L. Bell. Toronto: Women's Press, 100–3.

Smart, C. 1984. *The Ties That Bind: Law, Marriage and the Reproduction of Patriarchal Relations*. London: Routledge & Kegan Paul.

Smart, C. 1989. *Feminism and the Power of Law*. London: Routledge.

Smith, D.E. 1990a. "Femininity as Discourse." In *Texts, Facts, and Femininity: Exploring the Relations of Ruling*. Ed. D.E. Smith. New York: Routledge, 159–208.

Smith, G.W. 1992. "The Ideology of 'Fag': Barriers to Education for Gay Students." Ontario Institute for Studies in Education. Mimeographed.

Synnott, A. 1992. "Little Angels, Little Devils: A Sociology of Children." In *Sociology for Canadians: A Reader*. 2nd ed. Ed. A. Himelfarb and C.J. Richardson. Toronto: McGraw-Hill Ryerson, 191–202.

Tiger, L. 1969. *Men in Groups*. New York: Random House.

Valverde, M. 1987. "Too Much Heat, Not Enough Light." In *Good Girls/Bad Girls: Sex Trade Workers and Feminists Face to Face*. Ed. L. Bell. Toronto: Women's Press, 27–32.

Walkowitz, J.R. 1983. "Male Vice and Female Virtue: Feminism and the Politics of Prostitution in Nineteenth-Century Britain." In *Powers of Desire: The Politics of Sexuality*. Ed. A. Snitow, C. Stansell, and S. Thompson. New York: Monthly Review Press, 419–38.

Warskett, R. 1988. "Bank Worker Unionization and the Law." *Studies in Political Economy* 25 (Spring):41–73.

White, J. 1980. *Women and Unions*. Ottawa: Supply and Services Canada (for the Canadian Advisory Council on the Status of Women).

Wilson, S.J. 1986. *Women, the Family and the Economy*. 2nd ed. Toronto: McGraw-Hill Ryerson.

Chapter 6

Atkinson, J. 1978. *Discovering Suicide*. London: Macmillan.

Baldry, A.C. and F.W. Winkel. 2003. "Direct and Vicarious Victimization at school and at home as risk factors for suicidal cognition among Italian adolescents." *Journal of Adolescence* 26(6):703–716.

Balikci, A. 1970. *The Netsilik Eskimo* New York: Garden City. The Natural History Press.

Bannerji, Himani. 2000. *The Dark Side of the Nation: Essays on Multiculturalism, Nationalism and Gender* Toronto: Canadian Scholars Press.

Berkman, L.F., T. Glass, I. Brisette, T.E. Seeman. 2000. "From Social integration to health: Durkheim in the New Millennium." *Social Science and Medicine* 51(6):843–857.

Besnard, P. 2000. "The Fortunes of Durkheim's Suicide." In W.S.F. Pickering and G. Walford (eds) *Durkheim's Suicide: A Century of Research and Debate*. London and New York: Routledge, 97–125.

Besnard, P. "Marriage and Suicide. Testing the Durkheimian theory of marital regulation a century later." In W.S.F. Pickering and G. Walford (eds) *Durkheim's Suicide: A Century of Research and Debate*. London and New York: Routledge, 133–155.

Bhardwaj, Anita. 2001. "Growing up Young, Asian, and Female in Britain: A Report on Self-harm and Suicide." *Feminist Review* 68 Summer:52–67.

Bourke, Lisa. 2003. "Toward understanding youth suicide in an Australian rural community." *Social Science and Medicine* 57(12):2355–2365.

Boyer, R., G. Légaré, D.St-Laurent, and M. Préville. 1998. "Epidemiology of Suicide, Parasuicide, and Suicidal Ideation in Quebec. In Leenars, A.A., S. Wenckstern, I. Safinofsky, R.J. Dyck, M.J. Kral, R.C. Bland (eds) 1998. *Suicides in Canada*. Toronto: University of Toronto Press, 67–84.

Breault, K.D. and A.J. Kposowa. 2000. "Social Integration and Marital Status: A multi-variate individual-level study of 30,157 suicides." In W.S.F. Pickering and G. Walford (eds) *Durkheim's Suicide: A Century of Research and Debate*. London and New York: Routledge, 156–179.

Breton, J.J., R. Boyer, H. Bilodeau, S. Raymond, N. Joubert, M.A. Nantel. 1998. *Review of Evaluation Research on Suicide intervention and Prevention Programs for Young People in Canada: Theoretical context and Results.* Montreal: Government Documents.

Briggs, Jean. 1985. "Socialization, family conflicts and responses to culture change among Canadian Inuit." *Arctic Medical Research* 40:40–52.

Briggs, Jean. 1995. "Vicissitudes of attachment: Nurturance and dependence in Canadian Inuit family relationships, old and new. *Arctic Medical Research* 54. Suppl. 1:24–32.

Burr, J. 2002. "Cultural stereotypes of women from South Asian communities: mental health care professionals' explanations for patterns of suicide and depression." *Social Science & Medicine* 5595):835–845.

Charlton, J. 1995. "Trends and Patterns in Suicide in England and Wales." *"International Journal of Epidemiology of Suicide."* 24:45–52.

Cheung, F.M. 1996. "Gender Role Development" in S. Lau (ed) *Growing Up the Chinese Way.* Hong Kong: The Chinese University Press.

Cantor, C.H., P.J. Slater, J.M. Najman. 1995. "Socioeconomic Indices and Suicide rates in Queensland." *Australian Journal of Public Health* 19:417–420.

Cormier, H. and G. Klerman. 1985. "Unemployment and Male labour force Participation as Determinants of Changing Suicide Rates of males and Females in Quebec." *Social psychiatry* 20:109–14.

Davies, C. and M. Neal. 2000. "Durkheim's Altruistic and Fatalistic Suicide." In W.S.F. Pickering and G. Walford (eds) *Durkheim's Suicide: A Century of Research and Debate.* London and New York: Routledge, 36–52.

Davies, C., M. Neal, J. Varty, G. Walford, R.A. Jones, W. Ramp. 2000. "Teaching Durkheim's Suicide: A Symposium." In W.S.F. Pickering and G. Walford (eds) *Durkheim's Suicide: A Century of Research and Debate.* London and New York: Routledge, 180–200.

Dooley, D., R. Catalano, K. Rook, and S. Serxner. 1989. "Economic Stress and Suicde: Multilevel Analyses. Part 2: Cross-level Analyses of Economic Stress and Suicideal ideation." *Suicide and Life Threatening Behaviour* 19(4):337–51.

Douglas, J. 1967. *The Social Meaning of Suicide.* Princeton, NJ: Princeton University Press.

Dudley, M.J., N. Kelk, T. Florio, J. Howard, B. Waters, C.Haski, M. Alcock. 1997. "Suicide among young rural Australians 1964–1993. A Comparison with Metropolitan trends." *Social Psychiatry and Psychotic Epidemiology.* 32:251–260.

Eckersley, R. and K. Dear. 2002. "Cultural Correlates of Suicide." *Social Science & Medicine* 55(11):1891–1904.

Ferrada-Noli, M. 1997. "Social Psychological vs socio-economic hypothesis on the epidemiology of suicide." *Psychological Reports* 81:307–316.

Fullager, Simone. 2003. "Wasted Lives. Social dynamics of Shame and Youth Suicide." *Journal of Sociology* 39(3):291–307.

Gane, M. "The Deconstruction of Social Action. The 'reversal' of Durkheimian methodology from *The Rules* to *Suicide*." In W.S.F. Pickering and G. Walford (eds) *Durkheim's Suicide: A Century of Research and Debate.* London and New York: Routledge, 22–35.

Garroutte, E.M., J. Goldberg, J. Beals, R. Herrell, S.M. Manson. 2003. "Spirituality and attempted suicide among American Indians." *Social Science and Medicine* 56(7) April: 1571–1579.

Gove, W. 1979. "Sex Differences in the epidemiology of mental disorder." in E.S. Gomberg and V. Franks (eds.), *Gender and Disordered behavior.* New York: Brunner/Mazel.

Graham, M., H.P. Bergen, A.S. Richardson, L. Roeger, S. Allison. 2004. "Sexual Abuse and Suicidality: Gender Differences in a Large Community Sample of Adolescents." *Child Abuse and Neglect* 28(5):547–563.

Green, L. 1991. "A Cohort mortality study of forestry workers exposed to phenoxy acid herbicides." *British Journal of Industrial Medicine.* 48:234–238.

Hochschild, Arlie The Second Shift New York: Avon 1989.

Horwitz, A.V. 1984. "The Economy and Social Pathology." *Annual Review of Sociology* 10:95–119.

Jack, D. C. 2003, "The Anger of Hope and the Anger of Despair." in *Situating Sadness. Women and Depression in Social Context.* Eds. S.J. Stoppard and L.M. McMullen. New York & London: New York University Press, 62–87.

Jackson, P.R. and P.B. Warr. 1984. "Unemployment and Psycholgoical Ill-health: The Moderating Role of Duration and Age." *Psychological medicine* 14:605–14.

Johnson, B.D. 1965. "Durkheim's One Cause of Suicide." *American Sociological Review* 30:875–886.

Katt, M., P. Kinch, M. Boone, B. Minore. 1998. "Coping with Northern Aboriginal Youths' Suicides" chap 12 in Leenars, A.A., S. Wenckstern, I. Safinofsky, R.J. Dyck, M.J. Kral, R.C. Bland (eds) 1998. *Suicides in Canada.* Toronto: University of Toronto Press, 212–226.

Killias, M. J. van Kesteren, M. Rindlisbacher. "Guns, violent crime, and suicide in 21 countries." *Canadian Journal of Criminology* 43(4) October: 429–448.

Kirmayer, L.J., Malus, M. and Boothroyd, L. J. 1996. "Suicide attempts among Inuit youth: A Community survey of prevalence and risk factors. *Acta Psychiatrica Scandinavica* 94: 8–17.

Kirmayer, L.J., Boothroyd, L.J. and Hodgins, S. 1998. "Suicide in the northwest territories: A descriptive review. *Chronic Diseases in Canada* 19(4):152–156.

Kirmayer, L.J., Fletcher, C. and Boothroyd, L.J. 1998. "Suicide among the Inuit of Canada" in Leenaars, A.A., Wenckstern, S., Sakinosfky, I., Dyck, R.J., Kral, M. and Bland, R.C. (Eds) *Suicide in Canada* Toronto: University of Toronto Press, 179–188.

Kral, M.J. 1998. "Suicide and the internalization of culture: Three questions" *Transcultural Psychiatry* 35,(2):221–233.

Krull, C. and F. Trovato. 1994. "The Quiet Revolution and the Sex Differential in Quebec's Suicide Rates: 1931–1986." *Social Forces* 72(4):1121–47.

Kunce, Mitch and A.L. Anderson. 2002. "The Impact of Socioeconomic Factors on State Suicide Rates: A Methodolgoical Note." *Urban Studies* 39(1):155–162.

Lam, T.H., S.M. Stewart, P.S.F. Yip, G.M. Leung, L.M. Ho, S.Y. Ho, P.W.H. Lee. 2004. "Suicidality and Cultural Values among Hong Kong Adolescents." *Social Science & Medicine* 58(3):487–498.

Leenaars, Antoon A. and David Lester. 2004. "The Impact of Suicide Prevention Centres on the Suicide Rate in the Canadian Provinces." *Crisis. Journal of Crisis Intervention and Suicide Prevention.* 25(2):65–68.

Leenars, A.A., S. Wenckstern, I. Safinofsky, R.J. Dyck, M.J. Kral, R.C. Bland (eds). 1998. *Suicides in Canada.* Toronto: University of Toronto Press.

Lester, D., P. Wood, C. Williams, J. Haines. 2004. "Motives for Suicide: A Study of Australian Suicide Notes." *Crisis. Journal of Crisis Intervention and Suicide Prevention.* 25(1):33–34.

Lester, D. 2003. "Adolescent Suicide From an International Perspective." *American Behavioral Scientist.* 46(9) May: 1157–1170.

Lester, D. and A.A. Leenaars. 1998. "Suicide in Canada and the United States: A Societal Comparison." in Leenaars, A.A., S. Wenckstern,

I. Safinofsky, R.J. Dyck, M.J. Kral, R.C. Bland (eds). *Suicides in Canada*. Toronto: University of Toronto Press, 108–121.

Lester, D. 1997a. *Making Sense of Suicide. An In-depth look at why people kill themselves.* Philadelphia: The Charles Press.

Lester, D. 1997b. "Suicide in International Perspective." *Suicide and Life Threatening Behavior* 27:104–111.

Maltsberger, John T. "Letter Across the Pacific: The Conscience of Martyrs". *Crisis. Journal of Crisis Intervention and Suicide Prevention.* 25(2):88–90.

McMullen, Linda M. 2003. "'Depressed' Women's constructions of the Deficient Self." In *Situating Sadness. Women and Depression in Social Context.* Eds. S.J. Stoppard and L.M. McMullen. New York & London: New York University Press, 17–38.

Meng, L. 2002. "Rebellion and revenge: the meaning of suicide of women in rural China." *International Journal of Social Welfare* 11:300–309.

Middleton, N., D. Gunnell, S. Frankel, W. Whitley, D. Dorling. 2003. "Urban-rural differences in suicide trends in young adults: England and Wales 1981–1998." *Social Science and Medicine.* 57(7):1183–1194.

Morgan, Jenny and Keith Hawton. 2004. "Self-reported Suicidal Behavior in Juvenile Offenders in Custody: Prevalence and Associated Factors." *Crisis. Journal of Crisis Intervention and Suicide Prevention.* 25(1):8–11.

Neuringer C. and D.J. Lettieri. 1982. *Suicidal Women. Theoir Thinking and Feeling Patterns.* New York: Gardiner.

Nolan, P.D. 2003. "Questioning Textbook Truth: Suicide Rates and the Hawthorne Effect." *American Sociologist.* 43(3) **pages missing**.

Otsu, A., S. Araki, R. Sakai, K. Yokoyama, A.S. Voorees. 2004. "Effects of Urbanization, economic development, and migration of workers on suicide mortality in Japan." *Social Science and Medicine* 58(6) March: 1137–1146.

Pickering, W.S.F., and G. Walford. 2000. "Introduction." In W.S.F. Pickering and G. Walford (eds) *Durkheim's Suicide: A Century of Research and Debate.* London and New York: Routledge, 1–10.

Pickering, W.S.F. 2000. "Reading the Conclusion. *Suicide*, morality and religion." In W.S.F. Pickering and G. Walford (eds) *Durkheim's Suicide: A Century of Research and Debate.* London and New York: Routledge, 66–80.

Platt, S.D. 1984. "Unemployment and suicidal behavior." *Social Science and medicine* 19:93–115.

Platt, S.D. 1986. "Parasuicide and unemployment." *British Journal of Psychiatry.* 149:401–405.

Pope, W. 1976. *Durkheim's Suicide: A Classic Analyzed.* Chicago: University of Chicago Press.

Ramp, W. 2000. "The Moral Discourse of Durkheim's *Suicide.*" In W.S.F. Pickering and G. Walford (eds) *Durkheim's Suicide: A Century of Research and Debate.* London and New York: Routledge, 81–96.

Report of the Advisory Group on Suicide Prevention. 2003. *Acting on what we know: Preventing Youth Suicide in First Nations.* Government Documents.

Roberts, R., Y.R. Chen, and C. Roberts. 1997. "Ethnocultural Differences in Prevalence of Adolescent Suicidal Behaviors." *Suicide and Life Threatening Behaviour* 27:104–111.

Rossow, I. And G. Lauritzen 2001. "Shattered Childhood: A Key Issue in Suicidal behaviour among Drug Addicts." *Addiction* 96(2):.

Royal Commission on Aboriginal Peoples. 1995. *Choosing Life. Special report on suicide among Aboriginal people.* Canada Communication Group. Minister of Supply and Services.

Sakinofsky, I. And R. Roberts. 1987. "The Ecology of Suicide in the provinces of Canada: 1969–71 to 1979–81." In B. Cooper ed., *The Epidemiology of Psychiatric Disorders*, 27–42 Baltimore. John Hopkins University Press.

Sakinofsky, Isaac. 1998. "The Epidemiology of Suicide in Canada" Chap 2 in Leenars, A.A., S. Wenckstern, I. Safinofsky, R.J. Dyck, M.J. Kral, R.C. Bland (eds) 1998. *Suicides in Canada.* Toronto: University of Toronto Press, 37–66.

Sinclair, C.M. 1998. "Suicide in First Nations People" Chap. 9 in Leenars, A.A., S. Wenckstern, I. Safinofsky, R.J. Dyck, M.J. Kral, R.C. Bland (eds) 1998. *Suicides in Canada.* Toronto: University of Toronto Press, 165–178.

Smith, Linda Tuhiwai. (1999) *Decolonizing Methodologies* London: Zed Books.

Stack, S. 2001. "Occupation and Suicide." **journal missing** 82(2):384–396.

Stack., S. 1982. "Suicide: A Decade Review of the Sociological Literature." *Deviant Behaviour: An Interdisciplinary Journal* 4:41–66.

Statistics. Canada Health Reports Volume 15 Number 2, 2004.

Stillman, D. 1980. "The devastating Effect of Plant Closures." in *The Big Business Reader.* Ed. M. Green and R. Massie. New York: Pilgrim Press, 72–88.

Stoner, K.L. 2004. "Militant heroines and the Consecration of the Patriarchal State. The Glorification of Loyalty, Combat, and National Suicide in the Making of Cuban National Identity." *Cuban Studies.* 34:71–96.

Stoppard, Janet M. and Linda M. McMullen eds. 2003. *Situating Sadness. Women and Depression in Social Context.* New York & London: New York University Press.

Taylor, S. 1988. *Durkheim and the Study of Suicide.* London: Longman.

Tester, Frank J. and P. McNicoll. 2004. "Isumagijaksaq: mindful of the state: social constructions of Inuit suicide." *Social Sciences and Medicine* 58(12):2625–2636.

Tomasi, L. 2000. "Emile Durkheim's contribution to the Sociological Explanation of Suicide." In W.S.F. Pickering and G. Walford (eds) *Durkheim's Suicide: A Century of Research and Debate.* London and New York: Routledge, 11–21.

Travis, Robert. 1990. "Halbwachs and Durkheim: A Test of two Theories of Suicide." British Journal of Sociology 41(2):225–243.

Trovato, F. 1998. "Immigrant Suicide in Canada." Chap 4 in Leenars, A.A., S. Wenckstern, I. Safinofsky, R.J. Dyck, M.J. Kral, R.C. Bland (eds). *Suicides in Canada.* Toronto: University of Toronto Press, 85–107.

Varty, J. 2000. "Suicide, Statistics and Sociology. Assessing Douglas' critique of Durkheim." In W.S.F. Pickering and G. Walford (eds) *Durkheim's Suicide: A Century of Research and Debate.* London and New York: Routledge, 53–65.

Warr, P.B. and P.R. Jackson. 1987. "Adapting to the Unemployed Role. A longitudinal investigation." *Social Science and Medicine* 25:1219–24.

Wild, Lauren G., A.J. Flisher, C. Lombard. 2004. "Suicidal ideation and attempts in adolescents: Associations with Depression and six domains of self esteem." *Journal of Adolescence* 27(6):611–624.

Chapter 7

Adelberg, Ellen and Claudia Currie (eds.). 1987. *Too Few To Count: Canadian Women in Conflict with the Law.* Vancouver:Press Gang Publishers.

Adler, Freda 1975. *Sisters in Crime: The Rise of the New Female Criminal*. New York: McGraw Hill.

Alexander, B.K. 1990. *Peaceful Measures: Canada's Way Out of the 'War on Drugs.'* Toronto: University of Toronto Press.

Altheide, David L. 2002. *Creating Fear: News and the Construction of Crisis*. New York: Aldine De Gruyter.

Anderson, Kim and Bonita Lawrence (eds.). 2003. *Strong Women Stories, native Vision and Community Survival*. Toronto: Sumach Press.

Arat-Koc, Sedef. 1999. "'Good Enough to Work but Not good Enough to Stay': Foreign Domestic Workers and the Law." In *Locating law. Race/Class/Gender Connections*. Ed. E. Comack. Halifax: Fernwood, 125–159.

Artz, Sibylle. 1998. *Sex, Power and the Violent School Girl*. Toronto: Trifolium Books.

Artz, Sibylle and T. Riecken. 1994. The Survey of Student Life. In *A Study of Violence Among Adolescent Female Students in a Suburban School District*. Victoria: British Columbia Ministrey of Education, Education Research Unit.

Atcheson, M.E., M. Eberts, B. Symes, with J. Stoddart. 1984. *Women and legal action: Precedents, resources, and strategies for the future*. Ottawa:Canadian Advisory Council on the Status of Women.

Aylward, Carol. 1999. How to Engage in Critical Race Litigation" in C. Aylward (ed.) *Canadian Critical Race Theory: Racism and the Law*. Halifax:Fernwood, 134–173.

Arnup, K. 1994. "Mothers just like others: Lesbians, Divorce, and Child Custody in Canada." *Canadian Journal of Women and Law*. 3(1):18–32.

Bakan, Joel. 2004. *The Corporation: The Pathological Pursuit of Profit and Power*. Toronto: Viking Canada.

Beaman, Lori. 2002. "Legal Discourse and Domestic Legal Aid: The Problem of Fitting In." G. MacDonald (ed.) *Social Context & Social Location in the Sociology of Law*. Peterborough, ON: Broadview Press, 69–89.

Bell, Sandra. 2002. "Girls in Trouble." In Schissel, B. and C. Brooks, (eds.) *Marginality and Condemnation. An Introduction to Critical Criminology*. Halifax:Fernwood, 129–156.

Bernhard, Bo J. and Frederick W. Preston. 2004. "On the Shoulders of Merton: Potentially Sobering Consequences of Problem gambling Policy." *American Behavioral Scientist* 47(11):July:1395–1405.

Best, Joel. 1989. *Images of Deviance* New York: Aldine De Gruyter.

Best, Joel. 1987. "Rhetoric in Claims-Making: Constructing the Missing Children Problem" *Social Problems* 34(2):101–121.

Bland, Lucy. 1985. "In the name of Protection: The Policing of Women in the First World War." in J. Brophy and C. Smart (eds) *Women-In-Law. Explorations in Law, family, and Sexuality*. London: Routledge and Kegan Paul, 23–49.

Blomley, Nicholas. 2004. *Unsettling the City: Urban Land and the Politics of Property*. New York and London: Routledge.

Boldt, M. 1993. *Surviving as Indians: The Challenge of Self-Government*. Toronto: University of Toronto Press..

Bottomley, Ann. 1985. "What is happening in Family Law? A Feminist Critique of Conciliation." in J. Brophy and C. Smart (eds.) *Women-In-Law. Explorations in Law, family, and Sexuality*. London: Routledge and Kegan Paul, 162–187.

Bowker, Lee. 1993. "A Battered Woman's Problems are Social, not Psychological." in R. Gelles and D. Loseke (eds.) *Current Controversies on Family Violence*. Newbury Park:Sage, 154–165.

Boyd, Susan. 1987. "Child Custody and Working Mothers." in S. Martin and K. Mahoney (eds.) *Equality and Judicial Neutrality*. Toronto: Carswell, 168–183.

Boyd, Susan. 1989a. "Child Custody, Ideologies, and Employment." *Canadian Journal of Women and Law*. 3:111–134.

Boyd, Susan. 1989b. "From Gender Specificity to Gender Neutrality: Ideologies in Canadian Child Custody Law. In C. Smart and S. Sevenhuijsen (eds.) *Child Custody and the Politics of Gender*. London and New York: Routledge and Kegan Paul, 126–157.

Boyd, Susan. 1997. "Lesbian (and Gay) Custody Claims: What Difference Does Difference Make?" *Canadian Journal of Women and Law* 15:131–152.

Boyle, Christine and Susannah W. Rowley. 1989. "Sexual Assault and Family Violence: Reflections on Bias." in in S. Martin and K. Mahoney (eds.) *Equality and Judicial Neutrality*. Toronto: Carswell, 312–326.

Braun, Connie. 2002. "Seeking Alternatives to Segregation for Aboriginal Prisoners." in B. Schissel and C. Brooks (eds.) *Marginality & Condemnation: An Introduction to Critical Criminology*. Halifax: Fernwood, 355–380.

Bressette, Shelly E. 2003. "The truth about us: Living in the aftermath of the Ipperwash crisis. In *Strong Women Stories, native Vision and Community Survival*. Ed. K. Anderson and B. Lawrence Toronto: Sumach Press, 228–241.

Brooks, Carolyn. 2002. "New Directions in Critical Criminology." in Bernard Schissel and Carolyn Brooks, (eds.) *Marginality & Condemnation. An Introduction to Critical Criminology*. Halifax: Fernwood Publishing, 29–53.

Brophy, Julia. 1992. "Case Comments: New Families, judicial decision-making, and children's welfare." *Canadian Journal of Women and Law* 5:484–497.

Brophy, Julia. 1989. "Custody law, Child Care, and Inequality in Britain. In Boyd, Susan. 1989. In C. Smart and S. Sevenhuijsen (eds.) *Child Custody and the Politics of Gender*. London and New York: Routledge and Kegan Paul. 217–244.

Busby, Karen. 1999. "'Not a victim until a Conviction is Entered': Sexual violence prosecutions and legal 'truth'". In E. Comack (ed.) *Locating law. Race/Class/Gender Connections*. Halifax: Fernwood, 260–288.

Busby, Karen. 1994. "LEAF and Pornography: Litigation on Equality and Sexual Representations." *Canadian Journal of Law and Society*. 9(1):167–192.

Cheal, David. 1999. *New Poverty. Families in Postmodern Society*. Westport, Connecticut:Praeger.

Chamblis, William. 1986. "On Lawmaking." in S. Brickey and E. Comack. (Eds.) *The Social basis of Law* (1st Edition) Toronto: Garamond Press.

Chambliss, William. 1975. "Toward a Political Economy of Crime." *Theory and Society* 2(2) (Summer):149–70.

Chunn, Dorothy E. 1999. "Feminism, Law, and "the family": Assessing the Reform Legacy." In E. Comack (ed.) *Locating law. Race/Class/Gender Connections*. Halifax:Fernwood, 236–259.

Clark. L.M.G. and D.L. Lewis. 1977. *Rape: The Price of Coercive Sexuality*. Toronto: Women's Press.

Clark, Anna. 1992. "Humanity or Justice? Wifebeating and the Law in the Eighteenth and Nineteenth Centuries." in C. Smart (ed.) *Regulating Womanhood. Historical Essays on marriage, Motherhood and Sexuality* London and New York: Routledge, chap. 9.

Clegg, S. and D. Dunkerley. 1980. *Organization, Class, and Control*. London: Routledge and Kegan Paul.

Cloward, R. and Ohlin. 1960. *Delinquency and Opportunity: A Theory of Delinquent Gangs*. Chicago: Free Press.

Cockburn, A. and Cohen, A. 1991. "Explosive Mix." *New Internationalist* (Oct.):14–15.

Cohen, A.K. 1955. *Delinquent Boys: The Culture of the Gang.* New York: Free Press.

Comack, Elizabeth, Vanessa Chopyk and Linda Wood. 2002. "Aren't Women Violent Too? The Gendered Nature of Violence." in B. Schissel and C. Brooks, (eds.) *Marginality & Condemnation. An Introduction to Critical Criminology.* Halifax:Fernwood, 235–252.

Comack, Elizabeth. 1999. "Theoretical Excursions." in E. Comack (ed) *Locating law. Race/Class/Gender Connections.* Halifax:Fernwood, 19–68.

Comack, Elizabeth. 1996. *Women in Trouble: Connecting Women's Law Violations to Their Histories of Abuse.* Halifax: Fernwood.

Comack, Elizabeth A. 1985. "The Origins of Canadian Drug legislation: Labelling versus Class Analysis." In T. Fleming (ed.) *The New Criminologies in Canada.* Toronto: Oxford, 65–86.

Cote, Helen, Nino Mikana Ike Ka-Pimoset (Woman Who Walks Two Roads) and Wendy Schissel. 2002. "Damaged Children and Broken Spirits: A Residential School Survivor's Story." in B. Schissel and C. Brooks, (eds.) *Marginality & Condemnation. An Introduction to Critical Criminology.* Halifax:Fernwood, 175–192.

Crocker, Phyllis L. 1985. "The Meaning of Equality for Battered Women who Kill Men in Self-defence." *Harvard Women's Law Journal* 18:121–153.

DeKeseredy, Walter 2000. *Women, Crime and the Canadian Criminal Justice System.* Cincinnati:Anderson Publishing.

Dell, Colleen A. 2002. "The Criminalization of Aboriginal Women: Commentary by a Community Activist." in W. Chan and K. Mirchandani (eds.) *Crimes of Colour* Peterborough, ON:Broadview Press, 127–138.

Delorey, Ann M. "Joint Legal Custody: A Reversion to Patriarchal Power." *Canadian Journal of Women and Law* 3(1):33–44.

Diamond, Sara. 1985. "Pornography: Image and Reality." in V. Burstyn (ed.) *Women Against Censorship.* Vancouver:Douglas & McIntyre, 40–57.

Dick, Andrew J, Dan J. Pence, Randall M. Jones, H. Reed Geertsen. 2004. "The Need For Theory in Assessing Peer Courts." *American Behavioral Scientist.* 47,11 (July):1448–1461.

Doherty, Jason. 2000. "The Social Construction of Welfare Recipients as 'Lazy'" in L. Beaman (ed.) *New Persoectives on Deviance: The Construction of Deviance in Everyday Life.* Scarborough, ON: Prentice Hall Allyn and Bacon Canada, 150–162.

Doran, Chris 'Nob'. 2000. "'Growing Up' Under Suspicion: The Problematization of 'Youth' in Recent Criminologies." in L. Beaman (ed.) *New Perspectives on Deviance. The Construction of Deviance in Everyday Life.* Scarborough, ON: Prentice Hall Allyn and Bacon Canada, 192–207.

Doran, Chris 'Nob'. 2002. "Medico-legal Expertise and Industrial Disease Compensation: Discipline, Surveillance and Disqualification in the Era of the 'Social.'" In G. MacDonald (ed.) *Social Context & Social Location in the Sociology of Law.* Peterborough, ON:Broadview Press, 159–180.

Doran, Chris 'Nob'. 2002b. "'Making Sense' of Moral Panics: Excavating the Cultural foundations of the 'Young, Black Mugger'". In W. Chan and K. Mirchandani (eds.) *Crimes of Colour. Racialization and the Criminal Justice System in Canada.* Peterborough, ON:Broadview Press, 157–176.

Donzelot, Jacques. 1979. *The Policing of Families.* New York: Pantheon.

Du Mont, Janice. 2003. "Charging and Sentencing in Sexual Assault Cases: An Exploratory Examination." *Canadian Journal of Women and Law* 15: 305–341.

Dyck, Noel. 1992. "Negotiating the Indian problem." in D. Miller (ed.) *The First Ones: Readings in Indian/Native Studies.* Saskatoon: Saskatchewn Indian Federated College Press, 132–140.

Faith, Karlene and Yasmin Jiwani. 2002. "The Social Construction of 'Dangerous' Girls and Women." in B. Schissel and C. Brooks (eds.) *Marginality & Condemnation: An Introduction to Critical Criminology.* Halifax:Fernwood, 83–108.

Fedec, Kari. 2002. "Women and Children in Canada's Sex Trade: The Discriminatory Policing of the Marginalized." In B. Schissel and C. Brooks (eds.) *Marginality & Condemnation: An introduction to Critical Criminology.* Halifax:Fernwood, 253–267.

Fineman, M. 1989a. "The Politics of custody and Gender: Child Advocacy and the Transformation of Custody Decision-Making in the USA." in C. Smart and S. Sevenhuijsen (eds.) *Child Custody and the Politics of Gender* London and New York: Routledge and Kegan Paul, 27–51.

Fineman, M. 1989b. "Custody Determination at Divorce: The Limits of Social Science Research and the Fallacy of the Liberal Ideology of Equality." *Canadian Journal of Women and Law.* 3(1):88–110.

Foster, Janet. 1995. "Informal Social Control and Community Crime Prevention." *British Journal of Criminology* 35(4):563–583.

Foucault, Michel. 1978. *The History of Sexuality.* London: Allen Lane.

Foucault, Michel. 1977. *Discipline and Punish.* London: Allen Lane.

Gavigan, Shelley A.M. 1999. "Poverty Law, Theory, and Practice: The Place of Class and Gender in Access to Justice." In E. Comack (ed.) *Locating law. Race/Class/Gender Connections.* Halifax: Fernwood, 208–230.

Giddens, A. 1998. *The Third Way: The Renewal of Social Democracy.* Cambridge:Polity Press.

Gill, Sheila D. 2002. "The Unspeakability of Racism: Mapping Law's Complicity in Manitoba's Racialized Spaces. In S. Razack (ed.) *Race, Space, and the Law. Unmapping a White Settler Society.* Toronto: Between the Lines, 157–184.

Girdner, Linda K. 1989. "Custody Mediation in the United States: Empowerment or Social Control?" *Canadian Journal of Women and Law* 3:134–154.

Gordon, Jane. 1989. "Multiple Meanings of Equality: A Case Study in Custody Litigation." *Canadian Journal of Women and Law* 3:134–154.

Grace, Elizabeth K.P. and Susan M. Vella. 1994. "Vesting Mothers with Power they do not have: The non-offending Parent in Civil

Sexual Assault Cases: J. (L.A.) V. J. (H) and J.(J). *Canadian Journal of Women and Law.* 7:185–195.

Graycar, R. 1989. "Equal Rights v. Fathers' Rights: The Child Custody Debate in Australia." in C. Smart and S. Sevenhuijsen (eds.) *Child Custody and the Politics of Gender* London and New York: Routledge and Kegan Paul, 158–189.

Green, L.C. and Olive P. Dickason. 1989. *The Law of Nations and the New World.* Edmonton:University of Alberta Press.

Greenberg, D.F. 1981. "Delinquency and the Age Structure of Society." in D.F. Greenberg (ed.). *Crime and Capitalism: Readings in Marxist Criminology.* Palo Alto, CA: Mayfield, 118–139.

Hall, S. 1974. "Deviance, Politics and the Media" in P. Rock and M. McIntosh (eds.) *Deviance and Social Control.* London: Tavistock, 261–305.

Hermer, Joe and Moser, Janet (eds.) 2002. *Disorderly People. Law and the Politics of Exclusion in Ontario.* Halifax:Fernwood.

Hirschi, Travis. 1969. *Causes of Delinquency.* Los Angeles: University of California Press.

Holtrusst, N., S. Sevenhuijsen, A. Vebraken. 1989. "Rights for Fathers and the State: Recent Developments in Custody Politics in the Netherlands." In C. Smart and S. Sevenhuijsen (eds.) *Child Custody and the Politics of Gender.* London and New York: Routledge and Kegan Paul, 51–77.

Hughes, Patricia. 1993. "How Many Times a Victim?: L.(A) v. Saskatchewan (Crimes Compensation Board), and Pigeau v. Cromwell, P.C.J." *Canadian Journal of Women and Law.* 6:502–512.

Jacobs, B. 2004. "Stolen Sisters: A Human Rights Response to Discrimination and Violence Against Indigenous Women in Canada." *Amnesty International Report* 4 October 2004.

Jaffe, Peter, David Wolfe, & Susan Wilson. 1990. *Children of Battered Women* London: Sage.

Jakubowski, Lisa Marie. 1999. "'Managing' Canadian Immigration: Racism, Ethnic Selectivity, and the Law." In E. Comack (ed.) *Locating law. Race/Class/Gender Connections.* Halifax: Fernwood, 98–124.

James, Carl E. 2002. "'Armed and dangerous[1]': Racializing Suspects, Suspecting Race." in B. Schissel and C. Brooks (eds.) *Marginality & Condemnation: An Introduction to Critical Criminology.* Halifax:Fernwood, 289–308.

James, Adrian L. and Allison James. 2001. "Tightening the net: Children, community, and control." *British Journal of Sociology* 52(2) (June):211–228.

Jhappan, Radha. 1998. "The Equality Pit or the Rehabilitation of Justice." *Canadian Journal of Women and Law* 10:61–107.

Johnson, Kirsten. 1999. "Obscenity, Gender, and the Law." In E. Comack. (Ed.) *Locating law. Race/Class/Gender Connections.* Halifax:Fernwood, 289–316.

Johnson, Rebecca. 2002. "The Persuasive Cartographer: Sexual Assault and Legal Discourse in R. v. Ewanchuk." in G. MacDonald (ed.) In *Social Context & Social Location in the Sociology of Law.* Peterborough, ON:Broadview Press, 247–272.

Kawash, Samira. 1998. "The Homeless Body." *Public Culture* 10(2):319–339.

Keet, Jean E. 1990. "The Law Reform Process, Matrimonial Property, and Farm Women: A Case Study of Saskatchewan, 1980–1986." *Canadian Journal of Women and Law* 4(1):166–189.

Kelly, Katharine D. and Mark Totten. 2002. *When Children Kill: A Social-psychological study of youth homicide.* Peterborough, ON:Broadview Press.

Kelly, Katharine D. 1997. "'You must be crazy if you think you were raped': Reflections on the Use of Complainants' Personal and Therapy Records in Sexual Assault Trials." *Canadian Journal of Women and Law* 9:178–195.

King, Lynn. 1985. "Censorship and Law Reform: Will Changing the Laws mean a Change for the Better?" in V. Burstyn (ed.) *Women Against Censorship* Vncuver:Douglas & McIntyre, 79–90.

Klinenberg, Eric. 2001. "Bowling Alone, Policing Together." *Social Justice* 28(3):75–80.

Koggel, Christine M. 1994. "A Feminist view of equality and its implications for affirmative action." *Canadian Journal of Law and Jurisprudence* VII(1):43–60.

Kurz, Demie. 1993. "Physical Assaults by Husbands: A Major Social Problem." In R. Gelles and D. Loseke (eds.) *Current Controversies in Family Violence.* Newbury Park:Sage, 88–103.

Larsen, Nick. 2000. "Prostitition: Deviant Activity or Legitimate Occupation?" In L. Beaman (ed.) *New Perspectives on Deviance. The Construction of Deviance in Everyday Life.* Scarborough, ON: Prentice Hall Allyn and Bacon Canada, 50–66.

L'Heureux-Dube, Claire. 1997. "Making Equality Work in Family Law." *Canadian Journal of Family Law.* 14:103–127.

Liu, Mimi. 2000. "'A Prophet With Honour': An Examination of the Gender Equality Jurisprudence of Madam Justice Claire L'Heureux-Dube of the Supreme Court of Canada." *Queen's Law Journal* 25:417–478.

MacDonald, Gayle. 2002. "Critical Theory and the Sociology of Law: Contradiction and Currency." In G. McDonald (ed.) *Social Context & Social Location in the Sociology of Law.* Peterborough, ON:Broadview Press, 23–46.

Machum, Susan T. 2002. "The Farmer takes a Wife and the Wife Takes the Farm: Marriage and Farming.", in G. MacDonald (ed.) *Social Context & Social Location in the Sociology of Law.* Peterborough, ON: Broadview Press, 133–158.

MacKinnon, C. 1989. *Toward a Feminist Theory of the State.* Cambridge, Massachusetts: Harvard University Press.

MacKinnon, C. 1987. *Feminism Unmodified: Discourses on Life and Law.* Boston:Harvard University Press.

Mannette, Joy A. 1992. "The Social Construction of Ethnic Containment: The Royal Commission on the Donald Marshall Jr. Prosecution" in J. Mannette (ed) *Elusive Justice. Beyond the Marshall Inquiry.* Halifax:Fernwood., 63–77.

Martin, Melinda. 2002. "The Crown Owns All the Land? The Mi'gmaq of Listugui Resist." In G. MacDonald (ed.) *Social Context & Social Location in the Sociology of Law.* Peterborough, ON: Broadview Press, 229–246.

Marx, Karl. [1867] 1976. *Capital: A Critique of Political Economy:* Volume 1. Harmondsworth:Penguin Books.

McBean, Jean. 1987. "The Myth of Maternal Preference in Child Custody Cases" in S. Martin and K.E. Mahoney (eds.) *Equality and Judicial Neutrality.* Toronto: Carswell, 1184–192.

McCallum, Margaret E. 1994. "Caratun v. Caratun: It seems that we are not all realists yet." *Canadian Journal of Women and Law* 7:197–208.

McCarthy, M. and J.L. Radford. 1998. "Family Law for Same Sex Couples: Chart(er)ing The Course." *Canadian Journal of Family Law* 14:103–127.

McIntosh, Mary. 1985. "Who needs Prostitutes? The ideology of male sexual needs." **(incomplete reference)**.

McKendy, John 1997. "The Class Politics of Domestic Violence." *Journal of Sociology and Social Welfare.* XXIV (3):135–155.

Merton, Robert. 1968. *Social Theory and Social Structure. New York: Free Press.*

Mestemacher, Rebecca and Jonathan Roberti. 2004. "Qualitative analysis of vocational choice: a collective case study of strippers." *Deviant Behavior* 25:43–65.

Miller, W.B. 1958. "Lower Class Culture as a Generating Milieu of Gang Delinquency." *Journal of Social Issues* 14(2):5–19.

Monture-Angus, Patricia. 1999. "Standing against Canadian Law: Naming Omissions of Race, Culture, and Gender." In E. Comack (ed.) *Locating law. Race/Class/Gender Connections.* Halifax:Fernwood, 76–97.

Moon, Richard. 2002. "Keeping the Streets Safe from Free Expression." In Hermer, J. and J. Moser (eds.) *Disorderly People. Law and the Politics of Exclusion in Ontario.* Halifax:Fernwood, 65–78.

Morris, Ruth. 2000. *Stories of Transformative Justice.* Toronto: Canadian Scholars' Press).

Mossman, Mary Jane. 1986. "Feminism and Legal Method: The Difference it Makes." *Australian Journal of Law and Society* 3:30–52.

Naffine, Ngaire. 1990. *The Law and the Sexes: Explorations in Feminist Jurisprudence.* Sydney:Allen and Unwin.

Neilson, Linda C. 2003. "Putting Revisions to the Divorce Act Through a Family Violence Research Filter: The Good, The Bad and the Ugly." *Canadian Journal of Family Law.* 20:11–56.

Nelson, Jennifer J. 2002. "The Space of Africville. Creating, Regulating, and Remembering the Urban "Slum'" In S. Razack (ed.) *Race, Space, and the Law. Unmapping a White Settler Society.* Toronto: Between the Lines, 211–232.

Parnaby, Patrick and Vincent Sacco. 2004. "Fame and strain: the contributions of Mertonian deviance theory to an understanding of the relationship between celebrity and deviant behavior." *Deviant Behavior* 25(1):1–26.

Peace, K.A., L.G. Beaman, and K. Sneddon. 2000. "Theoretical Approches in the Study of Deviance." in L. Beaman (ed.) *New Perspectives on Deviance. The Construction of Deviance in Everyday Life.* Scarborough, ON:Prentice Hall Allyn and Bacon Canada, 2–17.

Pecora, Vincent P. 2002. "The Culture of Surveillance."*Qualitative Sociology* 25(3):345–358.

Quinney, R. 1975. "Crime Control in Capitalist Society: A Critical Philosophy of Legal Order." in I. Taylor, P. Walton, and J. Young. (Eds.) *Critical Criminology.* London: Routledge and Kegan Paul, 181–202.

Ramp, William. 2000. "Moral Spectacles: Norm and Transgression in the News Media." in L. Beaman (ed.) *New Perspectives on Deviance. The Construction of Deviance in Everyday Life.* Scarborough, ON:Prentice Hall Allyn and Bacon Canada, 18–49.

Ransom, D. 1991. "The Needle and the Damage Done." *New Internationalist.* (Oct.):4–7.

Rance, S. 1991. "Growing the Stuff." *New Internationalist* (Oct.):10–13.

Razack, Sherene 2002. "Gendered Racial Violence and Spatialized Justice: The Murder of Pamela George." In S. Razack (ed.) *Race, Space, and the Law. Unmapping a White Settler Society.* Toronto: Between the Lines, 121–156.

Razack, Sherene. 1998. "Race, Space, and Prostitution: The Making of the Bourgeois Subject." *Canadian Journal of Women and Law.* 10:276–338.

Razack, Sherene. 1991. *Canadian Feminism and the Law: The Women's Legal Education and Action Fund and the Pursuit of Equality.* Toronto: Second Story Press.

Reiman, Jeffrey. 2001. *The Rich Get Richer and the Poor get Prison: Ideology, Class, and Criminal Justice. Sixth edition .* Boston:Allyn and Bacon.

Richardson, C. James. 1996. *Family Life: Patterns and Perspectives.* Toronto: McGraw-Hill Ryerson.

Roots, Roger I. 2004. "When Laws Backfire. Unintended Consequences of Public Policy." *American Behavioral Scientist* 47,11(July):1376–1394.

Rosnes, Melanie. 1997. "The Invisibility of Male Violence in Canadian Child Custody and Access Decision-Making." *Canadian Journal of Family Law* 14:31–60.

Russell, Perry A. and Frederick W. Preston. 2004. "Airline Security After the Event. Unintended consequences and Illusions." *American Behavioral Scientist* 47(11):July:1419–1427.

Sacco, Vincent F. 2003. "Black hand outrage: a constructionist analysis of an urban crime wave." *Deviant Behavior.* 24:53–77.

Sandberg. 1989. "Best Interests and Justice." in C. Smart and S. Sevenhuijsen (eds.) *Child Custody and the Politics of Gender* London and New York: Routledge and Kegan Paul, 100–125.

Saner, Hilary, Robert MacCoun, Peter Reuter. 1995. "On the Ubiquity of Drug Selling among Youthful Offenders in Washington, DC, 1985–1991:Age, Period, or Cohort Effect?" *Journal of Quantitative Criminology* 11:362–373.

Schissel, Bernard. 1997. *Youth Crime, Moral Panics, and the Politics of Hate* Halifax:Fernwood.

Schissel, Bernard. 2002. "Youth Crime, Youth Justice, and the Politics of Marginalization." in Schissel, B. and C. Brooks, (eds.) *Marginality and Condemnation. An Introduction to Critical Criminology.* Halifax:Fernwood, 109–128.

Shaver, Frances M. 1994. "The Regulation of Prostitution: Avoiding the Morality Traps." *Canadian Journal of Law and Society.* 9:123–145.

Siegel, Larry J. and Chris McCormick. 2003. *Criminology in Canada: Theories, Patterns, and Typologies.* Scarborough, ON:Nelson, Thomson.

Smart, Carol. 1984. *The Ties That Bind: Law, Marriage and the Reproduction of Patriarchal Relations.* London: Routledge & Kegan Paul.

Smart, Carol. 1989. *Feminism and the Power of Law.* London & New York: Routledge.

Shaver, Frances. 1994. "The Regualtion of Prostitution: Avoiding the Morality Traps." *Canadian Journal of Law and Society.* 9(1):123–145.

Smart, Carol. 1989. "Power and the Politics of Child Custody." in C. Smart and S. Sevenhuijsen (eds.) *Child Custody and the Politics of Gender* London and New York: Routledge and Kegan Paul, 1–26.

Smart, C. 1992. "Disruptive Bodies and Unruly Sex. The Regulation of Reproduction and Sexuality in the Nineteenth Century." in C. Smart (ed.) *Regulating Womanhood. Historical Essays on marriage, Motherhood and Sexuality* London and New York: Routledge, 7–32.

Smith, Denis. 1988. "October Crisis" in M. Hurtig (Ed.) *The Canadian Encyclopedia.* Edmonton: Hurtig Publishers 1558.

Smith, Dorothy E. 1990. *The Conceptual Practices of Power: A Feminist Sociology of Knowledge.* Toronto: University of Toronto Press.

Sneider, Laureen. 2002. "'But They're Not Real Criminals': Downsizing Corporate Crime." in B. Schissel and C. Brooks (eds.) *Marginality & Condemnation: An Introduction to Critical Criminology.* Halifax:Fernwood, 215–234.

Snider, Laureen. 1999. "Relocating Law: Making Corporate Crime Disappear." In E. Comack (ed.) *Locating law. Race/Class/Gender Connections.* Halifax:Fernwood, 183–207.

Steel, Freda M. 1987. "Alimony and Maintenance Orders." in S. Martin and K.E. Mahoney (eds.) *Equality and Judicial Neutrality.* Toronto: Carswell), 155–167.

Straus, Murray A. And R.J. Gelles. 1986. "Societal Change and Change in Family Violence from 1975 to 1985. as Revealed by Two National Surveys." *Journal of Marriage and the family* 48:465–479.

Straus, Murray A. 1993. Physical Assaults by Wives: A Major Social Problem." in R. Gelles and D. Loseke (eds.) *Current Controversies on Family Violence.* Newbury Park:Sage, chap. 4.

Sutherland, E.H. and D. Cressey. 1960. *Principles of Criminology.* Philadelphia: Lippincott.

Sutherland, E.H. [1949] 1961. *White Collar Crime*. New York: Dryden.

Swift, K. 1995. *Manufacturing 'Bad Mothers': A Critical Perspective on Child Neglect*. Toronto: University of Toronto Press.

Thompson, E.P. 1975. *Whigs and Hunters: The Origin of the Black Act*. London: Allen Lane.

Thrasher, F.M. 1963. *The Gang: A Study of 1,313 Gangs in Chicago*. Chicago: University of Chicago Press.

Totten, Mark. 2000. *Guys, Gangs and Girlfriend Abuse*. Peterborough, ON:Broadview Press.

Wachholz, S. 2002. "Confronting the Construct of Child Neglect as Maternal Failure: In Search of Peacemaking Alternatives." in G. MacDonald (ed.) *Social Context and Social Location in the Sociology of Law*. Peterborough, ON:Broadview Press, 181–208.

Wacquant, Loïc. 2001. "The Advent of the Penal State is Not a Destiny" *Social Justice* 28(3):81.

Waldram, James B. 1997. *The Way of the Pipe. Aboriginal Spirituality and Symbolic Healing in Canadian Prisons* Peterborough, ON:Broadview Press.

Walker, Gillian A. 1990. *Family Violence and the Women's Movement. The Conceptual Politics of Struggle*. Toronto: University of Toronto Press.

Walker, Gillian A. 1992. "The Conceptual Politics of Struggle: Wife Battering, the Women's Movement and the State." *Studies in Political Economy* 33:66–90.

Walkowitz, Judith. 1982. "Male vice and Feminist Virtue: Feminism and the Politics of Prostitution in Nineteenth–century Britain." *History Workshop Journal* 1:79–93.

Wegner, Eldon L. and Sarah C.W. Yuan. 2004. "Legal Welfare Fraud Among Middle-Class Families." *American Behavioral Scientist* 47(11):July:1406–1417.

White, Rob. 2002. "Restorative Justice and Social Inequality".in Bernard Schissel and Carolyn Brooks (eds.) *Marginality & Condemnation. An Introduction to Critical Criminology*. Halifax:Fernwood Publishing, 381–396.

Willis, Paul. 1981. *Learning to Labour: How Working Class Kids Get Working Class Jobs*. New York: Columbia University Press.

Zedner, Lucia 2003. "Too Much Security?" *International Journal of the Sociology of Law* 31:155–184.

Chapter 8

Brenner, R. 1977. "The Origins of Capitalist Development: A Critique of Neo-Smithian Marxism." *New Left Review* 104 (July/Aug.):25–92.

Cohen, P. 1980. "Subcultural Conflict and Working-Class Community." In *Culture, Media, Language*. Ed. S. Hall, D. Hobson, A. Lowe, and P. Willis. London: Hutchinson, 78–87.

Eisenstein, Z. R. 1984. *Feminism and Sexual Equality: Crisis in Liberal America*. New York: Monthly Review Press.

Gulalp, H. 1990. "The State and Democracy in Under-developed Capitalist Formations." *Studies in Poltiical Economy* 32(Summer):145–166.

Marx, K. [1845] 1975. "Thesis on Feuerbach." in *Karl Marx, Frederick Engels: Collected Works*. Vol. 5. New York: International Publisehrs, 3–7.

Marx, K. [1856] 1975. "'Preface' to a Contribution to the Critique of Political Economy." in *Karl Marx: Early Writings*. Harmondsworth, Eng.: Penguin.

Marx, Karl and F. Engels. [1846] 1970. *The German Ideology*. New York: International Publishers.

Chapter 9

Abaidoo, Samuel and Harley Dickinson. 2002. "Alternative and Conventional Agricultural paradigms: Evidence from Farming in Southwest Saskatchewan." *Rural Sociology* 67(1) March:.

Anderson, Luke. 1999. *Genetic Engineering, Food, and our Environment*. Vermont: Chelsea Green Publishing.

Barlow, Maud. 2007. "Closed-door talks focusing on our water supply." *The Calgary Herald* Thur, 26 April A19.

Basok, Tanya. 2002. *Tortillas and Tomatoes: Transmigrant Mexican Harvesters in Canada*. Montreal and Kingston; McGill-Queen's University Press.

Bessant, Kenneth C. 2006. "A Farm Household Conception of Pluriactivity in Canadian Agriculture: Motivation, Diversification and Livelihood. *The Canadian Review of Sociology and Anthropology* 43(1):51–73.

Carroll, William K. 2004. *Corporate Power in a Globalizing World: A Study of Elite Social Organization* Don Mills, ON:Oxford University Press.

Carroll, William J. and R.S. Ratner. 2005. "The NDP Regime in British Columbia, 1991–2001: A Post-Mortem. *The Cdn Review of Sociology and Anthropology* 42(2):167–196.

Edin, Kathryn and Maria Kefalas. 2005. *Promises I Can keep: Why Poor Mothers Put Motherhood before Marriage*. Berkeley, Los Angeles, London: University of California Press.

Ferrie, Helke. 2004. Make Mine Organic: More people are rejecting GM foods, turning to organics instead." *CCPA Monitor* 11(4) Sept.:24–5.

Gillen, David W., Tae H. Oum, and Michael W. Tretheway. 1988. "Privatization of Air Canada: Why it is Necessary in a Deregulated Environment." *Canadian Public Policy* 15(3):285–299.

Hall, Alan and Veronika Mogyorody. 2001. "Organic farmers in Ontario: An Examination of the Conventionalization Argument." *Sociologia Ruralis* 41(4):3990422.

Hamilton, Eleanor. 2006. "Whose Story is it Anyway? Narrative Accounts of the Role fo Women in Founding and Establishing Family Business." *International Small Business Journal* 24(3) 253–271.

Hochschild, Arlie. 1989. *The Second Shift*. New York: Viking.

Hughes, Karen D. 2003. "Pushed or Pulled? Women's Entry into Self-Employment and Small Business Ownership." *Gender, Work & Organization* 10(4):433–445.

Hutton, Will. 2007a. "Don't Blame China: It's Western Business Practices That Widen the Pay Gap." *CCPA Monitor* April 2007:46.

Hutton, Will. 2007b. *The Writing on the Wall: Why We Must Embrace China as a Partner or Face it as an Enemy* Little, Brown and Co.

Jackson, Andrew. 2006. "Are Wage Supplements the Answer to Problems of the Working Poor? *CCPA Monitor* June:5–12.

Keet, Jean E. 1990. "The Law Reform Process, Matrimonial Property, and Farm Women: A Case Study of Saskatchewan, 1980–1986." *Canadian Journal of Women and Law* 4(1):166–189.

Kerstetter, Steve. 2002. *Rags and Riches: Wealth Inequality in Canada*. Canadian Centre for Policy Alternatives.

Klein, Naomi. 2000. *No Logo. Taking aim at the brand Bullies* Toronto: Vintage Canada.

Landon, Laura and Bruce Wark. 2004. Measuring food from land to Mouth. CCPA Monitor 11(1)May 32–34.

Lewis, Stephen. 1972. *Louder Voices: The Corporate Welfare Bums.* Toronto: James Lewis and Samuel.

Machum, Susan T. 2002. "The Farmer takes a Wife and the Wife Takes the Farm: Marriage and Farming.", in G. MacDonald (ed.) *Social Context & Social Location in the Sociology of Law.* Peterborough, ON:Broadview Press, 133–158.

Maxwell, Judith. 2002. "Smart Social Policy—'Making Work Pay'" Canadian Policy Research Networks.

McLaughlin, Darrell. 2007. "Introduction: The Global Context of the Canadian Wheat Board" in Pugh, Terry and Darrell McLaughlin (eds). 2007. *Our Board Our Business: Why Farmers Support the Canadian Wheat Board.* Halifax: Fernwood, 18–29.

Measner, Adrian. 2007. "The Global Grain Trade and the Canadian Wheat Board." in Pugh, Terry and Darrell McLaughlin (eds). 2007. *Our Board Our Business: Why Farmers Support the Canadian Wheat Board.* Halifax: Fernwood, 30–41.

Norberg-Hodge, Helena, Todd Marrifield, and Steven Gorelick. 2002. *Bringing the Food Economy Home: Local Alternatives to Global Agribusiness.* Halifax: Fernwood.

Novek, Joel. 2003a. "Intensive Livestock Operations, Disembedding, and Community Polarization in Manitoba." *Society and Natural Resources* 16:567–581.

Novek, Joel. 2003b. "Intensive Hog Farming in Manitoba: Transnational treadmills and Local Conflicts." *The Canadian Review of Sociology and Anthropology* 40(1):3–27.

Oliver, Christopher. 2005. "The Treadmill of production under NAFTA: Multilateral Trade, Environmental Regulation, and National Sovereignty." *Organization & Environment* 18(1):55–71.

Pinto, Laura. 2007. "The Donald Trump Illusion: Exploding the entrepreneurial myth in business education." CCPA Monitor 13(9):48–50.

Pugh, Terry and Darrell McLaughlin (eds). 2007. *Our Board Our Business: Why Farmers Support the Canadian Wheat Board.* Halifax: Fernwood.

Qualman, Darrin. 2004. Puncturing the "Farm Crisis" Myth: Farm crisis caused by greedy corporations, not inefficient farmers." CCPA Monitor 11(1) May1,6–7).

Reed, Maureen G. 2004. "Moral Exclusion and the Hardening of Difference: Explaining Women's Protection of Industrial Forestry on Canada's West Coast." *Women's Studies International Forum* 27(3) Aug/Sept.:223–242.

Reimer, Marilee. 1991–2. "Women's Invisible skills and gender segregation in the clerical-administrative sector." *Journal of Public Sector Management* 22(4):29–41.

Rothman, Laurel. 2005. "Campaign 2000: Submission to the Federal Labour Standards Review Re: Part III of the Canada Labour Code." 15 Aug.

Rubenstein, Hymie. 2003. "Marxist Class Warfare Lives On." *Fraser Forum.* June 30–31.

Sharma, Nandita. 2001. "On being Not Canadian: The Social organization of 'Migrant Workers' in Canada." *Canadian Review of Sociology and Anthropology* 38(4):415–39.

Schellenberg, Grant. 1995. "'Involuntary' Part-time Workers." *Perception* 28(3–4) Winter/Spring.

Canada Council for Social Development.

Shortall, Sally. 2001. "Women in the Field: Women, Farming and Organizations." *Gender, Work and Organization* 8(2):164–181.

Stanfield, Jim. 2003. "Alternative Federal Budget 2004. Paul Martin, The Deficit, and the Debt: Taking Another Look." Canadian Centre for Policy Alternatives Nov. 28 2003:1–16.

Statistics Canada. 2001. *Canada's International Investment Position,* 2000. Cat. No. 67–202. Ottawa: Ministry of Industry, Ueda, Yoko. 1995. "Corporate Wives: Gendered Education of Their Children." in M. Campbell and A. Manicom (eds) *Knowledge, Experience, and Ruling Relations: Studies in the Social Organization of Knowledge.* Toronto: University of Toronto Press, 122–134.

UNICEF. 2005. *Child Poverty in Rich Nations Report Card No. 6,* Innocenti Research Centre.

Veltmeyer, H. 1987. *Canadian Corporate Power* Toronto: Garamond.

Vasil, Adria. 2004. "What Teach is Smoking: Greenpeace Questions Ethics of Teachers' Pension Stake in Big Tobacco." *NOW Magazine Online Edition* Vol 23(25) Feb19–25, Wells, Stewart. 2007. "Comparing Apples and Oranges: The Canadian Wheat Board and the Ontario Wheat Producers Marketing Board." in Pugh, Terry and Darrell McLaughlin (eds). 2007. *Our Board Our Business: Why Farmers Support the Canadian Wheat Board.* Halifax: Fernwood, 58–63.

Werkerle, Gerda R. 2004. "Food Justice Movements: Policy, Planning, and Networks. *Journal of Planning Education and Research* 23:378–386.

Worth, Jess. 2007. "Overconsumption, ethical or not, is destroying the planet" CCPA Monitor 13(9):10–12.

Yainizyan, Armine. 2007. "Canada's huge income gap has widened to a 30-yr high" CCPA Monitor 13(10) April: 1,6–9.

Chapter 10

Adams, D. 1988. "Treatment Models of Men Who Batter: A Profeminist Analysis." In *Feminist Perspectives on Wife Abuse.* Ed. K. Ylló and M. Bograd. Beverly Hills: Sage, 176–99.

Armstrong, P. 1984. *Labour Pains: Women's Work in Crisis.* Toronto: Women's Press.

Armstrong, P., and H. Armstrong. 1985. "Beyond Sexless Class and Classless Sex: Towards Feminist Marxism." In *Feminist Marxism or Marxist Feminism: A Debate.* Ed. P. Armstrong, H. Armstrong, P. Connelly, A. Miles, and M. Luxton. Toronto: Garamond, 1–38.

Badgley, R.F., chair. 1984. *Sexual Offences Against Children.* Vol. 1. Ottawa: Canadian Government Publishing Centre.

Burtch, B.E. 1988. "Midwifery and the State: The New Midwifery in Canada." In *Gender and Society: Creating a Canadian Women's Sociology.* Ed. A.T. McLaren. Toronto: Copp Clark Pitman, 349–71.

Chesler, P. 1991. *Mothers on Trial: The Battle for Children and Custody.* New York: Harcourt Brace.

Crean, S. 1989. "In the Name of the Fathers: Joint Custody and the Anti-Feminist Backlash." *This Magazine* 22, 7 (Feb.):19–25.

Dobash, R.E., and R.P. Dobash. 1988. "Research as Social Action: The Struggle for Battered Women." In *Feminist Perspectives on Wife Abuse.* Ed. K. Ylló and M. Bograd. Beverly Hills: Sage, 51–74.

Dubinsky, K. 1985. "Lament for a 'Patriarchy Lost'? Anti-Feminism, Anti-Abortion, and REAL Women in Canada." *Feminist Perspectives Series No. 1.* Ottawa: Canadian Research Institute for the Advancement of Women.

Eichler, M. 1985b. "The Pro-Family Movement: Are They for or Against Families?" *Feminist Perspectives Series.* Ottawa: Canadian Research Institute for the Advancement of Women.

Eichler, M. 1988a. *Families in Canada Today: Recent Changes and Their Policy Consequences.* 2nd ed. Toronto: Gage.

Eisenstein, Z.R. 1979. "Developing a Theory of Capitalist Patriarchy and Socialist Feminism." In *Capitalist Patriarchy and the Case for Socialist Feminism.* Ed. Z.R. Eisenstein. New York: Monthly Review Press, 5–40.

Eisenstein, Z.R. 1984. *Feminism and Sexual Equality: Crisis in Liberal America.* New York: Monthly Review Press.

Engels, F. [1884]. 1978. "The Origins of the Family, Private Property, and the State." In *The Marx-Engels Reader.* 2nd ed. Ed. R.C. Tucker. New York: W.W. Norton, 734–59.

Firestone, S. 1971. *The Dialectic of Sex.* London: The Women's Press.

Forward, S., and J. Torres. 1987. *Men Who Hate Women and the Women Who Love Them.* New York: Bantam.

Goode, W.J. 1982. *The Family.* 2nd ed. Englewood Cliffs, NJ: Prentice-Hall.

Hale, S.M. 1988b. "Using the Oppressor's Language in the Study of Women and Development." *Women and Language* 11, 2 (Winter):38–43.

Kanter, R.M. 1977. *Men and Women of the Corporation.* New York: Basic Books.

Liddle, J., and R. Joshi. 1986. *Daughters of Independence: Gender, Caste and Class in India.* New Delhi: Zed Books.

Luxton, M. 1980. *More than a Labour of Love: Three Generations of Women's Work in the Home.* Toronto: Women's Press.

Miles, A. 1985. "Economism and Feminism: Hidden in the Household. A Comment on the Domestic Labour Debate." In *Feminist Marxism or Marxist Feminism.* Ed. P. Armstrong, H. Armstrong, P. Connelly, A. Miles, and M. Luxton. Toronto: Garamond.

Murdock, G.P. 1949. *Social Structure.* New York: Free Press.

O'Brien, M. 1981. *The Politics of Reproduction.* London: Routledge & Kegan Paul.

Parsons, T., and R.F. Bales, eds. 1956. *Family, Socialization, and Interaction Process.* London: Routledge & Kegan Paul.

Ptacek, J. 1988. "Why Do Men Batter Their Wives?" In *Feminist Perspectives on Wife Abuse.* Ed. K. Yllö and M. Bograd. Beverly Hills: Sage, 133–57.

Rafiq, F. 1988. "Women in Islam with Reference to Pakistan." Paper presented at Canadian Asian Studies Association meeting, Windsor, 9 June.

Reiss, I. 1976. *Family Systems in America.* 2nd ed. Hinsdale, IL: Dryden Press.

Shupe, A., W.A. Stacey, and L.R. Hazlewood. 1987. *Violent Men, Violent Couples.* Toronto: Lexington Books.

Smith, D.E. 1977. "Women, the Family, and Corporate Capitalism." In *Women in Canada.* Ed. M. Stephenson. Don Mills, ON: General, 32–48.

Smith, D.E. 1979b. "Women's Inequality and the Family." Department of Sociology, Ontario Institute for Studies in Education. Mimeographed.

Smith, D.E. 1983b. "Women, Class and Family." In *The Socialist Register.* Ed. R. Miliband and J. Saville. London: Merlin.

Spencer, M. 1976. *Foundations of Modern Sociology.* Englewood Cliffs, NJ: Prentice-Hall.

Tiger, L. 1977. "The Possible Biological Origins of Sexual Discrimination. In *Biosocial Man.* Ed. D. Brothwell. London: Eugenics Society, 23–40.

Yllö, K., and M. Bograd, eds. 1988. *Feminist Perspectives on Wife Abuse.* Beverly Hills: Sage.

Chapter 11

Archibald, W.P. 1978. *Social Psychology as Political Economy.* Toronto: McGraw-Hill Ryerson.

Armstrong, P., and H. Armstrong. 1990. *Theorizing Women's Work.* Toronto: Garamond.

Beechey, V. 1977. "Some Notes on Female Wage Labour in Capitalist Production." *Capital and Class* 3 (Autumn).

Boughey, H. 1978. *The Insights of Sociology: An Introduction.* Boston: Allyn & Bacon.

Bowles, S., and H. Gintis. 1976. *Schooling in Capitalist America.* New York: Basic Books.

Braverman, H. 1974. *Labor and Monopoly Capital: The Degradation of Work in the Twentieth Century.* New York: Monthly Review Press.

Brittan, A., and M. Maynard. 1984. *Sexism, Racism and Oppression.* Oxford: Basil Blackwell.

Cassin, A.M. 1979. *Advancement Opportunities in the British Columbia Public Service.* British Columbia Economic Analysis and Research Bureau. Ministry of Industry and Small Business Development.

Cassin, A.M. 1991. "Women, Work, Jobs and Value: The Routine Production of Inequality—A Report with Special Reference to Consumers Gas." Expert testimony before Ontario Pay Equity Tribunal. March.

Cassin, A.M. 1992. Expert testimony before Supreme Court of Ontario on behalf of the Federation of Women Teachers' Association of Ontario in the case between Margaret Tomen, Applicant, and Ontario Public School Teachers' Federation and Ontario Teachers' Federation, Respondents.

Clement, W. 1981. *Hardrock Mining: Industrial Relations and Technological Change at INCO.* Toronto: McClelland & Stewart.

Cockburn, C. 1981. "The Material of Male Power." *Feminist Review* 9 (Autumn):41–59.

Darrah, C. 1994. "Skill Requirements at Work: Rhetoric versus Reality." *Work and Occupations* 21, 1 (Feb.):64–84.

Davis, K., and W.E. Moore. 1945. "Some Principles of Stratification." *American Sociological Review* 10, 2:242–49.

Eisenstein, Z.R. 1984. *Feminism and Sexual Equality: Crisis in Liberal America.* New York: Monthly Review Press.

Friedan, B. 1981. *The Second Stage.* Fort Worth, TX: Summit.

Goffman, E. 1967. *Interaction Ritual: Essays on Face-to-Face Behavior.* Garden City, NY: Doubleday.

Gregor, F.M. 1994. "The Social Organization of Nurses' Educative Work." Ph.D. thesis, Dalhousie University, Halifax, NS.

Gyllenhammer, P. 1977. *People at Work.* Reading, MA: Addison-Wesley.

Hartmann, H. 1979. "Capitalist Patriarchy and Job Segregation by Sex." In *Capitalist Patriarchy and the Case for Socialist Feminism.* Ed. Z. Eisenstein. New York: Monthly Review Press, 206–47.

Himelfarb, A., and C.J. Richardson. 1979. *People, Power, and Process: Sociology for Canadians.* Toronto: McGraw-Hill Ryerson.

Kates, J. 1988. "The Quiet Revolution." *Report on Business Magazine* (July):58–64.

Lave, J., and E. Wenger. 1991. *Situated Learning: Legitimate Peripheral Participation.* New York: Cambridge University Press.

Liddle, J., and R. Joshi. 1986. *Daughters of Independence: Gender, Caste and Class in India.* New Delhi: Zed Books.

Morgan, K., and A. Sayer. 1988. *Microcircuits of Capital: "Sunrise" Industry and Uneven Development.* Cambridge, Eng.: Polity Press.

Reimer, M.A. 1987. "The Social Organization of the Labour Process: A Case Study of the Documentary Management of Clerical Labour in the Public Service." Ph.d. thesis, Ontario Institute for Studies in Education.

Ryten, E. 1994. "Getting into Medical School in the Nineties: Who's In? Who's Out?" *ACMC Forum* 26, 4 (June–July):13–26.

Sayer, A., and R. Walker. 1992. *The New Social Economy: Reworking the Division of Labour*. Cambridge, MA: Blackwell.

Tumin, M. 1953. "Critical Analysis of 'Some Principles of Stratification'." *American Sociological Review* 18, 4.

Tumin, M. 1973. *Patterns of Sociology*. Boston: Little Brown.

Veltmeyer, H. 1986. *Canadian Class Structure*. Toronto: Garamond.

Chapter 12

Anyon, J. 1980. "Social Class and the Hidden Curriculum of Work." *Journal of Education* 162, 1 (Winter):67–92.

Apple, M. 1986. *Teachers and Texts: A Political Economy of Class and Gender Relations in Education*. London: Routledge & Kegan Paul.

Apple, M. 1988. "Facing the Complexity of Power: For a Parallelist Position in Critical Educational Studies." In *Bowles and Gintis Revisited: Correspondence and Contradiction*. Ed. M. Cole. London: Falmer Press, 112–30.

Armour, M.A. 1988. "The WISEST Approach." *New Trial* 43 (Autumn):21–23.

Aronowitz, S., and H.A. Giroux. 1985. *Education Under Siege: The Conservative, Liberal, and Radical Debate Over Schooling*. Hadley, MA: Bergin and Garvey.

Basow, S.A. 1986. *Gender Stereotypes: Traditions and Alternatives*. 2nd ed. Monterey, CA: Brooks/Cole.

Becker, H.S. 1977. "Social Class Variations in the Teacher-Pupil Relationship." In *School and Society*. Ed. B.R. Cosin et al. 2nd ed. London: Routledge & Kegan Paul.

Bezucha, R.J. 1985. "Feminist Pedagogy as a Subversive Activity." In *Gendered Subjects: The Dynamics of Feminist Teaching*. Ed. M. Culley and C. Portuges. London: Routledge & Kegan Paul.

Bowles, S., and H. Gintis. 1976. *Schooling in Capitalist America*. New York: Basic Books.

Bowles, S., and H. Gintis. 1988. "Prologue: The Correspondence Principle." In *Bowles and Gintis Revisited: Correspondence and Contradiction*. Ed. M. Cole. London: Falmer Press, 1–4.

Braverman, H. 1974. *Labor and Monopoly Capital: The Degradation of Work in the Twentieth Century*. New York: Monthly Review Press.

Bunch, C. 1983. "Not by Degrees: Feminist Theory and Education." In *Learning Our Way: Essays in Feminist Education*. Ed. C. Bunch and S. Pollack. Trumansburg, NY: Crossing Press. 248–60.

Calvert, J., with L. Kuehn. 1993. *Pandora's Box, Corporate Power, Free Trade and Canadian Education*. Our Schools/Our Selves Education Foundation. Monograph series no. 13 (July/Aug.).

Cole, M. ed. 1988. *Bowles and Gintis Revisited: Correspondence and Contradiction*. London: Falmer Press.

Curtis, B. 1987. "Preconditions of the Canadian State: Educational Reform and the Construction of a Public in Upper Canada, 1837–1846." In *The Benevolent State: The Growth of Welfare in Canada*. Ed. A. Moscovitch and J. Albert. Toronto: Garamond.

Friedman, S.S. 1985. "Authority in the Feminist Classroom: A Contradiction in Terms?" In *Gendered Subjects: The Dynamics of Feminist Teaching*. Ed. M. Culley and C. Portuges. Boston: Routledge & Kegan Paul, 203–9.

Gabriel, J. 1986. "School and Stratification." Honours thesis, St. Thomas University.

Gaskell, J., and A.T. McLaren, eds. 1987. *Women and Education: A Canadian Perspective*. Calgary: Detselig.

Hall, R.M., and B.R. Sandler. 1984. "Out of the Classroom: A Chilly Campus Climate for Women?" Project on the Status and Education of Women. Washington, DC: Association of American Colleges.

Hammersley, M. 1990. *Classroom Ethnography: Empirical and Methodological Essays*. Toronto: OISE Press.

Hester, S. 1991. "The Social Facts of Deviance in Schools: A Study of Mundane Reason." *British Journal of Sociology* 42, 2 (Sept.):443–63.

Huston, A.C. 1983. "Sex Typing." In *Handbook of Child Psychology*. Ed. P.H. Mussen. Vol. 4. Ed. E.M. Hetherington. New York: John Wiley & Sons, 387–467.

MacDonald, P. 1988. "Historical School Reform and the Correspondence Principle." In *Bowles and Gintis Revisited: Correspondence and Contradiction*. Ed. M. Cole. London: Falmer Press, 86–111.

MacKay, R.W. 1974a. "Conceptions of Children and Models of Socialization." In *Ethnomethodology: Selected Readings*. Ed. R. Turner. Harmondsworth, Eng.: Penguin, 180–93.

Mackie, M. 1991. *Gender Relations in Canada: Further Explorations*. Toronto: Butterworths.

McHoul, A.W. 1978. "The Organization of Turns at Formal Talk in the Classroom." *Language and Society* 7:183–213.

McIntyre, S. 1986. "Gender Bias Within the Law School." Memo to all members of the Faculty Board. Queen's University, 28 July.

McRobbie, A. 1978. "Working-Class Girls and the Culture of Femininity." In *Women Take Issue: Aspects of Women's Subordination*. London: Hutchinson, 96–108.

Mehan, H. 1979. *Learning Lessons: Social Organization in the Classroom*. Cambridge, MA: Harvard University Press.

Moore, R. 1988. "The Correspondence Principle and the Marxist Sociology of Education." In *Bowles and Gintis: Correspondence and Contradiction*. Ed. M. Cole. London: Falmer Press, 51–85.

Muller, J. 1989. "Ruling Through Texts: Developing a Social Service Training Program for a Community College." *Community Development Journal* 24, 4 (Oct.):273–82.

Muller, J. 1990. "Co-ordinating the Re-organization of Ruling Relations: Management's Use of Human Resource Development for the New Brunswick Community Colleges." In *Political Economy of Community Colleges: Training Workers for Capital*. Ed. J. Muller. Toronto: Garamond.

National Council of Welfare. 1975. *Poor Kids. A Report by the National Council of Welfare on Children in Poverty in Canada*. Ottawa: National Council of Welfare.

National Council of Welfare. 1994. *Poverty Profile 1992*. Ottawa: National Council of Welfare.

Noble, J. 1982. "Fitting the Child to the Classroom: What Mothers Do." Paper prepared for Project 3648. Department of Sociology in Education, Ontario Institute for Studies in Education, Toronto.

Noble, J. 1990. "Social Class and the Under-Fives: Making the 'Differences' Visible." *Our Schools/Our Selves* 2, 2 (April):42–61.

Parsons, T. 1961. "The School Class as a Social System: Some of its Functions in American Society." In *Education, Economy and Society*. Ed. A.H. Halsey, J. Floud, and C.A. Anderson. New York: Free Press.

Payne, G.C.F., and D.E. Hustler. 1980. "Teaching the Class: The Practical Management of a Cohort." *The British Journal of Sociology of Education* 1, 1:49–66.

Porter, J., M. Porter, and B.R. Blishen. 1982. *Stations and Callings: Making it Through the School System*. Toronto: Methuen.

Richer, S. 1979. "Sex-Role Socialization and Early Schooling." *Canadian Review of Sociology and Anthropology* 16:195–205.

Richer, S. 1988. "Schooling and the Gendered Subject: An Exercise in Planned Social Change." *Canadian Review of Sociology and Anthropology* 25:98–107.

Rist, R.C. 1977. "On Understanding the Process of Schooling: The Contributions of Labelling Theory." In *Power and Ideology in Education*. Ed. J. Karabel and A.H. Halsey, New York: Oxford University Press, 292–305.

Rohner, R.P. 1967. *The People of Gilford: A Contemporary Kwakiutl Village*. Ottawa: National Museums of Canada.

Russell, S. 1987. "The Hidden Curriculum of School: Reproducing Gender and Class Hierarchies." In *Feminism and Political Economy: Women's Work, Women's Struggles*. Ed. H.J. Maroney and M. Luxton. Toronto: Methuen, 229–46.

Sadker, M., and D. Sadker. 1987. "Sexism in the Schoolroom of the '80s." In *Gender Roles: Doing What Comes Naturally*. Ed. E.D. Salamon and B.W. Robinson. Toronto: Methuen, 143–47.

Schneider, F.W., and L.M. Coutts. 1979. "Teacher Orientations Towards Masculine and Feminine: Role of Sex of Teacher and Sex Composition of School." *Canadian Journal of Behavioral Science* 11:99–111.

Shapiro, L. 1990. "Guns and Dolls." *Newsweek* 28 May:56–62.

Smith, D.E. 1975. "An Analysis of Ideological Structures and How Women Are Excluded: Considerations for Academic Women." *Canadian Review of Sociology and Anthropology* 12, 4:353–69.

Smith, D.E. 1992d. "Whistling Women: Reflections on Rage and Rationality." In *Fragile Truths: 25 Years of Sociology in Canada*. .

Ed. W.K. Carroll (and others). Ottawa: Carleton University Press, 207–26.

Smith, D.E., and the Wollestonecraft Research Group. 1979. "Educational Cutbacks and the Workload of Elementary Teachers." *Women in the Educational Workforce*. Status of Women Tabloid. Canadian Teachers' Federation. Sept.

Tumin, M. 1973. *Patterns of Sociology*. Boston: Little Brown.

Wax, M.L., R.H. Wax, and R.V. Dumont Jr. 1964. "Formal Education in an American Indian Community." *Social Problems* 11, 4(Spring) Supplement:1–126.

Weeks, P.A.D. 1985. "Error-Correction Techniques and Sequences in Instructional Settings: Toward a Comparative Framework." *Human Studies* 8:195–233.

Willis, P. 1981. *Learning to Labour: How Working Class Kids Get Working Class Jobs*. New York: Columbia University Press.

Wolcott, H.F. 1967. *A Kwakiutl Village and School*. Toronto: Holt, Rinehart & Winston.

Chapter 13

Abu-Laban, Yasmeen and Christine Gabriel. 2002. *Selling Diversity. Immigration, Multiculturalism, Employment Equity, and Globalization* Peterborough, ON; Broadview Press.

Adachi, Ken. 1978. *The Enemy That Never Was: A History of the Japanese Canadians*.

Afshar. Haleh and Mary Maynard. 2000. "Gender and ethnicity at the millennium: from margin to centre." *Ethnic and Racial Studies*. 23(5) September: 805–819.

Ahmadi, Nader 2003. "Migration challenges views on sexuality." *Ethnic and Racial Studies* 26(4) July:684–706.

Alfred, Gerald R. 1995. *Heeding the Voices of our Ancestors: Kahnawake Mohawk Politics and the Rise of Native Nationalism* Toronto, New York, Oxford: Oxford University Press.

Alleyne, Brian. 2002. "An idea of community and its discontents: towards a more reflexive sense of belonging in multicultural Britain." *Ethnic and Racial Studies* 25(4) July:607–627.

Amit-Talai, Vered and Caroline Knowles. 1996. *Resituating Identities. The Politics of Race, Ethnicity, and Culture* Peterborough, Ontario: Broadview Press.

Amit-Talai, Vered. 1996. "The Minority Circuit: Identity Politics and the Professionalization of Ethnic Activism" in Amit-Talai, Vered and Caroline Knowles (eds) *Resituating Identities. The Politics of Race, Ethnicity, and Culture* Peterborough, Ontario: Broadview Press. Pp. 89–114.

Andersson, Ruben. 2005. "The New Frontiers of America" *Race and Class* 46(3):28–38.

Augoustinos, Martha, Keith Tuffin, Danielle. Every "New Racism, meritocracy and individualism: constraining affirmative action in education." *Discourse and Society* 16(3):315–339.

Bannerji, Himani. 2000. *The Dark Side of the Nation* Toronto: Canadian Scholars' Press.

Bannerji, Himani. 1995. *Thinking Through. Essays on Feminism, Marxism, and Anti-Racism* Toronto: Women's Press.

Bauder, Harald. 2003. "'Brain Abuse', or the Devaluation of Immigrant Labour in Canada." *Antipode* 35(4) Sept: 699–717.

Beinin, Joel. 2004. "The new American McCarthyism: Policing thought about the Middle East." *Race and Class* 46(1):101–115.

Bissoondath, Neil. 1994. *Selling Illusions: The Cult of Multiculturalism in Canada*. Toronto: Penguin Books.

Bourne, Jenny. 2005. "Reviews: Anti-Semitism or anti-criticism? *Race and Class* 46(1):126–140.

Boyd, Monica. 1999. "Canadian, eh? Ethnic Origin Shifts in the Canadian Census." *Canadian Ethnic Studies* 31(3):1–19.

Brown, Jessica Autumn and Myra Marx Ferree. 2005. "Close your eyes and think of England. Pronatalism in the British Print media." *Gender and Society* 19(1) February: 5–24.

Bruno-Jofré, Rosa and Dick Henley. 2000. "Public Schooling in English Canada: Addressing Difference in the Context of Globalization." *Canadian Ethnic Studies* 32(1):38–54.

Carby, Hazel. 1999. *Cultures in Babylon. Black Britain and African America* : London and New York: Verso.

Chen, Zhongping. 2004. "Chinese Minority and Everyday Racism in Canadian Towns and Small Cities: An Ethnic Study of the case of Peterborough, Ontario 1892–1951." *Canadian Ethnic Studies* 36(1):71–92.

Chua, Peter, Kum-Kum Bhavnani, John Foran. 2000. "Women, Culture, development: a new paradigm for development studies?" *Ethnic and Racial studies* 23(5) Sept: 820–841, Cottle, Simon (ed) 2000. *Ethnic Minorities and the Media* Buckingham, Philadelphia: Open University Press.

Donnelly, Denise A., Kimberley J. Cook, Debra Van Ausdale, Lara Foley. 2005. "White privilege, Color blindness, and Services to Battered Women." *Violence against Women* 11(1) January:6–37.

Eid, Paul. 2003. "The Interplay between Ethnicity, Religion, and Gender among Second-Generation Christian and Muslim Arabs in Montreal." *Canadian Ethnic Studies* 35(2):30–55.

Essed, Philomena. 2000. "Dilemmas in leadership: Women of colour in the Academy." *Ethnic and Racial Studies* 23(5) Sept:888–904.

Fekete, Liz. 2005. Anti-Muslim racism and the European security state." *Race and Class* 46(1):3–29.

Fleras, Augie and Jean Leonard Elliott. 2003. *Unequal relations. An Introduction to Race ad Ethnic Dynamics in Canada 4th edition.* Toronto: Prentice Hall.

Franks, Myfanwy. 2000. "Crossing the borders of whiteness? White Muslim women who wear the hijab in Britain today." *Ethnic and Racial Studies* 23(5) September:917–929.

Gagnon, Julie E. Francine Dansereau, Annick Germain. 2004. "'Ethnic' Dilemmas?: Religion, Diversity and Multicultural Planning in Montreal." *Canadian Ethnic Studies* 36(2):51–70.

Grillo, Ralph. 2005. "'Saltdean can't cope': Protests against asylum-seekers in an English seaside suburb." *Ethnic and Racial Studies* 28(2) March:235–260.

Haggerty, Kevin D. and Amber Gazso. 2005. "Seeing beyond the Ruins: Surveillance as a Response to Terrorist Threats." *Canadian Journal of Sociology* 39(2):169–187.

Hartman, Andrew. 2004. "The Rise and fall of whiteness studies." *Race and Class* 46(2):22–38. Critiques whiteness studies for failing to take class into account.

Helly, Denise. 2004. "Are Muslims Discriminated Against in Canada Since September 2001?" *Canadian Ethnic Studies* 36(1):24–47.

Henderson, Jennifer. 2003. *Settler Feminism and Race making in Canada.* Toronto: University of Toronto Press.

Henry, Francis, Tator, C, Mattis, W., Rees, T. 1995. *The Colour of Democracy, Racism in Canadian Society* Toronto: Harcourt Brace and Co.

Hörnqvist, Magnus. 2005. "The birth of public order policy." *Race and Class* 46(1):30–52, 31).

bel hooks. 1992. *Black Looks. Race and Representation* ch 2 "Eating the Other".

Iganski, Paul and Barry Kosmin (eds). 2003. *A New Antisemitism? Debating Judeophobia in 21st-century Britain.* London: Profile Books.

Jedwab, Jack. 2001. "Leadership, Governance, and the Politics of Identity in Cda." *Canadian Ethnic Studies* 33(3):4–37.

Kelly, Lynnette. 2003. "Bosnian Refugees in Britain: Questioning Community." *Sociology* 37(1):35–49.

Kim, Claire Jean. 2004. "Imagining race and nation in multiculturalist America." *Ethnic and Racial Studies* 27(6) November:987–1005.

Kim-Puri, H.J. 2005. "Conceptualizing gender-sexuality-state-nation: An Introduction." *Gender and Society* 19(2) April:137–159.

Kundnani, Arun. 2004. "Wired for war: military technology and the politics of fear." *Race and Class* 46(1):116–125.

Lawrence, Bonita. 2004. *"Real" Indians and Others: Mixed-Blood Urban Native Peoples and Indigenous Nationhood.* Lincoln and London: University of Nebraska Press.

Lawrence, Errol. 1982. "Just Plain Common Sense: The 'roots' of racism." chap. 2 in *The Empire Strikes Back. Race and Racism in 70s Britain.* Centre for Contemporary Cultural Studies: University of Birmingham: Routledge.

Li, Peter. 1994. "A World Apart: The Multicultural World of Visible Minorities and the Art World in Canada."

Li, Peter. 2003. "The Place of Immigrants: The Politics of Difference in Territorial and Social Space. *Canadian Ethnic Studies* 35(2):1–13.

Liddle, Joanna and Rama Joshi. 1986. *Daughters of Independence: Gender, Caste, and Class in India.* London: Zed Books.

Massey, Douglas S. 2005. "Racial Discrimination in Housing: A Moving Target." *Social Problems* 52(2):148–151.

McAndrew, Marie. 2003. "School Spaces and the Construction of Ethnic Relations: Conceptual and Policy Debates." *Canadian Ethnic Studies* 35(2):14–29.

Monture-Agnes, Patricia. 1999. "Standing Against Canadial Law: Naming Omissions of Race, Culture, and Gender." Pp 76–97 in Comack, Elizabeth (ed) *Locating Law: Race/Class/Gender Connections.* Halifax:Fernwood, Ng, Roxana. "Multiculturalism as Ideology: A Textual Analysis." Pp 35–48 in Marie Campbell and Ann Manicom (eds) *Knowledge, Experience, and Ruling Relations: Studies in the Social Organization of Knowledge.* Toronto: University of Toronto Press.

Oberschall, Anthony. 2000. "The manipulation of ethnicity: from ethnic cooperation to violence and war in Yugoslavia." *Ethnic and Racial Studies* 23(6) November: 982–1001.

Radhakrishnan, Simitha. 2005. "'Time to show our true colours' The Gendered politics of "Indianness" in post-Apartheid South Africa." *Gender and Society* 19(2) April: 262–281.

Raj, Dhooleka Sarhadi. 2000. "'Who the hell do you think you are?' Promoting religious identity among young Hindus in Britain." *Ethnic and Racial Studies* 23(3) May:535–558.

Rajagopal, A. 2000. *Politics after Television: Religious Nationalism and the Retailing of Hindutva 1987–1993.* Cambridge: Cambridge University Press.

Razack, Sherene H. 2002. *Race, Space, and the Law: Unmapping a White Settler Society.* Toronto: Between The Lines.

Razack, Sherene H. 2000. "Gendered Racial Violence and Spatialized Justice: The Murder of Pamela George." *Canadian Journal of Law and Society.* 15(2):91–130.

Razack, Sherene. 1998. " Race, Space, and Prostitution: The Making of the Bourgeois Subject." *Canadian Journal of Women and Law* 10: 238– 276.

Reitz, Jeffrey G. and Raymond Breton. 1998. "Prejudice and Discrimination in Canada and the United States: A Comparison." In Satzewich, Vic (ed) *Racism and Social Inequality in Canada.* Toronto: Thompson.

Reynolds, Tracey. 2002. "Re-thinking a black feminist standpoint." *Ethnic and Racial Studies.* 25(4) July:591–606.

Reynolds, Tracey. 2001. "Black mothering, paid work and identity." *Ethnic and Racial Studies* 24(6) November:1046–1064.

Richmond, Anthony H. 2002. "Globalization: implications for immigrants and refugees." *Ethnic and Racial Studies* 25(5) September:707–727.

Richmond, Anthony H. 1988. *Immigration and Ethnic Conflict.* London Macmillan.

Scott, Ellen K. 2005. "Beyond Tokenism: The Making of Racially Diverse feminist Organizations." *Social Problems* 52(2):232–254.

Shaver, Frances M. 1994. The Regulation of Prostitution: Avoiding the Morality Traps." *Canadian Journal of Law and Society.* 9:123–145.

Simmons, Alan. 1998. "Racism and Immigration Policy" in Satzewich, Vic. (Ed) *Racism and Social Inequality in Canada* Toronto: Thompson.

Singh, S. 1995. "The Epic on Tube: Plumbing the Depths of History: A Paradigm for Viewing the TV Serialization of the Mahabharata" *Quarterly Review of Film and Video* 16(1):77–99.

Sivanandan, A. 2001. "Poverty is the new Black' in *The Three Faces of British Racism,* special issue of *Race and Class* 43(2) Oct–Dec.

Smart, Carol. 1984. *The Ties That Bind: Law, Marriage and the Reproduction of Patriarchal Relations.* London: Routledge and Kegan Paul.

Staub, Ervin, Laurie Anne Pearlman and Vachel Miller. 2003. "Healing the Roots of Genocide in Rwanda." *Peace Review* 15(3):287–294.

Stockden, Eric W. 2000. "Pluralism, Corporatism, and Educating Citizens." *Canadian Ethnic Studies* 32(1):54–71.

Sudbury, Julia. 2001. "(Re)constructing multiracial blackness: Women's activism, difference and collective identity in Britain." *Ethnic and Racial Studies* 24(1) January:29–49.

Sunahara, Ann. 1981. *The Politics of Racism: The Uprooting of Japanese Canadians During the Second World War.* Toronto: Latimer.

Thobani, Sunera. 2003. "War and the politics of truth-making in Canada." *Qualitative studies in education* 16(3) May–June: 399–414.

Thobani, Sunera. 2000. "Closing ranks: racism and sexism in Canada's immigration policy." *Race and Class* 42(1):35–55.

Verwimp, Philip. 2003. "The Political economy of coffee, dictatorship, and genocide." *European Journal of Political Economy* 19(2) June:161–181.

Thobani, Sunera 2000. "Closing ranks: racism and sexism in Canada's immigration policy." *Race and Class* 42(1):35–55.

Van Dijk, Teun A. 1993. *Elite Discourse and Racism* London: Sage.

Van Dijk, Teun A. 2000. "New(s) Racism: A Discourse Analytical Approach." Pp. 33–49 in Simon Cottle (ed) *Ethnic Minorities and the Media.* Buckingham, Philadelphia: Open University Press.

Walby, Kevin. 2005. "How Closed-Circuit Television Surveillance Organizes the Social: An Institutional Ethnography." *Canadian Journal of Sociology* 30(2):189–214.

Walling, Carrie Booth. 2000. "The History and Politics of Ethnic Cleansing." *International Journal of Human Rights* 4(3):47–67.

Wrench, John. 2005. "Diversity management can be bad for you." *Race & Class* 46(3):73–84.

Ye_eno_lu, Meyda. 2005. "Cosmopolitanism and nationalism in a globalized world." *Ethnic and Racial Studies* 28(1):January 103–131.

Young, Jon and Robert J. Graham. 2000. "School and Curriculum Reform: Manitoba Frameworks & Multicultural Teacher Education." *Canadian Ethnic Studies* 32(1):142–155.

Young, Judy. 2001. "No longer 'Apart'? Multiculturalism Policy and Canadian Literature." *Canadian Ethnic Studies* 33(2):88–97.

Mitchell, J. 1972. "Marxism and Women's Revolution." *Social Praxis* 1,1.

Panitch, L. 1992. "Beyond Communism and Social Democracy." *Studies in Political Economy* 38 (Summer):139–154.

Pentland, H.C. 1959. "The Development of a Capitalist Labour Market in Canada." *Canadian Journal of Economics and Political Science* 25(4)):450–461.

Resnick, S. And R. Wolff. 1993. "State Capitalism in the USSR? A High-Stakes Debate." *Rethinking Marxism* 6,2 (Summer):46–67.

Sayer, A. And R. Walker. 1992. *The New Social Economy: Reworking the Division of Labour.* Cambridge, MA: Blackwell.

Sayer, D. 1983. *Marx's Method, Ideology, Science and Critique in Capital.* Sussex, NJ: Harvester/Humanities Press.

Sayer, D. 1985. "The Critique of Politics and Poltitcal Economy: Capitalism, Communism and the State in Marx's Writings of the Mid-1840s." *Sociological Review* 33(2):221–253.

Sayer, D. Ed. 1989. *Readings from Karl Marx.* London: Routledge.

Smith, D.E. 1974. "The Ideological Practice of Sociology." *Catalyst* 8 (Winter):39–54.

Smith, D. E. 1990. "On Sociological Description: A Method from Marx." in *Texts, Facts, and Femininity: Exploring the Relations of Ruling.* Ed. D.E. Smith. New York: Routledge, 89–119.

Smith, D. E. 1992. "Feminist Reflections on Political Economy." in *Feminism in Action: Studies in Political Economy.* Ed. M.P. Connelly and P. Armstrong. Toronto: Canadian Scholars Press, 1–23.

Teeple, G. 1972. "Land, Labour, and Capital in Pre-Confederation Canada." in *Capitalism and the National Question in Canada.* Ed. G. Teeple. Toronto: University of Toronto Press, 43–66.

Thompson, E.P. 1978. "Eighteenth-Century English Society: Class Struggle Without Class." *Social History* 3,2 (May).

Chapter 14

Ashley, D. And M. Orenstein. 1985. *Sociological Theory: Classical Statements* Boston: Allyn & Bacon.

Gerth, H. And C.W. Mills. 1946. *From Max Weber: Essays in Sociology.* New Tork: Oxford University Press.

Giddens, A. 1971. *Capitalism and Modern Social Theory.* London: Cambridge University Press.

Leyton, E. 1986. *Hunting Humans: The Rise of the Modern Multiple Murderer.* Toronto: McClelland and Stewart.

Lee, D. And H. Newby. 1983. *The Problem of Sociology* London: Hutchinson.

Thompson, E.P. 1963. *The Making of the English Working Class* Harmondsworth, Eng: Penguin.

Weber, M. [1904] 1930. *The Protestant Ethic and the Spirit of Capitalism.* London: Unwin University Books.

Index

Credits

Photo Illustrations

Chapter 5

p. 98, Graham Harrop • p. 99, *The Markham Economist and Sun* • p. 104, © Danny Ogilvie • p. 108, Canapress • p. 111, *The Toronto Star*/P. Gower • p. 121, Drawing by Cheney; © The New Yorker Magazine, Inc.

Chapter 10

p. 244, Dick Hemingway • p. 248, © Danny Ogilvie • p. 258, Dick Hemingway • p. 259, Ministry of the Solicitor General, Ontario • p. 261, Fahmida Bhabha

Chapter 11

p. 268, Western Canada Pictorial Index • p. 270, National Archives of Canada/PA42949 • p. 278, © Punch/Rothco • p. 283, Pay Equity Commission, Ontario • p. 285, SALLY FORTH reprinted with special permission of King Features syndicate

Chapter 12

p. 297, Ontario Archives • p. 302, Calgary Herald Print Collection, Glenbow Archives, Calgary • p. 309, ABC Canada Literacy Commission • p. 310, HERMAN

Figures, Tables, and Excerpts

10-1, Statistics Canada (1994a), *Age, Sex, Marital Status, and Common-law Status*, Cat. 92-325E. • Figure 10-1, Statistics Canada, 1971 and 1986 Censuses of Canada • Figure 10-2, Statistics Canada, 1986 Census of Canada • Figure 10-3, National Council of Welfare (1994, 32) • Table 10-2, Adapted from Statistics Canada (1994h), *Marriage and Conjugal Life in Canada*, Cat. 91-534E. • Table 11-1, Statistics Canada (1994d), *Earnings of Men and Women*, Cat. 13-217. • Figure 11-1, Adapted from Statistics Canada, 1961 Census of Canada, Vol. III (Part 1) Labour Force, table 1, for 1911–61; for 1966–79; Cat. 71-201 Historical Labour Force Statistics, pp. 151, 153, 158; for 1981–84: Historical Labour Force Statistics, 1984, Cat. 71-201, p. 220, D767895, p. 225, D768005; for 1985–86, Cat. 71-001; for 1986–93, Cat. 71-201. • Table 11-2, Adapted from 1971 Census, vol. 3.2, table 8 and 1981 Census, Labour Force-Occupational Trends, Cat. 92-920, table 1. • Figures 12-1 and 12-3, Porter, Porter, and Blishen, *Stations and Callings* (Toronto: Nelson Canada, 1982), pp. 61, 193. Reprinted with permission of the authors. • Figure 12-2, Statistics Canada (1994e), *Education in Canada: A Statistical Review*, Cat. 81-229. • Table 12-1, Statistics Canada (1994b), *Canada Year Book 1992*, table 5, p. B-16. • Table 12-2, Indian and Northern Affairs Canada (1993), table 16, p. 41. • Figure 12-4, Indian and Northern Affairs Canada (1993), chart 17, p. 42. • Table 12-3, Adapted from Noble (1990, 54). • Figure 12-5, Statistics Canada, Cat. 81-222, p. 17. • Table 12-4, Adapted from Statistics Canada (1994e), *Education in Canada: A Statistical Review*, Cat. 81-229, table 13, pp. 84–87.

Note: Readers wishing additional information on data provided through the co-operation of Statistics Canada may obtain copies of related publications by mail from: Publication Sales, Statistics Canada, Ottawa, ON, K1A 0T6, or by calling (613) 951-7277 or toll-free 800-267-6677. Readers may also facsimile their order by dialing (613) 951-1584.